SO-ASK-589

Studies in Modern Capitalism · Etudes sur le capitalisme moderne
Past and Present Publications

Industrialization before Industrialization

Studies in modern capitalism · Etudes sur le capitalisme moderne

Editorial board · Comité de rédaction

Maurice Aymard, Maison des Sciences de l'Homme, Paris
Jacques Revel, Ecole des Hautes Etudes en Sciences Sociales, Paris
Immanuel Wallerstein, Fernand Braudel Center for the Study of Economies,
    Historical Systems, and Civilizations, Binghamton, New York

This series is devoted to an attempt to comprehend capitalism as a world-system.
It will include monographs, collections of essays and colloquia around specific
themes, written by historians and social scientists united by a common concern for
the study of large-scale long-term social structure and social change.
    The series is a joint enterprise of the Maison des Sciences de l'Homme in Paris
and the Fernand Braudel Center for the Study of Economies, Historical Systems,
and Civilizations at the State University of New York at Binghamton.

Other books in the series

Immanuel Wallerstein: *The capitalist world-economy**
Pierre Bourdieu: *Algeria 1960*
Andre Gunder Frank: *Mexican agriculture 1521–1630*
Folker Fröbel, Jürgen Heinrichs, Otto Kreye: *The new international division of labour*
Henri H. Stahl: *Traditional Romanian village communities*
Ernest Mandel: *Long waves of capitalist development*

This book is also published in association with and as part of Past and Present
Publications (Cambridge University Press and *Past and Present*), a series designed
to encompass a wide variety of scholarly and original works, monographs and
anthologies, primarily concerned with social, economic and cultural changes.

Volumes in the series

Family and Inheritance: Rural Society in Western Europe 1200–1800, edited by Jack
    Goody, Joan Thirsk and E. P. Thompson*
French Society and the Revolution, edited by Douglas Johnson
Peasants, Knights and Heretics: Studies in Medieval English Social History, edited by
    R. H. Hilton*
Towns in Societies: Essays in Economic History and Historical Sociology, edited by Philip
    Abrams and E. A. Wrigley*
Desolation of a City: Coventry and the Urban Crisis of the Late Middle Ages, Charles
    Phythian-Adams
*Puritanism and Theatre: Thomas Middleton and Opposition Drama under the Early
    Stuarts*, Margot Heinemann
*Lords and Peasants in a Changing Society: The Estates of the Bishopric of Worcester,
    680–1540*, Christopher Dyer
*Life, Marriage and Death in a Medieval Parish: A Social, Economic and Demographic
    Study of Halesowen, 1270–1400*, Zvi Razi

* Also issued as a paperback.

Industrialization before Industrialization

Rural Industry in the Genesis of Capitalism

PETER KRIEDTE, HANS MEDICK, JÜRGEN SCHLUMBOHM

Max-Planck-Institut für Geschichte, Göttingen

Translated by Beate Schempp

With contributions from
Herbert Kisch and Franklin F. Mendels

Cambridge University Press

Cambridge
London   New York   New Rochelle   Melbourne   Sydney

& Editions de la Maison des Sciences de l'Homme

Paris

Published by the Press Syndicate of the University of Cambridge
The Pitt Building, Trumpington Street, Cambridge CB2 1RP
32 East 57th Street, New York, NY 10022, USA
296 Beaconsfield Parade, Middle Park, Melbourne 3206, Australia
and
Editions de la Maison des Sciences de l'Homme
54 Boulevard Raspail, 75270 Paris Cedex 06

First published in German as *Industrialisierung vor der Industrialisierung*, Volume 53 of
Veröffentlichungen des Max-Planck-Instituts für Geschichte 1977 and © Vandenhoeck &
Ruprecht in Göttingen 1977

First published in English 1981 as *Industrialization before Industrialization*
English translation © Maison des Sciences de l'Homme and
Cambridge University Press 1981

Printed in Great Britain at the University Press, Cambridge

This book is published as part of the joint publishing agreement established in 1977 between
the Fondation de la Maison des Sciences de l'Homme and the Press Syndicate of the
University of Cambridge. Titles published under this arrangement may appear in any
European language or, in the case of volumes of collected essays, in several languages.

New books will appear either as individual titles or in one of the series which the Maison
des Sciences de l'Homme and the Cambridge University Press have jointly agreed to publish.
All books published jointly by the Maison des Sciences de l'Homme and the Cambridge
University Press will be distributed by the Press throughout the world.

British Library Cataloguing in Publication Data
Kriedte, Peter
Industrialization before industrialization.
 – (Studies in modern capitalism   ISSN 0144 2333).
1. Cottage industries – History
2. Home labor – History
3. Industrialization
I. Title   II. Medick, Hans   III. Schlumbohm,
Jürgen   IV. Schempp, Beate   V. Series
338.6′34′0941   HD2331   80-41644

ISBN 0 521 23809 9 hard covers
ISBN 0 521 28228 4 paperback

Contents

v

Contents

Preface

This book originated in a working paper, completed in the autumn of 1974. This paper was intended to lay out the theoretical problems before we embarked upon regional historical field studies. The course of our discussions, which produced that highly tentative paper, led us to revise it, extend it and publish it. The book which resulted gained much from discussions at the Max-Planck-Institut für Geschichte, at the Arbeitskreis für moderne Sozialgeschichte in Heidelberg, at the Institut für Wirtschafts- und Sozialgeschichte in Göttingen, at the Institut für Wirtschafts- und Sozialgeschichte in Münster, and with the Cambridge Group for the History of Population and Social Structure.

We are grateful for the encouragement and criticism which our project encountered in these centres. We are equally grateful to all the other people who helped us to improve our understanding of the problems by their interest, their arguments, and their questions. Only two names shall be mentioned: Herbert Kisch and Franklin F. Mendels. They contributed to our project both through extensive discussions and by allowing their own regional studies, which focus on some of the questions raised in this book, to be reprinted here. We are particularly grateful to Rudolf Vierhaus; he not only took an active interest in our work from the beginning, but without his concern, his criticism, and his help, especially at important turning-points, this book would not have been written.

Göttingen, August 1976   P. K., H. M., J. S.

ix

Abbreviations

Econ. Hist. Rev.	The Economic History Review
HMGOG	Handelingen der Maatschappij voor Geschiedenis en Oudheidkunde te Gent
Jb. Wirtsch. G.	Jahrbuch für Wirtschaftsgeschichte
Journ. Econ. Hist.	The Journal of Economic History
N. F.	Neue Folge
N. S.	New Series
VKVA	Verhandelingen van de Koninklijke Vlaamse Academie voor de Letteren, Wetenschappen en Schone Kunsten van Belgie
VSWG	Vierteljahrschrift für Sozial- und Wirtschaftsgeschichte
Z. Agrarg. Agrarsoziol.	Zeitschrift für Agrargeschichte und Agrarsoziologie
Zs.	Zeitschrift

Glossary

Brinksitzer Büdner Gärtner haricotiers Häusler Heuerlinge Köter, Kötter Kossäten manouvriers	cottagers or small peasants, who held little or no land
Einlieger	lodger
encomienda (Sp.)	estate granted by Spanish kings; commandery in one of the military orders; the lands or rents belonging to such a commandery
Grundherr(en) Grundherrschaft	feudal lord(s), feudal lordship in western and west-central Europe, in French 'seigneurie'; the economic, social and political organization of the landed property; the peasant is subject to the landlord only indirectly through the interposition of the soil; in distinction to the 'Gutsherrschaft' its mode of appropriation is through rents in kind or money rents, not through labour dues
Gutsherr(en) Gutsherrschaft	feudal lord(s), feudal lordship in east central and eastern Europe, the economic, social and political organization of the landed estates, the superstructure of the 'Gutswirtschaft'; the peasant is personally subject to the 'Gutsherr' as his serf and owes him extensive labour dues
Gutshof	demesne in east-central and eastern Europe, in German also 'Vorwerk', in Polish 'folwark', directly exploited by the 'Gutsherr' on the basis of labour dues from the peasant serfs
Gutswirtschaft	seigneurial economy in east central and eastern Europe, based on the extraction of forced labour from peasant serfs
Kaufsystem	a system of production where the petty producer owns the means of production (tools, raw materials etc.) and sells his product to a merchant
Verlagssystem	(putting-out system) a system of production where the producer works only upon being commissioned by a merchant or trader. Often in the *Verlagssystem* part of the means of production (the raw materials e.g.) are owned by the *Verleger*

xi

Part I

Introduction

It has long been known that industrial commodity production in the countryside for large inter-regional and international markets was of considerable importance during the formative period of capitalism. Contemporary travel accounts and geographies by authors interested in economics described the extent and variety of industrial activity in the countryside.[1] Spokesmen of the emerging science of political economy dealt with questions arising from this context, but their concerns were more practical and political rather than theoretical: mercantilist writers were interested in promoting export industries which they saw as an important means of achieving a favourable balance of trade as well as increasing the tax base and the economic power of the state. Not only did they discuss the advantages and disadvantages of urban guild privileges and various ways of organizing production and marketing, they also dealt with the relationship between the development of industry – not least of all rural industry – and the development of foreign trade, agriculture, and population.[2]

To be sure, ever since the Industrial Revolution the main interest of economists and social scientists in general has focused on factory industry. But they could not overlook the fact that, until well into the nineteenth century, in most European countries, more value was created and more people were employed in small workshops than in centralized and mechanized production units. However, once it constituted a mode of organization *alongside* the capitalist factory, 'domestic' or 'cottage' industry, while preserving a remarkable continuity in external appearance, differed in substance from the traditional 'rural export industries'. It was in this latter capacity that they were studied by economists and commissions of investigation and that they became the concern of political reformers during the nineteenth and early twentieth centuries. Karl Marx was one of the first to draw that dividing line and to point out the significance of both forms of domestic industry. On one hand, he characterized the 'so-called modern domestic industry' as 'an external department of the factory', as a further 'sphere in which capital conducts its exploitation against the background of large-scale industry'.[3] On the other hand, he assigned a position of epoch-making importance to the expansion of

1

rural industrial commodity production within the formative period of development of capitalist relations of production and capitalism as a social formation. 'The first presupposition' of the emergence of 'large industry' is 'to draw the land in all its expanse into the production not of use values but of exchange values'. This occurred when '*manufacture* proper', i.e. the production of 'mass quantities for export', or at least for a 'general market', seized the rural 'secondary occupations', not least 'spinning and weaving', and established itself 'on the land, in villages lacking guilds'.[4] But Marx never pursued these considerations systematically, just as he never gave a comprehensive account of the historical genesis of capitalism.[5]

A comprehensive attempt to acknowledge the 'debt which economic theory owes to domestic industry' (W. Sombart)[6] was undertaken by the Older and Younger Historical School of Political Economy in Germany.[7] Here, as elsewhere, the astonishing persistence of the domestic mode of production generated a growing public interest from the second half of the nineteenth century onward.[8] The development of the sweating system in modern, frequently urban domestic industry, which paralleled the final crisis of the old rural industry, aroused not only social and political concern, but – closely connected with this – also attracted the attention of social scientists. The beginnings of this concern were marked by the social conservatism of the middle classes. But despite its ideological character[9] this interest produced some real results. In Germany a systematic historical approach emerged relatively early in the course of the debate about 'domestic industry', 'domestic manufacture', and 'cottage industry'. Such an approach was less evident in the numerous investigations and 'enquêtes' about domestic industries and 'industries à domicile' in England, France, and other European countries.[10] But the German approach was paralleled in some respects by the far-reaching Russian discussion about kustar' industries.[11] The socio-statistical investigations in Germany were complemented by a considerable number of analyses dealing with the history of specific industries, among which the works of W. Troeltsch, E. Gothein, and A. Thun[12] stand out. In these works different degrees of emphasis were given to historical interests on one side and contemporary interests on the other. Still, even where the analysis of contemporary problems constituted the central theme, as in the work of A. Thun, the authors took a historical approach.

However, the historical interest in cottage industry developed by German political economists went beyond the writing of monographs about certain industries and individual industrial regions. It also found expression in numerous attempts to conceptualize 'cottage industry' systematically as a 'historical category'.[13] Among the exponents of the older historical school, especially W. Roscher[14] and A. Schäffle[15] – in his role as an 'outsider' – such attempts still suffered from a somewhat formal perspective. 'Domestic industry' and rural handicrafts were interpreted as a 'transitional stage between handicraft and the factory' (A. Schäffle)[16] and as 'household manufacture destined for trade', and consequently as an 'intermediate step between the factory proper and handicraft' (W. Roscher).[17] The origins and diffusion of domestic industry as a handicraft export or rural export industry were explained primarily by the expansion of trade during the early modern period and the resulting bottlenecks of supply which could no longer be overcome within the framework of the guild system. This older 'theory of craft export and by-occupation'[18] (W. Sombart) was considerably modified and redefined by the works of G. Schmoller, K. Bücher, and W. Sombart.[19] They emphasized the specific 'forms of social organization' which characterized domestic industry as a historically new 'system of production' (G. Schmoller).[20] As a 'unique mode of enterprise' it differed from the handicraft mode of production as much as from the factory system.

To them the decisive factor in this new 'mode of enterprise' was the 'interaction' of 'two social classes' within an asymmetrically structured basic relationship. A primarily domestic production process was dominated and organized by 'entrepreneurs' who were traders or putters-out. Schmoller and Bücher identified various historical phases of development and types of relations of production in domestic industry. They based their distinctions on the legal and political framework and the general socio-economic conditions under which cottage industry occurred. But they tended to see these development phases as modifications of the same basic structural relationship.[21] 'In essence, two different social classes interact with each other: the artisans are the body and the merchants are its head.'[22] Sombart, in his early works, radicalized the systematic approach which Schmoller had introduced. To him domestic industry was not a hybrid between old and new elements. The various types and phases of relations of production, for example the '*Kaufsystem*' and the 'putting-out system', differed only in degree. He applied Marx's interpretation of 'modern domestic industry' to the cottage industry of the past and regarded the latter as 'a manifestation of the modern capitalist mode of production', a 'form of capitalist enterprise' whose essential characteristic was the 'labourer's dependence on the capitalist entrepreneur'. Sombart maintained that 'in the case of domestic industry the "production factor" which the capitalist entrepreneur controls does not consist in the whole range of material means of production but rather in the market'.[23]

These different interpretations of early modern domestic industry as 'social modes of the organization' of production and marketing were related to the contrasting ideas which these exponents of the younger historical school of political economists developed in relation to contemporary economic questions. In particular they debated whether a 'division of labour' between domestic industry and 'large industry' continued to be economically advantageous and whether, therefore, the 'preservation of domestic industry' in their own time was desirable from the point of view of social welfare.[24]

Despite their diverging opinions, the exponents of the younger historical school of political economists agreed that domestic industry had been of great significance for economic development, especially during the early modern period. According to Schmoller, 'domestic industry was the predominant form of industry producing for mass markets from the fourteenth to the eighteenth century. Its development and flowering during that period were the primary indications of continuous economic growth and prosperity.'[25] And Sombart arrived at the following conclusion: 'The history of domestic industry is the history of capitalism. . . Disguised in the form of domestic industry capitalism likes to steal its way into an economic region. In economic history, therefore, there is at first a period of predominantly domestic industry.'[26]

The historical school of political economists, therefore, deserves credit for having focused on domestic industry as an historically relevant problem of 'political economy' and of society in general. Admittedly its members developed and discussed some of the themes which inspire the current discussion about 'proto-industrialization', but their perspective was limited insofar as they understood domestic industry primarily as a stage in the historical sequence of industrial 'modes of the organization of production', a bias which resulted from their strong focus on the institutional aspects of economic history. Despite comprehensive analyses in the best of their historical monographs, they did not systematically explore the relationship between this industrial development and other sectors of the socio-economic process, especially the development of agriculture and the growth of population.

After the turn of the century the interest in the history of domestic industry gradually became detached from the concern about the contemporary crisis of domestic industry. Moreover, as economic and social history began to emerge as a separate research area and as a special discipline, the study of domestic industry increasingly focused on the historical investigation of various branches of industry, which made the significance of domestic industry, especially for the emergence of the factory system, appear in a new light. This became most obvious when researchers turned specifically toward studying the history of rural industries; when they became interested in its agrarian context; and when they began to regard rural industry as part of the background of the Industrial Revolution. In this approach attempts at systematization receded behind empirical study. When the Russian economic historian J. Kulischer devoted a chapter in the second volume of his general economic history from the Middle Ages to the present (1929) – which is, incidentally, still worth reading – to early modern domestic industry,[27] he could already make use of a considerable amount of research. In 1910, his compatriot, E. V. Tarlé, had presented a survey of rural industries in France at the end of the Ancien Régime.[28] This basic study, valuable to this day, was continued in the work of H. Sée, especially in his little essay of 1923 about the nature of rural industry in France during the eighteenth century, where he discusses not only its agrarian preconditions but also links it to the factory system.[29]

This kind of research had developed most vigorously in England where it was stimulated by the interest in the origins of the Industrial Revolution.[30] The first efforts in this direction were made before World War I by W. J. Ashley, W. Cunningham, and G. Unwin. Then, during the 1920s and 1930s appeared a series of historical monographs on certain industries, most of which concentrated on individual regions. Because of the nature of their subject, the development of rural industries was at the centre of their concern: E. Lipson, C. Gill, A. P. Wadsworth and J. de Lacy Mann, W. H. B. Court.[31] The most important of these monographs is that of A. P. Wadsworth and J. de Lacy Mann about the rural cotton industry in Lancashire. The only work on the continent that matches it is the extremely detailed study of Hondshoote by E. Coornaert.[32] In Germany, the younger historical school of political economists, declining though it was, maintained its interest in the history of domestic industry mostly by writing regional industrial histories. But it did not produce a work comparable to that of Troeltsch.[33] No less important than the histories of specific industries were regional histories, especially when they aspired to the status of a '*histoire totale*' of a particular region. At the beginning of the twentieth century, this kind of research work experienced a precocious flowering in the great geographical theses which originated in the school of Vidal de la Blache and were of great significance for French historical scholarship: A. Demangeon, R. Blanchard, J. Sion, R. Musset.[34] These works devoted much space to the history of rural industry but nobody really followed up on this approach during the interwar period.[35]

A new phase in the study of rural industry began in the 1950s and early 1960s.[36] Decisive impulses came from the intensification of research in economic and social history. Not only was a new methodology applied to research in economic and social history, but new subject-matters were taken up as well, such as the history of population and the history of the family. Especially in studies of the early modern period, the region became the most favoured research unit, appropriate to the variety of questions that were asked and the subtlety of the methods that were used.[37]

At the same time, the problems of the underdeveloped world were increasingly discussed: economic growth, development and underdevelopment, modernization and backwardness. In this process there grew up a new awareness of the problems of transition to industrial capitalism in the European metropolitan areas. As early as 1954, Eric Hobsbawm put the emerging rural industries in the context of the seventeenth-century crisis and of the movements of concentration which it produced.[38] The interrelationship between agriculture and rural industry was given a new focus in the works of Joan Thirsk and Eric Jones.[39] Herbert Kisch, in a series of important studies, placed special emphasis on the social and institutional background of rural industry.[40] Eckard Schremmer studied the penetration of rural industry into the countryside and undertook to measure it quantitatively.[41] In Eastern Europe – despite a remarkable but discontinued initiative in the German Democratic Republic[42] – scholars have intensively studied industrial development in the countryside only since the end of the 1960s[43] (the 1950s and early 1960s had been devoted to the investigation and discussion of manufactures). The works of Rudolf Braun stand largely outside the context which has been delineated here; they reverse, so to speak, the former perspectives and take as their point of departure the everyday life-patterns of the petty producers.[44]

These new approaches were taken up by the American historians Franklin F. Mendels and Charles and Richard Tilly, who summarized them and raised them to a new level of conceptualization.[45] They not only coined the term 'proto-industrialization' to suggest a new research strategy, but also presented a comprehensive framework which made it possible to analyse areas of rural industry, that had emerged during the formative period of capitalism, within the context of socio-economic development in general and to determine their regional as well as supra-regional importance. Convinced that research strategies should be guided by explicit models, they overcame the isolation of individual historical disciplines, such as the history of population, of agriculture or of industry, and integrated them into a research concept whose spatial reach is, admittedly, limited but which makes some of the central questions of the transition from feudalism to capitalism appear in a new light.

The present study takes up the research concept developed by Franklin F. Mendels and Charles and Richard Tilly and develops it further. Proto-industrialization is here conceptualized as 'industrialization before industrialization', which can be defined as the development of rural regions in which a large part of the population lived entirely or to a considerable extent from industrial mass production for inter-regional and international markets.[46] The significance of the phenomenon becomes apparent when one tries to assign it a place in the socio-economic process. Viewed from the long-range perspective, it belongs to the great process of transformation which seized the feudal European agrarian societies and led them toward industrial capitalism. On closer inspection, however, it becomes clear that proto-industrialization could establish itself only where the ties of the feudal system had either loosened or were in the process of full disintegration.[47]

The first phase of the process of disintegration undergone by the feudal system dates back to the high Middle Ages. The manorial economy, the core of the feudal system, had to operate under fundamentally changed circumstances as a division of labour mediated by the market was established. The new division of labour found expression in the emergence of a dense network of towns. Its preconditions lay in sustained population increase as well as in the growing productivity of the agrarian sector. Owing to the penetration of market relations into the countryside, to the growth of towns, to the settlement movement, and to the class relations which changed under the influence of these processes, feudal lords came to consider it economically advantageous to relinquish the old system of appropriating social surplus labour, because the transaction costs (which arose from enforcing and supervising labour services) were too high. Moreover, seigneurial means of control weakened to such an extent that it became necessary to transform labour services into rents in kind and money rents, to dissolve the manorial estates, and, thus, to put the relations of appropriation on a new foundation, more consistent with the changed environment but also much more vulnerable.[48]

The division of labour between town and countryside, which had emerged during this first phase, and the process of differentiation and polarization within the rural population, which was fostered by this division of labour, determined the origins of proto-industrialization. While at first the division of labour between town and countryside had been the engine of the growth of industry, it turned into its crucial obstacle in the course of the historical process, because in the urban economy the supply of labour and materials was inelastic and was kept that way by the economic policies of the guilds. Merchant capital solved this problem by shifting industrial production from the town to the countryside where the process of differentiation and polarization had created a resource in the form of labour power which could easily be tapped by merchant capital.[49] Thus, proto-industrialization, due to its timing, belonged to the second phase of the great transformation from feudalism to capitalism. It was indeed one of the driving forces during this second phase. In conjunction with other factors it developed a dynamic which, by the end of the eighteenth century, enabled the most advanced and the most 'industrialized' agrarian societies of Europe to break away from the Malthusian cycle of population growth, declining income per head, and food crises.

Proto-industrialization, however, was not the only driving force during that phase. Changes in the agrarian sector, which continued to predominate over the industrial sector, at least when one considers the larger territorial units, can only partially be explained by proto-industrialization. To a considerable extent, they themselves constituted a factor which, in *its* turn, determined the course of proto-industrial development as well as the transformation process in general. Even within the secondary sector, other phenomena besides rural industry are relevant to the question of transition from feudalism to capitalism. It is true that the handicrafts which produced for local demand do not need to enter the discussion about the forces which propelled the great transformation process, even though in most countries such handicrafts probably still predominated quantitatively. Of greater importance as a dynamic force were the urban[50] crafts exports, despite the fact that they were largely displaced by rural industry, or at least deprived of their dominant position. The early centralized manufactures admittedly gave rise to capitalist relations of production more rapidly and more completely than did domestic mass production. But the latter was far more important both in terms of the number of labourers that it employed and in terms of the value it created. Such larger manufactures were often directly related to the dispersed rural production units, and complemented their production procedures or sometimes substituted for them. This is particularly true for the textile sector which, as a consequence of its mass-market potential, was the most important branch of industry before the period of industrial capitalism and which became the leading sector during the transition to industrial capitalism. Insofar as there existed a direct relationship between centralized manufactures and dispersed domestic workshops, 'manufactures' will be included in the following discussion of 'proto-industrialization'; manufacture as a 'work of economic artifice' will be viewed from its 'broad foundation' (K. Marx).[51]

In spite of these qualifications proto-industrialization is to be understood as one of the central elements which mark the second phase in the disintegration of the feudal system and the transition to capitalist society. This thesis is borne out by the fact that the relations of production in proto-industrial regions are of this transitional character. Since industrial commodity production could not be maintained under feudal modes of organization – at least not to the same degree as was possible for agricultural market production – a large segment of the population was only partially integrated into the feudal system or came to stand outside it. In addition, agrarian relations of production in regions of rural industry were affected by proto-industrialization. The development of proto-industry required not only a certain loosening of feudal ties, but it also advanced their disintegration. For example, in eastern European areas of rural industry labour services were more and more commuted into money rents.

Moreover, the very formation of proto-industrial regions meant a significant progress in the inter-regional division of labour, as ever larger parts of the population were drawn more deeply into inter-regional market relations. Proto-industrialization, therefore, necessarily had consequences for the entire society, for it affected the demand for and supply of raw materials, finished products, food, and labour power. Especially in the proto-industrially advanced countries, the development of industrial commodity production in the countryside contributed to the stimulation of agriculture which, in its turn, effected the transformation of the agrarian relations of production.

Finally proto-industrialization is closely related to the formation not only of inter-regional but also of international markets; indeed, to the development of a 'world system' dominated by those metropolitan countries of Europe which had advanced furthest on the road to capitalism and therefore came to constitute its core.[52] To be sure, the origins of this world system must not be sought in proto-industrialization. To the contrary, the world system, and especially the 'new colonialism' characterized by the plantation economy and the slave trade, can be regarded as a contributing factor to the formation of rural industrial regions. But as the world system took shape, the role of proto-industrialization grew ever larger and more active: industrial products constituted an increasing share of exports from the European core, and industry's demand for raw materials began to have economic and social consequences for the overseas world, as can be shown for the case of cotton, its newest and, in view of subsequent developments, its decisive branch. Thus, proto-industrialization contributed, at an early stage, to the development of a world-wide economic network of asymmetric relationships, which later – after the core had changed over to the factory system – made it inevitable that the backwardness of the periphery was continuously and massively reinforced by the economic progress of the core.

These are the perspectives that underlie the study that follows. They form a common point of departure for the substantive development of the concept of proto-industrialization. Nonetheless, the three authors have remained in disagreement over some questions, and their different interpretations did not arise arbitrarily. To some extent their different views are implicit in various research approaches that they have followed in the past, but they also appear in a debate which is now getting under way about the problems of the transition from feudally organized agrarian societies to industrial capitalism.

In many respects the question of the 'systemic' character of the basic structures of proto-industrialization provides a clue to the controversy. The exponents of the concept of a system (chapters 1, 2, 3, and 6) do not see the 'history of the system of proto-industrialization' in opposition to the 'history of its evolution'. To them the heuristic use of the concept of a system[53] seemed appropriate in order to analyse proto-industrialization as the specific 'asynchronous' set of socio-economic interrelationships which characterize a typical transformation period. The historical manifestations of the disintegration of the old pre-capitalist social formations became an essential, indeed sometimes structural, part of emerging capitalism.[54] These manifestations of disintegration gave to emerging capitalism a specifically historical character which distinguishes proto-industrial from industrial capitalism. During the proto-industrial transition phase, devolutionary and evolutionary forces, the '*post-histoire*' of feudal agrarian society, whose economy was based on domestic family units, and nascent capitalism merged into a unique social system. It gave to proto-industrialization its Janus face and its protean appearance,[55] that preclude any hasty identification of this transitional period as the 'first phase of the industrialization process' (F. Mendels).[56]

Marx distinguished two roads of 'transition from the feudal mode of production':[57] on one side he mentioned the emergence of merchant capital on the basis of pre-capitalist modes of production and on the other side the 'revolutionary' road of the capitalization of the production sphere itself. In the transition debate these two roads have been regarded as being in contrast with each other. The 'systemic' approach to proto-industrialization sees them as closely related to each other, indeed as forming two parts of the same historical process. Both modes of production were structural components of the proto-industrial system. Hence they formed a configuration of 'transitional modes of production', however much they differed in their historical importance. As long as proto-industrial capitalism had not exhausted its possibilities for expansion on the 'broad foundation' of the pre-capitalist mode of production, the second road was used only reluctantly. When, on occasion, it *was* taken it could quickly be left again in favour of the first road. Only when the problems arising in the process of proto-industrial growth could no longer be solved within the framework of the old production system did the process of circulation change into a mere element of the production process.

The third author (chapters 4 and 5) is in agreement with the first and second authors in that he does not consider proto-industrialization in its entirety as part of the old social formation of feudal agrarian society nor as part of the new formation of capitalism; but neither does he regard it as a unique third 'system' or as a system merged from these two. Behind the external appearance of *domestic* industry he sees quite divergent relations of production. They appear as different types of proto-industrialization when all regions and branches of proto-industry that existed at a given point in time are considered; but from a long-term perspective, they also reveal themselves as historical phases. For during the course of proto-industrialization the emphasis shifted from relations of production which were characterized by the independence of petty commodity producers in the sphere of production and the restriction of capital to the sphere of circulation, on one hand, to relations of production, on the other hand, where capital had entered into the sphere of production and increasingly limited the field of independent decision-making for the direct producers, turning them more and more into wage labourers. Thus, proto-industrialization contained within itself part of the great transformation process, during which the feudal system disintegrated and the capitalist system was formed. Within proto-industrialization, capitalist relations of production emerged, often haltingly, sometimes even subject to retrogression, pertinaciously and slowly, especially when compared with early centralized manufactures. But they developed on a much broader front than they did in centralized manufactures, indeed the broadest front within the secondary sector. The formation of such relations of production is seen as a factor of strategic importance for the breakthrough of the Industrial Revolution which forced all other societies either to industrialize as well or to succumb to increasing dependence.

This perspective implies the construction not of *one* system of proto-industrialization but of several models of its most important types and phases. These models will be constructed by further developing categories which, in rudimentary form, are implied in the critique of political economy.[58] In this way an attempt will be made to clarify a number of questions which appear essential but have hitherto been neglected: what specific laws underlie the functioning of each of these relations of production? How are they related to each other and under what conditions could a transition occur from one set of relations of production to another? Finally, how are specific relations of production connected with other aspects of the socio-economic process?[59]

According to this approach, the 'systemic' interrelationships as it were cut across the borderlines of proto-industrialization: on one hand, they do not include all proto-industrial regions, branches of industry, and development phases; on the other hand, they are not confined to proto-industrialization alone.[60] The non-systemic approach follows not only from the emphasis laid on the variety of relations of production within proto-industrialization and on viewing proto-industrialization as a process. It is also based on the fact that proto-industrial regions always constituted only a small part of larger socio-political units (though one that was relevant for the whole). Therefore proto-industrialization affected not only the societies in which it was embedded, e.g. their agrarian sector and their political and institutional structures; but proto-industrialization was, in its turn, strongly determined by the agrarian sector and by institutional structures.

The controversial nature of these perspectives is an indication of the tentativeness of this study and the open-endedness of the debate. The following contribution cannot hope to succeed where the historical research into proto-industrialization as well as the theoretical discussion about modernization, industrialization, and social evolution have failed to close the gaps both in empirical knowledge and in theory, just as they have failed to overcome the gulf between the two. Originally stimulated by an 'agenda', this contribution ends by suggesting another 'agenda'.

In this situation, the three authors deliberately chose a middle path which attempts to combine their theoretical interest with an empirical orientation. From a methodological point of view, this 'merger between narrative and theory' (J. Habermas)[61] may seem problematic to the social scientist and suspect to some historians. But it was hoped that this path might provide a sensible research strategy, not least with regard to the continuation of this work which will take the authors into regional field work and – as far as possible related to this – will aim at the continuation of this debate.

1 ✤ The origins, the agrarian context, and the conditions in the world market

1. The division of labour between town and countryside, and its dissolution

In the high Middle Ages the 'autarchic division of labour' (K. Modzelewski) based on closed social units, especially the manorial estate, came to an end. In its stead emerged a division of labour that was mediated by the market economy. This meant that agricultural production was assigned to the countryside and industrial production to the town. Two conditions underlay the emergence of the exchange economy based on this division of labour: an agrarian surplus had to be produced to feed that part of the population that no longer worked in the primary sector, and demographic growth had to be such that the emerging towns could be supplied with people. In the historical process these two conditions have turned out to be functionally related to each other: the increase in basic foodstuffs called forth a swifter population growth which, in its turn, decisively stimulated the intensification of agriculture. Population growth and agricultural transformation in conjunction with the revival of commerce lay at the basis of the flourishing towns which depended on the surrounding countryside to buy their industrial goods and to provide them with food.[1]

However, the extent of this division of labour between town and countryside was limited from the beginning. The market principle remained largely 'peripheral' to the peasant economy (P. Bohannan and G. Dalton),[2] which produced primarily use values and not exchange values. Only a small part of the total output of the peasant economy entered the market. A large part of its material needs – not only basic foodstuffs but also industrial products – was acquired not by purchase in the market but by home production.[3] Furthermore, certain crafts were indispensable in the countryside if the village economy was to function properly.[4] And finally, the iron industry and mining had to be located in the countryside.[5]

Then, as the social division of labour deepened and became the agent of the economic process, it ceased to be purely the division of labour between town and countryside. In fact, the division of labour between town and countryside, where it was upheld, increasingly turned into an obstacle to the further development of the forces of production. Economic growth could throw off its fetters only if the self-sufficient peasant production unit could be cracked open. This meant that the peasant household could become a relevant market factor only if it opened itself to specialization, limiting the making of agricultural or industrial products for home consumption and offering either agricultural or industrial goods for sale in the market. But the achievement of this new stage in the social division of labour required that the towns lost their privileged position in the overall production and exchange process and that rural centres of industrial commodity production as well as local markets were allowed to form.[6] Often the division of labour between town and countryside ceased to exist in the legal sense only when free trade was introduced, but in practice it had disappeared much earlier. It was swept away by the dynamic force of the socio-economic process that had already given birth to the simple market economy of the high Middle Ages and, since then, had been given additional strength by the emergence of merchant capital in the sphere of circulation. Guilds, city magistrates, and governments tried in vain to arrest this development and to save the urban monopoly on industrial production. Though the territorial state reaffirmed and expanded the control of the cities over trade and industry, and attempted to regulate rural industries, its measures were inadequate on both fronts.[7] The social and economic forces which promoted the expanding production of industrial goods in the countryside turned out to be stronger in the long run.

2. The emergence of rural industries in the countryside

In addition to the relatively undiversified handicrafts there emerged in some regions an extraordinarily concentrated industry which was organized on a domestic basis and produced for supra-regional markets.[8] Whilst rural handicrafts, as rural industry in the strict sense of the term, substantially owed their origin to an autonomous process, restricted to the agrarian sector, the origins of this other, newly-emerging industry were different. Here developments in the countryside and in the towns, in industry, as well as in inter-regional and international commerce converged. These developments lay outside the control of the two relevant systems, namely the agrarian economy and the industrial economy of the towns, and called for a new capacity for self-regulation.

(a) Factors operating within the agrarian sector

The forces which set in motion the process which is analysed here must first be sought in the agrarian sector, for at the beginning of the modern period the secondary and tertiary sectors were still insignificant by comparison.

Due to its dependence on nature, agriculture as an economic and social system is subjected to the rhythmic movement of the seasons. The social organization of agricultural labour is therefore characterized by heavy seasonal fluctuations in demand, which reach their peak at harvest time, and by corresponding fluctuations in the utilization of the existing labour supply. This accounts for the seasonal unemployment characteristic of the agrarian sector. Under the conditions of the family economy operating without wage labour seasonal unemployment remains 'hidden', but in an agricultural system dependent on wage labour it manifests itself openly during the less work-intensive season.[9] The situation of livestock-raising farms differs from that of arable farms. On the former, work is more evenly distributed over the entire year, but it is much less intensive, so that here hidden unemployment is likely to exist as well.[10]

Seasonal unemployment, however, was only a precondition for the expansion of industrial commodity production to the countryside. Production of industrial goods for the market, in contrast to production for home consumption, occurred only in situations of need. Whether a peasant family had to turn to an industrial side-occupation was determined by its economic situation which, in turn, depended above all on the quality and quantity of land at its disposal. In areas where the yield from the soil was meagre the peasant family had to acquire an additional income. It is no accident that the rural industries of Europe concentrated in barren mountain regions,[11] though it must be remembered that the prevalence of domestic industry in such regions was often a secondary phenomenon to be explained by the fact that industry was prevented from establishing itself in the valleys and on the plains by their firmly implanted and inflexible economic and social structures.[12]

The settlement of barren mountain regions and the emergence of peasant holdings insufficiently equipped with land are two aspects of the same socio-economic process. The trend-periods of the high Middle Ages and the sixteenth and eighteenth centuries were periods of large population increase. Demographic growth (which in the sixteenth and eighteenth centuries had, at first, a compensatory function after the population losses of the late medieval period and the seventeenth century) translated itself into economic growth which, in its turn, stimulated further population increase. However, in the course of this growth process the positive interaction between population growth and economic growth was dissolved and transformed itself into a negative relationship. Economic growth did not keep pace with population growth because the initially higher income-margin was not productively used but was largely consumed by population growth. The law of diminishing returns from the land took effect. Income per head fell as the marginal productivity of labour decreased. The relationship between the prices of labour and land shifted in favour of the latter.[13] In the countryside, owing to this change in the direction of the different secular trends, marginal soils were cultivated after the available good soils had been exhausted, but more importantly, a broad stratum of landless peasants emerged in regions of non-partible inheritance, while in the areas of partible inheritance the fragmentation of land took on extraordinary proportions. As a consequence of this trend, which repeated itself with increasing magnitude during each period, the rural social structure was completely changed. By the eighteenth century, the bulk of the rural population consisted not of full-scale farmers in control of enough land to feed their households but of a smallholding and occasionally landless substratum[14] which was made up of several groups: there were cottars, 'haricotiers', 'Söldner', 'Kötter', 'Kossäten', and 'Gärtner', and below these there were the cottagers, 'manouvriers', 'Brinksitzer', Büdner', and 'Häusler', most of whom possessed only a house and a small piece of land. And even lower on the social scale stood the day labourers, farmhands, and servants who lived on the estates of the feudal lords and farms of the peasants and were lucky if they managed to rent a piece of land. Occasionally, the boundaries between these classes, including the boundary which set them off against the full-scale farmers, were blurred.

The process of differentiation within the peasantry, which picked up momentum during the secular economic upswings and which was reinforced by wars and seigneurial pressure, had consequences similar to those of population growth. It often brought about the polarization of rural society. The intermediate peasantry declined; a group of large peasant proprietors and a peasant sub-stratum remained. On occasion, the entire economically viable peasantry was destroyed by the process of accumulation. Even though the sustained boom in grain prices did not cause the differentiation of rural society, it contributed to the acceleration of its differentiation, once that process had started. While smaller holdings did benefit from the price rise, larger farms profited much more, especially those which were more market-oriented. This necessarily strengthened their position within the village community vis-à-vis the small producers whose strength was impaired.

The latter were exposed to direct pressure during the short-term fluctuations in harvest yields caused by meteorological conditions. These upward and downward swings in the agrarian cycle were imbedded in its long-term conjuncture. Large farms were often strengthened by a bad harvest, since the rise in cereal prices more than compensated them for the reduced quantity that they could market, but small farms tended to be decisively and permanently weakened. Mostly they had nothing left to sell at all and might be forced to purchase food in the market in order to forestall starvation. The market quota of such farms fell to zero. Indeed, it could become negative. Families holding such farms were forced to go into debt and were often subject to extortion. In many cases they could not extricate themselves from debt even when the bad harvest was followed by a good one, and in the end they had no recourse but to sell part of their land. The effects of the long-term trend and the short-term fluctuations of the economic cycle were such that, together, they formed a cumulative process which reinforced the previously existing differences in land-holding and income and which transformed part of the peasantry into a rural proletariat.[15]

However, it must also be taken into account that in many cases the rapid growth of the smallholding and landless proletariat might well have resulted from the expansion of home industry and its reproductive pattern.[16] Once rural industry had established itself in a region it generated its own labour force. Smallholdings were made available precisely because it was possible to earn a living outside of agriculture. The social destabilization of the village was a pre-condition as well as a consequence of the spatial expansion of industrial commodity production.

Peasant families whose holdings did not yield enough for subsistence, due to the natural conditions or the insufficiency of their land, could adopt either of two strategies:

(1) They could try to secure their subsistence minimum by using their land more intensively. Under the pressure of 'unsatisfied demands' (A. V. Chayanov) the peasant family increased its labour input per unit of land.[17] However, as the holdings became smaller, the marginal returns decreased more rapidly and the point where the total yield could no longer be increased was reached faster.[18] Consequently, this strategy could not be adopted on very small holdings. To them only the second possibility was open.

(2) They could try to 'meet a shortfall in agricultural incomes by income from crafts and trade' (A. V. Chayanov).[19] Income from agriculture had to be supplemented by income from non-agricultural labour. The proportion of the latter, measured against the total income, depended on the quality of the soil, the size of the holding, and the intensity of cultivation, in addition to the existing possibilities for non-agricultural work.[20] While, at peak-season, smallholders and rural proletarians could find work on estates and large farms, especially since population growth had stimulated the intensification of agriculture, this did not solve the problem of seasonal unemployment. Here the adoption of rural industry provided the only solution.[21] Hence, households whose land–labour ratio was very unfavourable because of the small size of their holdings turned to industrial commodity production which was labour-intensive in contrast to land-intensive agricultural production. As the marginal product of their agricultural labour was rapidly approaching zero, they shifted part of their labour power to more productive activities, and rural industry provided them with an opportunity to do so.[22]

The processes of population growth, social differentiation, and specialization within the rural population largely paralleled the secular trends of growth in European agriculture. Admittedly, population pressure was alleviated during the depression periods of the late Middle Ages and the seventeenth century, partly because of a system of 'negative feedback' but partly also because of an 'autonomous' mortality rate, i.e. a rate which cannot be explained by the socio-economic process (J. D. Chambers). Indeed, occasionally, population figures were reduced sharply from their existing level. But the depression periods forced another group within rural society to search for additional income, for agrarian producers saw their incomes decline in the face of constant or even rising costs.[23] Especially those farms encountered difficulties which had begun to cultivate marginal soils during the previous trend period when the demand for food staples was increasing and prices were rising. Now these soils were hardly worth cultivating any longer since their yield stood in no relationship to the labour input they required. Many agricultural producers could get out of their difficulties only by extensifying their production, i.e. by making the transition to pastoral farming. This strategy was also furthered by the fact that prices for foodstuffs, like meat, for which the income elasticity of demand was high fell less rapidly than the prices of food staples, like cereals, whose elasticity of demand was low. Therefore underemployment developed in regions which turned to stock-raising and favoured, indeed necessitated, the expansion of industrial production.[24] In regions with poor soils, where the transition to stock-raising was impossible, the deterioration of the income of the agricultural population had similar effects.[25] Finally, the crisis in agriculture accelerated the process of differentiation in the countryside.[26] Those who became victims of the process of accumulation were forced to find a new subsistence base in industry. More and more industrial production came to be located in the countryside. Far from reversing this trend, the secular crises reinforced it.

The local distribution of power and the agrarian relations of production could restrict or promote the spatial expansion of industrial commodity production. Of central importance was the position which the local seigneur (either *Grundherr* or *Gutsherr*) and the village community adopted with regard to population growth and the differentiation process within the peasantry.[27] They could try to influence these processes by insisting on the indivisibility of holdings even in areas of partible inheritance. To this end, they might suppress the emergence of a land market, control the settlement of cottagers by withholding land, and judiciously manipulate their right of consent to marriages.[28] But such interference did not take place everywhere, especially not, if seigneurial authority and community cohesion were weak.[29]

Hence the most important precondition for industrial development in the countryside, namely the elasticity of the labour supply, depended not only on demographic developments and the social differentiation within the village population but also on the local constellation of seigneurial and communal power. This power-constellation was determined by many factors even if one disregards, for the moment, the *Gutsherrschaft* in east-central and eastern Europe where seigneurial authority was always very strong. Only one factor will be mentioned here. Inevitably, the community exercised powerful controls in areas of nuclear villages and three-field agriculture. The collective nature of the three-field system required a strong centralized institution to direct village affairs. In areas of individual farms and enclosed fields such an institution was unnecessary, and the preconditions for its development were lacking. Seigneurial authority, too, was most effective in areas where its subjects lived in closed communities rather than on dispersed farms.[30] To sum up, rural industrial regions could only develop where the village community and the lord did not have the power to enforce social cohesion. Where such cohesion still existed it had to loosen or dissolve altogether in order for population growth and the differentiation process among the peasantry to assert themselves.

The power-constellations and their impact on the spatial expansion of industrial commodity production were different in east-central and eastern Europe. Peasants were more directly and more firmly dominated by their lords, and there was little room for the development of rural industries. The few concentrations of industry which can be found in peripheral areas are not to be explained by the disintegration of the lord–peasant relationship. Instead, the feudal lords, for example those in Upper Lusatia or those of the Silesian–Bohemian border area, promoted industrial commodity production as an alternative to cereal production within the framework of the social relations of *Gutsherrschaft*. They released desmesne land and common meadows for the settlement of cottagers and consequently furthered population growth.[31] The lord–peasant relationship loosened only after the politics of the feudal lords had changed.

The rural relations of production contributed indirectly to the expansion of rural industries insofar as they often empowered the feudal lords to appropriate a large portion of the agrarian product. In the eighteenth century, the feudal quota, i.e. the portion extracted from the rural net income (gross yield minus expenses), amounted to between 38 and 46 per cent in central Europe.[32] During this time about 70–80 per cent of central European peasants rarely retained an income sufficient to assure a family's livelihood, after expenses and feudal dues had been deducted.[33] The majority of the rural population was consequently forced to look for a supplementary income outside of their farms.

But whether a region developed rural industries or not was determined not so much by the extent of feudal charges as by the form in which peasants paid them. And the form of payment was determined not only by the social relationship in the narrow sense between the feudal lord and his dependent peasants but also by the overall relations of production. Social surplus labour could be appropriated in the form of labour dues on one hand or in the form of payments in kind and money dues on the other hand, and either of these forms corresponded with a different set of relations of production.

The form in which social surplus labour was appropriated also marked a specific stage in the historical process, but this process did not occur simultaneously in the different parts of Europe. It generated regressive and devolutionary developments which made visible the structures of dependence that had emerged in Europe since the turn of the sixteenth century. The transition of *Gutsherrschaft* in east-central and eastern Europe can be interpreted as a devolutionary development in this sense. Several factors contributed to the process which resulted in the refeudalization of east-Elbian agriculture. The agrarian crisis of the late Middle Ages had produced deserted villages and had tied the peasants to the soil; it had thereby created the material and social pre-conditions for the expansion of the system of *Gutswirtschaft*. During the sixteenth century, the demand for cereals in western-European markets (in Russia the domestic market functioned like a foreign market because of its size) generated the forces which replaced the economy that had been based on money rents, with a manorial economy based on the extraction of forced labour from peasant serfs. This process was reinforced by the seventeenth-century crisis, a crisis which in Russia began as early as the 1560s, owing to the specific conditions of her autocratic system.[34] As the landlords imposed labour services on the peasant family, the time potentially available for domestic industry shrank, since a part of its labour time had to be given to the *Gutsherr*. Nonetheless, even when peasants had to render labour service six days a week, the agricultural work was subject to seasonal fluctuations and thereby to a *'limite technologique'* which prevented its exploitation by the lords to the *'limite sociale'* or even *'physiologique'* (W. Kula).[35]

The fact is that the fully developed *Gutswirtschaft* with its characteristic cereal monoculture and its labour system did not permit the development of industrial commodity production in the countryside. Demographic growth was compara-tively limited. In its demand for labour power the *Gutswirtschaft* resorted primarily to the labour dues of the peasant population. Consequently, only a small number of less than full-size holdings emerged which allowed their occupants to form families and be reproductively active. But a large number of servant positions were created so that the frequency of marriage and the birthrate remained relatively low.[36]

In contrast to money rents, labour dues arrested the process of social differentiation within the peasantry. The logic of the manorial system based on serf labour demanded that the lord had to preserve the peasant holding at all cost because it functioned as a supplier of labour power and of draft power. Therefore it was in his interest to assist peasants in emergencies which arose from harvest failures and other causes.[37] As a result he prevented their sliding into a rural sub-stratum. To be sure, such a sub-stratum did exist in manorial villages on a small scale, but since the lord prevented the differentiation process from taking its course, one of the sources of its growth was blocked. The reservoir of labour power necessary for the expansion of rural industry remained limited. Furthermore, since the *Gutsherr* exercised a secure monopoly in the labour market it remained inelastic. *Gutswirtschaft* was incompatible with the growth of rural industries because they both drew upon the same labour supply.

The expansion of industrial commodity production encountered less restrictive conditions in the mountain areas of east-central Europe and in that part of central Russia which does not belong to the black-earth belt. Here the development of *Gutswirtschaft* had stagnated because the soil was unfavourable to cereal production and market ties were lacking that might have joined these areas to the great consumer centres. Often it proved financially more feasible to divide up at least part of the area of existing estates and settle cottagers on the partitions, rather than to administer and cultivate them in their entireties. The *Gutswirtschaft* reverted to *Grundherrschaft*, but it preserved its characteristic legal system of 'second serfdom'.[38] Russia provides the clearest example of this phenomenon. In 1765–7, while 75 per cent of the manorial peasants of the black-earth belt of central Russia were charged with labour dues (*barshchina*) and only 25 per cent with money rents (*obrok*) (1858: 73.1 per cent and 26.9 per cent respectively), the equivalent percentages for the area outside the black-earth belt, i.e. for the industrial centre of early modern Russia, amounted to 40.8 per cent and 59.2 per cent (1858: 32.5 per cent and 67.5 per cent respectively). In the densely industrialized province of Jaroslavl', 64.1 per cent of manorial peasants had to pay '*obrok*' in 1765 (1858: 87.4 per cent).[39] In eighteenth-century Russia, '*obrok*' was practically synonymous with industrial employment and withdrawal from agriculture.[40]

The transition to money rents set in motion a process of differentiation which not only increased the number and size of rural groups who were dependent on industrial by-occupations, but occasionally also stimulated the emergence of rural entrepreneurship.[41] While the preconditions for the expansion of industrial commodity production thus existed in these regions, the continuing right of the *Gutsherr* to interfere with the personal freedom of his serfs had dysfunctional effects. To be sure, the feudal lords of the Silesian border area as well as those in Upper Lusatia and Bohemia favoured the shift of linen production to the countryside, but they thwarted its development by drawing the linen industry into the system of feudal obligations. They revived labour services (in the form of spinning and weaving) which probably dated back to the Middle Ages – the latter of which was commuted into the so-called *Weberzins* (weaver's rent) at the beginning of the seventeenth century. They apparently exercised the right of pre-emption on the remaining linen cloth produced by their subjects. They limited their serfs' mobility, though they granted them the right to buy their freedom.[42] Similar observations can be made in southern Poland and in Russia, even though the rise of such textile centres as Andrychów (southern Poland) and Ivanovo (northern-central Russia), to mention only two examples, could not be prevented in the long run.[43] All things considered, the incongruity between economic development and an inflexible legal system, between the disintegration of *Gutswirtschaft* and the continuation of 'second serfdom', constituted a severe impediment to the development of industrial commodity production in the countryside.

In Germany, west of the Elbe and in western Europe, the commutation of labour services into rents in kind and especially into money rents had begun with the dissolution of the manorial system. While this process was sometimes interrupted by the agrarian crises of the late Middle Ages, it was never seriously threatened until it reached its completion (though a few special cases do not fit into this pattern). In this respect nothing prevented the penetration of industry into the countryside. England was most deeply affected by the development of the rural relations of production. The appropriation of social surplus labour in the form of feudal rent was discarded and the adoption of short-term modern leases changed the feudal rent into a capitalistic ground rent. Since the sixteenth century, English agriculture became commercialized and the re-lations of production were increasingly determined by the laws of the market. Population growth, a deepening social division of labour, and the growing demand for wool generated by an expanding textile industry converged and destroyed the traditional agrarian structures.[44] The collectivism which had hitherto determined the village economy was replaced by 'agrarian in-dividualism' (Marc Bloch). This opened up the possibility to introduce modern agrarian methods like convertible husbandry. The enclosure movement, in which the emerging 'agrarian individualism' manifested itself, as well as the process of differentiation and polarization to which the peasantry was subjected, left a deep mark on the rural social system. The number of families who had to find some kind of side-occupation grew rapidly. The cottagers who lost their main source of income when the common land was partitioned and distributed among private owners were practically forced into rural industry. With the emerging stratification of English agrarian society into landowners, tenants, and rural labourers the traditional structures disintegrated completely.[45] No-where did the development of industrial commodity production in the countryside run so directly parallel to the re-organization of the rural relations of production according to the laws of the market as it did in England.

(b) Factors operating outside the agrarian sector

If industrial commodity production was to develop into full-scale proto-industrialization, the specific changes in the agrarian sector had to interact with the changes in supra-regional markets. Merchant capital had to develop and exploit the unutilized resources which existed in the countryside.

The secular growth-periods in European economic history broke the power of the towns.[46] Their productive potential did not meet the demand because the high labour intensity of pre-factory industrial commodity production required the involvement of large numbers of workers in the production process. Hence the rural labour force had to be mobilized. In view of the urban economy's low elasticity of supply, merchant capital had no choice but to shift production to the countryside. Often, foreign demand provided the incentive, and it could develop into a trend which – a few short-term interruptions not-withstanding – superseded even the secular growth-phases.[47] According to Adam Smith's classic theory of commerce, namely the vent-for-surplus theory, foreign demand made it possible for unutilized resources in the countryside – especially labour power and, to a lesser extent, natural resources – to find a different outlet. The opportunity costs of such factors were zero since their utilization did not imply that they were withdrawn from productive utilization elsewhere. When a country embarked upon foreign trade, an effective demand for its goods opened up which permitted the exploitation of resources whose previous utilization had been prevented by the inelasticity of domestic demand. In this way, a country which had been largely excluded from world trade could simultaneously strengthen its foreign trade position as well as its internal economic capacity without incurring 'costs'.[48]

Occasionally, opening a region to trade provoked arrangements between foreign merchants and feudal lords which resembled the 'classic pattern of colonial penetration' (H. Kisch).[49] The unutilized resources to be tapped did not only consist in labour power and raw materials but also in peasant skills. The 'nouvelles draperies', for example, as well as linen production can be viewed as the 'commercialization of peasant techniques' (D. C. Coleman).[50]

Not only was the urban economy's supply inelastic, but its productive relations were also constrained by guilds. They increasingly came into contradiction with the dynamic of the economy's growth, keeping the elasticity of supply low. The economic policy of the guilds was guided by the need of their members to earn a livelihood. Its goal was the adequate support of the individual guild members. It was unfavourable to growth insofar as it tried to control the expansion of individual workshops which necessarily threatened the existence of others. For this purpose the guilds limited the artisans' output, controlled the competition of price and quality, opposed the introduction of new production techniques and new products, and limited the access to the market.[51] In order to escape such limitations, merchant capitalists turned to the countryside. The urban crafts, unaccustomed to competition from rural industries, were unable to resist it and collapsed.[52] Occasionally, a division of labour arose between town and country in the course of the conflict.[53]

It must be admitted, however, that some cities succeeded in considerably expanding their internal field of economic operations, even if only temporarily. The most notable examples are the Italian cities of the late Middle Ages, but it applies to others as well. The Nürnberg putters-out manufacturers created a veritable industrial 'reserve army' by employing piece rate workers who, it has been estimated, amounted to one third of the labouring population (H. Aubin).[54]

Last but not least, there was the cost factor which favoured the shift of industrial production to the countryside. Raw materials were often cheaper in the countryside than in the town. The tax pressure which weighed on artisans tended to be lower in the rural areas than within the town walls.[55] The cost of living, too, was lower in the countryside. The important point, however, is the following: insofar as the rural artisans possessed a piece of land and thereby had a subsistence base in agriculture, they could forgo part of their wages, i.e. they could work under conditions where their remuneration did not suffice to cover the cost of reproducing their labour power as well as the renewal costs of their means of production. Merchants and putters-out exploited the dismal situation of the rural sub-stratum that was dependent on rural by-occupations but lacked the support of a guild. They drove down the rural wages far below the level that was customary under the conditions of guild production in the towns. A merchant or putter-out who utilized rural labour power thus obtained a differential profit, though it tended to disappear as the new production system became widespread.[56] Especially in times like the late Middle Ages and the seventeenth century, when industrial prices fell and wages tended to rise, merchant capital was necessarily more inclined to forestall the sinking of incomes by utilizing rural labour power.[57]

In east-central and eastern Europe, special conditions accounted for the rise of rural industries. The economic regression resulting from Poland's transition to *Gutswirtschaft* and the terribly destructive wars of the seventeenth and early eighteenth centuries had greatly diminished the towns' economic importance. At the end of the seventeenth century rural industries began to benefit from this situation.[58] In Russia, it was the weakness of the urban economy that accounted for the emergence of rural industrial regions.[59]

3. Proto-industrialization

(a) Origins, inter-regional connections, indicators

The first regions of relatively dense rural industry had developed in England, the southern Low Countries, and southern Germany in the late Middle Ages.[60] The decisive thrust which brought about the phase of proto-industrialization came at the end of the sixteenth and in the seventeenth centuries. The forces behind it did not differ from those which had operated since the end of the thirteenth century, but now they were gaining a new dimension. Quantitative changes in supply and demand combined to produce a cumulative process which led to a new phase.[61] A situation extremely favourable to the development of production centres in the countryside was created by a number of factors: the long waves of the agrarian cycle and the trend periods of population growth connected to these waves by a feedback system; the increasing underemployment in the countryside resulting from population growth; the crisis of agricultural incomes in the seventeenth and early eighteenth centuries which led to a differentiation in production. To this should be added a slight increase in domestic demand resulting from the recovery of real wages (on the continent, however, this was more than offset by the decline of agricultural incomes), as well as a greatly expanding international demand, not least of all in colonial markets whose demand for industrial products was rapidly gaining importance since the seventeenth century (Eric Hobsbawm: 'new colonialism').[62] The towns with their limited productive capacity could not respond to this new situation. Owing to developments in the markets for production factors and goods and to the advantages that could be gained from locating in the countryside, merchant capitalists now chose to utilize the rural resources.

When one considers the inner logic of the two systems under discussion, proto-industrialization constitutes the solution of two different sets of problems which had arisen in the agrarian sector on one hand, and in the industrial sector on the other hand, and which neither sector could solve on its own. These sets of problems concern, on one side, the demographic growth and differentiation process which the peasant population underwent and, on the other side, the low elasticity of supply of the urban economy. They became soluble only when both sectors interacted with each other. Increasing asymmetries in the economic structure were overcome by the formation of a new system which enhanced the capability of European societies to direct their economic affairs. In the long run, however, it generated new problems whose solution was to prove impossible under the conditions of a pre-industrial economy.

As was described above, rural industries producing for supra-regional markets developed in a large number of regions. Such proto-industrial zones contrasted with their agrarian environment, but they also became dependent on adjacent agrarian zones for basic foodstuffs and raw materials, as their labour force shifted to industrial commodity production. The gap between supply and demand which widened in the course of proto-industrial development had to be closed by provisions from outside. Only when proto-industry and commercial agriculture developed together could such regions preserve their self-sufficiency, but this occurred only rarely. The process which called forth a certain inter-regional division of labour was always initiated by industrial regions, but it required a positive response from their agrarian environment.[63] Only when such a response was forthcoming could proto-industrialization occur. Such inter-regional dependence could also arise from developments which originated in those agrarian regions that were linked to specific industrial regions. As was pointed out earlier, the reasons for relegation of proto-industry to harsh mountainous areas, which depended on food supply from outside, sometimes lie in the valleys and plains below. The rigid social order of the lowlands, characterized by the three-field-system, kept population-growth low and prevented rural industry from making significant inroads. It was forced to move to the mountains where a more open and more flexible social order prevailed.

East of the Elbe, cereal monoculture, based on *Gutswirtschaft*, dominated the fertile plains and pushed rural industries to the remoter regions that were remote from markets, such as the mountain zones of east-central Europe and that part of central Russia which lay outside the black-earth belt.[64] Rural industries which concentrated in stock-raising regions mostly stood at the end of a development that had begun during the seventeenth century crisis when agrarian production underwent significant changes in location. A number of regions had then turned to grazing because, owing to the general pressure on prices, they could not withstand the competition of the more efficiently producing cereal regions. Their soils were not suitable to the new methods of cultivation whose introduction, particularly in England, was favoured by the crisis.[65] Such stock-raising regions needed rural industries to compensate the population for their loss of employment that arose when grain cultivation was abandoned. Several lines of development crossed each other as the inter-regional structure of agrarian and industrial zones emerged. This structure took shape as a result of a series of often conflicting pushes and pulls, and it is not always possible to determine which of several factors carried the greater weight.

The introduction of a new term to characterize a specific stage in socio-economic development is justified only if it can be operationalized. It must be possible to assign to it empirically verifiable indicators. The most obvious are a micro-economic and a macro-economic indicator. From the viewpoint of agrarian producers, taking up an industrial occupation meant that an industrial income was added to their agricultural income. A gap opened between property and income which in peasant society had tended to be seen as a whole: income from industry was no longer related to the land and therefore to property.[66] In contrast to the agrarian income, it had to be almost totally realized in the market. In theory, a line could be drawn where the industrial income exceeded the agrarian income, or in other terms, where the supplementary occupation turned into the primary occupation.

This micro-economic indicator should be complemented by a macro-economic indicator: the share of the primary sector on one hand, and the secondary and tertiary sectors on the other hand, in creating the total national product and in employing the labouring population. But a clear dividing line cannot be drawn in either case; thus it cannot be maintained that the critical stage was reached either when the greater part of the household budget was earned in the secondary and tertiary sectors, or when the major part of the national product was created in these sectors and the majority of labourers employed in them. Therefore qualitative indicators must be added, such as the specific demographic pattern of proto-industrial populations, the destabilization of the traditional social structure of the villages, and the production for supra-regional and international markets.[67]

(b) The agrarian context

According to the model of agrarian specialization, those peasant holdings which were sufficiently equipped with land as their most important production factor concentrated on agricultural production and gave up the making of industrial products for home consumption, while those holdings which were poorly equipped with land and whose agriculturally employed labour therefore rapidly reached a marginal productivity of zero specialized in industrial products which they had always made for home consumption, but which they now began to produce for the market.[68] The assumptions of this model lead us to expect that agriculture in the first case approximates the commercial type and in the second case, comes close to the subsistence type.[69] But it is not necessarily true that commercial farms did not exist in proto-industrial regions; in fact, sometimes they were characteristic of the agriculture in those regions. Nonetheless, some of the factors which favoured the adoption of industrial occupations by groups of rural dwellers also pushed the entire agriculture in the direction of the subsistence type. Given the technological conditions of the period, poor soils and other unfavourable natural conditions prevented the commercialization of agriculture. Population pressure, especially where it generated extreme land fragmentation, restricted agriculture to the narrow confines of the subsistence holding. Owing to firmly implanted feudal controls, the peasant lacked the independence to respond positively to market impulses and to enter into the process of specialization.[70] And indeed, in many proto-industrial regions of Europe, for example in Brittany, Overijssel, the mountainous regions of central Germany, and the foothills of the Carpathians, proto-industrialization and subsistence agriculture went together.[71] We may therefore in principle conclude that the subsistence farm must be considered as the agrarian basis of proto-industrialization.

The concrete forms which agriculture took in regions with concentrated rural industries deserve to be elaborated. Despite what was said earlier, those forms could vary greatly. On one end of the scale, one finds the 'garden' agriculture of central Flanders, famous all over Europe, and a flourishing agriculture in the area above Zürich; at the other end, there is the poor agriculture of the area in which the Calwer Zeughandlungskompagnie operated (the eastern part of the Black Forest).[72] Several factors account for such stages of agricultural intensification in proto-industrial regions. First, it was important how much the agricultural income contributed to the family's total income. The smaller that proportion was, due to the small size of the family's holding, the more the petty industrial producers developed a tendency to neglect agriculture altogether and to devote their labour to industrial production. Forced by necessity, they had at first turned to the intensification of agriculture only to abandon it in favour of rural industry when the possibility had arisen. A Silesian cottar's family, for example, could generally survive only if it concentrated all its energy on the production of linen.

Secondly, the degree to which the petty industrial producers as a group shared in the total arable land must be taken into account. In general, they cultivated their land quite intensively, despite the marginal case mentioned above. But if their share in the total arable was small in a given region, only a small amount of land became subject to intensive tillage and their influence on the agrarian structure of that region remained insignificant. While in central Flanders the entire society and economy were characterized by intensive soil utilization owing to extreme fragmentation, in the Westphalian linen region it remained limited to the land cultivated by the cottars (Heuerlinge).

Thirdly, the social framework which regulated the utilization of the land must be considered. Where it was sufficiently flexible, agriculture could achieve a high degree of intensity despite its subsistence character. Where this was not the case and agriculture was made inflexible by a rigid three-field system with compulsive rotations, it maintained its extensive character. Under such conditions, domestic industry and agriculture were difficult to combine, and the proto-industrial family might 'prefer the easy work done inside the home to the arduous labour in the fields'.[73]

When proto-industrialization gained a foothold in a region of commercial agriculture despite these basic assumptions, special circumstances are usually responsible. First of all, commercial agriculture, generally, could only develop in a highly urbanized region. The concentrated demand of a large town or a whole network of towns was necessary in order to induce the self-sufficient peasant family holding to enter on the path of specialization.[74] Furthermore, it must be remembered that commercial agriculture generated a considerable demand for additional labour. It created a need for and promoted the development of specifically rural crafts and of transportation networks. A large proportion of the rural population surplus was also absorbed by the town which dominated a given agricultural region.[75] Consequently, the decisive precondition of proto-industrialization, namely the elasticity of the labour supply, was largely lacking. Labour was available only at 'opportunity costs' above zero. Rural industries could generally not establish themselves in such regions.[76]

If, despite all this, they did succeed, the explanation is likely to lie in the role of the cities. Here the decisive impulses for the commercialization of agriculture as well as for the spatial expansion of industrial commodity production originated – processes which occurred roughly simultaneously. Sooner or later competition for the rural labour power was bound to arise between agriculture and merchant capital.[77] Proto-industrialization became a burden for the agrarian sector, imposed upon it by merchant capital.

In commercial stock-raising regions, the situation was somewhat different. Here industrial commodity production had often made inroads before the seventeenth-century crisis had forced producers to give up grain cultivation in favour of stock-raising.[78] The latter system's low labour-intensity made the further expansion of industrial commodity production possible. Difficulties arose when stock-raising developed into dairy farming with its high labour-intensity.

The distinguishing feature between proto-industrial regions with subsistence farming and those with commercial agriculture was the fact that the latter were largely self-sufficient with regard to their food supply (not including stock-raising regions), whereas the former needed food imports. The agrarian surplus of other regions had to cover their food deficit. The feature which both had in common was the subsistence character of the agricultural pursuits of petty industrial producers. Their agricultural activities had no other goal but to contribute, in whichever form, to the food needs of the individual family and to the need for flax and hemp in the case of a family of spinners.

The agrarian sector made a four-fold contribution to proto-industrialization. It contributed labour, commercial as well as entrepreneurial skill and capital, products, and markets. But the comprehensive term 'agrarian sector' conceals a number of different territorial entities: first, the region which turned to industrial commodity production (it contributed labour, commercial and entrepreneurial skill and capital); secondly, the agrarian zones which were linked to the industrializing regions (they contributed products); and thirdly, the agriculture of the economic orbit to which the industrial regions belonged (it contributed the market). The agrarian sector laid the foundation for proto-industrialization by providing a surplus of labour power. But is it correct to say that the agrarian sector actually made all these contributions?

As far as the labour supply is concerned, it must be taken into consideration that the population did not grow in the seventeenth century and was even considerably reduced in some areas.[79] But as was shown earlier, no significant labour scarcity occurred because of the downward movement of the secular cycle; furthermore proto-industrial regions, due to their specific demographic pattern, were well equipped to generate their own labour supply. Any bottlenecks were almost certainly overcome by the rapid population growth of the eighteenth century. Still, three important qualifications must be made. The elasticity of the labour supply could be limited if population growth and the differentiation process within the peasantry were subject to heavy seigneurial and communal controls, if the *Gutsherr* exercised a monopoly in the labour market, or if a large part of the labour power was absorbed by commercial agriculture.[80] Disregarding these marginal cases, proto-industrialization can be described as 'economic development with unlimited supplies of labour' (W. A. Lewis).[81] Basically, the 'unlimited-supplies-of-labour' theory applies much more to proto-industrialization, especially during its early phase, than to the industrialization of today's underdeveloped countries. Under modern conditions of underdevelopment and industrialization, the withdrawal of labour power from the agrarian sector presents difficult problems even in cases where the marginal productivity of labour is near zero. The level of production can only be maintained when the relations of production are transformed and new agrarian techniques are introduced.[82] This was different in proto-industrialization. The rural industrial producer remained on his plot of land, and when the seasonal demand for agricultural labour rose he made himself available as farm labourer. Consequently, the agrarian product did not fall. In the labour market the requirements of agriculture and proto-industry – at least during its early phase – did not conflict.[83]

In addition to labour, the agrarian sector contributed commercial and entrepreneurial skill and capital to proto-industrialization. Of minor importance were the activities of the landed nobility in central and western Europe.[84] In east-central and eastern Europe, the nobility gradually withdrew from exercising entrepreneurial functions which they had initially attempted to do on the basis of their seigneurial power. They largely restrained themselves to solidifying a relationship which rested on the payment of tributes from proto-industrial producers.[85] Generally, it was a hindrance rather than a help for proto-industry when a feudal lord made an attempt to intervene, particularly when he organized commodity production on the basis of forced labour.

Wealthy, business-minded peasants, on the other hand, and members of the village 'bourgeoisie' often assumed a strategic function in the proto-industrialization process. They became the middlemen between domestic producers and the merchant. They constituted the personnel of the putting-out system's infrastructure. Occasionally, they became involved in the finishing of products, especially in bleaching if they had access to the necessary meadows. Often they, rather than the large putters-out in the cities, became the true agents of the industrialization process. They were closer to the production process and therefore more familiar with its requirements.[86] But this rural group of middlemen lacked a field of operations and did not develop where, as in eastern Westphalia, the quality of the products was controlled through organizations that were backed up by the community or the government. It was decisive for the formation of such a group that the agrarian relations should permit a maximum of social mobility within the rural population, and this condition was generally fulfilled in western Europe, but not in large parts of east-central and eastern Europe. The *Gutswirtschaft* did not promote the emergence of an economically viable village trade and of rural entrepreneurship. Such groups became established only in areas where the gradual disintegration of *Gutswirtschaft* and the transition to money rents had brought down the barriers against social differentiation within the peasantry.[87] Still, the very exceptional position which the peasant-merchants of Andrychów in Lesser Poland occupied, or the serf entrepreneurs in Russia like the Grachevs, Garelins, and Jamanskiis in Ivanovo, can be fully explained only by the weakness of the urban merchant capital.[88]

The production of an agrarian surplus had been the pre-condition for the development of the simple market economy of the high Middle Ages. But the rural industrial region did not depend on this prerequisite in quite the same way, and that fact constituted one of its characteristic features as well as an advantage over the town. Since the petty industrial producers usually continued to have some subsistence base in agriculture, no matter how limited, and since industrial employment was initially no more than a secondary occupation, the acquisition of food did not, at least in theory, present a problem. The – admittedly unstable – equilibrium between population and agrarian resources was put into question, however, as soon as the demographic growth-mechanisms characteristic of proto-industrialization took effect and population groups developed that were only insufficiently backed up by agricultural property, or not at all. The agrarian surplus had to be increased if the further expansion of proto-industrialization was not to find its end in recurrent food crises.[89]

It is true that the agrarian producer and the industrial worker – often they were the same – adjusted to the new situation by adopting more intensive methods of cultivation as well as new crops. The potato, for example, was introduced in many industrial regions after the subsistence crisis of 1771–4, if not earlier.[90] But that was rarely sufficient to close the gap between supply and demand. Many proto-industrial regions, especially those with subsistence agriculture, became dependent on adjacent regions for their basic foodstuffs.[91] A certain inter-regional division of labour became necessary, but if it was to survive crisis periods, agricultural productivity had to be high enough in order to generate regular large surpluses. Even in the eighteenth century, this was true only for a few areas of commercial agriculture in continental Europe.[92] The conclusion therefore seems to be that the level of the forces of production in agriculture set certain limits to proto-industrialization which could not be disregarded with impunity. In England, conditions were much more favourable. Here the agrarian crisis of the second half of the seventeenth and the first half of the eighteenth centuries was averted by decisive advances in productivity, namely the introduction of convertible husbandry. In the course of this development, agrarian regions emerged which sharply contrasted with each other, and proto-industrialization concentrated in those regions which turned to stock-raising.[93] The steadily progressing disintegration of the peasant economy opened the path for an agrarian production that was entirely market oriented.[94] Proto-industrialization therefore could expand without being significantly handicapped by bottlenecks of supply.

Not only did the agrarian sector have to supply food to the proto-industrial producers, it also had to provide such raw materials and fuels as flax, wool, and timber. The two tasks were not always compatible. Especially during the secular growth phases of the European economy they tended to conflict, for the growth of population implied that land under cereal crops had to be expanded at the expense of land cultivated with fibrous plants, meadows, pastures, and forests. This bottleneck was alleviated by the introduction of more intensive systems of cultivation and the import of raw materials from overseas. The bottleneck in the supply of fuel was not eliminated until wood was replaced by coal. Here as in so many other cases, England was ahead of her continental rivals.[95] And once again it can be observed that rural industrial regions became dependent on neighbouring regions for their supply of raw materials and semi-finished products.[96]

A similar difference between England and the continent, as it has just been described for the product contributions of the agrarian sector, existed with regard to direct and indirect market contributions. The crisis of the seventeenth century brought income reductions for agriculture on the continent, and it must be assumed that the sale of industrial products suffered as a consequence. In England, by contrast, the income reductions in the agrarian sector were more than compensated by advances in productivity.[97] Therefore the agrarian sector's market demands are unlikely to have fallen much. The agrarian trend of the eighteenth century did not substantially change this situation. While agricultural incomes rose on the continent, the size and structure of holdings as well as the constraints of the feudal system made it impossible for most agrarian producers to generate much domestic demand for industrial products.[98]

In east-central and eastern Europe, the peasant holding had been reduced by the resurgence of the manorial system based on serf labour, (W. Kula) to a 'parcelle de subsistence et de reproduction (simple)', and the market relations of the peasant population were radically reduced.[99] Here, as in many areas of central and western Europe, the relations of production did not permit the peasant economy to specialize. In no more than a few favoured regions was peasant labour power re-allocated to the production of agricultural goods for the market and pulled out of the production of industrial products for home consumption. Only where the peasant economy was thus seized and transformed by the social division of labour could it develop an effective demand in the domestic market.[100] With the disintegration of the peasantry as a social group the market economy penetrated into the agrarian sector.

The indirect market contributions of the agrarian sector, i.e. the income effects which it generated in other sectors and which affected their demand, stood more or less in opposition to the direct market contributions. But here, too, England occupied a special position. When the seventeenth-century crisis altered the terms of trade between agrarian and industrial products, purchasing power was released in favour of the seoondary sector. But only in England did the domestic market expand with the opening of the price scissors, for the gains in purchasing power among the wage earners and petty commodity producers were not offset by losses in purchasing power among agrarian producers, as it was the case in France and Germany.[101] To be sure, in England, too, the boom of agrarian prices exerted pressure on the income of the masses in the second half of the eighteenth century, but as far as we know, the expansion of domestic demand was not affected significantly thanks to the rapid increase of 'medium' incomes.[102]

The productivity advances of English agriculture not only secured a steadily growing domestic market for the products of proto-industry, but also contributed to the stabilization of that market. The intensification of the production process, i.e. the increasing input of labour and capital, not only improved the natural quality of the soil, but also made agrarian production less dependent on the vagaries of nature. The extremes of the harvest cycle became less pronounced and as a consequence the crises of the 'type ancien' (E. Labrousse), which used to determine the movements of the pre-industrial economy, declined in severity.

Crises of the old type were crises of shortage and not of overproduction. They began with a harvest failure which steeply raised the price of basic foodstuffs. They then moved from the agrarian sector to the industrial sector, because they redirected that part of the purchasing power normally concentrated on industrial products to the agrarian sector, where it benefited those few producers who could bring grain to the market despite the harvest failure. The drastic decline in the final purchasing power of consumers, brought about by the surge in subsistence costs, threw the industries into severe hardship. The 'crise de sous-production agricole', as Labrousse put it, gave rise to the 'sous-consommation de produits industriels', especially the under-consumption of textiles, and thus unleashed a 'crise de surproduction industrielle relative'.[103]

The fact that in agrarian societies the harvest cycle functioned as a regulator of the reproduction process can be explained, on the micro-economic level, by the large share of total expenses which individual households spent on food; on the macro-economic level, it can be explained by the large share which the agrarian sector comprised of the social product. The composition of the household budget and the social product determined the size of the margin that was available to counteract a sudden large increase in agrarian prices. If the share of food expenses and the agrarian product fell, this margin increased and the vulnerability of the economy declined. Therefore, countries such as England, where the agrarian sector's share of the social product declined to less than 50 per cent in the course of the eighteenth century,[104] were better shielded against harvest crises than those where agriculture still dominated. England, thus, had a double advantage: not only did the harvest crises decline in severity, the reduced importance of the agrarian sector also limited their effect. In the last analysis both advantages had their origin in the increased productivity of English agriculture. The short-term crises of the 'type ancien' almost precluded long-term planning within the industrial sector. Their decline was therefore of great importance for the development of industry. The possibility to plan the country's overall social and economic development improved decisively.

As far as the agrarian sector is concerned, then, the prerequisites for industrial commodity production in the countryside were much more favourable in England than they were on the continent, even though on the continent, as well, the crises of the old type lost some of their force in the course of the eighteenth century. Ultimately this divergence has its origin in the relations of production. Wherever the collective controls of the village were still unbroken

During the sixteenth century, few of the products manufactured in the European metropolitan countries found their way overseas, even though the periphery was gradually gaining importance as a market for industrial goods. England came to dominate the market for heavy cloth. Her cloth exports increased by 81 per cent during the first half of the sixteenth century (1498/1502–1550/52), then entered a crisis, and stabilized at 110,500 'short cloths' annually during the last quarter of the century. They lost ground again since the crisis of 1619–22 which was exacerbated by the Alderman-Cockayne project. The bulk of exported English cloth went to central Europe and, increasingly during the second half of the sixteenth century, the Baltic region as well as the Mediterranean countries. Here, during the seventeenth century, the 'new draperies' for the first time replaced the heavy cloth as the staple product of the English export trade.[114] During the sixteenth century the colonial regions seem to have been of importance only for the European linen production.[115] In 1553 the Spanish Netherlands exported 83,819 pieces of linen cloth to Spain via Antwerp.[116] In 1594, 980,710 'varas' of linen cloth found their way from Brittany to the West Indies.[117] Rouen confessed in 1601: 'Les toiles sont les vrayes mines de l'or et argent en ce royaume parce qu'elles ne s'enlèvent que pour estre transportées au pays d'où l'on apporte de l'or et de l'argent.'[118] And the cloth production of Lille has been shown to correlate with the fluctuations of the Spanish-America trade.[119]

Trade within Europe was heavily affected by the crisis of the seventeenth century. The east-central European share of international trade declined rapidly. The Mediterranean countries, which had traditionally been a region of growth, stagnated or declined.[120] Italy, Portugal, and Spain moved toward the periphery. The centre of the world economy shifted to north-western Europe, which was less heavily hit by the crisis. Only since the turn of the eighteenth century were there signs of a renewed upswing.[121] The fairs of Leipzig became the focal point of the west–east trade in central Europe and through these fairs, west- and central-European textiles found their way to the East.[122] Beginning in the 1720s, the passage of ships through the Danish Sound increased enormously.[123] France almost quintupled her trade with the European countries between the end of the reign of Louis XIV and the Revolution.[124]

Nevertheless, the crisis of the seventeenth century was mitigated by the surge in the Atlantic trade which – in turn – helped stimulate the upswing of the eighteenth century. The Atlantic system, based on unequal exchange and open violence, had its origins in the sixteenth century, but it became more clearly delineated during the seventeenth century as plantation economies developed in Brazil and on the West Indian islands, as well as settler colonies in America. Western and central Europe furnished finished products, means of transportation, and capital equipment; Africa contributed slaves who were needed on the labour-intensive plantations of Central America; tropical America contributed tobacco, sugar, and – since the eighteenth century – cotton; North America furnished timber, cattle, grain, and furs.[125] This market network became the most dynamic sector of the world economy which was dominated by the European core. Other sectors of the world economy were deeply affected. Russia and Asia, which had stood outside, were drawn into it as peripheral areas since the eighteenth century and subjected to the reproduction needs of the core.[126] The world market whose threads converged in Europe became all-inclusive. It became more difficult for countries outside of Europe henceforth to develop autonomously and according to laws of their own.

The foreign trade of the European core-countries was at first determined by the re-export of colonial products from the underdeveloped world. In the course of the eighteenth century, re-exports lost their pride of place to the export of finished products shipped to America, Africa, and Asia. In 1699–1701, only 16.4 per cent of the English domestic export of finished products went to those continents; in 1772–4, the figure had already risen to 55.0 per cent. The export of English finished products to the European continent, which comprised 81.2 per cent of the country's total domestic export in 1699–1701, stagnated because English cloth had to compete with growing 'national' textile industries.[127] France was less advanced than England. In 1787, only 31.5 per cent of her export of finished products went to colonial areas (1716: 11.0 per cent), and their share of total exports was only 34.2 per cent (1716: 36.8 per cent). But her foreign trade was growing faster than that of England. Her colonial trade grew tenfold between 1716 and 1787 alone.[128] Due to her colonial trade, textile exports, which rapidly lost ground in southern Europe during the 1760s, could preserve their absolute size; their relative size declined compared with the year 1750.[129]

Almost the entire European linen industry became an appendage to the Atlantic economy, and the economic indicators of that industry were entirely determined by the Atlantic system.[130] When in 1787, J. L. P. Hüpeden called the Hessian linen trade the 'Hessian Peru and East India' and said that it was 'the main channel through which Spanish gold and silver flows into our coffers',[131] he could have referred with equal justification to the Breton, Flemish, Westphalian, or Silesian linen trade. Between 1748–9 and 1789–90, an average of 75.6 per cent of the Silesian linen export went to western Europe and overseas.[132] In the second half of the eighteenth century, the 'bretañas', mostly produced in the area of the Bishopric of Saint-Brieuc (southwest of Saint-Malô), found their markets almost exclusively on the other side of the Atlantic, primarily in Spanish America.[133] The export quota of countries with proto-industrial regions could be extraordinarily large. During the eighteenth century, about one third of British industrial production was exported. Between 1695 and 1799, the share (by value) of the English woollen industry that was exported rose from about 40 to over 67 per cent; in West Riding alone it amounted to 72.3 per cent. In 1770, about 60 per cent of Irish linen production was sold abroad (1784: about 56 per cent). Bohemia, in 1796, exported about 51 per cent of her linen (1797: 43 per cent).[134]

Proto-industrialization stands between two worlds: the narrow world of the village and the world of trade that crosses all boundaries, between the agrarian economy and merchant capitalism. The agrarian sector contributed labour, commercial and entrepreneurial skill, capital, products, and markets. Merchant capital opened up foreign markets on whose capacity for expansion the rural handicrafts depended if they were to enter proto-industrialization. The dualistic structure of pre-industrial European societies thus became the soil on which capitalism could grow. Merchant capital, by drawing an essentially pre-capitalist social formation – namely peasant society – into its sphere, promoted the process of accumulation and became the pacemaker of the general acceptance of the market principle. If the process of accumulation was to continue, merchant capital needed the heretofore unused productive reservoir of the peasantry, once the urban production capacity had proved too inelastic. By changing peasant society into a supplier of either industrial or agricultural products, merchant capital opened it to specialization and created the precondition for sustained economic growth. The characteristic symbiosis of merchant capital and peasant society thus marks one of the decisive stations on the road to industrial capitalism.

This symbiosis was however to develop a dynamic all of its own. Although new, internal mechanisms of resolution pressed this symbiosis forward, it had its origin in the processes of accumulation, differentiation and polarization that had – as has been shown above – taken hold of the agrarian sector; the symbiosis nonetheless gave rise to new problems which were beyond the capacity of the system's potential for self-regulation. The 'structural hetero-geneity' which characterized the relationship between peasant society and merchant capital was not only perpetuated by the expansion of industrial commodity production to the countryside; it also increased.[135] The linkages between both sectors of the economy took on a new quality, but the polarization between the two sectors remained. The 'marginal pole'[136] within peasant society began to grow more rapidly as new demographic patterns were created by proto-industrialization and finally reached a scale which had to destroy the steering mechanisms of the entire system. The point was reached where a new system of social production and reproduction had to develop new steering mechanisms which would be adequate to the problem, or else the proto-industrial system would succumb to involution.

2 ❧ The proto-industrial family economy

1. Household and family in agrarian societies and in the proto-industrial system. An approach to the problem

In non-capitalist agrarian societies, the unity of production, consumption, and generative (i.e. biological) reproduction, which was the characteristic feature of the peasant household and family, formed the basis of the economic and socio-political order.[1] This unity, which characterizes the 'ganzes Haus' (literally: 'the whole house', O. Brunner),[2] remained a central element of the socio-economic system throughout the phase of proto-industrialization, even though it was modified by the fact that the family increasingly lost its land and its agrarian subsistence. As on the peasant farm, the production process in rural industry was based on the household economy of small producers. Proto-industrialization was quite literally 'cottage industry'. But the proto-industrial and peasant household not only had the same *productive forms*, but also had in common the unity of labour, consumption and demographic reproduction within the *social mode* of the 'ganzes Haus'. While these features are common to both types of household, differences between the proto-industrial and the peasant household result from the fact that they assumed different functions within the overall socio-economic system.

In the pre-capitalist agrarian societies of Europe, where the peasant economy was circumscribed by the productive relations of either *Grundherrschaft* or *Gutsherrschaft*, the peasant household and family played a central role in the process of the 'social reproduction' of the relations of property and the conditions of subsistence. The peasant household owed this role to its ownership of land, or at least to the control it exercised, through the work process, over land as the principal means of subsistence and production.

Politico-juridical interferences with the process of production and repro-duction, as well as the forced appropriation of a substantial part of the returns to peasant labour by 'powerful outsiders' (T. Shanin),[3] were constituent elements of the political economy of these societies. In fact, it is precisely here that the difference lies between them and less developed primitive societies, where 'the surpluses are exchanged directly among groups or members of groups; peasants, by contrast, are rural cultivators whose surpluses are transferred to a dominant group of rulers'.[4]

Still, as Robert Redfield put it: 'Landlords are not needed to establish the fact of a peasantry.'[5] The asymmetrical relationship between the lord and the peasant household meant that a considerable 'surplus' went to the holders of political power in the form of payments in labour, products, or money. But such 'charges' did not determine the production process and the distribution and redistribution of resources within the overall society, or even within the peasant 'part-society' (A. Kroeber),[6] to such an extent that they formed the only mechanism for the regulation of the socio-economic system. Within such dominant relations of production, the peasant household did not produce, consume, and reproduce itself in social isolation. A close connection existed between 'house' and 'land' which formed the peasant's 'family property', and its rootedness in the village community of peasant proprietors constituted a distinct system of rules and regulations, quite 'autonomous' in its specific local and regional forms. It directed the social process of peasant 'part-societies' in such a way that the distribution and redistribution of resources remained tied to the nexus given by the family cycle, by kinship relations, as well as by marriage and inheritance strategies.[7] This process of social reproduction manifested itself in an interaction between seigneurial controls and the 'socio-familial regulatory system' (W. Schaub) which in the long term tended toward an equilibrium between the unstable number of labourers and consumers on one hand and the existing, forever narrow subsistence base on the other.

In proto-industrial regions, this unity of production and the 'social reproduction' of the relations of domination, property, and subsistence disintegrated. Being simultaneously based on peasant land-ownership and seigneurial 'property', this unity was internally contradictory. When it came to an end, the heart of the system died. As the 'ganzes Haus' of the rural craftsmen lost its land and consequently its subsistence base, it was not only deprived of its rootedness in the traditional 'familial texture' (P. Laslett)[8] of the peasant 'part-society', it also came to stand outside, or at least on the fringes, of those feudal relations of production which found different expressions in *Gutsherrschaft* and *Grundherrschaft*.[9] The attempt to compensate for the growing insufficiency of land by increasing the exploitation of the family labour power in domestic industry had a double effect. It was the decisive factor which brought about the transition from a smallholder or sub-peasant household to the household that produced industrial commodities. It thereby generated changes in the internal structure of the family and in the distribution of roles; and it altered the function of the household within the total socio-economic system. Even where rural handicrafts remained tied to manorial estates, the function of the household within the manorial system changed as market relations and money rents were established. The lord, too, found it advantageous that the small producers had independent access to the market, though his reasons differed from theirs. For under the specific regional conditions which determined the development of rural industries (primarily a relatively ample labour supply and marginal resources in land which were difficult to exploit), the maximum increase in the work-effort as well as higher marginal productivity, and therefore higher rents, were most easily achieved if the relationship of domination was mediated by the market.[10]

In the peasant household the regulation of production and consumption was primarily geared to its own subsistence and its need to maintain self-sufficiency.[11] This regulation by no means excluded relationships of 'limited exchange'.[12] In the 'ganzes Haus' of the rural industrial producer this unity of the producing workshop and the consuming household lost its relative autarky. Generative reproduction among the landless and land-poor industrial producers was no longer tied to the 'social reproduction' of a relatively inflexible rural property structure. Production, consumption, and generative reproduction increasingly broke away from their agrarian base. They came to be entirely determined by the market, but, at the same time, they preserved the structural and functional connection that was provided by the family. The social mode of the 'ganzes Haus' still formed an effective socio-economic structural model, after its agrarian subsistence base had largely disappeared.[13]

For even under these new conditions, the household remained tied to the structural and functional prerequisites of the traditional 'family economy'.[14] As the 'marginal returns' of the agrarian subsistence economy sank, the small-holders and sub-peasant groups increasingly took up industrial commodity production without, however, participating fully in the logic of money earnings and exchange. It is true that the household economy of the weaver did not function like a peasant economy in which 'at bottom every individual household contains an entire economy, forming as it does an independent centre of production (manufacture merely the domestic subsidiary labour etc.)'.[15] But in many ways the weaver remained a peasant, even though he was more and more deprived of the foundation of his economic independence.[16] This seemingly paradoxical assertion needs to be explained. The thesis will be developed in the following sections. Here I will present an outline of the argument.

The attitudes of peasants and rural craftsmen were equally determined by the system of production, consumption, and generative reproduction within the 'ganzes Haus'. The categories of classic Political Economy[17] provide almost no basis for analysing this system, nor does the *Critique of Political Economy* do it complete justice.[18] This is true of its historical as much as of a systematic analysis. From the micro-perspective of social history, which must not lose sight of the macro-historical context,[19] the origin, course, and final crisis of industrial commodity production in the countryside appear to be largely a consequence of the 'marginal labour' and the 'self-exploitation' (A. V. Chayanov) of the traditional peasant family economy during its disintegration.

Especially from this perspective, proto-industrialization manifests itself as a transitional phase between pre-capitalist agrarian societies and industrial capitalism. To be sure, it developed within an overall socio-economic system which was increasingly determined by market and money relations, as well as by the capitalistic organization of trade and marketing. But capitalist exploitation and capitalist attitudes toward profit entered the sphere of production and reproduction only slowly and incompletely. And it was due to precisely this 'backwardness' that the family economy and its social mode of organization, the 'ganzes Haus' of the rural producer, became an historical force. A decisive structural element of pre-capitalistic social formations, the family economy was a condition of historical progress as well as of the contradiction which was inherent to the system of proto-industrial capitalism with its specific mode of production and its characteristic relations of production.

2. The model of the 'family economy'

The central feature of the 'rationality' underlying the family economy is the fact that its productive activity was not governed primarily by the objective of maximizing profit and achieving a monetary surplus.[20] The maximization of the gross produce rather than the net profit is the goal of family labour. The close functional connection between production and consumption in the 'ganzes Haus' means that the returns to family labour are realized as an indivisible 'total labour income' (Chayanov).[21] This attitude, which rests on the structure of the familial relations of production and consumption, precludes a cost-utility calculation which separates current 'income' from 'stock and property'.[22]

No separation is made between the shares of labour and income that individual members contribute to the family economy, nor are the returns of agricultural labour seen as distinct from those of industrial labour.[23] 'The family economy cannot maximize what it cannot measure.'[24] It may indeed use the chance to make a profit, but in doing so it pursues an economy of 'limited goals'.[25] Before it produces a surplus[26] – whether extracted by the political pressure of its superiors or by the process of capitalist exploitation – it will always strive to satisfy the traditional socio-culturally determined needs of familial subsistence.

The relationship of the domestic producer to the process of production and consumption is determined by his fundamental interest in the production of use values. Even when his products enter market and money relations and produce a 'surplus' for merchant capital, his own relationship to commodity production and commodity exchange remains that of a producer of use values. It is characterized by his interest in consumption, and his productive effort, on the whole, is geared toward guaranteeing his family's subsistence rather than toward earning a surplus through exchange values.[27] Even under capitalist relations of production, the family economy remains a pre-capitalist preserve.[28]

Its function within the capitalist process of growth and reproduction is largely determined by the fact that even under these conditions it behaves like an 'anti-surplus system' (M. Sahlins)[29] whose production goals are those of the self-regulating familial unit of labour, consumption, and reproduction. This situation also exists under restrictive conditions which may be produced by the pressure of political or seigneurial power, by the determinants of the social system (kinship and inheritance rules, marriage strategies), by macro-demographic factors, and especially by the arduousness of the work effort and the involvement of the family in market relations.

According to the internal functional relations of the family economy, the intensity of production as well as the size of the return to its labour and the level of consumption are regulated so as to strike a balance between the arduousness of the work effort[30] and the obligation to satisfy family needs. These two sides of the 'labour-consumer-balance' (D. Thorner)[31] are interdependent and affect each other in specific ways. An increase in the subsistence needs of the family leads to the intensification of the work effort. Subsistence needs tend to grow in the short or medium term primarily because of 'demographic differentiation' (Chayanov),[32] i.e. because the process of generative reproduction causes the number of consumers to increase relative to the number of labourers during the first phase of the family cycle. The increased work effort, in turn, results in an increase of the return to the labour expended by each worker and, therefore, of the family's total return to labour, but it does not increase the average return per consumer.

On one hand, the pressure of its needs demands of the family that it should exploit its labour power most severely, but on the other hand, the arduousness of the work restricts the expenditure of labour power and, in its turn, determines the degree to which needs are satisfied. The more arduous the work in relation to the returns, the lower the standard of living at which the family ceases to increase its work effort. Therefore, when the marginal work effort is increased, the family's standard of consumption falls.[33]

The marginal utility, marginal returns, and the marginal work-effort of the family economy depend decisively upon the equilibrium between these internal factors. But this equilibrium does not originate in the subjective preferences of the family members. Its logic rests on the structural and functional nexus of the 'ganzes Haus' as a socio-economic formation which organizes production, generative reproduction, and consumption and combines them into a way of life that is shared by the family members. The productive effort within the system of the family economy rises and falls according to specific rules which are not entirely determined by the external conditions of production, even though the latter do affect the balance of the internal factors in characteristic ways. As long as the internal balance has not been achieved, the unfulfilled subsistence needs strongly push the family to increase its work-effort. On the other hand, the intensity of the labour of the family economy, and therefore its 'productivity', decreases in inverse proportion to the size of the labour force and of the earning capacity of the production unit.[34] In 'normal' cases, this utilization of labour power may not be much different from what producers experience when well-developed wage labour and capital relations determine the allocation of resources. The characteristic features of the system, however, become obvious in limiting cases.[35]

A falling return on labour which results from the worsening of the external conditions of production, like an unfavourable market situation, land fragmentation, or population increase, drives the family to increase its work-effort. This increase can go beyond what is still profitable under developed wage labour and capital relations. In the family economy, marginal returns and marginal productivity are only to a limited extent influenced by 'outside' factors. The decisive factor is the preservation of the family's subsistence. When the traditional standard of subsistence is endangered, the 'self-exploitation' (Chayanov)[36] of the family through the labour process can easily exceed the 'exploitation from outside' which would be enforced under the relations of production of an 'integral capitalism' (Cl. Meillassoux). However, this does not prevent the pre-capitalist family economy from becoming a central structural element in the process of the development and continuous reproduction of capitalist societies. In fact, it assumes this role precisely because of its disposition toward 'self-exploitation'.[37]

When the subsistence of the familial production-unit is endangered, its behaviour is not determined primarily by considerations of productivity or by an interest in the high *average* return to each unit of labour. The family's main interest lies in a high '*total* labour income' which maximizes its chances of survival even under adverse conditions. As long as the familial subsistence is not assured and as long as the possibility of marginal returns exists, the work effort constitutes an inevitable 'fixed' cost factor for the family economy, regardless of its intensity and its potentially low productivity. This holds true even when the economic returns would yield a deficit in the framework of a net profit calculation based on comparable income scales for wage labour and when the net return calculated on this basis would appear to be below the cost of production.[38]

The reverse side of this self-regulatory function of the family economy's 'labour–consumer balance' shows itself when its earnings are increased by an improvement in the external conditions of production, for example an upswing in the economic cycle. Given the rationality of the family economy, this eliminates the need for an increased work-effort. The labour supply falls, and additional returns are converted into material, cultural, and ritual consumption.[39] These concepts were first developed by the Russian agrarian economist Alexander Chayanov[40] and set forth by him in an attempt to establish a theory of the pre-capitalist 'family economy'.[41] They may appear basic and abstract. But their considerable interpretive power is most clearly revealed when they are applied to that marginal case of family economy which became predominant during proto-industrialization.

3. The family economy of the rural artisans under market conditions

The peasant household in traditional agrarian societies lived from agriculture but did not limit itself to agricultural production. The manufacture of handicraft products for familial consumption and local demand was a characteristic feature of the 'year-round work' of the 'ganzes Haus'. But as long as such handicraft production was part of a subsistence economy, agriculture inevitably remained at its foundation. Handicraft production was the variable factor in the ensemble of 'combined agricultural and industrial family labour'.[42] Since it was considered as work that 'filled time',[43] it adapted itself to the requirements of the agrarian production process. Determined by the seasonal rhythm of the harvest year, it was mostly done by women and children during less work-intensive periods.

The production structure of the 'ganzes Haus', therefore, contained from the beginning the possibility of substituting labour-intensive craft production for land-intensive agricultural production.[44] But the peasant household made use of this 'possibility' only when its subsistence was no longer guaranteed by the 'self-exploitation' (Chayanov) of its labour force in agrarian production alone.

In the development of European agrarian societies, this situation arose in the course of, or following, the great waves of population expansion. In conjunction with the ups and downs of the agrarian cycle and assisted by seigneurial and governmental pressure in the form of rising feudal rents and/or taxes, such waves of population growth strongly promoted the class differentiation among the rural population. The class differentiation occurred as a process of 'discontinuous accumulation' (G. Bois) and 'peasant expropriation' and led to the emergence of a group of marginal smallholders and sub-peasant producers.[45] The *partial* integration of these marginal subsistence holdings into the market and money economy caused the incomes of small agrarian producers to decline; it drove down returns to agricultural labour below the level where their fall could be offset any longer by an increase in the work-effort. This integration into the market occurred as a *'commercialisation forcée'* (W. Kula).[46] The marginal producer, dependent on regular money returns from the sale of his products, was reduced to the subsistence level not only under the conditions of a medium- or long-term *fall* in agricultural prices; the parallel development of population expansion and *rising* agrarian prices was also to his disadvantage. Within the context of the subsistence economy which depended on 'partial exchange', these movements led to a fall in agricultural productivity which turned potentially advantageous terms of trade against the small producers. For them rising agrarian prices did not necessarily mean increasing incomes. Since their marginal productivity was low and production fluctuated, rising agrarian prices tended to be a source of indebtedness rather than affording them the opportunity to accumulate surpluses. The 'anomaly of the agrarian markets' (W. Abel) forced the marginal subsistence producers into an unequal exchange relationship through the market. They did not benefit from the market under these conditions; they were devoured by it. Instead of profiting from exchange, they were forced by the market into the progressive deterioration of their conditions of production, i.e. the loss of their property titles. Especially in years of bad harvests and high prices, the petty producers were compelled to buy additional grain, and, worse, to go into debt. Then, in good harvest years when cereal prices were low, they found it hard to extricate themselves from the previously accumulated debts; owing to the low productivity of their holdings they could not produce sufficient quantities for sale.[47]

When, due to these circumstances, the landless and land-poor agrarian producers took on labour-intensive industrial commodity production, they attempted, by earning an additional money income in the market-place, to close the subsistence gap which resulted from the loss or deficiency of the decisive production-factor 'land'. It is true that shifts in the terms of trade in favour of industrial products and against agrarian products (mostly due to the expanding demand from overseas) could be a strong stimulant even for non-marginal producers to make the transition.[48] But such shifts in the price relations were not necessarily the decisive factor that touched off rural industrial development. Normally it was set off by a structural factor: the marginal situation of petty agrarian producers under conditions of '*commercialisation forcée*'. Under these conditions their marginal productivity was higher in the handicraft sector than in agriculture. The transition to rural industry, thus, offered a relatively more favourable opportunity to survive. And it was also supported by the logic of the familial subsistence economy which submitted to an increased work-effort, even if the return per unit of labour fell, as long as the disequilibrium between an insufficient agrarian income and the minimal needs of the family could be held off.

On one hand, this shift of the family labour-force toward industrial production proved to be a suitable strategy to maintain its subsistence; for if the family increased its work effort in the industrial sector, it was not exposed to the dilemma of falling marginal returns in the same measure as in agrarian production. On the other hand, the market ties which industrial production required did not offer a lasting guarantee of subsistence either. Cyclical fluctuations of the economy, especially the unsteady demand for products and the irregular supply of raw materials, prevented this. But a structural factor was also of central importance: when the peasant family economy made the transition to industrial production, its labour power embodied in the good that it produced did not enter, or entered only incompletely, into their valorization by the market.

Even though the family's labour produced values which were realized in the market, it was not dominated completely by the law of value.[49] It still produced and reproduced itself partially outside the circle of commodity production. The exchange relationship of the 'ganzes Haus' did not necessarily cover the reproduction cost of the labour power nor the entire cost of production. If its monetary returns are compared with the wage rates of unskilled labourers, a deficit often shows up.[50] This can be explained by the fact that important parts of the production and consumption processes, and therefore also of the reproduction of the labour power, were not completely locked into that economic circle which rested on commodity exchange. While they were essential to industrial commodity production, they did not enter into the regulation and valorization of production costs by the market. Only under the conditions of this peculiar 'dual economy'[51] of 'pre-capitalist commodity production' (P. Sweezy)[52] did the producing family in the countryside have a chance to gain access to the market despite the competition of the guilds. The family had to produce below the cost of reproducing itself, or at 'individual unproductive costs of production' (Marx).[53] For the rural producers the opportunity of access to the market depended on the fact that only part of the actual production cost was realized in the value of the commodity and that the 'cost price' of their labour power was therefore higher than its actual market price.

The dualistic structure of the proto-industrial system divided, so to speak, the 'ganzes Haus' of the rural producer. On one hand, the peasant-artisan household needed industrial commodity production and capitalistically organized markets in order to maintain its subsistence. On the other hand, the modes of its production, reproduction and consumption had to be carried out at least in part in a pre-capitalist context if it wanted to compete successfully in the commodity markets.[54]

Thus, 'the survival value' which a money income had for the rural producer whose subsistence was endangered made possible the emergence of an unequal exchange relationship. But, what is more, that relationship became institutionalized due to its being structurally anchored in a pre-capitalist mode of production. While the income which the family earned, or rather received in the form of product prices, depended on fluctuations in the terms of trade, its size was not completely determined by the mechanisms of commodity exchange. For the work effort, independent of the fluctuations in the terms of trade, represented an unavoidable 'fixed' cost factor – though of variable size – as long as the familial labour power could not be alternatively employed.[55] Whenever in a situation of 'zero-opportunity-costs', involuntary leisure was the only alternative to increased expenditure of labour, the subjectively perceived cost of an increase in the work effort was almost always lower than its objectively measured benefit.

The domestic workers were immobile, a fact that resulted from the structural unity of production, reproduction, and consumption, as well as from the partial dependence of the family economy on its agrarian subsistence. This immobility prevented its full integration into supra-local labour markets and thus produced a flexible as well as a cheap labour supply. Comparable wage labour incomes were invariably higher than the money incomes of proto-industrial producers. Their differential costs, when they increased their work effort, always tended toward zero, at least in a 'survival situation' where the family was guided by the need to maintain its subsistence. At the same time, it was not possible for them to draw a differential benefit from their integration into the market and trading relationships. For their participation in the market occurred as a 'vent for surplus' (H. Myint),[56] i.e. under conditions which prevented the petty domestic producers from realizing comparative cost advantages.

Here a man lives more by the work of his hands than the fruits of the earth. When he has ended a part of his daily work, he goes home and takes up the spindle and distaff. He pulls the plant from the earth, he soaks it, dries it, beats it, breaks it, takes off the husk, he hackles the flax, spins it, weaves it, bleaches it, calenders it, he goes to market. This labour has no end and only on Sundays does he get a moment's rest. It is bread earned with sweat and toil. If everything were counted in money, one would find that the net return falls below zero. But it would be wrong to take his labour fully into account, for it mobilizes a capital which does not cost him anything and which, if unused, would be completely lost for the non-working person. This capital is time. (J. N. v. Schwerz)[57]

In this 'situation of precarious survival', the owner of property, who satisfied part of his needs from the land, still managed to 'earn' his subsistence, but the household which owned no property tended to be forced to produce below the subsistence level. Only if one understands the specific logic which the family unit of production had to follow under market conditions, will one be able to explain a paradox which has often been pronounced as the 'curse of cottage industry' (K. Bücher)[58] but rarely been systematically explained. This paradox shows up most clearly in the fact that the rural handicraft workshop based on the domestic system of production continued to exist as a commodity producing unit of labour even when it barely managed to meet the subsistence needs of its members.

The disadvantages of the capitalist mode of production, with its dependence of the producer upon the money-price of his product, coincide . . . with the disadvantages occasioned by the imperfect development of the capitalist mode of production. The peasant turns merchant and industrialist without the conditions enabling him to produce his products as commodities. (Marx)[59]

The dialectic of this system in which the combined peasant and handicraft producer could, on one hand, maintain his economic independence in a subsistence economy – indeed, had to maintain it if the proto-industrial system was to continue to reproduce itself – but where, on the other hand, 'a price had to be paid' for that independence, becomes particularly clear in the endemic trend toward indebtedness which was characteristic of the rural producers.

This indebtedness not only promoted the transition of landless and land-poor peasant producers to industrial commodity production, but also determined the course of proto-industrialization itself.

On one hand, owning or leasing a house and land as well as the industrial means of production was a pre-condition of the rural producers' production and subsistence; on the other hand, the holding-on to these pre-conditions, which was typical of the family economy, implied, by an almost 'inevitable law', the 'progressive deterioration of conditions of production and increased prices of means of production'.[60] These connections clearly emerge in a number of regions where the trend toward indebtedness and the acquisition of property has been more precisely studied and quantitatively charted. As proto-industrialization progressed, the percentage of house-owners and occupants of independent holdings among the total population increased. But this is paralleled by a decrease in the number of large properties as well as by a deterioration, because of indebtedness, of the average-size properties among handicraft producers.[61] Even though this regional development pattern does not necessarily apply everywhere,[62] it is highly suggestive. It outlines a basic secular trend toward increasing indebtedness among small producers which, during the course of proto-industrialization, developed quite independently of economic upswings and was accentuated during downswings.

But even more importantly, the regional development pattern shows up the immediate causes of indebtedness. They lie in the close connection of the familial mode of production with the 'ganzes Haus', which not only served as the physical place of production but as an encompassing 'way of life'.[63] The rural industrial producer, like the peasant producer in traditional agrarian societies, did not consider the possession or leasing of a house, fields, or the means of production as actual or potential capital, but as means to guarantee the familial subsistence. He treated his direct conditions of life and of production as his 'property' in the sense of an essential 'prerequisite for the labourer's ownership of the product of his own labour',[64] even when the material foundation of this property no longer offered him a sufficient base and when, furthermore, the products of his labour had largely lost their direct use value for him and could be counted toward his subsistence only in so far as they could assume the form of commodities and be turned into money. The rural producer's relationship to property continued to count on the traditional assumption of a unity between current income and stock and property[65] even when the economic pre-conditions of this unity no longer existed and when its original purpose could no longer be achieved through the acquisition of petty property.

This is the only way to explain the tendency among rural industrial producers to use their current income for the acquisition of real property, without having 'saved up', and to risk long-term indebtedness for the sake of a 'short-term' interest in acquisition, which was exclusively geared toward preserving the domestic subsistence unit. This tendency was condemned as 'irrational' by contemporary observers as well as subsequent social scientists, but within the domestic system of production it appears as completely 'rational'. The acceptance of excessive house and land prices can be explained by this 'striving for independence' (C. H. Bitter)[66] among the petty industrial producers, as can the possibility to impose 'hunger rents' (P. P. Maslow) for land, housing, and the means of production on those among them who had no property – rents, that is, which lay far above average capital rents.[67]

'The cottage tenant, abstemious and laborious, is enabled by the industry of his family to outbid the grazier. They cant [i.e. outbid] each other and give to land the monstrous price it now bears.'[68] The logic immanent to domestic handicraft production under market conditions finally demanded that the economic ties to the land give way to the 'propensity for buying a house or part of a house in order to have a stable centre around which work and the family can revolve' (W. Troeltsch).[69] This is what made it possible for the petty producers to realize, at least in the short run and if economic conditions were favourable, their 'drive for independence', even though, in the long run, the subsistence of the familial production unit was endangered precisely because its ties to the land loosened. 'The house is the last of his possessions that a man will sell. Even if he "doesn't have a shirt on his back", he will try to become or to remain part owner of a house' (R. Braun).[70]

A large part of the income of the family economy was consumed by interest on mortgages for land and real property and by excessive rents. In this fact lies not only the main element of the 'individually wrong production costs' under which the industrial family had to offer its labour in the market at times of normal economic conditions. It also became the direct source of new indebtedness as soon as production and marketing crises reduced the income of the family economy.[71] Furthermore, when the petty producers incurred debts and thus locked up their money, this did not mean that they invested their capital productively. Rather such investments functioned as 'anticipated rent' and reduced the amount of capital that the producers might have invested in the sphere of production. The surplus labour which was necessary to amortize these debts did not enter into the regulation of product prices through the market, nor did it enlarge the economic base of reproduction.[72] On the contrary, it functioned as an important impediment to the productive utilization of potential income in the form of investment capital, and it drove the family economy into a vicious circle of permanently having to rely on credit – a circle which it could not leave even when alternative occupational opportunities arose.[73]

This was true not only because the inheritance laws frequently obliged the heir to assume the considerable debts of his forebears so that the inheritance of a house, rather than being an assured source of subsistence, became one of the most frequent sources of indebtedness; it was also true because 'the habit of buying on credit necessarily became wide-spread' (Troeltsch)[74] and increasingly determined production as well as consumption. The lack of capital for the purchase of raw materials and the means of production contributed as much as the frequently necessary consumer credit, given by the baker, butcher, or innkeeper, to making the rural industrial producers dependent on the putter-out or the usurer. To sum up: the attempt to preserve the independence of the familial subsistence economy of the combined peasant-handicraft producer under the conditions of a capitalistically organized marketing system resulted in a mechanism of immiseration and indebtedness for the producers. This mechanism increasingly tore the 'ganzes Haus' away from its agrarian base, made the family dependent on a money income, and forced it to do (unpaid) surplus labour without, however, in the long run guaranteeing its subsistence.

4. The family economy as a macro-economic factor

The symbiosis between the 'stone-age economy' (Marshall Sahlins) and merchant or putting-out capital, which largely determined the social relations of production in rural industry, now reveals itself both in its internal dynamic and in its contradictions if one takes into account the macro-economic effect which the domestic mode of production had on trade, the organization of marketing and of the putting-out system. This macro-economic effect consisted primarily in the fact that the family economy of rural handicraft producers allowed the trader or putting-out capitalist to realize a specific 'differential profit'. This 'differential profit' exceeded both the profits that could be gained under the social relations of production in the guild system[75] as well as those that could be gained from comparable wage labour relations in manufactures.[76]

This paradox cannot be theoretically resolved by resorting to arguments about the different organic compositions of capital nor to the laws of supply and demand, nor can it even be resolved by analysis strictly in terms of surplus-value. This paradox parallels another, for, according to the logic of capitalism, capital ought to be invested in this sector of low productivity, where profits resulting from such investment would be highest. (Cl. Meillassoux)[77]

The specific mode of production and the marginal conditions of reproduction under which the domestic economy of small producers had to maintain its subsistence made it possible for the merchant-manufacturer or trader not only to establish relationships of 'unequal exchange', but also to save part of the costs which would have arisen in the simple reproduction of the labour power under wage labour relations or under the productive relations of the guild system. As long as the 'ganzes Haus' of the rural industrial producers, due to objective necessities as well as subjective preferences, had no alternative opportunities to employ its labour power and as long as the domestic unit therefore remained 'an indispensable field of employment',[78] the surplus labour which the family

members had to expend in order to maintain their subsistence did not
necessarily enter into the market price of the product that they produced. The
increased average utilization of the *total* familial labour power, which
distinguished rural industry from agrarian production, as well as from
comparable labour-relations in the guilds and in manufactures, did not find
expression in an increased 'total labour income' (Chayanov)[79] of the family.
This manifested itself particularly in the labour of women and children. Their
productive effort contributed a necessary share to the family wage[80] without
which the subsistence gap could never have been closed, but their labour did
not result in a proportional increase in income. The decisive marginal work
effort of the family therefore remained underpaid. The family did not receive a
wage for its labour power as it did in developed capitalist wage labour
relations; instead, it received a payment for its work effort in the form of the
price of the finished product.[81] The larger part of the volume of its increasing
labour-time fell to the merchant capitalist in the form of extra profit, so to
speak.

Industrial producers who still had a partial agrarian base could survive
under these relations of production even when they offered their labour 'below
cost'. Landless industrial families, on the other hand, worked under conditions
where the prices of products, but not the value of the labour power, were
equalized through general competition. Therefore, in order to have access to
the market, they had to work for an income which tended to be below the
subsistence threshold.[82] In order to survive they had to follow a dynamic – a
runway toward ruin (M. Mohl)[83] – which drove down the family incomes of all
industrial producers and which reduced even the subsistence base of the
property owners; but which increased the profits of the merchant-
manufacturers to the extent that and for as long as international competition
permitted.

Competition permits the capitalist to deduct from the price of labour power that which
the family earns from its own little garden or field. The workers are compelled to accept
any piece wages offered to them, because otherwise they would get nothing at all and
they could not live from the products of their agriculture alone, and because, on the
other hand, it is just this agriculture and landownership which chains them to the spot
and prevents them from looking around for other employment. . . . *The whole profit is
derived from a deduction from normal wages and the whole surplus value can be presented to the
purchaser.* (Fr. Engels)[84]

Just as was rural cottage industry, so the urban guild crafts were based on the
domestic mode of production regulated by the labour–consumer balance; the
guild economy, like the peasant economy, was founded on the custom of a
'livelihood' (W. Sombart).[85] The earning of a livelihood under these guild
relations of production was tightly controlled. As a consequence the family's
capacity to exploit its own labour force was limited. Women and children did
not directly participate in production.[86]

It will be found universally . . . where men have opposed the employment of women and children by not permitting their own family to work, or where work is such that women and children cannot perform it, their own wages are kept up to a point equal to the maintenance of a family. Tailors of London have not only *kept* up, but *forced* up their wages in this way, though theirs is an occupation better adapted to women than weaving. (Fr. Place)[87]

To the extent that the domestic mode of production was tied to the collective organization of the guild system, it imposed limits on the expansion of industrial commodity production by merchant and putting-out capital; such limits were set by guild regulations. The comparatively high labour incomes provided the guild-organized producers with a more adequate livelihood than those in rural industry; and they also prevented the realization of such high capital profits from trade and marketing as they could be made on the basis of the domestic mode of production in rural industry.

In the competing branches of manufacture, as well, the average profits of entrepreneurs were lower than those which could be realized in rural industry. Not only did the entrepreneur have to contribute, in the form of wages, a higher share to the cost of the simple reproduction of the labour power, but he also had fixed capital expenditures which were much higher than in rural industry. These disadvantages most severely limited the possibilities of substituting the manufacturing mode of production for the domestic and familial mode.[88] This, however, did not exclude the possibility of their complementing each other within the same industry. Frequently the domestic organization of the primary stages of the production process was combined with centralized forms of production in the more cost-intensive finishing and refining stages, when the product was closer to being sold. But even under these relations of production more labourers were employed in the domestically organized branches of production than in centralized manufactures. During the phase of proto-industrialization, the former always formed the 'broad basis of manufactures' (Marx).[89] 'The famishing Lilliputian cottage industry choked off large industry' (K. A. Wittfogel),[90] and prevented it from becoming the dominant form of production.

Considered from this viewpoint, the producing family of the rural industrial lower classes appears simultaneously as the passive object of exploitation by circulating capital as well as an agent in the growth-process of emerging capitalism. The family functioned *objectively* as an internal engine of growth in the process of proto-industrial expansion precisely because *subjectively* it remained tied to the norms and rules of behaviour of the traditional familial subsistence economy. In this perspective, the dominant impulse in the genesis of modern capitalism was less the 'Protestant ethic' and the labour discipline *subjectively* inherent in this ethic and enforced by capitalist wage-labour. The dominant impulse, rather, seems to have been the 'infinitely tenacious resistance . . . of pre-capitalist labour', anchored in the family economy, which

Max Weber,[91] himself a descendent of a family of linen merchants,[92] completely pushed to the edge of his consciousness.[93] Even though the family economy of rural producers could and would not realize capital 'for itself', it made it possible for merchant-manufacturers or capitalists to profit 'through it' from a special relation of capital in which the family economy largely bore the risks and costs of fixed capital without deriving any of its benefit. 'The employer in cottage industry, the merchant-manufacturer, has no fixed capital. The cottage workers are his machines. He can leave them unemployed whenever he wants without losing a penny' (K. Bücher).[94]

Rural industry was therefore the driving force within the growth-process of the proto-industrial system precisely because of this 'differential profit' which resulted from the conditions under which the family economy operated. The history of modern capitalism in its first, proto-industrial phase cannot be separated from the specific function which the 'ganzes Haus' of the small peasant household carried out in the final crucial stage of its own development which was also the period of its death struggle. For the proto-industrial relations of production contained, within their structural foundations, important contradictions. These prevented their continuously expanding reproduction and thereby became a decisive cause of the transition to industrial capitalism, once the proto-industrial system had reached an advanced stage.

The symbiotic relationship between the rural industrial family economy and merchant or putting-out capital appears to be a configuration characteristic of 'transitional modes of production'.[95] It was based on a relationship of dependence in which the growing capitalization of the sphere of production did not necessarily correspond with the destruction of the pre-capitalist base. The continuous transfer of values from the domestic to the capitalist sector did not result from the destruction but rather from the conservation of the family mode of production. The structural importance of the family economy, therefore, lies precisely in the fact that 'the independent and predominant development of capital as merchant's capital is tantamount to the non-subjection of production to capital, and hence to capital developing on the basis of an alien social mode of production which is also independent of it' (Marx).[96] The mode of production of rural industry thus acquired its characteristic features through its anchorage in the familial work-process. The domestic producer exercised a considerable degree of control over the production process even as the raw materials and finished products, as well as his land, house, and means of production increasingly became the property of the merchant or putting-out capitalist. In proto-industrialization, the accumulation of capital did not extend the control of the merchant capitalist over the production process; in most cases it only increased his control over the product.[97] The resulting contradiction between the social mode of production and a capitalist mode of appropriation[98] manifested itself symbolically in endemic theft among the rural handicraft producers. Even under capitalist relations of property, the domestic worker continued to regard the objective conditions and the products of his labour as his 'property'.[99]

Structurally, i.e. on the level of the social relations of production, this contradiction manifested itself in inertia regarding innovations and in a disproportionate rise in transaction costs.[100] The 'difficulty of motivating the spatially dispersed workers to follow the advances in techniques and fashion, according to the demands of the market' was the 'Achilles heel of the putting-out system' (Troeltsch).[101] This inflexibility of the social relations of production, caused by the spatial dispersion of the production units as well as by the control of the domestic producers over the work process, corresponded with the interests of the merchant capitalist who aspired to profiting mostly from gains in the sphere of circulation of his capital and therefore tended to stay away from the sphere of production as long as he could market the products at a reasonable profit. But the contradiction of this social system of production became particularly apparent in favourable conjunctural situations when the merchant capitalist could potentially make maximum profits. The contradiction arose from the fact that the family mode of production was opposed to productivity increases and to the production of a surplus. For when the demand for labour and the family income rose, the labour–consumer balance of the 'ganzes Haus' had the effect of reducing the productive work effort and of partially replacing it by consumption and leisure. A declining supply of labour set in precisely at the moment when merchant and putting-out capitalists needed additional labour in order to expand their production and maximize their profits.[102] In the long run, this contradiction could not be reconciled with the dynamic of reproduction and expansion of the proto-industrial system. It led the system either beyond itself to industrial capitalism or caused it to retreat into de-industrialization.

5. Household formation and family structure as elements of the process of production and reproduction

The nuclear family without servants was the predominant type of household in rural cottage industry.[103] This scarcely distinguished the proto-industrial household from other rural groups during the period of the disintegration of peasant society. It formed, rather, the common feature of the sub-peasant and land-poor classes.[104] Nevertheless, the average household size of the rural cottage workers was significantly higher than that of farm workers.[105] Previous analyses have shown that the decisive factor for larger household size was a greater number of co-residing children.[106] This does not appear to be the result of a higher level of legitimate fertility among cottage workers' families. Nor does a reduced level of infant mortality seem to have been a factor.[107] Instead the higher number of children is to be traced to the earlier age of marriage and possibly to an altered pattern of age-specific mobility in proto-industrial regions. R. Schofield, D. Levine, and L. Berkner[108] have demonstrated that the traditional status of servanthood as an age-specific precursor to adulthood amongst peasant populations largely lost its significance among the rural cottage workers. Children of rural cottage workers remained longer in their parents' house, and, nevertheless, married earlier than the members of peasant or sub-peasant classes. 'A family has a better bottom than formerly: residence is more assured and families are more numerous as increase of industry keeps them more together.'[109] For the children of weavers, spinners, and knitters, the work within their family of origin frequently took the place of work as servants in other households. But this alternative was not the result of free choice. Child labour, which both in its intensity and its duration went far beyond the corresponding labour of peasant households, was a vital necessity for the rural cottage workers' families.[110]

The extent to which the material existence of the proto-industrial family depended on child labour as the 'capital of the poor man' becomes clear in those cases in which children made no direct contribution to the 'working income' of the family. In case they left the house, children frequently were 'let out' as already trained workers, or they remained bound to the family by having to make regular payments to it.[111]

The longer residence of the youth in their parents' house and the relatively low age at marriage resulted in a higher average household size among rural artisans. However, family structures did not follow the pattern of the larger peasant stem families. That is, the more compelling integration of the child into the family work force, the prolonged period of his or her socialization in the parents' home, and his or her early marriage did not bring about a closer connection between the generations in the sense of providing a stimulus to form large, three-generational households. On the contrary, the increasing dissolution of the agrarian basis and the transition to the proto-industrial mode of production under market conditions rendered ineffective the very mechanisms which governed household and family formation among land-owning peasants.

Among peasant populations, the necessary connection between household formation and resources, which were principally scarce and which could be acquired only by inheritance, was the decisive structural determinant. It enforced restrictive marriage patterns[112] as well as the co-residence of the generations in the 'ganzes Haus'.[113] The iron 'chain of reproduction and inheritance' (Ch. Tilly and R. Tilly)[114] functioned as a system of 'reproduction and patriarchal domination'. By controlling access to land as the only basic source of subsistence the older generation controlled not only the pre-conditions of family formation on the part of the younger generation, but through inheritance it also controlled the structural extension of the family beyond the individual family cycle.[115]

Household formation and family structure of the cottage workers, on the other hand, grew out of fundamentally different pre-conditions. Inherited property as the 'tangible' determinant of household formation and family structure receded in the face of the overwhelming importance of the family as a unit of labour. The foundation and continuing existence of the family as a unit of production and consumption was no longer necessarily tied to the transmission of property through inheritance. It was replaced by the possibility of founding a family primarily as a unit of labour. This reduced not only the parents' control over the marital relations of the young, but it also loosened the structural connection between the generations, in so far as it had been guaranteed by property inheritance and patriarchal domination. It is true that the parents were more dependent on the labour of their children, but they possessed no sanctions against adolescent children who wanted to leave the house and found a nuclear family unit. Marriage and family formation slipped beyond the grasp of patriarchal domination; they were no longer 'tangibly' determined by property relationships, but they did not lose their 'material' foundation in the process of production.[116]

The 'beggars' marriages' between partners without a considerable dowry or inheritance, i.e. between 'people who can join together two spinning wheels but no beds',[117] were frequently criticized by contemporaries, and constitute evidence for the new conditions shaping household and family formation. They were based on the increasing exploitation of the *total* family labour force. As Martine Segalen has demonstrated, the extraordinarily high rate of occupational endogamy among weavers[118] in developed proto-industrial regions shows that household formation among rural artisans depended decisively on the highest possible work capacity of *both* marriage partners. A woman's ability to work as an artisan, demonstrated before marriage, determined her value as a marriage partner even more than her background as indicated by her father's occupation, property or social status.[119] 'The better the weaving maids can weave, the better able they are to find a husband' (J. N. v. Schwerz).[120] The new objective conditions of exploiting the family labour of rural cottage industry required the choice of marriage partners who possessed technical skills. In this way, these objective factors allowed, subjectively, a more individualized selection of partners, and they were also responsible for the relatively low marriage-age among rural industrial producers. They demanded the formation of a new family economy as early as possible in the life cycle of young men and women.[121] Maximum income opportunities were based on the maximum work capacity of *both* marriage partners, which reached its optimum at a comparatively early age.

This not only eliminated the conditions which had restricted the formation of new households among full peasants. The rural industrial family mode of production created new preconditions of household formation which were determined by market conditions on one hand and by the poverty of the rural producers on the other. These conditions shaped not only the process of family formation among the rural industrial class, but they were also the chief factor which determined family structure because they governed the entire life-cycle of the family.[122]

The constitution of the family economy primarily as a unit of labour had specific demographic consequences as well. The pressure for the maximal utilization of the family workforce brought about not only an early age at marriage and the teamwork of husband and wife; it also favoured a form of reproductive behaviour which, by 'producing' a maximal number of child labourers, raised the productive capacity of the family – and thereby its survival chances – beyond the critical threshold of poverty where the family often began its existence. Therefore it may be said that the demographic-economic paradox of proto-industrial systems[123] appears above all to be a consequence of the mode of production based on the family economy. 'Women's earnings set a premium on early marriage, while the employment available for children encouraged large families and increased the supply of labour out of all proportion to the demand of the trade.'[124] The imbalance, typical of proto-industrialization, between a fluctuating process of economic growth and a relatively constant process of demographic expansion rested on a central paradox of the social relations of production: precisely those people produced large numbers of children who were least capable of rearing them due to their material conditions and inherited possessions. This paradox can only be explained by the specific conditions of exploitation to which the entire family labour-force was subjected in proto-industrialization.[125] The drive toward early marriage and intensive reproduction tended to be independent – within certain boundaries – of the conjuncturally determined demand for labour. Even under worsening economic conditions, a retreat to a restrictive traditional marriage pattern, characteristic of peasants, and a corresponding mode of reproductive behaviour was no viable alternative for the rural artisans. For the adult proto-industrial worker, an existence separate from the family context was not possible. Especially under worsening 'material conditions of reproduction', he was increasingly dependent upon the 'cooperation' of his entire family. 'No single-handed man can live; he must have a whole family at work, because a single-handed man is so badly paid he can scarcely provide the necessaries of life. . . As soon as they [the children] are big enough to handle an awl, they are obliged to come downstairs and work.' (A domestic industrial shoemaker from Northampton.)[126]

The specific pattern of generative reproduction followed by industrial workers, which affected their household structure, family size, and work relations, was not only an exogenous variable dependent on the 'external conditions of reproduction'; it also acted as an endogenous variable shaping the family life cycle from within.[127] Functional and structural configurations of the working family were influenced by the reproductive process above all because that process determined the 'dependency ratio' throughout the various phases of the family cycle. The equilibrium between workers and consumers that existed at the founding stage of the family was endangered by the reproduction process before it was again brought into balance. Before children could contribute to the household economy, they both hindered its productive capacity and increased its consumption. Successive births reduced the mother's ability to participate in family labour and thereby narrowed the margin of survival for both parents. It was precisely this temporal disjunction between production and reproduction within the proto-industrial family which often trapped it between the Scylla of 'primary misery' (arising from the conditions of the proto-industrial system) and the Charybdis of 'secondary poverty' (brought on by the family life-cycle).

In bad times the longest working day does not suffice; the weavers who have between two and four dependent children fall heavily in debt and must regularly resort to poor relief. Only when two or three children sit at the loom can debts be repaid and savings be made. If the brothers and sisters remain within the family and conduct an orderly economy, a period is reached when savings are possible. It is obvious how important it is to the parents to make their children work as early as possible, for they will not remain with them long. The sons often marry at twenty-two to twenty-three, the daughters at eighteen to nineteen; both leave their parents and surrender them and their younger brothers and sisters to renewed destitution. *With the birth of children, the parents become poor; with their maturation, they become rich; and with their marriage, they fall back into poverty.* (A. Thun)[128]

This dilemma of the family cycle became particularly acute under bad conjunctural conditions. Nevertheless, rural industrial producers were exposed to the ambivalent effects of the reproductive process not only under marginal conditions of income. The independent, intra-familial dynamic of 'de-mographic differentiation' (A. V. Chayanov) manifested itself precisely in those cases where small- and medium-size peasant households had not yet become proto-industrialized on a permanent basis. In such cases, the pressure of the reproductive process could turn peasants into temporary rural artisans. A small- and medium-size household took on temporary industrial employment during these critical phases of its family life cycle when, owing to a large number of children, its subsistence could not be assured on the basis of agrarian production alone.[129]

The structural character of the dilemma to which the rural artisans were exposed under the marginal conditions of their existence – endangered as they were by their limited familial production capacity and an increased con-sumption brought about by their 'internal reproduction' – shows up above all in the formation of extended households. Such extended families may be seen as an attempt to counterbalance both the 'primary misery' caused by the social relations of production and the 'secondary poverty' generated by the family cycle in the absence of developed forms of trade-union organization and the incapacity to carry on an effective wage struggle.

Complex household forms extending beyond the nuclear family occurred occasionally among propertied proto-industrial producers. Depending on the kind of product, the stage of production, and the conditions of ownership, households with servants and apprentices were to be found more or less frequently. Such households sometimes belonged to traditional rural craftsmen[130] – some of them organized in guilds – or to small entrepreneurs who owned landed property and were simultaneously engaged in the production and distribution of industrial goods.[131] A third important group were the proto-industrial 'kulaks'.[132] The lines of demarcation between these extended household forms and yet another special type of rural work- and living-unit were blurred; in this special type, sub-peasant satellite households of industrial producers were grouped around a full-peasant farm as temporary tenants, providing the farm with seasonal labour and simultaneously serving as, so to speak, a proto-industrial buffer against seasonal fluctuations in the demand for labour power.[133] These households and settlement patterns should be considered as variants or mutations of the substantial farmer's or peasant's family. They must be distinguished from the main type of extended family to be found among the landless and land-poor proto-industrial producers.

This main type usually recruited its members above all from the closer circle of relatives or from a reservoir of non-related, paying or working lodgers.[134] Formally, therefore, its structure resembled that of the extended household of the full peasant classes. But the two types of 'extended family' differed fundamentally in their material, legal, and institutional determinants. Among the rural industrial workers the extended family arose as a result of pauperization, of increasing population pressure, of limited and congested living-conditions, and especially as a result of the secondary poverty engendered by the family life-cycle. The classic stem-family, by contrast, was formed essentially to preserve the peasant family property.[135]

Viewed from a comparative perspective, the extended family of the rural artisans was much more the forerunner of the proletarian household[136] than a variation of the peasant stem-family. Unlike the full peasant household, it did not function as an instrument for the preservation of property or for assuring the well-being and the care of the aged; it rather functioned as a private means to redistribute the poverty of the nuclear family by way of the family-and-kinship system. Such a situation of need could arise either temporarily during the critical stage of the family cycle or it could become a permanent condition of existence for the proto-industrial family, as was the case during the final stage of the proto-industrial system, i.e. the period of so-called de-industrialization.

The sparse data which have been made available so far indicate that even during the expansion period of rural industry in the eighteenth century, the classic three-generation stem-family, consisting of grandparents, parents, and children, no longer occurred to a significant extent.[137] The family-and-kinship system integrated its members in other ways. Nuclear family households which contained widows, unmarried sisters or brothers, nieces and nephews of the married couple occurred fairly frequently.

The conditions under which married couples co-resided in other households and then ceased to do so point toward the causes of the formation of such extended families: married couples who lived in another household – whether as relatives or lodgers – left it after the birth of their children began the process of 'demographic differentiation'.[138] Within their familial subsystem, the ratio of labourers to consumers worsened. Since the number of mouths to be fed increased and the family became poorer, the conditions which had originally favoured the co-residence of a young couple in their 'host's' house ceased to exist. For the host, his 'guests' counted above all as labourers or paying boarders who reduced the burdens and economic risks of his own family.

Extended household formations among rural artisans, therefore, aimed primarily at counteracting an unfavourable ratio of labourers and consumers. By having recourse to the kinship system or by recruiting lodgers, a partial substitute was created for those functions which had been fulfilled by servants in the traditional peasant households. Extended households seem to have been produced by primary misery and secondary poverty. But the conditions underlying their formation were fundamentally different from those that underlay the formation of extended peasant families, where property was a decisive precondition of family extension: here the care of the aged and other relatives was tied to family property and patriarchal domination, and so was the recruitment of servants, even though servants also functioned to maintain the evenness and regularity of production throughout the family life cycle.

However, the structural conditions and consequences of the specific connection between production and reproduction by which the proto-industrial family was formed, are only incompletely revealed by the changes in the composition of the domestic group. Marginal conditions of existence normally heavily restricted the possibilities of engineering the survival of the family within this context. The proto-industrial family was by no means as free as the peasant household in its decisions to recruit additional members into its labour force. The adaptation of the household to early marriage and high fertility, required by proto-industrialization, entailed above all a change in the organization of work within the nuclear family unit itself. The far-ranging effects of this 'inner structural change' (R. Braun),[139] which occurred in the organization of work, manifested themselves in the transformation of the division of labour between the sexes, of the configuration of roles within the family, and of social character of the whole family.

This 'inner structural change' was more than a process of 'structural differentiation' (N. J. Smelser) and 'role segmentation' – it was not just a prelude to the disintegration of the 'ganzes Haus'.[140] The history of the proto-industrial family economy forms part of the long post-history of peasant society, just as it is a part of the pre-history of industrial capitalism. Its historical significance, even if seen from the perspective of the history of a status-specific family type, cannot be reduced to that of an initial stage in the secular 'loss of function' (T. Parsons)[141] of the family, which is so often shortsightedly considered to be an immediate consequence of urbanization and industrialization and has been formally defined as the 'differentiation of occupational roles from the context of kinship structure' (T. Parsons).[142] To be sure, the proto-industrial family was drawn into the process of increasing social division of labour. On the level of the family unit, this led to a loss of individual functions of production and therefore to the specialization of the productive unit as a whole. As a structural unit of work, however, the family economy during proto-industrialization was very cohesive indeed and was not threatened by disintegration. On the contrary, the necessity to work together under adverse conditions called forth a higher degree of functional integration and thereby also of structural cohesion than was necessary in the peasant family. 'In case of emergency, one man may be recruited from two or three peasant families to protect the fatherland, and no harm to agricultural production would be done. This is hardly possible for families who weave woollen cloth. Their manufactures are like a machine consisting of many wheels which must not be touched' (J. P. Süssmilch).[143]

Even though the internal organization of family labour had to undergo substantial changes during proto-industrialization, and though these changes in the very foundation of work affected the role configurations and the role relations of the family members outside the immediate work process, they all took place within the framework of the 'ganzes Haus'. In fact, the restrictive conditions under which the family economy had to insure its survival necessitated a 'maximum . . . of familial cooperation' (K. Hausen).[144] This was achieved by optimally distributing and balancing the scarce labour power of the individual family members. Under certain market conditions and within certain industries this could go so far as to erase the traditional division of labour between the sexes and age groups. The domestic production process of the rural industrial workers was thus characterized by a greater flexibility in the role responsibilities of the family members than was customary among peasants, including smallholders and sub-peasant classes. Particularly noteworthy is the absence of the separation of work between men and women, as it was common, though not rigidly adhered to, in peasant households. Here, the men, as a rule, worked out of doors in the fields, while the women were occupied with 'housekeeping', which included making handicraft products for the personal needs of the family, cultivating the garden, dairying, caring for the smaller livestock, and marketing the surplus produce of the household.[145] Even when this sex-specific division of labour largely disappeared, as it did from the households of those small peasants and sub-peasants who continued to be mostly employed in agriculture, the men – whether they were day-labourers, migrant labourers, or cottagers – nevertheless remained excluded from domestic cottage production. The sphere of women's labour, on the other hand, expanded in this class and became increasingly important. Whether the woman became active as a spinner, engaging in the production of commodities for the market, or whether she increased the marginal returns from petty agrarian production by intensive cultivation and by tending the livestock on the common fields, it was often her activity that assured the vital margin of subsistence in the family economy.[146] 'A woman cannot get her living honestly with spinning on the distaff, but it stoppeth the gap.'[147]

The proto-industrial household continued this sub-peasant pattern and at the same time changed it by making the man, so-to-speak, return to the household. In the textile trades at least he moved into a work situation which had been traditionally pre-formed by women. But as long as the partial agrarian basis remained intact, he did not entirely give up his labour outside the house.[148] In this historical sense, it seems justified to describe women as the 'vanguard of the peasant household industries' (K. Wittfogel).[149] This holds true especially in those places where domestic industry was carried on in conjunction with a partial agrarian base. Generally, however, the proto-industrial situation was characterized by a strong degree of assimilation between the production functions of men and women. Women as cutlers, nailmakers,[150] and as organizers of the marketing of industrial products[151] were as common as men in the roles of spinners[152] and lace makers.[153] Occasionally, this adaptation of the organization of familial work to the conditions of survival went even further. It could lead to the reversal of traditional roles: where the necessities of production compelled women to neglect household 'duties',[154] this 'loss of function' could be compensated by the men's assuming traditional women's roles. To observers from the middle and upper social strata, such behaviour all too quickly appeared as a reversal of the 'natural order', but it posed no role problem for weavers and even less for specialized households of spinners. It was here that 'men . . . cook, sweep, and milk the cows, in order never to disturb the good diligent wife in her work' (J. N. v. Schwerz).[155]

The distribution of family labour without regard for sex and age group determined the behaviour of family members even outside the sphere of production. Social behaviour, especially consumption and sexual relations and attitudes, was also influenced by the ways in which men and women cooperated in their work and the external constraints upon this cooperation. As 'role-specific functions', the forms of social behaviour were not split off from the work process, even when, in their symbolic, socio-cultural 'meaning' they could not be reduced to simple expressions or 'extensions' of that process.[156]

Although precise investigations are lacking, there are indications that among rural artisans the role behaviour of the sexes in consumption was by no means constantly tied to a separation of labour in which men would function as privileged consumers, 'symbolizing the role of the chief breadwinner' (N. J. Smelser), and were thus entrusted with status consumption in public, whereas women would be restricted to housekeeping, to caring and to preparing the necessities of life.[157] As a matter of fact, status consumption came to symbolize the 'egalitarian' role of both sexes. This was true at home as well as in the wider

community. The 'plebeian sociability' of rural artisans gave frequent opportunity to both sexes to articulate their needs by drinking and smoking
together.[158] The similarity of their interests and behaviour manifested itself not
only in passive consumption but also in the active defense of traditional norms
of subsistence.[159] Women were publicly involved in food riots and actions
against excessive price rises. Very often it was the women who were 'more
disposed to be mutinous; . . . in all public tumults they are foremost in violence
and ferocity' (R. Southey).[160] Even in direct sexual encounters, the new
conditions of production led to changing social texture. Political and patriarchal
controls were loosened owing to the declining importance of property and
inheritance as pre-conditions of family formation. This resulted in a more
individual selection of partners and increased the freedom to form a family,
which, in turn, produced a gradual 'transformation of the world of erotic
feelings' (R. Braun).[161] Still, the choice of marriage partners and the initiation
of marriage and sexual behaviour continued to be grounded in the work
process. The individualization and personalization of the relationship between
husband and wife arose from the very necessities of domestic production. As the
agrarian basis was lost, the survival of the family economy no longer depended
on the transmission of inherited property, but on the 'capital of the working
power of *both* partners' (M. Segalen) and on the continuous regeneration of that
capital through the process of generative reproduction. Erotic expression,
however, was not confined to a separate sphere distinct from the work process,
but was bound in a specific way to household production itself.[162]

Where people of both sexes are always together in the warmth of the same room and
where they . . . carry out work that occupies their heads and their hearts so little', they
spend their time in idle intercourse, 'which is commonly concerned with gluttony and
lust, with fraud and theft' and those who have 'the dirtiest ideas imagine themselves to be
the heroes and are regarded as such by the others.'[163]

Not only at the symbolic level did the enlarged significance of sexuality in the
everyday life of the rural industrial workers change the position of the sexes and
age groups to each other. It led both to a lower age of sexual activity[164] and to
increasing similarities in the sexual behaviour patterns of men and women. The
'immorality' and 'shameless freedom of the sexes', which middle-class observers
noted about the rural artisans and which contrasted with the behaviour of
peasants,[165] was primarily a criticism of sex-specific role behaviour. Applying
their own behavioural standards, the upper classes considered the similarity in
the behaviour of men and women as reflecting an unbalanced relationship:

Among these classes of men, the male sex is the reserved one and the women are disposed
to go a-wooing . . . The common maid understands the art of coquetry in its various
forms just as well as the lady; she discloses her breasts without shame as well as certain
other enticing parts of her body, but just half way, because she knows that that is more
alluring than if she did it all the way. If the young man continues to resist, she spurs his
senses on with liquor, and if he doesn't respond to her invitation to her bed, she visits him
in his. The usual plot of the romantic novel is thus reversed. (J. M. Schwager)[166]

6. Plebeian culture and the proto-industrial family economy: articulation of needs and patterns of consumption

Even during the growth phase of proto-industry contemporaries considered the rural industrial producers to live in 'indigence'. Although 'different from complete poverty', this indigence meant that

despite hard work the means are often lacking for the necessities of life, let alone its comforts. There are never any savings and shortages exist everywhere. One can only earn one's barest necessities through the work of one's hands and live from hand to mouth, so to speak . . . This condition is directly opposed to that of comfortable wealth, since one does not save a penny and does not even earn one's subsistence in spite of much toil and pain . . . Most of our craftsmen nowadays are in this condition of indigence. And this is why few of them rise to any position of comfort, much less wealth. (G. H. Zincke)[167]

But although the rural handicraft producers largely lacked the 'means for a comfortable life', their 'way of life' (Lebenshaltung) was not reduced to the mere physical reproduction of their existence.[168] The 'indigence' of their material existence did not imply a lack of wants and needs or the inability to develop and articulate needs beyond the mere satisfaction of the needs of physical subsistence. On the contrary, the rural industrial producers defended their specific socio-cultural way of life with great vigour against the oppressions and denials which the proto-industrial relations of production imposed on them. They might even risk their physical survival in its defence. They articulated such needs in interaction rituals on feast days, at festivals and games, at athletic amusements and competitions, as well as by shaping the conditions of work and 'free time' in such a way as to gain leisure rather than money. Especially as consumers they exhibited certain characteristics: they developed new consumer habits, but they also defended the traditional consumption standards when they were threatened, and in doing so they did not shrink from violence or criminal action.

When the idleness and dissipation of rural industrial producers were criticized by contemporaries, as it often was by merchants, putters-out, clerics, doctors, government officials and journalists,[169] their disapproval turns out to be above all a convenient device of the mercantilist policy of discipline and supervision. It served to justify low wages and the enforcement of poverty as the supposedly only incentive toward diligence and asceticism.[170] 'A worker who earns too much is rarely a good worker.'[171] But this criticism was not entirely ideological, for it pointed – though in negative terms – toward a central element in the rural industrial producers' way of life. The specific combination of work and satisfaction of needs which they tried to achieve under the conditions of proto-industrial capitalism followed rules that differed from those of a rigorous work-discipline and the maximal commercial exploitation of their labour power. The rural artisans did not take it for granted that 'time is without any doubt the largest capital which nature has loaned to man and which melts away underneath his hands if he does not make use of it every moment' (J. N. v. Schwerz).[172] To the contrary, they offered 'an extremely tenacious resistance' (as even Max Weber conceded) to a 'work ethos' which endeavoured rigorously to subject the satisfaction and articulation of their needs to the demands of hard work and frugality and a correspondingly strict 'police'.[173] Their resistance was not confined to the realm of *norms*. Precisely because the producers' resistance was 'anchored in their everyday behaviour,'[174] it persistently took on practical forms. 'Many who can work don't want to do so. They prefer to be lazy, imitate their masters and indulge in idleness, or they rudely turn to drinking, gambling and get tied up with other things which they do not understand, or, even when they do understand them, they are kept away from their main occupation by them' (G. H. Zincke).[175]

Often the rural handicraft producers showed a tendency toward 'voluntary underemployment' (D. C. Coleman).[176] It resulted from the persistence of an economy where production was dominated by the producers' desire for consumption and for satisfying their needs. The core of this 'moral economy' (E. P. Thompson)[177] lay in the unity of 'work' and 'consumption' in the family mode of production. This is confirmed by frequent complaints 'from above' about 'bad domestic management'[178] among rural industrial producers as well as by the disapproval of the *consequences* of this bad housekeeping. Compared with the rationale of saving and provisioning for the future in a middle-class household economy 'whose riches consisted not so much in large incomes as in small expenditures' (J. Beckmann),[179] the householding of rural artisans was characterized by the fact that its short-term expenditures did not stand in a 'proper' relationship to its long-term income. In this respect, the rural artisan acted much more like a 'man of estate' than like a member of the 'genuine earning class', i.e. the 'middling estate':

Unaccustomed to a money economy, unfamiliar with the thousand . . . essential needs of life which await him, ignorant of their true worth and of the art of safeguarding with the greatest possible thrift and parsimony, alien to the task of book-keeping that is required in a good household economy, he does not think of preparing a clear budget or of placing his expenditures in relation with his income and to rank the expenditures from the largest to the smallest under separate headings; instead he spends money as long as he has any, he does not deny himself or others any of the joys of life nor the satisfaction of any whim of passion, he becomes a spendthrift and is exposed to deception everywhere. (J. A. Günther)[180]

When the rural industrial producers defined the goals of their labour in such consumption-oriented terms – in so far as economic conditions and governmental pressure permitted – their attitudes must be regarded as the other side of that logic of consumption and production which induced them to increase their work effort through self-exploitation when the returns to their labour sank. 'Tout ce qu'il gagne il le consomme, il le dissipe' (F. Galiani).[181] The producing family regulated its work-process primarily in accordance with the needs of familial subsistence, even though this was in contradiction to the purpose of the proto-industrial system as defined by the putter-out or merchant capitalist. The family continued to work until its subsistence was assured. It then gave in to leisure and worked to satisfy additional material or cultural needs which always took precedence over an expenditure of work to gain a purely monetary surplus.

Those who are best acquainted with the Nature and Customs of that sort of people tell us that they will not labour for any more than a bare subsistence and never think of making a Provision for Futurity. And tho' they do squander away much of their Gains at the Races, yet their Families have the same Subsistence Money as usual; and the only Difference is that they labour so much the harder to procure Money for their own extravagant Expenses at that Jubily.[182]

The 'labour–consumer balance' of the rural industrial family was by no means geared toward a purely physical subsistence minimum. Nor should it be understood as a mechanical relationship between work and leisure where less labour time was always preferred to higher earnings. Instead it was created within a way of life in which physical and emotional needs, work and pleasure were not yet separated from each other. While the rural industrial producer directed his daily work-effort and the organization of his work first and foremost at assuring his family's subsistence, he was equally concerned about his socio-cultural reproduction through public sociability as well as the display of luxury and conspicuous consumption.[183]

This close connection between work and socio-cultural reproduction manifested itself in the irregularity with which the working time was structured according to the worker's needs,[184] especially in the alternating rhythms of working days and holidays. For the annual cycle of the rural industrial producers was still very much tied to the agrarian cycle of the harvest year and – to a lesser extent – the calendar of the ecclesiastical year.[185] But the traditional calendar with its holy days and festivals was given a new rhythm based on the new 'conjunctural' conditions. The working week thus gained an importance of its own, to the extent that domestic producers were paid periodically, i.e. for the most part, every week.

However, the working week also constituted a measure of time that structured work and the satisfaction of needs: it spaced work and free time irregularly in accordance with specific tasks and needs. At one end of the work–leisure continuum, there was the time-honoured habit of celebrating 'the feast of Saint Monday', preceded by Sunday and followed, if possible, by a relaxed Tuesday and Wednesday; at the other end there was the concentrated work-effort of the second half of the week.[186] Finally, the close connection between production and socio-cultural reproduction could be observed during the individual working day and in the work-process: 'Weavers sang at their looms. A trip to the market combined business with social pleasures;

exchanging news and courtesies with a craftsman or dealer introduced sociability into an economic or service transaction.'[187]

The articulation and realization of needs not only functioned to provide the rural industrial producers with necessary physical relaxation or with a psychological compensation for and contrast to the burdens of uniform and monotonous work; beyond the regeneration of the labour power, the socio-cultural reproduction of the rural producers had a wider 'social' meaning. It was part of an independent 'plebeian culture' (E. P. Thompson),[188] with its great variety of forms of expression, in which the traditional, often 'archaic' and asynchronous customs and habits of rural everyday life formed a unique synthesis with new attitudes that grew out of the special working and living conditions of the proto-industrial producers and their location in a specific class structure.

Especially when economic conditions were favourable, the producers turned to the traditional leisure time rituals in which 'plebeian culture' found its expression. Rising money incomes and a decreasing inclination toward work resulted in an increased dynamic of socio-cultural reproduction. Holidays, fairs, and festivals served to combine amusement, sensuality, and sociability.[189] When they drank and danced, played skittles, and engaged in cockfights or public readings, the rural artisans articulated their sensual needs and bestowed meaning upon them as public and social symbols. To them, drinking[190] was not just a private pleasure, but a public act. A cockfight[191] involved more than the spectacle of a cruel and brutish blood-sport; it gained its significance from being a seriously conducted social game. The recreation of the labour power through festivals and festivities, through games and competitions, was a social act in which the desires and needs of rural industrial producers were expressed through collective acts on the level of symbolic representation. The symbolic form of their articulation gave a more complex and diverse 'public' meaning to these activities than was indicated by their manifest appearance.[192] Festivities did not just serve the purpose of shared pleasure. They expressed and affirmed the solidarity and the social cohesion of the village community. At the same time, they could highlight the everyday conflicts that existed despite this cohesion in the form of half-joking, half-serious simulations and parodies. And they could, on occasion, turn their world upside down by suspending its normal social controls through officially sanctioned temporary acts of political or sexual licence.[193]

The 'plebeian culture' of rural industrial producers was anchored in the common practice of the manners and customs of the peer group, the neighbourhood, the village community and the local market-place. Despite its spatial limitations, it realized itself in a 'plebeian public' (plebejische Öffentlichkeit).[194] It differed from the 'bourgeois public' not only because it tended to be local and because those who gave it expression were recruited in a different way, but also because of its different structure and meaning. It was 'public' in a very comprehensive, totalizing sense. For it did not separate public from private life, nor did it distinguish between an unpolitical sphere of consumption and production on one hand, and a public sphere of politics, education, and public discourse on the other. The forms of articulation underlying the 'plebeian public' had more in common with the 'representative public' of peasant populations or even of the aristocracy[195] than with the 'bourgeois public'. This became apparent when the rural industrial producers imitated, assimilated, or caricatured typical behaviour patterns of the 'representative public' as they manifested themselves in horse-races, cockfights, and dog-races.[196]

But in contrast to the 'representative public' the 'plebeian public' did not act out the rituals or adopt the symbols of political dominance. It was, instead, the socio-cultural reproduction of everyday life, through sensual experience and collective action. The reversal of roles and the temporary suspension of social controls could serve to reduce social distance and economic differences. Private affairs could be the object of public interest – for example in the punitive customs of rough music and charivari – just as seemingly unpolitical, elementary necessities of life could stir the 'plebeian public' into political action. The latently political character of the 'plebeian public' manifested itself especially in times of depression, when the 'moral economy of the crowd' defended its customary subsistence and thereby the very existence of its 'plebeian culture'. Whether this defence took the form of direct action during a hunger riot, or of a revolt against high prices,[197] or of habitual theft from merchant-manufacturers;[198] whether it manifested itself in counter-violence and anonymous threats against the merchant-capitalist or the government,[199] or in an exemplary punishment of those who violated the solidarity of the group:[200] the many faces of the 'plebeian public' were always expressions of a strictly regulated and socially mediated behaviour whose purpose was to articulate the needs of its participants. It was 'public' especially in so far as claims were not pursued as individual rights or as the 'spasmodic rebellion of the belly' but as a matter of customary solidarity and collective activity.

The rural artisans' patterns of daily consumption, too, were very much part of this public 'plebeian culture'. The rural industrial producers had a tendency – frequently criticized by contemporaries and perhaps prematurely judged as 'irrational'[201] even by historians – to consume 'superfluous' luxuries and delicacies, like coffee, alcohol, white bread, and sweets. They were also fond of fashionable clothing and jewelry,[202] which cannot be explained by the necessity of reproducing labour power. To the contrary, the physical reproduction of life was hindered rather than furthered by the asymmetry that characterized the consumption pattern of rural artisans. They found it more difficult than others to 'stay on an even path between indulgence and austerity'.[203] Their simple daily nutrition consisted of traditional stewed and mashed-up cereals and vegetables, of black bread and, soon also, potatoes, which were considered a 'hunger food'.[204] But this was often supplemented by the 'over-consumption' (K. Bücher) of sweets and other luxuries as soon as an additional money income permitted it.

There are many examples of girls who parade around their entire earnings by hanging fineries onto their bodies; and of young men . . . who spend their savings on a pocket watch, silver buckles, a Meerschaum pipe with silver decorations, i.e. on articles which the Jews know how to talk them into buying, and who use up the rest of their earnings on beer and brandy.[205]

This excess of consumption was not just a conjunctural but a structural phenomenon. It manifested itself in the everyday lives of rural artisans even under conditions of relative immiseration and pauperization, when, measured by the yardstick of the frugal bourgeois household, the satisfaction of such needs appeared highly irrational, since the subsistence could barely be assured despite the entire family's total involvement in the work-process.

It is beyond question that rural industrial producers developed this specific attitude toward consumption in response to the new opportunities of satisfying their needs – opportunities which were opened up to them, or forced upon them, by the market insofar as they had the money to benefit from this new supply of goods. The conditions of the work-process in many rural industries created an additional need: coffee, tea, and alcohol became necessary stimulants as the conditions of production deteriorated and work became more degrading. But neither the market stimulus nor the work-process by themselves were the decisive factors. The consumption of luxury goods, being a social means of expression, had an essentially 'public' purpose. For the rural artisans, it was the form of social competition *par excellence*, a competition operating among themselves as well as between them and other social groups and classes.[206] On one hand, luxury consumption made it possible for them to 'discover a new communal consciousness', on the other hand, it enabled them to experience and articulate their relationship to the outside world and helped them to establish a distance between themselves and their peasant and bourgeois environment. Rural artisans no longer disposed of the traditional means of peasant self-representation, namely landed property and material possessions. They had not yet acquired – or did not want to acquire – the symbols of bourgeois culture. 'Earlier, inherited status had determined the measure of luxury; now luxury determined status' (R. Braun).[207]

Household and family functioned as integral components of this 'public realm' in which needs were articulated and satisfied. For the rural industrial producers the family was by no means the protected place of emotional intimacy where, to the exclusion of all others, sensuality and elemental needs were satisfied. In plebeian socio-cultural reproduction, public and private life were not separated from each other, just as there was no distinction between working life and family life in the sphere of production.[208] To be sure, for the rural artisans the central pre-condition for enjoyment and sensuality was the unit of material production and reproduction, namely the household and family (see below), but they found their true expression only in public sociability. They had not yet been tamed by the informal constraints of bourgeois domesticity, but they were freed from the restrictions which dominated the community life of peasants and which arose from their necessity to preserve property as well as from seigneurial and governmental control over sexual and marital behaviour. The continuity of attitudes among rural artisans with those of peasants and sub-peasant groups, as well as the difference to the latters' attitudes, are exemplified in the socialization of the young.[209] Among the artisans, it was influenced only to a relatively small degree by parents and schools. Instead, the peer group of unmarried youth played an important role in their socialization. Such behaviour was part of the traditions of peasant usages and customs concerning the initiation of marriage, but their character changed once patriarchal controls had weakened under the social relations of the proto-industrial system. Thus, sensuality and sexuality could develop much more freely in the peer group socialization of rural artisans than was possible in a community of peasant proprietors.[210] This shows up clearly in the greater frequency of 'sexual anticipation of marriage' (D. Levine) as it manifested itself in illegitimate births and pre-marital pregnancies.[211] These behaviour patterns are indications of a greater freedom from traditional social controls, but they are not a step in the direction of an 'emancipated individuality' in sexual life, i.e. toward greater 'intimacy' and 'privacy' of feelings, as Edward Shorter claims.[212] Illegitimate births should rather be seen as a result of frustrated attempts to marry and set up a household – a frustration caused by poverty and unforeseeable fluctuations in economic conditions. The initiation of marriage still largely followed traditional patterns of courtship and pre-marital sexual behaviour, but the economic conditions and mechanisms of control had changed radically. The assurance no longer existed that sexual relations would lead to the foundation of a household. Women and men tended to be equally drawn into this 'public' sphere of the articulation of needs, just as they were drawn into the sphere of production. On the basis of her increased 'socio-economic independence' (A. Thun) as a labourer, the woman gained a greater degree of freedom to move about publicly. When a 'prudent' member of the upper classes stipulated: 'A daughter should go out only three times in her life: when she is baptized, when she gets married, and when she is buried', this statement could be countered by the 'atheistic' answer of a young girl: 'Why should I care, I want to have fun.'[213] Instead of withdrawing into private satisfactions, the rural artisans involved themselves in public pleasures; but the satisfactions in the private sphere did not need to stand in opposition to those. Even though governmental guardians of 'proper behaviour' tried to enforce the virtues of domesticity, frugality, and hard work via the church, school, and through state and police controls, the frequency of public appeals and admonitions only serves to demonstrate the strength of the resistance put forth by rural artisans who did not consider the family as a 'place of refuge' and who did not want to confine their 'everyday lives' to the privacy of their homes.

The proto-industrial household not only invested a considerable amount of 'emotional capital' into its socio-cultural reproduction, as has been emphasized by E. P. Thompson,[214] but also a remarkable portion of its monetary income. Especially from this 'economic' perspective, the family of the rural artisan was the pivotal point of 'plebeian culture'. It is true that household and family did not directly determine the total cultural milieu of the 'plebeian public realm', which was firmly tied up with the collective customs and behaviour of the peer group, the neighbourhood and the local market place. But the 'labour–consumer balance' of the household economy regulated and guaranteed the connection between the public and private spheres. Given the increasing dependence of the rural industrial producers on the money and exchange economy, this 'labour–consumer balance' caused the specific disequilibrium between the long-term scarcity of monetary incomes and their short-term rapid consumption which resisted all exhortations toward frugality and foresight and which found expression in a decisive preference among the rural artisans to develop new needs. This preference was a pre-condition of 'plebeian culture'.

The rural industrial producers continued to shape their lives according to the rules of the traditional peasant-artisan family economy, even though they could satisfy an increasing portion of their elementary subsistence-needs only with the help of a money income which they earned under the conditions of a capitalistically structured market and exchange economy. They acted within a relatively rigid set of preferences of needs in which money did not yet play the role of a common medium or of mediator. The marginal utilities of individual needs and goods were difficult to substitute for each other within this system of rules. An optimal satisfaction of needs, therefore, could hardly be achieved by foresight and by the attempt to balance the 'weighted utilities' of individual needs, for example by providential saving of money. 'Carelessness and frivolity, lack of concern for the future, the drive to spend their ample daily earnings on luxuries, all this is characteristic of this voluptuous class of people.'[215] The domestic producers insisted with remarkable pertinacity on the consumption of alcohol, tobacco, or white bread and preferred it to the effort of anticipating their future elementary needs and of making choices accordingly, even when they could hardly 'afford' any 'luxuries' owing to their low subsistence level.[216]

In this scheme of preferences, money was not used to compare the utilities of necessary everyday goods and balance these utilities against those goods which answered so-called luxury needs. Rather than exercising this 'universal' function cash income had its specific place within the hierarchy of uses and symbolic significance. As soon as the short-term necessities of life were assured, money became a surplus beyond subsistence needs. It could therefore be primarily oriented toward cultural expenditure for status, prestige and luxury consumption.[217]

Money as a means for storing supplies was as little known to the small producers as was money as an instrument for the long-term adjustment of all preferences. Even under enduring conditions of scarcity and poverty it could therefore make perfect 'economic' sense for the plebeian producers to devote a relatively large part of their income to short-term and intermittent expenditure for cultural needs.

The rural artisans counted on resolving the basic problems of their subsistence outside the conditions which exchange, competition, and economic fluctuations imposed on their existence. By living 'from hand to mouth', they thought that they would be able to maintain their subsistence through their own labour, just as the family economy of the peasant had always operated under that assumption. But there, under conditions of production which were in part controlled by the peasants themselves, a 'caloric minimum' and the storage of provisions were guaranteed by the household's agricultural production and its anchorage to a system of communal support and controls. Economic fluctuations as well as the basic conditions of the proto-industrial system prevented this kind of insurance for the rural industrial producers.[218]

The use of money as a means of acquiring provisions for storage was as unfamiliar to the rural artisans as was money as a means to balance choices which they made to satisfy their needs. 'It is as difficult to convince a peasant of the usefulness of a hail- or cattle-insurance as it is to explain to a cottage producer the significance of a savings bank or of health insurance.'[219] In many respects money as a return to the family's productive labour, as well as a medium of exchange, still had the same meaning for the rural artisan as it had for most members of pre-capitalist societies. It was a precious thing, a shiny coin to be exchanged, if possible, for other precious things or to be spent in the public sphere of socio-cultural reproduction. The money income which exceeded the expenses necessary for the direct subsistence needs might be invested in the acquisition of property; but primarily it served to acquire articles of conspicuous luxury and prestige or to incur demonstrative expenditures on the occasion of feast days, festivals and other interaction-rituals.[220]

Even in the twentieth century there exist parallels to this kind of behaviour pattern of rural artisans who were leaving behind the conditions of the peasant family economy. The Siane of New Guinea, the Tiv in northern Nigeria, or the Kwakiutl Indians in British Columbia, for example, have not realized the significance of the universal exchange of money and goods, which has been carried into their primitive environment by capitalist exploitation and market relations, and consequently, they have not been able to respond to the new conditions with the appropriate 'rationality'.[221] Even when the proto-industrial producers earned a sufficient income, their particular economic rationality prevented them, under the conditions of general exchange and capitalist market relations, from creating a balance between consumption and production which might have guaranteed them the greatest possible chances of survival given the precarious conditions of their lives. During proto-industrial capitalism this attitude toward money, in the long run, intensified and prolonged the misery to which the family was already exposed by the necessity of 'self-exploitation' in the work process. Nonetheless, the rural industrial producers intermittently *did* articulate a variety of needs which made use of the limited possibilities of the new capitalism, without, however, acknowledging its limitations.

3 ❧ The structures and function of population-development under the protoindustrial system

1. The demo-economic system of proto-industrialization

Because of its specific interrelationship with the economic growth-process, the dynamic of population development provided an essential impetus to proto-industrialization. It had a considerable influence not only on the emergence and development of rural industry, but also on its eventual stagnation and decline. In the early stages, the close connection between demographic and economic factors gained historical significance because population expansion and economic growth mutually reinforced each other. But their interaction not only promoted the emergence and early progress of the proto-industrial system; it was also one of the determinants of its internal contradictions. The stagnation, decline and ultimate end of the proto-industrial system appear to be bound up with a socio-economic problem inherent in the system itself, a problem which could not be resolved at the stage of socio-economic development characterized by proto-industrialization.[1]

Demographically, this problem manifested itself in a specific reproductive 'overreaction' by which the industrial producers responded to the constraints and opportunities of proto-industrialization. At the aggregate level, i.e. with regard to the total society, their overreaction resulted in rapid population-expansion[2] which had a tendency to exceed available resources. Such population growth seems particularly typical for the upswing of proto-industrialization, but, in changed form, it also appears in regions of de-industrialization, where the transition to industrial capitalism did *not* occur between the end of the eighteenth century and the second half of the nineteenth century. In such regions the 'overreaction' manifested itself not so much in an even, continuous population-expansion but in the delay with which the mechanisms of demographic growth 'adjusted' to the deteriorating economic conditions.[3] The intensification and localization of industrial commodity production in the countryside fostered population growth and simultaneously was fostered by it. The tenacity with which these conditions persisted even under de-industrialization, when they led the way to pauperism and pro-letarianization, constitutes evidence for a social nexus which lends a unifying structure to the different regional development patterns of proto-industrialization.

It would be premature to postulate a demo-economic system, in a strict sense of the word. But a hypothetical model can be suggested based on a synopsis of the research which has been done to date.[4] It is obvious from such investigations that proto-industrialization must be viewed as a regionally confined special phase in the history of the transformation of agrarian societies, whose course and structure, as expressed in its mode of production and its relations of production, were decisively shaped by demographic factors. Population growth affected the process and system of proto-industrialization primarily because it assured a large labour-supply. To be sure, that supply was a response to an increased demand for industrial labour power[5] which arose with the supra-regional and overseas demand for industrial products. But it did not rise linearly, simply as a function of demand and in response to market impulses. Instead, populations in regions of rural industry often displayed a 'Malthusian behaviour' (F. Mendels),[6] and it was due to this behaviour that population growth became a determining factor of the proto-industrial system. Given a certain demand for labour, the reproductive response of the artisans tended to produce an over-supply. At the expense of the producers' subsistence, this over-supply favoured extensive forms of industrial growth rather than the expansion of production based on increase in productivity through the investment of fixed capital. In the second half of the eighteenth century, the demand for labour increased by a revolutionary leap; the entire system of production changed, leading to a fundamental transformation of the demo-economic interrelation-ship. But until this happened, population expansion contributed to containing the development of the productive forces in proto-industrialization within a relatively 'static expansion' (J. H. Boeke).[7] The quantitative expansion of production and the number of producing units was combined with the perpetuation of a backward mode of production that was neither capital- nor technology-intensive.

The influence which population growth had on economic development became an 'interrelationship' of demographic and economic variables only because the proto-industrial mode of production affected the 'mode of population' (G. Mackenroth).[8] Population expansion in regions of rural industry appears to be a characteristic consequence of domestic family-based production under the specific macro-economic conditions of production in rural industry. In any case, the dynamic of proto-industrial population growth cannot be adequately explained with reference to those reproductive patterns which were typical for the traditional agrarian societies of Europe.[9] Those societies, too, had a considerable, though periodically interrupted growth dynamic. From the high Middle Ages onwards they exhibited a clearly structured long-term population development in which periods of great expansion alternating with periods of stagnation and contraction.[10] This development was of decisive importance for proto-industrialization, because rapid population growth brought about the underemployment of marginal smallholders and members of sub-peasant groups in agrarian regions, a process which frequently initiated the emergence of mono-industrially concentrated districts in such regions. But the intermittent dynamic of population growth inherent in agrarian societies must be contrasted with that which was inherent in the 'demographic hothouse of proto-industrialization' (R. Schofield).[11]

In fact, the agrarian 'mode of production' in European peasant societies was characterized by a set of 'social controls on growth', which tended to regulate the interplay between economic, demographic, and socio-structural variables and contain it at a status quo, thereby assuring the relative stability of the population and its adjustment to limited and relatively inflexible resources.[12] This regulatory system was structurally anchored to household and family as they existed under the conditions of the peasant-artisan mode of production. It was also upheld by the structures of domination and property within the respective agrarian societies. Thus, population was kept in balance with relatively scarce resources, because marriage and the founding of a family were normally tied to the ownership or inheritance of a full peasant holding or a craft shop.[13] This tie was enforced by governmental and seigneurial controls and resulted in a socially differentiated reproductive pattern. A relatively high marriage-age, which was even higher for the members of the lower classes, was the 'true weapon of birth control in the Europe of the Ancien Régime' (P. Chaunu).[14] It kept fertility within certain limits and could exclude the lower class from marriage and reproduction altogether. In this way, the population as a whole was kept back from the Malthusian abyss, in that a certain part of it was forced into temporary or enduring poverty, or into employment in domestic service, which largely ruled out the chances of legitimate procreation.

This reproductive system, upheld by property and patriarchal domination, was made flexible and adaptable mainly through changes in the age and frequency of marriage. Both variables, the age of marriage and – to a lesser extent – nuptiality, functioned as the decisive demographic regulators when the balance between population and resources shifted.[15] They reacted to short-term 'mortality crises', produced by epidemics, and to 'crisis mortality', brought about by harvest failures, as well as to long-term changes in the real income of the peasant and artisan classes. Such changes resulted from the interrelationship between the secular trends of population growth and the periodic trends of the agrarian economy which occurred in conjunction with the emergence of supra-regional markets and the transformation of institutions of domination since the high Middle Ages.[16] Even though this system contained a certain flexibility and considerable possibilities for development, 'pre-industrial societies were by definition in a position of negative feedback':[17] population growth and real income, fertility and mortality were tied to a mechanism of adaptation which permitted neither a continuous population growth on the basis of expanding resources nor permanent economic growth on the basis of a population development propelling that growth. Population expansion was the driving force behind the secular upward movements of the agrarian economic trends; but eventually the rising number of people, rising grain prices, on one hand, increasing feudal rents and falling marginal returns in agriculture on the other hand, 'cut short' each phase of population expansion, as well as 'each period of economic growth before the point at which they became self-sustained and progressive'.[18]

Proto-industrialization broke through this demo-economic system which regulated the feudal agrarian societies of Europe.[19] In its emergence, development, and final stagnation it can be considered both as cause and consequence of a new relationship between demographic and economic variables – a relationship which constitutes an 'institutionalized disequilibrium'. Population growth and economic expansion entered a relationship of mutual acceleration in which the critical demographic variables of the old feedback system ceased to be effective and became part of a new system.

If this new system was to take effect, the framework of political and governmental institutions, anchored to *Grundherrschaft* or *Gutsherrschaft* and the village community, had to disintegrate; at the very least this framework had to loosen the constraints controlling 'social growth' in the traditional agrarian societies of Europe by tying the opportunities of reproduction to property and inheritance. This development occurred even in regions where the growth of an industrial population was at first induced by seigneurial action, for example where cottagers were settled in the mountainous areas of east central Europe. Here, too, the expansion of industrial commodity production entailed the loosening of feudal ties and communal restrictions which originally had kept relatively constant the relationship between land ownership and the size of the working population.[20] But the growth dynamic of proto-industrial populations was not grounded alone in such negative pre-conditions as the loosening of seigneurial controls. It was based positively on the new conjunctural and structural conditions of the proto-industrial system itself.

To the extent that the rural industrial producers lost their agrarian base they became dependent on the fluctuating demand for industrial products in supra-local and overseas markets. Their income and survival opportunities remained tied to the returns from their production within the family economy, but they had to be realized under the new conditions and relations of production of proto-industrial capitalism. This twofold structural and functional dependence of production also determined the pattern of generative reproduction of the rural industrial populations. As reproductive behaviour lost its connection to land ownership, it became dependent on the market. But the special structural conditions of market dependence, under which the rural artisans were forced to utilize their labour power, called forth a specific response which made their reproductive behaviour quite inelastic in relation to price movements and shifts in the terms of trade.[21]

The demand for industrial products, generated by foreign markets, created new conditions for the demand for industrial labour. These prevented industrial populations from reaching the limit to growth that existed in agrarian societies in which the demand for *artisanal* labour depended on local and regional agrarian booms and crises. The greater elasticity of demand in international commodity markets changed the elasticity of demand for industrial labour.[22] To be sure, the interrelationship between population development and the periodic trends of the agrarian economy did not cease to function under proto-industrialization. Population growth still generated a rise in the demand for agrarian products and therefore a rise in agrarian prices which entailed a fall in the real income of rural industrial producers. But the traditional feedback mechanism between population and the economic growth process was interrupted at a decisive point: the demand for industrial labour was no longer necessarily tied to the short- and long-term movements of agrarian prices. The employment of rural industrial producers could be maintained even when the terms of trade deteriorated. It was strongly affected by the fluctuations in demand in foreign markets, but these were not negatively tied back to the population development in the industrial regions. So long as the demand curve for industrial products remained horizontal, the labour supply in proto-industrial regions, even if enlarged by population growth, could still be employed if the labourers accepted the conditions of international competition with its tendency to drive down wages.

The expansion of demand for industrial labour power and its relatively great elasticity was more than just a prerequisite for the growth of proto-industrial populations. Cyclical upswings had relatively direct impact upon the growth of 'industrious population' (H. Linde).[23] But this impact was directed and mediated by the structural conditions under which the labour power was exploited by merchant and putting-out capital as well as by mercantile policies.[24]

As long as industrial labour constituted the largest cost factor in the industrial production process and as long as the structural rigidity of the 'social relations of production' in rural industry handicapped the substitution of fixed capital for labour, the expansion of production could only take place on the basis of an increased dynamic of generative reproduction among the proto-industrial population. It was therefore one of the main goals of mercantilist policy to stimulate population growth. The achievement of a positive balance of population and employment became subject to political manipulation, for example through settlement projects. It became a concern equal to that for the achievement of a positive balance of trade.[25]

Marx's statement that the 'development of population ... summarized ... the development of all productive forces'[26] holds true much more fundamentally for the 'primitive accumulation' of proto-industrial capitalism than it does for industrial capitalism. Thus, population growth constituted a decisive 'valorization base' (Verwertungsbasis, H. Gorssmann)[27] for the proto-industrial progress. The expansion of the proto-industrial system of production could only occur on the foundation of a continuous growth of the number of labourers and/or a rise in the level of employment. 'Optimal' conditions existed only when the 'industrious population' grew at a pace which preserved the producers' marginal subsistence but at the same time *precluded* a lasting expansion of the food supply as well as a rise in real incomes. Population growth as a function of the effective demand for labour, therefore, was inherent in the expanded reproduction of proto-industrial capitalism because it was generated not only by upward economic trends but also by the structural conditions of production.

The precise measure of the population in a country . . . will not indeed be the quantity of food . . . but the quantity of employment.

The habitual practice of task work, and the frequent employment of women and children, will affect population like the rise in the real wages of labour . . . on the other hand the paying of every sort of labour by the day, the absence of employment for women and children, and the practice among labourers of not working more than three or four days in the week either from inveterate indolence or any other cause will affect population like a low price of labour. (T. R. Malthus)[28]

The translation of the effective demand for labour into the specific growth dynamic or proto-industrial populations occurred through the 'social mediation' (K. Marx)[29] of the family mode of production. The competition of supply and demand in international commodity markets regulated the prices of products but not the earnings of the individual producing family. Under the marginal conditions to which domestic production and reproduction in rural industry were usually subject, the economic flexibility of the family depended essentially upon the application of its *total* labour force. But the family could maximize the benefit from the application of its labour force only if it succeeded in achieving a large family income under relatively low costs of reproduction.

Therefore the very structure and course of the process of generative reproduction became essential elements in the rural producers' strategy to earn and maintain their subsistence.[30] For the household's production capacity and its chances for survival depended not only on the 'total labour income' (Chayanov) of the family but always also on the relationship of the total labour income to the cost of reproduction. If this relationship was to be favourable, it had to conform to a certain standard of generative reproduction, but it remained relatively independent from cyclical fluctuations. A comparatively early marriage age and a large number of children who survived to working age were its strategic variables.[31] They determined the 'economic strength of the household' (R. C. Geary)[32] under the external constraints under which the rural family reproduced itself. Since the subsistence of the family was not assured without the labour contributions which women and children made to the 'family income', and since the family was poor, so that inheritance and the maintenance of property did not exercise any restrictions on the process of generative reproduction,[33] an early marriage and an increasing number of children alleviated the burden of familial reproduction costs, because they raised the 'total labour income' which could be eventually obtained.

Early marriage became necessary particularly in view of the marginal conditions of subsistence of the rural industrial producers. The working capacity, and therefore earning capacity, of men and women were at their maximum at a relatively early age.[34] Still, the low marriage age of both sexes cannot be adequately explained by the desire to maximize the income of both partners; it also allowed them to overcome, as early as possible, the critical poverty phase of the family cycle which, in the process of 'demographic differentiation', was initiated by the birth of the first child.[35]

The benefit of a large number of children also resulted from the demo-economic dynamic of the family cycle in a marginal situation of reproduction. Children necessarily counted as labour power and as a means of production;[36] they were also 'living capital' that served to support the parents during their old age. They functioned to a much lesser extent to increase their parents' consumption. The first births, therefore, constituted primarily a cost factor that involved considerable risks since the children might not survive. Only after the considerable dangers of infant and child mortality had been overcome – dangers which increased disproportionately when the living conditions declined – could the children be employed in the familial production unit. Only then could the benefit derived from their labour exceed their (re)production cost.

If the considerable marginal utility of child labour for the 'total labour income' of the family suggested a strategy of relatively high fertility, such a strategy became virtually an economic necessity when it is taken into account that the children's chances to survive to working-age were small and fluctuated.[37] Since their survival was so uncertain it was hardly possible to determine the number of children through family planning. Especially with regard to the first children the risk of mortality implied that poverty might be perpetually reproduced through the demographic reproduction process. In order to assure the survival to working age of at least one or two children, a much larger number of births was necessary. In this situation the average social and economic costs of a single birth were relatively high, but the direct and indirect marginal costs of each additional child were much lower for the family. The costs of an n-th child were not substantially higher than those of an $(n-1)$th child. But the marginal utility of the n-th child rose considerably over that of the $(n-1)$th child. The family counted on the positive income effect which the prospective labour power of the child would have on its 'total labour income'. The entire family's chances of survival increased, not least because the parents' subsistence was more assured during the second precarious phase of the family cycle which began when old age caused their working capacity to decline and the children successively left home. In the 'survival situation' typical in rural industry, where the family was forced to gear its activities toward maintaining its subsistence, the positive income effect of increased fertility was considered more important than the negative effect of increased reproduction costs. The latter constituted an unavoidable burden for the proto-industrial family as long as it was compelled to utilize its labour power under conditions of 'zero-opportunity'.[38]

A historical and systematic model of the specific 'generative structure' (H. Linde)[39] of the proto-industrial household has been constructed here. It is characterized by the fact that 'not only the number of births and deaths, but the absolute size of families, stands in inverse proportion to the level of wages, and therefore to the amount of the means of subsistence at the disposal of different categories of worker' (K. Marx).[40] The high marginal utility which resulted from the enlargement of the familial labour force under the conditions of rural industry brought about an increased dynamic of generative reproduction at the level of the family; at the level of the entire society, however, it created a Malthusian labour supply. 'God has decreed that the men who carry on the most useful crafts should be born in abundant numbers' (F. Galiani).[41] This statement of a contemporary reflects the realities of the interrelationship between population and the economy in the proto-industrial system. The specific dynamic of reproduction among proto-industrial populations was the product of necessity; the necessity to ensure the survival of the industrial family with the aid of the one resource still left it in relative plenty despite the increasing loss of its agrarian base: namely its own labour power. The family engaged in domestic industry reproduced itself in such numbers in order to subsist through its labour, and not primarily to consume 'surpluses', still less to accumulate them.[42]

In a regional case study, Franklin Mendels for the first time systematically investigated the reproductive behaviour of proto-industrial populations under the influence of short-term cyclical price fluctuations (grain and linen).[43] This study shows that the dynamic of reproduction in proto-industrial families is anchored in a characteristic 'generative structure'. It is true that the income and consumption opportunities of rural artisans, as determined by fluctuating terms of trade, influenced their reproductive behaviour; an increased income and improved consumption opportunities, following a positive shift in the terms of trade, brought about an increased dynamic of generative reproduction, as Mendels proves on the basis of changes in nuptiality, which is a growth-related variable.[44] But the reproductive behaviour of rural artisans, though stimulated by the cyclical expansion of their incomes, was not *dominated* by it. Negative changes in the terms of trade and subsequent reductions in income did not necessarily lead to a reduced dynamic of reproduction.

This is not the only example which underlines the inelasticity of the reproductive behaviour of the rural artisans and the sluggishness of its response to fluctuations in income.[45] It draws our attention however to the fact that the growth of proto-industrial populations was determined by forces outside the cyclical changes which determined their latitude of choice in consumption. The generative reproduction of the labour force and the continuous regeneration of the productive capacity of the domestic unit turn out to be – within limits – independent variables in the maintenance of familial subsistence. This dynamic of reproduction, characteristic of rural industrial populations, which was based on the logic of familial production under marginal conditions of existence, constituted a central element of the demo-economic paradox of proto-industrialization. As a survival strategy for individual family economies it must be considered as perfectly rational: 'It may be quite rational for individual family units to be interested in as large a number of births as possible in an economy where life is lived close to the subsistence level, while the consequent high birth rate may be quite detrimental to the economy as a whole' (H. Leibenstein).[46] In the short run, the dynamic of reproduction of proto-industrial populations made it possible for the individual family to survive, but in the long run, the inelasticity of this dynamic produced a 'Malthusian' labour supply at the macro-social level. This dynamic was insufficiently adjusted to the fluctuations in the demand for labour and thus perpetuated the pauperization and marginalization of petty industrial producers, while, at the same time, it functioned as the driving force behind the expansion of proto-industrial capitalism.

2. Basic demographic patterns of proto-industrialization

Even a short comparison of the aggregate data for regions with strong concentrations of rural industry discloses a basic feature of proto-industrial demographic behaviour: their growth rates are frequently above those of agrarian regions, at least during the emergence and upswing of rural industry before the second half of the eighteenth century.[47] But this differentiation in population growth according to region and sector, observable from the agrarian crisis of the late Middle Ages, was by no means a linear historical process. It did not exclude the likelihood that the emergence of a rural industrial population was directly based on structural changes in the agrarian sector, nor did it rule out the long-term coexistence in the same district of a relatively stable farming population and an expanding proto-industrial population. For the secular trends of expanding proto-industrial population-growth in agrarian regions, especially during the late fifteenth and for the greater part of the sixteenth century and, later, during the second half of the eighteenth century, produced the landless and land-poor – underemployed classes of smallholders and sub-peasant groups who became the social foundation on which proto-industrialization was built.[48] The regional growth of proto-industrial populations was primarily a process of social regrouping at the local level. The rapid expansion of a class of industrially producing, smallholding and sub-peasant strata – landless 'Häusler', 'Gärtner', 'Einlieger', 'Heuerlinge', 'manouvriers', or cottagers – did not necessarily exclude the continued existence of a stable core of peasants,[49] who sometimes – being the dominant class in the village – controlled and restrained the reproductive behaviour of the industrial producers. But the process of social regrouping could also lead to 'industrial villages' from which the property-owning peasantry largely disappeared and which slowly turned into 'rural slums' (D. Levine).[50]

While the origin of proto-industrial populations was most closely tied to the secular agrarian cycles and their corresponding trends of population growth, its continuous expansion tended to become independent of the agrarian conjuncture. Here, the 'crisis of the seventeenth century' (E. Hobsbawm), in particular, constituted a break.[51] It initiated a new phase in which the division of labour deepened between commercialized agrarian production on the plains and industrial commodity production on the marginal soils of the uplands, in wooded country and in areas of sandy soils.[52] Subsequently, differences in the speed and rhythm of the growth of such regional populations developed along fairly specific lines. The demographic development of proto-industrial regions increasingly broke loose from the secular agrarian cycle and followed a relatively continuous growth-trend long before the transition to industrial capitalism.[53] But regions of commercialized agriculture, dominated by cereals, cattle, or dairy farming, had much lower rates of population growth,[54] at least as long as production and generative reproduction were grounded in an agrarian system of labour organization which was dominated by *Grundherrschaft* or *Gutsherrschaft* and the village community of peasant proprietors.[55]

The expansion of proto-industrial populations was carried into effect primarily by the self-sustained growth-process of a regional rural population base (Standbevölkerung, R. Braun). It was mostly the result of a surplus of births, to a lesser extent of an in-migration from agrarian regions.[56] The surplus of births had its origin in the demographic profile which is characteristic of proto-industrial populations: birth rates were consistently higher over long periods while death rates were lower, though also relatively high. This indicates that the persistent natural surplus of births was due to a rise in the number of births and not to a secular decline of the number of deaths.[57] The dynamic of growth of rural industrial populations is to be explained, then, by the dynamic of fertility rather than by a fall in mortality. Long-distance migration played a minor role, although the in-migration from neighbouring agrarian regions was not an unimportant factor in the growth of proto-industrial populations. The extent of such in-migration, however, greatly depended upon the existence of an 'open' and urban or quasi-urban centre in the industrial region.[58]

However, for the expansion of the proto-industrial system as a whole, urbanization was less important than the increasing concentration of an industrial population in the countryside. Therefore, it was typical of the population development in proto-industrial regions that the growth of its urban populations lagged behind or even stagnated, in comparison with its overall growth or the growth of proto-industrial villages.[59] The close demo-economic connection between the relatively slow growth of the cities and the expansion of intensive industrial production in the countryside is illustrated by the changes which the migration patterns underwent in proto-industrial regions. Proto-industrialization completely or partially abolished those migration patterns which until the nineteenth century balanced the 'natural' population losses of the cities with the population increases of the agrarian regions.[60] The increased demand for labour power in proto-industrial regions made it unnecessary for their surplus numbers to migrate to cities either within or outside of such a region.

It was mentioned earlier[61] that children stayed longer in the 'ganzes Haus' among industrial families than they did among peasant families. The reasons for this residential pattern become clear when one approaches it from the broader perspective of an entire local or regional population: proto-industrialization made unnecessary the extensive migrations which often characterized the lives of individuals and families of the landless and virtually landless classes in regions without industrial employment opportunities.[62] Such migrations resulted from endemic poverty and permanent underemployment, but also from temporary mortality crises. Their decline is exemplified by changes in the age-specific mobility which, among agrarian populations, controlled the labour supply at the regional and supra-regional level, as well as the choice of partners and the timing of the foundation of a household. The basic feature of this mobility pattern, namely the fact that unmarried youth regularly left their parental family unit and entered into service, was often modified by the employment of young people in rural industry. The industrial employment of unmarried family members and the relative freedom with which a new household could be formed at least partially replaced the traditional migratory movements.[63]

However, the aggregate data alone do not give precise information about the growth mechanisms of proto-industrial populations. For this purpose, demographic micro-analyses and calculations based on models are needed as well as local investigations of specific industries and of the class stratifications which they produced. So far, only a few of these exist.[64] But they are particularly valuable, since they include not only examples of 'normal cases', i.e. industrial villages, but also variants of partially proto-industrial populations in predominantly agricultural communities.[65] Many other preliminary results either confirm or supplement the findings of local case studies, and – despite some differences – consistent patterns and trends are becoming apparent.

The critical functional element in the growth-mechanism of proto-industrial populations appears to be their low age at marriage.[66] Not only did it tend to distinguish rural industrial producers from other social groups, like full peasants and guild artisans, as well as agricultural and day labourers; it emerges as the crucial variable of the demographic process: the decline of the marriage age could decisively determine the population rise in regions of rural industry. It influenced the demographic growth process in two ways: linearly by prolonging the duration of marriage and thereby allowing for the birth of a larger number of children; and structurally, by successively shortening the intervals between generations, which changed the age structure and led to a greater frequency of births within a given unit of time.[67]

This tendency toward a low marriage age seems to be a group-specific feature of the reproductive behaviour of rural artisans, which sets them off from other rural groups. It applies equally to men and women. But this does not exclude considerable local, regional, and sex-specific differences. Their structural and demographic significance becomes apparent if one takes into consideration the way in which they are conditioned by the work process and property relations, by governmental and institutional factors, as well as by regional and local customs: a low marriage age appears particularly typical where men and women were equally integrated into the production process as landless and land-poor domestic workers, and where industrial production had largely broken away from the institutional and economic context of the peasant village. Especially for an 'industrial population' of this kind did the marriage age exhibit a characteristic long-term downward trend, which on one hand corresponded to the expansion of demand for labour power and the growth of industrial production but was, on the other hand, relatively inelastic in its response to a deterioration of incomes and living conditions.[68]

Sex-specific differences in the behaviour with which men or women responded to short- or medium-term changes in their income situations could have important consequences for population growth. 'In response to deteriorating economic conditions men were deferring marriage. Their brides, however, displayed no such sensitivity to fluctuations in prosperity.'[69] The marital behaviour of brides, at least in this local case, continued the secular downward trend. This is precisely what distinguished it from the behaviour pattern of peasant populations where the marriage age of women tended to vary while that of men remained relatively constant over long periods of time.[70]

Similar behaviour patterns became evident when a proto-industrial population segment developed in a village where an agrarian labour organization and substantial land-owning peasants continued to play a dominant role. The rural artisans showed a strong trend toward a low marriage age, when compared with other local population groups.[71] But their age at first marriage was higher than that of comparable domestic producers in industrial villages and its trend was less consistent. Here the response of the rural artisans to the deterioration of their economic situation was relatively elastic; they did return to the traditional restrictive marriage pattern, i.e. they increased their marriage age.[72] Moreover, the sex-specific differences in marriage age clearly digressed from the behaviour pattern of a rural 'industrial population'. To be sure, compared with other rural social groups, a relatively small age difference between marriage partners was characteristic of all rural artisans; still, among the rural 'industrial population' the marriage age of the man was normally higher than that of the woman,[73] whereas among the proto-industrial part population in an agrarian environment, the marriage age of the woman was typically higher than that of the man and sometimes higher than that of women in the full peasant class, or in guild artisan or merchant families.[74]

This 'cottager marital age pattern' (M. Drake)[75] is evidence of an attitude toward marriage and household formation which followed the standards set by peasants without being materially based on property and the ownership of land which, through marriage and inheritance, determined the 'social reproduction' of the conditions of subsistence among peasant families. Among rural industrial producers, too, the concern for a 'good match' frequently dominated the choice of partners. It could lead to an industrial producer's marrying an older peasant daughter who was turning into an 'old maid'. But this was not the usual pattern. From the beginning, endogamy within the lower classes prevailed.[76] The absence of the material preconditions of peasant household formation was decisive for the emergence of a 'cottager marital age pattern': among 'cottagers' there was no more question of the expectation of an inheritance forcing late marriage-age on the man than of a parental dowry facilitating relatively early marriage for the woman. Only employment as a servant would allow the woman to acquire the marriage fund that was considered necessary to establish a family, and servanthood raised the marriage age above that of rural 'industrial populations'.

The 'cottager marital age pattern', being based on a partial integration into the peasant organization of work, life, and domination, made it possible for rural artisans to react with relative elasticity to fluctuations in the industrial economy, but the populations of purely industrial villages had no such opportunities to return to traditional behaviour patterns. Consequently, a change in their reproductive pattern and a lowering of the marriage age developed only very slowly during the periods of a downward trend and even after the onset of de-industrialization. The percentage ever married measured against the total population declined only gradually.[77] Rather than returning to the traditional demographic control-mechanisms of peasant society, the artisans in industrial villages reacted to the final crisis of the proto-industrial system by attempting – quite unsuccessfully – to check fertility within marriage,[78] as well as by forming sometimes very complex households which served to counterbalance their pauperization while simultaneously preserving the family economy.[79] The last resort was the emigration of entire families.[80] Not only had the institutional framework of patriarchal controls to demographic growth broken down, but the very structure and the socio-economic conditions of proto-industrialization, i.e. its specific family mode of production, prevented the return to traditional behaviour patterns. For early marriage, quite independently of the conjunctural conditions, was not only a fundamental prerequisite for achieving the optimal income of both partners; it was also a prerequisite of the total family's survival during those critical phases of its life cycle which it had to traverse during the process of 'demographic differentiation'.

An early marriage-age affected the expansion of proto-industrial populations primarily because it increased the rate of marital fertility.[81] The decline in the marriage age meant a prolongation of the woman's fertile period spent in marriage and consequently an increase in the number of births per completed marriage.[82] The growth effect of this extended fertile period was reinforced by the fact that the beginning of marriage at an earlier age was demographically more significant than a purely linear prolongation of the entire duration of marriage.[83] The accelerated succession of births, i.e. the reduction in the birth intervals, must be regarded as another factor which influenced the fertility of proto-industrial populations. Its extent differed according to industry and region, and occasionally it could compensate for the restraining effects which a late marriage age had on population growth.[84] But its significance as a variable in the demo-economic system is likely to have been smaller than that of the marriage age. The relative importance of both these factors for a typical rural 'industrial population' was calculated by David Levine. His comparison of the gross reproduction rates of individual marriage cohorts, which succeeded each other in the course of proto-industrialization, shows the demographic significance of both variables, i.e. of the low age at marriage and the increased birth intervals, for the population growth of regions of rural industry.[85] Levine then made a counterfactual calculation of the differences which the average family size of biologically completed marriages within each marriage cohort shows for the case that one of the two variables is held constant. He thereby succeeded in analysing and comparing the demographic effect of changes in age at marriage separately from those of age-specific marital fertility. The secular decline of the marriage age turns out to be the strategic variable which, during the phase of emerging proto-industrialization, was 'more than twice as important as the rise in fertility in promoting population growth'.[86]

The impact of mortality as a structural variable in the growth of proto-industrial populations is much less important than the marriage age. Rising fertility, and not a fall in mortality, was usually the dynamic agent in the growth process of rural 'industrial populations'. The reduction in the marriage age, the resulting increase in marital fertility, increased nuptuality, and an age-structure favourable to high fertility proved strong enough, even after de-industrialization had set in, to more than compensate the effects of high mortality.[87] The specific mortality experiences of rural 'industrial populations' were often characterized by an asymmetry which separated the development of infant and child mortality from that of the mortality of adults.[88] The phases of the origin, expansion, and the final ruin of intensive industrial commodity production in the countryside were accompanied by high infant and child mortality which surpassed that of primarily agrarian regions.[89] Its long-term significance consisted not only in considerably reducing the average expectation of life in comparison with other rural population strata; it also lowered the 'growing-up rate' and thereby reduced the percentage of individuals born who would reach the age of procreation. This mortality pattern was most clearly accentuated during the phase of de-industrialization, but even before then, it constituted a *differentia specifica* of 'industrial populations' which set their mortality experiences off against those of all social groups in primarily agricultural regions that contained proto-industrial part populations. Here too the 'inégalité sociale devant la mort' (H. Charbonneau) existed, but it was less pronounced than in mono-industrial regions and localities.[90]

The extremely high rate of infant mortality and the lower but still high rate of child mortality call attention to the socio-economic causes of this proto-industrial demographic pattern. These causes are to be found primarily in a deterioration of the living conditions of industrial producers and the downgrading of their environment, i.e. in insufficient nutrition as much as in unhealthy housing. The physical deprivation of children and young people through the work-process was of less – but still considerable – significance. The different mortality-experience of adults demonstrates that the harsh living conditions of proto-industrialization did not affect the different age groups in the same way. Contrary to some ideological propositions which, in search for social harmony, emphasized the 'ethical' and 'social' advantages of children working in the 'ganzes Haus' of rural industrial producers,[91] infants and children turn out to be the true victims of the proto-industrial system – a fact which is demonstrated beyond doubt by demographic analysis.

In contrast to infant and child mortality, the mortality of adults frequently declined during the phase of emerging proto-industrialization.[92] The deterioration of living conditions, working conditions, and incomes, which tended to accompany the emergence of a proletarianized rural 'industrial population', sometimes, but not consistently, lowered the expectation of life for adults even before the critical final phase of proto-industrialization set in. But this is relatively insignificant compared with the development of infant and child mortality. In any case, rural 'industrial populations' did not, as a rule, participate in that secular decline of mortality which was characteristic of agrarian populations since the middle of the eighteenth century.

In a few local case-studies it has been observed that the percentage of adult women who survived to the end of their childbearing period remained relatively constant during the entire proto-industrial phase.[93] This demographically decisive aspect of adult mortality suggests the same conclusion as do results from the calculation of the causal interrelationship between the decisive factors which shaped the growth process of the proto-industrial population in at least one potentially typical case: the 'net reproduction rate'[94] of successive generational cohorts of this population show that proto-industrialization departed from the demographic equilibrium of traditional agrarian societies, unstable and precarious though it was; but industrial producers were unable to develop mechanisms which might have restored an equilibrium within the demo-economic nexus of the proto-industrial system. They were prevented from doing so by the constraints which the social relations of production under the domestic system imposed upon them, and this situation persisted even when their minimal subsistence needs were no longer guaranteed. A decline in the expectation of life and the attempt at controlling fertility within marriage might reduce the 'natural' growth rate of the population during the phase of de-industrialization, but a demographic equilibrium did not re-emerge. Seen from this perspective, one is tempted to support E. A. Wrigley's statement: 'Industry came just in time to save the day',[95] even though the horrors of early factory-industry hardly warrant such a positive assertion.

3. Remarks on the change in the structure and course of demographic conjunctures and crises

An analysis of the connections between economic and demographic conjunctures and crises is helpful toward an understanding of the interrelationship of economic and demographic variables in regions of proto-industrialization.[96] Up to now, the study of short-term cycles and changes has predominated,[97] not least because these were easier to handle methodologically. For the short-term economic and demographic fluctuations in the period before industrial capitalism constitute relative precise and limited phenomena which recur with a certain regularity; their causes and the interrelationship of various factors which determine their course can therefore be calculated with precision.[98]

Even though there still exists much controversy on this subject and even though historical case-studies and regional developments are sometimes difficult to fit into a simple interpretive framework, a starting point for analysis is provided by Ernest Labrousse's theory of economic crises[99] to which has been added the concept of a 'crise démographique de type ancien'[100] by Jean Meuvret[101] and Pierre Goubert.[102] On the basis of these theories, central aspects of the interrelationship between economic and demographic variables in agrarian societies can be understood, and perhaps it will eventually be possible to explain the deviation of proto-industrial regions from this 'classic' pattern.

Labrousse's study of the price- and wage-movements of the eighteenth century French economy show the pattern of a basic pre-industrial cycle whose short-term upswings and downswings were largely controlled by changing harvest-yields and consequent price and wage fluctuations.[103] The changes in grain production, mostly caused by natural, i.e. climactic factors, called forth fluctuations in cereal prices, because the demand for basic foodstuffs remained relatively inelastic in the face of a changed supply situation. These were the crucial factors which regulated the 'agriculturally determined business cycle' (D. Landes)[104] through the complex structures of local, regional, supra-regional (though not necessarily national), and international agrarian markets.[105]

The conjunctural effects of harvest fluctuations depended on the *extent* of the oscillation in grain prices. W. Abel has rightly emphasized that minimal as well as maximal grain prices generated economic crises.[106] But the economy as a whole was only affected during crises produced by food shortages and price rises. Only they resulted in the subsistence crisis of the 'type classique' or 'type ancien', and in rural and urban famines. In the countryside its main victims were small producers and those members of the lower classes who, even when economic conditions were normal, closed the subsistence gap by taking up a side-occupation either as day labourers or as industrial producers. The latter were affected by the crisis in two ways. The 'agrarian crisis' deprived them of their bread, and the 'industrial crisis' of their income. For the 'industrial crisis of the old type', too, was determined by the movement of cereal prices. During the months when grain prices were very high, the purchasing power especially in cities and large urban centres was shifted toward food products on a short-term basis. Consequently the demand for industrial products declined and industrial incomes were reduced relative to other wages and incomes or sometimes completely eliminated. Thus, the crisis of the 'type ancien' threatened the industrial producers' subsistence base in a double sense.[107]

The social power of the subsistence crises manifested itself in their de-mographic consequences. The 'crise social des subsistences' (P. Goubert),[108] i.e. the classic crisis of food shortages and high prices, did not merely parallel the 'demographic' crisis, i.e. it had more than a superficial functional relationship to it. It *was* the 'crise démographique de type ancien'. On the one hand, it originated in the cause–effect relationship of harvest failure, rise in grain prices and general economic and food crises; on the other hand, its demo-economic results became a dynamic element in this basic economic cycle and its effects. This was due to the fact that the combination of the medium-term growth and decline of population, characteristic of traditional agrarian societies, and, on the other hand, a generally narrow margin of resources, quite independent of the accidents of nature, exercised an influence on the decisive variable, namely the grain prices.[109]

Although this demographic crisis occurred only rarely in its 'pure' form, in the sense that people simply starved to death without being also afflicted by epidemics and diseases resulting from malnutrition, it could be distinguished quite clearly from that second 'autonomous' variant of the demographic crisis, namely the 'mortality crisis', which occurred as a consequence of epidemic diseases without a crisis-like deepening of the subsistence problem.[110] Not only was there a regular correlation between crisis-like fluctuations in cereal prices and the so-called 'crisis-mortality'; the 'crise démographique de type ancien' can be identified as a 'crisis of the social substance' only when its structural effects are taken into account. Owing to these effects, it acted as a regulator of long-term demographic conjunctures and, consequently, as an impulse of secular economic processes of growth and contraction.[111]

The structural effect of the demographic crisis is visible in the reaction of its primary 'conjunctural' demographic variables: the birth, marriage, and death figures. Their contrasting curves describe the crisis as a cyclical movement in covariance with the rhythm set by the conditions of the harvest year and the sudden rise of cereal prices. The crisis found expression in the acute rise of the number of deaths and a simultaneous decline in marriages and conceptions. It reached its climax in close correlation with the peak in cereal prices, before the demographic variables finally returned to their 'normal position', which, however, would be importantly modified by the changes in the demographic structure.

In the proto-industrial system, the harvest year lost its decisive influence on reproductive behaviour as well as on the economic growth process. The new dynamic arising from the interrelationship between economic and demographic variables is largely due to this fact. Even contemporaries considered proto-industrialization as a self-regulating process of 'growing manufactures' (A. Smith) where – contrary to 'stationary manufactures' – the economic 'variations' no longer showed 'sensible connections with the dearness or cheapness of seasons'.[112]

This change in the configuration of demographic and economic variables shows up systematically in an important detail: the traditional seasonal fluctuations of demographic variables were often modified during proto-industrialization.[113] Here the extent to which the reproductive behaviour of proto-industrial populations had detached itself from the rhythms of the agricultural year becomes apparent.

In particular, the birth curve changed, at least in the only example of a population of rural artisans which has been studied so far with regard to this question.[114] The example constitutes a significant marginal case insofar as it concerns a population in which intensive domestic commodity-production was adopted mostly by women and children while the men continued their agricultural work on tiny holdings and, at most, took up industrial work during the winter.[115] Here the marriage-age of rural producers to a large extent continued to follow the ecclesiastical calendar and the rhythms of the agricultural year, and the seasonal distribution of mortality did not deviate from the mortality pattern of agrarian societies. But the births very clearly showed an 'oubli des rhythmes ruraux' (J. B. Bardet)[116] similar to what has been found for the populations of larger cities since the seventeenth century. The original pattern of the distribution of births over the year showed a large number of births during the winter and a relatively low birth-frequency during the harvest months of the summer. As rural producers adopted industrial pursuits, winter births and summer births were 'equalized'. The original pattern which regulated sexual behaviour, conceptions, and births lost its pertinence. It had been determined, among other factors, by the necessity to free the labour power of women from the burdens of childbirth during the critical time of the working year, in order to assure the total application of their work-effort in the interest of the family economy. The secular tendency for winter births and summer births to become equalized shows that generative reproduction among proto-industrial populations became divorced from its determination by the agricultural year, as production became dependent on supra-regional and overseas demand for industrial products and on the resulting demand for labour.

The structural relevance which these conjunctural changes in demand had for the growth of proto-industrial populations particularly shows up in cases where proto-industrialization softened the impact of crises of the 'old type'. Even when the 'classic' economic circumstances prevailed, i.e. when grain prices fluctuated greatly, the demographic effect did not take hold with full severity:[117] 'The famine came but the holocaust halted' (J. D. Chambers).[118]

To be sure, even in agrarian regions, the violence and the demographic effects of short-term local food crises declined as a consequence of the growing supra-regional integration of agrarian markets and the formation of an 'économie céréalière' (J. Meuvret),[119] controlled and directed by market forces and the state. But this may not be the decisive causal factor in the decline of really severe mortality crises in proto-industrial regions. For a characteristic feature of the new 'conjunctural' behaviour-pattern of proto-industrial populations is the simultaneity of demographic crises of the 'type ancien' in the agrarian regions and their weakness or occasional absence in neighbouring regions with intensive rural industry.[120] The decisive economic determinant of these changes appears to lie in the growing weight of the overseas demand for industrial products,[121] which tended to make the conjunctural trends in proto-industrial regions and in agrarian regions independent of each other. It did not necessarily bring about an increase in the real incomes of rural industrial households which would have raised them above those of the land-poor and landless peasant classes in agrarian regions, but it made the incomes of industrial producers relatively more stable, especially in times of harvest failures. In any case, the increase in the level of employment, despite lower incomes, was demographically more important than an increase in an income which was received only intermittently.[122] Although the former did not raise the average life-expectancy of the individual (since the secular decline of mortality occurred in agrarian and not in proto-industrial regions),[123] the proto-industrial population reacted to their relative independence from the agrarian cycle with an increased dynamic of growth.

The structural conditions of this new dynamic and its conjunctural implications manifested themselves in marginal cases. A food crisis might still be followed by signs of crisis mortality, but the births and marriages no longer fluctuated according to the classic pattern. They remained relatively inelastic even when conditions deteriorated.[124] One of the causes of the changed demographic conjunctures of proto-industrial populations lies in this new demo-economic configuration. Among rural artisans, the structural conditions of permanent growth persisted, even though the population *figure* was reduced by an increase in mortality.

4 ❧ Relations of production–productive forces–crises in proto-industrialization

1. The phases and types of relations of production: the precarious independence of the industrial family and emerging wage–labour relations[1]

The existing literature on the emergence of capitalism misses two important points. First, it fails to develop explicit models of pre-capitalist and transitional relations of production. Secondly, it does not analyse systematically the reasons why capital, which had long been present in the form of merchants' and usurers' capital, penetrated into the sphere of production. These shortcomings have significant consequences. To begin with, the differences between various types and phases of relations of production are minimized or simply overlooked. Wallerstein's book provides a recent example. He calls every form of production 'capitalist' that is pegged for the emerging world market, and therefore underestimates the gulf that separates a mechanized industrial plant in the European metropolitan country from an *encomienda* or *Gutswirtschaft* in the periphery.[2] Other authors, instead of explaining why capital advanced into production, simply assume that capital has an inherent interest in doing so. The following chapter does not try to cover the whole problematic of the transition from feudalism to capitalism, but focuses on the proto-industrial sector. It outlines specific models for the various types and stages of relations of production in this sector and tries to analyse the specific 'rationality' of direct producers and capitalists. One of the major conclusions from these models is that capital does not have a built-in tendency to penetrate into production, but merely an inherent interest in profit. What follows from this assertion is that in order to explain the emergence of capitalist relations of production it is not enough to quote some passages from Marx's chapter on the 'So-Called Primitive Accumulation' concerning the non-economic conditions of, and the violent methods used in, this process. Rather it is necessary to make a theoretical effort to understand the inner logic of pre-capitalist and transitional relations of production about which Marx made interesting remarks, but which he never really analysed. Furthermore, the theoretical models have to be based on, and confronted with, the empirical data collected in the descriptive historical literature. For neither the merely descriptive scholarship nor quotations from the classics provide an explanation of the emergence of capitalism.

(a) Feudal organization of industrial commodity production

Industrial commodity production in the countryside originated in the agrarian economy. This is true not only in the sense that industrial work was carried out by peasants, especially smallholders, before the development of a large non-land-owning class; it is also true for the work techniques and work processes. In particular the most important branch, the textile industry, was built on the traditional skills and production tools of the rural population. Furthermore, production was usually carried on in the family, which therefore functioned as a 'unit of production',[3] though sometimes the familial core was supplemented by one or two extra-familial labourers. While within the cities guilds increasingly limited and largely prevented the artisanal work of women and children,[4] in the countryside women and children were integrated into the production process.[5] Here a limited division of functions and a certain cooperation arose between family members when women and children tended to perform the preparatory and auxiliary tasks. But the division of labour practised within the family does not seem to have gone very far.[6]

Despite these connections concerning origin and form, the structural conditions of intensive industrial production in the countryside differed from those of agrarian production in important respects. First the marketed share of this industrial production was much higher than that of peasant agricultural production, i.e. home consumption absorbed much less of the industrial output than of the agricultural output. Second and more importantly, the surplus which exceeded the consumption of the direct producers (either direct consumption of their own products or consumption mediated by exchange) was largely appropriated in a different manner and by a different class than the surplus of peasant agricultural production. Industrial commodity production in the countryside, as a rule, was integrated less directly and less comprehensively into the feudal system than was agrarian production. This is most clearly illustrated by the fact that rent in kind and labour services could remain viable in agricultural production for the market, but rarely did either of them form the basis of industrial commodity production.

Let us examine the reasons more closely. Before proto-industrialization – and in most parts of Europe even during proto-industrializ-ation – the peasant economy was integrated into the feudal organization of agriculture, i.e. the agrarian producer had to turn over to his lord a portion of his labour time or of his products, or their value, owing to the lords' 'extra-economic' power particularly his power over the principal means of production, namely land. Originally, this was true not only for primary production but also for all things that peasants processed. As long as markets had been minimally developed and products could only with difficulty be circulated by trade, use-value had been the goal of peasant production as well as the goal of the appropriation, by the feudal lord, of the surplus which the peasant produced beyond his own needs. This appropriation, therefore, had a basic, though elastic, limit in what the lord's household could consume.[7] When markets emerged and expanded substantially, this limit ceased to exist. The consequences of an increased integration into the market affected the lord–peasant relationship in fundamentally different ways depending on the entire structure of the society and economy (which will not be analysed here).[8] These differences became visible during the agrarian crisis of the late Middle Ages and the growth-phase of the sixteenth century. In parts of western Europe, the commutation of labour services and rents in kind into money rents paved the road toward the weakening and final disintegration of feudal ties. East of the Elbe, on the other hand, the possibility of marketing grain in large quantities brought about the establishment of the *Gutswirtschaft* which was based on 'second serfdom', and extensive labour services.[9]

While in the entire eastern half of Europe the production of grain for the market was dominated by this feudal system until the nineteenth century,[10] it was much less widespread in industrial commodity production.[11] To be sure, when the opportunity arose to market large quantities of industrial products, the feudal lords made some efforts to appropriate such products by increasing labour-services or rents in kind, i.e. in exactly the same way in which they appropriated grain.[12] But they often gave this up after a short time.[13] Even in eastern Europe, a strictly feudal mode of organization did not predominate in the production of industrial goods for the market. Why this was so, is still far from clear, but the reasons ought to shed light on the problems of the way in which, and of the extent to which, the growth of industrial commodity production stood in opposition to the feudal system and in the long run undermined it. Whatever the answer, the social norms of the nobility and its mentality do not, by themselves, provide a sufficient explanation. First, narrow and quite rigid constraints were imposed upon the concentration of industries as long as the feudal lord appropriated the industrial goods to be marketed simply in the form of labour services and rents in kind, without any compensation to his subjects. For this required that the agrarian base of the direct producers remained sufficient for their livelihood, which precluded the emergence of a large class of landless and near-landless people who were mainly employed in industry. Secondly, it is likely that the more highly developed technology of industrial production and the considerable diversification of industrial products demanded a higher quality of workmanship than could be enforced under feudal relations of production, at least as long as they rested chiefly on labour services and rents in kind. With regard to agricultural labour, it was well known that the peasant applied more effort to the work on his own farm than to the services he performed on the manor.[14] This is part of the reason why in the countries of *Gutswirtschaft* the productive forces in agriculture remained at a low level during this period so that the lord could content himself with extracting a certain amount of labour or quantity of products, without being much concerned about their quality. But differences in quality seem to have affected the marketability of industrial goods to a much greater extent than that of the standard agrarian products which were being exported from eastern to western Europe. It can perhaps be formulated as a rule that the more highly developed the production techniques in an industry were, and the fiercer its competition in international markets with products from 'freer' regions, the less that industry was based on feudal labour services or rents in kind.[15]

The feudal lord could try to overcome both these barriers by paying his subjects for their work with part of the money which he received when selling their products. Their agrarian base could shrink to the extent that they received an income from their industrial labour, and the spatial concentration of industry could progress. And if the direct producers' incomes were linked to the quantity and quality of their products through the payment they received, this would give them economic incentives to increase and improve their output. If, in this way, the feudal lord who sold his subjects' products became a merchant or putting-out entrepreneur, he would not have to share the quota, which he appropriated, with a capitalist. He could also use his extra-economic power as feudal lord to keep the price or piece-wages low which he paid as a merchant or putting-out entrepreneur. A number of examples exist from different parts of eastern Europe for this kind of incorporation of industrial commodity production into the feudal system. But in general, feudal lords did not follow this route. In fact, in some important regions they left it during the course of proto-industrialization.[16] This can perhaps be explained by a lack of liquid capital. As long as, in the agrarian sector, the lord could still increase his income by shifting more burdens onto his peasants rather than by making investments,[17] and could therefore spend his money income almost entirely for purposes of consumption, he had little incentive to act differently in the industrial sector – namely to invest his money in commerce or industrial production. This assumption is supported by the fact that the lords acted in their industrial enterprises, as they did in their grain production: they purchased very few of the required elements in the market but attempted to produce them all on their estates.[18] Thus they sought to complete the entire production process from raw material to finished product on the estate – a procedure for which the boundaries of a *Gutswirtschaft*, or even of a complex of estates, were often too rigid.

Thus, in eastern Europe, it was apparently the rule, or at least it became the rule during the course of proto-industrialization, that the feudal lord appropriated his portion of the industrial commodity production of his subjects in the form of money rents, concessions, and similar indirect means,[19] leaving the production and marketing of industrial goods to the interaction between direct producers and merchants or putting-out entrepreneurs. But this could not occur unless merchant or putting-out capital existed in the region. It could either originate in the country itself, or the country could open itself to capitalists from outside. Once this had occurred, the commutation of industrial labour-services and rents in kind into money rents could mean an increase in the lord's income, for it turned out that production increased and its quality improved when the direct producers' incomes were linked to the quantity and quality of their labour. Observers noted that they produced more and better goods than they did under the conditions of obligatory labour services, when they received 'regular' payments for their work from merchants or putting-out entrepreneurs.[20]

As a rule, then, even in the area of second serfdom, industrial commodity production was not *feudally* organized, in the narrow sense of the word. Such an organization was the exception though it increased in frequency the further to the East one went. Nonetheless, the money rents which the feudal lords drew from the industrial employment of their subjects usually continued and could cause them to take a lasting interest in the expansion of rural industry and of the population. Important centres of proto-industry were built on this foundation. But together with the undiminished strength of feudal relations in agriculture, even this parasitic method of the feudal system of integrating the rural industrial producers limited the possibilities of industrial growth,[21] as long as the dynamic of these new socio-economic forces could not shake off the fetters of the feudal order.

(b) The Kaufsystem: petty commodity-production and its interaction with merchant capital

Even in the areas of *Gutsherrschaft* east of the Elbe, and much more so in the western parts of Europe, it was the exception rather than the rule that the rural population delivered the products of their industry, without receiving an equivalent compensation, to feudal lords who would market them. Instead, the direct producers themselves entered into market relationships. But their situation was significantly different from that of other petty commodity producers. While many urban artisans and some peasants who produced for the market sold their products directly to the consumer, this was impossible once a specialized industry concentrated in a certain 'proto-industrial' region. Since mass-produced goods could only be sold in relatively large markets and since there are economies of scale to be gained in long-distance trade (so that the marketing cost per unit decreases considerably as the scale of transaction increases) the attempts of producers to maintain the direct sale to consumers as the regular form of exchange had to fail in the long run. Industrial concentration in the countryside was made possible only where merchants opened up distant markets.[22] Either merchants bought the products from the rural producers and arranged for their sale, or some of the producers themselves, as well as other wealthy villagers, assumed that function for all producers. This intervention of commerce between production and consumption was more than just a division of functions. It gave rise to an economic dependence which gradually undermined the formal independence of the petty commodity producer and in the end destroyed it. For the successful trader could achieve considerable profit at the expense of the small producer who had no direct access to the distant market. In times of crisis and personal difficulty he was in a position to extend credit to the producer against the unfinished product and thereby obligated him to sell to nobody else. The big traders were in a strong position anyway *vis-à-vis* the small dispersed producers, but where they succeeded in limiting the competition among buyers by mutual agreements or through public institutions, they could make that position even stronger and lower the purchase prices. Consequently, the *Kaufsystem*, while not attacking the formal independence of the petty producer in the area of production, nonetheless entailed a considerable amount of 'exploitation through trade'.[23]

[margin, handwritten: Producers exploited by merchants, traders in distant markets]

Two different and in many ways contrasting elements interacted with each other but each retained a certain degree of autonomy within their own sphere as long as this type of industrial organization lasted.[24] The sphere of production was ruled by the laws of petty commodity production. The direct producer owned the product which he made. For its manufacture he used home-made or purchased raw materials, his own tools, his own labour power as well as the labour power of his family, though not – or at least to a much smaller extent – wage labour. He took the product to market as a commodity and exchanged it for money in order to buy other commodities. For part of the money he exchanged commodities needed to replace his means of production, i.e. new raw and auxiliary materials as well as replacements for worn out production tools. The remainder constituted the net income of the family,[25] which cannot be divided further, since there was no wage labour. A division into wages and profit is not appropriate under these conditions.[26] This net income was also converted into commodities, namely those which the family needed for its livelihood. With this reproduced labour power and with his replaced means of production the petty producer could start the production process from the beginning.

The sphere of circulation, on the other hand, was ruled by the laws of capital. The trader brought his money to the market and exchanged it for the products of many petty commodity producers. But he made this exchange only in order to exchange those commodities for money somewhere else. This circuit achieved a purpose only if the quantity of money which he received at the end exceeded that which he had had at the beginning. The trader was not interested in the type of commodity (as long as he could resell it somewhere) but only in its exchange value. Profit was the driving force behind this circuit, and depending

[margin, handwritten: hopefully at a profit]

on the economic power constellations, it could be made either at the expense of the small producer in the act of purchase or at the expense of the consumer in the act of sale or at the expense of both.

It was different for the petty commodity producer. He carried his product to the market because he could not use the quantities produced in his own household and because he needed money to buy other goods which he could not produce himself due to his specialization (which, in turn, was forced upon him by the insufficiency of his agrarian base). His real goal when he went to market was not the money which he temporarily held in his hands, but the use value of the goods which he could buy with it. The fact that the goods obtained at the end of this exchange process were qualitatively different from those which he had carried to the market constituted the meaning of this circuit for him. It was therefore not necessary that the exchange value of the purchased goods should be greater than that of the sold goods; rather, if this occurred, it was by 'chance'.[27] One reason why the circuit took on these characteristics for the petty commodity producer lies in the fact that he earned his income purely through his own and his family's physical work-effort without utilizing the work of others. Moreover, on the average and in the long run the returns to a person's or a family's labour could not substantially exceed the means necessary for their livelihood and for the repetition of the production process. The purpose of production was limited to assuring the producers' livelihood as long as production was dominated by the average petty producers. Although their needs and therefore the volume of production varied, they could not constitute the engine of – in principle – unlimited growth.

The phenomenon of a 'backward-bending supply of labour' can be interpreted as a consequence of this determination of production by the producer's needs; he slowed down production when an economic boom increased his real income per unit of product. Whether and to what extent a backward-bending supply of labour actually occurred, depended on a number of conditions. It was the more likely to occur, the more the existing relations of production made it possible for the direct producers to determine the course of production, i.e. the less capital had penetrated into the sphere of production and subjected the labourers to its interests by way of suppression or consumer incentives.[28] In addition, the incomes of the direct producers had to suffice, under average conjunctural conditions, to satisfy their needs; for only then did a rising real income per unit allow them to satisfy their needs by working less and to lower their output. And even that depended on the condition that their consumption needs remained relatively constant.[29]

The laws which regulated the sphere of circulation, dominated by merchant capital, were different:[30] no limit existed, in principle, to the quantitative augmentation of value. Since the capitalist's profit was based on using the products of other people's physical labour and since this involved the labour of a large number of people, his consumption needs were not a decisive factor that determined the extent of his economic activity. That portion of his profit which entered into his personal consumption was of minor importance and was therefore not the driving force behind his activities *as a capitalist*.

For this reason, capitalists could take an interest in the expansion of commodity production when demand rose. Since the pursuit of profit was not limited to the capitalist's capacity for consumption, he would wish to invest profitably whatever he earned beyond his needs. Unless there clearly existed more attractive alternatives,[31] he would try to step up the quantity of his trade, i.e. to always buy and sell again a larger quantity of goods during the following turnover than he had bought and sold during the previous one. If the output of the individual producers was not increased, this was only possible when the products of an ever greater number of producers could be bought. In a situation of rising demand this goal was not just pursued by a few merchants to the disadvantage of others, but by capital in general. For competition tended to equalize and drive down profit rates, which the merchants could only compensate for by enlarging the turnover and thereby the quantity of their profits, as well as their individual market power. This meant that the total number of industrial producers had to grow. And this is precisely what the merchants tried to achieve during proto-industrialization, whenever marketing opportunities opened up. Under such circumstances merchant capital had tapped the rural labour power, which was larger and cheaper than that of the cities, for industrial production.[32] And under such circumstances, capital continued to seize the opportunities offered by the changes in the social stratification of the village[33] and by the demographic growth-process[34] to enlarge the number of industrial producers.[35] This is how the concentrated industrial regions came into existence, which specialized in the mass production of one or a small number of products for far-away markets,[36] and which are encompassed by the term 'proto-industrialization'. When the labour power in a region became insufficient, or when the growing demand for labour made the producers try to improve their situation to such an extent that the merchant-entrepreneurs could employ labour more cheaply elsewhere, they opened up neighbouring as well as more distant regions in order to tap their labour reserves.[37] This kind of spatial expansion was favoured by the fact that, in newly industrializing regions, either more producers than in the old regions cultivated a plot of land and could supplement their industrial incomes, or the price of food was lower.[38] This tendency toward extensive expansion was the main reason why the quantity of industrial goods grew considerably during the period of proto-industrialization.[39]

(c) The putting-out system: the penetration of capital into the sphere of production

When the petty producer worked only upon being commissioned by a trader under the putting-out system (*Verlagssystem*),[40] he lost the formal equality with which he had offered his products to the merchant under the *Kaufsystem*. For the trader, the opportunity to bind numerous petty producers exclusively to himself arose either from his economic superiority, especially when the producers were indebted to him or depended on his raw materials.[41] It could also arise from institutional privileges which gave him a monopoly position.[42] Such putters-out came either from the class of merchants or, sometimes, from the ranks of producers, and in the latter case often from the ranks of the 'finishers', i.e. those who carried out the last stages of the production process.[43]

Within the putting-out system the step toward the penetration of capital into the sphere of production could be a very small one. Once the petty producers were indebted and received their raw materials from the same putter-out to whom they had to deliver their finished products, no great barrier separated them from the situation where the putter-out remained owner of the raw materials throughout the production process. This form of enterprise did not become widespread in the European linen industry, at least not before the nineteenth century and especially not where linen production depended on locally or regionally produced raw materials.[44] In the other branches of the rural textile industry as well as in several of the metal industries this variant of the putting-out system predominated.[45] Quite often the system here described also involved a centralized plant where some part or parts of the production process were carried on.[46]

In the form of the putting-out system where the putter-out owned the raw materials, capital had clearly begun to go beyond the sphere of circulation, i.e. of trade, and penetrated into the sphere of production. Some of the means of production no longer belonged to the direct producers but had been transformed into capital, i.e. into a value that was to create surplus value for its owner. Out of the total cost of replacing the means of production the expenses for raw materials, which were paid for by the putter-out, often constituted the largest part.[47] For, the development of the productive forces being low, the instruments of production must have been quite durable as well as relatively inexpensive to acquire;[48] sometimes, indeed, they were manufactured in the households of the very producers. The expenses for workshops could not have been very high either, especially since production was often carried on in the producers' homes.

In industries which used new and expensive machinery the instruments of production often became the property of the putter-out as well.[49] In this case, capital dominated the sphere of production almost completely.[50] The direct producers no longer manufactured commodities which they sold as their property; they merely sold their labour power for piece-wages (which included the upkeep of the workshops which were also their homes).[51] When capital was invested in the instruments of production, part of it became fixed and could no longer be transferred to other businesses as quickly as had been possible for merchant capital or even for that part of the putting-out capital which was invested in raw materials. But the burdens and risks involved largely fell upon the direct producers when the instruments of production were 'leased out' to them in return for a fixed, often excessive payment. For the direct producers this meant that they preserved a remnant or – at least the semblance – of power over the instruments of production.[52]

In dealing with the problems of organizing and directing the dispersed domestic producers, the putter-out often employed agents and middlemen whose position and authority varied greatly depending on local conditions. They could be mere employees who carried out orders and received fixed commissions; or they could be quite independent businessmen. But the subordinacy and weakness of the mass of producers was increased rather than reduced by this system, since these middlemen often reduced their incomes even further.[53]

To the extent that the ownership of the means of production passed from the domestic producer to the putter-out, the power to decide whether, what, how, and how much should be produced also shifted from the former to the latter. The direct producer, for example, who was no longer the owner of the raw materials that he processed could not even begin his work unless these materials were provided by the putting-out capitalist.[54] But in order to achieve this additional economic power, the putter-out, in contrast to the mere trader, needed an additional capital. The trader needed only enough capital to cover the price which he paid the petty commodity producer, and he needed it only from the moment when he purchased the finished products until the moment of their sale. The putter-out on the other hand, who owned part of the means of production, was obliged to apply part of his capital before the production process was started. It is true that the piece-wage which he paid to the labourer upon completion of the product was correspondingly lower than the price which the independent petty commodity producer received; but since part of his capital turned over more slowly, he needed a larger total capital in order to carry on business on the same scale as the mere trader.[55] Therefore, in order to derive the same profit per unit of time as the mere trader derived from his capital, the putting-out capitalist had to realize a larger profit per unit of product. It is true that capital has an inherent interest in maximizing profit,[56] but it would be wrong to assume that it likewise has an inherent tendency to penetrate into the sphere of production. Therefore, it needs to be explained how and under what conditions an interest in the maximization of profit brought about the penetration of capital into the sphere of production. For this to occur, the profit rate that could be expected from production had to be not only equal to, but greater than, the profit rate common in trade alone. Put briefly, unless such a putter-out could sell his goods at higher prices than the mere merchant – which appears plausible only if they were of better quality – the production costs per unit must have been clearly lower than the purchase prices which the mere trader had to pay to the small commodity producers.[57] How was this possible?[58]

One explanation might be that the independent petty commodity producer received a larger net income than was necessary for the reproduction of his labour power – his net income being the difference between the prices of his products and his expenses for the replacement of the means of production. He therefore could keep at least part of the 'surplus product' to himself. By contrast, under capitalist production which began within the putting-out system, the 'surplus product' fell to the capitalist entrepreneur.

If thinking along these lines is to help explain the historical transition from the former to the latter system, a number of circumstances must be taken into account which will modify it to no small degree. Apparently, it is not always true that the petty commodity-producers achieved a larger net income than was necessary for their own and their family's livelihood, even if one includes the produce from a plot of land that they might cultivate. In some regions, feudal levies siphoned off everything procured above that minimum. Elsewhere an abundant labour supply, perhaps enlarged by institutional limitations on mobility, permitted traders – without becoming involved in production – to drive down purchase prices so low that the direct producers were reduced to the subsistence minimum. Institutional arrangements and agreements among the buyers, which limited the competition between them,[59] artificially produced such a situation, while measures and institutions which were to cut down the competition among producers, like guilds and the exclusion of outsiders, attempted to produce the opposite effect.[60] An incentive for capital to penetrate from the sphere of circulation into that of production could therefore have existed only if the incomes of industrial producers were relatively high – a situation most often brought about by an expansion of the demand for their products which exceeded the growth of that part of the population which was dependent on industrial employment for its livelihood.[61] For only in this case could the producers' incomes be reduced and in this way production costs be lowered.

But what would have induced them, under such circumstances, to give up their independence and to use the means of production belonging to a putting-out capitalist instead of their own? Often these seem to have been workers who were newly drawn into industrial commodity-production during an expansionist phase, or who had been employed in the workshops of others and now wanted to become 'independent'. In both cases, the start was easier if a putter-out gave them the means of production and lessened their marketing risk by giving them commissions.[62] In addition, the succession of economic booms and depressions, in conjunction with the petty producers' indebtedness, must often have irreversibly shifted power from them to the merchant entrepreneur. If, during bad times, they had become indebted to him, he could make their seemingly temporary dependence on him permanent; anticipating an expansion of sales in the long run despite the momentary crisis, he invested part of his capital into raw materials and had them processed by producers who lacked the means to buy them. He thus strengthened his economic position, which, under improved economic conditions, made it easier for him to keep the piece-wages low; it was more difficult for a merchant to keep the purchase prices low in a situation of free play of supply and demand between him and the petty commodity producers.[63]

These mechanisms must have been reinforced by the fact that fewer and fewer industrial producers owned even a small piece of land. It is true that where agricultural incomes were too small for a family's subsistence and where the supply of labour exceeded the demand, the combination of agriculture with industry had originally made it possible, indeed necessary, for petty rural producers to accept lower industrial incomes per unit of labour time than those producers who had to earn their incomes exclusively by industrial work.[64] But this additional agrarian source of income must also have constituted a barrier that made them less susceptible to the fluctuations of the industrial cycle and must have reduced their structural dependence on merchant entrepreneurs. This must have been particularly the case where they remained small independent producers in their agrarian production, even if that was confined to home consumption.[65] During the course of proto-industrialization, the pieces of land in the possession of industrial labourers became smaller and smaller, and the number of landless labourers rose,[66] so that this barrier lost its effectiveness.

An investigation of the reasons which made putting-out capitalists enter the sphere of production, by bringing about a more favourable cost–profit balance in these relations of production than existed in petty commodity production, must consider the relationship between capital and the direct producers under the concrete and changing conditions in the markets for raw materials, on one hand, and for finished products on the other. Finally, this investigation must also deal with the conditions, and especially the changes, in the sphere of production itself. Raw materials which came from relatively distant markets could be bought much more easily by the putter-out than by the individual petty producers. The latter had an approximately equal chance only when the raw materials were produced in small, nearby farms or workshops.[67] Whenever the demand for a certain product changed rapidly owing to changes in fashion[68] or when entirely new articles were to be produced and sold, all the advantages fell to that supplier who could bring the new product to market first. This was easiest for the entrepreneur who owned the raw materials, and possibly the means of production, and therefore could most effectively prescribe the type of article which the direct producers were to manufacture. Finally, it is important to consider the connection between the capital–labour relationship on one hand, and the possibilities for the development of the productivity of labour, on the other. The introduction of new techniques, tools, or forms of organization might mean that capitalists had to assume the cost for some or all of the means of production;[69] but if such a step promised to lower production costs and to increase profit, a strong incentive was provided for capital to undertake the innovations and enter the sphere of production.

The petty producers fought against these newly-arising relations of production as best they could. They resisted being cut off from the markets for their products and being tied to a trader.[70] Those who were not crushed by the sheer impossibility of continuing to produce refused to process the raw materials of a putter-out and even tried to prevent him from distributing raw materials to impoverished and indebted producers and thereby entering the sphere of production.[71] If they had preserved some independence as producers, they resisted the introduction of those new production instruments which they found too large and too expensive to purchase and whose ownership would further strengthen the superiority of the putter-out.[72]

At all these stages the resistance of organized urban guild artisans had greater chances of success than that of the dispersed rural industrial producers who could be, and often were, played off against the former.[73] The rural petty-producers were conscious of the importance of being organized in groups, for they tenaciously held on to the remains of guild and corporative rights – as far as they existed in the countryside.[74] They also repeatedly attempted to form new guilds.[75] As long as they could hope that a deterioration in their situation was caused by a temporary crisis, they refused to work with the capitalist's means of production in order to prevent their dependence on him from becoming permanent and irreversible. But if, in fact, as a result of the economic ascendancy of the new relations of production, this resistance was unsuccessful,[76] the workers turned toward fighting for their wages and working conditions within the framework of the new form of industrial organization. And strikes assumed a prominent place in the new struggle.[77]

As the petty industrial producers became more and more dependent on commerce, and particularly as capital penetrated deeper into the sphere of production, the social division of labour advanced. Consequently, the autonomy of the petty producers and of their 'family economy' declined not only in terms of their control over the material means of production, but also of their power to structure the processes of production.[78] While in the making of products for home consumption all steps of the production process from the raw material to the finished article were often carried on within the household, this hardly applied to those geographically 'concentrated' industries which produced for the market. Even in those linen-producing regions which were based on local flax and hemp cultivation, it was the exception rather than the rule that the cultivation and the processing of the raw material into yarn, as well as weaving were all done successively in the same household.[79] In the putting-out system, apparently, this no longer occurred at all.[80] Here several family members might do the same work side by side,[81] or if the man, woman, and children performed different tasks, these were not necessarily successive steps in the production process; instead, the putter-out, who was also the owner of the raw material, could interfere, apparently because the specialization of individual labourers was so advanced that is was more rational to recruit the workers for different parts of the production-process among the entire workforce employed by a putter-out rather than within a single family.[82] In such cases the family and household were no longer a production *unit* in the sense that the work process required the cooperation of all its members and all earned an indivisible income through their common labour; instead, each family member could earn an individual wage by separate labour. The family and household was merely the *location* where production took place. The family continued to be a unit only with regard to consumption and reproduction. The production process, on the other hand, which was dispersed among many domestic work places, was given its unity by the entrepreneur's direction and control.[83]

(d) Tendencies to centralize production: capitalist manufactures

Even during the phase of proto-industrialization, some and occasionally all[84] the steps of the production process could be centralized in a single production centre where a larger number of labourers – mostly wage-labourers –worked together (*Manufaktur*: centralized manufacture).[85] Such centralized workshops often supplemented rural domestic industry, but under certain conditions they could replace them as well. When production was thus shifted to a central workshop owned by the entrepreneur, the economic functions of family and household were reduced to consumption and the reproduction of the labour power. This centralization was initiated either by the merchant or the putter-out who added some workshops to his counting-house and his stock-rooms with their workers, and, as a consequence, directly supervised some of the productive labour. Alternatively, a few of the petty producers succeeded in expanding their workshops and employing a considerable number of wage-labourers. They thereby broke through the limitations of the family work-unit, eventually gave up productive work altogether, and concentrated their efforts on the supervision of the work of others and on marketing.[86] Last but not least, some who established centralized workshops rose from the heterogeneous group of middlemen and agents in the putting-out system. In such centralized workshops, new, more complex, and more expensive production-procedures could be implemented, as well as larger and more expensive machinery installed. But often enough, the same production-processes which were being performed in small dispersed workshops were simply centralized.

No matter how they had come about, all the means of production in large workshops were normally the property of the entrepreneur. His capital provided the means to pay for raw materials, auxiliary materials, the replacement of the instruments of production, and the work space. To this were added the wages of the labourers. Only after the entrepreneur had acquired all these production-factors in the market could the production process begin. And now it had no other goal than to sell the products, which it generated, at a higher price than that which the entrepreneur had had to lay out. Profit, i.e. the increase of the capital with which the entrepreneur had begun the production process, had become the sole purpose of the process. The direct producers, on the other hand, no longer had to bear any of the cost of the means of production out of their incomes; but this also meant that they now no longer had anything to sell to capital but their labour power. Their goal in selling this commodity was in principle limited and was the same as that of the independent petty commodity-producers. It consisted in the use-value of the commodities which they exchanged for the money which they earned.[87] (And their opportunity to earn an income in excess of the socially necessary reproduction-cost of their labour power was even smaller than in the case of the small commodity-producers who depended on merchant capital to sell their goods.) Industrial capital and merchant capital, on the other hand, had a common motivation in the increase – in principle unlimited – of the exchange value of the commodity. Neither the goals of the direct producers nor those of capital were different in the higher forms of the putting-out system or in centralized manufactures from what they had been in the *Kaufsystem*. The distinguishing feature between the two systems lay in the distribution of power between direct producers and capital. Owing to the change in their objective positions within the production process, capital was stronger in the higher forms of the putting-out system than in the *Kaufsystem* and the direct producers were weaker.[88]

There exists, therefore, a basic distinction between the two forms of commodity production: either its goals are in principle limited to satisfying the needs of the producers, or its goals consist in the essentially unlimited maximization of profit. This distinction is identical with the difference between, on one hand, the production of petty commodity producers who use their own labour power and their own means of production, and, on the other hand, capitalist production which rests on the separation of labour in the form of wage labour, from the ownership of the means of production, in the form of capital.[89] Questions concerning the participation of several members in the production process,[90] the identity of residence and work-place in the 'ganzes Haus',[91] or the combination of industry with agriculture[92] are not central to this basic distinction, even though in other respects they provide important causal explanations for a series of concrete social manifestations, especially those of proto-industry.

The producers forcefully resisted even the last step which deprived them of the rest of their independence, namely the shift of work from their homes to a location under the direct control of the entrepreneur. For long as they continued to hope that their distressed conditions might improve, they tried to avoid this step and survive by other means. When some of them had from sheer necessity taken it, the others often enough tried to defend their existence, which was all the more threatened by the new competition, through protests and even physical violence against the large workshops.[93]

But despite such resistance, and despite the failure of many manufactures, the number of centralized workshops grew which operated profitably even without being supported by privileges and monopolies. The reason why lies in their economic superiority. Although the establishment of a centralized manufacture required more capital than needed to be invested even in the most highly developed forms of the putting-out system – especially more fixed capital[94] which could not be suddenly withdrawn or increased according to economic fluctuations – the profit rate must have been larger in these successful manufactures than either in commerce or in putting-out. This was likely to be the case where new production methods and instruments, which could only be applied in larger workshops, greatly increased the productivity of labour.[95] Moreover, given the spatial dispersion of domestic production, sometimes the problems of transportation, and especially those of controlling the producers' attempts of improving their low piece-rates by embezzling material and botching their work, grew to the point where the centralization of production in large workshops became profitable for the entrepreneur. But in general, the benefit to be derived from centralization without new methods and instruments which increased productivity was worth the investment of a larger amount of fixed capital only in the case of particularly valuable materials and products, and even here usually only for those steps of the work-process which decisively determined the quality and marketability of the finished product.[96] The other steps of the production process were frequently combined with the centralized workshop through the putting-out system, so that the whole enterprise formed a partially centralized manufacture.[97] This must have strengthened further the position of the putter-out. For he now exercised complete control over strategically important parts of the production-process in his manufacturing workshop, and the domestic producers he employed became dependent on him not only for raw materials and the marketing of their products, but also for the finishing of their products into marketable commodities. During the course of proto-industrialization, this form of enterprise became common in many industries.[98]

Centralized manufactures, then, superseded the domestic rural industries, as well as the urban crafts, not in their entirety but only in parts; more often the dispersed and centralized parts of the production process continued to supplement each other.[99] The reason for this was that the capitalist centralized manufacture before the factory was based essentially on handicraft work and did not bring about any revolutionary progress in productivity. Only when this situation changed in one industry after another, due to the Industrial

Revolution and the factory system, did the large plants begin to decisively replace the small workshops. Even here, dispersed production continued in industries that had not yet been seized by mechanization; indeed, depending on the needs of industrial capitalism, it could even expand, usually under conditions of extreme dependence and misery. This lasted until even these industries and these steps of the production process were reached by the revolution of the productive forces.[100]

The stages in the development of the relations of production, which have been described here, do not constitute a sequence in the sense that they necessarily *had* to follow each other. In the course of the historical development of an enterprise or of a region or industry, stagnation or even retrogression could occur, e.g. development might be arrested at the stage of the *Kaufsystem* or at a low stage of the putting-out system. On the other hand, a stage could be omitted, e.g. development might proceed directly from the *Kaufsystem* to a type of centralized manufacture or from some form of putting-out system to the mechanized factory.[101] Nonetheless, the trend in proto-industrialization, though slow and irregular, is clearly recognizable: capital increasingly penetrated into the sphere of production, and relatively independent petty producers, who owned the means of their production, were transformed into dependent wage-labourers. This trend could manifest itself in two forms: either the relations of production in an older proto-industrial region or industry changed, or new industries and regions which were more capitalistically organized grew in importance.[102]

To recapitulate, the explanation of this trend must begin with an analysis of the interests of capital as manifested under conditions of competition, on one hand, and with the constraints under which the direct producers had to earn their livelihood, on the other hand. The type of relations of production, however, that emerged from the interplay between these interests and constraints, also depended on the total set of conditions which originated not only in the relatively narrow limits of a proto-industrial region, but in the society at large. Therefore, the agrarian sector, a region's position in the world market, as well as political and institutional factors have to be taken into account if this process within proto-industrialization is to be explained. (It may be remembered that these factors are equally important for an explanation of the origins of proto-industrialization.)

The new relations of production were a decisive precondition for revolutionizing the productive forces. Proto-industrialization made an important contribution to the emergence of these new relations of production; their complete and exhaustive development in all areas of material production was the definitive sign of the emergence of industrial capitalism, in which proto-industrialization, now 'transcended' or 'anulled', met its end. On the other hand, there were regions and industries where the trend of capital to penetrate into the sphere of production was weak or arrested at an early stage: this was an essential reason why they industrialized late or not at all.[103] In the extreme case a region de-industrialized under the pressure of competition from regions that had progressed from proto-industrialization to industrialization.

2. The development of the productive forces: stagnation and progress

The growth of proto-industrial commodity production rested primarily on the employment of an ever-larger number of labourers. Compared with industrial capitalism, therefore, the growth of proto-industry took on an 'extensive' form. But not exclusively so, for the productivity of labour progressed as well. Compared with earlier centuries such progress appears considerable[104] but it is unspectacular when compared with that under industrial capitalism.

Most likely the chief factors in the growth of productivity were changes in organization, especially the progress in the division of labour. In general, the kind of mass production which was practised in the regions of rural industry and which specialized in a few articles must have been more efficient than the occasional production of an article for home consumption in a peasant household, as well as the production of an artisan who produced a variety of goods on commission by the consumer. If urban guild-artisans, on the other hand, mass-produced a single product, for example cloth or needles, they in the long run competed unsuccessfully with rural industry, not so much because their productivity was lower, but because rural producers could – or had to – content themselves with a lower remuneration for their labour. This was so partly because they obtained some food from a plot of land, or because food prices were lower in the countryside; but partly, too, because they and their families were more vulnerable to exploitation by merchants or entrepreneurs because of the existence of a large rural labour-supply and the absence of protective guild regulations.

The putting-out system by itself did not entail an increased labour productivity either. Rather, the putting-out capitalist adopted existing work-processes and tools. Yet the management of different steps of the production process by a single entrepreneur opened up important opportunities for innovations. When attempts were made to increase efficiency, the division of labour could be manipulated with greater flexibility than was possible when different production stages were divided up among autonomous guild corporations. The division of labour could also increase far beyond what was possible within a single artisan's workshop or industrial family.[105]

When parts of the production-process were successfully centralized, this must have meant a considerable advance in productivity over the dispersed rural production. Only under this condition did the entrepreneur – in contrast to the merchant or putter-out – have any incentive to tie up a considerable part of his capital in a manufacturing building and in tools and machinery; and only under this condition could he try – by offering higher and more assured wages – to entice the reluctant petty producers to leave their domestic workshops and enter his premises, thereby giving up their last vestige of independence. The advantage of the large centralized workshop was finally realized in the fact that the use of transportation routes – which had tended to lengthen with the growth of dispersed rural production – was minimized. Furthermore, control and direction were substantially more effective than was possible even where the small workshops were supervised by a well-developed system of middlemen; embezzlement and fraud, with which the merchant-manufacturer had endlessly to contend, became more difficult. Last but not least, the division of the production-process among cooperating workers could be carried much further than before, once the labourers were spatially concentrated in a centralized manufacture.[106]

However, the advances in productivity, achieved during proto-industrialization, were not brought about exclusively by such improvements in organization. New and improved production techniques and instruments were introduced, others were more widely applied. The water-wheel, for example, which had been known in Europe for centuries was applied to more and more stages and branches of iron-making, processing, and finishing. It was used in forging and cutting iron and steel, for drawing wire, making scythes, grinding blades, tools, needles and pins. In textile production, the most important industry according to the number of workers it employed and the value of its output, technological progress occurred in the production of yarn as well as in weaving and various preparatory and finishing processes.[107] For example, the treadle-operated spinning-wheel with the flyer, probably invented at the beginning of the sixteenth century, replaced the hand spindle in north-western Europe during the sixteenth and seventeenth centuries and was developed further. In the eighteenth century, it moved into eastern and southern Europe. The Dutch loom, on which several ribbons could be woven simultaneously, and the knitting-frame emerged around 1600 and were gradually adopted in the seventeenth and eighteenth centuries, against heavy resistance put up by the guilds. The throwing-mill, which was equipped with a large number of spindles and operated by water-power or a whim-gin, had been developed in the northern Italian silk industry in the late Middle Ages, but was hardly adopted elsewhere in Europe until the seventeenth and eighteenth centuries. The flying shuttle, invented in 1733, spread widely from about the middle of the eighteenth century; it made the second man in weaving broad webs unnecessary, considerably shortened the production time of narrow cloth, and improved the quality of products. In many places, improved bleaching, dyeing, and finishing methods were introduced.

But the importance of these European productivity-increases must not be overestimated. In contrast to the advances in productivity made in England at the end of the eighteenth century they were revolutionary neither in extent nor in character. For example, the water-driven scythe-hammer raised the output per unit of labour to five times that of a hand forge. The treadle-operated spinning-wheel with the flyer may have increased yarn production per spinner and time unit by a third compared to the hand spindle. The Dutch loom increased the productivity of labour perhaps four-fold, the knitting-frame perhaps ten-fold, the flying shuttle probably doubled it. The spinning machines of the late eighteenth century, by contrast, immediately increased the productivity of labour ten-fold, and after a few more years of development, at the end of the century, they exceeded the efficiency of the spinning-wheel a hundred-fold.[108]

Some of these technical innovations had considerable repercussions for the relations of production. The Dutch loom and knitting-frame, for example, were so expensive that the direct producers could often not buy them, so that a putter-out had to provide them and the direct producers became wage labourers who did not own the means of production.[109] This often led to the installation of several such tools in one workshop, which clearly went beyond the boundaries of a single family work-unit.[110] Other items of equipment, especially the water-driven machinery in the metal and textile trades, from the outset required the cooperative labour of just such a larger number of workers concentrated in a central workshop. They thereby brought about the separation of the home from the workplace and the subjection of the worker to the direct control of the entrepreneur. Often the introduction of new or improved finishing processes had similar consequences, for example in bleaching, dyeing, and the printing of calico.[111]

Nonetheless, during the phase of proto-industrialization such economic and social effects of technological progress were not nearly as sweeping as they became during the Industrial Revolution. First, the instruments of production used by the large majority of proto-industrial labourers remained such in size, complexity, and motive power that they could be installed in the direct producers' homes. Secondly, the important innovations, including those which led to centralized production, tended to occur in specialty and luxury industries, rather than in industries with mass markets like the linen and later the cotton trades. When they did occur in the latter, they affected the finishing processes more than spinning and weaving, but these were more significant because they employed more workers. Only when innovation seized the main stages in those branches of industry whose mass markets had a vast potential for expansion, were other production stages and branches affected as well; and so, indeed, was the entire economy and society. Then each innovation brought another in its wake.[112] In this regard the flying shuttle was an important step which increased the productivity of weaving for a variety of fabrics and thereby created a bottleneck in the provisioning of weavers with yarn. But it did not have the revolutionary character of the spinning-machines of the late eighteenth century. Compared with these, the productivity increase of the flying shuttle was small, and moreover, it could be introduced in the workshops of domestic producers and did not require a large centralized plant.[113]

Just as certain innovations which increased productivity stimulated a change in the relations of production, these, in turn, are of fundamental importance in the overall configuration of economic, social, and cultural factors which determined the development of productive forces. Especially during the phase of proto-industrialization, when stagnating regions and industries existed beside others which progressed, an explanation of such differences appears possible only when it is taken into consideration that the relations of production differed through time and space. These questions can be further illuminated by a comparison with older and simultaneous feudal conditions in the agrarian sphere, as well as with urban guild structures and with the subsequent conditions of industrial capitalism.

First a comparison with feudal conditions: it has been pointed out earlier that as long as markets had been undeveloped a fundamental barrier existed to the interests which the feudal lord had in enriching himself, this barrier being the consumption capacity of his household. The barrier fell when markets opened up for the goods which his serfs produced. But this did not usually mean that he took measures to increase productivity, for there were other ways of expanding his income, which he preferred because they did not require that he use part of his revenue for investments. He was far more likely to try to increase his share of the total product at the expense of his serfs than to enlarge the volume of the total product. Or he simply profited from changes in the terms of trade. In any case, the growing income of feudal lords during this time is hardly the result of increasing labour-productivity.[114] The interests of the serfs, too, prevented it. If they performed labour services and produced goods which had to be turned over to their lord, they obviously had no interest in increasing their efficiency.[115] If their services and rents in kind were commuted into money rents, the participation of the feudal lord in the economic process took on more parasitic forms so that his interest in, as well as his possibilities for, improving production are unlikely to have increased. The position of serfs who took their own products to market approached that of petty commodity producers, but it remained distinct insofar as serfs were economically weakened by feudal dues.

For the average petty commodity-producers, the use value of the commodities which they exchanged for their products was the goal of production, rather than the unlimited maximization of their income.[116] Nonetheless, the expectation of improving their living conditions might have stimulated their interest in increasing their productivity. Since consumption, at any given time in history, could be increased only by a limited amount, it could not provide the incentive that would permanently revolutionize the productive forces. (This became possible only with industrial capitalism, when production was dominated not by consumption needs, but by the interest in, and – as a result of competition – the necessity of, the maximization of profit and the continuous accumulation of capital.) In addition, for a number of reasons, the limited interest which the mass of petty commodity-producers might have in developing the productivity of their labour could change into a lack of interest or even resistance. This effect was produced, in particular, by the fear that a considerable increase in production through the improvement of tools and machinery would in the long run lead to unemployment.[117] Often enough, too, the average petty industrial producer must have been prevented from adopting technological innovations which required additional expenditures, because his economic base was too weak. This is most likely one of the reasons why new and improved tools and techniques found acceptance much more slowly in eastern Europe, where the petty industrial producers in the countryside were dependent not only on merchants or putters-out but were also subject to considerable feudal burdens.[118] But even in England, the resistance of weavers was apparently directed not so much against the innovation of the flying shuttle *per se* as against the payments that had to be made under patent law for its use.[119] Finally, resistance appeared when innovations threatened to restrict or eliminate the independence of the direct producers, for example when a new tool was too expensive for the petty producer and he had to 'rent' it from a capitalist, or when it could be operated only in the central production facility of the entrepreneur.

A fundamental interest as well as these specific reasons for resistance united all types of petty commodity-producers in contrast to the industrial capitalist. In this respect, no difference existed between, let us say, urban guild artisans and rural families of industrial producers. Nonetheless, some innovations, which were most violently and to some extent successfully combated by urban guilds, were introduced into rural industry. This applies, for example, to the Dutch loom and the knitting-frame.[120] While, in the event of conflict arising, all petty producers were more interested in assuring the adequacy of their incomes as well as tolerable living and working conditions than they were in increasing output through innovation, the town artisans had their guild organization which could be used as a rather powerful means of defending their interests against deviant individual producers as well as against merchants, putters-out, or entrepreneurs.[121] The rural industrial population, on the other hand, usually had no such strong organization but lived and worked dispersed in the villages. They were more dependent on distant markets, with their economic fluctuation, and therefore on merchants, putters-out, or entrepreneurs. Wherever effective guild organizations did exist in the countryside, the forms and effects of resistance against threatening innovations were quite similar to those in towns. The scythe-smiths' guild in the region of Remscheid (Rhineland), for example, fought quite successfully against the introduction of water-driven scythe-hammers.[122]

In contrast to the mass of petty commodity-producers, the merchant had the capital necessary for innovations. Moreover, his interest in enlarging his capital by maximizing his profit was in principle unlimited.[123] As long as he remained only a merchant, however, he did not try to achieve this goal by increasing the productivity of labour. Rather, he responded to expanding demand by buying up the products of an increasing number of industrial producers in ever more distant rural areas, and, if possible, in such areas where the industrial incomes did not have to cover the entire livelihood of the producers.[124] And he responded to contracting demand and falling profits by lowering the prices paid for the products of petty producers[125] and by limiting, even discontinuing, the purchase of their products. To a crisis of long duration he might respond by trading in different products and by investing his capital elsewhere. In addition, a part of mercantile profits must often have arisen from the legal and social dependency and the inexperience of producers and consumers. As long as capital remained within the sphere of circulation and the capitalist as merchant expended his money only when the product was finished, he must have had little interest in interfering with the production-process in order to increase productivity. In any case, he was hardly in a position to do so. Commerce promoted the growth of the national product only indirectly, in particular by contributing to an advancement of the social division of labour and regional specialization, as well as by the lowering of the transaction costs per unit of product which resulted from the distribution in bulk.[126]

The situation changed when – and to the extent that – capital entered the sphere of production. In this way the structural conditions emerged which, for the first time, could direct the interest which capital has in accumulation and expansion – an interest which had existed in earlier periods as well and also applied to merchant capitalists and usurers – toward a systematic development of the productive forces. Already the putting-out capitalist, who owned the raw materials, profited from the shortening of production time as well as from the economizing of materials, for his profit rate was increased by them. This was even more true for the entrepreneur who owned the instruments of production: he profited, in addition, from the improved utilization and from the improvement of the production tools. Even if he gave his labourers an incentive to accept the use of new or improved instruments in the form of higher wages per unit of labour time, nobody could prevent him from drawing the main advantage from the utilization of such instruments since he was their owner. As the direct producers' dependence on capital increased, so their chances declined of benefiting directly from increases in productivity. Their motivation to adopt such advances, therefore, cannot have become more lively. Their power, however, to resist them, when they saw their interests threatened, tended to decline as production became more and more dominated by capital and the workers were subjected to its discipline.[127]

The penetration of capital into the sphere of production, effected either by merchants or by individual petty commodity-producers who did not adhere to the norms of their fellow producers, was a long-lasting process conditioned by many factors.[128] By the same token, the potentiality for the development of the productive forces which was created by this process became reality only slowly. To a growth or decline in demand, for example, the putter-out who owned the raw materials is likely to have reacted, in the beginning, much like the merchant, that is by enlarging or reducing the number of his labourers and thereby adjusting his wage expenditures.[129] If he also owned the instruments of production and the building where work took place, his opportunity to enlarge or reduce his capital investment in the short run was limited. But he gained power to reshape the production process when the situation in the factor or product markets promised higher returns from the introduction of an innovation. The advance of capital into the sphere of production created the possibility for capital to profit from cost-saving improvements of the process of production. If this potentiality was to become reality, i.e. if the interest of capital was to become an active force which increased productivity, a situation must be assumed in which the demand for industrial products grew continuously and much faster than the available labour power,[130] and in which, therefore, given a relatively free play of supply and demand, wage costs rose,[131] but in which all capitalists strove, under the pressure of competition, to sell their products as cheaply as possible in order to achieve as large a market share as possible. Under such circumstances, capitalists, in order to lower their wage costs and thereby undersell their competitors, had to increase productivity. But this mechanism could only take effect and lead to the cumulative process of the Industrial Revolution, after capital had entered the sphere of production and subjected the direct producers to its control. Only to the extent that this occurred did capital profit from changes in the production process which raised productivity, and only then did it have the power to effect such changes.

3. The character of economic fluctuations: crises of the 'type ancien' caused by harvest failures – crises resulting from political causes – beginnings of a cyclical movement of the economy generated by capital

Industrial commodity-production in the countryside had a twofold origin. It rested, on one hand, on the special conditions in certain regions which prevented part of the rural population from earning a sufficient income from agriculture and, on the other hand, it depended upon the opening up of markets in other regions, countries, and continents. Consequently, the economic fluctuations in proto-industrial regions were conditioned both by the circumstances within the region or in nearby regions as well as by developments in international markets and in the competing proto-industrial regions of other countries. In addition, the economic fortunes of proto-industrial regions were influenced by the emergent capitalism as well as by the agrarian sector, for such regions remained integrated into predominantly agrarian societies.

Nevertheless, during the course of the proto-industrial phase, depending on the stage of development in individual countries and regions, the weight of the factors which determined economic fluctuations shifted and as a consequence the character, extent, and effects of the crises changed.

Natural conditions still exercised a great influence on the course of the economy. The climate in particular directly influenced the fluctuations between normal, good and bad harvests which led to the crises of the 'old type'. Yet the effects of such natural factors were also socially determined. Fluctuations in the weather could produce the disastrous consequences of the crises of the 'old type' only because the productive forces in agriculture were little developed, which, in turn, must be seen in connection with the relations of production which failed to stimulate their development or even prevented it.[132] The fact that such crises weakened under the progressive conditions in England helps to prove this point.[133] The shift between good and bad harvests still had considerable importance for the proto-industrial regions. This was true, first of all, because the industrial population needed to be provided with food. Even local harvest-fluctuations continued to influence the fortunes of petty rural industrial producers in areas where many of them worked a piece of land to provide for their own needs. Still, as long as the harvest did not fail completely, the agrarian base was a buffer against the effects of dearth for the small producer. But since the percentage of producers without sufficient land grew during proto-industrialization, their provisioning with food was more and more dependent on the price fluctuations in the grain markets, which took on an increasingly inter-regional, indeed international, character, due, in part, to improvements in transportation.[134] The fact that proto-industrial regions participated in social unrest during times of dearth shows that the situation of petty industrial producers was strongly influenced by the price movements of their basic foodstuffs.[135]

The raw-material basis, too, remained dependent on the regional fluctuations of the harvest cycle, if the raw materials that were processed in a particular proto-industrial region were produced within that or a neighbouring region; this often applied to flax and hemp, and sometimes to wool. However the harvest-fluctuations of foodstuffs and those of industrial raw materials did not necessarily run parallel,[136] and since the raw-material prices usually constituted only a small portion of the cost of the finished product, the harvest-fluctuations and the price-movements which they entailed for raw materials are likely to have affected the industrial cycle less severely than the movement of grain harvests and grain-prices did.[137] On the other hand, the prices for raw materials and semi-finished products were by no means consistently determined by the market opportunities of the finished product.[138]

Crises of the old type had a disastrous effect on the industrial population in a double sense. Not only did the prices of the most basic foodstuffs rise precipitously, but the bulk of the population was forced to spend all available income on food which caused the demand for industrial products to shrink drastically so that sales and employment opportunities in industry declined – and that probably more steeply than prices and wages. Contemporary reports and historical statistics indicate not only that this vicious circle affected the urban crafts, but that numerous rural industrial regions were also subject to it. A small agent of the Swiss cotton industry, whose family was hard hit by the food crisis of 1770, wrote: 'Trading declined as the food prices rose, and the poor spinners and weavers had no other recourse but to borrow and borrow again.'[139] In 1740 and 1752, when grain prices peaked, the index of woollen-cloth production in the area of Rouen declined by 16 and 30 per cent respectively of the average volume of the 1740s and 1750s. Similarly, when in 1770 and 1772 grain prices in Brittany rose by 31 and 38 per cent respectively, linen production decreased by 18 and 19 per cent compared with the average of the surrounding one-and-a-half decades.[140] During food crises, proto-industrial regions were not only hit by the contraction of demand, but could be subject to disastrous demographic consequences as well: in Electoral Saxony, mortality doubled in 1772, while simultaneously births declined by almost one third, and the population losses in the industrial regions of the Erzgebirge and the Vogtland were significantly higher than this average for the entire state.[141]

But there was a difference between the industries which worked for distant markets and those whose products catered for the local demand. In times of dearth the former could avoid the additional negative effects on the demand for their products, if the regions where their products were consumed remained unaffected by the rise in cereal prices.[142] Those industries which worked for overseas markets escaped the worst consequences of the great food-crises that swept through large parts of Europe. In 1771–2, for example, the value of linen-exports from Silesia increased by 29.7 per cent above the average of the previous five years, even though sales in the Prussian provinces and the Empire had fallen perceptibly because of the harvest-failures. The reason was that the chief markets for Silesian linen products were to be found overseas in 'England, Holland, France, Spain, Portugal, the West Indies, and other parts of the world', and these exports rose by 58.6 per cent. Even during the hunger-year of 1772–3, according to census figures – incomplete though they are – this level was maintained and it was slightly exceeded again during 1773–4.[143] This, however, should not lead to the conclusion that such regions no longer felt the effects of the food crisis at all, for contemporary reports testify to the contrary.[144] Even though the continuing uptake-capacity of the distant markets prevented industrial prices and wages from falling and unemployment from spreading, the prices of foodstuffs far outstripped the incomes of petty producers. Still, the effects of the crisis were mitigated and its disastrous demographic consequences limited or prevented.[145]

But while the interaction of proto-industrial regions with the world market offered the chance to escape the negative effects of food crises upon industrial demand, the new network of international dependencies contained new risks as well. Competition in distant markets became international. Not only did several German linen-regions compete with each other for outlets in the American colonies, but Flemish, French, Scottish, and Irish ones competed as well. The fortunes of proto-industrial regions, their rise, stagnation, and ruin, were all determined in this international network. The prices of their products became international.[146] But the efficiency of the individual region participating in this international competition, i.e. the question whether its producers could or could not produce at the price fixed in the international market while maintaining their subsistence, was primarily determined by the economic, social, and institutional conditions within that region.

Proto-industrial regions were drawn not only into international competition, but also into the fluctuations of world trade. These frequently had political causes: changes in the economic and tariff policy of other countries, political upheavals, and military conflicts. Especially during this period, economic causes and goals, in addition to directly political and military ones, tended to lie at the root of conflicts.[147] Politics and war in Europe and its colonial dependencies were often determined by the competitiveness of the emerging national economies. If the stimulating and the crisis-producing effects of politics and war upon industrial production are to be analysed, differentiations must be made according to time period, country, and industry, and short-term effects must be distinguished from long-term consequences. The direct influences of war could be extremely harsh, as the Silesian linen weavers had to realize on several occasions during the eighteenth and early nineteenth centuries. When enemy forces marched through the province in 1761–2 and at the same time overseas connections suffered because England turned away from Prussia, the value of linen exports from Silesia fell by 78 per cent from one year to the next, according to official statistics. Exports to 'England, Holland, France, Spain, Portugal, the West Indies, and other parts of the world' were reduced by as much as 88 per cent. (It should be mentioned, though, that the census for that crisis year may be incomplete.[148]) Exports were sharply reduced in 1793 during the wars of the French Revolution,[149] and the Continental Blockade was a severe blow that lasted for years. According to the export table of the Landshut linen trade, the annually-exported quantity of linen products fell by 67 per cent during 1807–13 compared with the average of the years 1800–6; indeed, during the worst year, 1813, it declined by 85 per cent.[150]

It needs to be carefully investigated whether and, if so, to what extent an 'endogenous' economic and specifically industrial cyclical movement was at the root of fluctuations during the phase of proto-industrialization, instead of or in addition to harvest fluctuations or political events. Proto-industry obviously contained some of the structural conditions of such a cyclical movement[151] which leads from expansion to over-production, i.e. to the expansion of production beyond the effective demand of those who have enough money to buy, and thereby to a crisis. To what extent these conditions existed, depended on the concrete relations of production.

Already, with commodity production and the severance of the unmediated relationships of natural exchange between producers, and their replacement by money-mediated trade, the possibility arose of the interruption of the circulation process. This happened when a producer sold a product without buying another one thereafter, so that another producer was prevented from converting *his* product into money. The larger and more distant the markets – taking into consideration the poorly developed communications-system – the more importance would attach to the fact that, at the beginning of the production-process, the effective demand was an unknown quantity, one that would emerge only 'a posteriori', that is to say only after the commodities produced were offered in the market. Under contemporary transport-conditions, a long period of circulation elapsed between the finishing of the product and its final consumption,[152] which made industry susceptible to disturbances, especially when credit was used.[153] Since in proto-industrialization, capital mediated the commodities between the direct producers and consumers, an interest was added to these structural factors that could set off a cycle of crises. For the petty commodity-producers, the basic purpose of production lay in the satisfaction of their needs, and they had no interest in interrupting the social process of circulation by withholding the money obtained for their products instead of exchanging it for the products of others; nor did they wish to increase the quantity of their products without limit. Moreover, their economic weakness did not permit them either of these courses of action. But for the trader, the purpose of economic activity consisted in the basically unlimited accumulation of capital.[154] Given favourable marketing-expectations, this interest in accumulation led to the expansion of his business activity, which always included the possibility that the capacity of markets would be over-estimated, so that stores of goods piled up, prices declined, and the goods could only be sold at a loss. For expansion was often overheated due to speculation, financed by extensive credit, and carried on simultaneously by many merchants in a number of competing regions. In this situation, there existed an interest, indeed the necessity, for the merchant to limit or even interrupt the reconversion of his money into products. He lowered the purchasing-prices so that the sales prices again covered his purchasing-prices plus his overhead and profit, and his business restored to health. In addition, since he was overstocked, he limited his purchases, either because he was forced to do so in order to meet his obligations or because he preferred to trade in goods that were not affected by the marketing crisis. He could easily switch to another commodity, since his capital was not tied up in the sphere of production and, more likely than not, was already invested in trading in a variety of products.[155] And indeed, there exist reports of such booms and 'trading-goods crises' for the period of proto-industrialization.[156] These crises, however, did not originate endogenously in the interaction between merchant capital and commodity production. Rather, they were caused by political and military events or by fluctuations in the money and credit situation, which, in turn, did not originate primarily in the sphere of industrial production. Consequently, the cyclical movement of commodity-production, mediated by merchant capital, was a contributing factor to the crisis but cannot be regarded as its fundamental characteristic nor as its intrinsic cause.

If, during the period of expansion and under the condition of a relatively free play of supply and demand between petty industrial producers and merchants, the real income per unit rose above the consumption-needs of the producers,[157] and if the producers could therefore reduce their working hours and the volume of their production, this should have brought about an anticyclical effect that counteracted the danger of overproduction. For it must have been difficult and costly for the merchant to offset this decline in supply by employing new labourers in distant areas at short notice. In fact, he had to overcompensate the decline in supply if he wanted to benefit from the increasing sales opportunities. But once a marketing crisis existed, the attitudes of petty independent commodity-producers must have reinforced it. Most likely, they tried to compensate for the fall in prices for their products by enlarging the volume of their production as far as their own and their family's physical strength permitted.[158] The quality of their production, however, might have deteriorated.[159] As long as they had no other opportunities to gain an income, they had no choice but to sell their products even at the lowest price, even if it covered only the cost of their means of production and a minute net return for their subsistence, for – as has been pointed out – the item 'wages' did not enter their calculation.[160] In extreme situations, it is reported, the petty producers did not even recover the costs of their means of production. But even for petty producers such pro-cyclical behaviour had limits beyond which they could not go. First, there were limits to their capability and willingness to endure such distress. In 1793, for example, the weavers rebelled in Silesia, and – something conceivable only among petty commodity-producers – they rebelled more fiercely against the yarn traders (who had raised the yarn-prices by 11–13 per cent in the course of a year ending February 1793) than against the linen merchants who, due to marketing problems caused by the war, had lowered their purchase-prices by between one sixth and one third. These opposite movements of prices went so far that the weavers could not even cover the cost of yarn with the money that the merchants paid them for their products.[161] A further barrier against the expansion of production under very low net incomes was the fact that the petty industrial producers could not – or could only to a limited extent – continue to work when their gross income covered less than the cost of their livelihood at minimum subsistence level plus the cost of replacing their means of production, and when their credit was exhausted[162] – something that happened all too quickly unless they owned a house or land. Furthermore, it must be remembered that in a crisis in which the merchants had few liquid assets and their stores were full of unsaleable goods, they limited their purchases even when prices were falling so that the petty producers were unable to sell anything at all. When, finally, their misery outlasted their capacity to survive or when no prospect of improvement remained, the petty producers must have turned to other kinds of work, if any existed, rather than starve to death. But such alternatives were not available at all times and in all regions of proto-industrialization. It was often only during the course of proto-industrialization and as a consequence of it that it became possible to find employment at piece-wages for a putter-out, or as a wage labourer in a centralized manufacturing facility.

To the extent that capital gained ground in the sphere of production, the distinctive features of the economic behaviour of independent petty producers were whittled away. This tendency was at its most obvious in crisis situations. Already in the putting-out system, where the raw materials were owned by the capitalist, the entrepreneur not only lowered the piece-wages when he encountered marketing problems – as the merchant lowered the purchasing prices; he also distributed fewer, and in extreme cases, no raw materials to his labourers, as soon as his sales prices no longer sufficed to cover the price of the raw material, plus the piece-wages, plus his profit. Since they lacked the necessary means of production, the direct producers could no longer attempt to offset their reduced income per unit by increasing the volume of their production. It was the capitalist who determined how much, if anything, could be produced. This means that ever since capital had entered the sphere of production, the immediate consequence of a crisis was unemployment.[163] However, if a considerable amount of fixed capital was invested in the instruments of production and possibly also in centralized manufactures, it could in the long run be less detrimental for the entrepreneur to maintain, rather than interrupt, at least that special part of his production, provided his financial situation permitted this and an end of the crisis could be expected[164] – particularly when he employed specialized labourers, who were hard to find.

To protect themselves against a potential reduction in the supply of labour when demand was rising, the putters-out, when business was normal, might give out raw materials to a slightly larger number of producers, all of whom remained slightly underemployed. In this way, the merchant-manufacturer tied a reserve labour force to himself in case demand should increase. But greater opportunities to control the labour-supply arose only in centralized manufactures. To the extent that independent petty producers tended to reduce the volume of their production when the prices per unit rose, and to the extent that the effects of this behaviour – or the behaviour itself – were contained by the emergence of capitalist relations of production, a factor was eliminated which had tended to curtail overproduction.

Other conditions which furthered the crisis arose when means of production were transformed into capital. Whereas the business of the merchant could only be disturbed in the marketing of the finished products, the enterprise of the putter-out was exposed to additional disturbances when he bought raw materials to give to his labourers. Moreover, the capital of the putter-out turned over even more slowly than the merchant's capital. If the former tied up his capital in production-tools and a centralized manufacturing plant, he could no longer respond with the same flexibility to fluctuations in demand. To the extent that the advancement of capital was tied to innovations that raised productivity and favoured such innovations, the tendency to expand production beyond effective demand must have been strengthened.

In sum, the beginnings of a cyclical movement of industrial commodity production became more marked when capital was no longer limited to circulation but had entered the sphere of production. This cyclical movement, however, could not become the dominant feature of economic fluctuations until the transition to industrial capitalism had been made; only then did economic crises generally take on the form of periodic over-accumulation, i.e. of investment of more capital than could profitably be employed.[165] For all through proto-industrialization, the capital that was tied up in the instruments of production and manufacturing plants constituted a small portion of the total national capital. Its elements were rarely the object of capitalist production: a capital-goods industry did not exist or was of no significance for the economy as a whole. Therefore speculative booms and crises occurring in the consumer-goods industry could not have a multiplier effect on the entire economy. Since the forces of production were not yet being systematically developed, a sudden crisis of overproduction was less likely. Admittedly, under the contemporary conditions of production and transportation, the turnover of capital was slow, thus making the cycle more vulnerable; but since this slowness also forestalled short-term reactions to boom-situations, it must surely also have contributed toward flattening the curve. Finally, since throughout proto-industrialization the agrarian sector far exceeded the industrial sector in the value of its production and the number of labourers it employed, the movements in industry could not dominate the entire economy.

Thus, proto-industrial regions were affected by the economic fluctuations of their closer and more distant environment as well as by those of distant countries. The various fluctuations could counterbalance each other so that their effect was weakened, but they could also reinforce each other. The harvest crises of the 'type ancien' still had considerable effects on people in proto-industrial regions, even though their impact tended to be less pronounced than it was on the inhabitants of agrarian regions and on industrial producers who supplied the nearby markets. On the other hand, the former felt the influence of international political and military changes much more keenly than the latter. Already the fluctuations of proto-industrial commodity production showed signs of a cyclical movement generated by capital.

The degree to which proto-industrial regions were susceptible to crises could therefore vary considerably. As the severity of agrarian subsistence-crises was gradually reduced, as in England, by a strengthening of the productive forces, which resulted from the advance in the relations of production, the domestic demand could expand and achieve greater continuity. The stabilizing effect of such a domestic demand was lacking, for example, in the German linen regions,[166] which were therefore most severely hit by all dislocations in international trade. In most parts of Germany the great majority of the rural population were so poor that they could only buy what was absolutely necessary.[167] The demand for luxury goods, generated by princes and large landowners, who siphoned off so much of the agrarian income,[168] might offer a certain compensation for the lack of purchasing power among the masses during the proto-industrial phase,[169] but sooner or later such an expansion in the demand for luxuries *instead of* the expansion of a stable demand for mass consumer products turned out to be a dead end. The revolutionizing of the productive forces, in any case, could only be brought about by those industries which produced mass goods.[170] On the other hand, the demand generated by the state, particularly by the army, could call forth standardized commodities in large quantity, but it never reached either the volume or the continuity of a broad general mass demand and therefore could only supplement but not replace it.[171] Those regions which were particularly closely tied to the world market because of their raw material imports or their sales of the finished products were better protected against political and military upheavals if the state occupied a strong international position.

All these factors, in addition to a relatively well-ordered currency and credit situation, contributed to England's being less vulnerable than her competitors on the continent. Based on a steadily growing domestic market, which enabled her to overcome temporary export problems,[172] as well as on the enormous potential for expansion of her foreign trade[173] which, owing to her political and military supremacy at sea and in colonial areas, was usually not interrupted during wars,[174] the long-term demand for industrial products could grow relatively undisturbed, and even faster than the industrial population. This demand stimulated organizational and technical progress and gave to English industry the head-start which was decisive for the transition from proto-industrialization to industrialization.[175]

5 ❧ Excursus: the political and institutional framework of proto-industrialization

Neither the producers nor the capitalists could directly create and guarantee the basic institutional conditions for the continuous development of market production and commodity exchange. With the separation of production and consumption, with the emergence and expansion of commodity exchange mediated by money, and with the development of socio-economic relations in which part of the direct producers' surplus was siphoned off by persons who had no 'extra-economic' power over them, the need arose for a political power which guaranteed the legal basis of such socio-economic relations. This power had to be permanent and institutionalized; it had to formally stand above the producers and those who appropriated the 'surplus product'. Property in the commodities designated for exchange must be acknowledged and guaranteed by the state, and the buyer and seller recognized as free and equal in their capacity as owners of commodities and money respectively. This is the basic condition of commodity exchange in the markets for products and 'factors'.[176] However, the period of which proto-industrialization was one of the features had two important characteristics. First, the legal order based on formal freedom and equality as well as on bourgeois property was only emerging. Its course of development differed greatly from one society to the next. Secondly, the fundamental importance of violence was more clearly visible during the period when this new legal order was created than during the later period when it functioned regularly. Later, the process of production reproduced its own social conditions as well, and violence, therefore, could more often – though by no means always – remain latent in 'normal' times. But during the earlier period, power tended much more to assume the form of direct physical action and violence. It did so in the interior of countries as well as in their relations with other states.[177]

The expansion of market relations in spatial range as well as in depth, i.e. in the extent to which individual farms and workshops produced and consumed commodities, contributed to making the 'modern' state both necessary and possible.[178] But neither the origin of the modern state nor its goals and activities were directly determined by economic interests; nor did the governments and state officials pursue such interests in the form of consistent and conscious political actions. Rather, political power should be viewed as being to a certain extent autonomous. During the period under discussion, this shows up in the fact that governments were directly interested in increasing their political and military power and their tax revenues and the economic policy was only a means to that end.[179] From the point of view of the results achieved, governments often wasted their resources on luxuries and military expenditures which turned out to be burdensome and did not promote the economic development of their countries.[180] Countries differed, however, with regard to the ease with which such fiscal goals could be pursued and such an 'uneconomic' policy be developed. They also differed with regard to the economic and social policy which was most likely to increase the power and the tax revenue of the state, i.e. the policy which produced the greatest effect while involving the least cost and risk. These differences depended on the structure of the state's decision-making organs[181] and – more basically – on the structure of the society and economy to be governed and taxed.[182]

An analysis of the interrelationship between the economy and the political system, and of the mechanisms for their mediation during the period under discussion, must not be limited to proto-industrialization, but would have to include the entire society, especially the still predominant agrarian sector. It would have to reveal general features as well as the differences between states. In fact, it would have to become a theory of the state for this period. This, however, far exceeds the intentions and possibilities of this study.[183] Nonetheless, since the political and institutional conditions clearly were of considerable importance for the origin and development of proto-industrialization, some of them will be briefly outlined. This outline will mainly consider the consequences which certain political and institutional configurations had for proto-industrialization, i.e. the question what sort of politics and which institutions proved to be beneficial for proto-industrialization, and which detrimental to it. An attempt will be made to analyse the purely economic measures taken by governments against the background of the economic consequences of other government actions as well as the background of the structure of the respective state and its society. It is hoped that the understanding of 'mercantilist' politics will be deepened by this approach and that its assessment can be differentiated according to country and time period.[184] On the other hand, the extent to which proto-industrialization in its turn contributed to changing or maintaining the political and institutional order can hardly be analysed here. For it can only be determined if the contributions of the other sectors are evaluated at the same time.

On the whole, there tended to be a correlation between economic and institutional development: a more developed organization of the production and marketing of industrial commodities as well as improved instruments and methods of production spread more quickly and more widely in those countries where the old legal framework of agriculture and industry was weaker, the protection of property and mobility on factor- and product-markets was greater, and where political institutions gave more weight to the interests of trade, industry and modernizing agriculture.[185] This correlation is apparent in the conflict between emerging proto-industrialization and the exclusive rights of the urban guilds.

The monopoly which the towns exercised in industrial commodity-production, and the regulations which limited competition by controlling the volume, organization, and techniques of production within the guilds had to be abolished or at least weakened and circumvented, if the reservoir of cheap rural labour was to be tapped for industrial commodity production, in order to satisfy the strongly expanding demand in sixteenth- and seventeenth-century European and in overseas markets. The merchants, putters-out, and sometimes feudal lords who were all interested in shifting industry to the countryside, by and large persuaded the political powers, against the resistance of urban guilds, to legalize or at least tolerate rural export industries. The governments, in their turn, were usually interested in integrating the urban economy into a 'territorial economy'[186] that more or less comprised the entire area under their control. In several city republics of the Holy Roman Empire, however, where guild interests directly determined governmental policies, putting-out firms and partially centralized manufactures left the territory directly controlled by city governments.[187]

The corporate monopolies of the towns, against which the emerging proto-industry had to assert itself, were quite similar in all European countries, but the legal situations which merchant capital encountered in the countryside varied considerably.[188] Still, the utilization of rural labour power for industrial commodity-production turned out to be possible not only in those parts of western Europe where the feudal ties and burdens of the producers and of the soil had weakened since the late Middle Ages, but also in the area of second serfdom. Here, however, it was a precondition of proto-industrialization that the feudal lords developed an interest in export industries, in expectation of higher rents. Otherwise, they would use their power of controlling new settlements in order to prevent industries from establishing themselves in the countryside.[189] As a rule, proto-industrialization did not emerge in those regions where the lords appropriated the surplus labour of the rural population most directly and most thoroughly, particularly in regions where labour services predominated.[190] A certain incentive, apparently, had to be given to rural producers so that they could count firmly on at least a portion of the return to their industrial labour and did not need to fear its being mostly or entirely siphoned off.

In these areas, then, as well as in western Europe, some degree of freedom and security among the producers was an indispensable prerequisite of proto-industrialization. Those feudal constraints and charges which continued to exist in eastern Europe put pressure on the incomes of producers in the industrial regions and prevented the development of a strong domestic market. Owing to this situation, these regions, even more than others, were vulnerable to crises and provided fewer opportunities and incentives for petty producers and merchants or putters-out to increase their productivity through innovations. Compared with many parts of western Europe, these regions therefore suffered.[191] The limitations upon mobility that were connected with serfdom increasingly turned into an obstacle to industrial growth, a fact which apparently contributed to the abolition of serfdom.[192]

Since proto-industrialization was mass production for relatively distant markets, it required improved conditions of commodity exchange. Basically, states of sufficient size and strength guaranteed a legal situation which enabled buyers and sellers to make business calculations largely without being subjected to 'arbitrary' interferences.[193] All European states attempted to create this kind of legal situation with more or less success during this period. In the advanced countries, the incentive as well as the possibility increased to create a larger, more integrated domestic market by eliminating internal tariffs, especially those on trade routes, as well as staple rights and other impediments to free trade.[194] The development of money and capital markets was important for the trade in the products as well as sometimes the raw materials of rural industry. Trade with distant countries and continents could only be carried on if credit institutions were developed and supported by governments, especially in view of the relatively long transportation periods. In the absence of such preconditions, sales to overseas areas tended to be effected only upon commission by merchants in more developed areas.

Thus it was one aspect of the role of political power in proto-industrialization that legal freedom, formal equality, and the protection of private property more and more took the place of arbitrary exploitation in the form of unlimited feudal levies, unpredictable confiscations, piracy, and robbery. The other aspect – no less important – is revealed by the fact that economic inequality, which was an essential condition of the progress of industry and trade, was established and maintained with the support of political power – in fact, often with open brutality. This is apparent in the relationship between petty producers and merchants, especially during crises. Unfavourable economic conditions were aggravated for the petty producers by the economic superiority of the merchants and often also by agreements among the merchants to limit competition. The police and military forces interfered when the petty producers tried to ameliorate the unfavourable market situation by rioting and bringing joint pressure upon the merchants, thereby violating the rules which protected the freedom and property of their exchange-partner.[195] The economic inferiority of the petty commodity-producers in relation to merchant capital was thus sanctioned by the very application of the principles of freedom under the law and formal equality between buyer and seller.

The fact that the general norms of legal freedom, equality, and the protection of property had a class-specific effect was even more apparent where the relations between direct producers and the entrepreneurs had changed from the *Kaufsystem* to the putting-out system or even to manufacture and to wage labour. For as long as the petty producers owned their instruments of production, purchased their raw materials, and sold their own products, economic necessity forced them to expend a large work-effort to gain a low return, at least outside economic boom periods; they were poor because the margin between the market-price that they paid for their raw materials and the price their products fetched was small. The only problem for merchant capital was the control over the quality of products, but even here they were often supported by state regulations and institutions which controlled the quality of products.[196] However, when capital penetrated into the sphere of production, for example when the raw material as well as the finished product remained the property of the putter-out, the embezzlement of material was always a grave obstacle to a rational organization of production by the putter-out, i.e. one that was favourable in terms of costs and profits. 'Normal' property-laws turned out to be inadequate to handle the problem; special ordinances were passed everywhere and particularly harsh punishments inflicted, including long jail sentences.[197] When the labourers tried to improve their position vis-à-vis the putters-out and entrepreneurs by coalitions and strikes, by demanding higher wages and the exclusion of outsiders from work, they came up against laws and special decrees as well as the intervention of the police and military forces. It is true that the entrepreneurs were legally prevented from forming coalitions too – a regulation which upheld the principle of formal equality; but owing to their economic superiority and their smaller number, they found it much easier to circumvent such regulations. In some places, governments openly accepted the closed organizations of entrepreneurs while suppressing the coalitions of workers.[198] The poor laws, too, contributed to the creation of a cheap labour force for the entrepreneurs and to the disciplining of the workers. This is most apparent in houses of correction and poorhouses, where beggars, vagabonds, and convicted criminals were subjected to forced labour.[199]

The economic role of coercive power and violence is even more obvious in the relations of the European states among each other and especially vis-à-vis the rest of the world. The establishment and guarantee of a legal framework, the development of an international law, and the signing of mercantile treaties between countries admittedly constituted an important foundation for economic exchange, especially among the European countries.[200] But on the other hand, economic rivalry was a cogent factor among the causes of the numerous wars of the period: the ultimate aim therefore was to snatch away some part of one's rival's trade, his productive capacity, his raw materials or his markets.[201] For the governments the incentive lay in the possibility of increasing their military and tax bases and thereby strengthening their position in the international power struggle. But the tendencies of economic development pointed in the same direction. Since production for the market was growing and market relations were being spatially extended, the legal, political, and military guarantee of the conditions of production and of foreign as well as domestic exchange became increasingly important. Moreover, such guarantees could be more effectively and more cheaply provided by larger rather than smaller political units.[202] This is not to say that the economic benefit of the wars exceeded their costs for all European states; in fact, it is only of England that this statement can be made with some certainty.[203] The extent to which the growth of proto-industry rested on the foundation of unequal exchange and open violence is evidenced by the manner in which overseas colonies and dependent regions were drawn into the circle of the European economy – a process which began during the growth phase of the sixteenth century and became increasingly important for the expansion of European trade and industry after the crisis of the seventeenth century and the new colonialism. The slave trade and the slave economy, as well as the severe exploitation of colonial and dependent regions developed in close connection with the use of such regions as markets and sometimes providers of raw materials.[204] The continental European countries needed the colonies as much as the maritime colonial powers did, though countries such as Prussia or Austria had access to overseas markets only because this was tolerated and mediated by the maritime powers. For England, which was politically and militarily the most successful country, the 'virtual monopoly among European powers of overseas colonies', established during the phase of proto-industrialization, was one of the central preconditions which carried proto-industrialization beyond itself into the Industrial Revolution.[205]

The revenues which the rulers derived from crown estates and other traditional sources no longer sufficed to finance the legal, administrative, and military apparatus which guaranteed the conditions of production and exchange – an expense that increased particularly during the course of proto-industrialization. While military, administrative, judicial, and police institutions were primarily designed to expand and secure control over the people for those in power, they also served economic purposes, though in a manner and to an extent which must be carefully analysed for each individual country. The necessity to find new sources of revenue called forth a system of taxes, levies, and tariffs, which, in turn, had far-reaching consequences for the economic development of a country. Where the rulers succeeded in casting aside the estates' right of consent and in establishing 'absolute' governments, they could simply impose the forms of taxation whose collection was the least costly but which promised the largest revenues while avoiding, if possible, the risk of unrest and violent opposition among their subjects. The individual choices that were made on the basis of such a calculation depended on the respective country's socio-economic structure and its level of development.[206] It was increasingly recognized, despite the ever-present short-term need for money, that the long-term tax-paying capacity of a country and its economic strength must be upheld and developed. From this awareness arose a conscious economic policy as well as the theoretical interest of the cameralists in politics, finances, and economics. But it was always difficult to create a balance between the governments' momentary financial need (which, after all, not only arose from the luxuries of the courts but also from the rivalry among the states) and the desire to make far-sighted fiscal and economic plans for the future.

Wherever estates managed to uphold their right of consent to the imposition of taxes and duties that exceeded the traditional revenues from royal holdings, explicit negotiations were carried on about the fiscal claims made by the rulers and the economic interests of the country, which were represented by the estates. An agreement had to be achieved, and in return for their consent to taxes which provided the resources to meet the ruler's requirements and for governmental functions, the estates insisted that their views on judicial, administrative, and political matters be taken into account. Whether the result of such negotiations furthered or hindered economic development, crucially depended on the social composition of the country's estates.[207] If it reflected older economic structures, the estates usually became an instrument that rigidified the political and legal basis of such structures. If the estates were more open to new interests – if not necessarily as a result of explicit changes in the constitutional arrangements then at least in practice – they could contribute to the modernization of government policies. Again, the effects of the institutionalized mechanism of mediation between the claims of the ruler's treasury and the economic interests of the country, depended in the final analysis on the country's socio-economic structure and its level of development.

A brief comparison of the course of development in various European countries during proto-industrialization sheds light on the tax system's function as a connecting link in the interrelationship between the socio-economic process and politico-judicial institutions.[208] England, where foreign trade assumed considerable importance at an early stage, began to create a national system of import and export tariffs in the late Middle Ages; this was favoured, of course, by her insular location. As English foreign trade grew, the export tariffs soon became an important part of her government revenues, while the tolls on trade routes and other internal tariffs in general no longer played a large role.[209] In the sixteenth and early seventeenth centuries, the English kings, like rulers everywhere, tried to benefit as conveniently as possible from the growth of commerce and industry: they sold privileges and monopolies to individuals and corporations. At an early stage of development, such exclusive rights might sometimes have benefited not only their holders but the country in general, especially as long as England still had to catch up with the Netherlands. For they created a sufficient incentive to undertake pioneering ventures in overseas trade which involved considerable risks; they promoted the adoption of new instruments and methods of production; and they initiated the manufacture, in

England, of new products that had been imported up to that point. But when trade and industry grew on a broader front, monopolies and privileged corporations no longer benefited the economy as a whole. They became a hindrance and therefore an important object of dispute between the Crown and Parliament in the seventeenth century.[210] The mobility in the factor- and product-markets grew, a development which favoured not only the progress of agriculture but also the expansion of trade and industry.

In other countries, the state debt was responsible for many political and economic crises. But in England, under the influence and guarantee of Parliament, it was regulated in such a way that, since the seventeenth century, it became not only a source out of which political and military undertakings could be financed – which, in turn, promoted economic growth – but also an essential factor contributing to the emergence of a capital market and credit institutions.[211] From the second half of the seventeenth century onwards, and even more in the course of the eighteenth century, export tariffs were no longer determined only by fiscal considerations; protection of English trade and industry took on a more and more important role. In conjunction with a number of import restrictions they helped secure the unified and growing domestic market for some sectors of English industry that were crucial for further development.[212] This policy could be implemented because, after Parliament had gained its victory over the Crown in the revolutions of the seventeenth century, power on the local level as well as in Parliament was in the hands of a coalition of landowners, who lived not on feudal rents but on the leasing out of modernized farms operated by wage labour, and of merchants, financiers, and increasingly also industrial entrepreneurs.

In continental Europe, on the other hand, most rulers throughout the eighteenth century clung to their revenues from internal tariffs, staple rights, and the sale of monopolies, which were relatively cheap to raise, but which hindered the development of factor- and product-markets. When new taxes were introduced, they could not be distributed equally, because of the exemptions claimed and upheld by the feudal lords. This was true not only in countries where *Grundherren* and *Gutsherren* exercised strong political power through the estates which they dominated, but also in countries where absolutism had curtailed their political power – an act which was usually accompanied by the acknowledgement, and sometimes the reinforcement, of their economic and social pre-eminence. The tax exemptions of the class whose property and income were the largest in agrarian societies increased the tax burden for all other classes, which may have forced them into industrial market production,[213] but almost certainly made them more susceptible to crises. Furthermore, the tax system acquired certain structural peculiarities which hindered the expansion of commerce and industry. The situation in Prussia provides a good example. Here the aristocracy regarded the plan of a general indirect tax, namely the *Akzise* (excise), as an infringement upon their tax privileges and mounted a staunch resistance against it, which led to the fiscal separation between city and countryside. This, in turn, thwarted commodity exchange inside the country and, in the central and eastern provinces, led to far-reaching prohibitions of industrial commodity production in the countryside. In the western provinces and in Silesia, where it was already firmly established, the trade with its products was confined to the towns which prevented the rural producers from becoming traders and capitalists and ultimately restricted industrial growth in general.[214]

On the other hand, in the seventeenth and eighteenth centuries some states in continental Europe implemented a particularly active mercantilist policy that was to promote industry and trade. It is interesting, though, to note that those countries where the estates, dominated by feudal lords, still occupied a strong position adopted a mercantilist policy only late or not at all. Mercantilist policy involved numerous regulations affecting trade and industry, such as prohibitions, directives, limitations, and premiums; capital contributions such as government credit and subsidies were made by the state, or firms were owned by the state; entrepreneurs and skilled workers were recruited; there was regulation and control of the quality of products, as well as privileges and monopolies for the production and sale of certain products. This 'interventionist' policy of continental mercantilist states appears as an attempt to overcome their backwardness, especially when compared with England which, at this time, was already making the transition to a more 'global' economic policy, changing from the preferential treatment of individual enterprises to the creation of a general framework. Mercantilism payed special attention to large centralized manufactures,[215] but was concerned with rural industry as well. And it appears that the more backward the country, the more rigorous the attempt of its government to plan the growth of its economy.[216] Many examples demonstrate the profitability of privileged enterprises; but these countries could not in this way catch up with the English development, as long as they maintained the basic institutions of the old, essentially feudal order, which were increasingly in conflict with the dynamic of agrarian and industrial growth.[217] The continental states, however, were firmly committed to the old order, and their commitment was upheld by the mechanisms of the tax system, the revenues from royal estates which made the rulers themselves into feudal lords, the structure of political institutions especially at the lower level, and even the military system.[218] This attachment to the old order could only be terminated by the pressure of peasants, petty industrial producers and sometimes entrepreneurs, on one hand, and on the other, by the necessity to enlarge the resources of the state in order to strengthen it in the competitive struggle with other European powers; this necessity was impossible to ignore after the political and social upheaval of the French Revolution and the beginning of the Industrial Revolution in England.

6 ❧ Proto-industrialization between industrialization and de-industrialization

Proto-industrialization, as the term indicates, is functionally related to industrialization. When Charles and Richard Tilly described it as 'industrialization before the factory system',[1] they implied not only that it predates the factory system, but also that it constitutes a transitional stage on the road to it, at least for those countries which first entered the process of capitalist industrialization. Upon closer examination, however, the connection between proto-industrialization and industrialization turns out to be extremely complex.

(1) A direct connection can only be established for the first phase of industrialization, i.e. essentially the textile phase. The connection is largely lacking for the phase of heavy industry or, where the two *phases* occurred simultaneously, the *sector* of heavy industry. Despite many ties to pre-industrial development, the growth of heavy industry, which as a production goods industry is dependent on derived demand, could accelerate only when the process of industrialization had advanced and thereby created that derived demand.[2]

(2) Under the conditions of delayed industrialization the link between proto-industrialization and industrialization could loosen or break altogether. Here the impetus toward industrialization came from outside rather than from the fact that the proto-industrial system had lost the capacity to resolve the problems which faced it during its growth process. It also turned out that the preconditions for industrialization which proto-industrialization had brought about could be created in other ways or be replaced by others.[3]

(3) Not all proto-industrial regions made the transition to the factory system. In a number of regions, proto-industry, instead of being subsumed ('aufgehoben') into factory industry, went into decline. Proto-industrialization could be replaced by industrialization only where certain socio-economic and institutional conditions existed. In their absence stagnation and de-industrialization threatened in as much as those countries with which the region or country in question competed in the world market might be successful in crossing the threshold to industrialization.

Despite these reservations, which should constantly be borne in mind, we may take it that, in the classical industrialized countries of western and central Europe at any rate, the preconditions for the introduction of the industrialization process came to the fore, in so far as the transition to industrialism had not been, as in England, directly made.

1. From proto-industrialization to capitalist industrialization

In England, owing to the pressure of a greatly increasing domestic and foreign demand, the internal contradictions of the proto-industrial system erupted earlier and more violently than elsewhere. In fact, it became doubtful whether these contradictions could be 'controlled' (M. Godelier) any longer. While, on the one hand, the laws of the family economy functioned as the engine of proto-industrial growth, on the other hand, they stood in fundamental contradiction to the growth-dynamic of the overall system. Because of this contradiction, which became particularly apparent during boom phases, when the merchant or putter-out would try to mobilize every last production-reserve, and which manifested itself in a backward-bending labour-supply curve, the proto-industrial system eventually had to end and make the transition to a different system as the forces of production reached a new level.[4] Particularly in late eighteenth-century England, a backward-bending labour-supply curve could no longer fully be remedied by the mobilization of additional labour, since the production-factor labour was becoming scarce. In so far as the family economy was inimical to growth under the conditions which prevailed in England at the end of the eighteenth century, it limited the possibilities of the proto-industrial system and made its transformation ('Aufhebung') into the system of factory-production inevitable.

There were other equally serious problems. Since proto-industrialization was essentially geared toward the quantitative expansion of production, but not toward a qualitative change in the *mode* of production, progress in productivity remained limited, and a point was eventually reached where the marginal cost, and – somewhat later – the average cost, of each product rose.[5] The further a putter-out extended his operations, the more difficult the supervision of domestic producers became. The misappropriation of raw materials could hardly be controlled, and there were never-ending complaints about this issue. Threats of heavy punishment were ineffective. A genuine black market in misappropriated raw materials developed. Similarly, the spatial expansion of the putting-out system made it more and more difficult to control the quality of domestically-produced goods. The time that a merchant had to wait between handing out the raw material and having the finished product returned to him became longer and longer so that he encountered difficulties in meeting his delivery-dates.[6] Simultaneously, the turnover of capital, which was slow anyway due to the – admittedly weakening – interrelation between domestic production and the seasonal rhythm of agricultural labour, slowed down even more. Profits in the putting-out system declined.

Furthermore, as distances increased, transportation costs rose disproportionately. The textile industry suffered in particular, for the disequilibrium between spinning and weaving, which had traditionally made one loom dependent upon the yarn of five spinning-wheels – and even more since the invention of the flying shuttle – made it necessary to transform ever more distant regions into 'yarn country'. In fact, the limited elasticity in the supply of yarn threatened to become a serious obstacle to the further expansion of the textile industry. Labour power was no longer available in unlimited quantity in textile regions, and wages rose.[7] Other production-factors, too, were becoming scarce (water-power and timber for example), so that marginal costs rose. In England, the proto-industrial system had reached a point in its development where the preservation of its basic structures threatened to bring about its stagnation and eventually its turning in upon itself.

The putter-out/merchant could try to counteract some of these difficulties by attaching the domestic producers more closely to himself in the course of the capitalization of the production-sphere. But this too was usually not completely successful. Even though the putter-out gained control of the product, notwithstanding certain modifications in the production process, this process continued to be controlled by the direct producers.[8] Only the centralization of production could bring a lasting solution. Only in centralized installations could the production-process be supervised, the traditional irregular work rhythms be combated, and the producer be subjected to a rigorous work-discipline. In the case of complete centralization, moreover, the turnover of capital could be increased and the transaction costs lowered.

Nevertheless, the advantages of manufacture as a mode of production did not ususally outweigh its disadvantages, except in the preparatory and final stages of the production-process and in cases where the raw material was particularly expensive and, consequently, fixed capital investments constituted a relatively small share of the total cost. The increase in productivity in the large manufacturing plant was too low, in the light of the expenditure on fixed capital and wages it necessitated, the latter usually being above the wages in rural industry. It was impossible to eliminate the bottleneck in yarn-production by organizing spinning on the basis of manufacture. Production had to be mechanized in addition to being centralized. Since the manufacturing mode of production remained at the same level of technology as the domestic mode, its potential for solving problems was limited. It was not to become the dominant mode of production.[9]

There was only one way out of the crisis of the proto-industrial mode of production: mechanization coupled with centralization. It was the latest branch of the English textile industry, the one most closely connected with the colonial trade, namely the cotton industry, which embarked upon this course, starting in the 1760s. The cotton industry became the 'pacemaker' (E. J. Hobsbawm) of the first phase of the Industrial Revolution.[10] The invention of the spinning machines of the 1760s and 1770s, Hargreaves's 'jenny', Arkwright's water-frame, Crompton's mule, and their installation in central buildings made it possible not only to control part of the production process, but also to eliminate the disequilibrium between yarn- and cloth-production. To be sure, exactly the reverse disequilibrium appeared owing to the increased production of yarn, especially after the steam engine came into use. The preponderant mode of organization of the *processing* of yarn continued however to be domestic, and failed to keep pace with production; as a consequence a large proportion of the yarn produced had to be exported. Only when, between 1820 and 1850, weaving was itself mechanized did this new disequilibrium come to an end.[11] Machine spinning called forth machine weaving. Due to the increasing supply of yarn and the immensely growing demand for cotton goods, domestic looms multiplied at the end of the eighteenth and the beginning of the nineteenth centuries. But this expansion can no longer be called proto-industrialization, for it occurred under the conditions set by capitalist industrialization. 'The handloom weavers and others who were starved out were not simply "survivals from the middle ages", but a class multiplied, and largely created as part of capitalist industrialization in its early phases just as the factory workers were.'[12] Handloom weaving was the integral part of an economic sub-system, namely the cotton industry, and was subject to its conditions of valorization. Expansion and contraction of handloom weaving can thus be explained systematically by the development of the cotton industry. In other branches of the textile industry, the replacement of the proto-industrial system began one generation later, but here, too, the factory organization of spinning preceded that of weaving by a fairly long interval. Even by the middle of the nineteenth century factories did not yet dominate the entire textile industry.[13] In the metal goods industry, as well, the factory system won ground only slowly.[14]

In eighteenth-century England, the development of the forces of production had met with an obstacle which could only be surmounted by the introduction of innovative processes and the adoption of a new system of production. The capacity of the proto-industrial system for solving its own problems had become exhausted. New mechanisms were needed in the areas of technology and the social organization of labour. The emerging class of industrial capitalists met the difficulties which confronted it by replacing relatively scarce resources, like labour, water power, and timber, with relatively abundant resources, like capital, steam power, and coal. The domestic system of production gave way to the factory system.[15] Since the continuation of proto-industrialization involved rising marginal costs, it had to yield to the application of capital-intensive techniques and of a new organization of social labour. The proto-industrial system was replaced by the system of industrial capitalism, a system which was decisively to increase the range of possibilities for economic growth.

On the European continent, industrialization assumed a different pattern from that in England. It did not develop independently but was primarily a response to the English challenge. Compared with England, the continent industrialized late. There was no pressure upon resources corresponding to that in England which would have required a search for substitutes. Neither domestic nor foreign demand produced the cumulative effects which steered England into the Industrial Revolution. By the end of the eighteenth century, the continental states had not yet reached the point where it would have become necessary to abandon the traditional channels of growth. The old system of production had not yet exhausted its potential for expansion.[16] To be sure, in some regions, such as the Rhineland, developments were such that they might have led to an autonomous industrialization if given the chance.[17] Putters-out, for example, tried to deal with the contradictions of the domestic system of production by concentrating all phases of cloth production, except spinning and weaving, in manufactures.[18] Resources did become scarcer. In order to assure an adequate supply of yarn it became necessary to take recourse to ever more distant regions of production.[19] The limited availability of water power created bottlenecks not only in the iron industry, but also for the production of fine cloth.[20] But before these developments reached maturity, an exogenous element changed the situation entirely: the Industrial Revolution in England. Endogenous developments were cut off, and the continental European states were confronted with the necessity of making the transition from proto-industrialization to factory industry by adopting the technology developed in England. If they failed to do so, they stood to lose their domestic and foreign markets to English competition. Given the conditions of the world market, industrialization became imperative for the European states on the continent.

However, since the overturn of the proto-industrial system was not brought about by endogenous economic necessities, i.e. by the fact that the regulative mechanisms of the system ceased to function, the transition from proto-industrialization to factory industry was extended over a longer period. In fact, proto-industrialization could continue to expand in the nineteenth century,[21] and it can be shown for a number of industries that this expansion resulted not only from population growth.[22] It was comparative costs that favoured the continued existence and even expansion of domestic industry on the continent. While in England, under the pressure of supply and demand, the relations between the factor-costs of labour and capital, i.e. between the wage costs and the costs of capital goods, had already shifted in favour of the latter, on the continent this process had not yet begun. Labour power was abundant and cheap in comparison with England, a fact which led France and Germany to concentrate on labour-intensive production, especially on finished goods where they had cost-advantages over England. The French and German merchant-manufacturers and industrialists recognized early that they could assert themselves against English superiority only if they specialized in the secondary production processes in which human skill rather than machines still predominated.[23] Moreover, the secondary processes contributed much more than the primary ones to the value that was created in the respective industries.[24] Thus emerged a constantly changing 'system of complementarity' (S. Pollard)[25] determined by comparative costs.

France managed to stabilize her position in the world market by supplying products of superior quality.[26] Germany imported yarn and pig-iron from England and processed them (between 1820 and 1850, Germany produced only about 30 per cent of the cotton yarn which she processed).[27] Trading primarily with backward economies, she managed to fortify her position in the world market through the sale of finished products which were based on the combination of cheap German labour and semi-finished products imported from the centres of the world economy.[28] Apart from a few completely centralized factories, the continental states, under the pressure of comparative costs, turned chiefly to those products whose manufacture was still domestically organized.[29] That was the very condition of their competitiveness in the world market. Insofar as their expansion was determined by the quantity of semi-finished products that were brought to market by the advanced capitalist sectors of the world economy, both national and international, they approached the type of *modern* domestic industry which is integrated in and functionally a part of the capitalist industrialization process.

On the continent, then, industrialization penetrated into the secondary production processes only hesitantly and had not yet conquered them by the end of the nineteenth century. This is true, above all, for the production of textile fabrics.[30] It was due, as pointed out earlier, to the competitive conditions in the world market which were determined by comparative costs, and to the fact that the textile industry grew relatively autonomously when compared with heavy industry. Its autonomous growth resulted from the fact that the traditional cyclical movements of the economy were modified only very slowly and continued to be influenced by harvest fluctuations.[31] But most importantly, industrialization on the European continent was late industrialization and took on special features for that reason. The degree of backwardness was reflected in a specific pattern of industrialization.[32] The acceleration of industrial growth that can be observed in Germany since the middle of the 1840s, and that was to eventually bring the industrial breakthrough, was induced by heavy industry, especially the railroad sector.[33] Consumer goods, especially the textile industry, came to play a subordinate role in the process of industrialization. Other domestically-organized industries, such as metal goods, toys, musical instruments, and clocks, remained alive far into the twentieth century. As late as 1887, Friedrich Engels called the rural domestic industry 'the broad basis of Germany's new large-scale industry'.[34]

In many ways, problems internal to the proto-industrial system, i.e. problems which could no longer be controlled within the limits of the system, pushed it beyond itself, directly or – through impulses from out-side – indirectly, and brought about industrial capitalism. But they could not have had the effect they did, had not the system as such created certain preconditions for the transition to industrial capitalism.[35] These may be summarized as follows.

(1) During proto-industrialization, a broad stratum of skilled handicraft-workers was formed, which grew rapidly because of the pattern of demographic behaviour characteristic of this group. It constituted a reserve of labour power which the founders of the early factories could draw upon.[36] Nonetheless, a wide gap separated the domestic producer from the industrial worker. Only reluctantly did he give up the '*ganzes Haus*', i.e. the domestic unit where production and consumption were combined, in order to become a factory worker. And the new factory-masters had to apply harsh discipline in order to make the workers accept the constraints of the industrial mode of production.[37]

(2) A group of merchant-manufacturers, middlemen, and sometimes small artisans emerged who became the agents of industrialization, backed by capital which they had accumulated during proto-industrialization.[38] But the differ-ence between the putter-out and the industrial entrepreneur must be em-phasized. The latter operated in the sphere of production, the former in the sphere of circulation. If the putter-out did enter the production sphere and began to capitalize it, he did so under conditions that allowed him to withdraw from it without great loss whenever the business cycle reversed itself.[39] This explains why a large proportion of the industrial entrepreneurs were recruited, not from the city-based group of merchant manufacturers, but from the rural intermediate strata, such as the 'Tüchler', 'Fabrikanten', 'Fergger', and artisans of the Zürich Oberland, or else from the group of small producers, much as was the case with the better-off 'clothiers' in West Riding.[40] The social basis of early industrial entrepreneurship consisted not only of merchants who operated as putters-out, but was proto-industrial in a broader sense of the word.

(3) With regard to the organization of production, the putting-out system – though older than rural industry itself – had brought unquestionable advances. It connected merchant capital with the sphere of production and permitted it to direct commodity production from the vantage point of the sphere of circulation. (The 'really revolutionizing path' which Marx refers to was only taken when the petty producer developed into a putter-out or an industrialist and the production process became the centre of his activity and concern. But often this road was not followed to the end; it had a tendency to lead to the renewed predominance of the circulation process.)[41] When the petty producers were organized under the putting-out system, production could be more responsive to market demand; changes in the structure of demand could be more quickly absorbed and technical improvements more easily imposed. The putter-out who began to capitalize the production sphere by supplying

raw materials and tools and by erecting centralized manufactures for the starting and finishing phases of the production process, anticipated some of the crucial elements of the capitalist relations of production. But he could not completely do away with the family economy, i.e. the economic foundation upon which proto-industrialization was built. Yet, here too, it must be remembered that the putters-out did not pursue strategies of capitalization with resolute consistency. In view of the uncertainties of the market, they avoided sinking all their investments into a single product. Instead they followed a 'policy of diversification' (S. D. Chapman) in order to have alternative sources of income in the case of a crisis.[42] The process of circulation remained the decisive factor. It was reduced to a 'mere element' of the production process only after the mechanisms to regulate the proto-industrial system had become exhausted.

(4) During proto-industrialization, a symbiotic relationship developed between agrarian regions and densely industrial regions (except where proto-industrialization and commercial agriculture developed side by side). As proto-industrialization advanced, the latter became dependent on surrounding agrarian regions for their food supply. Agriculture in such surrounding regions had to become more efficient if it was to respond to the demand generated in proto-industrial regions. A development was introduced – though not completed – which was to make it possible to provide the rapidly expanding secondary sector with food, once industrialization had started.[43]

(5) A network of local, regional, national, and international markets developed during the course of proto-industrialization; in fact, partly because of it. The development of proto-industrialization as a system of mass production not only presupposed such markets and the demand they generated, but it also brought them into existence. Needs were aroused which had hitherto simply gone unsatisfied, or had been satisfied in other ways. The peasant production-unit could become a relevant factor, generating demand, when it specialized in producing either agrarian or industrial goods. Overseas, markets for the products of European proto-industries seemed to be without limit.[44] It was in this way that the current of demand came into being which helped give rise to the new system of production.

In these five areas proto-industrialization laid the foundation for capitalist industrialization; the contradictions which were inherent to the proto-industrial system but escaped the system's regulating mechanisms forced it into existence. The possibilities of socio-economic evolution were however limited by the proto-industrial environment. The overthrow of this mode of production could succeed only where certain socio-economic and institutional conditions were fulfilled.

Proto-industrialization established itself within a labour system that was still essentially feudal, though to a declining degree as one moved from east to west, and in which 'property rights' were not fully assured. Seen from a long-term perspective, proto-industrialization did indeed contribute to the undermining of the feudal system; but it did not wholly succeed in ousting it. Industrialization, on the other hand, presupposes that the production factors land, labour, and capital should be 'freed' from their feudal constraints. Labour had to be formally free and the 'appropriation of all physical means of production as disposable property of autonomous private industrial enterprises' (M. Weber)[45] had to be assured if the process of capitalist exploitation was to take its course. 'Property rights', here understood in a more comprehensive sense, needed to be guaranteed so that the 'private rate of return' did not lag behind the 'social rate of return', i.e. that no part of the profit from a 'private' economic activity should fall to a third party – for if it did, the activity might not be undertaken at all, especially if the costs should exceed the anticipated profit.[46]

In eighteenth-century western Europe, as distinct from east-central and eastern Europe, the feudal system was only a shadow of its former self. But that shadow was still enough to restrain – though not to block – the development of the forces of production in agriculture and industry. Agrarian progress remained limited for as long as relations of production in the countryside, and the utilization of land, remained subject to traditional feudal and collectivist restrictions and 'property rights' were not fully guaranteed. But industrialization demanded the maximization of agricultural contributions, and the agrarian sector, therefore, came to play a key role.[47]

The securing of 'property rights' outside the agrarian sector required a whole bundle of institutions and institutional arrangements, some of which were already part of the infrastructure. These included the formulation of a body of patent law which guaranteed intellectual property in the form of inventions and thereby stimulated inventive activities. Such institutional requirements had a parallel in certain social changes. The status-hierarchy of the feudal system, which assigned social rank according to the ownership of land as the predominant means of production in pre-industrial society, needed to be modified and supplemented by professional status-hierarchies open to the social ambition of those who belonged to the lower ranks of the 'feudal' hierarchy. The fact that these professional hierarchies constituted themselves as independent status-hierarchies and closed rank with the traditional 'feudal' hierarchy was the precondition for the mobilization of entrepreneurial potential and for the productive investment of the social surplus.[48]

England's lead was due, in part, to the fact that her agriculture had early on thrown off the feudal and collectivist bonds and had opened itself to commercialization. Her status system had adjusted relatively quickly to the new conditions. In the absolutist continental states, only the French Revolution, as well as subsequent revolutions from above, cast aside the barriers against sustained economic growth.

The specific relations of production are closely connected with the general conditions of production. Capitalist industrialization could begin only where available capital met a material, institutional, and human infrastructure which would relieve it of costs that it was unable to assume.[49] Most of that infrastructure had to be created, maintained and guaranteed by the state. It was up to the state to provide the general conditions of production, i.e. the prerequisites for the production process. The acceleration of the turnover of capital was dependent upon a well-developed trade and communication network. Furthermore, in the sphere of circulation, the legal system had to provide institutional guarantees for the freedom of trade; in the sphere of production it had to be able to enforce and maintain wage-labour relations. In general, the law had to be consistent and predictable for the owners of capital. Finally, it had to be possible to recruit skilled personnel, though only for the late industrializers did the state's function as educator and trainer of industrial skills take on greater importance.[50] Whether or not the state exercised these functions, i.e. whether it used the wealth obtained by taxation productively, was determined not only by the total social context; it also depended upon whether the state was an integral part of that context or whether it had become independent of it and stood in opposition to it.[51]

Thirdly, capitalist industrialization presupposed expanding markets, or at least markets that were capable of expansion. Whether they existed or not depended on a country's internal socio-economic structure. While in England, from the seventeenth century, the agrarian sector rapidly became more important as a market for industrial goods, on the continent agriculture was inefficient in many regions owing to its dominant relations of production and the agrarian sector did not generate a large demand. This heritage from the past survived revolutions and reforms and was felt until far into the nineteenth century. In France, the development of a domestic market was inhibited by the small-peasant structure of agriculture and its reinforcement by the Revolution; in central Europe, by the burdening of the peasantry with high commutation-payments, and in east-central and eastern Europe by the restrictions to mobility imposed upon the economy by a vigorously developing agrarian capitalism.[52] In the towns, just as in the countryside, the emergence of a dynamic demand was largely a function of the socio-economic structures and the opportunities for mobility that they provided.[53] It is true that the foreign markets offered the possibility of compensating for sluggish domestic markets, but if this opportunity was to be seized, a certain social foundation was needed, as well as the support of political institutions. England achieved a quasi-monopolistic position in the world market because her power-élites, in conducting foreign policy, promoted her commercial interests. Their attitudes stood in contrast to that of the élites in the absolutist regimes. The foreign policy of the English élites created a vast potential demand for the domestic industries of the country.[54] This supremacy, which developed into a monopoly during the wars of the French Revolution, robbed the other states of the opportunity to compensate their own sluggish domestic demand in the same way. They became 'inward looking' (F. Crouzet) and were faced with the necessity of expanding their domestic markets and removing existing restrictions to economic freedom.[55]

An attempt has been made, in the preceding pages, to explore the connections between proto-industrialization and industrialization on three different levels: the direct connection, the preconditions created by proto-industrialization, and the general socio-political framework. As we come closer to the last level – disregarding, for a moment, the other two – the connection between proto-industrialization and industrialization seems to evaporate. But even in the case of late industrialization, an indirect connection exists because of the demonstration-effect of English industrialization.

2. Industrialization: its retarded beginnings and troubled development; de-industrialization

De-industrialization was not unique to the transition period from proto-industry to factory industry. Even during proto-industrialization, its beginnings can be observed in the towns as well as in the countryside. Whether a region lagged behind or advanced rapidly was determined by the conditions of inter-regional and international competition. Given the persistent struggle between various proto-industrial regions for international markets, product-diversification became an important factor. D. C. Coleman has shown that, alongside the spatial expansion of industrial commodity-production, the diversification of products constituted a second potentiality for growth in the textile industry.[56] Regions which did not adapt early enough to new trends fell behind. Beginning in the sixteenth century, for example, the demand for cheap linen increased rapidly in international markets, and the industry in Upper Swabia was forced into recession because the putters-out of Augsburg failed to make the transition from fustian to pure linen.[57] In the seventeenth century, when the English textile industry underwent a painful structural change, trying to weather the crisis of the 'old draperies' and adjust to the rise of the 'new draperies', some industrial regions did much better than others.[58] A variety of other factors, such as the availability of raw materials, relative costs, and tariff discrimination by importing countries, contributed to the stagnation and decline of rural industrial areas.

But it was during the period of industrialization that the full scope of the problem of de-industrialization became apparent.[59] When a region entered on the industrialization process, it gained a competitive advantage over those regions which had been its rivals in the world market. The latter fell behind if they did not catch up quickly by industrializing in their turn. But here lay the problem. Proto-industrialization did indeed provide certain conditions for a capitalistic industrialization; they were not however sufficient to actually introduce the process of industrialization. For the domestic system of production to be pushed into industrialization, a certain general framework was necessary, in addition to the internal contradictions or an impetus from outside. If that framework was lacking or insufficiently developed, the mechanisms which regulated the proto-industrial system could break down under the combined pressure of its internal contradictions and the outside thrust. The system would collapse altogether, without succeeding at industrialization, or become subject to a succession of severe crises. This, in different degrees of intensity, was the lot of western and southwestern France, Flanders, east Westphalia, Hesse, Württemberg, and Silesia.

The proto-industrial system was marked by internal contradictions which confronted it with serious problems during its growth-phase and put into question its capacity for self-regulation; but they also complicated its transition to the factory mode of production. They can to some extent be attributed to the fact that the conditions of the family economy and its specific demographic pattern inclined the proto-industrial system toward the extension of production, rather than toward its intensification. Technological progress remained largely external to the system of domestic production.[60] This was not due only to the economic behaviour of small producers. The rapid growth of proto-industrial populations, whilst guaranteeing the elasticity of the labour supply which the expansion of proto-industry required, also determined the mode of production as such. Where it resulted in an over-supply of labour power, it arrested the introduction of capital-intensive techniques; and because it favoured the extension of production, it threatened to freeze the forces of production at the existing level. The merchant-manufacturers did not need to substitute capital for labour as long as the demand for labour did not rise faster than its supply.

This permanent over-supply of labour power, in conjunction with a very unfavourably developing demand for goods, locked the linen industry of the European mainland into a vicious circle of poverty. But demographic mechanisms, inherent in the linen industry as part of the proto-industrial system, were not alone responsible for maintaining this over-supply of labour. Forces from outside played a role as well. In many parts of Europe, linen production was the peasants' traditional by-occupation. At a time when many peasants came under pressure because they lost their land or had to make commutation payments, and when alternative sources of income were unavailable due to the lag in the development of industrial capitalism, there was an inevitable rise in the number of those who hoped to earn a supplementary income from linen work.[61] The crisis in agriculture affected the linen industry and increased its problems of adaptation. A similar situation occurred in England. In the framework knitting industry of the Midlands, wages and living-conditions declined drastically in the first half of the nineteenth century because of an over-supply of labour as well as sluggish sales in foreign markets.

Framework knitting had always been heavily dominated by putting-out capital, but the factory system made inroads into the industry only from the middle of the century.[62] As it turned out, the specific demographic pattern which had had important regulative functions within the system of proto-industrialization continued to exist during the critical phase of its transition to industrial capitalism. But now it furthered the involution of the system. Proto-industrialization perpetuated itself and thereby invited its death sentence, for its environment had changed.

To these endogenous factors which account for the death of proto-industry must be added an exogenous factor: British competition had become a serious threat to the industries on the continent.[63] England had gained an advantage by revolutionizing her production apparatus and further consolidating it between 1790 and 1814, as well as by pushing her rivals out of overseas markets during the Wars of the Coalition. As early as 1792, when the British blockade robbed the Atlantic economy of its function as 'engine of growth', whole areas of France, Spain, and Portugal succumbed to 'pastoralization' (F. Crouzet).[64] The German linen industry, too, entered into a severe crisis after the turn of the century, especially after the Continental Blockade had been proclaimed.[65] The linen exports from Landeshut in Silesia (now Kamienna Góra) fell from 167,713 pieces in 1805 to 90,414 pieces in 1807 (1813: 24,234), and those of the districts of Eschwege and Hersfeld in Hesse fell from 192,769 in 1805/06 to 89,114 pieces in 1807/08.[66] After the Blockade, when English goods were sold on the continent at dumping prices, many industries that had been artificially supported faced severe difficulties in domestic markets as well.[67] England had gained the upper hand over them in the struggle for the 'appropriation of "foreign" purchasing power' (W. Hofmann); now the 'national' purchasing-power itself was at stake.

The crisis of the continental linen industry continued. In the long run, it could not stand up to Irish and Scottish competition in international markets.[68] The Irish and Scots were superior largely because, even before the middle of the century, they used machine-made yarns, as well as better bleaching and finishing processes.[69] But for the countries that lagged behind, the consequences of the British lead could be ambivalent. Some regions were stimulated by the British challenge and adjusted their production apparatus to the new conditions. Others failed to make the connection and their industrial structures regressed. Sometimes they succeeded in entering the industrialization process only after a long crisis-ridden transition period. The width of the gap must have been crucial, for too large a shortfall in development must often have made it impossible for the retarded region to catch up. The dialectic of backwardness could not then work itself out.

This takes us back to the general framework of capitalist industrialization. De-industrialization did not simply arise out of the crisis of domestic industry caused by internal and external factors. In order to analyse it, we need a more comprehensive frame of reference that includes the entire industrialization process. We need to know about the physical environment, the level of socio-economic development, the general conditions of production as well as the relations of production in the region under consideration. It is here that explanations will be found for those cases where the proto-industrial system did not undergo the fundamental structural changes which had become necessary once its self-regulating mechanisms could no longer cope with its increasing internal contradictions and the rapidly changing environment. In our analysis, individual factors will have to be treated as parts of an interdependent structural whole.

If a region lacked those natural resources which industrialization 'actualized' (K. A. Wittfogel),[70] its stagnation and decline often became inevitable, since subsidiary industries did not establish themselves. Seen within the wider context of proto-industrial regions, 'quasi-horizontale démographique' robbed the economy of Normandy and in particular lower Normandy of – as Pierre Chaunu sees it – one of its most important stimulants toward growth, namely population increase, and subjected it to stagnation. But such a demographic pattern needs to be explained. In Normandy, it seems to have resulted from agricultural specialization, i.e. from the expansion of a labour-extensive pastoral economy and contraction of the arable, in response to the proximity to the Parisian consumer centre. The specialization process, according to Chaunu, entailed 'une réduction brutale de l'optimum de peuplement'.[71]

Even apart from such secondary effects, the agrarian sector assumed a strategic function in the process of industrialization and de-industrialization. Where an unfavourable structure of farm-sizes, high commutation-payments, and an overwhelmingly powerful agrarian-capitalist sector pushed the peasant economy into subsistence farming and, as a result, there was no reallocation and specialization of peasant labour power, agriculture failed to develop a demand for industrial products. The formation of a domestic market was thus impeded. At the same time these products, needed for the expansion of the industrial sector, were not forthcoming – a circumstance which does not, however, apply in the case of the agrarian capitalism in east-central and eastern Europe.[72] Finally, a region's level of socio-economic development influenced the investment-decisions of the owners of capital. In the absence of subsidiary and service industries, which would have made possible external savings, investments were not made because their profitability was not assured.[73]

Where the general conditions of production were not guaranteed, the prerequisites for the necessary renewal of the production-apparatus were lacking. Bad transportation and communication networks meant competitive disadvantages in relation to other more favourably equipped regions. Capital invested in such regions involved comparatively large risks.[74] Where the state interfered with the relations of production, trying to regulate and control them, it could conjure up a constellation of events and circumstances which immobilized the old productive system and contributed to its stagnation and final death. Where government institutions which controlled the quality of products took their place between petty producers and merchant capital, they hindered not only the formation of the putting-out system; they also prevented a situation in which the better-situated domestic producers could become agents and middlemen between their co-producers and the putters-out – a situation, i.e. which elsewhere gave rise to that intermediate social stratum where the impetus toward industrialization often originated. Monopolies and privileges granted by governments could successfully guide and regulate economic development at the time they were awarded, but they could become dysfunctional if they outlived their usefulness. By protecting against competition the enterprises to which they were granted, they promoted their involution and at the same time prevented the rise of potentially more efficient rivals. This can be observed in the area dominated by the Calwer Zeughandlungskompagnie, whose liquidation in 1797 came much too late.[75]

Finally, industrialization encountered barriers wherever remnants of the feudal relations of production continued to exist. They constrained the markets for labour, capital, and goods and thereby hindered adaptation to new economic circumstances. Merchant capital remained attached to the status system of pre-industrial societies. It avoided the sphere of production and favoured investments in the agrarian sector which continued to enjoy high social prestige. When serfdom was abolished in Silesia in 1807, the lords continued to impose a series of servile levies, not least of all the *Weberzins* (weaver's tax).[76] According to contemporary reports, the weavers were obliged to give up to one fourth of their income to their lord and the state.[77] Such conditions paralysed all initiative for technical or organizational progress on the part of the petty producers. Instead they had to resort to fraudulent practices if they wanted to survive, and this further damaged the competitiveness of Silesian linen in domestic and foreign markets.[78] All this, combined with the economic attitudes of the Silesian merchant capitalists, the underdeveloped regional market constricted by the rural relations of production, the insufficient infrastructure, the unfavourable geographic location, and the overpowering competition of west-German textile industries, formed a vicious circle from which it seemed impossible to break out.[79]

In Russia, the belated abolition of serfdom (1861) heavily burdened the transition from proto-industrialization to industrialization. The harshness of Russian serfdom not only restricted the mobility of labour but also the field of operations of the entrepreneurs, especially if they were serfs. Their uncertain legal status, which exposed them to the arbitrary power of their lords, severely limited the 'time horizon of entrepreneurial decisions'. The servile dues of proto-industrial producers, of the labourers in centralized manufactures, and of the serf-entrepreneurs took on – as A. Gerschenkron put it – the form of a 'tribute' from industry to the land-owning classes.[80] And the modalities of the abolition of serfdom, especially the preservation of a system of land-redistribution within the community, the *obshchina*, by no means cleared the road for capitalist industrialization. During the following decades, substitutes had to be found to offset the failure of the abolition laws to create the appropriate preconditions. To a considerable extent the violence of Russian industrialization can be attributed to these substitutes.[81]

But the determining factors of de-industrialization cannot all be found within the region which succumbed to it. Underdevelopment was, and still is, the result of a process of 'circular causation with cumulative effects' (G. Myrdal). In this process, the beginning capitalist industrialization and the dynamic of socio-economic change which it unleashed were of decisive importance. The emergence of an industrial centre produced (negative) 'backwash effects' in other regions which could usually not be offset by the (positive) 'spread effects' (G. Myrdal) from the industrial centre since these were spatially limited. A district where factory industries were concentrated already had important advantages of concentration (external savings etc.) for the settlement of more industries and consequently developed such a strong pull that other regions could not remain unaffected. Interregional migrations, movements of capital and trade all converged on the industrial centre. In the other regions deficits arose as a consequence of these centripetal movements which, in conjunction with the existing restrictive elements, formed a cumulative process. The gap between development and underdevelopment widened. 'The evolutionary growth of industry produced a devolutionary counter-current' (Ch. Tilly).[82]

From the theoretical perspective, the industrialization process represents an immense reallocation of resources compressed into a relatively short time-period. In this connection industrial locations were reassigned. Traditional but outmoded locations went into decline as the development of the material and institutional infrastructure increasingly made it possible to mobilize production-factors and goods. Labour, once it was legally free, lost its power to determine the location of industries.[83] Instead the spatial distribution of raw materials and fuel, as well as transport costs, became the factors which determined the location of industries. The sites of new resources to be tapped greatly influenced the infrastructure to be developed, and both resources and infrastructure together might give a competitive advantage to one region while causing others to fall back. Mountainous areas, where proto-industries had been attracted by the easily available raw materials and fuel when pushed out of the plains with their relatively rigid social structure, lost their importance as centres of industrial activity when those factors ceased to be determinants of industrial location.[84] When an industrial region, relatively protected by its isolation from the outside world, was opened up by the completion of new transportation routes, its industries which had been geared toward a limited market often could not stand up to the competition that now confronted it.[85] On the other hand, the full utilization of the advantages inherent in agglomerations of population became possible through improvements in the supply of food.[86]

The phenomenal rise of the woollen industry in the West Riding and its relatively rapid mechanization left behind all the other English production centres, such as the wollen-cloth industry in the West country – and more especially that of East Anglia whose production-structures regressed before they disappeared entirely during the nineteenth century. The woollen industry of the West Riding triumphed not only because of its superior production and sales organization but also because it was supported by a bundle of subsidiary industries.[87] The Irish linen industry underwent a similar reallocation process as the English woollen industry. In the first half of the nineteenth century it was concentrated in the north-east, i.e. in Ulster, which offered the most favourable conditions for the mechanization of yarn production. The declining northern Irish cotton industry, which was itself a child of the linen industry, had laid the foundation for its mechanization. Now linen could enter on the cotton industry's inheritance. Belfast, moreover, had good connections with England which was important when the northern Irish linen industry, in making the transition to steam-driven spinning-machines in the 1830s, became dependent on English coal.[88] But the rise of linen in the north-east entailed its decline in other parts of the country. The spinning-wheel was replaced by the spinning-machine and handloom-weavers moved to northern Ireland attracted by the spinning factories. The South was subject to a process of industrial decay and fragmentation helped along by the decline of its woollen industry which was unable to stand up to English competition. The points were switched, and the country set on a collision course for the catastrophic food crisis of 1846–50.[89]

Occasionally, this process of reallocation and concentration took on the form of a division of labour, assigning the production of industrial goods to one region and that of agrarian goods to another. The specialization in agrarian production, brought about by the demand that a large industrial centre or big city generated, could turn a region into a 'désert industriel' (F. Crouzet).[90] De-differentiation resulted from specialization. Processes like this can be observed in Normandy, in parts of Lancashire and Cheshire.[91]

No less important than the changeover in the locations of industrial activity and, to some extent, not without a feedback-effect upon it, was the process of substitution or replacement that affected raw materials and fuels. As a result of the substitution of coke for charcoal, for example, the iron industry migrated to coal-bearing areas. The linen industry was heavily hit by the competition of cotton. Since the beginning of the nineteenth century, the terms of trade between linen and cotton rapidly shifted in favour of the latter. Around 1900, the production-cost (including the cost of the raw material) of a unit of linen cloth amounted to double the production-cost of the same unit of cotton cloth.[92] Cotton, therefore, became a most dangerous competitor for linen.

Mechanization was introduced into linen very slowly and followed far behind the mechanization of cotton. This was primarily due to the nature of the fibre. Many more difficulties had to be overcome to produce linen yarn than cotton yarn, and the situation in weaving was similar.[93] But there were other reasons, too. As discussed earlier, the close connection between the linen industry and peasant life, caused by the lack of alternative income-opportunities, engendered a persistent surplus of labour as well as of finished and semi-finished goods during the first half of the nineteenth century which, for quite some time, hindered the mechanization and factory organization of linen yarn production.[94]

One last point must be taken into consideration. The linen industry's incapacity to adjust to the new circumstances says something about its organizational structure. The predominance of the Kaufsystem – characteristic of the linen industry – meant that the industry was turned in upon itself, that it lacked the link provided by the putter-out/merchant which, in the circumstances, could have initiated the process of adaptation leading to the change-over to cotton.[95] Only in the 1850s, probably much too late for most regions, did the putting-out system come to dominate the German linen industry. In order to keep German linen competitive the merchants were forced to impose stricter controls on the production-process and to organize the producers under the putting-out system. At the same time the first signs of labour scarcity appeared, and the merchants thought it wise to tie the weavers more closely to themselves.[96] Yet the linen industry survived only where they succeeded in mechanizing yarn-production and specialized in quality products. This was the foundation of the – admittedly relative – success of production centres in northern Ireland, in the département du Nord (Lille), in Flanders (Ghent), in east Westphalia (Bielefeld), in Upper Lusatia (Zittau), in Silesia (Kamienna Góra, formerly: Landeshut), and in northern and north-eastern Bohemia.[97] Other production regions, such as western France, Hesse (including the Rhön), the former County of Tecklenburg, and the area around Osnabrück, failed to adjust.[98] Their industrial structures collapsed.

The regions of de-industrialization on the European continent, then, tended to be those which specialized in the production of linen during the proto-industrial phase. But it would be going too far to attribute the relative backwardness of continental Europe as compared with England to the predominant position of linen within its industrial structure on the eve of the Industrial Revolution. Nor can the failure of the industrialization process in certain regions be attributed to its predominance. Instead it was of crucial importance that no close bond was formed between linen and cotton which, as in Lancashire, might have facilitated the transition to cotton production but would also have stimulated technical progress in linen after its success in the cotton industry.[99] There is no need to trace the reasons why such a bond did not develop, for they are largely identical with the factors described above.

Actually, the terms 'industrialization' and 'de-industrialization' do not do justice to the variety of developments undergone by proto-industrial regions during the Industrial Revolution. What is needed is to replace this rigid dichotomy with a scale of empirically verifiable paths of development.[100] This will be attempted here.

(1) Industrialization, including the autonomous industrialization in England as well as late industrialization in the continental states: the industrialization process, as it entered a proto-industrial region, gradually brought about the concentration of factory production in a few places. The 'country mills' disappeared as soon as steam-power took the place of water-power.[101] Certain subsidiary industries and service industries sometimes managed to survive in the countryside, but their contribution was mostly limited to agricultural products.

(2) A difficult transition to industrialization, often combined with a temporary and partial de-industrialization: some proto-industrial regions, especially Flanders, eastern Westphalia, and Silesia, succeeded in introducing the industrialization process only after a long crisis-ridden transition period. They were drawn into de-industrialization and are therefore often grouped with the de-industrialization regions.[102] But their industrial structures proved so resistant that factory industry finally managed to establish a foothold, even if sometimes only marginally so, as in Lower Silesia.

(3) De-industrialization and simultaneous concentration on commercial agriculture: in such regions the proto-industrial base proved too weak to be developed during the phase of industrialization; however, advantage was taken of the presence of a nearby city or cluster of towns to specialize in agrarian production, above all dairy products. De-industrialization, on occasion resulted from this process of specialization.

(4) De-industrialization due to the loss of contact with supra-regional markets: when their industries declined, such regions were thrown back upon themselves. Since agriculture was no alternative, many people were forced to emigrate and population declined.

With entry upon the process of capitalist industrialization and the consequent acceleration of socio-economic change, the international system of competition between centres of industrial commodity production got under way. One country took the lead, others followed, yet others fell behind. The distance increased between countries that revolutionized their production-apparatus and those that lagged behind; eventually, this distance far exceeded anything ever observed during proto-industrialization. The gap, in particular, which was now opening between the European metropolitan countries and the countries on the periphery widened dramatically. The proto-industries of the great agrarian societies of Asia were destroyed when their traditional markets were flooded by machine-made finished products from the metropolitan countries, cheap because they were machine-made. The countries on the periphery were defenceless against this invasion and had to yield to it since they were either formally or informally dependent on the metropolitan countries. It is true that some countries, by making use of the advantages of backwardness, succeeded relatively quickly in closing in on the leader of the Industrial Revolution, i.e. in catching up with it and sometimes even overtaking it. But aside from Japan, late industrialization was initially confined to Europe. Here the distance between the two poles of development narrowed in the long run, but in the world at large it increased and there is no end to this process in sight.

3. Decline of proto-industrialization, pauperism and the sharpening of the contrast between city and countryside

The decline of the proto-industrial system of production and its replacement by the factory system left deep impressions on the lives of hundreds of thousands of people. The peasant with insufficient land to support his family was deprived of the opportunity to earn a supplementary income in rural industry. The rural producer who earned his living primarily through industrial labour was forced to enter the factory, no matter how long he resisted it. This might not have caused him too much hardship if he lived in a region which succeeded in making the transition to the factory system without much delay, for then he did not have to leave his familiar environment even if he had to cover long distances to and from the factory. But the situation of small producers became almost desperate if the industrialization process began only haltingly and was accompanied by severe crises, and especially if it failed or did not get started at all, leaving the industrial structures of the region to collapse. Penury became general. Many joined the great trek to the industrial centres, others emigrated overseas. For many the threat to the foundations of their existence was particularly harsh because they had lived in a fairly paternalistic and communal environment which now broke down. There was a decline in the traditional notion of a moral economy which had shaped not only the expectations of the dependent social classes but also to some extent informed the economic decisions of governments. It was pushed aside by the laissez-faire economy which made the individual defenceless against the anonymous mechanisms of the market.[103] The crisis of material existence became an all-encompassing crisis of human relationships. The death of the proto-industrial system conjured up a great social crisis. Its disintegration threatened the integration of society and plunged those who were directly affected into an identity-crisis of heretofore unknown proportions.

These are the causes of the pauperism of the first half of the nineteenth century. Although its history goes far back into the pre-industrial period,[104] it took on a new quality during the transition from the agrarian society interwoven with proto-industries to industrial capitalism. Three elements coincided: the crisis of proto-industry, the change in agrarian structures, and population-growth.[105] The third European wave of population increase, which began in the eighteenth century, was at first not much different from its predecessors, being primarily caused by a reduction in mortality. But during its progress, the growth of population picked up speed. Authority-patterns that had kept fertility under control broke down. Pre-marital conceptions and illegitimate births accounted for a rapidly increasing percentage of the total number of births and inflated the overall birth figure.[106] The specific reproductive pattern of proto-industrial populations had a powerful influence on population growth. Even during the decline of proto-industrialization it was not significantly modified. The reduced growth in those proto-industrial regions which had become subject to de-industrialization seems to be traceable to an increase in mortality and to out-migration rather than to a change in reproductive behaviour.[107] In the areas of *Gutsherrschaft*, population-growth was induced by the capitalization of large estates, i.e. the transition from the manorial system based on servile labour to the type of estate farming whose labour was freely contracted.[108]

As the traditional peasant society disintegrated – a process that was accelerated by the agrarian reforms of the late eighteenth and early nineteenth centuries – the deterioration in the situation of those who lived on its fringes was particularly marked. The enclosures and partitions of communal property often decisively diminished the subsistence-margin of the smallholders. Once the common fields and the right to glean had been abolished, they were forced to limit their livestock and indeed, often enough, to give up their last cow. They found it almost impossible to meet their need for wood.[109]

The accelerated demographic growth and the transformation of the agrarian structures that occurred in the first half of the nineteenth century fell upon a socio-economic system which had reached the limits of its capacity for the absorption of such shocks, and which could no longer assure the subsistence of the population which carried that system. Proto-industrialization had been that part of the production-system which had absorbed most of the rural population-surplus, but by now it had entered upon its death struggle. Admittedly the number of domestic production-units continued to increase – at first at a rate even faster than that of the population – but that increase took place at the expense of those who were already domestic producers and whose situation was already precarious as a result of the crisis of domestic industry.[110] Not only did the subsistence-value of an individual domestic production-unit shrink, but it was also systematically reduced by merchants and putters-out who turned the situation to their advantage and profited from the overmanning of industries. In addition to increasing their profit-rate, they had also to concern themselves about their competitiveness in national and international markets. The overmanning in proto-industrial occupations and the inter-regionally and internationally uneven progress of capitalist industries had the effect of narrowing down the subsistence-margin of the proto-industrial family economy. The factory system was for the most part still too little developed for it to be able to play a large compensatory role. Such was the constellation of causes that produced the pauperism of the first half of the nineteenth century.

Three factors determined the chronological, inter-regional, and inter-national course of the pauperization-process.
1) the industrialization of a particular sub-system of the social organization of labour (e.g. spinning);
2) the falling back of the sub-system (e.g. weaving) which, in the course of the production-process, follows next upon the first sub-system;
3) the falling back of entire regions and states behind those regions and states where industrialization had begun earlier.

The process of pauperization which seized the proto-industrial population began when the first cotton-spinning factories were built. The livelihoods of many who had earned their subsistence as spinners was threatened.[111] The demand for hand-spun yarn declined rapidly and yarn prices fell.[112] The spinning-mills in particular presented the hand-spinners with no alternative employment-prospects, and this was not only on account of their subjective attitudes but also for objective reasons. The mill-owners employed mainly women and children, because they were easier to discipline. In acting thus, the employers were not primarily following their own inclinations but were rather pressured by the situation on the labour market or were following pre-industrial employment patterns. Many spinners, of necessity, turned to handloom-weaving.[113]

The number of handloom-weavers multiplied. In Great Britain, the number of cotton weavers more than trebled between 1795 and 1833.[114] The domestic system expanded, but instead of being a relatively autonomous part of the proto-industrial system, it was now an integral component of the process of capitalist industrialization.[115] Consequently its utilization was subject to the conditions of exploitation which characterized that process. As soon as it became possible to close the gap between yarn and cloth production, and the entrepreneurs realized that greater profits could be made if they abandoned the domestic mode of production in weaving, the piece-rate which the weavers could command came under pressure. In times of crisis, they were the first to lose their livelihood. From then on handloom-weaving played a different role in the strategies of exploitation used by textile capitalists. Having lost their freedom of movement by sinking capital into fixed investments, they regarded handloom-weaving as an additional resource which could be tapped or left idle depending on market trends.[116] For the English handloom-weavers, however, the golden age came to an end, not in the 1820s when a larger number of power looms were first installed, but with the beginning of the Continental Blockade. An overcrowded labour-market, subject to severe fluctuations, made it possible for putters-out to lower the price rate. The price-index for muslins fell to 40 in 1820 (1805:100), the index for calicos fell to 30 in 1840 (1815:100).[117]

Abandoned by their governments, and having no recourse to trade-union-like organizations, the handloom-weavers were doomed. Some died, others turned to different occupations.[118] On the continent, the lag in the development of mechanized weaving behind mechanized spinning had similar effects on the working- and living-conditions of the handloom-weavers. But the situation was complicated by the fact that their number often muliplied in response to the quantity of English yarn that appeared on the domestic market. Furthermore, they were at first not so much exposed to the competition of domestic as to that of the English weaving-mills.[119]

On the continent, the technological lag behind Great Britain, as well as the occasional development-gap between individual regions, was much more relevant to the explanation of pauperism than was the mechanization of a part of an industry and subsequent attempt to close the rift between the two stages of production by increasing the number of domestic production-units. The causes of pauperism in continental Europe lie in the general crisis of proto-industry which was brought about by British competition in the world market, and deepened by the rapid population-growth, and in the late development of the factory system which lagged not only behind Great Britain but also behind more rapidly progressing regions on the continent. In 1844, the *Deutsche Vierteljahrsschrift* (German Quarterly), citing a newspaper report, wrote: 'The main cause of the great misery that has affected the Fichtelgebirge, the Saxon Voigtland, and the Bohemian Erzgebirge lies in the total depression of all branches of industry that is common to these areas.'[120] And this applied to many other regions as well. Another article, about the upper Erzgebirge, in the same journal is more analytical:

The cause of this sudden impoverishment does not only lie in a temporary slowing down of trade, as we have often experienced in the past, but in the circumstance that the factories in England have encroached upon our manufacture. The making of lace is the first industry to have received its death blow, and this affects thousands of people for whom the bobbin had been the milk-giving cow all the year round.[121]

The linen-producing regions were the hardest hit. Demand lagged far behind supply. Yarn prices fell, for ever since cheap British machine-spun yarn flooded the market, the price of hand-spun yarn was determined by that of machine-spun yarn. The income of spinners fell, since the margin between rising flax-prices and falling yarn-prices shrank.[122] In regions where hand-spinning was the livelihood of its inhabitants, the misery was extraordinary. In 1853, the Prussian government official, C. H. Bitter, wrote a 'Report about the state of distress in the Senne region between Bielefeld and Paderborn', i.e. about that district which Georg Weerth, in 1845, had called a 'desert' and about which he had said that it 'is now populated by the most unfortunate inhabitants of the once mighty Westphalia'.[123] Bitter, in his report, could show that the yearly income of a spinner's family of five had fallen from 82 to 49 *Reichstaler*, and he estimated the deficit in their household budget at 31 to 36 *Reichstaler*.[124] The days when a whole family could derive the main part of its subsistence from hand-spinning were gone for ever.[125]

The income of the handloom-weavers, though higher than that of the spinners and sustained by the fall in yarn prices, was also adversely affected during the first half of the nineteenth century. The loss of foreign markets, the general overcrowding of the craft, and the competition of cotton robbed it of its vitality and drove the weavers into unbelievable misery.[126] They tried to increase their output in order to compensate for their diminishing incomes, according to the laws of the family economy, and thereby entered a *circulus vitiosus* from which there was no escape.[127] Their patience was finally exhausted when they found themselves dependent on merchants who put pressure on their incomes and subjected them to all kinds of harassment. This is the background to the revolt of the Silesian weavers in 1844. The violence of that eruption can be explained by the fact that the weavers of Peterswaldau (now Pieszyce) and Langenbielau (now Bielawa) had already made the switch to cotton and, through the putting-out system, were chained to merchant-manufacturers whom they hated, namely the Zwanzigers and others. Some of the weavers had come from the completely depressed linen-industry hoping for a scanty subsistence. The merchant-manufacturers took advantage of their plight and cut their pay wherever possible. Thus the storm that burst over the premises of the Gebrüder Zwanziger establishment in Peterswaldau on 4 June 1884 had been some considerable time in the brewing.[128]

During the crisis of 1846–7 which preceded the Revolution of 1848 and was the last crisis of the 'type ancien' in central and western Europe, the misery among the proto-industrial population reached its peak. Outside of England, therefore, it became in some respects the final crisis of the proto-industrial system, though not of domestic industry.[129] The reasonable harvest of 1845 was followed by a catastrophic one in 1846: the rapidly spreading potato-blight destroyed large parts of the crop, and to that was added the failure of the grain harvest. In the period leading up to the Spring of 1847, the prices of potatoes and bread-grains multiplied many times over.[130] The high prices of basic food stuffs produced a chain-reaction. The crisis, caused by the deficiency of agrarian products, brought in its wake an underconsumption-crisis for the consumer goods industries, which inevitably hit particularly hart at the proto-industrial producers.[131] The situation was already so depressed that they could do little to counteract the crisis. During the heyday of proto-industrialization foreign, and especially overseas, markets had often made it possible to weather the contraction of domestic demand that followed harvest failures; but now most of the foreign markets were lost. Those of the petty producers who competed with factories or manufactures and who were regarded by industrial capitalists as an industrial reserve army were the first to lose their work. In Silesia, the misery took on such proportions that on 17 May 1847, troops were once again transferred to Reichenbach (now Dzierżoniów) 'because of the concern about anticipated unrest'.[132]

The misery of the Flemish spinners and weavers was beyond description. The linen sold in Flemish markets fell from 208,826 pieces in 1845 to 129,674 pieces in 1848, and the exports fell from 2,789,304 kilograms in 1845 to 1,448,485 kilograms in 1848. In 1843, 18.4 per cent of the population were on public assistance and the number had risen to 32.0 per cent in 1847. In eastern Flanders 37.8 per cent of the rural poor were spinners and weavers in 1847.[133] But the poverty on the continent was completely overshadowed by the events in Ireland where the hunger-crisis culminated in a mortality-crisis of extraordinary proportions. Between the Autumn of 1846 and the Spring of 1851, Ireland lost almost one tenth of her population. Another 10 per cent emigrated. The western counties had by far the highest mortality losses. In this region the decline of the rural textile industry, resulting especially from the concentration of the linen industry in the north-east, had thrown many people into destitution and thereby laid the groundwork for the catastrophe of 1846–51.[134] In Ireland, the crisis of proto-industry literally destroyed its social base.

Elsewhere the adjustment of the social structures, which proto-industrialization left behind, to the realities of industrial capitalism was less violent, but it could still involve great suffering. The concentrations of population which had developed during proto-industrialization in various regions could only to a small extent be smoothly integrated into industrial capitalism. Even in regions where the transition to the factory system was made without great delays, human labour needed to be reallocated. If the process of industrialization failed in a once proto-industrial region or if it advanced only slowly, a new equilibrium between population and resources had to be established and the population had to bear the brunt. Agriculture could absorb only a limited number, even though its demand for labour still rose during the agrarian revolution. The growth of the agrarian population remained far behind that of the total population.[135] The attempts to ward off the social consequences of the decline of proto-industrialization by new domestic industries such as basket-making or cigar-making had no lasting success.[136] Numerous petty producers were forced to join the trek into the centres of factory industry or to try their luck overseas. Many proto-industrial regions thus turned into a reservoir that fed not only domestic migration but also the emigration to America.[137] Those parts of the population who lived by the work of their hands felt utterly, physically powerless, faced with the violence of the enormous reallocation-process into which they were being drawn. Nascent industrial capitalism treated them with complete disregard and subordinated them to its own utilitarian interests. The industrial system was claiming its first tribute.

As industrial capitalism developed, industrial activity was once more concentrated in towns. To be sure industrial centres also arose in the countryside, but they soon grew and became towns or town-like communities. The productive structure of the countryside, on the other hand, was subject to de-differentiation: the manufacture of industrial goods declined and the relative weight of agriculture increased. In many cases, agriculture remained the only important production-sector. This is why many areas in the countryside were much more rural around 1900 than they had been a century earlier, even if they belonged to regions into which industrial capitalism had penetrated.[138] The original division of labour between town and country-side had been restored, but the emphasis had shifted. Agriculture had lost its primacy to the secondary and tertiary sectors. Its contribution to the national product, as well as the percentage of the total population that it employed, had declined rapidly.

In addition, since the beginning of the – still continuing – world agricultural crisis, the terms of trade between agrarian and industrial products have – to all appearance finally – shifted in favour of the latter. The countryside has come under the economic dictate of the city. The social consequences of re-agrarianization were immense. No longer was it possible to earn a living in the countryside outside the agrarian economy.[139] This affected not only the proto-industrial population-groups as such, but also the smallholders who were dependent on additional incomes to be earned outside of agriculture. If their village was situated near a large town or industrial district, they could find work and commute between city and countryside. But that was the exception rather than the rule. The more the agrarian incomes of smallholders came under pressure, the more they had to face the necessity of giving up agriculture and starting a new life in the town. As the process of the accumulation of capital progressed, so also the depopulation of the countryside got under way, as the inhabitants increasingly converged on a few districts.

Part II

Agriculture and peasant industry in eighteenth-century Flanders

Well before the coming of modern industrialization in the nineteenth century, a large section of the population of Flanders was involved in industrial occupations. A large export-oriented linen industry – outside the framework of the city or factory – had developed in the countryside during the seventeenth and eighteenth centuries to complement agricultural production on many farms. Of the 600,000 inhabitants of East Flanders in 1800, more than 100,000 adults and an undetermined number of children were spinning flax, while another 22,000 adults were engaged in weaving linen, mostly on a part-time basis.[1] This essay will discuss the impact of industry on agrarian organization and agricultural growth in Flanders in some of its spatial, economic, and demographic dimensions.

Industry

Producing linen had become the principal industrial activity in Flanders by 1800. The older woolen industry, which was the basis of Flemish industrial preeminence during the Middle Ages, had almost entirely vanished. Other industries, such as leather, paper, brick, glass, beer, gin, and linseed oil, although not negligible, were devoted only to the needs of the local population, and employed relatively few people.

Linen production was largely a rural activity. In Ghent, Bruges, Lille, Courtrai, and other cities, linen production stagnated or declined in the eighteenth century, while production in the rural hinterland increased. The number of looms in rural Vieuxbourg doubled from 4,976 to 8,868 between 1730 and 1792[2] but decreased in Ghent from 400 to 300 between 1700 and 1780 (Figure 1). Although Ghent was declining as a center of manufacturing, it was becoming a more important commercial center. The number of pieces brought to the Ghent market doubled between 1700 and 1780 (Figure 2), and while there were only 39 linen manufacturers in the city in 1792, there were 69 merchants who dealt primarily in goods produced in the countryside.[3] The growth of rural industry is also attested in the probate inventories (*staten van goed*). They show a steady increase in the percentage of households that owned

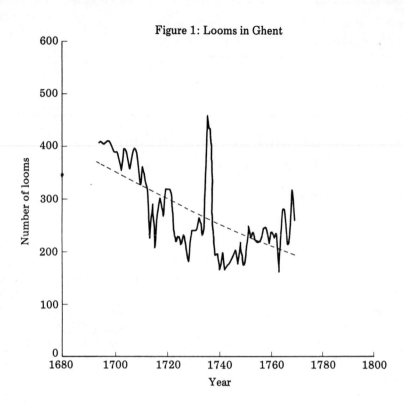

Figure 1: Looms in Ghent

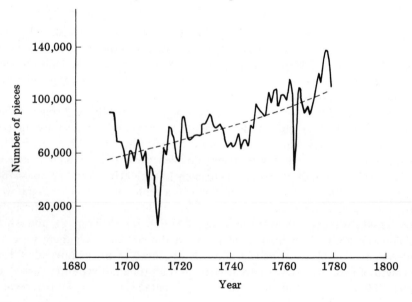

Figure 2: Pieces Brought to Market in Ghent

163

Figure 3: Map of Flanders

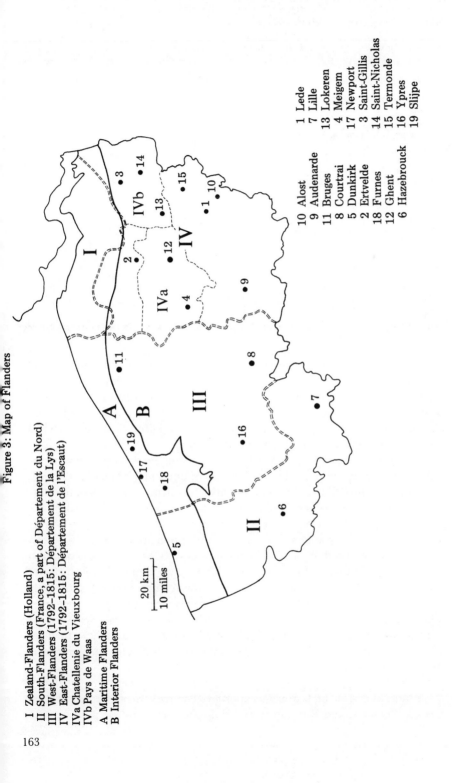

I Zealand-Flanders (Holland)
II South-Flanders (France, a part of Département du Nord)
III West-Flanders (1792–1815: Département de la Lys)
IV East-Flanders (1792–1815: Département de l'Escaut)
IVa Chatellenie du Vieuxbourg
IVb Pays de Waas

A Maritime Flanders
B Interior Flanders

10 Alost
9 Audenarde
11 Bruges
8 Courtrai
5 Dunkirk
2 Ertvelde
18 Furnes
12 Ghent
6 Hazebrouck

1 Lede
7 Lille
13 Lokeren
4 Meigem
17 Newport
3 Saint-Gillis
14 Saint-Nicholas
15 Termonde
16 Ypres
19 Slijpe

Table 1. *Incidence of Spinning Wheels and Handlooms in Lede and Ertvelde*

	1656–1705[a]	1706–1755	1756–1795
Number of Inventories			
Lede	259	378	439
Ertvelde	292	237	221
Percentage with Spinning Wheels			
Lede	68	80	80
Ertvelde	77	77	85
Percentage with Handlooms			
Lede	43	48	50
Ertvelde	31	30	47
Percentage with Spinning Wheels and Handlooms			
Lede	33	39	41
Ertvelde	23	25	42
Percentage with Spinning Wheels or Handlooms			
Lede	83	90	91
Ertvelde	85	81	90

[a] Ertvelde, 1642–1705
Sources: J. de Brouwer, *Geschiedenis van Lede* (Lede, 1963), p. 246; A. de Vos, *Geschiedenis van Ertvelde* (Ertvelde, 1971), p. 456.

looms or spinning wheels in the eighteenth century.[4] By the end of that period, that proportion had become very high indeed (Table 1), reaching 90 percent in some cases. The proportion of households that owned a loom or a spinning wheel was much higher than the proportion of heads of households who were classified as weavers or spinners in the census.[5] This reflects the extent to which the linen industry provided an income supplement.

The value of the annual output of linen cloth in the first years of the nineteenth century amounted to 25.7 million francs. In East Flanders the value of the production of linen cloth was roughly equivalent to one-half of the value of the potato harvest, or one-third of the value of the harvest of all cereals.[6] Only a fraction of this linen cloth was consumed regionally. It was estimated in the department of West Flanders that local consumption amounted to 16 percent (1.2 million for a production of 7.3 million francs).[7] Only the production from the area of Courtrai and from southern Flanders was exported to France, and the principal market for the rest of the Flemish linen industry during the seventeenth and eighteenth centuries was Spain and her American colonies.[8] The *presillas* were used for packing coffee and indigo, the *brabantes* were used for the clothing of negro slaves, for packing, and for draperies, and the striped and checkered cloth (*toiles rayées* and *toiles à carreaux*) were used in making mattresses, drapes, and clothing for negro slaves.[9]

In the Spanish and Spanish-American market. Flanders competed with other large and growing European exporters. The Irish, Scots, Bretons, Dutch, Saxons, Silesians, and Russians were striving to improve their position, and, judging from the production and trade statistics, were successful.[10] Flanders thus had a significant place in the world market but essentially remained a price-taker: it was faced with an elastic demand for its linens at a world price it could not affect. On the contrary, the prosperity of its merchants, farmers, wage laborers, and landlords was affected by the world price, and many contemporaries were quite aware of this.[11]

The income of a large part of the Flemish population, particularly the peasantry, had thus come to depend on the vagaries of international trade. For many – probably most – of the peasants in question, working in the linen industry was a part-time activity. The weavers and spinners took up their instruments only at times when agriculture did not demand their labor. Essentially, weaving and spinning were winter activities. In a full working day (5 A.M. to 8 P.M.), 5 to 6 els, that is, about 4 to 5 yards, of average quality linen cloth could be woven.[12] Thus it took 12 to 15 days of full-time work to weave one standard "piece" of 75 els (about 60 yards). On the basis of the census of 1792, 12 pieces of linen were calculated as the average output of an operating loom in the industrial villages near Ghent,[13] which means that the weavers worked an equivalent of 140 to 200 days per year.

According to the same source, each loom occupied one weaver, four spinners, and one and one-half other auxiliary workers, who could be children. In a household of this size and composition (a self-contained production unit), 5 els of linen could be obtained by working full time for one day. For this quantity, 3.75 pounds of flax were needed. Unless a peasant spinner grew it himself, the flax cost him 26 groten in the market at the middle of the century, while the final product (5 els of ordinary linen cloth) had a sales price of 60 groten. A full day's work for a five-person household could thus bring an income of 34 groten. This sum was very low, even compared with the average wage of unskilled workers, which was 20 groten per day in the winter. The daily income of a five-person household engaged in linen work was thus less than the wage of two unskilled workers.[14] The family probably persisted in producing linen because it could not earn more elsewhere. As we shall see, winter wage employment was very hard to find, and a family needed cash to supplement the insufficient food that could be extracted from the land it rented. In this sense, the colonial linen trade served as a vent for a surplus resource which, in Flanders, was a seasonal labor surplus.[15]

Most of the labor force engaged in the linen trade was of the kind described above: family labor with very low opportunity cost. But there were also landless wage workers and servants involved in the industry and receiving income from it. These were not usually employed directly by a merchant-manufacturer since, in Flanders, the peasants owned their tools until the nineteenth century, and merchants were therefore not directly engaged in production. Rather, these laborers worked during the dead season for cloth-working peasant families that, owing to their size or composition, did not possess the correct mix of labor inputs. The wages they could earn in this way were always comparatively low. In 1765, they amounted to four-fifths of the winter wages of other unskilled rural workers.[16] In 1800, the wages of a full-time adult weaver were 0.94 francs per day in the countryside, and 1.26 francs in the city, compared to 1.36 for the urban tailor and 1.81 for a mason.[17] The alternative to low-paying winter weaving was unemployment, which was heavy in Flanders (and with which the numerous urban charitable institutions were unable to cope). Fifteen percent of the population of Ghent was on relief in 1772, when the government opened the first 'modern' European prison, a thick-walled workshop where the inmates paid for their upkeep by working linen. Fourteen years later (1786), 20 percent were on relief in Ghent (9,480 out of about 45,000). For East Flanders, 57,000 persons were said to be on relief in 1801 in a population of 600,000.[18]

Poverty and unemployment thus coexisted with the form of industrial growth described above. This was not because industry produced impoverishment. Rather it appears on first analysis that an already impoverished population was forced to turn to industrial by-occupations to save themselves from destitution. In 1733 an observer wrote of Wasquehall, South Flanders, that the inhabitants were becoming 'too numerous for all to apply themselves to agriculture; three-quarters of the inhabitants of the countryside are now occupied in manufacturing, with which they can pay their taxes and maintain their families, who would be reduced to mendicity without this help.'[19] The relationship between agriculture and industry was more complex, however, than is implied by this statement. As we shall see, agricultural technology in fact permitted some degree of labor intensification. But before one can attempt to analyze the relationships between this industrial growth and the agricultural sector, the spatial distribution of the linen industry must be examined (see Figure 3).

The linen industry of Flanders was confined to the interior of the region; it was bounded on the west by the maritime strip along the English Channel. For instance, the area (*Métier*) of Furnes near the coast had 4,532 persons in the labor force in 1697, only 70 of whom (1.5 percent) were engaged in the textile industry. A century later (1796) there were still only 5.0 percent.[20] Indeed, the hinterland of Furnes (and Ypres) had shed its old woolen industry by the end of the seventeenth century, almost precisely when other areas of Flanders were acquiring international significance in linen production.[21]

The industrial interior was bounded on the east by the flaxgrowing Pays de Waas and the hinterland of Termonde, with their markets in Saint-Nicholas, Lokeren, and Termonde. 'The Pays de Waas and the area of Termonde do not have a large linen manufacture. The thousand to fifteen hundred looms there do not merit much consideration when in a single village of the Châtellenies of Vieuxbourg, Alost, Courtrai or Audenarde, there are more than a thousand.'[22] A number of spinners and only a few weavers worked there; but the flax harvest was large, larger than the quantities consumed domestically by the linen industry Indeed, a handsome surplus of more than one-fourth of the total output was sent abroad in normal years.[23] This commercial flax production was supplemented by the limited amount that peasants could grow on their own, and by the production that originated in the maritime areas.[24]

Finally, the degree of industrialization in the southeast of Flanders, particularly the area immediately east of Audenarde, is difficult to ascertain. The proportion of weavers in the labor force appears to have fallen in the second half of the eighteenth century, but there is some doubt as to the quality of the data used by De Rammelaere in establishing this fact.[25]

To summarize, the linen industry was located in the interior. Its labor was local, its raw materials mainly came from the northeast (Pays de Termonde and Pays de Waas). It must nevertheless be remembered that every village of the industrial area did not have a large number of weavers. One can easily find in the local censuses of the Revolutionary period areas where two almost contiguous villages had entirely different occupational structures. For example, the village of Balegem southeast of Ghent had as many weaving household heads as there were farmers, while neighboring Lemberge did not shelter a single weaver or spinner.[26]

Land and Labor in Maritime Flanders

There is a counterpart to the spatial distribution of industry in the spatial organization of Flemish agriculture. The lack of rural industrial development in the maritime strip was related to the development there of a commercial agriculture with large, up-to-date farms and a scattered and sparse population. This is in contrast to the agriculture and settlement pattern of the interior, which was marked by subsistence peasant agriculture, small farms, and a very dense population.

Maritime Flanders is a strip of polders (land reclaimed from the sea and below sea level), bordered by a fringe of dunes that extends from Artois through Zealand-Flanders to the Scheldt. Its soil, reclaimed between the ninth and nineteenth centuries, consists of a layer of heavy loam resting on a sandy foundation in the subsoil. In contrast to the rest of Flanders, it is extremely fertile and able to support soil-exhausting crops. Its dense fabric, however, requires very sturdy, heavy, and costly ploughs and other implements pulled by teams of horses. The nature of the soil thus required a large amount of fixed capital.[27] This region, not surprisingly, was one of large capitalistic farms, a region of *grande culture* (Table 2). It produced wheat, butter, and cheese for sale in foreign as well as domestic markets. Some of the land in the dunes or along the dikes and highways, however, was fragmented and owned or rented by peasants and part-time agricultural workers. In contrast to the rest of Flanders, a large proportion of the soil was held by successful farmers, who employed a

168   Franklin F. Mendels

Table 2. *Size of Farms, Polder Area, Métier of Furnes, 1697*

Hectares	Number of Farms	Percent of Farms
20 and above	14	28.6
15–19	5	10.2
10–14	13	26.5
5–9	14	28.6
Less than 5	3	6.1
Total	49	100.0

Source: D. Dalle, 'De bevolkstelling van 1697 in Veurne-Ambacht en de evolutie van het Veurnse bevolkingscijfer in de 17e eeuw', *Handeligen van het Genootschap voor Geschiedenis, Société d'Emulation, te Brugge* 90 (1953), 97–130.

large number of agricultural laborers or servants, or both. Almost 38 percent of the labor force was classified as wage workers in 1697 in the métier of Furnes.[28] It was an agrarian structure similar to the English style.

Maritime Flanders was never as densely settled as the rest of the region. The maritime section of the department of Escaut (Zealand-Flanders) had a density of 53 persons per square kilometer in 1800, compared to 191 in the rest of the department.[29] The maritime arrondissement of Dunkirk had a density of 117 at about the same date, while the area around Lille in the interior had 272.[30] Similarly, maritime Furnes had 71, but Courtrai in the interior had 200.[31] The population density of the whole region was high (West Flanders, 115; Nord, 141; East Flanders, 165; as opposed to England and Wales, 45; France, 50; the Netherlands, 60; Belgium, 88), but the aggregate statistics conceal the marked contrast between maritime and interior Flanders. The density was extreme in the interior, and there was a marked internal differentiation of high- and low-density zones. As a consequence of the sparse local population, the large farms depended on migrant labor to meet the seasonal needs of agriculture. Wages in the maritime areas were reputed to be higher than in the rest of Flanders, as one would expect under such conditions.[32] In the maritime region, however, there was little permanent immigration of surplus labor from the rest of the country; in fact, there is evidence of measures taken by the local authorities to prevent this from happening.[33]

The population growth of villages in the maritime region was generally slower in the eighteenth century than in interior villages. In sample areas taken from the maritime region of Furnes, population only increased from 6,600 to 9,600 persons between 1700 and 1800.[34] In other areas the population completely stagnated, while villages a few miles away, situated in the sandy zone, experienced rapid growth. A prefect once wrote that the death rate was higher in the very low and humid areas of the polders, where the climate tended to be unhealthy.[35] But other literary evidence links the slow population growth to late marriages and widespread celibacy. The marriage and migration patterns are related to the persistence of large commercial farms.[36] Since it would have been uneconomical to divide them, because the soil required heavy ploughs that were only practical on large plots,[37] the farms remained unfragmented and all the farmers' sons could not become farmers in turn. They had to enter into other occupations or migrate. Little is known about emigration, but it is my hypothesis that it differed in the maritime regions from the experience of the interior, where no such curbs to fragmentation existed.

Land and Labor in the Interior

The interior of Flanders experienced a comparatively high average population growth rate in the eighteenth century. In spite of very slow growth in the first two or three decades, the population doubled by the end of the century. (The population of England and Wales only increased by 55 percent, that of Holland by 10 percent.) The population density of the Flemish interior was comparatively high in 1700 – it had already been high in the Middle Ages in comparison with the rest of Europe – and the trends in the eighteenth century only served to increase the contrast. It has already been noted above that, on first analysis, demographic pressure directly promoted rural industrialization. This is supported by the fact that those sections of the countryside where population growth was curbed did not industrialize. But it is premature to speak of demographic 'pressure' until one has learned more about the agricultural response to population changes.

First, the rapid population increase created incentives both to clear new land and to reduce the amount of fallow. The former seems to have been undertaken by bankers, financiers, the nobility, and church landowners.[38] It is impossible to say how much of this took place in the course of the eighteenth century. We do know that toward the end of this period, woods, marshes, and heaths added up to approximately one seventh of the total surface of the department of East Flanders,[39] and a later inquiry expressed pessimism about the possibility of further reclamation.[40] The possibilities of reducing the amount of fallow land had been almost exhausted, too; a famous trait of Flemish agriculture, which impressed foreign visitors so much in this period, was farming without fallow.[41] Instead, farmers used long and complex rotation sequences, including an occasional year under clover, and made use of various types of manure purchased at the market, such as the refuse from gin distilleries.

Besides expanding the total area under cultivation, the number of farms increased in the interior, particularly among the smallest sizes (Table 3). The village of Lede, east of Ghent, approximately doubled its population between 1701 and 1791 (from ca. 1300 to ca. 2600 persons), but the number of its smallest farms more than doubled. The same was true of neighbouring Saint-Gilles (Table 4). It is possible both that small tenures were further divided,

Table 3. *Size of Farms, Lede*

Hectares	Number			
	1695	1701	1751	1791
20 and above	4	5	4	3
10–19	20	23	11	5
5–9	15	23	28	43
2–4.9	85	88	120	120
1–1.9	73	82	122	131
0.3–0.9	86	74	76	121
less than 0.3	130	52	89	169
Total	350	345	450	472

Source: J. de Brouwer, *Geschiedenis van Lede* (Lede, 1963), p. 219.

Table 4. *Size of Farms, Saint-Gilles*

Hectares	Number	
	1691	1797
15 and above	5	4
10–14	21	5
5–9	38	45
1–4	95	180
0.6–0.9	12	21
less than 0.6	19	105
Total	190	360

Source: M. Bovyn, *St-Gillis bij Dendermonde in 1571–1800* (Ghent, 1958).

and that some large blocks were split up by their owners. (In Tables 3 and 4, note the decrease in farms above 10 hectares.)[12]

It would appear that population growth was directly responsible for the fragmentation, but this relationship was in fact mediated by the land tenure system. Tenancy was more common than proprietorship among small as well as large farms, both in the interior of Flanders and in the maritime region. In Meigem, for instance, of the 111 holdings counted in 1765, 79 were held in tenancy, 11 were owned by their occupiers, and 21 were mixed. Of the 11 that were held in proprietorship entirely, none was larger than 4 hectares, while all of the 6 farms that were larger than 25 hectares were farmed by tenants. Tenancy was thus the usual form of land tenure, and the more so among the larger farms.[43] The same was true in the maritime area.[44] The exception to this Flemish pattern was found along the eastern border of the interior, where peasant proprietorship was predominant.

In Lede, which belonged to this area, of the 350 holdings counted in 1695, 63 were held in tenancy, 253 were owned by their occupiers, while the others were mixed.[45] The eastern boundary of the area of proprietorship has been mapped by Paul Deprez, but his source was not indicated.[46] It shows the Pays de Waas, the Pays de Termonde, and the Pays d'Alost to the south of Audenarde as the areas of ownership. Much of this area of peasant proprietorship does not seem to have been heavily industrialized, but the tantalizing correlation breaks down when one remembers that the Pays d'Alost (where Lede is located) had many weavers and spinners.

But the Pays d'Alost differed in one other respect – it was the only area of Flanders where open fields still prevailed. The fields were divided there into minuscule strips, sometimes no larger than 30 by 300 feet[47] (about one-tenth of a hectare). In fact, in Lede there were 27 'farms' in 1695, 28 in 1701, 46 in 1751, and 106 in 1791 that were smaller than one-thirteenth of one hectare.[48] Within the same Pays, however, there coexisted large blocks of land tilled by wealthy farmers.

The causes for such differences in both the ownership and layout of land probably could not be found in soil conditions. They lay, rather, in the conditions and period of initial settlement in the Middle Ages.[49]

The number of peasant proprietors may have increased slightly in the course of the eighteenth century.[50] Some writers have, in fact, explained the astounding increase in land prices by attributing it to the peasants' strong taste for proprietorship, even if their purchases were accompanied by great indebtedness, made possible by the development of a mortgage system.[51] Although peasant demand undoubtedly helped drive up the price of land, there were other reasons as well. Much of the land in Flemish villages was owned by landlords from neighboring cities. Jan Frans Hopsomer, a bourgeois of Ghent, owned one-fifth of the surface of Meigem.[52] Jacobus F. Maelcamp, another Gentenaar, was worth 70,000 gulden in real property at the time of his second marriage, and his possessions were spread over thirty-four different localities in Flanders. His rental income was estimated at 6654 gulden[53] for a rate of return of 9.5 percent at the time of his death in 1741.

Such handsome returns on land did not persist. As is shown in Table 5, the price of land increased much faster than land rents in the interior, driving down the rate of return to 1.5 percent in the 1780s. Mortgage rates fell continuously from an average of 6 percent at the beginning of the eighteenth century to 4.5 percent toward the end.[54] If the principal source of the increase in land prices had been peasant demand, one would have expected mortgage rates to rise as well, because peasants were presumably the ones who had to borrow in order to purchase land. But in reality they fell. This suggests that the supply of loanable funds increased faster than the demand for them from the so-called land-hungry peasantry. This in turn suggests that the urban merchants, manufacturers, and magistrates who injected money in the mortgage market were also responsible for most of the increase in land prices.

Why did these land purchasers allow the rate of return on their landed investment to fall so low, lower even than what they could earn on mortgages?

Table 5. *Prices, Rent, and Population*

	1690–99	1700–09	1730–39	1750–59	1780–89
Interior					
1) Price of Land	1.26	1.00	1.34	2.57	10.22
2) Rent of Land	0.69	1.00	1.02	1.02	2.31
3) Rate of Return on Land	3.6%	6.6%	5.0%	2.6%	1.5%
4) Price of Rye	1.67	1.00	0.78	0.85	1.10
5) Price of Linens	1.13	1.00	0.79	1.28	1.96
6) Population	n.a.	1.00	1.16	n.a.	1.67
Maritime Area					
7) Rent of Land	1.11	1.00	1.30	1.07	1.89
8) Price of Wheat	1.32	1.00	0.76	0.91	1.19
9) Population	n.a.	1.00	1.01	n.a.	1.30

Sources:
1) Land prices from the area of Nevele; Paul Deprez, 'De boeren in de 16de, 17de, en 18de eeuw', in J. L. Broeckx *et al.*, *Flandria Nostra* (Antwerp, 1957), Vol. 1, 144. Base 1700–1709 = 100.
2) Land rents from the same as (1); *ibid.*, p. 147. Church and poor administration property.
3) Rent ÷ price, from the data for (1) and (2).
4) Ghent *mercuriale*. Base 1699–1708 = 100, 1709 being extraordinarily high, in Charles Verlinden *et al.*, *Dokumenten voor de geschiedenis van prijzen en lonen in Vlaanderen en Brabant, XVe–XVIIIe eeuw* (Bruges, 1959), pp. 64–65.
5) Linen prices in Spain deflated by the Spanish/Flemish silver price ratio, in Earl J. Hamilton, *War and Prices in Spain, 1651–1800*, (Cambridge, Mass., 1947), pp. 34, 53, 77, 233ff., and Verlinden, *Dokumenten*, p. 21.
6) Sample taken from villages in the neighbourhood of Ghent. Source: Franklin Mendels, 'Industrialization and Population Pressure in Eighteenth-Century Flanders,' Ph.D. dissertation, University of Wisconsin, 1969, p. 144. 1696–1705, 1716–1745, and 1786–1795.
7) Rent from the polder village of Slijpe. Church and poor administration property. Base 1700–1709 = 100. Verlinden, *Dokumenten*, pp. 237–38.
8) Wheat is a more representative product than rye in the polders. Mercuriale of Newport. Base 1699–1708 = 100. Verlinden, *Dokumenten*, pp. 67ff.
9) Sample taken from ten villages in the neighborhood of Furnes by D. Dalle, *De bevolking van Veurne-Ambacht in de 17^{e} eeuw*, Verhandelingen van de Koninklijke Vlaamse Academie voor de Letteren, Wetenschappen en Schone Kunsten van België 49 (Brussels, 1963), 24–25, 227. Years: 1693, 1704, 1735, 1794.

The reason was that this form of investment paid non-monetary dividends in the form of security and prestige. Land rents also increased, although less than land prices. The fact that they increased faster than food prices, however, could be explained by a combination of an increase in population, land-saving agricultural changes, the development of the linen industry, and land fragmentation. Finally, land rents did not increase as fast in the maritime area as in the interior because of a slower population increase, fewer land-saving agricultural changes, the lack of development of a rural industry, and barriers to land fragmentation.

The rapid fragmentation of the land could have been induced by the prevalence of an egalitarian system of inheritance customs.[55] However, the latter probably had more effect on transfers of land titles among absentee owners than on their tenants. It is often forgotten that the legal rules of inheritance deal with the ownership of real property and not its rental, and that therefore they should not be expected to affect the subdivision of the land in an area of tenancy if the owners live away from the villages. It is true that, in one of the rare concrete descriptions of Flemish succession practices, subdivision of the land among the offspring when the parents are deceased is mentioned.[56] A contrast is noted between the polder areas, where such practices never occur, and the interior, where they do. The study in question deals, however, with the Pays de Waas, which is precisely an area of ownership. If, therefore, the old Flemish inheritance customs could have had an effect on the evolution of the countryside, it would have been in the eastern border, where peasant ownership predominated.

Elsewhere, that is in most of Flanders, economic-demographic rather than legal causes must be sought. Fragmentation was ultimately caused by population growth, but it came about through the response of landlords to the price mechanism. The fragmentation of the land was a market phenomenon – the result of the fact that higher unit rents could be drawn from smallholdings than from the large ones in the interior.[57]

Small self-contained family units with no wage labor only sought to maximize output, even if the marginal productivity of labor was thereby driven to very low levels.[58] When marginal productivity fell low enough, mostly in the winter, they started their seasonal textile occupation. Large holdings, on the other hand, required wage labor, and would not continue operating to the point where the marginal productivity of labor was lower than the set wage. Output per hectare on large holdings was therefore lower and commanded lower unit rents as well, as shown in Table 6.

Although the interior of Flanders stands out as an area of great fragmentation, the statistics show that many large plots remained in commercial operation, and must have been able to generate surpluses. If we follow the productivity and diet estimates made by the Prefect Faipoult and recently by Vandenbroeke, it would seem that two-thirds of one hectare were sufficient to feed a family of five on the diet that prevailed at the end of the eighteenth century.[59] If this was so, one farm family in four in Meigem, one in three in Saint-Gilles, and one in two in Lede, would have had to purchase food at the market. These numbers represent *minimum* estimates of the proportion of farms that needed supplementary, nonagricultural sources of income, for one must add rent and taxes to the minimum subsistence requirement. In fact, the probate inventories for Lede show that in the period 1786–1795, 88 percent of households had spinning wheels or looms.[60]

Another response that can be related in many ways to the growth of population, to the spread of industry, and to the fragmentation of the land is the

Table 6. *Relation of Rent to Farm Size*[61]

Parish	Farm Size (roeden)	Total Rent (groten)	
		1731	1743
Landegem	33	24	72
id.	36	9	7
id.	37	12	16
id.	37	36	16
id.	40	56	96
id.	40	14	96
id.	50	21	21
id.	75	140	162
Meigem	100	37	n.a.
Landegem	150	72	74
id.	150	192	192
Meigem	150	24	n.a.
Landegem	150	96	108
id.	150	180	126
id.	160	180	180
id.	200	168	192
id.	200	96	96
Meigem	300	48	n.a.
id.	400	162	n.a.
Landegem	400	200	246
id.	450	120	120
id.	1350	18	76

1 roede = 0.00147 hectares
Data source: Paul Deprez, 'Pachtprijzen in het Land van Nevele (17^e en 18^e eeuw)', in *Dokumenten*, I, 181ff.
Correlations between rent *per* roede and farm size:
1731: $R = .39$ (signif. 95%) Sample size: 22 cases
1743: $R = .42$ (signif. 90%) Sample size: 18 cases

progressive diffusion of the potato in the course of the century. It first appeared near Bruges in 1709, and spread rapidly to the small farms of the interior;[62] but there was little or no trade in potatoes until much later. The peasants grew this crop for their own consumption as an inferior substitute for rye, which could then be sold in the market for the cash they needed to pay their rising rents. In 1801, about 14.5 percent of the surface planted with food crops in East Flanders was given to potatoes. (According to a recent article, this figure would represent the maximum ever reached there.)[63] In Flanders, as in many other European regions, the potato played an important role in changing the balance between population and the means of subsistence, for the weight yield per hectare of a potato crop was ten times larger than that of land planted with bread cereals. It is easy to exaggerate this development, however. The nutritive value of potatoes is five times smaller than that of rye or wheat for a given weight. Assuming no change in caloric consumption per capita and no increase in the land effectively under cultivation, we may estimate that the population increase allowed by the substitution of potatoes for rye and wheat would have been not more than 14.5 percent[64] in the eighteenth century.

In reality, the population of Flanders almost doubled in that century and, furthermore, toward the middle of this period the region became a net food exporter for the first time since the Middle Ages.[65] Moreover, a considerable amount of grains went into non-human consumption: rye, barley, hops, and oats were used to feed animals and to supply the breweries and genever distilleries. So even though Flanders was already very advanced in its agricultural techniques in 1700, other changes must have taken place besides the spread of the potato. Knowledge of improved rotation cycles probably spread. In the village of Lede for example, only 3.6 percent of the probate inventories from the early seventeenth century mention clover on the field. This grew to 56.8 percent in the late seventeenth century, and peaked at 84.8 percent in the late eighteenth century.[66] The surplus of food that was produced by Flanders above domestic human consumption did not entirely originate in the maritime area. The calculations in the Appendix lead to the conclusion that the maritime area of East Flanders produced a theoretical surplus which was equal to 78.6 percent of total output. The theoretical surplus from the interior was 26.5 percent. Although the relative sizes of these surpluses cannot be checked against independent evidence, their sum (36%) can and seems realistic.[67] It might seem paradoxical that the interior of Flanders could generate a food surplus, although much evidence points to population pressure in this region. But the surplus most probably originated from the large capitalistic farms that coexisted with the smallholdings. Furthermore, some of it may even have come from peasant farms, in spite of the fragmentation taking place at the time. The existence of a surplus is not incompatible with other evidence pointing to low standards of living, nor is impoverishment impossible in the midst of agricultural progress and industrial expansion.[68] The engine of this growth was the pressure of rising debts and rents, which ultimately can be traced back to demographic pressure, mediated by the existing system of land ownership and distribution.

The progress of agriculture and the growth of industry can be related in one more way. Innovations in Flemish agriculture had both a labor-using and a seasonal bias. It was noted by a contemporary that on one acre of a Flemish farm, wheat demanded 25 man-days of work, while rye required 21 man-days. But the potato patch required 77 man-days per acre, of which 50 were needed for the deep digging and repeated ploughing necessary to cultivate this crop. When flax was grown, the requirement was 82 man-days for pulling the weeds.[69] While the new crops undoubtedly increased employment per acre, thereby facilitating the reduction of the size of family farms, they also reinforced the seasonal peaks of employment and accentuated the winter slack.

Flax cultivation also had high seasonal labor peaks, since weeding and harvesting required a large number of workers within a few days. A flax stalk

that has become ripe very quickly becomes over-ripe, resulting in a considerable deterioration in the quality of the fiber. In the eighteenth century 12 to 15
adult workers could harvest one hectare of flax in one day. The flax crop
covered 14,000 hectares of land in East Flanders alone, requiring 170,000 to
210,000 man-days of labor within a very few days of the calendar.[70] As other
crops came to maturity and competed for the same labor in the same season,
there was a shortage of labor at certain times of the year. For big farmers this
was a reason to hire servants and laborers on half-year contracts, long before the
peak season, to insure their harvest labor.

In summary, during the eighteenth century, the aggregate amount of land
under cultivation did not keep up with the increase in the number of farm
households. Households of roughly constant size had to live on holdings of
diminishing dimensions. This was made possible by the increased output per
acre and rising labor intensity. Labor intensity did not rise evenly across the
annual cycle, however, and this provided periods of slack during which
nonagricultural activities, above all the linen industry, could be carried out.

Summary and Conclusion

The economic history of Flanders from the late seventeenth to the late
eighteenth century adequately fits what I have called elsewhere a phase of
'proto-industrialization' – a period of rural industrialization with simultaneous
bifurcation between areas of subsistence farming with cottage industry and
areas of commercial farming without it.[71]

The linen industry was only a by-occupation for the Flemish countryside, a
subsidiary income for an essentially agricultural population. Yet it is striking
how much the story of its organization and growth is intimately connected with
other aspects of the agrarian economy in the eighteenth century. I have tried to
show that its spread resulted from forces that can be traced back ultimately to
population pressure. Rural industry, like the diffusion of the potato and of new
agricultural techniques, permitted the multiplication of people on the land
through the fragmentation of farms. Without it, such a rate of natural increase
of population as was experienced in Flanders would have necessitated
emigration to cities or other regions.

But this is only one side of the coin, for the rate of natural increase of the
Flemish population was not determined exogenously. Elsewhere I have shown
that in rural-industrial areas, improvement in the relative price of linen
produced surges in the number of marriages.[72] Rural industry itself thus helped
to accelerate the rate of population growth. It not only permitted population
growth, but actively promoted it. The role of cottage industry was therefore
perverse in the sense that it perpetuated the dismal pressures that had first
induced its penetration into the countryside. As long as an outlet was readily
found for the output of the cottage industry, this dismal high-pressure

equilibrium remained feasible. It was destroyed in the nineteenth century, when competition from machine-made yarn and cloth and from the new urban cotton industry threw the Flemish rural economy and society into a dreadful crisis.[73]

Appendix: Estimated Food Surplus in 1804

The surface of the polder zone in East Flanders (at the time when this province included Zealand Flanders) was 65,300 hectares; that of the interior, 292,400 hectares. The former had a population of 34,750 persons (1805), the latter, 558,750.[74] Assuming that the diet was the same for the inhabitants of both areas, 0.618 liter of grain per person per day and 1.3 kg. of potatoes were consumed.[75] If the net yields in quintals per hectare were also the same, that is, 33 for wheat, 36 for rye, and 347 for potatoes,[76] a family of five needed for subsistence 0.47 hectares of wheat *or* 0.44 hectares of rye and 0.10 hectares of potatoes.[77]

To feed the polder zone at subsistence level, one would therefore need to have 695 hectares planted with potatoes and 3,266 hectares with wheat (or 3,058 hectares of rye). Assuming that no rye was grown there and that wheat and potatoes together constituted the same proportion (28.3 percent) of total land surface as devoted to food crops in the province as a whole, approximately 3,695 hectares should have been planted with potatoes (20 percent of foodcrop surface assumed) and 14,783 hectares with wheat (80 percent assumed).

The difference between the estimates of consumption needs and of crops production is an excess of 3,000 hectares for potatoes and 12,000 for wheat. Theoretically, the surplus as a proportion of output was therefore 78.6 percent. In the interior 558,750 inhabitants would have needed 11,175 hectares of potatoes and 52,522 hectares of wheat (or 49,170 hectares of rye). It was estimated, however, that 16,521 hectares were planted with potatoes, 17,378 hectares with wheat, and 49,229 with rye. The surplus produced here was therefore approximately equal to the output of 22,000 hectares, or 26.5 percent.

The textile industries in Silesia and the Rhineland: A comparative study in industrialization

HERBERT KISCH

I

The gradual yet cumulative advance of West European capitalism was in large part epitomized by the developments of its textile trades.[1] They were the first to carry the seeds of economic change into the stagnant preserves of guild conservatism, and subsequently they again proved to be the pioneers of the new factory system. In Germany the sequence of economic change was not quite as uniform. Each German textile district emerged as a specific case of economic growth with contours of industrial evolution that manifested unique deviations from the broad pattern of development. The heterogeneity of the German lands, particularly marked before the advent of the railways, was both cause and effect of this diversity.

The contrasting fortunes of Silesian and Rhineland textile trades are extreme cases of this divergence. Nevertheless both these areas share certain common features that need to be emphasized before continuing with a comparison of their disparate ways. In both instances the textile trades assumed within the regional economy a position of sufficient importance to render the welfare of the local population dependent upon the prosperity of these trades. In each case the share of exports bulked large within total output, thus exposing the two regions: at a very early stage, to the structural and cyclical vagaries of international trade. In both instances the textile trades antedated by centuries the industrial revolution, providing evidence for those adjustments generally called forth once the factory system tended to exert its dominance, within the world economy, upon an older industrial structure. Finally, both districts in their own way affected and were affected by the composite of German economic development.

To render these regional differences in any way meaningful it becomes necessary to delineate the character of the institutional setting. Only against the background of its relevant industrial framework and social structure is it possible to understand why the Silesian textile trades of the nineteenth century were subjected to such difficulties while the same industry in the Rhineland was to enjoy, with relatively minor interruptions, steady expansion.

178

II

The Silesian textile industry, the linen manufacture in particular, merits a special place in a study of German nineteenth-century economic development, even though it affords no insights into the processes of industrial evolution. Confronted, since the second half of the eighteenth century, by the rise of foreign competition and the appearance of cotton as a substitute product, the linen trades relapsed into a state of helpless resignation. Advantages of a once flourishing industry ran to waste. External economies of the past, a tradition of skills, and availability of ancillary trades were left untapped for purposes of development. Given its inability to adapt to changing circumstances, the Silesian linen industry becomes a case study in economic stagnation. What was it that made the Silesian scene so peculiar as to inhibit economic growth and condemn its inhabitants to a state of indescribable misery?

Lujo Brentano was able to provide an interesting explanation for this unfortunate sequence of economic change. Referring to the then (1892) standard work on the Silesian linen industry (Alfred Zimmermann, *Blüthe und Verfall des Leinengewerbes in Schlesien* (Oldenburg and Leipzig: Schulzesche Buchhandlung, 1885), Brentano wrote that '. . . the industrial organization of the ordinary weavers and their plight remained unintelligible to me, as often as I read the book, until I came upon an idea that unravelled all that had hitherto remained mysterious: the organization of Silesia's rural linen industry was based upon a feudal order'.[2] Apart from its importance to the present study, the hypothesis endows this account with some topical relevance as it raises issues that may be of interest to those who concern themselves with the problems of underdeveloped economies.

The emergence of the Silesian linen manufacture as an industry working for the world market dates back to the sixteenth century. At that time foreign merchants entered the Silesian countryside and organized a domestic industry in order to tap the labor services of the rural population that had been spinning and weaving on a part-time basis and mostly for its own use.[3] These traders deliberately bypassed the urban crafts because the corporate fetters made the guild artisans quite incapable of adjusting to the requirements of the new production as demanded by the foreign markets.[4]

The feudal lords approved and supported the creation and subsequent extension of local industry. As the principal estate owners, they welcomed the more intensive utilization of local resources, particularly timber, and the consequent rise in land values. In the same way they were to profit from the increased capacity of their serfs to bear the burden of feudal dues as a result of the latter's improved employment opportunities. Above all, this new industrial expansion meant that the lords were able to turn into cash the flax, the yarn, and the linen which, since times immemorial, they had been receiving as part of the feudal tribute.[5]

In the subsequent wranglings over the extension of a rural manufacture, the guilds and their artisans naturally opposed these industrial developments as a threat to their existence. It was equally obvious that the lords (the Junkers), as an interested party, sided with the rural crafts settled on their estates and influenced the Imperial government accordingly. Initially, the Habsburg authorities also supported the rural industrialists against the complaints of the urban guilds. After sometime, however, they had second thoughts and attempted to save the corporate system from complete collapse. By then, however, the economic forces aided and abetted by the power of the aristocratic landowners made such attempts quite futile.[6]

In the struggle waged between resident and foreign traders over the continuance of existing trading privileges, the lords once again sided with those disruptive of the old order; these were the English and Dutch merchants who were the principal customers of the Junkers' feudal stores. This commercial alliance, of local landowner and foreign merchant, so important from the very inception of the Silesian linen industry, was thus continually strengthened. In 1601 the local traders complained to the authorities that the Dutch and English competitors were undermining their traditional privileges and thus their very existence. The lords, bribed by the foreigners, promptly submitted a counter petition opposing monopoly rights and extolling the benefits, including the higher sales prices received for their products, accruing to the area from the activities of the foreign traders and from the expansion of free trade.[7]

Given these circumstances surrounding their origins and early history, the Silesian linen trades reflected, in many ways, a classic pattern of colonial penetration. Compradores allied themselves with the local rulers in order to open up a territory and together the two groups mobilized underemployed resources for the so-called 'vent of surplus'.[8]

Industrial growth continued unabated during the early decades of the seventeenth century. The weavers in the countryside already numbered in the thousands, and urban artisans were supposedly leaving the cities to settle in the rural areas where the conditions for expansion seemed more propitious. The prosperity prevailing in the textile centers reflected the continuous expansion of linen exports. Even the destruction and devastation of the Thirty Years' War interrupted only temporarily the advance of the industry, secure in its rural setting. The post-war period enhanced this resilience by increasing the supply of available labor. Thousands of Czech and Moravian Protestants, driven from their homes by the Counter-Reformation, fled into Silesia. Without means or property, these refugees were as happy to turn to spinning and weaving as the lords were eager to settle them on their estates in order to enlarge their sources of feudal revenue.[9]

This industrial labor force was also augmented by native hands. Since the lords preferred to enlarge their own demesne by enclosure rather than by reconstructing the holdings destroyed by the war, many a peasant was reduced to a landless proletarian. At best he became a cotter who was compelled to eke out his existence by spinning and weaving.[10] This development in turn led to a reduction in labor costs which constituted the basis for the success of local industry. Silesian linen remained unchallenged in world markets, and many historians claimed that the late seventeenth and early eighteenth century were the brightest periods of Silesian development.

Apart from the Junkers, the linen merchants were the main beneficiaries of this expansion. They were able to gather the fruits of commercial progress, once they had come to terms with the foreign factors who had previously pressed them so hard. While traveling through Silesia early in the eighteenth century, a German Cameralist noted that in those mountain towns resided 'very wealthy and distinguished merchants' who entertained commercial relations with all parts of the world.[11] The comforts of the merchants contrasted almost as sharply as the luxuries of the lords with the miserable existence of the rural inhabitants.[12]

Subjected to increasing pressure, the exasperated serf was driven to the verge of mutiny. This mounting social tension manifested itself in frequent refusals on the part of the peasants and cotters to meet their feudal obligations. On several occasions the disturbances erupted in violence and could only be put down by military force.[13] These difficulties, however, did not seem to interfere with industrial progress. Silesian linen continued to enjoy a favorable market in Holland, England, Spain, and their respective colonies.[14] Thus the local lords could easily satisfy their desire for more serfs by increasing the number of weavers and spinners on their estates.[15] Even the Austrian authorities came to acknowledge the importance of the linen manufacture for the regional economy and its advantage for the Imperial treasury.[16]

The feudal basis of the linen trades was not affected when Silesia became part of the Prussian kingdom in 1742. Frederick the Great pursued a policy of industrial encouragement which was but a continuation of the mercantilist practices initiated by the Austrian authorities. Several hundred new colonies of foreign spinners and weavers were established.[17] Spinning for all rural youth became mandatory, and special schools were opened to teach the young facility with the spindle. Generally, new edicts and laws were promulgated by the Prussian government to assure an increase in the supply of linen without a deterioration in quality or a rise in price.[18] Because these measures were to their advantage, the privileged merchants and the Junkers acclaimed Frederician policy with enthusiasm. The support of the lords was crucial, for without their active co-operation no royal program stood any chance of success.[19]

Taking advantage of the growth in world commerce during the second half of the eighteenth century, the lords and the King succeeded in their efforts at industrial expansion. According to the first census takers in Silesia, there were 19,810 looms in use in 1748. By 1790 the number of looms stood at 28,704, with more than 50,000 people working them.[20] Without doubt, the linen trades had become one of the decisive factors in the regional economy, and they were in large part responsible for encouraging the population increase which occurred during this period, (which was one million in 1741 and 1,747,000 in 1791).[21]

A shift in location accompanied the expansion of the linen trades. The use of timber as fuel for the bleaching of raw linen led to a deforestation in the original centers of manufacture and therefore compelled the industry to move into the mountains where wood was still at hand.[22] This industrial relocation was a boon to the lords who owned the scraggy land at the foot of the 'Giant Mountains'. Unlike elsewhere, many a landlord of hilly land carried on no agriculture characteristic of the feudal estate. Instead he lived off the sale of timber and from the dues and rents which the industrial population, settled on this estate, owed him. A serf-weaver had to pay a fee for carrying on his trade, the *Weberzins*. He paid a further sum as a commutation for the labor services to be rendered and for having his children, needed as ancillary labor, exempt from having to do service in the house and on the land of the lord. On marriage, on death, when selling the inventory of his holding, and when removing himself from the domain, the serf was obligated to pay more.[23]

As long as industrial conditions were propitious, this feudal burden may have been bearable. However, despite industrial expansion, the second half of the eighteenth century was fraught with difficulties. The frontier changes following the incorporation of Silesia into Prussia tore asunder a delicate network of economic interdependence.[24] At the same time, English cotton fabrics made their appearance. As a material, cotton was popular and well suited for a tropical climate. It consequently came to encroach upon those spheres, especially as garments for the slaves on colonial plantations, which hitherto had been the exclusive preserve of linen.[25] Moreover there developed in Northern Ireland and Scotland, under the auspicious circumstances of a free economy, a linen industry which was to offer serious competition to Silesian exports.[26]

At home in Silesia conditions became equally pressing. The population increase and the extension of the industry had enhanced the world rise in the prices of foodstuffs and industrial raw materials far above the increase in the price of linen. In the absence of any technical improvements, such a 'scissor movement' was to hit the weaver hard.[27] Consequently, weavers and serfs became ever more discontented with the growing pressures exerted upon them by the lords. Throughout the 1770s and 1780s, frequent peasant revolts occurred. When the message of 1789 spread through Europe, Silesia did not remain immune. Apart from the weavers who rioted in the Spring of 1793, the peasants and the city journeymen also rose in revolt.[28]

During the 1790s conditions in world markets further aggravated the economic and social situation. The increase in exports, because of the inflation, was more apparent than real. The perverse relative price movements left no margins for absorbing a temporary setback, such as occurred in 1798 when sea warfare paralyzed the linen trade. The sombre government reports provided a detailed account of the difficulties suffered by the industry because of the disturbances of war.[29]

The subsequent return to peace offered no improvements. Severance from traditional markets had only hastened the decline of the linen and linen yarn manufacture at the expense of the Irish competition.[30] The rise in food prices during the first decade of the nineteenth century aggravated the situation as the weavers and spinners had to buy most of their food in the market. Only the timely appearance of the potato staved off what otherwise might have been a famine of major proportions. The spinners in particular were condemned to utter destitution in view of the competition of English and Scottish mechanized spinning mills. By the 1820s the export market in this branch of the business had come to a complete standstill, and English merchants were heard to comment that Silesian yarn had become 'unsaleable'.[31] Even the export of linen had declined considerably. During the 1830s and 1840s the linen exports from Silesian towns, once flourishing centers of this industry, dwindled to almost nothing. At the same time the woolen trades faced a similar decline and offered no alternative sphere of employment.[32] Thus the misery of the local population increased, and during the famine years of the 1840s thousands of these spinners died from hunger.[33]

Only the cotton trades enjoyed a secular expansion. In 1830 a local magistrate observed that the linen manufacture was being supplanted by the cotton industry. A census of 1849 showed that in Silesia the ratio of linen weavers to cotton weavers was 7:12, while the number of cotton looms plied on a full time basis was double that of those weaving linen.[34] Nevertheless, the expanding cotton industry was not spared its full share of difficulties. Though the principal outlets were within Germany, English products offered serious competition, especially throughout the deflationary decades following the end of the Napoleonic Wars. Not even the 1818 tariff and the *Zollverein* of 1834 proved to be unmixed blessings as Saxon and Rhineland products were able to increase their competitive pressures.[35]

The Silesian cotton industry could continue to hold its own only by paying low wages to its work force, particularly the weavers. Coming out of the declining linen and woolen trades, the weavers offered themselves to cotton mill operators in relatively large numbers, a circumstance the merchant-manufacturers dominating the industry were not loath to exploit. The workers in turn were rendered increasingly desperate by this misery and came to vent their wrath upon those who seemed to them responsible for this distress.[36] In 1844 the weavers of two cotton centers attacked the most hated local cotton manufacturers as well as their factors, and destroyed their plant and inventory. The rioting quickly spread throughout the textile districts of Silesia. Eventually, the brute force of the military established the supremacy of the law.[37]

Furthermore, the textile workers continued to be oppressed by feudal obligations. The all pervasiveness of feudal dominance had remained un-impaired despite the Stein-Hardenberg Reforms (1807–1812), since the lords had been able to shape the new 'freedoms' in such a way as to strengthen their social and economic preeminence.[38] Thus one might say that in the Prussia of the first half of the nineteenth century feudalism had not been abolished, but only modernized. Under one pretext or another feudal tribute continued to be levied from the local population right up to 1850.[39]

Even the state taxes paid by the rural inhabitants were high in view of the almost total exemption from all taxation of the aristocracy. According to contemporary reports, the pauperized weaver cotter paid, throughout the 1830s and 1840s, in the form of dues, tithes, and taxes, no less than one third of his annual income.[40] This is why the Silesians were among the first in the German lands to submerge themselves in the revolutionary tide of 1848. Once again the weavers stood in the forefront of violent action. In this instance, unlike 1844, they directed their anger against the feudal system and the lords who were taking from them what little the manufacturer may have left them.[41]

Capital accumulation within the industrial sector was most adversely affected by these feudal pressures. The potential drives of the craftsmen were stifled. Burdened by feudal tributes and heavy taxes, they were unable to accumulate those first few pennies that might have sparked their en-trepreneurial initiative and turned them into innovators within their trade. More important, the extra-economic pressures characteristic of a feudal society inhibited changes in the investment flow and thereby prevented steady industrial progress. The specific nature of these pressures became most apparent during the depression at the end of the Seven Years' War in 1763. At that time the price of estates had collapsed, and the fabric of feudal society seemed in jeopardy. Many lords were reduced to ruin, having borrowed excessively in order to partake in the speculative mania of the preceding land boom.[42] In their desperation the Silesian lords appealed to Frederick the Great. They pleaded, though the claim was most dubious, that the ravages of war had been responsible for their plight. The King heard them with sympathy and granted them their principal demand, the establishment of a land mortgage bank, the so-called *Landschaft*, meant to restore the lords' credit standing and channel the flow of capital once more in their direction.[43]

To achieve its purpose and raise the relative profitability of the feudal estate against the competing alternatives of industry and trade, the new credit institution was endowed with privileges typical of the pressures imposed upon the market forces within this setting. For one, the Junkers alone could partake of the facilities of this credit scheme, thus assuring them of monopsony in the capital market. Secondly, to reduce risks and enhance the attractiveness of the *Landschaft* as an investment outlet to the potential lender, particularly the local bourgeois, the landed estates, grouped within the *Landschaft* collectively, were to serve as security for all loans. The general acceptability of these mortgages was thus assured, and they circulated, in addition to cash, as part of the existing money supply. Given these advantages, the new credit institution easily gathered, on behalf of the Junkers, most available funds in the area and thereby contributed to the subsequent rise in land values.[44] In view of the cumulative increase in the supply of capital offering itself to the *Landschaft*, the existing mortgages enjoyed a steady capital appreciation. This in turn meant that the rate at which the Junkers were borrowing declined throughout this period from 6 per cent in 1769 to 4 per cent in 1791.[45]

The same non-economic pressures were evident in the labor market. On the one hand the ever increasing exploitation of the serfs was part of the over-all efforts to maintain and even raise the profitability of feudal agriculture. On the other, the system of compulsion imposed by the Junkers and privileged merchants upon the serfs, in their capacity as weavers and spinners, caused the supply conditions of labor to be very much akin to those in the model of a colonial labor market elaborated by Hla Myint in his recent essay.[46] In this instance the existing industrial structure, based on cheap labor and in no way reflecting 'real costs', was rendered a permanent and nearly unalterable feature of the linen trades.[47] Moreover, the authorities opposed all improvements since the Junkers feared that labor saving devices would cause unemployment among their serfs. Capital to pioneer innovations therefore did not flow into the industry as it might have done in a different setting. Adam Smith must have had a case of this nature in mind when he wrote '. . . Whatever obstructs the free circulation of labor from one employment to another, obstructs those of stock likewise . . .'

Silesian industrial conditions, especially in the linen trades, were aggravated by the continued drain of industrial and mercantile capital into agriculture. As soon as a merchant accumulated some capital, he invested it in mortgages of the *Landschaft*. If, however, the merchant became rich, as some of the privileged traders did during the eighteenth century, they purchased landed estates outright. Such a propensity was understandable considering the character of Silesian society. The rich merchants sought emancipation from their serf status through elevation into the circle of the elite.[48] But apart from social and political considerations, sound economic reasons prompted the merchants to invest in land. For the Junker estate, endowed with privileges, remained the most profitable investment outlet throughout the second half of the eighteenth century.

Frederick the Great was included among the vociferous critics of this investment flow. Yet he did nothing, and probably could do nothing, to alter the institutional setting which was responsible for this investment flow. When criticizing Brentano for his hypothesis regarding the deterrents of feudalism and Frederican policy upon the linen trades, Sombart argued that investment possibilities in linen towards the end of the eighteenth century were poor, and therefore could not have attracted new savings.[49] Indeed, the relative profitability of the linen trades must have been low, but not, as Sombart suggested, because of an inadequate resource pattern nor because technical improvements were unavailable at the time for innovation. Rather, the linen trades remained starved of capital because of the peculiar laws and customs prevailing in Silesian industry.

Unlike in the cotton trades, the general absence of a *Verlag* system in the Silesian linen trades was an index of the industry's anemic condition. Even as late as the 1820s the *Kaufsystem*, the original system of production, was very much in evidence.[50] By then this form of economic organization, based on the independence of those working in the trade, seemed rather primitive and inefficient.

The best contemporary account of this system written in English came from the pen of John Quincy Adams who toured Silesia in 1801 while United States Minister to the Prussian Court. At first Adams noted with great satisfaction the absence of 'extensive manufacture'. But his enthusiasm for Silesian industry waned once he realized the wretchedness of the working population associated with it.[51] For the *Kaufsystem* had become, in the last decades of the eighteenth century, the worst of all possible worlds. As independent producers, the weavers, had to bear risks of market fluctuations which they were in no way capable of assuming.

At the same time the Frederican legislation regulating the linen trades reinforced the monopsony power of the privileged merchants, while the growing wealth of the yarn jobbers gave them a pre-eminent position in the raw material market. Since the poor weaver usually bought his yarn on credit, and at usurous interest rates, he had to accept whatever yarn he was given, even if it was short of the requisite reels. Oppressed as a borrower and defrauded as a buyer and seller, it was not surprising that the weaver resorted to defraudation and adulteration of the product. These abuses progressively expanded to all stages of production, however strict the rules against them.[52] Overseas customers complained more vocally of faulty production. As early as the 1780s, a contemporary observer noted that the new Irish linen trades, developing in freedom, could produce a material of superior quality.[53]

The impact of the past upon Silesian industrialization appeared clearly in a report published in 1850 by a Commission set up by the Prussian Diet to investigate the causes of the distress in the German linen trades. While the report of this Commission, also meant to suggest ways for improvement, revealed little that was startling,[54] it offered some interesting insights on the relative degree of industrial development in Germany and England. Despite high transportation costs, the Commission found that imported English linen yarn was almost 10 per cent cheaper than the same yarn produced in Breslau. The investigation also revealed that costs in general were much higher in Germany than in England. The costs of constructing a linen yarn spinning mill were 40 per cent higher and the differential in operating costs almost 20 per cent.

The reasons for this disparity were varied: 1. The higher cost of iron in Germany; 2. Higher coal costs (in a Silesian spinning mill these costs were $2\frac{1}{2}$ times greater than in England); 3. The greater price of capital (4 per cent in England and 6 per cent in Germany); 4. Installation and initial utilization of the machinery was more costly in Germany because skilled mechanics and operatives were lacking; 5. Higher costs of steam engines, the cost per horse power being £30 in England and £45 in Germany; 6. Other factory equipment, such as water pipes, belts, cans, lamps and the like, were 20 per cent more expensive. The Commission commented upon those differences with Marshallian insight: 'In England the procurement of all factory equipment is cheaper because of the lower costs of the basic constituent, iron. Also, in England almost every individual piece of equipment is manufactured in large and specialized factories, close to the spinning mills, in a faultless and inexpensive manner.'

Given these conditions, it was not surprising that the statistician Freiherr von Reden during the 1850s found local capitalists unwilling to set up modern textile mills.[55] Bad transportation, the absence of social overheads, the almost total lack of supporting industry, which Scitovsky refers to as the 'pecuniary external economies', rendered the marginal efficiency of investment in the textile sector very low, a state of affairs not untypical of an underdeveloped area.[56]

In many ways the Silesian linen trades corroborate the contention of a Japanese historian that domestic industry was not always, as might be generalized from the English case, an agent of progress; rather, where domestic trades have been appendices of the feudal order they have had the opposite effect.[57]

III

Rhineland society, in contrast to Silesian, was not subject to such stresses and strains. Advantageously situated at the crossroads of European trade, it had enjoyed since early medieval times an entrepôt trade that prompted local industry and commercial endeavor. This was particularly so because the Rhine river and an extensive network of roads linked the Rhineland with the contiguous Netherland economy, where in the sixteenth and seventeenth centuries the emerging forces of capitalism manifested their greatest vitality.[58] The specific gains of this geographic propinquity were: firstly, the integration of Rhineland industry, by way of the Dutch ports, into the most buoyant part of the world economy; secondly, mobility of labor, capital and entrepreneurship across political borders, enhancing the movement of goods and services; thirdly, absorption of Dutch and Belgian techniques, which gave Rhineland industry a dynamic all its own.[59]

The political fragmentation of the Rhineland economy was equally pro-pitious for its economic advance. The various small states that dotted its political map were unable to press measures of forced industrialization as practiced in the larger political entities. This was all to the good, since the majority of these mercantilist schemes proved to be abortive and led to a misallocation of resources. The most any of those petty Rhineland potentates could do was to create an environment of freedom and tolerance so as to rouse dormant initiative and, above all, attract from the outside experienced entrepreneurs and competent workmen.[60]

Benefitting from the favorable circumstances, the Rhineland escaped the depression that had set in before the Thirty Years' War and continued to plague most regions in Germany. Towns in this area expanded and prospered. The structure of Rhineland agriculture equally reflected the development of a money economy as it shifted from self sufficiency to production for a market. Beginning with the fifteenth century, feudal bonds, were thus progressively weakened as manorial estates were reduced in size and tenant holdings consolidated and enlarged at their expense.[61] These changes in agricultural organization in turn provided the basis for the emergence of a prosperous class of tenants, relatively independent and forever jealous of their rights. This is a social phenomenon of some significance, for these tenants proved to be not only agents of agricultural progress but the nuclei of rural capital accumulation as well. This was particularly the case once the industrial center of gravity was to shift from the old urban centers, hemmed in by guild restrictions and other kinds of monopoly, to the more liberal environment of the countryside.[62]

This then was the unique feature of the Rhineland at the end of the seventeenth century: while in the rest of Germany the feudal system was being strengthened, here it increasingly disappeared. As a result, during the eighteenth and nineteenth centuries, the course of economic progress of the Rhineland seemed more akin to the pattern of English and West European development than to the type of economic growth that was to be observed in most other parts of Germany.[63]

Towards the end of the eighteenth century the textile districts of this region were hives of industrial endeavor. In Crefeld a thriving silk industry had taken root. Drawing upon the labor of the underemployed linen weavers in the vicinity, it was able to keep costs low and thus could successfully compete in foreign markets. The von der Leyen, the founders of this local industry, were by far the richest people of this region. Employing by 1790 more than 3,000 workers, many of them residing in outlying districts, the von der Leyen produced $\frac{3}{4}$ million thalers worth of goods, accounting for 90 per cent of Crefeld's total output.[64] 'This place', wrote Wilhelm von Humboldt, 'gives an impression totally different from all other towns in Westphalia and from most other towns in Germany',[65] while the Comte de Mirabeau observed that '. . . it is precisely because they are unencumbered and left to run along natural lines . . . these factories enjoy continuous prosperity'.[66]

Industrial progress in the Duchy of Berg, centering upon the Wupper Valley towns of Elberfeld and Barmen, was even more impressive. Although they originally specialized in the manufacture of linens, the local industrialists branched out into the production of silks and cottons. The Duchy's increase in population from about 140,000 in 1730 to 260,000 in 1792 reflected this economic expansion.[67] Where a hundred years before, according to contemporaries, had been hamlets and peasant holdings, there now stood densely populated areas. 'Shacks and dilapidated houses were torn down and palaces created in their places.' The Wupper Valley merchants were very wealthy, some of them being reputed to be millionaires.[68]

In the 25 years following the Seven Years' War, some localities in this area experienced a 50 per cent increase in the volume of manufacture. By 1790 the Berg textile trades claimed some 30,000 workers whose rising wages prompted Wupper Valley merchants to 'put out' the manufacture of cruder fabrics into ever more distant districts. This is how, in the period 1770–1790, cotton production was introduced into the Gladbach-Rheydt district.[69]

While Aachen's woolen trades, impeded by guild restrictions, did not share in the secular expansion, the townships of the surrounding countryside fully enjoyed the advantages of the Rhineland environment. The rise of the Montjoie fine cloth industry, utilizing the labor of the resident artisans who had been producing coarse cloth for a local market, was quite typical of industrial developments in the Aachen district. Founded by Bernard Scheibler, a Protestant immigrant, this fine cloth achieved great renown in foreign markets during the eighteenth century. In 1787 annual production stood at $1\frac{1}{2}$ million thalers, a larger output than the sum total of all production in the other cloth manufacturing centers of the Duchies of Jülich and Berg. At the time the Scheiblers were reputed to possess assets valued at 680,000 thalers. In the Lower Rhine region only the von der Leyen were said to be wealthier. When asked to account for Montjoie's success, Scheibler stressed freedom from guild restrictions as the mainspring of local progress.[70]

On the eve of the French Revolution the Lower Rhine textile trades had become an integral part of the 'Atlantic Economy' and fully shared the benefits of its buoyancy. Low costs of production, making it possible to meet the challenge of foreign competition, assured the industries of the region this favorable position. This was essentially due to a loose social structure which the Rhineland textile manufacturers could easily adapt to their needs in order to exhaust the existing potential of a cheap and plentiful labor supply.[71]

During the period of the Revolutionary Wars the unique and distinct lines of Rhineland development, in contrast to those of the other German lands, were further accentuated as large parts of this region were incorporated into France and thereby brought under its reformed system of government. French occupation policy in the Rhineland was by no means uniform in its effects upon all the various districts. Nor was this vacillating policy always consistent with the best interests of this region. But once these qualifications have been made, it can safely be said that French domination provided, in its long-run effects, a true blessing.[72]

By sweeping away the last vestiges of feudalism, French administrative zeal helped to accelerate the pace of economic progress. On the land the peasant's property rights and his general condition were improved as monastic estates were broken up and the sale and inheritance of land freed from all limitations. In the towns, guild and monopoly restrictions were declared null and void. All were proclaimed equal before the law, and the jury system was made the cornerstone of justice. Legislation pertaining to joint stock companies and the regulation of industrial regulations clearly strengthened the position of the entrepreneurial class. Finally, Chambers of Commerce and Industry, as established by the French authorities, gave the merchants and manufacturers means for active participation in public affairs commensurate with their rising importance.[73] Friedrich Engels, who, as a native of the area, was well acquainted with local conditions, once remarked that 'over the rest of the German states revolutionized by the French, Rhenish Prussia has the advantage of *industry*, and over the rest of the German industrial areas (Saxony and Silesia) the advantage of the French Revolution'.[74]

Within the economic sphere proper, incorporation of its industry into the French market gave the Rhineland economy, including the Duchy of Berg before 1807, a special and prompt impetus. This was particularly true of the Imperial city of Aachen. Freed from the noxious guild restrictions that so far had held back its advance, the Aachen woolen industry enjoyed its close ties to the buoyant Paris market. New techniques, including mechanized spinning mills of the English type, were introduced. Between 1784 and 1806, the number of employed within this textile sphere increased from 3000 to 6000.[75]

Rates of growth that were almost as impressive were evident in the vicinity of Aachen. There, between 1800 and 1811, several woolen textile centers almost doubled their population. The same demographic pattern manifested itself in Crefeld, reflecting the town's expanding silk manufacture.[76] During the same period the increase in the Berg area exports was staggering. In the Wupper Valley and its surrounding villages more than 30,000 people worked in the textile industries, and Joachim Murat, whom Napoleon had made Grand Duke of the Duchy of Berg, boasted of his new principality that 'l'industries dans mon petit pays est semblable a celle de L'Angleterre'.[77] Also, the tendency of concentrating the cotton trades in the Gladbach-Rheydt area was accelerated. Between 1802–1803 and 1812 the population of Gladbach increased from 2304 to 6932, that of Rheydt, between 1794 and 1814, from 277 to 3555.[78]

This rapid industrial expansion came to an abrupt halt with the coming of peace. The post-war period brought havoc in the Rhineland textile districts as the various branches of manufacture very suddenly lost their main customers in the territory of the former Napoleonic Empire. English competition and the post-war depression aggravated the plight. The Aachen woolen trades were especially hard hit, having been cut off from the Paris market upon which they had so overwhelmingly relied. Similarly, the industries of Crefeld and the Wupper Valley suffered from the difficulties plaguing the world economy at that time.[79]

However, many an observer of the contemporary scene stressed not the problems facing the Rhineland economy but the intensity of local industrialization and its resilience. 'The richest and most remarkable of all the countries in the Rhineland with respect to its industrial activity', was the reaction of one visitor to the Wupper Valley. Another writer, who showed the obliviousness to the needs of the working people that was characteristic of the educated during this period, was impressed 'by the beehive like activity where children from five to six years of age already earn a living'.[80] Even the studies of such authorities as the Statistician Viebahn and State Secretary Kunth conveyed the same general impression of industrial vigor.[81]

Indeed, the rapidity with which the various textile trades subsequently adapted themselves to a Prussian government by no means friendly towards industrial endeavor and to a world economy of high tariffs was a tribute not only to the ability of its inhabitants but also to the propitious social framework which elicited such responses. In the Berg area, for example, the manufacture of linen fabrics, which for some time had been a declining industry, disappeared completely. Instead the manufacture of linen ribbons, lace, and cords was not only combined but greatly expanded. Despite its protectionist policy France soon became once more one of the Wupper Valley's principal customers.[82] In the same way, Crefeld's silk producers turned to those silken fabrics, silk ribbons and velvet in which they enjoyed the greatest comparative advantage. Even the Aachen woolen trades that had been so closely tied to the French, particularly the Paris market, turned from their traditional products, woolen cloth and cashmere, to a lighter material with a pattern weave which was in great demand by overseas customers.[83]

While the cotton spinning mills, which had been established on the most questionable foundations during the period of the Continental System, collapsed with the return of peace-time conditions, the situation in the cotton weaving sector was by no means as serious. The partial loss of the French market was quickly offset by production for German, European, and even American customers. By 1826–1828 the Gladbach district employed 10,000 workers using 6000 cotton looms. The rise in population clearly revealed its industrial expansion. Between 1803 and 1834 the number of inhabitants in Gladbach increased from 2304 to 8034, the corresponding figures for Rheydt being 2753 and 5069.[84]

Slowly but surely the technical innovations already in use in England and neighboring Belgium were being absorbed by Rhineland industry. The increasing importance of the American market as a customer for the Rhineland textile wares, particularly marked since the 1830s, accelerated this trend.[85] The rapidly expanding American market provided the larger manufacturers with the opportunities of reaping huge profits with which to finance the construction of large establishments and the introduction of up-to-date techniques.[86]

In the Aachen of the 1830s and 1840s a high degree of concentration became a prominent feature of the local woolen trade.[87] The average size of the cloth mill continued to grow as the ancillary branches of manufacture were being integrated into the production process of the new cloth spinning mills whose tall chimneys came to dominate the landscape as much as the local economy.[88] Technical innovations were equally forthcoming in the Gladbach cotton industry as the newly opened railways widened the market and reduced the costs of raw material imports, particularly fuel. By the late 1840s this district possessed 16 cotton mills, three of which were steam driven. At the same time, large cotton mills were being set up in the Berg area. This tendency towards mechanization was indispensable; without it the Rhineland cotton trades would have been unable to survive '. . . the competitive struggle waged against them', as Marx put it with reference to the older European nations, 'by the English both on the home as well as on the world market'.[89]

A positive response to many challenges remained a characteristic of the Rhineland textile industry. When, upon the formation of the *Zollverein*, Saxon cottons came to press the products of Gladbach, the manufacturers in the latter area turned from the making of stripes and bedding to the manufacture of cotton materials for men's coats, trousers, and vests.[90] Prompted by similar considerations, the Elberfeld-Barmen manufacturers turned to the production of fashion articles, mostly imitations of French goods, for which in the next half century these Wupper Valley towns were to become famous.[91] Henceforth, the Rhineland textile trades, including the silk industry of the Crefeld area, concentrated upon those goods requiring especially skilled labor in order to compete successfully against the cheap labor of Saxony and the more highly mechanized production of England.[92] Such resourcefulness in turn enabled the Rhineland manufacturers, particularly the larger ones, to overcome the serious though temporary difficulties created by the depression of the 1840s.

Despite secular expansion, social conditions in the textile trades remained dismal throughout the first half of the nineteenth century, particularly in the period 1815–1850. In the crowded working-class quarters of the industrial towns, filth, disease, and vice were rampant. Exposed to continuous pressures, the wage earners and artisans were the victims of all the malpractices well known to a period of incipient industrialization.[93] Yet it is not always appreciated that these abuses were part and parcel of the prevailing order. The very vitality and resilience of the Rhineland textile trades in large part depended upon their ability to utilize the human factor of production to an extent that was at times inconsistent with the maintenance of its long run supply. The entrepreneur took so 'short run' a view of his principal factor of production not only because the emphasis on quick gain was typical of early periods of capitalist development, but also because he was assured of being able to tap seemingly inexhaustible, fresh labor supplies in the neighboring countryside.

The brutal treatment which the workers suffered at the hands of their employers was to manifest itself in mounting class antagonism. Conflict not eschewing force loomed large in the sphere of industrial relations. This was to be fatal to the whole course of the 1848–1849 Revolution in Germany, for the bourgeoisie that was destined to lead the struggle for a democratic state became quickly frightened by the menacing tone of the working class clamoring for social rights. The Rhineland merchants and industrialists in particular stood horrified by the forces that had been unleashed by the Revolution. Preoccupied with safeguarding their property, these large businessmen and manufacturers became increasingly willing to come to terms with absolutist authorities which they were supposed to overthrow.[94]

When eventually autocracy triumphed and the Junkers and their army re-established law and order, the rich as well as the petty bourgeoisie once again felt sufficiently secure to pursue their commercial endeavors. From then on, the middle class was 'to postpone indefinitely' according to Hans Rosenberg, 'any claims upon direct political power',[95] and Marx wrote that henceforth '. . . [the bourgeoisie was] thrown back upon [its] real resources – trade and in-dustry. . . .'[96] The Junkers welcomed this trend, hoping that the bourgeoisie, with its energies absorbed in commercial ventures, would permanently be diverted from any interest in government.

The attitude was to be further strengthened by Prussia's post-revolutionary legislation favoring industrial development and those associated with it. The Junkers now were to encourage rather than oppose industrial growth because they came to appreciate that it was more expedient to harness these new forces for their own purpose than to oppose them indiscriminately. At the same time, German industrialization became increasingly important for their own agricul-tural interests. No longer able to compete in the English market, which so far had been the most important outlet for the products of their estates, against such products as Australian wool and North American wheat and timber,[97] the Junkers realized that the profitability of their future agricultural production depended upon a thriving and protected home market which industrial development alone could sustain and expand.

This *rapprochement* and eventual alliance between the aristocratic estate owners of the East and the captains of trade and industry in the Western area was to be characteristic of subsequent German development. The new political conjucture in turn strengthened, in most respects, the resilience of the German, particularly West German, economy.[98] Accelerating the rate of regional industrialization, the vigorous boom of the 1850s once again testified that the Rhineland continued to enjoy an environment that was most propitious for economic progress.

IV

By focussing upon such extreme cases of diverging development as the textile trades of Silesia and the Rhineland, this investigation purports to stress the importance of the social setting upon economic progress. How social institutions affect the economic process and how in turn they are affected by it, remains, in many respects as yet, an 'empty economic box'. Nevertheless, this particular relationship stands at the center of economic history. Those of us who concern ourselves with problems of industrialization and the classical long run will have to continue to wrestle with this issue, and by doing so hope to shed further light upon these unresolved aspects of economic growth.

Postscriptum

Last year a friend and I spent several weeks away from our respective homes doing archival work. The provincial inn we stayed in was noisy and the room we shared was small and poorly lit. Nevertheless, every night, just before we turned in, my friend persisted in reading some part of a recently published economic-history series. And as he diligently turned the pages, he would, from time to time, look towards me, quote a passage and then say: 'This reeks of the (nineteen) Fifties'.[1]

By this, he, of course, meant that the majority of the chapters in that particular series is cast in terms of the development perspective: increases in per capita income, rates of industrialization and urbanization, commercialization of agriculture. These are some of the factors with which the distinguished authors in this series wrestle in order to highlight the determinants of economic advance. To generalize in this way about an important scholarly undertaking may seem unfair. However, it does serve one purpose: it defines (stereotypes?) a whole generation of economic historians who reached academic maturity during the post-World-War-II era, a period when the maintenance of sustained growth in the industrialized countries and the elimination of the vicious circle of poverty in the Third World became the dominant issues among economists.[2]

Economic historians (especially Anglo-Saxon ones) were quick to join the development bandwagon. They promptly rearranged their research projects in order to make the most of the tools of dynamic economics and more importantly, to coax from the past answers that bore upon the predicaments of the present. The result of these efforts proved to be most fruitful. During the Fifties and early Sixties, economic history achieved a vitality and relevance which the discipline had not enjoyed for years.[3]

There is, of course, another side to this reorientation. By setting themselves new sights and by adopting a framework to match these ambitions, economic historians turned their backs upon what had been their traditional preserve within the historic landscape – the evaluation of the social dimension of economic change. For decades, economic historians were the ones who had spent a major portion of their professional activity assessing the human costs of material advance and reminding students, colleagues in the other social sciences and also lay audiences about the blood, sweat and tears that are the usual concomitants of capital accumulation.[4]

But economic historians were to change their attitude once they had become converted to growthmanship. Following the economics profession at large, economic historians became preoccupied with the purely economic mechanism of development. As a corollary to this stance, they came to emphasize the benefits rather than the backwash of capitalist advance. Though few expressed it aloud, many economic historians were to accept (as it were by implication) some version of the trickle down theory. At the time, even some of those scholars who should have known better, left readers and listeners with the distinct impression that 'if you feed the horse, the sparrows would eat too'.[5]

In due course, unrealistic expectations of this sort were bound to be disappointed. First, in many underdeveloped areas where, during the 1950s and early 1960s, material advance occurred, it proved a kind of 'flash in the pan' that left the basic institutional setting unaltered and therefore did nothing to bring about sustained economic development. Secondly, even in those regions enjoying longer periods of economic progress, large sections of the population continued in grinding poverty. Eventually, it was this type of confrontation with stark reality that dampened the economists' fondest hopes about being able to manipulate certain key variables in order to help lift at least part of the Third World out of stagnation. And in turn, economic historians were to have second thoughts as well, especially about perceiving growth in purely economic terms without giving the social scene and welfare considerations their proper due.

Such expressions of doubt on the part of established economic historians were to be grist for the mill of the younger generation of scholars coming to the fore during the upheavals of the late 1960s. At the time, many of these younger people were already in revolt against the value system of their parents, against what they perceived as the crass materialism, careerism and hypocrisy of middle class existence. And consequently, *qua* economic historians, these young men and women have also come to view the past through their own particular prism.

To dwell on the key differences: these young veterans of protest are no longer primarily interested in investigating the mainsprings of economic growth nor in elaborating its achievements. Instead many of these up-and-coming economic historians have returned to emphasizing those concerns which excited scholars when economic history was in its infancy. Specifically, the young researchers are trying to devise new methods and discover new data in order to retrieve as it were from the anonymity of history (by way of detailed accounts) the pain and suffering of the little people caught up in the process of change.

For example, what has been the impact upon attitudes toward work and religion among those involved in the early commercialization of agriculture, or the penetration of the domestic trades into the countryside?; how did this, in turn, affect relations within the family as reflected in changing demographic trends to be shown by the family reconstruction technique? These are some of the topics at present very much under discussion – and to anyone who has been following this literature, it has become quite clear that during the last six or seven years, on both sides of the Atlantic, a new *genre* of historiography has been in the making. In some ways, nothing highlights this new era more glaringly than the books which presently Clio's apprentices desire to emulate above all: Edward Thompson's *The Making of the English Working Class* and Rudolf Braun's two volumes about the social changes following the commercialization and industrialization of the züricher Oberland (*Industrialisierung und Volksleben* and *Sozialer und Kultureller Wandel in einem ländlichen Industriegebiet*).

In terms of these novel perspectives, the above essay has little to commend itself. It contains no innovations in methodology and offers no new insights that serve to enrich the historical imagination. Indeed, 'Textile Industries in Silesia and the Rhineland' is standard pre-computer-age economic history. More specifically, it is vintage nineteen-fifties, reflecting above all the aforementioned concerns and interests of social scientists in general and economists in particular, as to how to initiate and sustain economic development in the Third World.

In the course of these development debates, economists elaborated growth strategies based on their respective assessments regarding the causes of underdevelopment. Some stressed programs for a new and optimal investment pattern. Others emphasized projects for a more effective use of the existing resource base and others again, educational reforms, birth-control schemes and measures to improve the overall quality of manpower. And finally there were those economists (and other social scientists) who insisted that above all, the prerequisite for expansion was a change – some said a radical change – in the institutional setting.[6] Drawing upon a time-honored tradition in political economy, these latter scholars (usually of a more leftish political orientation) insisted that in most instances the basic reasons responsible for backwardness and stagnation in the Third World were those historic circumstances that had created political and social structures incompatible with progress. The key factors to which they pointed as perpetuating the vicious circle of poverty and retrogression were not lack of raw materials nor unfavorable geographic location (as conservatives would have it), but perverse class and power relationships.[7]

This, then, was the intellectual asmosphere into which, during the early nineteen-fifties, I came to do economic history, German economic history, to be exact. Joining a large development project that was being carried out at the time at the University of California at Berkeley, I was asked to investigate the sources of German industrialization.[8] And as I immersed myself in all this eighteenth- and nineteenth-century material and tried to make sense of it, I quite naturally turned for guidance and illumination to the many propositions emerging from the discussions raging all around me.[9]

Eventually, I tried to select from this 'development-tool box' those concepts which, I thought, might help in transforming my inchoate thoughts into an operational framework. Specifically, I opted for the aforementioned hypotheses emphasizing interaction of institutional setting and economic process. I did so because I had become convinced that to understand Germany's sequence of economic development after 1750 called for a careful consideration of Germany's regional differences with respect to economic change. In turn, these striking differences, so it seemed to me, could be accounted for only after making a detailed inquiry into the particular responses to economic stimuli (as evidenced by saving habits, labor supply, elasticities, entrepreneurial initiatives and investment patterns) by the respective regional factors of production within their uniquely regional settings.[10]

Having finally decided to view some facets of German economic history in this way, I tried to adapt for my own purposes the findings and insights of those scholars who, under similar circumstances, had reached similar conclusions. At the time, for example, one author resurrected, and elaborated on, the old theme that in the United States the contrast in development between dynamic North and less prosperous South was primarily due to the existence of the institution of slavery and its aftermath in the latter region.[11] At the same time – i.e. during the nineteen-fifties, several development economists insisted that – viewed from a long-run perspective, the poverty and stagnation so widespread in many regions of Latin America had not, for the most part, been caused by lack of resources, but were, above all, due to a system of economic and social organization dominated by *latifundia*.[12]

Therefore the next step, to make the feudalism-*latifundia* hypothesis the main theme of the above essay, seemed easy. I had no difficulty in marshalling evidence to support my original hunch: that the inexorable decline of the Silesian linen trades, from their erstwhile position of world renown, could be most effectively explained in terms of the survival into modern times of an agrarian setting incompatible with industrial progress. This, of course, had been Lujo Brentano's thesis sixty years before, and it was his original interpretation which strengthened my resolve to elaborate on his hypothesis by use of the comparative method. I hoped that by demonstrating the difference in the secular evolution of the two German textile districts, I would be able to establish my case concerning the relevance and effectiveness of my approach.[13]

My position was challenged by Ursula Lewald.[14] She promptly took me to task for what she considered a simplistic and one-sided interpretation on my part of a complex historic phenomenon. She then proceeded to drive home an important point, by showing that the center of gravity of the Silesian linen manufacture, and especially its export sector, was located in the Giant Mountains, in picturesque burghs and villages along the Bohemian border where the lord–serf relationship was always weak and where, by the eighteenth century, it had ceased to exist.[15] This, of course, is a significant observation and it shows that as elsewhere in Europe, manorial discipline was usually weakest in forest and swamp areas and isolated mountain territories.[16]

Interesting as these latter facts are, I do not think they invalidate the argument put forth by Brentano and those who followed in his footsteps. Indeed, Lewald, in her critique, is prevented from coming to grips with the essence of the Brentato position because of a somewhat narrow and literal interpretation of feudalism – a state of affairs, as she understands it, where, in a juridical sense, serfdom can be shown to exist. This, of course, is not the way political economists, social scientists in general and modern development economists in particular have traditionally viewed the matter. They did not perceive feudalism merely as a legal institution to be described on the basis of legal documents – i.e. a world where serfs are still *de iure* tied to the land. Indeed they defined (and continue to define) feudalism as a social system in which *minfundia* coexisting with *latifundia* are the dominant modes of production and where consequently the big landlords constitute an oligarchy, a ruling group that puts its unique stamp upon virtually all aspects of life, including the pace and pattern of industrial change.[17]

Given her approach, Lewald may not agree with the way in which many German, and after the Second World War, most Polish scholars have surveyed pre-1848 Silesia. Based on contemporary accounts,[18] these historians have frequently enumerated the various tributes and charges demanded from the rural textile workers without specifically probing to what extent these payments were the contractual obligations arising out of a tenant relationship, or whether these were taxes, to defray the costs of administration and justice, or outright feudal dues. The reason why these distinctions were not spelled out is quite obvious. Many of the writers took the view that most of these payments were parts of a totality, of a scheme of things where the lords by virtue of their virtual monopoly of the land and by their almost exclusive access to the machinery of state, were in a position to impose upon the helpless weavers and spinners burdens which, whatever their origin, were clearly excessive.[19]

Lewald has also taken me to task for comparing what to her does not seem comparable since, as she points out, by 1800 the two textile centers were engaged in radically different types of endeavors. I must reject this criticism. To be sure, at that time, Silesia continued, almost exclusively, in its traditional manufacture of linen goods while the various Rhenish textile districts (which once had been linen producers, too), had already gone beyond that stage to concentrate, especially since the 1750s, on making various assortments of silken and cotton wares.[20] But as I see it, it is precisely this glaring contrast in levels of industrial performance and organization and the divergent routes of economic evolution by which, since the mid eighteenth century, these different levels of industrial activity were reached (in Silesia and in the Rhineland respectively) that call for an explanation.

It may not say much for my intellectual development; but even though almost twenty years have elapsed since I wrote the above article, there is little that I can add to my erstwhile interpretation. I continue to put the blame for the secular stagnation of the Silesian textile trades – i.e. their inability to adapt to the requirements of a changing world economy – on the perverse institutional arrangements of that society in general and its outmoded industrial structure in particular. At the same time, I continue to believe that in an account of these difficulties plaguing the Silesian linen industry, lack of resources and unfavorable geographic location are not to be assigned decisive significance.

However, if after two decades of reading and ruminating about these matters I were to rewrite this paper I would want to put greater emphasis upon the so-called *Kaufsystem* and its *modus operandi*. Specifically, I would want to focus on this antiquated system as the proximate cause and as the most obvious symptom of the demise of the Silesian linen trade. As suggested above, the *Kaufsystem* saddled the weaver with an independence he could ill afford. In fact he was to have the worst of all possible worlds. Given the prevailing conjucture, under the *Kaufsystem*, he suffered the full impact of the price scissors that, after the 1770s, were most of the time working against him. In other words, within this particular industrial structure, the poor weaver was forced to assume commercial risks which, during the last quarter of the eighteenth century, he should no longer have had to bear.[21]

The consequences of such an arrangement were soon to prove disastrous. Having been caught in a squeeze of rising yarn prices and simultaneously falling linen prices, the hard-pressed weaver had no alternative but to stave off starvation by offering inferior wares. Quantity at the expense of quality seemed to him the only way to survive. In the long run, such a practice was bound to be the kiss of death. It destroyed the reputation of Silesian goods in export markets which, in turn, spelled the industry's irrevocable ruin.[22]

Given the weaver's chronic plight, these abuses and frauds had become endemic within the trade. Consequently, no regimen of controls, however strictly enforced, could have prevented such defects as damaged materials and short measure from eroding Silesian linen's erstwhile good name. Only the timely emergence of the putting-out system, with a merchant-manufacturer at the center of the web of production, could have turned matters around and saved this domestic manufacture from ruin.[23]

Within the framework of that capitalist mode of production, the Silesian linen trades might have had a chance of regaining their vitality. For a start, the *Verleger* would have put the industry on a sounder basis by assuming the risks associated with supplying the raw materials and with marketing the finished product. Secondly, in order to improve the declining reputation of this trade, the capitalist entrepreneur would have made the necessary arrangements to assure quality-control by providing his weaver-employees with an adequate subsistence and also with an incentive system that puts a premium on careful work.[24]

Finally, and most importantly, by virtue of his close and continuous contacts with world markets, the *Verleger* would undoubtedly have developed great sensitivity to the requirements of international demand. Combined with adequate funds at his disposal, this awareness of rapidly changing consumer tastes in export markets would have surely made the *Verleger* – the prototype of the early capitalist buccaneer – both able and willing to revamp the Silesian textile trades. Specifically, he would have streamlined the traditional linen manufacture by concentrating on those few products he believed still had a fighting chance of meeting the challenge of foreign, especially Irish, competition in third markets. At the same time, he would, in all likelihood, have closed down all the other branches of the linen industry and instead have started upon what promised to be the wave of the future – local silk and cotton industries.[25]

Why then, did this progressive force – the putting-out system – not take root here during the second half of the eighteenth century? Why indeed did the local textile trades not replicate the development-path of some of the more fortunate West European manufacturing districts? My answer now would be the same I gave almost twenty years ago. On the one hand, the feudal exactions imposed upon the rural population, and the *ambiance* that went with it, prevented, on both economic and social grounds, the emergence of the Kulak type capitalist who, in his own remoreseless way, would have pioneered capital accumulation and thus economic development throughout the countryside.[26] On the other hand, the continuation throughout the eighteenth century (and well into the nineteenth) of these feudal pressures (that is the other side of the same coin) preserved and bolstered the relative profitability of feudal agriculture. Consequently trade and industry suffered from a continuous bloodletting as *latifundia* agriculture attracted a large part of entrepreneurial savings. Characteristically, this particular investment pattern was buttressed by the aristocratic monopoly with respect to the real estate mortgage banks – the so-called *Landschaften*.[27,28]

Notes

Notes to the Introduction

1 Classical examples are D. Defoe, *A Tour through the Whole Island of Great Britain*, 1st edn. (1724–6) and the travel accounts by Arthur Young. Such writings often contain interesting general reflections about problems of rural industry, for example J. Tucker, *Instructions for Travellers* (1757) cited in A. P. Wadsworth and J. de Lacy Mann, *The Cotton Trade and Industrial Lancashire 1600–1780* (Manchester, 1931; rpt. 1965), pp. 384f. about the effects of different relations of production upon the development of the industry; H. -G. V. Riquetti Comte de Mirabeau, *De la monarchie prussienne sous Frédéric le Grand* (London, 1788), vol. 3, p. 109 about the advantages and disadvantages of centralized manufacturers and of rural industries carried on by independent petty producers; A. Young, *Travels during the Years 1787, 1788 and 1789 . . . of the Kingdom of France* (London, 1792), vol. 1, pp. 503–11 about the effects of rural industry upon agriculture.

2 The treatment of rural industry in the writings of mercantilists, physiocrats, and classic political economists deserves closer study. There are a few references to German-speaking authors in W. Stieda, *Litteratur, heutige Zustände and Entstehung der deutschen Hausindustrie. Nach den vorliegenden gedruckten Quellen*, Schriften des Vereins für Socialpolitik, vol. 39, pt. 1 (Leipzig, 1889), pp. 129–34; also Stieda, pp. 1–55 about some nineteenth-century authors; C. Böhle, *Die Idee der Wirtschaftverfassung im deutschen Merkantilismus*, Freiburger Staatswissenschaftliche Schriften, vol. 1 (Jena, 1940), pp. 40ff., 46ff., 112ff.; also cf. the writings by Justi and Süssmilch quoted on p. 257f. In the systems developed by the physiocrats and the classic political economists questions concerning rural industries are occasionally discussed. The physiocrats supported the complete freedom of industry in order to achieve as favourable terms of trade as possible for large farmers and especially estate owners. But they also discussed the more specific question of whether the expansion of industry in the countryside promoted agriculture or hindered it: G. Weulersse, *Le mouvement physiocratique en France de 1756 à 1770* (Paris, 1910; rpt. 1968), vol. 1, pp. 290–304, 391–4, 588–604. Adam Smith, in tracing the emergence of export industries in the history of European society since the Middle Ages, distinguished between a 'violent' way and a 'natural' way. The first came about when merchants and entrepreneurs introduced export industries in imitation of foreign crafts and usually based on imported raw materials; they were the 'offspring of foreign commerce'. The latter consisted in the further development of export industries out of 'household . . . manufactures' and was mostly based on the working up of domestic raw materials. This kind of export industry was an 'offspring of agriculture' and had in turn a positive effect on the progress of commercial agrarian production. Smith regarded the first way as an earlier phase and a historical precondition of the second, but he did not clearly identify the difference between the violent and natural way with that of urban and rural export industry: A. Smith, *An Inquiry into the Nature and Causes of the Wealth of Nations*, Book 3, Ch. 3, The Glasgow Edition of the Works and Correspondence of Adam Smith, 2, ed. R. H. Campbell et al. (Oxford, 1976), pp. 407ff. In book 1, Ch. 10, pp. 133ff., 135ff., where Smith discusses the reasons behind different levels of wages, he mentions as two important factors urban guild privileges on the one hand and the combination of agriculture with industrial activity among cottagers on the other hand; the latter appears to be an indication of a relatively backward economy.

3 K. Marx, *Capital*, vol. 1, introd. by E. Mandel, transl. by B. Fowkes (Harmondsworth, 1976), Ch. 15, pp. 590f., 595f., Ch. 19, p. 695; on p. 590 the dividing line between 'modern' and 'old-fashioned' domestic industry is described.

4 K. Marx, *Grundrisse. Foundations of the Critique of Political Economy*, transl. by M. Nicolaus (Harmondsworth, 1973), pp. 510f.; cf. also *Grundrisse*, pp. 277f., 505, 507ff. and K. Marx and F. Engels, *The German Ideology*, pts. 1 and 3, ed. by R. Pascal (New York, 1947), pt. 1, Ch. 1, pp. 43–58, esp. 50ff. Here the term 'manufacture' comprises mass industrial commodity production in large centralized production units as well as in rural domestic industry.

5 Instead, especially in *Capital*, he made use of some essential elements of the transition phase in order to illuminate different aspects of the developed capitalist system, and the same is true for his references to pre-capitalist social formations. See L. Althusser and E. Balibar, *Reading Capital* (London, 1970), pp. 196f., 269ff.; B. Hindess and P. Q. Hirst, *Pre-capitalist Modes of Production* (London etc., 1975), pp. 221f., 226f., 287f. Thus, in *Capital*, vol. 1, Ch. 14, pp. 455–91, Marx used '*manufacture*' – here in the narrower sense meaning a large plant essentially based on handicraft production – in order to explain historically the possibilities for capital to produce relative surplus value (i.e. the maximization of profit through an increase in labour productivity) by applying the principle of the division of labour. He nevertheless emphasized that manufacture in this sense was during no period in history the quantitatively predominant mode of organization in industry, but stood rather 'as a work of economic artifice' (wrongly translated as 'artificial . . . construction') on the 'broad foundation of the town handicrafts and the domestic industries in the countryside': Marx, *Capital*, vol. 1, p. 490; see also vol. 1, Ch. 30, pp. 911ff.; similarly in Marx, *Grundrisse* (cf. n. 4 above), p. 510. He also gave occasional references elsewhere in *Capital* to the importance of rural domestic industry, e.g. in vol. 1, Ch. 16, p. 645; vol. 1, Ch. 30; vol. 3 (London and Moscow, 1971), Ch. 20, pp. 334ff.; vol. 3, Ch. 47, pp. 795f. and 807ff.

6 W. Sombart, 'Die Hausindustrie in Deutschland', *Archiv für soziale Gesetzgebung und Statistik*, 4 (1891), 103–56.

7 Generally: Stieda, *Litteratur* (cf. n. 2 above), pp. 1–14; Sombart, 'Hausindustrie in Deutschland' (cf. n. 6 above), pp. 105ff.; W. Troeltsch, 'Das neuzeitliche territoriale Gewerbewesen bis 1800', in: *Die Entwicklung der deutschen Volkswirtschaftslehre im 19. Jahrhundert. Gustav Schmoller zur 70. Wiederkehr seines Geburtstags* (Leipzig, 1908), vol. 2, Ch. 24, 1–20, here: pp. 2ff.; cf. also M. Simon, *Der wissenschaftliche Streit um die Berechtigung der Heimarbeit*, Heimarbeit und Verlag in der Neuzeit 19 (Jena, 1931), pp. 11–55. This 'apologetic' study supports the continuation of domestic industry

8 For the beginnings and the course of this development in Germany cf. especially two conferences of the 'Verein für Socialpolitik': the discussion of a presentation by Fr. J. Neumann about factory legislation in *Verhandlungen des Vereins für Socialpolitik 1873*, Schriften des Vereins für Socialpolitik 4 (Leipzig, 1874), pp. 41ff., and the presentations by A. Weber and E. v. Philippovich about 'Die Hausindustrie und ihre gesetzliche Regelung' in *Verhandlungen des Vereins für Socialpolitik 1899*, Schriften des Vereins für Socialpolitik 88 (Leipzig, 1900), 12–35 and 36–50, especially the discussion on pp. 50–99.

9 Cf. W. Roscher, *System der Volkswirtschaft* (Stuttgart, 1881), vol. 3, pp. 544f.; G. Schmoller, *Zur Geschichte der deutschen Kleingewerbe im 19. Jahrhundert. Statistische und nationalökonomische Untersuchungen* (Halle, 1870), pp. 202–10; G. Schmoller, 'Die geschichtliche Entwicklung der Unternehmung 5: Hausindustrie', *Jahrbuch für Gesetzgebung, Verwaltung und Volkswirtschaft*, 14 (1890), 1053–76, esp. pp. 1061, 1070f., 1075; G. Schmoller, *Grundriss der allgemeinen Volkswirtschaftslehre*, 4th edn. (Munich, 1919), vol 1, p. 496; Schmoller, in his writings between 1870 and 1917, shows an increasingly realistic assessment of contemporary domestic industry.

10 There is an international bibliography up to 1908 divided according to countries: *Bibliographie générale des industries à domicile*, Royaume de Belgique. Ministère de l'industrie et de travail. Office du travail (Bruxelles, 1908); also see: W. Sombart, 'Hausindustrie', in *Handwörterbuch der Staatswissenschaften*, 2nd edn. (1900), vol. 4, pp. 1138–69, esp. 1158–69; continued in W. Sombart and R. Meerwarth, 'Hausindustrie', in *Handwörterbuch der Staatswissenschaften*, 4th edn. (Jena, 1923), vol. 4, pp. 179–207, esp. pp. 204–7.

11 For the contemporary literature cf. *Bibliographie générale* (cf. above, n. 10), pp. 154ff. The intensity and range of this discussion can be explained by the relatively greater economic importance of rural *kustar'* industries in the context of Russia's 'backwardness'. The debate did not view rural domestic industry in pre-revolutionary Russia primarily as a 'historic' or as a problem of social policy. To a much larger extent than in Germany and in western Europe, it formed part of a larger controversy about the advantages of a capitalist versus a non-capitalist road toward industrialization. But even the advocates of the non-capitalist road disagreed in their assessment of rural domestic industry. For the populist and neo-populist economists, the state-directed further development of *kustar'* industry, co-operatively organized on the basis of peasant society, was to be the crucial development in Russia's transition to a higher non-capitalist social formation. The first systematic approaches were made by V. V. (pseud. for V. P. Vorontsov), *Sud'by kapitalizma v Rossii* (The fate of capitalism in Russia) (St Petersburg, 1882) and Nikolai-on (pseud. for N. Danielson), *Ocherki nashego poreformennogo obshchestvennogo khozyaistva* (Outlines of our social economy after the reform) (St Petersburg, 1893); also A. Walicki, *The Controversy Over Capitalism. Studies in the Social Philosophy of the Russian Populists* (Oxford, 1969), pp. 109ff. For those writers who assumed a dominating tendency toward capitalist development in contemporary Russia *kustar'* industries were relevant because they constituted one of the origins of capitalist relations of production, but *kustar'* industries did not occupy a strategic position in their political perspectives for the future. Cf. Lenin's assessment of rural industries and his debate with the populist economists, esp. Vorontsov and Danielson: V. I. Lenin, *The Development of Capitalism in Russia* (Moscow, 1956), pp. 407ff., 414ff., 480ff., 487ff., 589ff. Cf. also the position of the 'legal' Marxist M. Tugan-Baranovsky, *Geschichte der russischen Fabrik*, Sozialgeschichtliche Forschungen, vols. 5 and 6 (Berlin, 1900), pp. 526–88: 'Der Kampf der Fabrik mit dem Kustari'; cf. also P. Kropotkin, *Fields, Factories and Workshops* (London, 1899).

12 W. Troeltsch, *Die Calwer Zeughandlungskompagnie und ihre Arbeiter. Studien zur Gewerbe- und Sozialgeschichte Altwürttembergs* (Jena, 1897); E. Gothein, *Wirtschaftsgeschichte des Schwarzwaldes und der angrenzenden Landschaften* (Strassburg, 1892), vol. 1; A. Thun, *Die Industrie am Niederrhein und ihre Arbeiter*, 2 vols. Staats- und socialwissenschaftliche Forschungen vol. 2, pts. 2 and 3, (Leipzig, 1879); A. Thun, *Landwirtschaft und Gewerbe in Mittelrussland seit der Aufhebung der Leibeigenschaft*, Staats- und socialwissenschaftliche Forschungen, vol. 3, pt. 1 (Leipzig, 1880).

13 Sombart, 'Hausindustrie in Deutschland' (see n. 6 above), p. 112.

14 W. Roscher, 'Die grosse und kleine Industrie', *Die Gegenwart*, 10 (1855), 688–739; changed versions of this article in: W. Roscher, *Ansichten der Volkswirtschaft aus dem* *geschichtlichen Standpunkte* (Leipzig, 1861), Ch. 4, pp. 117–72 and W. Roscher, *System der Volkswirtschaft* (see n. 9 above), vol. 3, pp. 521–56.

15 A. Schäffle, 'Hausindustrie' in *Deutsches Staatswörterbuch*, eds. J. C. Bluntschi and K. Brater (Stuttgart, 1860), vol. 5, pp. 7–12.

16 Schäffle, 'Hausindustrie' (see n. 15 above), p. 7.

17 Roscher, *System der Volkswirtschaft* (see n. 9 above), p. 541.

18 Sombart, 'Hausindustrie in Deutschland' (see n. 6 above), pp. 105ff., esp. p. 112.

19 Schmoller, *Geschichte der deutschen Kleingewerbe* (see n. 9 above), pp. 203ff., pp. 540ff. (here Schmoller still argues in terms of the older export craft theory); Schmoller, 'Geschichtliche Entwicklung der Unternehmung' (n. 9), pp. 1035–76; Schmoller, *Grundriss* (n. 9), vol. 1, pp. 487–96; K. Bücher, 'Gewerbe' in *Handwörterbuch der Staatswissenschaften*, 3rd edn. (Jena, 1909), vol. 4, pp. 847–80; K. Bücher, 'Die gewerblichen Betriebssysteme in ihrer geschichtlichen Entwicklung', in K. Bücher, *Die Entstehung der Volkswirtschaft. Vorträge und Aufsätze*, 7th edn. (Tübingen, 1922), vol. 1, pp. 163–96, esp. pp. 185ff.; Bücher, 'Hausfleiss und Hausindustrie' in *Handelsmuseum*, 5 (1890), Nos 31, 32, 33; Bücher, 'Die Hausindustrie auf dem Weihnachtsmarkte' in K. Bücher. *Die Entstehung der Volkswirtschaft. Vorträge und Aufsätze*, 7th edn. (Tübingen, 1922), vol. 2, pp. 161–94; Sombart, 'Hausindustrie in Deutschland' (see n. 6 above), esp. pp. 105ff.; Sombart, 'Hausindustrie' (see n. 10 above); Sombart, 'Zur neuerem Literatur über Hausindustrie (1891–1893)', *Jahrbücher für Nationalökonomie und Statistik*, 61 (1893), pp. 738–81, 894–936. Sombart did not pursue this approach in his later systematic works. See already: Sombart, 'Die gewerbliche Arbeit und ihre Organisation', *Archiv für soziale Gesetzgebung und Statistik* 14 (1899), 1–52, 310–405.

20 Schmoller, 'Geschichtliche Entwicklung der Unternehmung' (see n. 9 above), p. 1058.

21 Schmoller, 'Geschichtliche Entwicklung der Unternehmung' (n. 9), pp. 1058f., Schmoller, *Grundriss* (n. 9), vol. 1, pp. 487ff.; Bücher, 'Gewerbe' (see n. 19 above), pp. 867ff. On pp. 869ff. he introduces, based on his ethnological perspective, an interesting distinction between 'primary' and 'secondary' branches of domestic industry, i.e. those which are rural from the beginning and those which arose out of urban crafts. Bücher considers 'primary' rural domestic industry as 'perhaps the most important group'. He describes them as originating in peasant 'housework' and as having developed into an export industry under the 'putting-out' system (pp. 869–70); cf. also Weber, 'Hausindustrie' (see n. 8 above), pp. 12ff. who, in deliberate contrast to Sombart (see n. 6 above), introduces a historical and systematic distinction between different development stages of the relations of production in domestic industry. He separates the 'pure domestic industry', i.e. the *Kaufsystem*, from 'domestic work within the putting-out system' as well as from outwork in modern domestic industry under advanced capitalism. Cf. Weber, 'Die volkswirtschaftliche Aufgabe der Hausindustrie', *Jahrbuch für Gesetzgebung, Verwaltung und Volkswirtschaft*, 25 (1901), 383–405; a similarly differentiating analysis about contemporary – though not historical – domestic industry had been made much earlier by O. Schwarz, 'Die Betriebsformen der modernen Grossindustrie', *Zeitschrift für die gesamte Staatswissenschaft*, 25 (1869), 535–629, esp. pp. 546–9 and 615–23.

22 Schmoller, 'Geschichtliche Entwicklung der Unternehmung (see n. 9 above), p. 1059.

23 Sombart, 'Hausindustrie in Deutschland' (see n. 6 above), pp. 110, 116, 117, where he also defines 'domestic industry' as 'that form of private capitalist enterprise where the labourers are employed in their homes'. On p. 109 he expresses himself positively about Marx's interpretation of domestic industry which Sombart considers as a 'completely new perspective'. According to Sombart, Marx was 'the first to fully recognize domestic industry as a variant of the mode of production of modern large-scale capitalism'. Cf. Sombart, 'Hausindustrie in Deutschland' (n. 6 above), p. 109; generally about Sombart's reception of Marx's ideas D. Lindenlaub, *Richtungskaempfe im Verein für Sozialpolitik* VSWG, Beiheft 53 (Wiesbaden, 1967), vol. 2, pp. 316ff.

24 Cf. Schmoller's ideas about the 'proper division of labour' between 'domestic industry' and 'large industry' in Schmoller, 'Geschichtliche Entwicklung der Unternehmung' (see n. 9 above), p. 1071, also p. 1061; Schmoller was becoming increasingly sceptical, and, in the last edition of *Grundriss*, called domestic industry 'convenient for the putter-out but undesirable from the point of view of social policy'. Nevertheless, his overall assessment remained fairly positive: *Grundriss* (see n. 9 above), p. 487, also pp. 495ff. Sombart's perception stood in contrast to Schmoller's: Sombart, 'Hausindustrie in Deutschland' (n. 6 above), pp. 154ff. He characterized domestic industry as an economic and social 'evil'; see also the disguised polemic of K. Bücher against Sombart in Bücher, 'Die gewerblichen Betriebssysteme' (see n. 19 above), pp. 195ff. and the answer: Sombart, 'Zur neueren Literatur' (n. 19), p. 742; also the controversial discussion at the conference of the 'Verein für Socialpolitik' in 1899 which followed the presentations by A. Weber and E. von Philippovich about 'domestic industry and its regulation by the law' (see n. 8 above); on the concept of a 'mode of social organization' cf. Sombart, 'Hausindustrie in Deutschland' (see n. 6 above), p. 116.

25 Schmoller, *Grundriss* (see n. 9 above), vol. 1, p. 487.

26 Sombart, 'Hausindustrie' (see n. 10 above), p. 1141; cf. also the remark concerning the 'rusticalization of industry' since the end of the Middle Ages in Sombart, *Der moderne Kapitalismus*, 2nd edn. (Munich, 1916), vol. 2, pt. 2 p. 803.

27 J. Kulischer, *Allgemeine Wirtschaftsgeschichte des Mittelalters und der Neuzeit* (Munich etc., 1929), vol. 2, pp. 113ff.; also Kulischer, 'La grande industrie aux XVIIe et XVIIIe siècles: France, Allemagne, Russie', *Annales d'histoire économique et sociale*, 3 (1931), 11–46, esp. pp. 25ff.

28 E. Tarle, *L'industrie dans les campagnes en France à la fin de l'Ancien Régime*, Bibliothèque d'histoire moderne, vol. 11 (Paris, 1910) and Tarle, *Rabochii klass vo Francì v epochu revoljutsii* (The working-class in France during the period of the Revolution), Zapiski istorisko-filologicheskago fakul'teta Imperatorskago S. -Peterburskago Universiteta, vols. 91 and 100 (St Petersburg, 1909–11), vols. 1 and 2.

29 H. Sée, 'Remarques sur le caractère de l'industrie rurale en France et les causes de son extension au XVIIIe siècle', *Revue Historique*, 142 (1923), 47–53; Sée, *L'évolution commerciale et industrielle de la France sous l'Ancien Régime* (Paris, 1925); Sée, *Histoire économique de la France* (Paris, 1939), vol. 1, and many other writings.

30 Already P. Mantoux, *La révolution industrielle au XVIIIe siècle. Essai sur les commencements de la grande industrie moderne en Angleterre* (Paris, 1906) and the extended English translation *The Industrial Revolution in the Eighteenth Century. An Outline of the Beginnings of the Modern Factory System in England*, (London, 1928, 2nd edn. 1961). In the first chapter of the first part, the 'domestic system' is delineated as the point of departure for the Industrial Revolution.

31 W. J. Ashley, *The Early History of the English Woolen Industry*, Publications of the American Economic Association, vol. 2, pt. 4 (Baltimore, Md., 1887); Ashley, *An Introduction to English Economic History and Theory* (London, 1893), vol. 2; W. Cunningham, *The Growth of English Industry and Commerce in Modern Times. The Mercantile System*, 5th edn. (Cambridge, 1910–12, 1st edn. 1882); G. Unwin, 'The History of the Cloth Industry in Suffolk' (1907), in G. Unwin, *Studies in Economic History. The Collected Papers of . . .*, ed. by R. H. Tawney (London, 1927), pp. 262–301; E. Lipson, *The History of the Woolen and Worsted Industries* (London, 1921); C. Gill, *The Rise of the Irish Linen Industry* (Oxford,

1925); A. P. Wadsworth and J. de Lacy Mann, *The Cotton Trade and Industrial Lancashire* (Manchester, 1931); W. H. B. Court, *The Rise of the Midland Industries, 1600–1838* (London, 1938), here especially the chapters about the production of nails; W. G. Hoskins, 'The Rise and Decline of the Serge Industry in the South West of England with Special Reference to the Eighteenth Century', unpbl. thesis (M. Sc. University of London, 1929); also the important study by the American economic historian H. Heaton, *The Yorkshire Woolen and Worsted Industries*, Oxford Historical and Literary Studies, vol. 10 (Oxford, 1920); a comprehensive account is given in E. Lipson, *The Economic History of England* (London, 1931 and 1956), vol. 2.

32 E. Coornaert, *Un centre industriel d'autrefois. La draperie-sayetterie d'Hondschoote (XIVᵉ–XVIIIᵉ siècles)* (Paris, 1930).

33 Of special importance was the school of G. Aubin of Halle, from which the works by A. Kunze stand out. The basic account of the east-central European linen trade, jointly authored by G. Aubin and A. Kunze, only marginally touches on the shift of industrial production to the countryside because it is limited to an earlier time period: G. Aubin and A. Kunze, *Leinenerzeugung und Leinenabsatz im östlichen Mitteldeutschland zur Zeit der Zunftkäufe. Ein Beitrag zur industriellen Kolonisation des deutschen Ostens* (Stuttgart, 1940).

34 A. Demangeon, *La plaine picarde. Picardie, Artois, Cambrésis, Beauvaisis. Etude de géographie sur les plaines de craie du Nord de la France* (Paris, 1905); R. Blanchard, *La Flandre. Etude géographique de la plaine flamande en France, Belgique et Hollande* (Lille, 1906); J. Sion, *Les paysans de la Normandie orientale. Etude géographique sur les populations rurales du Caux, du Bray, du Vexin normand et de la vallée de la Seine* (Paris, 1908); R. Musset, *Le Bas Maine. Etude géographique* (Paris, 1917); about this school of geographers cf. also L. Febvre, *La terre et l'évolution humaine* (Paris, 1922 and 1970), pp. 29f.

35 English examples are J. D. Chambers, *Nottinghamshire in the Eighteenth Century. A Study of Life and Labour under the Squirearchy* (London, 1932); G. H. Tuplin, *The Economic History of Rossendale* (Manchester, 1927).

36 The interest, enriched by new perspectives, became apparent at the Second International Conference of Economic History in 1962 in Aix-en-Provence (Section: Industries et artisans ruraux) as well as at the fifth conference of the Gesellschaft für Sozial – und Wirtschaftsgeschichte in 1973; see *Deuxième conference internationale d'histoire économique Aix-en-Provence 1962*, (Paris etc., 1965), vol. 2, pp. 363–484; H. Kellenbenz, ed., *Agrarisches Nebengewerbe und Formen der Reagrarisierung im Spätmittelalter und 19./20. Jahrhundert*, Forschungen zur Sozial – und Wirtschaftsgeschichte, vol. 21 (Stuttgart, 1975).

37 The great 'thèses' on regional history which originated in the Annales school do not explicitly deal with rural industry although they do contain a number of references to it (cf. the theses by P. Goubert, E. Le Roy Ladurie and P. Deyon). E. Le Roy Ladurie stated in the conclusion of his thèse about the peasants of Languedoc: 'Ce livre est d'histoire rurale et il n'est pas possible d'y étudier en detail le cas des industries languedociennes, qui mériterait un ouvrage particulier', E. Le Roy Ladurie, *Les paysans de Languedoc* (Paris, 1966), vol. 1, p. 646; an important exception is P. Bois, *Paysans de l'Ouest. Des structures économiques et sociales aux options politiques depuis l'époque révolutionnaire dans la Sarthe* (Le Mans, 1960); B. H. Slicher van Bath, on the other hand, devoted a great deal of space to rural industry in his great study of Overijssel: B. H. Slicher van Bath, *Een Samenleving onder spanning: Geschiedenis van het platteland in Overijssel, Historische sociografieen van het platteland*, vol. 1 (Assen, 1957). If the regional histories of his students J. A. Faber and A. M. van der Woude about Friesland and Noorderkwartier do not deal with concentrated rural industries, this is due to the fact that they did not exist in those regions.

38 E. J. Hobsbawm, 'The General Crisis of the European Economy in the 17th Century', *Past and Present*, 5 (1954), 33–53, 6 (1954), 44–65, rpt. with a postscript in T. Aston, ed., *Crisis in Europe, 1560–1660* (London, 1965), pp. 1–58.

39 J. Thirsk, 'Industries in the Countryside', *Essays in the Economic and Social History of Tudor and Stuart England in Honour of R. H. Tawney*, ed. F. J. Fisher (Cambridge, 1961), pp. 70–88; J. Thirsk, 'The Farming Regions', *The Agrarian History of England and Wales, 1500–1640*, ed. J. Thirsk (Cambridge, 1967), vol. 4, pp. 1–112; E. L. Jones, 'Agricultural Origins of Industry', *Past and Present*, 40 (1968), 58–71; a more detailed Italian version under the title 'Le origini agricole dell' industria', *Studi storici*, 9 (1968), 564–93.

40 H. Kisch, 'The Textile Industries in Silesia and the Rhineland: A Comparative Study in Industrialization', *Journal of Economic History*, 19 (1956), 517–37 (rpt. below, pp. 178–200 with a post-scriptum); H. Kisch, 'Das Erbe des Mittelalters ein Hemmnis wirtschaftlicher Entwicklung: Aachens Tuchgewerbe vor 1790', *Rheinische Vierteljahresblätter*, 30 (1965), 253–308 (a short English version in *Journ. Econ. Hist.*, 24(1964), 517–37; H. Kisch, *Prussian Mercantilism and the Rise of the Krefeld Silk Industry: Variations on an Eighteenth-Century Theme*, Transactions of the American Philosophical Society N.S. 58, 7 (Philadelphia, 1968); H. Kisch, 'From Monopoly to Laissez-faire: The Early Growth of the Wupper Valley Textile Trades', *Journal of European Economic History*, 1 (1972), 298–407.

41 E. Schremmer, 'Standortausweitung der Warenproduktion im langfristigen Wirtschaftswachstum. Zur Stadt-Land-Arbeitsteilung im Gewerbe des 18. Jahrhunderts', *VSWG*, 59 (1972), 1–40. The term 'territorialization of industry', coined by Schremmer, emphasizes the 'diversification of rural crafts into a great number of occupations'; consequently, Schremmer p. 6f. contrasts 'territorialization of industry' to the emergence of regions dominated by a single industry. The latter, however, are the subject matter of the present volume.

42 'Forschungsseminar J. Kuczynski 1952' (unpubl. working papers): J. Kuczynski and D. Lösche, 'Einleitung'; R. Berthold, 'Zur Geschichte der Entwicklung der Produktionsverhältnisse in der württembergischen Zeugmacherei von der Mitte des 16. bis zur Mitte des 18. Jahrhunderts', report 1; P. Stulz, 'Zur Geschichte der Entwicklung der Produktionsverhältnisse in der ländlichen westfälischen Leinenproduktion von 1450 bis 1750', report 2; D. Lösche, 'Zur Geschichte der Entwicklung der Produktionsverhältnisse in der Leinen- und Barchentproduktion oberdeutscher Städte von 1450 bis 1750', report 3; G. Heitz, 'Die Entwicklung der ländlichen Leinenproduktion Sachsens in der ersten Hälfte des 16. Jahrunderts', report 4; H. Hoffmann, 'Diskussion über den gesellschaftlichen Charakter des Verlages'. The 4th report was further developed into G. Heitz, *Ländliche Leinenproduktion in Sachsen 1470 bis 1555*, Schriften des Instituts für Geschichte vol. 2, pt. 4 (Berlin, 1961).

43 For example L. L. Murav'eva, *Derevenska a promyshlennost' central'noi Rossii vtoroǐ XVII v.* (The rural industry of central Russia in the second half of the seventeenth century) (Moscow, 1971); A. Klima, 'The Role of Rural Domestic Industries in Bohemia in the Eighteenth Century', *Econ. Hist. Rev.*, 2nd ser., 27 (1974), 48–56; M. Kulczykowski, 'En Pologne au XVIIIᵉ siècle: Industrie paysanne et formation du marché national', *Annales E.S.C.*, 24 (1969), 61–9; M. Kulczykowski, *Andrychowski ośrodek płócienniczy w XVIII i XIX wieku* (The linen centre of Andrychow in the eighteenth and nineteenth centuries), Prace komisji nauk historycznych, vol. 31 (Wrocław etc., 1972). Because of the subtlety with which it poses its problems and the precision with which the statistical analysis is conducted this monograph about Andrychów is one of the best studies that exist about rural industry.

44 R. Braun, *Industrialisierung und Volksleben. Veränderungen der Lebensformen unter*

Einwirkung der textilindustriellen Heimarbeit in einem ländlichen Industriegebiet (Züricher Oberland) vor 1800 (Erlenbach-Zürich, 1960; rpt. Goettingen 1979); continued in R. Braun, *Sozialer und kultureller Wandel in einem ländlichen Industriegebiet (Züricher Oberland) unter Einwirkung des Maschinen- und Fabrikwesens im 19. und 20. Jahrundert* (Erlenbach-Zürich etc., 1965). An important beginning was made by W.-E. Peuckert, *Volkskunde des Proletariats*, vol. 1. *Aufgang der proletarischen Kultur*, Schriften des volkskundlichen Seminars der Pädagogischen Akademie Breslau, vol. 1 (Frankfurt, 1931, rpt. and extended in W.-E. Peuckert and E. Fuchs, *Die schlesischen Weber* (Darmstadt, 1971), vols 1 and 2.

45 F. F. Mendels, 'Industrialization and Population Pressure in Eighteenth Century Flanders', (Ph.D. Diss., University of Wisconsin, 1970); F. F. Mendels, 'Proto-industrialization: The First Phase of the Industrialization Process', *Journ. Econ. Hist.*, 32 (1972), 241–61; Charles Tilly and Richard Tilly, 'Emerging Problems in the Modern Economic History of Western Europe' (1971, unpubl.), printed in a shortened version under the title 'Agenda for European Economic History in the 1970s', *Journ. Econ. Hist.*, 31 (1971), 184–98.

46 A distinction must be made between proto-industrialization and early industrialization (Frühindustrialisierung). Early industrialization means the first phase of industrialization and, in central Europe, dates to the first half of the nineteenth century; cf. W. Fischer, ed., *Wirtschafts- und sozialgeschichtliche Probleme der frühen Industrialisierung*, Einzelveröffentlichungen der Historischen Kommission zu Berlin, vol. 1 (Berlin, 1968); O. Büsch, ed., *Untersuchungen zur Geschichte der frühen Industrialisierung vornehmlich im Wirtschaftsraum Berlin/Brandenburg*, Einzelveröffentlichungen der Historischen Kommission zu Berlin, vol. 6 (Berlin, 1971).

47 More detailed esp. with regard to the situation in east-central and eastern Europe, see below, p. 17f.

48 D. C. North and R. P. Thomas, *The Rise of the Western World. A New Economic History* (Cambridge, 1973), pp. 19–45; North and Thomas, 'The Rise and Fall of the Manorial System: A Theoretical Model', *Journ. Econ. Hist.*, 31 (1971), 777–83, esp. pp. 780–96; the criticism by A. Jones, 'The Rise and Fall of the Manorial Economy: A Critical Comment', *Journ. Econ. Hist.*, 32 (1972), 938–44 and St Fenoaltea, 'The Rise and Fall of a Theoretical Model: The Manorial System', *Journ. Econ. Hist.*, 35 (1975), 386–409, is only partly justified (Fenoaltea is correct in criticizing the 'non-exploitative' interpretation of feudalism). In this context and with regard to the shortcomings of the North–Thomas theory see the studies about the origins and development of capitalism by Maurice Dobb and the controversy they raised at the beginning of the 1950s in the journal *Science and Society*. M. Dobb, *Studies in the Development of Capitalism* (London, 1946, 2nd ed. 1963), pp. 37–50 and P. Sweezy et al., *The Transition from Feudalism to Capitalism* (New York, 1954); here the new edition introduced by R. Hilton (London, 1976) is cited, extended, pp. 34–46, 59–61, 74–83, 103–6, 109–17, 123f. and 130–4; the opposing positions taken in this volume (internal versus external causes of the decline of feudalism) need to be synthesized and that synthesis should include the positive elements of the North–Thomas theory. Hilton's introduction (pp. 9–30) does not yet achieve this synthesis. Any theory of socio-economic change must analyse the individual factors of the historical process as parts of an interdependent whole. In the context of the present debate this has been attempted by E. J. Nell, 'Economic Relations in the Decline of Feudalism: An Examination of Economic Interdependence and Social Change', *History and Theory*, 6 (1967), 313–50, esp. pp. 327–31. If this precondition is not fulfilled, i.e. if one factor is singled out as decisive and all other factors are reduced to it, the perspective will be too narrow. Such an approach is taken by R. Brenner, 'Agrarian Class Structure and Economic Development in Pre-industrial Europe', *Past and Present*, 70 (1976), 30–75, who singles out the class structure as the decisive factor. Brenner and others sometimes cite the example of east-central Europe in order to disprove the relevance of market relations for the decline of feudalism: Dobb, pp. 39–41; Sweezy et al., pp. 61 and 76f., Brenner, pp. 43, 53f., 60. But this view overlooks the fact that the socio-economic impact of the integration into international markets (as in east-central Europe in the fifteenth and sixteenth centuries) can only to a limited extent be compared with the impact of the emergence of regional markets (as during the high Middle Ages). It is significant that in east-central Europe the penetration of international trade went in parallel with the drying-up of regional exchange. This point has been made by, among others, M. Małowist, *Wschód a zachód Europy w XIII–XVI wieku. Konfrontacja struktur społeczno-gospodarczych* (The east and the west of Europe from the thirteenth to the sixteenth century. A comparison of socio-economic structures) (Warsaw, 1973), pp. 275–83. Not only the market factor has to be taken into consideration here but also the specific function of the great secular trends in prices, real wages, and feudal rents, as well as the cycles of population growth and contraction which were tied to them through a feedback system. For example, the change in class structure during the high Middle Ages can be adequately explained only when it is seen in the context of the first great growth phase of the European agrarian economy. Class structure, in *its* turn – though it needs to be explained just as do market relations and secular trends – can, in conjunction with other factors, determine the direction of the historical process. This argument, though overdrawn, is made in the article by Brenner.

49 See below, pp. 14–23.

50 It must be emphasized that the dividing line between 'urban' and 'rural', especially during the period treated here, cannot be sharply drawn. Town privileges, guild organization, great population density, and the relatively small significance of the agrarian sector did not always coincide; conversely, the absence of town privileges, the absence of guilds, low population density and the importance of the agrarian sector did not always go together. In fact, proto-industrialization itself sometimes generated new agglomerations, quasi-towns without town or guild privileges. For this reason, the present study cannot make a schematic distinction between 'rural' and 'urban' industries.

51 See above, n. 5 for the quotation. Among these larger centralized enterprises which will not be dealt with in this study, but ought to be included in a comprehensive treatment of the contribution which the secondary sector made to this phase of the socio-economic transformation process, the mines and ironworks are probably the most important. Since they were often closely linked to agriculture, their inclusion into the complex 'proto-industrialization' might be illuminating.

52 For the genesis of the capitalist world system in the fifteenth and sixteenth centuries see I. Wallerstein, *The Modern World System. Capitalist Agriculture and the Origins of the European World-Economy in the Sixteenth Century* (New York etc., 1974), vol. 1. Despite its refreshing provocativeness, the reconstruction of the formation period of the capitalist world system Wallerstein attempts, raises considerable doubts. In the context of the present work the most important objections are: (1) The European expansion into other continents was not directly caused by the 'crisis of feudalism' in the fourteenth and fifteenth centuries, as Wallerstein maintains. In this connection it is well to remember that the late medieval agrarian crisis was not in its origins the crisis of feudalism, but rather became the crisis of feudalism during its course and termination. It is true that the late medieval agrarian depression drove some nobles who were hurt by it to promote the overseas expansion, cf. for Portugal: M. Małowist, *Europa a Afryka zachodnia w dobie wczesnej expansji kolonialnej* (Europe and West Africa during the period of early colonial expansion) (Warsaw, 1969), pp. 52f. and 71–90; but this should not lead to the conclusion that 'the territorial expansion of Europe was a key prerequisite to a solution for the crisis of feudalism' without which Europe could have fallen 'into relative constant anarchy and further contraction' (Wallerstein, p. 38, also p. 24). Neither had the 'internal Americas' of Europe been exhausted, nor is it true that 'the nascent and potentially very violent class war' could only be held in check in this way (Wallerstein, p. 57 and p. 51). (2) One cannot interpret all parts of the socio-economic process in terms of the emerging capitalist world system. The price revolution of the sixteenth century was only partially caused by 'the emergence of capitalism as the dominant mode of social organization of the economy' (Wallerstein, pp. 69–77, n. p. 77). First and foremost it was an expansion of disparities which arose in the structure of the European agrarian societies during the course of the growth process. The 'second serfdom' in east-central Europe and the Latin American *encomienda* were related to developments at the European core, but they cannot therefore be classified as 'capitalist' (Wallerstein, pp. 90–100); they were essentially feudal. (3) The industrial development of the European core and the shift of industrial production from the towns to the countryside are insufficiently integrated into the emergence of the capitalist world system. However, it is important to interpret the emergence of the capitalist world system in the light of proto-industrialization, for the question of whether a country made the transition to proto-industrialization or not was of strategic importance not only for the relation between European metropolitan countries and the extra-European periphery but also for the development within Europe. The successful or non-successful outcome of this transition to proto-industrialization determined whether a country rose to become part of the core or whether it lapsed to the semi-periphery, like southern Europe.

53 Interesting suggestions for the introduction of such a historically reformulated concept of system into a theroy of social evolution and into a 'historically directed analysis of social systems' have been made by J. Habermas and K. Eder on the basis of their critical assessment of functionalist systems' theory: Habermas, 'Geschichte und Evolution', in Habermas, *Zur Rekonstruktion des Historischen Materialismus* (Frankfurt, 1976), pp. 200–59, esp. pp. 226ff.; cf. also Habermas, 'Geschichte und Evolution', pp. 242ff.; where he attempts to explain the problems of transition from feudalism to capitalism in an 'outline' which is based on a somewhat generous reading of Dobb; K. Eder, 'Einleitung' to *Seminar: Die Entstehung von Klassengesellschaften* (Frankfurt, 1973), pp. 7ff.; Eder, *Die Entstehung staatlich organisierter Gesellschaften. Ein Beitrag zu einer Theorie sozialer Evolution* (Frankfurt, 1976), pp. 119ff.

54 Cf. concerning the significance of devolutionary factors in the developmental process of social formations in history: Ch. Tilly, 'Clio and Minerva', *Theoretical Sociology*, eds. J. C. Kinney and E. A. Tiryakin (New York, 1970), 434–66; Ch. Tilly and R. Tilly, 'Agenda' (see n. 45 above), p. 187.

55 E. Hobsbawm, 'Crisis of the Seventeenth Century' (see n. 38 above), p. 38; the putting-out system is here referred to as a 'protean stage of industrial development'.

56 Mendels, 'Proto-industrialization: The First Phase' (see n. 45 above).

57 Marx, (see n. 5 above), vol. 3, Ch. 20: 'Historical Facts about Merchant's Capital', pp. 323–37, esp. p. 334; this aspect of the transitional problems between feudalism and capitalism was discussed among Dobb, Sweezy, Takahashi and Lefèbvre, and their discussion summarized by G. Procacci, 'A Survey of the Debate', in Sweezy et al., *Transition from Feudalism* (see n. 48 above), pp. 128–42, esp. pp. 137–41.

58 According to this view, Marx's methodology and his categories have the advantage that they were developed for the purpose of analysing the capitalist system from the perspective of its historicity: Marx's main point is that the laws ruling the capitalist system do not have timeless validity but are limited to this specific socio-economic formation which has emerged and will be overcome in the course of history. If this is so, then Marx laid the foundation for statements about the range within which specific economic categories are valid. This is why the categories for an analysis of pre-capitalist socio-economic formations or for the genesis of capitalism can be more fruitfully developed from Marx's point of view than from theories like marginalism which deny, or treat as peripheral, the historicity of the laws which underlie the socio-economic system.

59 In dealing with these problems, the expectation arose that, beyond the questions treated in Chs. 4 and 5, other aspects of proto-industrialization could be illuminated by this approach as well.

60 See for example Ch. 4, n. 82.

61 Habermas, 'Geschichte und Evolution' (see n. 53 above), p. 246.

Notes to Chapter 1

1 Cf. W. Abel, *Agrarkrisen und Agrarkonjunktur. Eine Geschichte der europäischen Landwirtschaft seit dem hohen Mittelalter*, 2nd ed. (Hamburg etc., 1966), pp. 17–20; B. H. Slicher van Bath, *The Agrarian History of Western Europe A.D. 500–1850* (London, 1963), pp. 132–7; G. Duby, *Guerriers et paysans VIIe–XIIe siècle. Premier essor de l'économie européenne* (Paris, 1973), pp. 292–300; J. le Goff, *Das Hochmittelalter*, Fischer Weltgeschichte, vol. 11 (Frankfurt, 1965), pp. 37–54; see also n. 48 of the Introduction above. For 'autarchic division of labour' see K. Modzelewski, 'La division du travail à l'échelle d'un état: L'organisation "ministérielle" en Pologne médiévale', *Annales E.S.C.*, 19 (1964), 1125–38. Concerning the theory which underlies this chapter and Ch. 6 see J. Habermas, N. Lumann, *Theorie der Gesellschaft oder Sozialtechnologie. Was leistet die Systemforschung?* (Frankfurt, 1971); J. Habermas, *Legitimationsprobleme im Spätkapitalismus*, Edition Suhrkamp, vol. 623 (Frankfurt, 1973), pp. 9–49; Habermas, 'Zum Thema: Geschichte und Evolution', *Geschichte und Gesellschaft*, 2 (1976), 310–57; K. Eder, 'Komplexität, Evolution, Geschichte', *Theorie der Gesellschaft oder Sozialtechnologie. Beiträge zur Habermas-Luhmann-Diskussion*, ed. F. Maciejewski, Theorie-Diskussion Supplement, vol. 1 (Frankfurt, 1973), pp. 9–42; Eder, ed., *Seminar: Die Entstehung von Klassengesellschaften*, Suhrkamp Taschenbuch Wissenschaft, vol. 30 (Frankfurt, 1973); Eder, *Die Entstehung staatlich organisierter Gesellschaften. Ein Beitrag zu einer Theorie sozialer Evolution* (Frankfurt, 1976); M. Godelier, *Rationality and Irrationality in Economics* London, 1972, Eng. tr of *Rationalité et irrationalité en économie* (Paris, 1966); especially concerning the crucial role of disequilibriums in the historical process: G. Myrdal, *Economic Theory and Under-developed Regions* (London, 1957), pp. 12–38.

2 P. Bohannan and G. Dalton, 'Introduction', *Markets in Africa*, eds. P. Bohannan and G. Dalton, Northwestern University Studies, vol. 9 (Evanston, Ill., 1962), pp. 1–26, here pp. 2, 7–9, 12; their classification follows K. Polanyi et al., eds., *Trade and Market in Early Empires. Economies in History and Theory* (Glencoe, Ill., 1957), esp. part 3, and met with unduly harsh criticism by G. Dupré and P.-Ph. Rey 'Reflections on the Pertinency of a Theory of the History of Exchange', *Economy and Society*, 2 (1973), 131–63, here 132–44; cf. also E. R. Wolf, *Peasants* (Englewood Cliffs, N. J., 1966), pp. 40–8; T. Shanin, 'The Nature and Logic of the Peasant Economy', *Journal of Peasant Studies*, 1 (1973–4), 63–80 and 186–206, here 73–5; B. Galeski, *Basic Concepts of Rural Sociology* (Manchester, 1972), pp. 10f.

3 Cf. e.g. F. Hähnsen, *Die Entwicklung des Ländlichen Handwerks in Schleswig-Holstein*, Quellen und Forschungen zur Geschichte Schleswig-Holsteins, vol. 9 (Leipzig, 1923), pp. 105–141; Wolf, *Peasants* (see n. 2 above), pp. 37–9.

4 A. Skalweit, *Das Dorfhandwerk vor Aufhebung des Städtezwangs*, Abhandlungen des europäischen Handwerks-Instituts Frankfurt/M., vol. 1 (Frankfurt, 1942), pp. 17–34; concerning the rural crafts that meet 'basic needs' cf. also F. W. Henning, 'Die

Wirtschaftsstruktur mitteleuropäischer Gebiete an der Wende zum 19. Jahrundert unter besonderer Berücksichtigung des gewerblichen Bereichs', *Beiträge zu Wirtschaftswachstum und Wirtschaftsstruktur im 16. und 19. Jahrhundert*, ed. W. Fischer, Schriften des Vereins für Socialpolitik n.F. 63 (Berlin, 1971), pp. 101–67, here 136–49.

5 M. Mitterauer, 'Produktionsweise, Siedlungsstruktur und Sozialformen im östereichischen Montanwesen des Mittelalters und der frühen Neuzeit', *Osterreichisches Montanwesen. Produktion, Verteilung, Sozialformen*, ed. M. Mitterauer (München, 1974), pp. 234–315.

6 Especially H. Otsuka, 'The Market Structure of Rural Industry in the Early Stages of the Development of Modern Capitalism', *Deuxième conférence internationale d'histoire économique. Aix-en-Provence 1962*, Congrès et colloques, vol. 8 (Paris etc., 1965), vol. 2, pp. 457–72; and J. de Vries, 'Labour/Leisure Trade-off', *Peasant Studies Newsletter*, 1 (1972), 45–50, esp. 47f.; concerning the city as a retarding factor in the formation period of capitalism see J. Merrington, 'Town and Country in the Transition to Capitalism', *The Transition from Feudalism to Capitalism*, ed. P. Sweezy (London, 1976), pp. 170–95, esp. 180–91.

7 Skalweit, *Dorfhandwerk* (see n. 4 above), pp. 11–15 and 56–71; Hähnsen, *Entwicklung* (see n. 3 above), pp. 13–100; for Saxony cf. G. Heitz, *Ländliche Leinenproduktion in Sachsen (1470–1555)*, Schriften des Instituts für Geschichte 2.4 (Berlin, 1961), pp. 77–107; for Bavaria cf. E. Schremmer, *Die Wirtschaft Bayerns. Vom hohen Mittelalter bis zum Beginn der Industrialisierung. Bergbau, Gewerbe, Handel* (München, 1970), pp. 127f.; for England cf. A. P. Wadsworth and J. de Lacy Mann, *The Cotton Trade and Industrial Lancashire 1600–1780* (Manchester, 1931), pp. 54–70, and H. Heaton, *The Yorkshire Woolen and Worsted Industries*, Oxford Historical and Literary Studies, vol. 10 (Oxford, 1920), pp. 54–8. In France, textile production in the countryside was only permitted after 1762, but attempts were made to subject it to the usual regulations. Cf. E. Tarlé, *L'industrie dans les campagnes en France à la fin de l'Ancien Régime*, Bibliothèque d'histoire moderne, vol. 11 (Paris, 1910), pp. 4f. and 52–78; a somewhat different view is taken in P. Bois, *Les Paysans de l'Ouest. Des structures économiques et sociales aux options politiques depuis l'époque révolutionnaire dans la Sarthe* (Le Mans, 1960), pp. 527–41.

8 Concerning village crafts cf. E. Schremmer, 'Standortausweitung der Warenproduktion im langfristigen Wirtschaftswachstum. Zur Stadt-Land-Arbeitsteilung im Gewerbe des 18. Jahrhunderts', *VSWG*, 59 (1972), 1–40; Skalweit, *Dorfhandwerk* (cit. 4); Skalweit, 'Der Werdegang des Landhandwerks', *Z. Agrarg. Agrargsoziol.*, 2 (1954), 1–17; K. H. Kaufhold, 'Umfang und Gliederung des deutschen Handwerks um 1800', *Handwerksgeschichte in neuer Sicht*, ed. W. Abel, Göttinger handwerkswirtschaftliche Studien, vol. 16 (Göttingen, 1970), pp. 26–64, here 51–8. Concerning rural industry cf. H. Kellenbenz, 'Ländliches Gewerbe und bäuerliches Unternehmertum in Westeuropa vom Spätmittelalter bis ins 18. Jahrhundert', *Deuxième conférence*, vol. 2 (see n. 6 above), pp. 376–427; an excellent survey through one for the linen industry in France, Silesia and Russia is M. Kulczykowski, *Andrychowski ośrodek płócienniczy w XVIII i XIX wieku* (The linen centre of Andrychów in the eighteenth and nineteenth centuries), Prace komisji nauk historycznych, vol. 31 (Wrocław etc., 1972), pp. 6–20.

9 A. V. Chayanov, 'Peasant Farm Organization', in: A. V. Chayanov, *The Theory of Peasant Economy*, ed. by D. Thorner, B. Kerblay and R. E. F. Smith (Homewood, Ill., 1966), pp. 29–269, esp. 74–76; N. Georgescu-Roegen, *The Entropy Law and the Economic Process* (Cambridge, Mass., 1971), pp. 250–3; H. A. Luning, *Economic Aspects of Low Labour-income Farming*, Verslage van landbouwkundige onderzoekingen, vol. 699 (Wageningen, 1967), pp. 26f. and 31–53; F. F. Mendels does not emphasize sufficiently that seasonal unemployment became a social problem only under certain conditions which have their origin in the historic process: F. F. Mendels, 'Proto-industrialization: The First Phase of the Industrialization Process', *Journ. Econ. Hist.*, 32 (1972), pp. 241–61, and in this volume pp. 16f.

10 The connection between pastoral farming and rural industry has often been observed; cf. J. Thirsk, 'Industries in the Countryside', *Essays in the Economic and Social History of Tudor and Stuart England in Honour of R. H. Tawney*, ed. E. J. Fisher (Cambridge, 1961), pp. 70–88, esp. 86f.; Thirsk, 'The Farming Regions', *The Agrarian History of England and Wales 4. 1500–1640*, ed. J. Thirsk (Cambridge, 1967), pp. 1–112, esp. 12–14; E. L. Jones, 'Agricultural Origins of Industry', *Past and Present*, 40 (1968), 58–71, here the extensive Italian version has been used: 'Le origini agricole dell 'industria', *Studi Storici*, 9 (1968), 564–93, esp. 571–5 and 585–7; A. Klíma, 'The Role of Domestic Industry in Bohemia in the Eighteenth Century', *Econ. Hist. Rev.*, 2nd ser., 27 (1974), 48–56, esp. 50.

11 For an evaluation of the factor of natural conditions cf. the controversial viewpoints of the two Russian historians Tarle, *Industrie* (see n. 7 above), pp. 16–25 and J. Loutchisky (I. V. Luchiskii), *La propriété paysanne en France à la veille de la Révolution (principalement en Limousin)*, Bibliothèque de la Révolution et de l'Empire, N.S. 2 (Paris, 1912), pp. 80–99; Tarle puts too much emphasis on natural conditions; see also H. Sée, 'Remarques sur le caractère de l'industrie rurale en France au XVIIIe siècle', *Revue Historique*, 142 (1923), 47–53 and Kulczykowski, *Ośrodek* (see n. 8 above), p. 225; also Klíma, 'Role' (see n. 10 above), p. 150.

12 In this connection see especially R. Braun, *Industrialisierung und Volksleben. Veränderung der Lebensform unter Einwirkung der verlagsindustriellen Heimarbeit in einem ländlichen Industriegebiet (Zürcher Oberland) vor 1800* (Erlenbach and Zürich, 1960), pp. 49–53.

13 M. Reinhard et al., *Histoire générale de la population mondiale*, 3rd ed. (Paris, 1968), pp. 67ff., 108ff. and 197ff. Concerning the secular trend-periods cf. Abel, *Agrarkrisen* (see n. 1 above), pp. 27ff., 97ff. and 182ff.; Slicher van Bath, *History* (n. 1 above), pp. 132ff., 144, 195ff. and 221ff.; recently as part of a theory of institutional change in D. C. North and R. P. Thomas, *The Rise of the Western World. A New Economic History* (Cambridge, 1973), pp. 11–17, 19ff. and 91ff. Concerning the factor of population growth see G. Hohorst, 'Bevölkerungsentwicklung und Wirtschaftswachstum als historischer Entwicklungsprozess demo-ökonomischer Systeme', *Dynamik der Bevölkerungsentwicklung. Strukturen, Bedingungen, Folgen*, eds. R. Mackensen and H. Wewer (München, 1973), pp. 91–118. The 'quasi-stable equilibrium system' in H. Leibenstein, *Economic Backwardness and Economic Growth. Studies in the Theory of Economic Development* (New York etc., 1957), pp. 15–37 is helpful for an understanding of the process delineated above. All attempts, especially those by Marxists, to refute the system of secular economic changes, developed primarily by Abel, are ultimately flawed by their neglect of the importance of the demographic factor in the historical process. Cf. e.g. the discussion about the agrarian crisis of the late Middle Ages to which especially R. Hilton and the Polish Marxists, M. Małowist, B. Geremek, and B. Zientara, have opposed the theory of a crisis of feudalism. The same is true for the unsatisfactory attempt by E. J. Nell, 'Economic Relations in the Decline of Feudalism: An Examination of Economic Interdependence and Social Change', *History and Theory*, 6 (1967), 313–50. Neither is the work of J. Topolski, *Narodziny kapitalizmu w Europie XIV–XVII wieku* (The birth of capitalism in Europe from the fourteenth to the seventeenth centuries) (Warsaw, 1965) convincing; this is a description of agrarian pre-conditions which does not touch on the problems which are central to the present study. In the final analysis, the activities of the nobility became the 'primum movens', according to Topolski, but he does not place this argument into the socio-economic context. The model of secular economic changes needs to be integrated into a comprehensive theory of socio-economic change. An attempt was made in R. Brenner, 'Agrarian Class Structure and Economic Development in Pre-industrial Europe', *Past and Present*, 70 (1976), 30–75, but Brenner's treatment of the subject, in my opinion, is too rigid, and retrogressive when it rejects the demographic and commercialization models. In particular, his attempt to explain the secular crises by way of the 'property or surplus-extraction relationship' (pp. 37, 50 and 66) is unacceptable, at least in this formulation.

14 Slicher van Bath, *History* (see n. 1 above), pp. 128f. and 314–18; for Germany see Schremmer, 'Standortausweitung' (n. 8), pp. 4–22; Schremmer, *Wirtschaft* (see n. 7 above), pp. 125–37 and 349–81; K. Blaschke, *Bevölkerungsgeschichte von Sachsen bis zur Industriellen Revolution* (Weimar, 1967), pp. 174–95; J. Peters, 'Ostelbische Landarmut. Sozial-ökonomisches über landlose und landarme Agrarproduzenten im Spätfeudalismus', *Jb. Wirtsch. G.* (1967), pt. 3, 255–302; Peters, 'Ostelbische Landarmut. Statistisches über landlose und landarme Agrarproduzenten im Spätfeudalismus', *Jb. Wirtsch. G.*(1970), pt. 1, 97–126; R. Heck, *Studia nad położeniem ekonomicznym ludności wiejskiej na Śląsku w XVI w.* (Studies on the economic situation of the rural population in Silesia in the sixteenth century) (Wrocław, 1959), pp. 57–78; Heck, in: *Historia Śląska. Opracowanie zbiorowe* (History of Silesia. Collected Essays) 1, 2 (Wrocław etc., 1961), pp. 62–8; St. Inglot, in: *Historia Śląska* 1, 3 (Wrocław, 1963), pp. 90–103; St. Michalkiewicz, in: *Historia Śląska* 2, 1 (Wrocław, 1966), pp. 134–42; a summary is provided by G. Franz, *Geschichte des deutschen Bauernstandes*, Deutsche Agrargeschichte, vol. 4 (Stuttgart, 1970), pp. 214–27; for England see A. Everitt, 'Farm Labourers', *Agrarian History*, ed. Thirsk (see n. 10 above), pp. 369–465, esp. 399ff.; for France see E. Labrousse, 'Aperçu de la repartition sociale de l'expansion agricole', *Histoire économique et sociale de la France*, vol. 2: *Des derniers temps de l'âge seigneurial aux préludes de l'âge industriel, 1660–1789* (Paris, 1970), pp. 473–97, esp. 489f.; there also exist numerous regional studies for France; for Poland see St. Inglot, ed., *Historia chłopów polskich* 1. *Do upadku rzeczypospolitej szlacheckiej* (A History of the Polish Peasants 1. Until the decline of the Noblemen's Commonwealth (Warsaw, 1970), pp. 295f. and 376–82; for Bohemia see O. Placht, *Lidnatost a společenska skladbá českého státu v 16.–18. století* (Population and Social Structure of the Czech State from the Sixteenth to the Eighteenth Centuries) (Prague, 1957), pp. 119–56; concerning this development at the level of landownership see F.-W. Henning, 'Die Betriebsgrössenstruktur der mitteleuropäischen Landwirtschaft im 18. Jahrhundert und ihr Einfluss auf die ländlichen Einkommensverhältnisse', *Z. Agrarg. Agrarsoziol.*, 17 (1969), 171–93. It would be shortsighted to explain population growth and therefore the emergence of rural industries on the basis of inheritance practices, here partible inheritance, as has been done, though very cautiously, in Thirsk, 'Industries', (see n. 10 above), pp. 77ff. Many regions with impartible inheritance practices could be held against this interpretation and, furthermore, inheritance practices vary over time; cf. L. Berkner, 'Rural Family Organization in Europe: A Problem in Comparative History', *Peasant Studies Newsletter*, 1 (1972), 145–56, esp. 149.

15 R. Tawney, *The Agrarian Problem in the Sixteenth Century* (Oxford, 1912), pp. 55–97; M. Spufford, *Contrasting Communities. English Villagers in the Sixteenth and Seventeenth Centuries* (Cambridge, 1974), pp. 49–119 and 165–7; E. le Roy Ladurie, *Les paysans de Languedoc* (Paris, 1966), vol. 1, pp. 248–57; J. Jacquard, *La crise rurale en Ile-de-France* (Paris, 1974), pp. 213–20, 232–45, 248–53; concerning the effects of harvest fluctuations on the monetary incomes of farms of different sizes see W. Abel, 'Landwirtschaftliche Wechsellagen' *Berichte über die Landwirtschaft* N.F. 21 (1937), 1–17, esp. 7–9; Abel, *Agrarkrisen* (see n. 1 above), pp. 23–6.

16 See below, Ch. 3, part 2.

17 Chayanov, *Peasant Farm Organization* (see n. 9 above), p. 87.

18 Due to the cultivation of cabbage, turnips, and especially potatoes, whose calorie content per unit of land is much higher than that of grain, this point was considerably delayed, i.e. the apogee of the total yield curve was not only moved upward, but also to the right; but the village institutions which regulated the cultivation of crops at first often prevented their introduction; cf. Henning, 'Betriebsgrössenstruktur' (see n. 14 above), pp. 188–91.

19 Chayanov, *Peasant Farm Organization* (see n. 9 above), pp. 101 and 107–10; Luning, *Aspects* (n. 9), pp. 42–5.

20 Cf. F.-W. Henning, Industrialisierung und dörfliche Einkommensmöglichkeiten. Der Einfluss der Industrialisierung des Textilgewerbes in Deutschland im 19. Jh. auf die Einkommensmöglichkeiten in den ländlichen Gebieten', *Agrarisches Nebengewerbe und Formen der Reagrarisierung im Spätmittelalter und 19./20. Jahrhundert*, ed. H. Kellenbenz, Forschungen zur Sozial- und Wirtschaftsgeschichte, vol. 21 (Stuttgart, 1975), pp. 155–75, esp. 156. The relationship between agrarian and non-agrarian income was closest when a family not only grew flax but also processed it to yarn; cf. W. Achilles, 'Die Bedeutung des Flachsanbaus im südlichen Niedersachsen für Bauern und Angehörige der unterbäuerlichen Schicht im 18. und 19. Jahrhundert', *Agrarisches Nebengewerbe*, ed. Kellenbenz, pp. 109–24; Achilles (p. 111) found a correlation between the percentage of the total arable under flax and the percentage of the total population of a village who belonged to the sub-peasant group (in southern Lower Saxony, the cottars were permitted to grow flax on a piece of land in compensation for helping estate-owners and farmers with their harvest work; Achilles, pp. 118f.).

21 Schremmer, 'Standortausweitung' (see n. 8 above), pp. 5 and 7–22; Braun, *Industrialisierung* (see n. 12 above), pp. 23–7; Everitt, 'Labourers' (see n. 14 above), pp. 425–9; Sée, 'Remarques' (see n. 11 above), pp. 48–51; H. Sée, *Französische Wirtschaftsgeschichte* (Jena, 1930), vol. 1, pp. 331f.

22 St. Hymer and St. Resnick, 'A Model of an Agrarian Economy with Nonagricultural Activities', *American Economic Review*, 59 (1969), 493–506, esp. 500f.; De Vries, 'Trade-off' (see n. 6 above), pp. 47f.; De Vries, *The Dutch Rural Economy in the Golden Age, 1500–1700* (New Haven, Conn. etc., 1974), pp. 19–21.

23 Slicher van Bath, *History* (see n. 1 above), pp. 217f.; Slicher van Bath, 'Historische ontwikkeling van de textielnijverheid in Twente', *Textielhistorische Bijdragen*, 2 (1960), 21–39, esp. 23. For Languedoc, Le Roy Ladurie, *Paysans* (see n. 15 above), vol. 1, pp. 645f. wrote: 'Les deux courbes, agriculture et draperie, se croisent. Le fléchissement agraire est très partiellement compensé par l'essor textile, où les éléments de croissance sont indéniables.' Concerning the crises of the late Middle Ages and the seventeenth century see Abel, *Agrarkrisen* (see n. 1 above), pp. 42ff. and 142ff.; Slicher van Bath, *History* (n. 1), pp. 160ff. and 206ff.; concerning negative feedback see E. A. Wrigley, *Population and History* (London, 1969), pp. 108–11; concerning the 'autonomous mortality rate' see J. D. Chambers, *Population, Economy, and Society in Pre-industrial England* (Oxford etc., 1972), pp. 77–106.

24 See n. 10 above.

25 See n. 11 above.

26 Le Roy Ladurie, *Paysans* (n. 15), vol. 1, pp. 567–81; Jacquart, *Crise* (see n. 15 above), pp. 700–15, 723–8, 753–6; P. Goubert, 'The French Peasantry of the Seventeenth Century: A Regional Example', *Crisis in Europe, 1560–1660. Essays from Past and Present*, ed. T. Ashton (London, 1965), pp. 141–65, esp. 162–5.

27 See especially L. K. Berkner, *Family, Social Structure, and Rural Industry: A*

Comparative Study of the Waldviertel and the Pays de Caux in the Eighteenth Century (Unpubl. Diss., Harvard University, 1973), pp. 286–93.

28 For Waldviertel see Berkner, 'Family' (see n. 21 above), pp. 164–72 and 194–6; only when, due to the commutation of labour services under Joseph II, the lords' demesnes were dissolved and the land distributed could a larger number of cottagers settle here. Concerning the Züricher Oberland, R. Braun, *Industrialisierung* (see n. 12 above), pp. 38–54 could show that the tendency of the valley communities to exclude outsiders caused the domestic industry to establish itself in the infertile mountain communities. The resistance of landlords who feared a rising poor-rate prevented the ribbon-weaving industry from establishing a foothold in the villages to the west and south of Coventry; see J. Prest, *The Industrial Revolution in Coventry* (Oxford, 1960), p. 45. In Bavaria, land was divided into the so-called 'walzende Stücke', i.e. plots which could be bought and sold, and plots which constituted the foundations of individual farms and were excluded from the land market; see G. Hanke, 'Zur Sozialstruktur der ländlichen Siedlungen Altbayerns im 17. und 18. Jahrhundert', *Gesellschaft und Herrschaft. Forschungen zu sozial- und landesgeschichtlichen Problemen vornehmlich in Bayern. Eine Festgabe für K. Bosl zum 60. Geburtstag* (München, 1969), pp. 219–69, esp. 247–54.

29 Concerning the Pays de Caux see Berkner, 'Family' (see n. 27 above), pp. 240f.; for Wigston Magna, which became a stocking-knitters' village around the end of the seventeenth century, see W. G. Hoskins, *The Midland Peasant. The Economic and Social History of a Leicestershire Village* (London, 1957), pp. 62f. and 97f.

30 Braun, *Industrialisierung* (see n. 12 above), pp. 51–3; Thirsk, 'Industries' (see n. 10 above), p. 86; Thirsk, 'Regions' (n. 10), pp. 6–12, where she contrasts the 'highlands' and 'lowlands' in England; Berkner, 'Family' (see n. 27 above), p. 291.

31 R. Gottwald, *Das alte Wüstewaltersdorf Ein Beitrag zur Geschichte des Eulengebirges* (Breslau, 1926), pp. 21, 28, 40f. and 43; R. Lauterbach, 'Die Ansiedlung der Weber auf den Dorfauen der Dörfer des Kreises Reichenbach', *Schlesische Geschichtsblätter* (1932), 43–6; H. Jahn-Langen, *Das böhmische Niederland. Bevölkerungs- und Sozialstruktur einer Industriedorflandschaft*, Forschungen zur deutschen Landeskunde, vol. 117 (Bad Godesberg, 1961), p. 16; E. Wauer, *Die Geschichte der Industriedörfer Eibau und Neueibau. Eine Studie über die wirtschaftliche Bedeutung der südlausitzer Industriedörfer* (Dresden, 1913–15), vol. 1, pp. 96f., 378–81, 396–8. vol. 2, pp. 429f. and 463–5; A. Kunze, 'Vom Bauerndorf zum Weberdorf. Zur sozialen und wirtschaftlichen Struktur der Waldhufendörfer der südlichen Oberlausitz im 16., 17. und 18. Jahrhundert', *Oberlausitzer Forschungen. Beiträge zur Landesgeschichte*, ed. M. Reuther (Leipzig, 1961), pp. 165–92 and 350, esp. 180, 182f. and 191.

32 F.-W. Henning, *Dienste und Abgaben der Bauern im 18. Jahrhundert*, Quellen und Forschungen zur Agrargeschichte, vol. 21 (Stuttgart, 1969), pp. 151–60.

33 Henning, *Dienste* (see n. 32 above), p. 173.

34 The following works should be mentioned: B. Zientara, 'Z zagadnień spornych tzw. "Wtórnego poddaństwa" w Europie Środkowej' (Comments concerning the so-called 'second serfdom' in central Europe), *Przegląd Historyczny*, 47 (1956), 3–47; S. D. Skazkin, 'Problèmes fondamentaux du "deuxième servage" en Europe centrale et orientale', *Le deuxième servage en Europe centrale et orientale*, Recherches internationales à la lumière du marxisme 63–4 (Paris, 1970), pp. 15–64; J. Blum, 'The Rise of Serfdom in Eastern Europe', *American Historical Review*, 62 (1956/57), 807–36; J. Blum, *Lord and Peasant in Russia. From the Ninth to the Nineteenth Century* (Princeton, N. J., 1961), pp. 106–276; C. Goerke, *Die Wüstungen in der Moskauer Rus'. Studien zur Siedlungs-, Bevölkerungs- und Sozialgeschichte*, Quellen und Studien zur Geschichte des östlichen Europas, vol. 1 (Wiesbaden, 1968), pp. 63ff., 96ff. A model of the manorial economy in Poland: W. Kula, *Teoria ekonomiczna ustroju feudalnego* (Warsaw, 1962), here somewhat the expanded French edition has been used: *Théorie économique du système féodal. Pour un modèle de l'économie polonaise aux 16ᵉ–18ᵉ siècles*, Civilisations et sociétés, vol. 15 (Paris etc., 1970); from the broad discussion which this book stimulated: W. Rusiński, 'Kilka uwag o istocie ekonomiki feudalnej w XV–XVIII wieku' (Some remarks on the essence of the feudal economy in the fifteenth to eighteenth centuries), *Roczniki dziejów społecznych i gospodarczych*, 27 (1965), 9–31. W. Kula's functional model has as its object the export-oriented cereal monoculture of the east-central European manorial economy.

35 Kula, *Théorie* (see n. 34 above), pp. 30f., concerning by-occupations p. 53.

36 H. Harnisch, 'Bevölkerung und Wirtschaft. Über die Zusammenhänge zwischen sozialökonomischer und demographischer Entwicklung im Spätfeudalismus', *Jb. Wirtsch. G.* (1975), vol. 2, 57–87, esp. 73f.; G. Mackenroth, *Bevölkerungslehre. Theorie, Soziologie und Statistik der Bevölkerung* (Berlin etc., 1953), pp. 422f.; here the term 'peasant population' includes not only the full farmers but also the smallholders and 'Gärtner' who owed simple labour-services without a plough team to their lords. The number of smallholders increased greatly since the manorial estates began at the end of the sixteenth century to discontinue the hiring of permanent servants. This has been demonstrated quantitatively by A. Wyczański, *Studia nad gospodarką starostwa korczyńskiego 1500–1660* (Studies of the economy of the Starosty Korczyn 1500–1660) (Warsaw, 1964), pp. 127–34, 153f., 177–84 and 217–21.

37 Kula, *Théorie* (see n. 34 above), pp. 43–8, very succinctly on p. 48: 'En Pologne, après une mauvaise année, l'escargot [i.e. the peasant] ressortait prudemment de sa coquille et tout rentrait dans l'ordre.' Concerning the dissolution of this system in the nineteenth century see W. Kula, *Kształowanie sie kapitalizmu w Polsce* (The development of capitalism in Poland) (Warsaw, 1955), pp. 30–53. But in many territories east of the Elbe, this process began earlier, namely in the eighteenth century, when the estates that were partly based on labour services (Teilbetriebe) made the transition to wage labour (Eigenbetriebe), cf. e.g. H. Harnisch, *Die Herrschaft Boitzenburg. Untersuchungen zur Entwicklung der sozialökonomischen Struktur ländlicher Gebiete in der Mark Brandenburg vom 14. bis zum 19. Jahrhundert*, Veröffentlichungen des Staatsarchivs Potsdam, vol. 6 (Weimar, 1968), pp. 162–96.

38 Kunze, 'Bauerndorf' (see n. 31 above), pp. 182–4, 166f. concerning the contrasting developments in upper and lower Lusatia; Wauer, *Geschichte* (n. 31), vol. 1, pp. 372–81, vol. 2, pp. 429f. and 463–5, vol. 1, pp. 373–5 contains a list from 1707 about the advantages of the dissolution of a manorial estate and the leasing out of its land in small plots for the village of Eibau; Jahn-Langen, *Niederland* (see n. 31 above), p. 16; J. Ziekursch, *Hundert Jahre schlesischer Agrargeschichte. Vom Humbertusburger Frieden bis zum Abschluss der Bauernbefreiung*, 2nd ed. (Breslau, 1927), pp. 132–8 and 305 with n. 3; St. Michalkiewicz, in: *Historia Śląska 2*, 1 (n. 14), p. 123; Michalkiewicz, *Gospodarka magnacka na Śląsku w drugiej połowie XVIII wieku na przykładzie majątku Książ* (The economy of the magnates in Silesia in the second half of the eighteenth century: the example of the estate Książ) (Wrocław etc. 1969), pp. 10–12 (the linen industry only spread in the south-eastern part of the Hochberg estates, p. 136. Here there was only one manorial estate, but 22 villages); H. Madurowicz and A. Podraza, *Regiony gospodarcze Małopolski zachodniej w drugiej połowie XVII wieku* (The economic regions in western Little Poland in the second half of the eighteenth century), Studia z historii społeczno-gospodarczej Małopolski, vol. 1 (Wrocław etc., 1958), pp. 184–97, esp. p. 184, table 74; W. Urban, *Poddani szlacheccy w województwie krakowskim w drugiej połowie XVIII wieku i ich opór antyfeudalny* (The noble subjects of the voivodeship Cracow in the second half of the eighteenth century and their anti-feudal resistance), Studia z historii społeczno-gospodarczej Małopolski, vol. 2 (Wroclaw, 1958), pp. 14f. and 38–50; A. Falinowska-Gradowska, *Świadczenia poddanych na rzecz dworu w królewszczyznach województwa* *krakowskiego w drugiej połowie XVIII wieku* (The feudal obligations of the subjects on the royal domains of the voivodeship Cracow in the second half of the eighteenth century), Studia z historii społeczno-gospodarczej Małopolski, vol. 7 (Wrocław, 1964), pp. 56–66, 98–108, esp. p. 57, table 20 and pp. 98f., table 55/6; I. Rychlikowa, *Klucz wielkoporębski Wodzickich w drugiej połowie XVIII wieku* (The complex of estates Poręba Wielka of the Wodzicki in the second half of the eighteenth century), Studia z historii społeczno-gospodarczej Małopolski, vol. 4 (Wrocław etc., 1960), pp. 25f. and 55–8. In Great Poland, a dense rural industry only developed after serfdom had been abolished, see W. Sobisiak, *Wiejskie włókiennictwo w Wielkopolsce. Porównawcze studium historyczno-etnograficzne* (The rural textile industry in Great Poland. A comparative historical and ethnographic study), Prace komisji etnograficznej vol. 1, 1 (Poznań, 1968), pp. 26–9. It should also be emphasized that, once rural industry had established itself in a region, it could prevent the development of manorial estates, or – if the latter existed already – their possibilities were limited and finally stifled; cf. Heitz, *Leinenproduktion* (see n. 7 above), pp. 56f. and R. Wuttke, *Gesindeordnungen und Gesindezwangsdienst in Sachsen bis zum Jahre 1835. Eine wirtschaftliche Studie*, Staats- und socialwissenschaftliche Forschungen, vol. 12, 4 (Leipzig, 1893), pp. 50f., 69, 129 and 159.

39 I. D. Koval'chenko, *Russkoe krepostnoe krest'janstvo v pervoi polovine XIX v.* (Russian peasant serfs in the first half of the nineteenth century) (Moscow, 1967), pp. 62f. table 7 and pp. 60–7; this work has been partially translated without the table: 'Zur sozialökonomischen Entwicklung des russischen Dorfes in der ersten Hälfte des 19. Jahrhunderts', *Wirtschaft und Gesellschaft im vorrevolutionären Russland*, ed. D. Geyer, Neue wissenschaftliche Bibliothek, vol. 71 (Cologne, 1975), pp. 110–32, esp. 113–16; M. Confino, *Domaines et seigneurs en Russie vers la fin du XVIIIᵉ siècle. Etudes de structures agraires et de mentalités économiques*, Collection historique de l'Institut d'Etudes slaves, vol. 18 (Paris, 1963), pp. 168–254. According to V. I. Semevskii, whose figures are less reliable, 76.5% of manorial peasants in the black-earth belt of central Russia performed labour services in 1782, and 23.5% paid rent. In the non-black-earth region, 38% performed labour services and 62% paid rent (calculated according to Confino, p. 187, table 1). The importance of mixed charges grew and is not expressed in these figures, but see Confino, *Domaines*, pp. 196–201 and 232–51 and Confino, 'Le système des redevances mixtes dans les domaines privés en Russie (XVIIIᵉ–XIXᵉ siècle)', *Annales E.S.C.*, 16 (1961), 1066–95, esp. 1082–95, also Koval'chenko, pp. 64–7 with table 8 (German text: pp. 115f., but without the table).

40 Confino, *Domaines* (see n. 38 above), pp. 218 and 225–8.

41 H. Rosovsky, 'The Serf Entrepreneur in Russia', *Explorations in Entrepreneurial History*, 6 (1953/54), pp. 207–33, esp. 209–11; concerning the greater 'freedom of choice' of the 'obrok' peasants to make 'decisions of a purely economic nature', see A. Kahan, 'The Infringement of the Market upon Serf-economy in Eastern Europe', *Peasant Studies Newsletter*, 3 (1974), 7–13, esp. 8.

42 The older controversy about the *grundherrlich* character of the Silesian linen industry (L. Brentano, C. Grünhagen, and W. Sombart) was taken up by H. Kisch, 'The Textile Industry in Silesia and the Rhineland: A Comparative Study in Industrialization', *Journ. Econ. Hist.*, 19 (1959), 541–64, esp. 543–7 (this essay also appears in this book, pp. 178–200) and U. Lewald, 'Die Entwicklung der ländlichen Textilindustrie im Rheinland und in Schlesien. Ein Vergleich', *Zeitschrift für Ostforschung*, 10 (1961), 601–30, esp. 604–17. In his controversy with Ziekursch, *Agrargeschichte* (see n. 37 above), pp. 104–13, Lewald asserts that a considerable part of the weaving population were not serfs, which is true: in the south-eastern part of the Hochberg estates, where the linen industry was concentrated, about 37.5% of the Häusler and 39.9% of the Gärtner were no longer serfs as early as 1745. This was calculated according to Michalkiewicz, *Gospodarka* (see n. 37 above), pp. 43−6, 195f. and also p. 44f. But this did not undermine the system of serfdom altogether. The *Weberzins* cannot be regarded as a charge for protection, as is done by Grünhagen; cf. the succinct remark by L. Brentano, 'Über den Einfluss der Grundherrlichkeit und Friedrichs des Grossen auf das schlesische Leinen-Gewerbe. Eine Antwort auf meine Kollegen Grünhagen und Sombart in Breslau', *Zeitschrift für Social- und Wirtschaftsgeschichte*, 2 (1894), 295−379, esp. 323; concerning the origin of the *Weberzins* cf. H. Aubin, 'Die Anfänge der grossen schlesischen Leineweberei und -handlung', *VSWG*, 35 (1942), 105−78, esp. 165−74; concerning the commercial policies which form the background to the commutation of labour services in weaving to the *Weberzins*, see E. Zimmermann, 'Der schlesische Garn- und Leinenhandel mit Holland im 16. und 17. Jahrhundert', *Economisch-historisch Jaarboek*, 26 (1956), 193−254, esp. 204−29. Important as a summary of our state of knowledge is W. Rusiński, 'Tkactwo lniane na Śląsku do 1850 roku' (Linen-weaving in Silesia down to 1850), *Przegląd Zachodni*, 5, 2 (1949), 369−419, 639−66, esp. 376f., 383−7 and 397−400; also B. Kan, *Dva vosstaniya silezskich tkachei 1793−1844* (Moscow, etc., 1948), here according to the Czech translation under the title: *Dvě povstání slezských tkalců 1793−1844* (Two revolts of the Silesian weavers 1793−1844), Socialistická věda, vol. 23 (Prague, 1952), pp. 42−8. For Upper Lusatia see G. Aubin and A. Kunze, *Leinenerzeugung und Leinenabsatz im östlichen Mitteleuropa zur Zeit der Zunftkäufe. Ein Beitrag zur industriellen Kolonisation des deutschen Ostens* (Stuttgart, 1940), pp. 15−17; Kunze, 'Bauerndorf' (see n. 31 above), p. 175; Wauer, *Geschichte* (n. 31), vol. 2, pp. 533f., 697, 701−3, 712−15 and 801−3; Kunze, *Zittaus Weg in die Welt* (Zittau, 1955), pp. 47−60; for Bohemia see A. Kunze, *Die nordböhmisch-sächsische Leinwand und der Nürnberger Grosshandel. Mit besonderer Berücksichtigung des Friedland-Reichenberger Gebietes*, Forschungen zur sudetendeutschen Heimatgeschichte, vol. 1 (Reichenberg, 1926), pp. 44−8; A. Klima, *Manufakturní období v Čechach* (The period of manufactures in Bohemia) (Prague, 1955), pp. 131−3; A. Klima, 'Role' (see n. 10 above), pp. 51−3. In Moravia, the feudal lords possessed the right of preemption for the yarn spun by their subjects until far into the eighteenth century. By selling the better yarn to Silesia, they hindered the development of the Moravian linen industry, cf. F. Mainuš, *Plátenictví na Moravě a ve Slezsku v XVII a XVIII stoleti* (The linen trade in Moravia and Silesia in the seventeenth and eighteenth centuries) (Ostrava, 1959), pp. 28−42; also, with new details, M. Dohnal, 'Rozwój handlu przędzą lnianą w okręgach płócienniczych śląskim i pólnocnomorawskim w XVI−XVIII w., (The development of the trade with linen yarn in the Silesian and north Moravian linen regions in the sixteenth to eighteenth centuries), *Śląski Kwartalnik Historyczny Sobótka*, 27 (1972), 531−44, esp. 537−42.

43 For Poland cf. Inglot, ed., *Historia* (see n. 14 above), pp. 302f. and 371f.; concerning labour services in spinning, see E. Trzyna, *Położenie ludności wiejskiej w królewszczyznach województwa krakowskiego w XVII wieku* (The condition of the rural population of the royal domains of the voivodeship Cracow in the seventeenth century), Prace Wrocławskiego Towarzystwa Naukowego A, vol. 92 (Wrocław, 1963), pp. 251f. Urban, *Poddani* (see n. 37 above), pp. 43f.; Falinowska-Gradowska, *Świadczenia* (n. 37), pp. 161−4, and this is supplemented by a significant detail in W. Kula, *Szkice o manufakturach w Polsce XVIII wieku* (notes on the manufactures in Poland in the eighteenth century), Badania nad dziejami przemysłu i klasy robotniczej w Polsce, vol. 1 (Warsaw, 1956), pp. 710f.; concerning the struggle over the labour services in weaving in Gorlice 1784−6, see Madurowicz and Podraza, *Regiony* (see n. 37 above), p. 210; here is an example of linen production on a largely feudal basis in Rychlikowa, *Klucz* (n. 37), pp. 160−6, according to table 92 on page 37, the following percentage of the feudal income were derived from the trade, with linen cloth: 6.3% in 1755−6, 3.2% in 1782−5,

1% in 1785–7, and 0% in 1787–9; cf. also F. Kotula, 'Łancucki ośrodek tkacki w XVII i XVIII wieku' (The weaving centre of Łańcut in the seventeenth and eighteenth centuries), *Kwartalmk historii kultury materialnej*, 2 (1954), 664–75, esp. 671f. and W. A. Serczyk, *Gospodarstwo magnackie w województwie podolskim w drugiej połowie XVIII wieku* (The economy of the magnates in the voivodeship Podole in the second half of the eighteenth century), Prace komisji nauk historycznych, vol. 13 (Wrocław etc., 1965), pp. 123f.; for Russia cf. Blum, *Lord* (see n. 34 above), pp. 289–92. In Andrychów, the feudal lord withdrew from yarn and linen cloth production as early as the first half of the eighteenth century; the yarn and cloth rents were converted into a money rent, labour services largely abolished, and the peasant-merchants could build up a huge trading network involving large parts of Europe, without having to fear much interference from the estate-owners; see Kulczykowski, *Ośrodek* (see n. 8 above), pp. 145, 74–8, 176–82; for Ivanovo cf. R. Portal. 'Aux origines d'une bourgeoisie industrielle en Russie', *Revue d'histoire moderne et contemporaine*, 8 (1961), 35–60, esp. 44–53; V. K. Jacunskii, 'Formation en Russie de la grande industrie textile sur la base de la production rurale', *Deuxième conférence*, 2 (see n. 6 above), pp. 365–76, esp. 366–73. In east-central and eastern Europe, the desire of estate owners to be autarchic often promoted the village crafts, cf. Kula, *Théorie* (see n. 34 above), pp. 106–10; Inglot, ed., *Historia* (see n. 14 above), pp. 302f. and 370f.; H. Samsonowicz, *Rzemiosło wiejskie w Polsce XIV–XVI w.* (The village crafts in Poland in the fourteenth to the sixteenth centuries), Badania z dziejów rzemiosła i handlu w epoce feudalizmu, vol. 2 (Warsaw, 1954), pp. 106–63 and 179f.; Schremmer made similar observations for the south-east German *Grundherrschaft*; E. Schremmer, 'Agrarverfassung und Wirtschaftstruktur. Die südostdeutsche Hofmark – Eine Wirtschaftsherrschaft?' *Ž. Agrarg. Agrarsoziol.*, 20 (1972), 42–65.

44 B. Moore, *Social Origins of Dictatorship and Democracy. Lord and Peasant in the Making of the Modern World* (London, 1967), pp. 4–13; still unsurpassed Tawney, *Problem* (see n. 15 above), pp. 184ff.; L. Stone, *The Causes of the English Revolution, 1529–1642* (London, 1972), pp. 67–76.

45 Spufford, *Communities* (see n. 15 above), pp. 45–167; H. J. Habakkuk, 'La disparition du paysan anglais', *Annales E. S. C.*, 20 (1965), 649–63; this is modified by F. M. L. Thompson. 'The Social Distribution of Landed Property in England since the Sixteenth Century', *Econ. Hist. Rev.*, 2nd ser., 19 (1966), 505–17; Hoskins, *Midland Peasant* (see n. 29 above), pp. 247–76; Ch. Tilly, 'Food Supply and the Public Order in Modern Europe', *The Formation of National States in Western Europe*, ed. Ch. Tilly (Princeton, N. J., 1975), pp. 380–455, esp. 402–4; like Hoskins, Tilly questions the assumption of social harmony which underlies the view of the enclosure movement put forth by J. D. Chambers and E. G. Mingay. In general: Everitt, 'Labourers' (see n. 14 above), pp. 425–9 and 462–5.

46 See the literature listed under n. 13 above. The so-called *Zunftkäufe*, i.e. collective sales-contracts with the guilds of a town, constituted an intermediate stage. These existed between south German merchant capitalists and the guilds of the east-central German towns in the sixteenth and early seventeenth centuries; cf. Aubin and Kunze, *Leinenerzeugung* (see n. 41 above). It should be mentioned that evidence for a movement from the cities to the countryside has not been found for all industries in all regions. On occasion, an industry clearly originated in the countryside. A fairly recent example is the clock-making industry of the Black Forest, but it also applies to the rural textile industry in Flanders which was apparently tied to the manorial economy. Still, the conditions for its subsequent expansion were created by the urban economy and merchant capital. Cf. R. van Uyten, 'Die ländliche Industrie während des Spätmittelalters in den südlichen Niederlanden', *Nebengewerbe*, ed. Kellenbenz (see n. 20 above), pp. 57–77, esp. 63f., 67–9 and 72.

47 D. Sella, 'European Industries, 1500–1700', *The Fontana Economic History of Europe*, vol. 2: *The Sixteenth and Seventeenth Centuries*, ed. C. M. Cipolla (London, 1974), pp. 354–426, esp. 360–5.

48 H. Myint, 'The "Classical Theory" of International Trade and the Underdeveloped Countries', *Economic Theory and the Underdeveloped Countries*, ed. H. Myint (New York etc., 1971), pp. 118–46, esp. 120 and 124–8 and in addition R. E. Caves, '"Vent for Surplus" Models of Trade and Growth', *Trade, Growth, and the Balance of Payments. Essays in Honor of G. Haberler* (Chicago etc., 1965), pp. 95–115. Caves shows that the 'staple' theory and the 'unlimited-supplies-of-labour' theory can be understood as versions of the 'vent-for-surplus' theory. Concerning the application of this theory to proto-industrialization, see H. Kisch, 'The Development of the Domestic Manufacture in the Lower Rhine Textile Trades Prior to the Industrial Revolution. Introductory Comments' (Unpubl., 1974), pp. 34f.; also H. van der Wee and Th. Peters, 'Un modèle dynamique de croissance interséculaire du commerce mondial (XIIᵉ–XVIIIᵉ siècles)', *Annales E.S.C.*, 25 (1970), 100–26, esp. 123f. The theory of comparative costs cannot be applied since it presupposes the complete utilization of all available resources.

49 Kisch, 'Textile Industries' (see n. 41 above), p. 544 (below, p. 180); A. Kunze, 'Die Oberlausitzer Leinenausfuhr nach England, Holland und Spanien im 17. und zu Beginn des 18. Jahrhunderts', *Zittauer Geschichtsblätter*, 7 (1930), 3–6; Klíma, *Období* (see n. 41 above), pp. 143–53.

50 D. C. Coleman, 'An Innovation and its Diffusion: The "New Draperies"', *Econ. Hist. Rev.*, 2nd ser., 22 (1969), 417–29, esp. 421–3.

51 Cf. the systematic survey in R. Ennen, *Zünfte und Wettbewerb. Möglichkeiten und Grenzen zünftlerischer Wettbewerbsbeschränkungen im städtischen Handwerk und Gewerbe des Spätmittelalters*, Neue Wirtschaftsgeschichte, vol. 3 (Cologne etc. 1971) and Schremmer, *Wirtschaft* (see n. 7 above), pp. 33–6.

52 Cf. e.g. for Aachen, H. Kisch, 'Das Erbe des Mittelalters, ein Hemmnis wirtschaftlicher Entwicklung: Aachens Tuchgewerbe vor 1790', *Rheinische Vierteljahrsblätter*, 30 (1965), 253–308, esp. 264–70 and 295ff.; for Cologne, see H. Kisch, *Prussian Mercantilism and the Rise of the Krefeld Silk Industry: Variations upon an Eighteenth-Century Theme*, Transaction of the American Philosophical Society n.s. 58, 7 (Philadelphia, 1968), p. 26; G. Croon, 'Zunftzwang und Industrie im Kreise Reichenbach', *Zs. des Vereins für Geschichte Schlesiens*, 43 (1909), 98–130, and this is supplemented by T. Bieda, 'Z życia cechu płócienników w Dzierzoniowie w latach 1742–1800' (Concerning the life of the linen weavers' guild in Reichenbach 1742–1800). *Uniwersytet Wrocławski im. Bolesława Bieruta*. Zeszyty Naukowe A 30 = Historia 5 (1961), 53–80 (I am grateful to Professor M. Wolański, Wrocław, for pointing this article out to me); for England, see J. D. Chambers, 'The Rural Domestic Industries during the Period of Transition to the Factory System with Special Reference to the Midland Counties of England', *Deuxième conférence*, 2 (see n. 6 above), 429–55, esp. 431 and Wadsworth and Mann, *Cotton Trade* (see n. 7 above), pp. 54–70; in general M. Dobb, *Studies in the Development of Capitalism*, 2nd ed. (London, 1963), pp. 151–76. Often the competition of a rural industry brought about the decline of that urban industry, not only on the regional, but also on an international level; examples are the Italian and Spanish cloth industry which did not stand up to the competition of the 'new draperies' from England. Cf. C. M. Cipolla, 'The Economic Decline of Italy', *The Economic Decline of Empires*, ed. C. M. Cipolla (London, 1970), pp. 196–214 and R. Davis, *English Overseas Trade, 1500–1700* (London, 1973), pp. 21f. The decline of Leiden, the largest industrial centre in Europe in the seventeenth century, can be explained in the same way: at first the Leiden 'nieuwe draperie' were pushed aside by English competition in the seventeenth century, and the 'oude Leidsche draperie' which replaced it and prospered in the seventeenth century succumbed to the competition of the rural cloth industry situated on the Vesdre river in the eighteenth century; cf. Ch. Wilson, 'Cloth Production and International Competition in the Seventeenth Century', in Ch. Wilson, *Economic History and the Historian. Collected Essays* (London, 1969), pp. 94–113, esp. 102–13 and N.-W. Posthumus, 'De industrieele concurrentie tusschen Noord- en Zuid-Nederlandsche nijverheidscentra in de XVIIe en XVIIIe eeuw', *Mélanges d'histoire offerts à H. Pirenne* (Brussels, 1926), pp. 369–78, esp. 376–8.

53 P. Deyon, Amiens, capitale provinciale. Etude sur la société urbaine au 17e siècle, Civilisations et sociétés, vol. 2 (Paris, 1967), pp. 214f. Concerning the functional relationship of the development of urban and rural textile trades, see especially P. Deyon, 'La concurrence internationale des manufactures lainières aux XVIe et XVIIe siècles', *Annales E. S. C.*, 27 (1972), 20–32.

54 H. Aubin, 'Die Stückwerker von Nürnberg bis ins 17. Jahrhundert', *Beiträge zur Wirtschafts- und Stadtgeschichte. Festschrift für H. Ammann* (Wiesbaden, 1965), pp. 333–52.

55 Skalweit, *Dorfhandwerk* (see n. 4 above), pp. 13–15 and J. A. van Houtte, 'Stadt und Land in der Geschichte des flandrischen Gewerbes im Spätmittelalter und in der Neuzeit', *Wirtschaftliche und soziale Probleme der gewerblichen Entwicklung im 15.–16. und 19. Jahrhundert*, ed. F. Lütge, Forschungen zur Sozial- und Wirtschaftsgeschichte, vol. 10 (Stuttgart, 1968), pp. 91–101, esp. 97f.

56 See also below, p. 50. There are many examples that prove that the returns on labour were lower in the countryside than in the cities; here only Deyon, *Amiens* (see n. 53 above), pp. 209f. (in 1698, accordingly to Deyon, they were apparently by 50 to 73% lower).

57 E. J. Hobsbawm, 'The Crisis of the Seventeenth Century', *Crisis*, ed. Aston (see n. 26 above), pp. 5–58, esp. 38. The expansion of the rural, and crisis of the urban textile industry in the seventeenth century, which can be especially observed in France, must be seen in this context; cf. P. Goubert, *Beauvais et le Beauvaisis de 1600 à 1730. Contribution à l'histoire sociale de la France du XVIIe siècle*, Démographie et sociétés, vol. 3 (Paris, 1960), pp. 127–32 and 585–97 and Deyon, Amiens (see n. 52 above), pp. 205–15. For the late Middle Ages, see M. Małowist, *Studia z dziejów rzemiosła w okresie kryzysu feudalizmu w zachodniej Europie w XIV i XV wieku* (Studies in the history of handicrafts during the period of the crisis of feudalism in western Europe in the fourteenth and fifteenth centuries) (Warsaw, 1954), pp. 112–16, 203–6, 274–8 and 450–5 and Nell, 'Relationships' (see n. 13 above), p. 345.

58 J. Topolski, 'La régression économique en Pologne du XVIe au XVIIIe siècle', *Acta Poloniae Historica*, 7 (1962), 28–49; M. Kulczykowski, 'En Pologne au XVIIIe siècle: Industrie paysanne et formation du marché national', *Annales E.S.C.*, 24 (1969), 61–9, esp. 66–8 and Kulczykowski, *Ośrodek* (see n. 8 above), p. 222. For surveys of the rural industries in Little Poland cf. Madurowicz and Podraza, *Regiony* (see n. 38 above), pp. 94–124 and M. Kulczykowski, *Kraków jako ośrodek towarowy Małopolski zachodniej w drugiej połowie XVIII wieku* (Cracow as the commercial centre of the western part of Little Poland in the second half of the eighteenth century), Studia z historii społeczno-gospodarczej Małopolski, vol. 6 (Warsaw, 1963), pp. 89–99, 108–16 and 140–3.

59 A short survey in Jacunskii, 'Formation' (n. 42); cf. also M. Tugan-Baranovskii, *Geschichte der russischen Fabrik*, Sozialgeschichtliche Forschungen 5/6 (Berlin, 1900), pp. 43–62.

60 E. Carus-Wilson, 'The Woolen Industry', *The Cambridge Economic History of Europe*, vol. 2 (Cambridge, 1952), pp. 355–428, esp. 411–28; E. Carus-Wilson, 'An Industrial Revolution of the Thirteenth Century', *Medieval Merchant Ventures. Collected Studies*, ed. E. Carus-Wilson (London, 1954), pp. 182–210 and in addition E. Miller, 'The Fortunes of the English Textile Industry during the Thirteenth Century', *Econ. Hist.*

Rev., 2nd ser., 18 (1965), 64–82, concerning the role of the woollen-mill which has been too strongly emphasized by Carus-Wilson in her discussion of the cloth production's move to the countryside; E. Carus-Wilson, 'Evidences of Industrial Growth on some Fifteenth-Century Manors', *Econ. Hist. Rev.*, 12 (1959/60), 191–205 (Stoudwater and Castle Combe); E. Coornaert, *Un centre industriel d'autrefois. La draperie-sayetterie d'Hondschoote (XVIe–XVIIIe siècles)* (Paris, 1930), pp. 1–21; Coornaert, 'Draperies rurales, draperies urbaines. L'évolution de l'industrie flamande au moyen âge et au XVIe siècle', *Revue belge de philologie et d'histoire*, 28 (1950), 59–96, esp. 79–90; van Houtte, 'Stadt' (see n. 54 above), pp. 90–101; van Uytven (see n. 45 above), pp. 63–76; H. van der Wee, 'Structural Changes and Specialization in the Industry of the Southern Netherlands, 1100–1600', *Econ. Hist. Rev.*, 2nd ser., 28 (1975), 203–21, esp. 211–15; E. Sabbe, *De belgische vlasnijverheid 1. De zuidnederlandsche vlasnijverheid tot het verdrag van Utrecht (1713)*, Rijksuniversiteit te Gent. Werken uitgegeven door de Faculteit van de wijsbegeerte en letteren, vol. 95 (Brugge, 1943), pp. 140–62; for south Germany see B. Kirchgässner, 'Der Verlag im Spannungsfeld von Stadt und Umland', *Stadt und Umland*, eds. E. Maschke and J. Sydow, Veröffentlichungen der Kommission für geschichtliche Landeskunde in Baden-Württemberg, vol. 82 (Stuttgart, 1974), pp. 72–128, esp. 85–97 and H. Ammann, 'Die Anfänge der Leinenindustrie des Bodenseegebietes', *Alemannisches Jahrbuch* (1953), 251–313, esp. 254–7. Concerning the development of rural industries in the area of Nürnberg and Cologne cf. H. Amman, 'Die wirtschaftliche Stellung der Reichsstadt Nürnberg im Spätmittelalter,' *Nürnberger Forschungen*, vol. 13 (Nuremberg, 1970), pp. 194–226 and H. Kisch, 'From Monopoly to Laissez-faire: The Early Growth of the Wupper Valley Textile Trades', *Journal of European Economic History*, 1 (1972), 298–402, esp. 298–306 and F. Petri, 'Das bergische Land in der älteren deutschen Siedlungs- und Wirtschaftsgeschichte', *Rheinische Vierteljahrsblätter*, 20 (1955), 61–79, esp. 71–5. Especially in England, where the woollen industry 'possessed a rural character' (Carus-Wilson, 'Evidences', p. 190) at the end of the Middle Ages, and in the southern Netherlands, it is very difficult to distinguish this early phase from the later development, since adequate quantitative data are missing. It seems that the criteria which will be mentioned below applied to individual villages, though not to entire regions as early as the late Middle Ages (but only the latter case can be called proto-industrialization); cf. Carus-Wilson, 'Evidences', pp. 197–205 and van Uyten (see n. 45 above), p. 67. In Hondschoote, the decisive change came at the beginning of the sixteenth century (Coornaert, *Centre*, pp. 335–8).

61 The following authors are in approximate agreement about the timing of this new phase: Jones, 'Origini' (see n. 10 above), Mendels, 'Proto-industrialization' (see n. 9 above), pp. 247f., and Hobsbawm, 'Crisis' (see n. 56 above), p. 38; for the northern Netherlands, France, Spain, Italy, Poland, and Russia cf. Z. -W. Sneller, 'La naissance de l'industrie rurale dans les Pays-Bas aux XVIIe et XVIIIe siècles', *Annales E.S.C.*, 23 (1968), 759–87, esp. 782; J. Gentil da Silva, *En Espagne. Développement économique, subsistence, déclin* (Paris, 1965), pp. 27–31 and 125f. and P. Vilar, *La Catalogne dans l'Espagne moderne. Recherches sur les fondements économiques des structures nationales* (Paris, 1962), vol. 1, pp. 594–8; Cipolla, 'Decline' (see n. 51 above), pp. 201f. and G. Luzzato, *Storia economica dell'età moderna et contemporanea*, vol. 2, 3rd ed. (Padua, 1955), p. 155; for the Mediterranean countries in general, see F. Braudel, *La Méditerranée et le monde méditerranéen à l'époque de Philippe II*, vols. 1 and 2, 2nd ed. (Paris, 1966), vol. 1, pp. 391f.; Kulczykowski, 'Pologne' (see n. 58 above), pp. 61–9 and L. L. Murav'eva, *Derevenskaya promyshlennost' central' noi Rossii vtoroi poloviny XVII v.* (The rural industry of central Russia in the second half of the seventeenth century) (Moscow, 1971) and in addition B. Widera, 'Die ländliche Kleinindustrie in Russland im 17. Jahrhundert. Ein Beitrag zur Genesis des Kapitalismus in Russland', *Jb. Wirtsch. G.* (1972), pt. 4, 223–30. For

224   Notes to pp. 24–6

England and the southern Netherlands cf. the qualifying remarks under n. 59. In the literature about the crisis of the seventeenth century (W. Abel, P. Chaunu, A. Mączak, R. Romano, J. Topolski, A. Wyczański), the emergence of rural industries was linked to that crisis only occasionally, namely by E. J. Hobsbawm and B. H. Slicher van Bath in particular.

62 Hobsbawm, 'Crisis' (see n. 56 above), pp. 50–3.

63 This regional connection was for the first time systematically explored by Jones, 'Origini' (see n. 10 above); also Mendels, 'Proto-industrialization' (see n. 9 above), pp. 248f.; individual examples are Jones (n. 10); R. Blanchard, *La Flandre. Etude géographique de la plaine flamande en France, Belgique et Hollande* (Lille, 1906), pp. 117–21 and 294–408; F. F. Mendels, *Industrialization and Population Pressure in Eighteenth Century Flanders* (Ph.D. Diss., University of Wisconsin, 1970) and F. F. Mendels 'Agriculture and Peasant Industry in Eighteenth Century Flanders', *European Peasants and their Markets. Essays in Agrarian Economic History*, eds. W. N. Parker and E. L. Jones (Princeton, N.J., 1975), pp. 179–204 (this article is reprinted in this book, pp. 161–77); J. Petráň, 'A propos de la formation des régions de la production spécialisée en Europe centrale', *Deuxième conférence*, 2 (see n. 6 above), pp. 217–22 and Koval'chenko, *Krest'janstvo* (see n. 38 above), pp. 67–73 (in the German translation: pp. 116–20).

64 See above, pp. 14–19f.

65 Jones, 'Origini' (see n. 10 above), pp. 568–75.

66 Cf. K. Bücher, 'Die Entstehung der Volkswirtschaft', in K. Bücher, *Die Entstehung der Volkswirtschaft. Vorträge und Aufsätze*, vol. 1, 14th ed. (Tübingen, 1919), pp. 83–160, esp. 115 and 153 and Schremmer, 'Standortausweitung' (see n. 8 above), p. 15.

67 See below, Ch. 3, §I, 2a and 3c.; Mendels, 'Proto-industrialization' (see n. 9 above), p. 248 sees in the formation of specifically agrarian and specifically industrial regions a 'quasi-empirical definition of proto-industrialization'. Two objections can be raised against this definition: (1) This criterion does not apply to those proto-industrial regions where agriculture was carried out on a commercial basis. (2) Despite a number of qualifications, the separate but complementary development of agrarian and industrial regions – though it constituted a basic precondition of proto-industrialization – was a secondary phenomenon.

Attention should also be paid to the attempt of E. Schremmer to reach a correct assessment of the criteria as well as their combinations and their groupings – for the development of proto-industrialism in a region, see E. Schremmer, 'Überlegungen und Bestimmungen des gewerblichen und agrarischen Elements in einer Region. Fragen und Probleme – auch zum Thema Werturteile', *Nebengewerbe*, ed. Kellenbenz (see n. 20 above), pp. 1–23.

68 De Vries, *Economy* (see n. 22 above), pp. 7–10 and de Vries, 'Trade-off' (see n. 6 above), pp. 47f.

69 Concerning the division between subsistence and commercial agriculture cf. C. L. Wharton, 'Subsistence Agriculture: Concepts and Scope', *Subsistence Agriculture and Economic Development*, ed. C. L. Wharton (Chicago, 1969), pp. 12–20 and Ch. Nakajima, 'Subsistence and Commercial Family Farms: Some Theoretical Models of Subjective Equilibrium', *Subsistence Agriculture and Economic Developmemt*, ed. C. L. Wharton (Chicago, 1969), pp. 165–85.

70 De Vries, Economy (see n. 22 above), pp. 13 and 15f.

71 Dauphiné: P. Léon, *La naissance de la grande industrie en Dauphiné (fin du XVIIᵉ siècle–1869)*, vols. 1 and 2, Université de Grenoble. Publications de la Faculté des lettres, vol. 9 (Paris, 1954), vol. 1, pp. 56f.; western France: Ch. Tilly, *The Vendée* (London, 1964), pp. 35f., 113–18, 132–40; Bois, *Paysans* (see n. 7 above), pp. 449–69 and 495–574; R. Musset, *Le Bas-Maine. Etude géographique* (Paris, 1917), pp. 256–312;

H. Sée, *Les classes rurales en Bretagne du XVI* siècle à la Révolution (Paris, 1906), pp. 379–405 and 446–56 and in addition F. Bourdais and R. Durand, 'L'industrie et le commerce de la toile en Bretagne au XVIII* siècle', *Notices, inventaires et documents*, vol. 7 (Paris, 1922), pp. 1–48; Flanders (the interior): Blanchard, *Flandre* (see n. 62 above), pp. 341–64 and 370–8; Overijssel: B. H. Slicher van Bath, *Een samenleving onder spanning. Geschiedenis van het platteland in Overijssel*, Historische sociografieen van het platteland, vol. 1 (Assen, 1957), pp. 200–10, 508–88 and 729–32; Württemberg: W. Troeltsch, *Die Calwer Zeughandlungskompagnie und ihre Arbeiter. Studien zur Gewerbe-und Handelsgeschichte Altwürttembergs* (Jena, 1897), pp. 263–7; Silesia (the borderland): St. Michalkiewicz, in: *Historia Śląska* 2, 1 (see n. 14 above), pp. 88f.; the foothills of the Carpathian mountains: Madurowicz/Podraza, *Regiony* (see n. 37 above), pp. 40–87, esp. 85. Proto-industrialization did not penetrate into every region with subsistence agriculture. In the Waldviertel, for example, the labour supply was too inelastic. Here it was not the small number of *Häusler* who were employed as weavers, but the farmers instead, and, as a consequence, the social effects of the expansion of commodity production remained insignificant; cf. Berkner, 'Family' (see n. 27 above), pp. 25–32, 196–212 and n. 28 above.

72 Blanchard, *Flandre* (see n. 62 above), pp. 341–64; Braun, *Industrialisierung* (see n. 12 above), pp. 176–80; Troeltsch, *Zeughandlungskompagnie* (see n. 70 above), pp. 263–8.

73 Here especially Braun, *Industrialisierung* (see n. 12 above), pp. 176–80, the quotation on p. 179.

74 De Vries, *Economy* (see n. 22 above), pp. 2f. and Tilly, *Vendée* (see n. 70 above), pp. 18f. Here it is well to remember the 'free economy' of von Thünen's 'first circle' (around the city); cf. J. H. von Thünen, *Der isolierte Staat in Beziehung auf Landwirtschaft und Nationalökonomie*, 4th ed. (Stuttgart, 1966), pp. 12–15.

75 De Vries, *Economy* (see n. 22 above), pp. 8–10.

76 The best example is the northern Netherlands with the exception of Overijssel; cf. de Vries, *Economy* (see n. 22 above), pp. 224–35. For the surroundings of Paris see Tarlé, *Industrie* (see n. 7 above), p. 19f.; for the light soils of the English 'Lowland Zone' see Jones, 'Origini' (see n. 10 above), pp. 568–75.

77 The best investigations of this problem have been made for thePays de Caux; cf. J. Sion, *Les Paysans de la Normandie orientale. Etude géographique sur les populations rurales du Caux et du Bray, du Vexin normand et de la Vallée de la Seine* (Paris, 1908), pp. 166–89 and 224–58 and in addition Berkner, 'Family' (see n. 27 above), pp. 232–81. Concerning complaints from agriculture about the lack of labourers due to domestic industry see Sion, pp. 176 and 186–9, and Berkner, p. 270. A higher level of wages than in other French textile regions for the first half of the nineteenth century is mentioned in M. Lévy-Leboyer, *Les banques européennes et l'industrialisation internationale dans la première moitié du XIX* siècle, Publications de la faculté des lettres et sciences humaines de Paris. Série Recherches, vol. 16 (Paris, 1964), p. 73. Already H. Sée has contrasted the rural industry in regions with subsistence agriculture with that in regions with commercial agriculture; cf. H. Sée, 'Remarques' (see n. 11 above), pp. 47–51.

78 Jones, 'Origini' (see n. 10 above), pp. 571–4 and J. Ruwet, *L'agriculture et les classes rurales au Pays de Herve sous l'Ancien Régime*, Bibliothèque de la Faculté de philosophie et lettres de l'Université de Liège, vol. 100 (Liège etc., 1943), pp. 44–68, 157–79 and 270-4 and in addition P. Lebrun, *L'industrie de la laine à Verviers pendant le XVIII* et le début du XIX* siècle. Contribution à l'étude des origines de la révolution industrielle*, Bibliothèque de la Faculté de philosophie et letters de l'Université de Liège, vol. 114 (Liège, 1948), pp. 75–84 and 216–19. L. Dechesne, *Industrie drapière de la Vesdre avant 1800* (Paris etc., 1926), pp. 229f., this work claims that the cloth industry on the Vesdre river found its labourers in the area around Limburg more than in Franchimont, because the latter's natural resources did not suffice to maintain a growing population; the author then asserts that a 'flourishing agriculture' like that of the area around Limburg is the prerequisite of domestic industry. This thesis (though it is partially supported by H. Kisch who assumes a 'critical minimum level': Kisch, 'Development' [see n. 47 above], pp. 84–6) must be questioned. Not only does Deschesne underestimate the importance of the Franchimont (cf. Lebrun, pp. 216f. and 271), his thesis is also contradicted by the development in the Silesian mountain area.

79 Reinhard et al., Histoire (see n. 13 above), pp. 146–96.

80 See above pp. 17f., 19, 27.

81 W. A. Lewis, 'Economic Development with Unlimited Supplies of Labour', *The Economic Underdevelopment. A Series of Articles and Papers*, eds. A. N. Agarwala and S. P. Singh (London etc., 1958), pp. 400–49; for the theory of 'disguised unemployment' which is part of Lewis's theory, cf. Ch. H. C. Kao, K. R. Anschel and C. K. Eicher, 'Disguised Unemployment in Agriculture: A Survey', *Agriculture in Economic Development*, eds. C. Eicher and L. Witt (New York, etc., 1964), pp. 129–44 and W. C. Robinson, 'Types of Disguised Unemployment and some Policy Implications', *Oxford Economic Papers* NS 21 (1969), 373–86; comprehensively J. C. H. Ranis and G. Fei, *Development of the Labour Surplus Economy. Theory and Policy* (Homewood, Ill., 1964); this has been criticized by H. Myint, *The Economics of Developing Countries*, 4th ed. (London, 1971), pp. 68–74; Luning, *Farming* (see n. 9 above), pp. 38–41 and G. Myrdal, *Asian Drama. An Inquiry into the Poverty of Nations*, vols. 1–3 (New York, 1968), vol. 2, pp. 961–1012 and vol. 3, 2041–61.

82 Myint, Economics (see n. 81 above), pp. 69 and 74.

83 Mendels, 'Proto-industrialization' (see n. 9 above), pp. 253f.; cf. also Fei/Ranis, 'Development' (see n. 81 above), p. 168. Only for this case is the optimism justified which stands behind the 'disguised unemployment' theory; Myrdal, in *Asian Drama* (n. 81), vol. 3, pp. 2058–61, appropriately speaks of an 'escapist approach'.

84 Scotland and Ireland were exceptions to some extent. This was due, first of all, to the relative backwardness of both countries compared with England, and in the case of Ireland also to her colonial structure; see T. G. Smout, 'The Landowner and the Planned Village in Scotland, 1730–1830', *Scotland in the Age of Improvement. Essays in Scottish History in the Eighteenth Century*, eds. N. T. Phillipson and R. Mitchison (Edinburgh, 1970), pp. 73–106; W. H. Crawford, 'Ulster Landowners and the Linen Industry', *Land and Industry. The Landed Estate and the Industrial Revolution*, eds. W. T. Ward and R. G. Wilson (Newton Abbot, Devon, 1971), pp. 117–44.

85 See above, p.20f. Aside from their importance in mining, the Silesian estate owners also preserved a certain significance as owners of bleaching establishments; cf. Z. Kwaśny, *Rozwój przemysłu w majatkach Schaffgotschów w latach 1750–1850* (The development of industry on the estates of the Schaffgotsch in the years 1750 to 1850), Prace Wrocławskiego Towarzystwa Naukowego A, vol. 10 (Wrocław, 1965), pp. 21–26; the percentage of bleaching establishments owned by the feudal lords, however, declined between 1749/50: 41.2% and 1799/1800: 26.1%; see also St. Michalkiewicz, 'Z dziejów wykańczalni tkackiej w Gluszycy na Pogórzu Sudeckim' (The history of the cloth-finishing establishment in Głuszyca in Silesia), *Studia i materialy z dziejów Śląska*, 4 (1962), 64–114 and Michalkiewicz, *Gospodarka* (see n. 38 above), pp. 142–7 (on the estates of the Hochberg family, most of the bleaching establishments were owned by mayors, farmers and cottars, Michalkiewicz, *Gospodarka*, p. 139). The Russian nobility owned a relatively large number of manufactures; cf. Tugan-Baranovskii, *Geschichte* (see n. 59 above), pp. 35f., 103f. and 120–28 and W. L.

Blackwell, *The Beginnings of Russian Industrialization, 1800–1860* (Princeton, N. J., 1968), pp. 25–7 and 198–201.
86 Wadsworth/Mann, *Cotton Trade* (see n. 7 above), pp. 36–48, 261–73 and 321–3 and R. Braun, *Sozialer und kultureller Wandel in einem ländlichen Industriegebiet (Zürcher Oberland) unter Einwirkung des Maschinen- und Fabrikwesens im 19. und 20. Jahrhundert.* (Erlenbach and Zürich etc., 1965), pp. 66–108. H. Kisch has repeatedly pointed out the importance of these peasants whom he called kulaks; cf. Kisch, 'Development' (see n. 481 above), pp. 37–9 and 61f.; Kisch, 'Monopoly' (see n. 601 above), pp. 301f. and 331–4; Kisch, *Mercantilism* (see n. 52 above), p. 16; cf. also Heitz, *Leinenproduktion* (see n. 7 above), pp. 67f.
87 See above pp. 17f., 19f.
88 Kulczykowski, *Ośrodek* (see n. 8), pp. 144–217 and 221f.; J. Kulischer, 'Die kapitalistischen Unternehmer in Russland (insbesondere die Bauern als Unternehmer) in den Anfangsstadien des Kapitalismus', *Archiv für Sozialwissenschaft und Sozialpolitik*, 65 (1931), 309–55, esp. 327–55; Rosovsky, 'Serf Entrepreneur' (see n. 41 above); Portal, 'Origines' (see n. 43 above); Portal, 'Du servage à la bourgeoisie: La famille Konovalov', *Revue des etudes slaves*, 38 (1961), 143–50 and Blackwell, *Beginnings* (see n. 85 above), pp. 205–11. There existed an active village trade in Upper Lusatia and Silesia as well, but its potential was severely limited by the cities, especially in Silesia; cf. Kunze, 'Bauerndorf' (see n. 31 above), pp. 176f. and 180f.; W. v. Westernhagen, *Leinwand-manufaktur und Leinwandhandel der Oberlausitz in der zweiten Hälfte des 18. Jahrhunderts und während der Kontinentalsperre* (Diss. phil., Leipzig, 1932), pp. 29–37; Wauer, *Geschichte* (see n. 31 above), vol. 2, pp. 433–62 and S. Kühn, *Der Hirschberger Leinwand- und Schleierhandel von 1648–1806*, Breslauer Historische Forschungen, vol. 7 (Breslau, 1938), pp. 26–32.
89 Jones, 'Origini' (see n. 10 above), pp. 564–93; Jones is of course in danger of laying an altogether undue stress on the income-and-demand effect of an agrarian 'surplus' (pp. 566–8 and 585–7); concerning the aspect that is stressed here see pp. 569f. and 585f.; cf. also the review by B. R. Mitchell in *Econ. Hist. Rev.*, 2nd ser., 22 (1969), pp. 584f.
90 Braun, *Industrialisierung* (see n. 12 above), pp. 97–9; Troeltsch, *Zeughandlungskompagnie* (see n. 71 above), pp. 296f.; J. Janczak, *Rozmieszczenie produkcji roślinnej i zwierzęcej na Śląsku na przełomie XVIII i XIX wieku* (The location of plant and animal production in Silesia at the turn from the eighteenth to the nineteenth centuries) (Wrocław etc., 1964), pp. 34–8; generally about the cultivation of potatoes Slicher van Bath, *History* (see n. 1), pp. 266–71.
91 Dechesne, *Industrie* (n. 78), pp. 182f.; Braun, *Industrialisierung* (see n. 12 above), pp. 49–51; K. Winkler, *Landwirtschaft und Agrarverfassung im Fürstentum Osnabrück nach dem Dreissigjährigen Krieg*, Quellen und Forschungen zur Agrargeschchte, vol. 5 (Stuttgart, 1959), pp. 111 and 129 and Janzcak, *Rozmieszczenie* (see n. 90 above), pp. 142f.
92 W. Abel, *Geschichte der deutschen Landwirtschaft*, 2nd ed. Deutsche Agrargeschichte, vol. 2 (Stuttgart, 1967), pp. 201ff.; F.-K. Riemann, *Ackerbau und Viehhaltung im vorindustriellen Deutschland*, Beihefte zum Jahrbuch der Albertus-Unversität zu Königsberg/Pr., vol. 3 (Kitzingen, 1953); D. Saalfeld, 'Die Produktion und Intensität der Landwirtschaft in Deutschland und angrenzenden Gebiten um 1800', *Z. Agrarg. Agrarsoziol.*, 15 (1967), 137–75; E. Labrousse, 'L'expansion agricole: La montée de la production', *Histoire*, eds. E. Labrousse et al. (see n. 14 above), pp. 417–71; M. Morineau, *Les faux-semblants d'un démarrage économique: agriculture et démographie en France au XVIIIᵉ siècle*, Cahiers des Annales, vol. 30 (Paris, 1971). For the Netherlands,

on the other hand, cf. Slicher van Bath, 'The Rise of Intensive Husbandry in the Low Countries', *Britain and the Netherlands*, eds. J. S. Bromley and E. H. Kossmann (London, 1960), pp. 130–53 and de Vries, *Economy* (see n. 22 above), pp. 119ff. Concerning the social mechanisms which enforced the rise in the product contributions of the agrarian sector, see Tilly, 'Food Supply' (see n. 45 above), pp. 417–24.

93 E. L. Jones, 'Introduction', *Agriculture and Economic Growth in England, 1650–1750*, ed. E. L. Jones (London, 1967), pp. 1–48, here 8–11; E. L. Jones, 'Agriculture and Economic Growth in England, 1660–1750: Agricultural Change', *Agriculture and Economic Growth in England, 1650–1750*, ed. E. L. Jones (London, 1967), pp. 152–71; E. L. Jones, 'English and European Agricultural Development, 1650–1750', *The Industrial Revolution*, ed. R. M. Hartwell, Nuffield College. Studies in Economic History, vol. 1 (Oxford, 1970), pp. 42–76, esp. 48–76; A. H. John, 'The Course of Agricultural Change, 1660–1760', *Essays in Agrarian History*, vol. 1, ed. W. E. Minchinton (Newton Abbot, Devon, 1968), pp. 223–53; Jones, 'Origini' (see n. 10 above), pp. 568–75; cf. also J. D. Chambers and G. E. Mingay, *The Agricultural Revolution, 1750–1880* (London, 1966).

94 Thompson, 'Distribution' (see n. 45 above), p. 517 and Tilly, 'Food Supply' (see n. 45 above), pp. 402f.

95 E. A. Wrigley, 'The Supply of Raw Materials in the Industrial Revolution', *The Causes of the Industrial Revolution in England*, ed. R. M. Hartwell (London, 1967), pp. 97–120; P. Léon. 'La réponse de l'industrie', *Histoire*, eds. E. Labrousse et al. (see n. 14 above), pp. 217–66, esp. 230–3; W. Abel, *Massenarmut und Hungerkrisen im vorindustriellen Europa. Versuch einer Synopsis* (Hamburg etc., 1974), pp. 308f.

96 Cf. e.g. the extent of flax cultivation in Silesia: Janczak, *Rozmieszczenie* (see n. 90 above), pp. 57–61 with a map on page 59 (also *Historia Śląska* 2, 1 [n. 14 above], p. 105).

97 Jones, 'Agriculture' (see n. 93 above), pp. 169f. and A. H. John, 'Agricultural Productivity and Economic Growth in England, 1700–1760', *Agriculture*, ed. Jones (n. 93 above), pp. 172–93, esp. 174f.

98 Henning, *Dienste* (see n. 32 above), 166–8 and Labrousse, 'Aperçu' (see n. 14 above), pp. 485f. and 495–7.

99 Kula, *Théorie* (see n. 34 above), pp. 32f., 48f. and 100–10.

100 See above, pp. 12f. with n.6.

101 A. H. John, 'Aspects of English Economic Growth in the First Half of the Eighteenth Century', *Essays in Economic History*, ed. E. Carus-Wilson (London, 1962), vol. 2, pp. 360–73; A. H. John, 'Productivity' (see n. 97 above), pp. 172–93; Jones, 'Introduction' (see n. 93 above), pp. 36–46.

102 D. C. Eversley, 'The Home Market and Economic Growth in England, 1750–1780', *Land, Labour and Population in the Industrial Revolution. Essays presented to J. D. Chambers*, eds. E. L. Jones and G. E. Mingay (London, 1967), pp. 206–59 and in addition Jones, 'Introduction' (see n. 93 above), pp. 40f.

103 C. -E. Labrousse, *Esquisse du mouvement des prix et des revenues en France au XVIIIe siècle*, vols. 1 and 2, Collection scientifique d'économie politique, vol. 3 (Paris, 1933), vol. 2, pp. 243–67; C. -E. Labrousse, *La crise de l'économie française à la fin de l'Ancien Régime et au début de la Révolution* (Paris, 1944), vol. 1, pp. xiii–xvi and 172–84 (the quotation on p. 175); C. -E. Labrousse, 'Les ruptures périodiques de la prospérité: les crises économiques du XVIIIe siècle', *Histoire*, eds. Labrousse et al. (see n. 14 above), pp. 629–63 and in addition D. S. Landes, 'The Statistical Study of French Crises', *Journ. Econ. Hist.*, 10 (1950), 195–210; Abel, *Agrarkrisen* (see n. 1 above), pp. 22–6; Abel; *Massenarmut* (see n. 95 above), pp. 267–301. Concerning the connection between harvest failures and the demand for industrial products in England in the first half of the seventeenth century cf. B. Supple, *Commercial Crisis and Change in England, 1600–1642. A Study in the Instability of a Mercantile Economy* (Cambridge, 1959), pp. 14–19; for the eighteenth century T. S. Ashton, *Economic Fluctuations in England, 1700–1800* (Oxford, 1959), pp. 1–48 and J. D. Gould, 'Agricultural Fluctuations and the English Economy in the Eighteenth Century', *Journ. Econ. Hist.*, 22 (1962), 313–33. W. G. Hoskins, 'Harvest Fluctuations and English Economic History, 1480–1619', *Agricultural History Review*, 22 (1964), 28–46 and Hoskins, 'Harvest Fluctuations and English Economic History, 1620–1759', *Agricultural History Review*, 26 (1968), 15–31; the grain-price series on which these articles are based have not been statistically investigated so that conclusions cannot be derived from them either about the consistency of harvest fluctuations – as Hoskins does – or about their weakening between 1480 and 1759. Evidence for heavier fluctuations in France than in England is provided in J. Meuvret, 'Les oscillations des prix des céréales au XVIIe et XVIIIe siècles en Angleterre et dans les pays du bassin parisien', in J. Meuvret, *Etudes d'histoire économique. Recueil d'articles*, Cahiers des Annales, vol. 32 (Paris, 1971), pp. 113–24. The works of L. H. Bean, G. Brandau, E. Graue, S. A. Pervushin, and V. P. Timoshenko, which deal with the connection between the agrarian and industrial cycles in the late nineteenth and early twentieth centuries, are useful, though of limited value for an analysis of the crises of the 'old type'. Concerning the significance of different levels of intensity see G. Brandau, *Ernteschwankungen und wirtschaftliche Wechsellagen 1874–1913*, Beiträge zur Erforschung der wirtschaftlichen Wechsellagen. Aufschwung, Krise, Stockung, vol. 14 (Jena, 1936), p. 20.

104 1770: 45%; 1801: 32.5%; 1811: 35.7% (Ph. Deane and W. A. Cole, *British Economic Growth, 1688–1959. Trends and Structure*, 2nd ed. [Cambridge, 1969], pp. 156–61), 1688: ca. 56% (S. Pollard and D. W. Crossley, *The Wealth of Britain, 1085–1966* [London, 1968], p. 155; this corrects the data given by Deane and Cole, p. 156).

105 A. Klíma, 'The Domestic Industry and the Putting-out System (Verlags-System) in the Period of Transition from Feudalism to Capitalism', Deuxième conférence 2 (see n. 6 above), pp. 477–84 and Kunze, 'Bauerndorf' (see n. 31 above), pp. 182–4.

106 Ch. Tilly and R. Tilly, 'Emerging Problems in the Modern Economic History of Western Europe' (Unpubl., 1971), pp. 13f.; Braun, *Industrialisierung* (see n. 12 above), pp. 176–80; for Saxony, though this connection is not made explicit, see R. Gross, *Die bürgerliche Agrarreform in Sachsen in der ersten Hälfte des 19. Jahrhunderts. Untersuchungen zum Problem des Übergangs vom Feudalismus zum Kapitalismus in der Landwirtschaft*, Schriftenreihe des Staatsarchivs Dresden, vol. 8 (Weimar, 1968), pp. 38–56.

107 I. B. Kravis, 'Trade as a Handmaiden of Growth: Similarities between the Nineteenth and Twentieth Centuries', *Economic Journal*, 80 (1970), 850–72 (Kravis objects to the 'engine-of-growth' hypothesis of Ragnar Nurkse).

108 W. Hofmann, *Europa-Markt und Wettbewerb*, Volkswirtschaftliche Schriften, vol. 45 (Berlin, 1959), pp. 10–12, 16 and 20–25, the quotation on p. 10.

109 Myint, *Theory* (see n. 48 above), pp. 120–8; van der Wee and Peters, 'Modèle' (n. 48), pp. 123f.; above pp. 21f.; D. C. North, 'Location Theory and Regional Economic Growth', *Journal of Political Economy*, 63 (1955), 243–58, the quotation p. 257.

110 The role of foreign demand has mostly been discussed in connection with the Industrial Revolution; cf. K. Berrill, 'International Trade and the Rate of Economic Growth', *Econ. Hist. Rev.*, 2nd ser. 12 (1959/60), 351–9; E. J. Hobsbawm, 'Le origini de la rivoluzzione industriale britannica', *Studi storici*, 2 (1961), 496–516, esp. 508–12; Hobsbawm, *Industry and Empire*, The Pelican Economic History of Britain, vol. 3 (Harmondsworth, 1969), pp. 42–54; Ph. Deane and H. J. Habakkuk, 'The Take-off in Britain', *The Economics of Take-off into Sustained Growth. Proceedings of a Conference held by the*

International Economic Association, ed. W. W. Rostow (London, 1963), pp. 63–82, esp. 77–80; important qualifications have recently been voiced especially by P. Bairoch, 'Commerce international et genèse de la révolution industrielle anglaise', *Annales E.S.C.*, 28 (1973), 540–71.

111 Carus-Wilson, 'Introduction', in Carus-Wilson, *Merchant Venturers* (see n. 60 above), pp. xi–xxxii, esp. xvi–xxi and in addition Carus-Wilson and O. Coleman, *England's Export Trade 1275–1547* (Oxford, 1963), pp. 122f. and 138f.

112 Ammann, 'Anfänge' (see n. 60 above), pp. 258f.

113 I. Wallerstein, *The Modern World System*, vol. 1. *Capitalist Agriculture and the Origins of the European World-Economy in the Sixteenth Century* (New York etc., 1974), pp. 84–129 (about this book see above, n. 52 of the Introduction); in general: D. Senghaas, 'Elemente einer Theorie des peripheren Kapitalismus', *Peripherer Kapitalismus. Analysen über Abhängigkeit und Unterentwicklung*, ed. D. Senghaas, Edition Suhrkamp, vol. 652 (Frankfurt, 1974), pp. 7–36, esp. 15–31; F. Fröbel, J. Heinrichs and O. Kreye, *The New International Division of Labour* (Cambridge, 1980), pp. 24–33; concerning the theory of unequal exchange see A. Emmanuel, *L'échange inégal. Essai sur les antagonismes dans les rapports économiques internationaux*, 2nd ed. Economie et socialisme, vol. 12 (Paris, 1972); S. Amin, *Accumulation on a world scale: Critique of the Theory of Underdevelopment* (London and New York, 1974), 2 vols., vol. 1, pp. 44–90; cf. the critical assessment of these works in K. Busch, 'Ungleicher Tausch. Zur Diskussion über internationale Durchschnittsprofitrate, ungleichen Tausch und komparative Kostentheorie anhand der Thesesn von Arghiri Emmanuel', *Probleme des Klassenkampfs*, 8/9 (1973), 47–88.

114 Davis, *Trade* (see n. 52 above), pp. 11–25 and 52f. tables 1 and 2; Davis, 'England and the Mediterranean, 1750–1670', *Essays*, ed. Fisher (see n. 10 above), pp. 117–37, esp. 117–26; H. Zins, *England and the Baltic in the Elizabethan Era* (Manchester, 1972), pp. 160–91 (transl. from Polish); Supple, *Crisis* (see n. 103 above), pp. 33ff. and 135ff.

115 E. Schäfer, 'Spaniens koloniale Warenausfuhr nach einer Preisliste des 16. Jahrhunderts', *Ibero-Amerikanisches Archiv*, 12 (1938–39), pp. 313–32; Sella, 'Industries' (see n. 47 above), pp. 362–4; Aubin and Kunze, *Leinenerzeugung* (see n. 42 above), pp. 4f. and 248–52.

116 Sabbe, *Vlasnijverheid* (see n. 60 above), vol. 1, pp. 179–84 and 278–83.

117 J. Tanguy, 'La production et le commerce des toiles "bretagnes" du XVIe au XVIIIe siècle. Premiers résultats', *Actes du 91e Congrès national des Sociétés savantes. Rennes, 1966. Section d'histoire moderne et contemporaine*, vol. 1 (Paris, 1966), pp. 105–41, esp. 109; cf. also A. Girard, *Le commerce français à Séville et Cadiz au temps des Habsbourg. Contribution à l'étude du commerce étranger en Espagne aux XVIe et XVIIe siècles* (Paris, 1932), pp. 344f.

118 H. Lapeyre, *Une famille de marchands: les Ruiz. Contribution à l'étude du commerce entre la France et l'Espagne au temps de Philippe II*, Affaires et gens d'affaires, vol. 8 (Paris, 1955), p. 503.

119 P. Deyon and A. Lottin, 'Evolution de la production textile à Lille aux XVIe et XVIIe siècles', *Revue du Nord*, 49 (1967), 23–33, esp. 26f.; for Amiens and other textile centres see P. Deyon, 'Variations de la production textile aux XVIe et XVIIe siècles: Sources et premiers résultats', *Annales E.S.C.*, 18 (1963), 939–55, esp. 946f.; P. Deyon, 'Concurrence' (see n. 53 above), pp. 26f.

120 Van der Wee and Peters, 'Modèle' (see n. 48 above), pp. 115–17; Zs. P. Pach, 'Diminishing Share of East-central Europe in the 17th Century International Trade', *Acta Historica*, 16 (1970), 289–306; Cipolla, 'Decline' (see n. 52 above).

121 P. Léon, *Economies et sociétés préindustrielles*, vol. 2: *1650–1780. Les origines d'une accélération de l'histoire* (Paris, 1970), pp. 170ff.

122 J. Reinhold, *Polen/Littauen auf den Leipziger Messen des 18. Jahrhunderts*, Abhandlungen zur Handels- und Sozialgeschichte, vol. 10 (Weimar, 1971).

123 P. Jéannin, 'Les comptes du Sund comme source pour la construction d'indices généraux de l'activité économique en Europe (XVIe–XVIIIe siècle)', *Revue Historique*, 231 (1964), 55–102 and 307–40, esp. 331–5.

124 P. Léon, 'Structure du commerce extérieur et évolution industrielle de la France à la fin du XVIIIe siècle', *Conjoncture économique, structures sociales. Hommage à E. Labrousse*, Civilisations et sociétés, vol. 47 (Paris etc., 1974), pp. 407–32, esp. 423–6, tables 1–5.

125 F. Mauro, 'Towards an "Intercontinental Model"': European Overseas Expansion between 1500 and 1800', *Econ. Hist. Rev.*, 2nd ser., 14 (1961/62), 1–17; D. A. Farnie, 'The Commercial Empire of the Atlantic, 1607–1783', *Econ. Hist. Rev.*, 2nd ser., 15 (1962/63), 205–18; Hobsbawm, 'Crisis' (see n. 57 above), pp. 50–3.

126 F. Mauro, *L'expansion européenne 1600–1870*, Nouvelle Clio, vol. 27 (Paris, 1964), pp. 140f.; concerning the status of Russia and Asia as 'external area' to the world economy in the sixteenth and early seventeenth centuries, see Wallerstein, *World System* (see n. 113 above), pp. 300–44.

127 R. Davis, 'English Foreign Trade, 1600–1700', *The Growth of English Overseas Trade in the Seventeenth and Eighteenth Centuries*, ed. W. E. Minchinton (London, 1969), pp. 78–98; R. Davis, 'English Foreign Trade, 1700–1774', *The Growth of English Overseas Trade in the Seventeenth and Eighteenth Centuries*, ed. W. E. Minchinton (London, 1969), 99–120 (the calculation is based on the table on p. 120); cf. R. Davis, *A Commercial Revolution. English Overseas Trade in the Seventeenth and Eighteenth Centuries*, Historical Association Pamphlets, vol. 64 (London, 1967) and Deane and Cole, *Growth* (see n. 104), pp. 41–50. From 1663 to 1669, America, Africa, and Asia provided markets for 10.1% of the export of finished products from London (calculated according to Davis, 'Trade, 1660–1700', p. 97).

128 Léon, 'Structures' (see n. 124 above), pp. 423–6, tables 1–5 and pp. 411–15; J. Tarrade, *Le commerce colonial de la France à la fin de l'Ancien Régime. L'évolution du régime de 'l'Exclusif' de 1763 à 1789*, vols. 1 and 2, Publications de l'Université de Poitiers. Lettres et science humaines, vol. 12 (Paris, 1972), pp. 713–78. For the seventeenth century J. Delumeau, 'Le commerce extérieur français au XVIIe siècle', *XVIIe siècle*, 70 and 71 (1966), 81–105 and Girard, *Commerce* (see n. 117 above), pp. 337–91. Of the total English export, the percentage of finished products constituted 54.2% in 1772/74 and 55.8% in 1699/1701, calculated according to Davis, 'Trade 1700–1774' (see n. 127 above), p. 119f.

129 Léon, 'Structures' (see n. 124 above), pp. 415–22 and especially M. Morineau, 'Trois communications au Colloque de Göttingen 2. 1750, 1787: Un changement important des structures de l'exportation française dans le monde saisi d'après les états de la balance du commerce', *Vom Ancien Régime zur Französischen Revolution. Forschungen und Perspektiven*, eds. E. Hinrichs et al., Veröffentlichungen des Max-Planck-Instituts für Geschichte, vol. 55 (Göttingen, 1978), pp. 395–412; this work is the first to contain figures for 1750.

130 F. Dornic, *L'industrie textile dans le Maine et ses débouchés internationaux (1650–1815)* (Le Mans, 1955), pp. 79–90; Tanguy, 'Production' (see n. 117 above), pp. 109–11 and 119–23; V. Prévot, 'Une grande industrie d'exportation. L'industrie linière dans le Nord de la France, sous l'Ancien Régime', *Revue du Nord*, 39 (1957), 205–26, esp. 225; Sabbe, *Vlasnijverheid* (see n. 60 above), pp. 375–400; Sabbe, *Histoire de l'industrie linière en Belgique*, Collection Nationale, vol. 6, 67 (Brussels, 1945), pp. 41–49; E. Schmitz, *Leinengewerbe und Leinenhandel in Nordwestdeutschland (1650–1850)*, Schriften zur rheinisch-westfälischen Wirtschaftsgeschichte, vol. 15 (Cologne, 1967), pp. 81–95; Aubin und Kunze, *Leinenerzeugung* (see n. 42 above), pp. 248–52; v. Westerhagen, 'Leinwandmanufaktur' (see n. 88 above), pp. 41ff., Kisch, 'Textile Industries' (see n. 42 above), pp. 543–6 and below, pp. 179–82; Kühn, *Leinwand- und Schleierhandel* (see n. 86 above), pp. 43–56; M. Kossok, 'Die Bedeutung des spanischamerikanischen Kolonialmarktes für den preussischen Leinwandhandel am Ausgang des 18. und zu Beginn des 19. Jahrhunderts', *Hansische Studien H. Sproemberg zum 70. Geburtstag*, Forschungen zur mittelalterlichen Geschichte, vol. 8 (Berlin, 1961), pp. 210–18; O. Dascher, *Das Textilgewerbe in Hessen-Kassel vom 16. bis 19. Jahrhundert*, Veröffentlichungen der historischen Kommission für Hessen und Waldeck, vol. 28 (Marburg, 1968), pp. 12 and 143–56.

131 C. L. F. Hüpeden, 'Vom Linnenhandel in Hessen', in A. L. Schlözer, *Staats-Anzeigen*, 41 (1787), pp. 3–12, here 3, partially cited by Dascher, *Textilgewerbe* (see n. 130 above), p. 1.

132 Standard deviation: 7.1, calculated according to: 'Nachweisung, wie viel leinene Ware von 1748/9 bis 1789/90 in Schlesien, und zwar in beiden Cammer-Departments ausser Landes versandt worden', *Schlesische Provinzialblätter*, 31 (1800), 9–12, rpt. with small errors and a minor disarrangement in the production figures after the years 1783/84 in: A. Zimmermann, *Blüthe und Verfall des Leinengewerbes in Schlesien. Gewerbe- und Handelspolitik dreier Jahrhunderte*, 2nd ed. (Oldenburg, 1892), pp. 460–7 and supplement 5, the figures for 1772/73, 1783/84 and 1785/86 are missing; in explanation of this table: H. Fechner, 'Friedrich's des Grossen und seiner beiden Nachfolger Garnhandelspolitik in Schlesien 1741–1806', part 2, *Zs. des Vereins für Geschichte und Altertum Schlesiens*, 36 (1902), 318–64, esp. 357, cit. 1.

133 Tanguy, 'Production' (see n. 117 above), pp. 119–25 and 139f. table 2. On the average, between 1746 and 1789 (with the exception of the years 1748, 1759, 1781–8, for which the figures are missing), 89.9% of the 'bretañas' which were exported from Saint-Malo, Morlaix and Saint-Brieuc went to Spain, and from there most of them probably made their way to Spanish America; 4.5% went to Portugal, 0.9% to the French West Indian Islands, and 4.6% to northern and north-western Europe. 80–90% of the entire export of 'bretañas' was shipped out via Saint-Malo, Morlaix, and Saint-Brieuc, the rest via Nantes. Apparently, very few of them were sold in France.

134 Deane and Cole, *Growth* (see n. 104 above), p. 42; Ph. Deane, 'The Output of the British Woollen Industry in the Eighteenth Century', *Journ. Econ. Hist.*, 17 (1957), 207–23, esp. 220f.; R. G. Wilson, *Gentlemen Merchants. The Merchant Community in Leeds, 1700–1830* (Manchester, 1971), pp. 42f.; C. Gill, *The Rise of the Irish Linen Industry* (Oxford, 1925), p. 161;]. Purš, 'Struktur und Dynamik der industriellen Entwicklung in Böhmen im letzten Viertel des 18. Jahrhunderts', *Jb. Wirtsch. G.* (1965), part 1, pp. 166–96 and part 2, pp. 103–24 and Supplement, esp. Suppl. Tables 13, 41 and 42.

135 In recent years, the concept of 'structural heterogeneity' has largely replaced the concept of a 'dual economy'; see especially J. H. Boeke, *Economics and Economic Policy of Dual Societies as exemplified by Indonesia* (Haarlem, 1953). While the concept of the 'dual economy' separated sharply between different sectors, the concept of 'structural heterogeneity' highlights their dynamic interrelationship. See among others A. Cordova, *Strukturelle Heterogenität und wirtschaftliches Wachstum. Drei Studien über Lateinamerika*, Edition Suhrkamp, vol. 602 (Frankfurt, 1973) and Senghaas, 'Elemente' (see n. 113 above), pp. 22–4.

136 A. Quijano Obregón, 'The Marginal Pole of the Economy and the Marginalised Labour Force', *Economy and Society*, 3 (1974), 393–428.

Notes to Chapter 2

1 Discussion of peasant production, reproduction and life-styles, and of how these relate to household and family in peasant 'part-societies' (A. L. Kroeber) in their relationships of dependence with government, economy and society at large has received fresh impetus from the research of anthropologists, agrarian sociologists, and economists. Cf. Th. Shanin, 'The Nature and Logic of the Peasant Economy', *Journal of Peasant Studies*, 1 (1973–4), 65–80, 186–206, esp. 67ff.; Th. Shanin, ed., *Peasants and Peasant Societies* (London, 1971), pp. 11–19; E. R. Wolf, *Peasants* (Englewood Cliffs, N. J., 1966), pp. 2–17; H. Mendras, *Sociétés Paysannes. Eléments pour une théorie de la Paysannerie* (Paris, 1976); J. D. Powell, 'On Defining Peasants and Peasant Society', *Peasant Studies Newsletter*, 1 (1972), 94–99 and the discussion pp. 156–62; Cl. Geertz, 'Studies in Peasant Life: Community and Society', *Biennial Review of Anthropology 1961*, ed. B. Siegel (Stanford, Calif., 1962), pp. 1–41; G. Dalton, ed., *Tribal and Peasant Economies. Readings in Economic Anthropology* (Garden City, 1967); G. Dalton, 'Peasantries in Anthropology and History', *Current Anthropology*, 13 (1972), 385–407; J. M. Potter, M. N. Diaz, and G. M. Foster, eds., *Peasant Society. A Reader* (Boston, Mass., 1967); R. Redfield, *Peasant Society and Culture. An Anthropological Approach to Civilization* (Chicago, 1967); B. Galeski, *Basic Concepts of Rural Sociology* (Manchester, 1972). The questions, models, and typologies, which were developed during this discussion, primarily grew out of an interest in non-European societies and cannot simply be transformed into 'historical categories' to be applied to European societies; see R. Hilton, 'Medieval Peasants – Any Lessons?' *Journal of Peasant Studies*, 1 (1973–4), 207–19 and E. P. Thompson, 'Anthropology and the Discipline of the Historical Context', *Midland History* (Spring, 1972), 41–55. Nevertheless, when these models and typologies are used thoughtfully and – if necessary – are modified, they open new perspectives for historical research; cf. the exemplary studies by J. W. Cole and E. R. Wolf, *The Hidden Frontier. Ecology and Ethnicity in an Alpine Valley* (New York, 1974); Th. Shanin, *The Awkward Class. Political Sociology of the Peasantry in a Developing Society. Russia 1910–1925* (Oxford, 1972); H. Wunder, 'Zur Mentalität aufständischer Bauern. Möglichkeiten der Zusammenarbeit von Geschichtswissenschaft und Anthropologie, dargestellt am Beispiel des samländischen Bauernaufstandes von 1525', *Der Deutsche Bauernkrieg*, ed. H. U. Wehler, Geschichte und Gesellschaft, Sonderheft 1 (Göttingen, 1975), pp. 9–37 and E. Le Roy Ladurie, *Montaillou* (New York, 1978). The close connection between theoretical conceptualization and practical research promises to open new approaches toward a re-interpretation of European development. These are likely to stand outside the biased and often sterile analytical categories which underlie the debate about modernization and industrialization theories, and they may inject new vitality – from below so-to-speak – into the older debate of Marxist development theorists which focuses on the transition from feudalism to capitalism. It could be particularly fruitful to base these new approaches on the investigation of peasant society and peasant economy, because these concepts do not start from the assumption that European development necessarily had to have its goal (or *terminus ad quem*) in industrial capitalism and do not define the origin (or *terminus a quo*) accordingly. Instead the new approaches take into consideration the conscious alternative attempts of today's developing countries to achieve their own 'Great Transformation' (K. Polyani) independent from the Euro-American model. Daniel Thorner's appeal of 1962 remains valid: 'The time has arrived to treat European experience in categories derived from world history, rather than to squeeze world history into Western European categories. D. Thorner, 'Peasant Economy as a Category in Economic History', *Deuxième conférence internationale d'histoire économique. Aix-en-Provence, 1962*, Congrès et Colloques, vol. 8 (Paris, 1962), pp. 287–300, esp. 300.

2 O. Brunner, 'Das "ganze Haus" und die alteuropäische "Ökonomik"' (1950), in O. Brunner, *Neue Wege der Verfassungs- und Sozialgeschichte*, 2nd ed. (Göttingen, 1968), pp. 103–27, esp. 107ff.

3 Th. Shanin, 'Peasantry. Delineation of a Sociological Concept and a Field of Study',*European Journal of Sociology*, 12 (1971), 189–300, esp. 296.

4 Wolf, *Peasants* (see n. 1 above), p. 3.

5 Redfield, *Peasant Society* (see n. 1 above), p. 28.

6 A. Kroeber, *Anthropology* (New York, 1948), p. 284; concerning the concept of peasant 'part-societies' cf. Powell, 'On Defining Peasants' (see n. 1 above), pp. 94ff.; also Wunder, 'Zur Mentalität' (n. 1), pp. 16f.

7 J. Goody, 'Strategies of Heirship', *Comparative Studies in Society and History*, 15 (1973), 3–20; Goody, 'Inheritance, Property and Marriage in Africa and Eurasia', *Sociology*, 3 (1969), 55–76; Goody, 'Inheritance, Property and Women: Some Comparative Considerations', *Family and Inheritance*, eds. J. Goody, E. P. Thompson, and J. Thirsk (Cambridge, 1976), pp. 10–36; D. Sabean, 'Notes on Kinship Behaviour and Property in Rural Western Europe before 1800', *Family and Inheritance*, 96–111; L. Berkner and Fr. Mendels, 'Inheritance Systems, Family Structure and Demographic Patterns in Western Europe 1700–1900', *Historical Studies of Changing Fertility*, ed. Ch. Tilly (Princeton, N. J., 1978), pp. 209–25; for a masterly anthropological case-study of the contrast between peasant inheritance strategies on one side and the official inheritance customs as well as government attempts at regulation, on the other, in a present-day enclave of traditional peasant family economies (South Tyrol), see Cole and Wolf, *Hidden Frontier* (see n. 1 above), pp. 175–205; for the function of marriage circles among peasant proprietors see M. Ségalen, *Nuptialité et alliances. Le choix du conjoint dans une commune de l'Eure* (Paris, 1972), pp. 99ff.; for the area of east European *Gutsherrschaft* cf. the interesting case studies: A. Plakans, 'Seigneurial Authority and Peasant Family Life: The Baltic Area in the Eighteenth Century', *Journal of Interdisciplinary History*, 5 (1974/75), 629–54, esp. 651ff. and A. Plakans, 'Peasant Farmsteads and Households in the Baltic Litoral, 1797', *Comparative Studies in Society and History*, 17 (1975), 2–35; W. Kula explains marriage and inheritance practices entirely on the basis of seigneurial authority and control: W. Kula, 'La seigneurie et la famille paysanne en Pologne au XVIIIᵉ siècle', *Famille et société*, special issue of *Annales E.S.C.*, 27, (1972), 949–58; concerning the role which the village community played in determining the divergent development of the relationship between peasant and lord in western Europe as opposed to east of the Elbe, see R. Brenner, 'Agrarian Class Structure and Economic Development in Pre-industrial Europe', *Past and Present*, 70 (1976), 30–75, esp. pp. 56ff., but see also the criticism of Brenner's too narrow approach in n. 48 of the Introduction above.

8 P. Laslett, *The World We Have Lost*, 2nd ed. (London, 1971), p. 20.

9 See pp. 18ff., 96ff.

10 Cf. the literature cited above, pp. 18ff. and 96ff. esp. A. Kahan, 'The Infringement of the Market upon the Serf-Economy in Eastern Europe', *Peasant Studies Newsletter*, 3(1974), 7–13; G. Heitz, *Ländliche Leinenproduktion in Sachsen*, Deutsche Akademie der Wissenschaften. Schriften des Instituts für Geschichte. Reihe 2: Landesgeschichte, vol. 4 (Berlin, 1961), pp. 43–57, 70ff., 112ff.; G. Bois, *Crise du Féodalisme. Economie rurale et démographie en Normandie orientale au début du XIVᵉ siècle*, Cahiers de la fondation nationale des Sciences politiques, vol. 202 (Paris, 1976), pp. 339ff., 346.

11 Shanin, 'Nature' (see n. 1 above), pp. 67ff.; K. Bücher, *Die Entstehung der Volkswirtschaft*, vol. 1 (Tübingen, 1893), pp. 15ff.; contrary to what is generally assumed, Bücher's typology does not refer to a completely autarchic form of domestic economy, but claims to apply particularly to peasant households under conditions of 'limited exchange'. See Bücher, *Volkswirtschaft*, pp. 37ff.

12 P. Bohannan and G. Dalton, 'Introduction', *Markets in Africa*, eds. P. Bohannan and G. Dalton (Evanston, Ill., 1962), pp. 2ff., esp. 7ff.; cf. G. Dalton, 'Theoretical Issues in Economic Anthropology', *Current Anthropology*, 10 (1969), 63–80; Shanin, 'Nature' (see n. 1 above), pp. 73ff.

13 Cf. the general perspectives discussed in connection with the present developments in the peripheral societies of Africa in the important work Cl. Meillassoux, *Femmes, greniers et capitaux* (Paris, 1975), pp. 7ff., 14ff., esp. 139ff., 209ff. (English Translation *Maidens, Meal and Money* (Cambridge, 1981), pp. xijj., 3jj., 91jj., 138jj.)

14 The determinants which underlie the familial mode of production as analysed on the following pages are based on A. V. Chayanov, *On the Theory of the Peasant Economy*, ed. by D. Thorner, B. Kerblay and R. E. F. Smith (Homewood, Ill., 1966), pp. 29–269. Chayanov's ideas rest on empirical investigations of the peasant economy in Russia before 1914. He hoped that his concepts would lead to a comprehensive theory of pre-capitalist peasant economies which would include crafts and rural industries as well (cf. Chayanov, 'Peasant Farm Organization; in: A. V. Chayanov, *On the Theory of the Peasant Economy*, ed. D. Thorner, B. Kerblay and R. E. F. Smith, pp. 29–269, esp. 110ff.). The comprehensive theoretical perspective of his 'economic paleontology' is visible in A. V. Chayanov, 'On the Theory of Non-capitalist Economic systems', in Chayanov, *The Theory of Peasant Economy*, pp. 1–28, but he does not sufficiently consider the problems of transition from pre-capitalist to capitalist social formations. Concerning Chayanov's approach, cf. the literature under n. 20 below.

15 K. Marx, *Pre-capitalist Economic Formations*, transl. by J. Cohen (London, 1964), p. 79.

16 Cf. the interesting reconstruction in W. Peuckert, *Volkskunde des Proletariats*, vol. 1, *Aufgang der proletarischen Kultur*, Schriften des volkskundlichen Seminars der Pädagogischen Akademie Breslaus, vol. 1 (Frankfurt, 1931), rpt. in Peuckert and E. Fuchs, *Die schlesischen Weber*, vols. 1 and 2 (Darmstadt, 1971), here the 1931 ed., esp. pp. 24ff.: 'The Weaver is a Peasant' (Der Weber ist ein Bauer). In his case study of the Silesian weavers, Peuckert anticipates in a number of respects the later, much more thorough studies of R. Braun (see n. 57 below).

17 In contrast to the basic assumptions of classical political economy, the theory of the family economy assumes that the rules of familial production cannot be explained with reference to the functional interrelationship of the basic categories of commodity price, wage-labour, capital, interest, and ground rent. For the 'family economy without wage-labour' (Chayanov), the capitalist calculation of profitability is irrelevant; Chayanov, *Theory*, pp. 86ff.; Chayanov, 'Non-capitalist Systems' (see n. 14 above), pp. 1ff. This fact must be taken into consideration if one wants to determine the functional role which the family economy played within the relations of production of an entire society; see below pp. 42f.

18 Cf. W. Seccombe, 'The Housewife and her Labour under Capitalism', *New Left Review*, 83 (1974), 3–24, esp. 4ff.; Meillassoux, *Femmes, greniers et capitaux* (see n. 13 above), pp. 8ff., 14ff., 139ff., 150ff., Eng. Tr. pp. xiff., 3ff., 91ff., 99ff.

19 See above, pp. 12ff., 94ff.

20 In general cf. Chayanov, *Theory* (see n. 14 above), pp. 70–89; Chayanov, 'Non-capitalist Systems' (n. 14), pp. 1–28; concerning Chayanov's approach see D. Thorner, 'Chayanov's Concept of Peasant Economy', in Chayanov, *Theory* (n. 14), pp. xi–xxi; for a bibliography see B. Kerblay, 'A. V. Chayanov: Life, Career, Works', in Chayanov, *Theory* (n. 14), pp. xxv–lxxv; an interesting aspect of Chayanov's approach is illuminated by J. R. Millar, 'A Reformulation of A. V. Chayanov's Theory of the Peasant Economy', *Economic Development and Cultural Change*, 18 (1969), 219–29, although this article does not really provide a 'reformulation' of Chayanov's theory; Chayanov's model has been empirically applied and partially reformulated by T. G. Kessinger, 'The Peasant Farm in North India, 1848–1968', *Explorations in Economic History*, 12, No. 3 (1975), 303–31; for a critical examination of Chayanov's categories and statistical results see M. Harrison, 'Chayanov and the Economics of the Russian Peasantry', *Journal of Peasant Studies*, 2 (1975), 389–417; Chayanov's central categories are confirmed for a case analysed by J. H. Boeke, *Economics and Economic Policy of Dual Societies as Exemplified by Indonesia* (Haarlem, 1953), pp. 39–49; Chayanov's approach and his perspective of the family economy have been accepted in an early essay by A. Gerschenkron, 'A. Čajanovs Theorie des landwirtschaftlichen Genossenschaftswesens', *Vierteljahresschrift für Genossenschaftswesen*, 8 (1930–1), 151–66, 238–45; the first German historian who, as far as I know, pointed out the pioneering character of Chayanov's works was O. Brunner, but he did not make intensive use of Chayanov's concept: O. Brunner, *Adeliges Landleben und Europäischer Geist. Leben und Werk Wolf Helmhards von Hohberg 1612–1688* (Salzburg, 1949), p. 359; Brunner, 'Das "ganze Haus"' (see n. 2 above), p. 107; O. Brunner, 'J. J. Bechers Entwurf einer Oeconimia ruralis et domestica', *Sitzungsberichte der Phil. Hist. Klasse der Österreichischen Akademie der Wissenschaften*, vol. 226, 3 (Vienna, 1949), 85–91, esp. 85; M. M. Postan's works appear to be influenced by Chayanov as well; see M. M. Postan and J. Titow, 'Herriots and Prices on Winchester Manors' (1959), now in M. M. Postan, *Essays on Medieval Agriculture and General Problems of the Medieval Economy* (Cambridge, 1973), p. 174, n. 35; but this is the only time that Chayanov is mentioned in Postan's works, and in this instance, Postan misunderstood the German text of Chayanov's essay; this is overlooked in the cautious remarks about the usefulness of Chayanov's approach in R. H. Hilton, *The English Peasantry in the later Middle Ages* (Oxford, 1975), pp. 6f., esp. 6.

21 Chayanov, *Theory* (see n. 14 above).

22 Concerning the structural and functional foundations of the unity of 'income' and 'property and stock' in the 'domestic' and 'family economy', see Bücher, *Entstehung der Volkswirtschaft*, vol. 1 (see n. 11 above) pp. 41f., 79; also Bücher, 'Verbrauch', in *Die Entstehung der Volkswirtschaft*, vol. 2 (Tübingen, 1918), pp. 250ff.

23 Chayanov, *Theory* (see n. 14 above), pp. 98f., 102; cf. also the interesting review of this book by Colin Clark in *Soviet Studies*, 19 (1967–8), pp. 292f.

24 Chayanov as paraphrased by Millar, 'A Reformulation' (see n. 20 above), p. 220.

25 M. Sahlins, *Stone Age Economics* (Chicago, 1972), p. 84.

26 The surplus concept which is used here is described in C. Keyder, 'Surplus', *Journal of Peasant Studies*, 2 (1975), pp. 221–4.

27 Sahlins, *Stone Age Economics* (see n. 25 above), pp. 74–99, here 82–6; cf. K. Polanyi, *The Great Transformation. The Political and Economic Origin of Our Time* (Boston, Mass., 1957), pp. 53ff.

28 Cf. the discussion about modern housework which, admittedly, deals with a different historical context, but is useful here because housework can be considered as a residual element of the family mode of production: Seccombe, 'Housewife and her Labour' (see n. 18 above), pp. 3–24, esp. 8ff.; J. Gardiner, 'Women's Domestic Labour', *New Left Review*, 89 (1975), 47–58, esp. 53ff.; M. Coulson, Br. Magaš, H. Wainwright, 'The Housewife and her Labour under Capitalism. A Critique', *New Left Review*, 89 (1975), 59–71; W. Seccombe, 'Domestic Labour – Reply to Critics', *New Left Review*, 94 (1975), 85–96; cf. also L. Müller, 'Kinderaufzucht im Kapitalismus – wertlose Arbeit; über die Folgen der Nichtbewertung der Arbeit der Mütter für das Bewusstsein der Frauen als Lohnarbeiterinnen', *Probleme des Klassenkampfs*, 22 (1976), 13–65 – the article is interesting and suggests a number of new perspectives, but it gives too little detail when attempting to historically explain the preoccupation of housewives and mothers with the 'use value' as a 'pre-capitalist attitude'; cf. also Meillassoux, *Femmes, greniers et capitaux* (see n. 13 above), pp. 139ff. (Eng. Tr., pp. 91ff.).

29 Sahlins, *Stone Age Economics* (see n. 25 above), p. 82.

30 Chayanov, *Theory* (see n. 14 above), pp. 77–85; cf. Thorner, 'Chayanov's Concept' (see n. 20 above), pp. xv–xviii.

31 Thorner, 'Chayanov's Concept' (see n. 20 above), pp. xv–xviii.

32 Chayanov, *Theory* (see n. 14 above), pp. 53–69.

33 Chayanov, *Theory* (see n. 14 above), pp. 77–81, esp. 80f.

34 Sahlins, *Stone Age Economics* (see n. 25 above), pp. 87–92: 'Chayanov's Rule'.

35 Chayanov, *Theory* (see n. 14 above), pp. 195–223, 231–5.

36 Chayanov, *Theory* (see n. 14 above), Ch. 2: 'Measure of Self-exploitation of the Peasant Family Labor Force. The Concept of Advantage in the Labor Farm', pp. 70–89.

37 See the literature under n. 27, but esp. Meillassoux, *Femmes, grenier et capitaux* (see n. 13 above), pp. 139ff., 150ff., (Eng. Tr. pp. 91ff and 99ff.), and below pp. 50ff.

38 Chayanov, *Theory* (see n. 14 above), p. 88f.

39 Chayanov, *Theory* (see n. 14 above), pp. 79–80, 83–4.

40 Concerning Chayanov's empirical case-studies, see Kerblay, 'A. V. Chayanov' (see n. 20 above), pp. xxxff. and, from a critical point of view: Harrison, 'Chayanov' (n. 20), pp. 396ff.

41 See above, n. 14.

42 Karl Marx, *Capital*, vol. 3, (London and Moscow, 1971) Ch. 47, sect. 3, p. 795.

43 H. Riepenhausen, *Die Entwicklung der bäuerlichen Kulturlandschaft in Ravensberg* (Diss. mat. nat., Göttingen, 1936)(Münster, 1938), p. 107.

44 Cf. the theoretical model in S. Hymer and St. Resnick, 'A Model of an Agrarian Economy with Non-agricultural Activities', *American Economic Review*, 59 (1969), 493–506; this model has been made concrete by J. de Vries, 'Labour/Leisure Trade-off', *Peasant Studies Newsletter*, 1 (1972) 45–50, esp. 47ff.; de Vries, *The Dutch Rural Economy in the Golden Age 1500–1700* (New Haven, Conn. and London, 1974), pp. 4ff.

45 Cf. below pp. 14ff. concerning the concept of 'discontinuous accumulation', cf. Bois, Crise du Féodalisme (see n. 10 above), pp. 343ff., 361.

46 W. Kula, *Théorie économique du système féodal. Pour un modèle de l'économie polonaise 16ᵉ–18ᵉ siècles*, Civilisations et Sociétés (Paris, 1970), p. 27.

47 Concerning the cumulative effect of short-term harvest fluctuations and long-term conjunctural changes upon marginal peasant producers, see M. Spufford, *Contrasting Communities. English Villagers in the Sixteenth and Seventeenth Centuries* (Cambridge, 1974), pp. 46–7; P. Goubert, 'The French Peasantry in the Seventeenth Century: A Regional Example', *Past and Present*, 10 (1956), 55–77, esp. 71ff.; a satisfactory systematic consideration is still lacking though it has been attempted by W. Abel, *Agrarkrisen und Agrarkonjunktur*, 2nd ed. (Hamburg, 1966), pp. 22ff.; C. E. Labrousse, *Esquisse du mouvement des prix et des revenues en France au xviiiᵉ siècle* (Paris, 1932), vol. 2, pp. 407ff.; C. E. Labrousse, *La crise de l'économie française à la fin de l'ancien régime et au début de la révolution* (Paris, 1944), vol. 1, pp. 173ff.; J. D. Gould, 'Agricultural Fluctuations and the English Economy in the Eighteenth Century', *Journ. Econ. Hist.*, 22 (1962), 313–33, esp. 320ff.

48 Chayanov, *Theory* (n. 14), pp. 107–9.

49 On the categories which determine this relationship, though developed in a different historical context, cf. Seccombe, 'Housewife and her Labour' (see n. 18 above), pp. 3ff.; Müller, 'Kinderaufzucht' (see n. 28 above), pp. 20ff.

50 See Fr. Mendels, 'Agriculture and Peasant Industry' in this volume, part 2, pp. 161–77; cf. W. Achilles, 'Die Bedeutung des Flachsanbaus im südlichen Niedersachsen für Bauern und Angehörige der unterbäuerlichen Schichten im 18. und 19. Jahrhundert', *Agrarisches Nebengewerbe und Formen der Reagrarisierung im Spätmittelalter und 19./20. Jahrhundert*, ed. H. Kellenbenz (Stuttgart, 1975), pp. 109–39, esp. 116ff.; see also below, n. 80.

51 The concept of a dual economy, which was originally developed in order to analyse and explain the simultaneous existence, in colonial societies, of economic growth in a few sectors and general underdevelopment, can be applied to proto-industrialization only with considerable modifications; cf. esp. Boeke, *Economics and Economic Policy* (see n. 20 above); W. A. Lewis, 'Economic Development with Unlimited Supplies of Labour', *Manchester School of Economics and Social Studies*, 2 (1954), 139–91; Lewis, 'Unlimited Labour, Further Notes', *Manchester School*, 26 (1958), 1–32; Lewis, *The Theory of Economic Growth* (London, 1955). In W. A. Lewis's model, in particular, the 'unlimited supplies of labour' of the pre-capitalist sector entirely determine the relationship between the pre-capitalist sector, where the domestic economy predominates, and the sector of commodity exchange, i.e. the sector of capitalist relations of production in the proper sense; the function of the 'dualistic' system lies in the preservation of the separation between both sectors; but in proto-industrialization, the close interconnection between both sectors in the structural nexus of the 'ganzes Haus' appears to be the crucial element in the emergence, growth, stagnation, and final decline of rural industry and its social relations of production. The systematic aspects of this problem are hinted at in Boeke, *Economics and Economic Policy* (see n. 20 above), pp. 10ff., a study which provides much factual detail but is highly questionable in its political conclusions. For a criticism of Lewis's approach see Kula, *Théorie économique* (see n. 46 above), pp. 9f. The following modification of the 'dual-economy' approach was derived from Meillassoux, *Femmes, greniers et capitaux* (see n. 13 above), pp. 139ff., esp. 149 (Eng. tr pp. 91ff., esp 97f.); cf. also E. Laclau, 'Feudalism and Capitalism in Latin America', *New Left Review*, 67 (1971), 19–38; about Boeke's study: W. F. Wertheim, 'Dual Economy', *International Encyclopedia of the Social Sciences*, vol. 4 (New York, 1968), pp. 495–500; Cl. Geertz, *Agricultural Involution. The Process of Ecological Change in Indonesia* (Berkeley and Los Angeles, Calif., 1963), pp. 48–62; H. Myint, 'Dualism and the International Integration of the Underdeveloped Economies', in H. Myint, *Economic Theory and the Underdeveloped Countries* (London and Toronto, 1971), pp. 315–47, esp. 318ff.; based on the Irish experience of the eighteenth and early nineteenth centuries, the hypothesis has been challenged that the separation between the subsistence sector and the commodity producing sector is the constituent feature of the dual economy: R. Lee, 'The Dual Economy in Ireland, 1800–1850', *Historical Studies*, 8 (1969), 191–201.

52 See n. 54 below.

53 Marx, *Capital* 3 (see n. 42 above), Ch. 47, sect. 5, p. 808; cf. K. Bücher, 'Die Hausindustrie auf dem Weihnachtsmarkte', in Bücher, *Die Entstehung der Volkswirtschaft* (see n. 22 above), vol. 2, pp. 147–77, esp. 175f.

54 P. Sweezy's concept of 'pre-capitalist commodity production', which he developed in his debate with M. Dobb, seems more appropriate for this context than Marx's rudimentary and quite abstract model of 'simple commodity production', which assumes the exchange in the market of equivalent units of labour between independent producers. Cf. P. Sweezy, 'A Critique' [of M. Dobb, *Studies in the Development of Capitalism* (London, 1964)]. *The Transition from Feudalism to Capitalism*, ed. R. H. Hilton (London, 1976), pp. 33–56, esp. 49f.; among the critics of Dobb's approach, K. Polyani – based on the concrete analytical investigation of pre-capitalist societies – has been most relevant; K. Polyani, 'Review of: M. Dobb, *Studies in the Development of Capitalism*', *Journ. Econ. Hist.*, 8 (1948), 206f.; Polyani especially criticizes Dobb's 'introduction into precapitalist economy of the concept of a labour market . . . Mr. Dobb is keeping what is bad and discarding what is good in Marxism . . . [he] is drifting away from its fundamental insight into the historically limited nature of market organization'; cf. also R. Hilton, 'Introduction', *The Transition*, ed. R. Hilton, p. 9; the non-applicability of the concept of 'simple commodity production' to the family mode of production is emphasized in Gardiner, 'Women's Domestic Labour' (see n. 28 above), pp. 47ff.

55 Millar, 'A Reformulation' (see n. 20 above), pp. 219ff., esp. 222ff.

56 This concept is explained in H. Myint, 'The "Classic Theory" of International Trade and Underdeveloped Countries', in Myint, *Economic Theory* (see n. 51 above), pp. 118–46; R. Caves, '"Vent for Surplus" Models of Trade and Growth', *Trade, Growth, and the Balance of Payments. Essays in Honour of Gottfried Haberler* (Amsterdam, 1965), pp. 95–115.

57 J. N. v. Schwerz, *Beschreibung der Landwirtschaft in Westfalen und Rheinpreussen* (1816) (Stuttgart, 1836), vol. 1, pp. 129f.; cf. also R. Braun, *Industrialisierung und Volksleben. Die Veränderung der Lebensform in einem ländlichen Industriegebiet vor 1800 (Zürcher Oberland)* (Erlenbach und Zurich 1960 reprinted Göttingen 1979), p. 32.

58 Bücher, 'Hausindustrie auf dem Weihnachtsmarkt' (see n. 53 above), p. 175.

59 Marx, *Capital* 3 (see n. 42 above), Ch. 47, sect. 5 p. 812.

60 Marx, *Capital* 3 (see n. 42 above), Ch. 47, sect. 5, p. 80.

61 W. Troeltsch, *Die Calwer Zeughandlungskompagnie und ihre Arbeiter: Studien zur Gewerbe- und Sozialgeschichte Altwürttembergs* (Jena, 1897), pp. 247–90; K. H. Blaschke, *Bevölkerungsgeschichte von Sachsen bis zur Industriellen Revolution* (Weimar, 1967), p. 195; cf. also Mendels, 'Agriculture and Peasant Industry', below, p. 161.

62 Between 1675 and 1758 (a period of mostly favourable economic conditions) B. Slicher van Bath's study of the Dutch province Overijssel shows that the number of industrial producers grew considerably faster than the number of house-owners; simultaneously, there existed a strong trend toward indebtedness and pauperization: B. Slicher van Bath, 'Historical Demography and the Social and Economic Development of the Netherlands', *Population and Social Change*, eds. D. V. Glass and R. Revelle (London, 1972), pp. 331–46, esp. 343ff.

63 Cf. the significant 'detail' in Peuckert, *Volkskunde* (see n. 16 above), p. 67.

64 Marx, *Capital* 3 (see n. 42 above), Ch. 47, sect. 5 p. 807; concerning the concept of 'functional property' in pre-capitalist modes of production, which is relevant to the proto-industrial context as well and which is founded on the 'privileged position of domestic groups, whatever the coexisting tenures', cf. Sahlins, *Stone Age Economics* (see n. 25 above), pp. 92–4: 'Property'; cf. also Marx, *Pre-capitalist Economic Formations* (see n. 15 above), pp. 67–120.

65 Concerning the structural foundations of this unity in the 'domestic economy', see Bücher, *Entstehung der Volkswirtschaft* (see n. 11 above), vol. 1, pp. 41f., 79; Bücher, 'Verbrauch', in Bücher, *Entstehung der Volkswirtschaft* (see n. 22 above), vol. 2, pp. 250ff.

66 C. H. Bitter, 'Bericht über den Notstand in der Senne zwischen Bielefeld und Paderborn, Regierungsbezirk Minden, und Vorschläge zur Beseitigung desselben, aufgrund örtlicher Untersuchungen dargestellt' (1853), *Jahresbericht des historischen Vereins Ravensberg*, 64 (1965), 1–108, here p. 23.

67 W. H. Crawford, 'Landlord-Tenant Relations in Ulster 1609–1820', *Irish Economic and Social History*, 2 (1975), 5–21, esp. 14ff.; E. Lipson, *The Economic History of England* (London, 1931), vol. 2, p. 80; A. P. Wadsworth and J. de Lacy Mann, *The Cotton Trade and Industrial Lancashire 1600–1780* (Manchester, 1931, rpt. 1965), p. 318; G. Adelmann. 'Strukturelle Krisen im ländlichen Testilgewerbe Nordwestdeutschlands zu Beginn der Industrialisierung', *Wirtschaft and Arbeitsmarkt*, ed. H. Kellenbenz (München, 1974), p. 113; cf. K. A. Wittfogel, *Wirtschaft und Gesellschaft Chinas. Versuch der wissenschaftlichen Analyse einer grossen asiatischen Agrargesellschaft*, Schriften des Vereins für Sozialforschung an der Universität Frankfurt/M., vol. 3 (Leipzig, 1931), p. 667f.; for a theoretical treatment cf. Chayanov, *Theory* (see n. 14 above), pp. 234ff.

68 Charles O'Hara, *Account of Sligo 1760* (1766), cited in W. H. Crawford, 'Economy and Society in South Ulster in the Eighteenth Century', *Clayton Record* (1973), p. 253.

69 Troeltsch, *Calwer Zeughandlungskompagnie* (see n. 61 above), p. 246.

70 Braun, *Industrialisierung* (see n. 57 above), p. 33.

71 L. Schneider, *Der Arbeiterhaushalt im 18. und 19. Jahrhundert. Dargestellt am Beispiel des Heim- und Fabrikarbeiters* (Berlin, 1967), p. 85; Braun, *Industrialisierung* (see n. 57 above), p. 230; cf. the eloquent account given by a contemporary: U. Bräker, 'Lebensgeschichte und natürliche Ebenteuer [sic.] des armen Mannes im Tockenburg' (1789), in U. Bräker, *Werke in einem Bande*, ed. by H. G. Talheim (Berlin and Weimar, 1964), pp. 221, 223. (Eng. tr. U. Bräker, *The Life Story and Real Adventures of the Poor Man of Toggenburg* (Edinburgh, 1970), pp. 162–5).

72 For a systematic explanation see Marx, *Capital* 3 (see n. 42 above), Ch. 47. sect. 5 pp. 808ff.

73 Bücher, 'Hausindustrie auf dem Weihnachtsmarkte' (see n. 53 above), p. 176.

74 Troeltsch, *Calwer Zeughandlungskompagnie* (see n. 61 above), p. 278; for the 'loan system' cf. Peuckert, *Volkskunde* (see n. 16 above), p. 75f.; W. G. Hoskins, *The Midland Peasant* (London, 1965), pp. 273f.; Bücher, 'Hausindustrie auf dem Weihnachtsmarkte' (see n. 53 above), pp. 162f., 170, 176; A. Thun, *Die Industrie am Niederrhein und ihre Arbeiter*, vols. 1 and 2 (Leipzig, 1879), vol. 1, p. 149.

75 See above p. 22f.

76 Troeltsch, *Calwer Zeughandlungskompagnie* (see n. 61 above), pp. 224–33; H. Krüger, *Zur Geschichte der Manufakturen und der Manufakturarbeiter in Preussen* (Berlin, 1958), pp. 308f., 311f.

77 Meillassoux, *Femmes, greniers et capitaux* (see n. 13 above). p. 145. (Eng. tr. p. 95).

78 Marx, *Capital* 3 (see n. 42 above), Ch. 47, sect. 5, p. 805.

79 The 'family income' is not so much defined formally by the manner in which the income is earned, i.e. it is not important whether it consists of the individual wages of man, woman and children or of the joint income of all the family members, which is derived from the sale of a product jointly produced in the household. The concept of 'family income' derives its significance from a custom which originates in the pressure of the social relations of production in rural industry and in the structural unity of production, consumption, and generative reproduction within the family. The returns on the labour of women and children contribute decisively to this marginal 'equilibrium of family earnings' (Wadsworth and Mann).

80 I. Pinchbeck, *Women Workers and the Industrial Revolution 1750–1850*, 2nd ed. (London, 1962), pp. 1f., 122f., 313f.; D. Bythell, *The Handloom Weavers. A Study in the English Cotton Industry during the Industrial Revolution* (Cambridge, 1969), pp. 136f.; E. W. Gilboy, *Wages in Eighteenth Century England* (Cambridge, Mass., 1934), pp. 196ff., 221ff.; Wadsworth and Mann, *Cotton Trade* (see n. 67 above), pp. 403f.; J. D. Chambers, *Nottingham in the Eighteenth Century. A Study of Life and Labour under the Squirarchy*, 2nd ed. (London, 1966), pp. 295f.; cf. also Braun, *Industrialisierung* (see n. 57 above), pp. 81ff. and below p. 61f.

81 This has up to now been a rather neglected problem; concerning the categories under which it might be investigated, cf. also B. Rowthorn, 'Die neoklassische Volkswirtschaftslehre und ihre Kritiker, eine marxistische Beurteilung', *Seminar: Politische Ökonomie. Zur Kritik der herrschenden Nationalökonomie*, ed. W. Vogt (Frankfurt, 1973), pp. 268f.; also W. Sombart, 'Die Arbeitskräfte im Zeitalter des Frühkapitalismus', *Arhiv für Sozialwissenschaft und Sozialpolitik*, 44 (1917/18), 19–51, esp. 19ff.

82 Wadsworth and Mann, *Cotton Trade* (see n. 67 above), pp. 316f.

83 M. Mohl, *Über die Württembergische Gewerbs-Industrie* (Stuttgart, 1828), p. 85.

84 Fr. Engels, 'Preface to the Second German Edition', in Fr. Engels, *The Housing Question* in Karl Marx and Fr. Engels, *Selected Works* (London and Moscow, 1958), vol. 1, p. 553.

85 W. Sombart, *Der moderne Kapitalismus*, 2nd ed. (Munich, 1928), vol. 1, pp. 29ff.

86 Concerning the question of 'women's work', and the exclusion of women and children from guild production, which did not begin until the late Middle Ages, especially in the textile trades, cf. K. Bücher, *Die Frauenfrage im Mittelalter* (Tübingen, 1882), pp. 10–17; R. Wissel, *Des alten Handwerks Recht und Gewohnheit*, vol. 2, ed. by E. Schraepler, 2nd ed., Einzelveröffentlichungen der Historischen Kommission zu Berlin, vol. 7 (Berlin, 1974), pp. 439ff.; Pinchbeck, *Women Workers* (see n. 80 above), pp. 125f.; concerning women's guilds and the activity of masters' widows, cf. also H. Hauser, *Ouvriers du temps passé*, 5th ed. (Paris, 1927), Ch. VIII: 'Le travail des femmes', pp. 141ff.

87 Fr. Place, 'A Letter to Jas. Turner, Cotton Spinner', cited by Pinchbeck, *Women Workers* (see n. 80 above), p. 179, n. 1.

88 A basic work continues to be J. Kulischer, 'La grande industrie aux XVIIe et XVIIIe siècles: France, Allemagne, Russie', *Annales d'histoire économique et sociale*, 3 (1931), 11–46, esp. 25ff.; J. Kulischer, *Allgemeine Wirtschaftsgeschichte des Mittelalters und der Neuzeit* (Munich, 1929; rpt. Darmstadt, 1976), vol. 2, pp. 113ff., esp. 146ff.; but cf. also below pp. 103ff, 137.

89 Marx, *Pre-capitalist Economic Formations* (see n. 15 above), p. 116; for this insight, which was not systematically pursued by Marx, cf. also the further remarks in n. 5 to the Introduction, above.

90 Wittfogel, *Wirtschaft und Gesellschaft Chinas* (see n. 67 above), pp. 669–75, here 670.

91 M. Weber, *The Protestant Ethic and the Spirit of Capitalism*, translated by T. Parsons (New York, 1958), pt. 1, Ch. 2, pp. 47ff.

92 M. Weber's grandfather, on his father's side, Karl August Weber, was a linen-merchant in Bielefeld, the urban centre of the Minden – Ravensberg region of linen production; he was also co-owner of the firm 'Weber, Laer und Niemann', which M. Weber's great-grandfather had founded and which was the leading merchant establishment 'through which Bielefeld linen became famous'; cf. Marianne Weber, *Max Weber: a Biography* (New York and London, 1975), esp. p. 24. Weber's occasional pointed and peculiarly nostalgic remarks about the corresponding characteristics in the mentality of Pre-capitalist producers and the rentier-mentality of the merchant-capitalist putters-out who were anxiously concerned to lead a 'respectable and stately life' (The German word 'Standesgemäss' contains both these aspects) (M. Weber, *Protestant Ethic* [n. 91 above], pp. 65ff.) grew out of his personal experiences in his grandfather's house during the period when the rural industry declined; cf. Marianne Weber, *Max Weber*, p. 25.

93 Weber, *Protestant Ethic* (see n. 91 above), p. 60.

94 Bücher, 'Hausindustrie auf dem Weihnachtsmarkte' (see n. 53 above), p. 176; cf. Thun, *Industrie am Niederrhein* (see n. 74 above), vol. 1, p. 130; Wadsworth and Mann, *Cotton Industry* (see n. 67 above), pp. 404f.; Troeltsch, *Calwer Zeughandlungskompagnie* (see n. 61 above), pp. 319f.

95 Concerning the concept of transitional modes of production, the ideas of P. P. Rey, *Les Alliances des classes* (Paris, 1973) have been developed and specified, and the structural importance of the factor of the family economy taken into account by Meillassoux, *Femmes, greniers et capitaux* (see n. 13 above), pp. 146ff. (Eng. tr. pp. 96ff.); cf. also E. Balibar, 'The Basic Concepts of Historical Materialism', in L. Althusser and E. Balibar, *Reading 'Capital'* (London, 1970), pp. 302ff., but see the qualification in n. 98 below.

96 Marx, *Capital* 3 (see n. 42 above), Ch. 20, pp. 327–8.

97 In general: H. Freudenberger and F. R. Redlich, 'The Industrial Development of Europe: Reality, Symbols, Images', *Kyklos*, 17 (1964), 372–403, here 378: 'what was shifted was the control of the product while that of the process remained in the hands of the producer . . . strategic decision-making as to what to produce shifted to an outsider, while managing and manual labour still remained in the old hands'; concerning the problem of control over the work-process during the beginning stages of industrialization properly speaking, see the important article by G. Stedman-Jones, 'Class Struggle and the Industrial Revolution', *New Left Review*, 90 (1975), 35–69, esp. 63ff.

98 Cf. Balibar, 'Basic Concepts' (see n. 95 above), pp. 212ff., 233ff., 302ff. Balibar's structuralist approach rightly rejects a reified, 'verdinglicht' conception of the 'relations of production' and emphasizes that this contradiction, which is situated within the 'social' relations of production, is important for the relatively autonomous character of the transitional phase to industrial capitalism. He does not manage, however, to discard entirely the orthodox hypotheses centring on 'manufactures'. Much less sophisticated is the conception of P. Q. Hirst and B. Hindess, *Pre-Capitalist Modes of Production* (London, 1975), pp. 260ff., since it schematically assumes a dichotomy between pre-capitalist and capitalist modes of production.

99 Cf. above, p. 68.

100 Cf. below, pp. 136ff.

101 Troeltsch, *Calwer Zeughandlungskompagnie* (see n. 61 above), p. 318.

102 See below, pp. 136f.

103 The following section orginated from a discussion with Peter Laslett and from the author's critical assessment of Laslett's work, esp. P. Laslett, *The World We Have Lost*, 2nd ed. (London, 1971); P. Laslett and R. Wall, eds., *Household and Family in Past Time* (Cambridge, 1972): P. Laslett, 'Introduction: The History of the Family', pp. 7–73; P. Laslett and E. A. Hammel, 'Comparing Household Structure over Time and between Cultures', *Comparative Studies in Society and History*, 16 (1974), 73–109; cf. also my comments in 'Zur strukturellen Funktion von Haushalt und Familie im Übergang von der traditionellen Agrargesellschaft zum industriellen kapitalismus', *Sozialgeschichte der Familie in der Neuzeit Europas. Neue Forschungen*, ed. W. Conze, Industrielle Welt, vol. 21 (Stuttgart, 1976), pp. 254–82, esp. 254ff. Laslett's abstract concept of the structure of household and the family based on co-residence and kinship relations is too 'formal and narrow' (H. Rosenbaum). It is here replaced by a substantive concept of the structure of household and the family which is limited to a specific social group and to a specific historical period, but which regards the structure of household and the family as an element within the functional interrelationships of those 'basic processes' from which structures originate. For the 'ganzes Haus' of the rural industrial producers this interrelationship consists primarily in the specific connection between production and generative reproduction which constitutes itself through the social relations of production in proto-industry as a precondition of the family's survival. For a critical assessment of Laslett's work see: E. P. Thompson (anon.), 'Under the Rooftree', *Times Literary Supplement*, no. 3713 (4 May 1973), 485–7; L. K. Berkner, 'The Use and Misuse of Census Data for the Historical Analysis of Family Structure', *Journal of Interdisciplinary History*, 4 (1975), 721–38; H. Rosenbaum, 'Zur neueren Entwicklung der historischen Familienforschung', *Geschichte und Gesellschaft*, 1 (1975), 210–25; M. Mitterauer, 'Familiengrösse – Familientypen – Familienzyklus. Probleme quantitativer Auswertung von österreichischem Quellenmaterial', *Geschichte und Gesellschaft*, 1 (1975), 226–55; T. K. Hareven, Review of *Household and Family in Past Time*, in *History and Theory*, 14 (1975), 242–51; C. Lasch, 'The Family and History', *The New York Review of Books*, 22 (13 Nov. 1975), 33–8.

104 Among the few quantitative and status-specific investigations of household sizes and family structures for regions and locations of rural industry the following must be mentioned: L. K. Berkner, *Family, Social Structure, and Rural Industry: A Comparative Study of the Waldviertel and the Pays de Caux in the Eighteenth Century* (Ph.D. Harvard University, 1973), pp. 294–346, esp. 307–9 and the table on pp. 310, pp. 329, 347ff.; D. Levine,

Family Formation in an Age of Nascent Capitalism, Studies in Social Discontinuity (New York, 1977), pp. 45ff.; M. Mitterauer, 'Zur Familienstruktur in ländlichen Gebieten Österreichs', *Beiträge zur Bevölkerungs- und Sozialgeschichte Österreichs*, ed. H. Helczmanovski (Vienna, 1973), pp. 168–222, esp. 181, 190ff.; M. Mitterauer, 'Vorindustrielle Familienformen. Zur Funktionsentlastung des "ganzen Hauses" im 17. und 18. Jahrhundert', *Fürst, Bürger, Mensch. Untersuchungen zu politischen und sozio-kulturellen Wandlungsprozessen im vorrevolutionären Europa*, eds. F. Engel-Janosi et al.(Vienna, 1975), pp. 123–85, here 133, 157, 160ff.; also the references in R. Braun's pioneering study *Industrialisierung* (see n. 57 above), pp. 59–89, esp. 89; 155–80, esp. 162ff.

105 Levine, *Family Formation* (see n. 104 above), pp. 49ff.; the same situation is indicated by a comparison of the findings in R. Wall, 'Mean Household-Size in England from Printed Sources', *Household and Family in Past Time*, eds. P. Laslett and R. Wall (Cambridge, 1972), pp. 159–203, where the mean household-sizes for settlements in the heavily proto-industrialized areas of Lancashire (esp. the region around Manchester) are decisively larger than those for agrarian regions: pp. 178f. and 180f.; cf. also E. J. Walter, *Zur Soziologie der alten Eidgenossenschaft. Eine Analyse zur Sozial- und Berufsstruktur von der Reformation bis zur Französischen Revolution* (Berne, 1966), pp. 78–82.

106 Levine, *Family Formation* (see n. 104 above), p. 50.

107 Levine, *Family Formation* (see n. 104 above), pp. 68ff.

108 R. Schofield, 'Age-specific Mobility in an Eighteenth Century Rural English Parish', *Annales de Démographie historique* (1970), 261–74; Levine, *Family Formation* (see n. 104 above), p. 46f.; Berkner, 'Family, Social Structure' (see n. 104 above), pp. 200, 323–47, esp. 331ff.

109 Charles O'Hara, *Account of Sligo 1760* (referring to changes in family structure following the transition of the small and sub-peasant population of north-west Ireland to linen weaving), as quoted by W. H. Crawford, 'Economy and Society in South Ulster in the Eighteenth Century', *Clayton Record* (1973), 241–58, esp. pp. 253–4.

110 Pinchbeck, *Women Workers* (see n. 80 above), pp. 122, 160, 168, 179, 232ff., 272ff.; E. P. Thompson, *The Making of the English Working Class* (Harmondsworth, 1970), pp. 366ff.; Thun, *Die Industrie am Niederrhein* (see n. 74 above), vol. 1, pp. 109, 150; Braun, *Industrialisierung* (see n. 57 above), pp. 24ff., 183, 192ff.

111 See the precise description in Braun, *Industrialisierung* (see n. 57 above), pp. 83ff.; cf. also v. Schwerz, *Beschreibung der Landwirtschaft* (see n. 57 above), vol. 1, p. 111; Pinchbeck, *Women Workers* (see n. 80 above), pp. 273, 278–9.

112 J. Hajnal, 'European Marriage Patterns in Perspective', *Population in History: Essays in Historical Demography*, eds. D. V. Glass and D. E. C. Eversley (London, 1965), pp. 101–46; J. D. Chambers, *Population, Economy and Society in Pre-industrial England* (London, 1972), pp. 34–50; Braun, *Industrialisierung* (see n. 57 above), pp. 60f., 155ff.; G. Mackenroth, *Bevölkerungslehre. Theorie, Soziologie und Statistik der Bevölkerung* (Berlin, 1953), pp. 421ff.

113 Concerning the connection between inheritance, peasant property, and family structure as determined by the developmental cycle of domestic groups, see the exemplary study by L. K. Berkner, 'The Stem Family and the Developmental Cycle of the Peasant Household: An Eighteenth-Century Austrian Example', *American Historical Review*, 77 (1972), 398–417; Mitterauer, 'Zur Familienstruktur' (see n. 104 above), pp. 197ff.; Mitterauer, 'Familiengrösse – Familientypen – Familienzyklus' (see n. 103 above), pp. 243ff.; Mitterauer, 'Vorindustrielle Familienformen' (n. 104), pp. 134ff.; cf. also M. Anderson, *Family Structure in Nineteenth Century Lancashire* (Cambridge, 1971), pp. 79ff.

114 Ch. and R. Tilly, 'Agenda for European Economic History in the 1970s', *Journ. Econ. Hist.*, 31 (1971), 184–98, esp. 189.

115 Berkner, 'Stem Family' (see n. 113 above), pp. 400ff.; Anderson, *Family Structure* (n. 113), pp. 81ff.; Segalen, *Nuptialité* (see n. 7 above), pp. 99ff.

116 The transitional character of the marriage behaviour of rural industrial producers which stands between the behaviour of peasants, determined by material (*sachhaft*) constraints of property relationships, and that of the modern individualistic 'companionate marriage' is rightly stressed by M. Ségalen, *Nuptialité* (see n. 7 above), p. 106; R. Braun puts too much emphasis on 'sublimation' and 'intimization' as characteristics of rural industrial marriage customs: cf. Braun, *Industrialisierung* (see n. 57 above), pp. 64ff.; an even more one-sided interpretation in the direction of a unilinear concept of 'modernization' and 'emancipation' is to be found in E. Shorter, 'Female Emancipation, Birth Control, and Fertility in European History', *American Historical Review*, 78 (1973), 614ff.; E. Shorter, *The Making of the Modern Family* (New York, 1975), pp. 255–68.

117 J. Hirzel, *Rede über den physischen, ökonomischen und sittlich religiösen Zustand der östlichen Berggemeinden des Kantons Zürich, Synodalrede 1816* (Zürich, 1816), p. 16, as quoted by Braun, *Industrialisierung* (see n. 57 above), p. 66.

118 Segalen, *Nuptialité* (see n. 7 above), pp. 75ff.

119 Segalen, *Nuptialité* (see n. 7 above), pp. 99ff.

120 v. Schwerz, *Beschreibung der Landwirtschaft* (see n. 57 above), vol. 1, p. 111.

121 Cf. Levine, *Family Formation* (see n. 104 above), pp. 61ff. Chambers, *Population, Economy and Society* (see n. 112 above), pp. 49f.; J. D. Chambers, *The Vale of Trent 1670–1800: A Regional Study of Economic Change*, Economic History Review, Supplement 3 (Cambridge, 1978), pp. 51–3; Troeltsch, *Calwer Zeughandlungskompagnie* (see n. 61 above), p. 405; Braun, *Industrialisierung* (see n. 57 above), pp. 59–80; see below, pp. 85ff.

122 For a systematic discussion of the relationships between household cycle and family structures see M. Fortes, 'Introduction', *The Development Cycle in Domestic Groups*, ed. J. Goody (Cambridge, 1958), pp. 1–14; the same essay is reprinted as 'The Developmental Cycle in Domestic Groups' in *Kinship*, ed. J. Goody (Harmondsworth, 1971), pp. 85–98; making a critical assessment of Laslett's 'narrow' concept of 'structure', Berkner has applied Fortes's approach to the analysis of peasant households in 'Stem Family' (see n. 113 above), pp. 405ff.; cf. Mitterauer, 'Familiengrösse–Familientypen–Familienzyklus' (see n. 103 above), pp. 243ff.

123 See below, pp. 79ff.

124 Pinchbeck, *Women Workers* (see n. 80 above), p. 179.

125 This aspect has been stressed in the unduly neglected work of S. Coontz, *Population Theories and the Economic Interpretation* (1957), Ch. 7, pp. 145ff.; 'The Evolution in the Economic Function of the Family', esp. pp. 150ff.; cf. J. M. Stycos and R. Weller, 'Female Working Roles and Fertility', *Demography*, 4 (1967), 210–17.

126 'Statement of a Working Man', in *Meliora*, ed. Ingestre (London, 1852), pp. 226f., as quoted by J. Foster, *Class Struggle and the Industrial Revolution. Early Industrial Capitalism in Three English Towns* (London, 1974), p. 94.

127 This is overlooked in K. Hausen, 'Familie als Gegenstand historischer Sozialwissenschaft. Bemerkungen zu einer Forschungsstrategie', *Geschichte und Gesellschaft*, 1 (1975), 171–209, esp. 200f., even though the author correctly assesses the problems with regard to proto-industrial conditions.

128 Thun, *Die Industrie am Niederrhein* (see n. 74 above), vol. 1, p. 150; cf. the interesting statistical information for linen and cotton weavers' families in the Saxon district of Upper Lusatia for the year 1832 in F. Schmidt, *Untersuchungen über Bevölkerung, Arbeitslohn und Pauperism in ihrem gegenseitigen Zusammenhange* (Leipzig, 1936), pp. 296ff., esp. 298f.; Bythell, *Handloom Weavers* (see n. 80 above), p. 136; Pinchbeck, *Women Workers* (n. 80), p. 179.

129 E. R. R. Green, 'The Cotton Handloom Weavers in the North-east of Ireland', *Ulster Journal of Archaeology*, 7 (1944), 30–41, esp. 35; cf. the observations about the age specific participation of women in the industrial production process in Levine, *Family Formation* (see n. 104 above), p. 29; cf. J. Knodel and V. Prachuabmoh, *The Fertility of Thai Women. Results of the First Rural and Urban Rounds of the Longitudinal Study of Social, Demographic and Economic Change in Thailand*, Institute of Population Studies, Chulalongkorn University (Bangkok, 1973), p. 49; S. Bucher, *Bevölkerung und Wirtschaft des Amtes Entlebuch im 18. Jahrhundert* (Luzern, 1974), p. 228 (table), 229.

130 On the conditions in the lower Rhine small metal trades (Remscheid) see Thun, *Die Industrie am Niederrhein* (see n. 74 above), vol. 2, pp. 148ff., 150f.; v. Schwerz, *Beschreibung der Landwirtschaft* (see n. 57 above), vol. 1, pp. 110f. (weavers of linen cloth in the district of Ravensberg). One of the effects which home-industrial production had on the guild-organization of certain trades seems to have been that children increasingly remained in the households of their parents as apprentices, which brought about the gradual disappearance of the traditional tramping habits of the artisan; cf. Troeltsch, *Calwer Zeughandlungskompagnie* (see n. 61 above), pp. 208ff.; Berkner, 'Family, Social Structure' (see n. 104 above), p. 200; because of the specific requirements of the work, extended households with apprentices and servants were especially frequent among those who were employed in the finishing stages of the textile trades.

131 A good example of this household type is provided by the clothiers in the West Riding of Yorkshire, cf. H. Heaton, *The Yorkshire Woollen and Worsted Industries* (Oxford, 1920), pp. 295f.; E. Lipson, *The Economic History of England* (see n. 67 above), vol. 2, pp. 69ff.

132 For this household type as it existed in the linen industry of north-western Germany, where the full peasant household of 'Kolonen' and 'Meier' had male and female servants who wove and span, cf. the description in v. Schwerz, *Beschreibung der Landwirtschaft* (see n. 57 above), vol. 1, p. 128; the peasant 'manufacturers' in the northern-Irish linen industry provide a parallel to the German situation described by v. Schwerz: cf. A. Young, *A Tour of Ireland*, 2 vols. (London, 1780), vol. 1, pp. 149f. For the entrepreneurial functions of this social group cf. C. Gill, *The Rise of the Irish Linen Industry* (Oxford, 1925), pp. 145ff.; for the domestic workshops organized by kulaks cf. Wittfogel, *Wirtschaft und Gesellschaft Chinas* (see n. 67 above), pp. 652f.

133 This 'Heuerlingssystem' was very common in the north-west German linen-producing areas; cf. H. Riepenhausen, 'Die Entwicklung der bäuerlichen Kulturlandschaft' (see n. 43 above), p. 107ff.; H. Wrasman, 'Das Heuerlingswesen im Fürstentum Osnabrück', *Mitteilungen des Vereins für Geschichte und Landeskunde von Osnabrück*, 42 (1919), 53–171, continued in vol. 44 (1921), 1–154; parallels can be found in the linen producing areas of Northern Ireland, cf. Crawford, 'Economy and Society in South Ulster' (see n. 68 above), p. 253, and in the 'masure' system of the Pays de Caux in Upper Normandy as described by Berkner, 'Family, Social Structure' (see n. 104 above), pp. 238ff.

134 For the data-base of the following remarks about the 'extended family', but not necessarily for its interpretation, cf. Levine, *Family Formation* (see n. 104 above), pp. 45ff. and Berkner, 'Family, Social Structure' (see n. 104 above), pp. 294–346.

135 Analytically, it does not make sense to apply the same categories to both forms of 'extended' family in a comparative regional or class-specific investigation or in a study of long-term trends. Such an attempt would falsely reflect a continuity of family structures where basic differences in socio-economic conditions as well as in demographic growth-mechanisms had changed the conditions under which extended family forms emerged and functioned. P. Laslett's concept of structure, which is primarily based on kinship relations and co-residence, supports this 'optical illusion', see above, n. 103; cf. also Mitterauer, 'Familiengrösse – Familientypen – Familienzyklus' (n. 103), pp. 231ff., 241f.

136 See Foster, *Class Struggle* (see n. 126 above), pp. 91ff. and Anderson, *Family Structure* (see n. 113 above), pp. 79ff., 111ff., but esp. the illuminating remarks about the 'half-open family structure' of proletarian households in L. Niethammer in collaboration with F. Brüggemeier, 'Wie wohnten der Arbeiter im Kaiserreich?', *Archiv für Sozialgeschichte*, 16 (1976), 61–134, esp. 122ff.

137 Levine, *Family Formation* (see n. 104 above), pp. 52ff., Berkner, 'Family, Social Structure' (n. 104), pp. 296ff., esp. 298, 307ff.

138 In confirmation of M. Anderson's thesis this has been stressed by Levine, *Family Formation* (see n. 104 above), pp. 53; Anderson, *Family Structure* (see n. 113 above), pp. 50ff. and Foster, *Class Struggle* (see n. 126 above), pp. 91ff.; contrary to Anderson's own assumptions (pp. 166f.) it is possible that his views contradict those of Foster only on the surface. In any case, the contradictions between the two authors seem to be founded not so much on different empirical findings but on divergent interpretive perspectives. Foster places his emphasis on the 'cycle of poverty' and the critical life-phases of the 'host family', and sees its extension beyond the nuclear unit through the formation of complex households and the falling back on the kinship system ('sharing', 'huddling') as an effort to solve the problem of 'secondary poverty' of the working-class family. Anderson, on the other hand, fixes his attention primarily on the co-residing 'guest family' and the moment of its separation from the host family (pp. 48ff.). What seems to be necessary is a combination of both perspectives. It is interesting to note in this connection that a status-specific interpretation of Anderson's own data shows for the group of 'lower factory, labourer, and handloom weaver' (p. 51, table 14) a tendency to extend their families by 'sharing' during exactly those critical phases of the family life-cycle which are characterized by a high ratio of dependent children. This behaviour stands in clear contrast to other social groups, such as 'high factory and artisan'.

139 Braun, *Industrialisierung* (see n. 57 above), p. 83.

140 This is the problematic thesis of the works of N. J. Smelser which is in need of historical critique. Within the straightjacket of structural-functionalist theory ('empty theoretical boxes', 'filling the boxes', 'refilling the boxes') Smelser assumes all too quickly a convergence of family economy and *industrial* capitalism and sees a tendency in this direction already during proto-industrialization: N. J. Smelser, *Social Change and the Industrial Revolution: An Application of Theory to the Lancashire Cotton Industry 1770–1840* (London, 1959), esp. pp. 50–60, 129–43, 158–79, 180–212; N. J. Smelser, 'Sociological History: The Industrial Revolution and the British Working-class Family', *Essays in Social History*, eds. M. W. Flinn and T. C. Smout (Oxford, 1974), pp. 23–38; for a recent critique of Smelser's hypothesis of a successful 'adaptation' by the family workforce to the conditions of factory industry during the initial phase of machine spinning: M. M. Edwards and R. Lloyd-Jones, 'N. J. Smelser and the Cotton Factory Family: A Reassessment', *Textile History and Economic History. Essays in Honour of J. de Lacy Mann*, eds. N. B. Harte and K. G. Ponting (Manchester, 1973), pp. 304–19.

141 T. Parsons, 'The American Family: Its Relations to Personality and the Social Structure', in T. Parsons and R. F. Bales, *Family, Socialization and Interaction Process* (London, 1956), pp. 3–33, esp. 16.

142 T. Parsons, 'Das Problem des Strukturwandels: eine theoretische Skizze', *Theorien des sozialen Wandels*, ed. W. Zapf, 3rd ed. (Köln and Berlin, 1971), pp. 35–74, esp. 48. Parsons here explicitly refers to Smelser's study of the cotton industry.

143 J. P. Süssmilch, *Die göttliche Ordnung in den Veränderungen des menschlichen Geschlechts, aus der Geburt, dem Tode und der Fortpflanzung desselben erwiesen*, 2 vols., 3rd ed. (Berlin, 1765), vol. 2, p. 67.

144 Hausen, 'Familie als Gegenstand historischer Sozialwissenschaft' (see n. 127 above), p. 200.

145 Pinchbeck, *Women Workers* (see n. 80 above), pp. 7ff.; J. Scott and L. Tilly, 'Women's Work and the Family in Nineteenth-Century Europe', *Comparative Studies in Society and History*, 17 (1975), 36–64, esp. 43ff., esp. 44f., n. 26; R. H. Hilton, 'Women in the Village', in R. H. Hilton, *The English Peasantry in the Later Middle Ages* (Oxford, 1975), pp. 95–110; cf. H. Schmidlin, *Arbeit und Stellung der Frau in der Landgutswirtschaft der Hausväter* (Phil. Diss. Jena, 1940, published Heidelberg, 1941) which is confusing on the whole but contains some useful observations and interesting contemporary illustrations.

146 Pinchbeck, *Women Workers* (see n. 80 above), pp. 19ff.; cf. the compelling and precise observations of the Norwegian ethnographer and demographic sociologist Eilert Sundt about the central position of the woman in Norwegian cottager households, as well as the comments of M. Drake about these observations: M. Drake, *Population and Society in Norway 1735–1865* (Cambridge, 1969), pp. 138ff., esp. 143ff.; cf. – despite its lack of sufficient attention to status-specific differences – E. Richards, 'Women in the British Economy since about 1700: An Interpretation', *History*, 59 (1974), pp. 342ff.; on the essential marginal returns from women's work see Pinchbeck, *Women Workers*, pp. 20f.; for a later period cf. the interesting findings of J. Kitteringham, 'Country Work-Girls in Nineteenth-Century England', *Village Life and Labour*, ed. R. Samuel, History Workshop Series (London, 1975), pp. 73–138, esp. 113ff.

147 J. Fitzherbert, *The Book of Husbandry* (1534) ed. by W. W. Skeat (1882), p. 96, as quoted by Lipson, *Economic History* (see n. 67 above), vol. 2, p. 50.

148 On the division of labour in rural industrial households, cf. Pinchbeck, *Women Workers* (see n. 80 above), pp. 111ff. (cotton industry), pp. 129ff. (spinning), pp. 157ff. (weaving), pp. 202ff. (smaller domestic industries) and pp. 270ff. (small metal trades); Lipson, *Economic History* (see n. 67 above), vol. 2, pp. 50f. (wool industry); even in the textile trades the division of labour within the family showed no uniformity; it varied according to the branch of production, its development stage, and its market conditions. It frequently deviated from the 'classical' pattern – described for example in Smelser, *Social Change* (see n. 140 above), pp. 54f., 183 – in which the man wove, the wife span, and the children were occupied with subsidiary tasks such as the preparation of materials for the production process; cf. the variants mentioned in Braun, *Industrialisierung und Volksleben* (see n. 57 above), p. 210; Thun, *Die Industrie am Niederrhein* (see n. 74 above), vol. 1, pp. 108f., 148. An important form of domestic division of labour, resulting from the combination of a partial agrarian subsistence base with industrial production, has been carefully observed by C. H. Bitter: 'When one enters the cottages of rural dwellers who do not hold large plots of land and who must earn their basic subsistence by spinning, one often finds the whole family sitting at the spinning wheel. It is by no means rare that the grandmother, mother, and grandchild are occupied with spinning, while the father and his grown-up son work in the field or do other jobs around the house, such as preparing meals, cleaning turnips, or peeling potatoes – if and as long as they have any. In the weavers' cottages the father is busy preparing the yarn, unless he is out to buy yarn or to sell the linen that the family has produced or to cultivate the plot of land together with his grown-up son. The mother is occupied at the hearth or tends the animals. The older daughters sit at the loom and the younger children who still go to school have to wind yarn onto bobbins in their spare time', C. H. Bitter, *Bericht* (see n. 66 above), pp. 1–108, here 22; cf. the general remarks relevant to this context in Pinchbeck, *Women Workers* (see n. 80 above), p. 159.

149 Wittfogel, *Wirtschaft und Gesellschaft Chinas* (see n. 67 above), p. 656.
150 Pinchbeck, *Women Workers* (see n. 80 above), pp. 270ff.; W. H. B. Court, *The Rise of the Midland Industries 1600–1838*, 2nd ed. (Oxford, 1953), pp. 100f.; M. B. Rowlands, *Masters and Men in the West Midland Metalware Trades Before the Industrial Revolution* (Manchester, 1975), pp. 160f.
151 C. L. Ziegler, 'Nachricht von der Verfertigung der Spitzen im Erzgebirge', *Beyträge zur Ökonomie, Technologie, Polizey und Cameralwissenschaft*, ed. Joh. Beckmann (Göttingen, 1779), vol. 1, pp. 108–14, esp. 110f.; Scott and Tilly, 'Women's work' (see n. 145 above), p. 47; Thun, *Industrie am Niederrhein* (see n. 74 above), vol. 2, p. 154 (small-metalware trades of the Lower Rhine area).
152 Ziegler, 'Nachricht' (see n. 151 above) contains numerous pieces of evidence, esp. pp. 108f. and 114.
153 Süssmilch, *Die göttliche Ordnung* (1765) (see n. 143 above), vol. 2, p. 47 (cotton spinners); Bitter, *Bericht* (see n. 66 above), p. 27 (men as spinners of course yarn and women as spinners of fine yarn); v. Schwerz, *Beschreibung der Landwirtschaft* (see n. 57 above), vol. 1, p. 128f. (manufacture of a coarse quality of linen, called 'Löwendlinnen', under conditions of part-time agrarian employment of males, taking place in the Tecklenburg region of Westphalia: weaving here is considered as the appropriate occupation for women. Spinning, on the other hand, is carried out by men as well, and it seems strange that they spin the finest yarn while women and children spin the coarser qualities [p. 128f.]).
154 Braun, *Industrialisierung* (see n. 57 above), pp. 97, 175, 195f.; E. Sax, *Die Thüringische Hausindustrie*, 3 vols. (Jena, 1888), vol. 3, p. 58, n. 2.
155 V. Schwerz, *Beschreibung der Landwirtschaft* (see n. 57 above), vol. 1, p. 111.
156 See also below, p. 65f.
157 This assumption is made by Smelser, *Social Change* (see n. 140), pp. 161f., 342ff., esp. 345.
158 Cf. Anon. (G. W. Chr. Consbruch), *Medicinische Ephemeriden, nebst einer medicinischen Topographie der Grafschaft Ravensberg* (Chemnitz, 1793), pp. 44f.; Pinchbeck, *Women Workers* (see n. 80 above), p. 237; interesting source material is quoted in H. Strehler, *Beiträge zur Kulturgeschichte der Zürcher Landschaft* (Phil. Diss., Zürich, 1934), p. 37: 'women and men . . . frequently smoke on their way to church and the sacrilegious sort of people even do so during the sermon'.
159 Cf. E. P. Thompson, 'The Moral Economy of the English Crowd in the Eighteenth Century' *Past and Present*, 50 (1971), 76–136, esp. 115ff.; on the question in which social groups these protests originate see *ibid.*, p. 108 and in particular E. P. Thompson's review of J. W. Shelton, *English Hunger and Industrial Disorders: A Study of Regional Conflict during the First Decades of George III's Reign* (London, 1973) in *Econ. Hist. Rev.*, 27 (1974), 480–4, esp. 483.
160 R. Southey, *Letters from England* (1807) (London, 1814), vol. 2, p. 47, as quoted by Thompson, 'Moral Economy' (see n. 159 above), p. 116.
161 Braun, *Industrialisierung* (see n. 57 above), p. 68.
162 E. Shorter has repeatedly tried to explain the changes, which appeared since the end of the eighteenth century, in terms of the sexual behaviour as well as the family life of the lower classes; see e.g. Shorter, *The Making of the Modern Family* (see n. 116 above), pp. 225ff., Shorter, 'Female Emancipation' (n. 116), pp. 614ff. The central weakness of their approach lies in the fact that he tries to trace these changes back, in a rather abstract way, to the emergence of a capitalist market and the resulting 'market mentality', which affected lower-class behaviour, as well as to the 'liberating' influence which the new wage-labour relations exercised on women. Shorter does not sufficiently locate these changes in the concrete conditions of production and reproduction,

which – even under the impact of emerging capitalist markets – continued to be determined by the family mode of production. These conditions exerted their formative influence not only amongst the 'rural artisans' but also amongst the industrial working class until well into the nineteenth and twentieth centuries. Cf. the interesting remarks by Tilly and Scott, 'Women's Work' (see n. 145 above), pp. 55ff.

163 J. Schulthess, *Beherzigung des vor der Zürcher Synode gehaltenen Vortrags* (Zürich, 1818), p. 54, as quoted in Braun, *Industrialisierung* (see n. 57 above), p. 131.

164 Braun, *Industrialisierung* (see n. 57 above), pp. 68ff., 119ff., esp. 123.

165 J. M. Schwager, 'Über den Ravensberger Bauer', *Westfälisches Magazin zur Geographie, Historie und Statistik*, 2 (1786), no. 5, 49–74, esp. 56f.; cf. Anon. (Consbruch), *Medicinische Ephemeriden* (see n. 158 above), pp. 44f.; Braun, *Industrialisierung* (see n. 57 above), pp. 65ff.

166 Schwager, 'Über den Ravensberger Bauer' (see n. 165 above), pp. 56f.

167 The article 'Dürftigkeit' in G. H. Zincke, *Deutsches Real-, Manufaktur- und Handwerkslexikon*, vol. 1 (only A – F appeared) (Leipzig, 1745), p. 578. According to his 'Preface', Zincke's information is based on 'observations which I made over the course of many years in my intercourse with merchant-manufacturers and workers and which I wrote down . . . [and in addition] on renewed research and conversations with merchants, manufacturers, and workers'. Cf. R. Engelsing, 'Probleme der Lebenshaltung in Deutschland im 18. und 19. Jahrhundert', in R. Engelsing, *Zur Sozialgeschichte deutscher Mittel- und Unterschichten* (Göttingen, 1973), pp. 11–25, esp. 13, who attributes the passage quoted above to the later J. G. Krünitz, *Ökonomische Enzyklopädie*, vol. 2 (1773), p. 788; cf. for the concept of 'Dürftigkeit' (indigence) also G. H. Zincke, *Abhandlung von der Wirtschaftskunst der Armen und Dürftigen, sammt denen allgemeinen Regeln ihrer Wirtschaft* (Düsseldorf, 1759), pp. 14ff.

168 Cf. the important article by Engelsing, 'Probleme der Lebenshaltung' (see n. 167 above), p. 11, although questions concerning rural industry are referred to only in passing. Despite Engelsing's justified critique of the narrow perspective with which consumer-habits have been studied in the past, he does not give enough consideration to the socio-cultural determinants which shaped the way of life of the lower classes; he puts too much emphasis on their imitation of the consumption-patterns of the nobility and on the worker's striving for a bourgeois life-style; Engelsing, p. 21.

169 Cf. E. S. Furniss, *The Position of the Labourer in a System of Nationalism. A Study in the Labour Theories of the Later English Mercantilists* (Boston, Mass., 1920; rpt. New York, 1965), esp. pp. 117ff.; Sombart, 'Arbeiterverhältnisse' (see n. 81 above), pp. 19–51, esp. 26ff.; Braun, *Industrialisierung* (see n. 57 above), pp. 181ff.

170 For an evaluation of this criticism see D. C. Coleman, 'Labour in the English Economy of the Seventeenth Century', *Econ. Hist. Rev.*, 8 (1956), 280–95; Furniss, *Position* (see n. 169 above), pp. 230ff.; Braun, *Industrialisierung* (see n. 57 above), pp. 213ff.

171 G. Jars, *Metallurgische Reisen zur Untersuchung der vornehmsten Stahl-, Blech- und Steinkohlenwerke in Deutschland, Schweden* [. . .] *vom Jahr 1759 bis 1769*, 4 vols. (Berlin, 1777–85), esp. vol. 4, p. 135.

172 V. Schwerz, *Beschreibung der Landwirtschaft* (see n. 57 above), vol. 1, p. 78.

173 Weber, *The Protestant Ethic* (see n. 91 above), p. 60.

174 This conception of 'everyday life' as the sphere which encompasses the economic and socio-cultural 'reproduction' of social life, is treated in H. Lefèbvre, *Kritik des Alltagslebens* (München, 1974), vol. 1, pp. 37ff., 203ff.; for the basic categories of this concept, cf. the interesting study by Th. Kleinspehn, *Der Verdrängte Alltag. Henri Lefèbvres marxistische Kritik des Alltagslebens* (Giessen, 1975), pp. 67ff.

175 Zincke, 'Dürftigkeit' (see n. 167 above), p. 587.

176 Coleman, 'Labour' (see n. 170 above), p. 290.

177 Thompson, 'Moral Economy' (see n. 159 above), pp. 76–136; Thompson, however, does not deal with the ways in which the dynamic of the family economy influences that of the moral economy; he emphasizes instead the moral economy's origin in a communal way of life and in the symbiotic relationship which obtains between the social patriarchalism and 'welfare police' of the nobility and gentry and the traditional 'consumer conciousness'.

178 Wadsworth and Mann, *Cotton Trade* (see n. 67 above), p. 387; cf. Sombart, 'Arbeiterverhältnisse' (see n. 81 above), pp. 27 and 28; Braun, *Industrialisierung* (see n. 57 above), pp. 175, 237; cf. also O. Rühle, *Illustrierte Kultur- und Sittengeschichte des Proletariats* (Berlin, 1930), pp. 300f.

179 J. Beckmann, *Anweisung die Rechnungen kleiner Haushalte zu führen. Für Anfänger aufgesetzt*, 2nd ed. (Göttingen, 1800), p. 3.

180 J. A. Günther, *Versuch einer vollständigen Untersuchung über Wucher und Wuchergestze (und über die Mittel, dem Wucher ohne Strafgesetze Einhalt zu thun; in politischer, justizmässiger und mercantilischer Rücksicht)* - only vol. 1 appeared (Hamburg, 1790), p. 162.

181 F. Galiani, 'Dialogues sur le commerce des blés' (1770), *Mélange d'Economie politique*, vol. 2, ed. M. de Molinari (Paris, 1848), p. 22.

182 Anonymous, 'Remarks upon the Serious Dissuasive from an Intended Subscription for continuing the Races' (1733), cit. in Wadsworth and Mann, *Cotton Trade* (see n. 67 above), p. 392, n. 1.

183 In general: R. W. Malcolmson, *Popular Recreations in English Society 1700–1850* (Cambridge, 1974), where explicit references to a proto-industrial context are made on pp. 15, 29, 49, 52, 81, 84 and elsewhere; Thompson, *Making of the English Working Class* (see n. 110 above), pp. 441ff.; Wadsworth and Mann, *Cotton Trade* (see n. 67 above), pp. 384ff; the classic source for a weaving village in Lancashire is S. Bamford, *Passages in the Life of a Radical* and *Early Days*, ed. by H. Dunckley, 2 vols. (London, 1893), Ch. 1, pp. 14–16; Braun, *Industrialisierung* (see n. 57 above), pp. 90ff.; cf. also the evidence in Sombart, 'Arbeiterverhältnisse' (see n. 81 above), pp. 26f.

184 E. P. Thompson, 'Time, Work Discipline, and Industrial Capitalism', *Past and Present*, 38 (1967), 56–97, esp. 70ff.; Thun, *Industrie am Niederrhein* (see n. 74 above), vol. 1, p. 150. Here are two accounts from periods of favourable economic conditions: in the weaver's town of Paisley, near Glasgow, at the end of the eighteenth century, everyday work was stopped upon the arrival of the newspapers from London; the papers were read jointly and the news discussed in the streets: T. C. Smout, *A History of the Scottish People* (London, 1969), p. 423. Arthur Young made similar observations about the northern-Irish linen weavers in the second half of the eighteenth century: 'As to health, they rarely change their possession on account of their sedentary life; they take exercise of a different sort; keeping packs of hounds, every man one, and joining hunt hares; a pack of hounds is never heard, but all the weavers leave their looms, and away they go after them by the hundreds. This much amazed me, but I was assured it was very common'; Young, *Tour of Ireland* (see n. 132 above), vol. 1, p. 141.

185 Thompson, 'Moral Economy' (see n. 159 above), p. 135; E. P. Thompson, 'Patrician Society, Plebeian Culture', *Journal of Social History*, 7 (1974), 382–405, esp. 391f.; cf. also Braun, *Industrialisierung* (see n. 57 above), pp. 117f.

186 Thompson, 'Time' (see n. 183 above), pp. 72f.; Thun, *Industrie am Niederrhein* (see n. 74 above), vol. 1, p. 150; Braun, *Industrialisierung* (see n. 57 above), pp. 100, 118.

187 Malcolmson, *Popular Recreations* (see n. 183 above), p. 15.

188 Concerning the concept of plebeian culture and its forms of articulation, cf. Thompson, 'Patrician Society' (see n. 184 above), pp. 390ff.

189 Cf. Braun, *Industrialisierung* (see n. 57 above), pp. 117ff.; Thompson, *Making of the*

English Working Class (see n. 110 above), pp. 441ff.; Thompson, 'Patrician Society' (see n. 184 above), pp. 390ff.; generally: Malcolmson, *Popular Recreations* (see n. 183 above), p. 15ff., 52ff.

190 Concerning drinking-habits cf. Bamford, *Passages* (see n. 183 above), vol. 1, pp. 127, 135, 136; E. Strübin, *Baselbieter Volksleben*, 2nd ed. (Basel, 1967), p. 93; Malcolmson, *Popular Recreations* (see n. 183 above), pp. 76f.

191 Wadsworth and Mann, *Cotton Trade* (see n. 67 above), p. 391; concerning the social function, see the interesting evidence in Malcolmson, *Popular Recreations* (see n. 183 above), p. 49 for the weaving town of Halifax; an exemplary analysis of a Third World society: C. Geertz, 'Deep-Play: Notes on the Balinese Cock-Fight', in C. Geertz, *The Interpretation of Cultures. Selected Essays* (New York, 1974), pp. 412–53.

192 Concerning the logic of socio-cultural reproduction and its forms of articulation, see C. Geertz, 'Thick Description: Toward an Interpretative Theory of Culture', in C. Geertz, *The Interpretation of Cultures* (see n. 190 above), pp. 3–30; Geertz, 'Ideology as a Cultural System', in Geertz, *The Interpretation of Cultures* (n. 190), pp. 193–233, esp. 208ff.; concerning the neglect, in Geertz's concept of culture, of the structural significance of socio-economic factors, see M. Douglas, 'The Self-Completing Animal', *The Times Literary Supplement*, 3830, 8 August 1975, p. 886f.

193 As examples, see the evidence in Bamford, *Passages* (see n. 183 above), vol. 1, pp. 119ff., 130ff.; cf. Malcolmson, *Popular Recreations* (see n. 183 above), pp. 75ff.; Lefèbvre, *Kritik des Alltagslebens* (see n. 174 above), vol. 1, pp. 204f.

194 There is no adequate translation for the German word 'Offentlichkeit'. In ordinary English language-usage the equivalent word 'public' functions primarily as an adjective and needs some noun, such as 'public realm', 'public space', 'public arena' to render the full meaning of the German word. But since the word is here taken up in the specific sense articulated by Jürgen Habermas in his work *Strukturwandel der Öffentlichkeit. Untersuchungen zu einer kategorie der bürgerlichen Gesellschaft* (Neuwied, 1962) it is translated as 'public' so that the reader is aware of the complex, specific meaning behind my usage. The concept 'plebeian public', which is given concrete social substance here, draws attention to the wide gap between the works of J. Habermas, *Strukturwandel der Öffentlichkeit* and O. Negt and A. Kluge, *Öffentlichkeit und Erfahrung. Zur Organisationsanalyse von bürgerlicher und proletarischer Öffentlichkeit* (Frankfurt, 1972). Habermas first coined the term in the Introduction to *Strukturwandel* where he briefly mentioned the 'variant of a plebeian public which has been suppressed in the historical process' (p. 8). According to Habermas, the 'plebeian public' is contradictory within itself, since, on the one hand, it stands in opposition to the 'bourgeois public', but on the other hand remains oriented toward it. Negt and Kluge also speak of the 'plebeian public', but consider it to be a mere variant of the 'bourgeois public'. They distinguish it – perhaps too sharply – from the 'proletarian public' which 'essentially has its roots in the production process' (*Öffentlichkeit und Erfahrung*, pp. 8f., n. 1). The thesis advanced here follows neither Habermas nor Negt and Kluge; in my view, the 'plebeian public' historically preceded the 'proletarian public' and is relatively independent of it. Both differ from each other according to their origins in the differing social relations of production of proto-industrial and industrial capitalism respectively. But there are also strong historical continuities in the forms of articulation and consciousness, in the symbols, norms, traditions and self-understanding of both publics. Above all they have in common the concrete relationship which they create, within everyday life, between the articulation of needs, the close experience of production, the production of social experiences, and their specifically 'public' realization.

195 For the 'representative public realm' cf. Habermas, *Strukturwandel* (see n. 194 above), pp. 17ff.; E. P. Thompson, 'Patrician Society, Plebeian Culture' (see n. 185

above) does not examine the 'public' character of 'plebeian culture' explicitly and systematically, but he emphasizes the latter's relative autonomy while simultaneously pointing out its interrelationship with the 'public theatre' presented by the nobility and gentry.

196 Concerning horse-races and cockfighting, see above, pp. 66 and 67, and concerning the beginnings of dog-races, see above, n. 184.

197 Thompson, 'Moral Economy' (see n. 159 above), pp. 76ff.

198 Braun, *Industrialisierung* (see n. 57 above), pp.196ff.; Thun, *Industrie am Niederrhein* (see n. 74 above), vol. 1, pp. 94f.; Lipson, *Economic History* (see n. 67 above), vol. 2, pp. 48f., 59ff.; Heaton, *Yorkshire Woollen and Worsted Industries* (see n. 131 above), pp. 405–37; for the higher 'crime rate' of districts with domestic industry in comparison with districts of factory indusry, see W. Roscher, *Nationalökonomie des Handels- und Gewerbefleisses* (Stuttgart, 1881), vol. 3, p. 535.

199 Cf. E. P. Thompson, 'The Crime of Anonymity', *Albion's Fatal Tree. Crime and Society in Eighteenth Century England*, eds. D. Hay et al. (London, 1975), pp. 255–34, esp. 260, 272ff., 318ff.; concerning the 'public' character of the anonymous threatening letters which he analyses, Thompson remarks poignantly: 'The great majority adopt a similar tone and manner of address, distinguished by the collective pronoun "we". What is offered is rarely a personal grievance, but the common sense of injustice of the poor as a whole'; (The Crime of Anonymity', p. 273).

200 Thompson, *Making of the English Working Class* (see n. 110 above), pp. 562f.

201 Braun, *Industrialisierung* (see n. 57 above), pp. 203, 205, 229, 231f.; Braun repeatedly speaks about the traditional irrational mental attitude of the domestic producers. But he seems caught up in a modern frame of reference when he juxtaposes this mentality to the 'rationality' with which they approached their work (pp. 193–203). 'Though the approach which the domestic producers took to their work is rational, their attitude toward their "dynamic and technical existence" is quite irrational and traditional' (p. 203). Baun's perception seems to be somewhat limited by the intellectual categories of his own times, and he does not quite do justice to the proto-industrial producers. His use of the term 'rationality', which is synonymous with 'rationalism' in his writings, is somewhat ambiguous ('The domestic worker's mentality is influenced by economic rationalism, ... but he [remains] attached to the system of beliefs of a traditional popular culture'; p. 203); but it is quite clear which criteria underlie his own understanding of a 'rational' action, and he measures the attitudes of the domestic workers according to these criteria. They originate in a specific type of economic rationality ('rational division of labour', 'economic rationalism') which has only asserted itself during the course of the victory of modern capitalism. Braun judges the rural industrial producers according to this 'capitalist' rationality. It is no wonder that their attitudes and behaviour appear to him semi-rational, if not irrational. The fact is that their's is a different rationality, but within their own system of beliefs and values, they do use 'rational' means to achieve coherent purposes, just as the 'rational' attitudes of entrepreneurs, a 'rational' division of labour and 'optimal' consumer attitudes achieve such goals under capitalism. Braun's attempts to analyse the behaviour of the rural artisans are subtle, but his understanding of the dichotomy rationality – irrationality is subjective. For a more objective approach to this concept see M. Godelier, *Rationality and Irrationality in Economics* (London, 1972), pp. 7–30, 303–19, esp. 303ff. W. Sombart speaks even more emphatically than Braun about the 'complete irrationality in their attitude toward life and in their organization of life', referring in particular to the consumer behaviour of the rual industrial producers; Sombart, 'Arbeiterverhältnisse' (see n. 81 above), p. 26.

202 Braun, *Industrialisierung* (see n. 57 above), pp. 95ff.; Wadsworth and Mann, *Cotton*

Trade (see n. 67 above), pp. 384–95; Schneider, *Arbeiterhaushalt* (see n. 71 above), pp. 51ff.; Troeltsch, *Calwer Zeughandlungskompagnie* (see n. 61 above), pp. 315ff.

203 Mohl, *Württembergische Gewerbs-Industrie* (see n. 83 above), p. 52, cited in Troeltsch, *Calwer Zeughandlungskompagnie* (see n. 61 above), p. 317, n. 2.

204 See the regional comparisons in G. Wiegelmann, 'Volkskundliche Studien zum Wandel der Speisen und Mahlzeiten', in H. J. Teuteberg and G. Wiegelmann, *Der Wandel der Nahrungsgewohnheiten unter dem Einfluss der Industrialisierung* (Göttingen, 1972), esp. pp. 225ff., 267ff., 276ff., 315ff.

205 V. Schwerz, *Beschreibung der Landwirtschaft* (see n. 57 above), vol. 1, p. 103.

206 Braun, *Industrialisierung* (see n. 57 above), pp. 101ff.; B. Mandeville, *The Fable of the Bees* (1714) (Harmondsworth, 1970), pp. 151ff.; cf. the important systematic remarks in P. Bourdieu, 'Klassenstellung und Klassenlage', in P. Bourdieu, *Zur Soziologie der symbolischen Formen* (Frankfurt, 1974), pp. 43–74, esp 57ff.

207 Braun, *Industrialisierung* (see n. 57 above), p. 115.

208 Bamford, *Passages* (see n. 183 above), pp. 119ff., esp. 132f. about the display of household objects in festive parades; cf. in general: Chr. Lasch, 'What the Doctor Ordered', *New York Review of Books*, 22 (Dec. 11 1975) No. 20, pp. 50ff.

209 Braun, *Industrialisierung* (see n. 57 above), pp. 119ff.; J. R. Gillis, *Youth and History, Tradition and Change in European Age Relations 1770–Present* (New York, 1974), pp. 37ff.

210 Gillis, *Youth* (see n. 209 above), pp. 45ff.; in general cf. also E. Shorter, *Making of the Modern Family* (see n. 116 above), pp. 121ff.

211 See D. Levine, *Family Formation* (n. 104 above), Ch. 8: 'Illegitimacy: Marriage Frustrated not Promiscuity Rampant'; also see the observations about a Silesian weaving village in Peuckert, *Volkskunde* (see n. 16 above), pp. 35f.; see also the interesting data on illegitimacy as a consequence of poverty and immiseration in a study which is useless otherwise, since it is dominated by racist prejudices: B. Richter, *Burkhards und Kaulstoss. Zwei Oberhessische Dörfer. Eine rassenkundliche Untersuchung* (Jena, 1936), pp. 18, 31ff.

212 Shorter, *Making of the Modern Family* (see n. 116 above), pp. 80ff., esp. pp. 255ff.; cf. Shorter, 'Illegitimacy, Sexual Revolution and Social Change in Modern Europe', *Journal of Interdisciplinary History*, 2 (1971), 237–72; Shorter, 'Female Emancipation' (see. n. 116 above), 605–40; for a critique of Shorter's works cf. Lasch, 'What the Doctor Ordered' (see n. 208 above), pp. 50ff.; cf. also above, n. 116 and n. 162.

213 Cited in Strehler, 'Beiträge zur Kulturgeschichte der Zürcher Landschaft' (see n. 158 above), p. 61.

214 Thompson, 'Patrician Society' (see n. 185 above), p. 392.

215 Braun, *Industrialisierung* (see n. 57 above), p. 160.

216 Thompson, *Making of the English Working Class* (see n. 110 above), pp. 347ff.; Thompson, 'Moral Economy' (see n. 159 above), pp. 80ff.; Braun, *Industrialisierung* (see n. 57 above), pp. 95f., 99, 100.

217 Concerning the hierarchy of uses and goods in traditional societies as well as the function of money in this connection see Godelier, *Rationality and Irrationality* (n. 201 above), pp. 28ff.; M. Godelier, '"Salt money" and the circulation of commodities among the Baruya of New Guinea', in M. Godelier, *Perspectives in Marxist Anthropology* (Cambridge, 1977), pp. 127–51; P. Bohannan and G. Dalton, 'Introduction', in P. Bohannan and G. Dalton, *Markets in Africa* (see n. 12 above), pp. 4ff.

218 Braun, *Industrialisierung* (see n. 57 above), pp. 100ff., 202ff.; concerning the storage of food in peasant households, its structural conditions, and the changes in consumer attitudes which result from its discontinuation, see Bücher, 'Verbrauch', in Bücher, *Die. Entstehung der Volkswirtschaft* (see n. 22 above), vol. 2, pp. 251ff.

219 Braun, *Industrialisierung* (see n. 57 above), p. 203.

220 Concerning the meaning and function of money in the socio-economic system of traditional societies, see the literature under n. 217 above. See the interesting remarks in P. Bourdieu, 'The Attitude of the Algerian Peasant toward Time', in J. Pitt-Rivers (ed.), *Mediterranean Countrymen* (Paris/The Hague, 1964), pp. 55–72. The often criticized disinclination among rural industrial producers to accumulate savings seems to arise from this traditional attitude toward money and from its socio-structural precondition in the family economy so that their 'deficit spending' cannot be adequately explained by the superficial reference to a mentality of 'insufficient frugality'.

221 For the Siane: R. F. Salisbury, *From Stone to Steel. Economic Consequences of a Technological Change in New Guinea* (Melbourne, 1962) and the review of this work by M. Godelier in *L'Homme*, 4 (1964), No. 3, pp. 118–32; also E. K. Fisk, 'Planning in a Primitive Economy, Special Problems of Papua New Guinea', *The Economic Record*, 38 (1962), 462–78; for the Tiv: P. and L. Bohannan, *Tiv Economy* (London, 1968), pp. 220ff.; P. Bohannan, 'The Impact of Money on an African Subsistence Economy', *Journ. Econ. Hist.*, 19 (1959), 491–503; P. Bohannan and G. Dalton, 'Introduction' (see n. 12 above), p. 57; for the Kwakiutl Indians: I. Goldman, 'The Kwakiutl Indians of Vancouver Island', *Cooperation and Competition among Primitive Peoples*, ed. M. Mead (New York and London, 1937), pp. 180–209 and F. B. Steiner, 'Notes on Comparative Economics', *British Journal of Sociology*, 5 (1954), pp. 118–29; cf. also the interpretation in Godelier, *Rationality and Irrationality* (see n. 201 above), pp. 298ff.

Notes to Chapter 3

1 This 'systemic' aspect was first emphasized by E. A. Wrigley, *Population and History* (New York and Toronto, 1969), pp. 136–41; also E. A. Wrigley, 'The Process of Modernization and the Industrial Revolution in England', *Journal of Interdisciplinary History*, 3 (1972–3), 225–59, esp. 250–3; R. Schofield, 'The Relationship between Demographic Structure and Environment in Pre-industrial Western Europe', *Sozialgeschichte der Familie in der Neuzeit Europas. Neue Forschungen*, ed. W. Conze, Industrielle Welt, vol. 21 (Stuttgart, 1976), pp. 147–60. In contrast to Wrigley and Schofield the following interpretation attempts to explain the specific interrelationships between demographic and economic factors within the proto-industrial system by looking at their socio-structural mediation: the social relations of production in rural industry. For a limited social stratum it thus tries to achieve what is often missing from the work of the Cambridge Group: the fusion of the 'history of population' with that of 'social structure'.

2 This behaviour of proto-industrial populations was first statistically analysed and systematically explained by Fr. Mendels, *Industrialization and Population Pressure in Eighteenth Century Flanders* (PhD. Diss., University of Wisconsin, 1970), esp. Ch. 5, pp. 220–77; Fr. Mendels, 'Proto-Industrialization: The First Phase of the Industrialization Process', *Journ. Econ. Hist.*, 32 (1972), 241–61; Fr. Mendels, 'Industry and Marriages in Flanders before the Industrial Revolution', *Population and Economics: Proceedings of Section V of the Fourth Congress of the International Economic History Association 1968*, ed. P. Deprez (Winnipeg, 1970), pp. 81–93; a short summary in Fr. Mendels, 'Industrialization and Population Pressure in Eighteenth century Flanders', *Journ. Econ. Hist.*, 31 (1971), 169–71; cf. in partial contradiction of Mendels's results: G. Hohorst, *Wirtschaftswachstum und Bevölkerungsentwicklung in Preussen 1816–1914* (New York, 1977), Ch. 5, sects. 1 and 2, pp. 208ff.; G. Hohorst, 'Bevölkerungswachstum als historischer Entwicklungsprozess demo-ökonomischer Systeme', *Dynamik der Bevölkerungsentwicklung. Strukturen – Bedingungen – Folgen*, eds. R. Mackensen and H. Weber (Munich, 1973), pp. 91–118.

3 See below, p. 86; a particularly clear example of the delayed adaptation of population growth to worsening economic conditions is provided by the deindustrialization zones of Ireland before the catastrophic onset of the famine in 1845. Especially in the provinces with the highest industrial density, Ulster and Connaught, a growth-pattern existed that was characterized by a 'growth in population, accompanied by a decline in domestic industries'; see L. M. Cullen, *An Economic History of Ireland since 1660* (London, 1972), pp. 118ff., esp. 121; cf. the numerical data given in K. H. Connell, *The Population of Ireland* (Oxford, 1950), pp. 247ff., according to which the population in the provinces of Connaught and Ulster expanded more rapidly than that in the rather more agrarian provinces Leinster and Munster. Connaught, which was most severely hit by deindustrialization, had the highest rate of population growth; for Connell cf. below n. 66.

4 The following works stand out: S. Blaschke, *Bevölkerungsgeschichte von Sachsen bis zur Industriellen Revolution* (Weimar, 1967), but see the useful and critical review of this book: H. Harnisch, 'Über die Bedeutung der Bevölkerungsgeschichte als Teil der Wirtschafts- und Sozialgeschichte', *Jb. Wirtsch. G.*, IV (1973), 205–20, and – containing numerical data about Prussian and Saxon regions – H. Harnisch, 'Bevölkerung und Wirtschaft. Über die Zuammenhänge zwischen sozialökonomischer und demographischer Entwicklung im Spätfeudalismus', *Jb. Wirtsch. G.*, II (1975), 57–87; R. Braun, *Industrialisierung und Volksleben. Veränderungen der Lebensformen in einem ländlichen Industrie gebiet vor 1800 (Zürcher Oberland)* (Erlenbach and Zurich 1960, reprinted Göttingen 1979), Ch. 2, pp. 59–89: 'Wandel der Familien- und Bevölkerungsstruktur in den Industriegebieten' : an English version of this chapter has been reprinted: R. Braun, 'Proto-industrialization and Demographic Changes in the Canton of Zürich', *Historical Studies of Changing Fertility*, ed. Ch. Tilly (Princeton, N.J., 1978), pp. 289–334; J. D. Chambers, *Population, Economy and Society in Pre-industrial England* (London, 1972); J. D. Chambers, *The Vale of Trent, 1670 to 1800: A Regional Study of Economic Change*, Econ. Hist. Rev. Supplement, vol. 3 (Cambridge, 1958), pp. 19–35: 'The Course of Popultaion Change'; P. Deprez, 'The Demographic Development of Flanders in the Eighteenth Century', *Population in History*, eds. D. E. C. Eversley and D. V. Glass (London, 1965), pp. 608–31; greater emphasis is placed on the functional interaction between population growth and the expansion of rural industries in P. Deprez, 'Evolution démographique et évolution économique en Flandre de dix-huitième siècle', *Troisième conférence internationale d' histoire économique*, 4, Congrès et Colloques, vol. 10 (Paris, 1972), pp. 49–53; N. Friberg, 'The Growth of Population and its Economic Geographical Background in a Mining District in Central Sweden 1650–1750. A Methodological Study', *Geografiske Annaler*, 38 (1956), 394–439; Hohorst, *Wirtschaftswachstum* (see n. 2 above); a pioneering work: D. C. Levine, *Family Formation in an Age of Nascent Capitalism*, Studies in Social Discontinuity (New York, 1977); D. C. Levine, 'The Demographic Implications of Rural Industrialization: a Family Reconstitution Study of Shepshed, Leicestershire, 1600 to 1851', *Social History*, 1 (1976), 177–96; Mendels, 'Industrialization and Population Pressure' (see n. 2 above); B. H. Slicher van Bath, *Een samenleving onder spanning. Geschiedenis von het platteland in Overijssel*, Historische sociografien van het platteland, vol. 1 (Assen, 1957); B. H. Slicher van Bath, 'Historical Demography and Economic Development – the Netherlands', *Population and Social Change*, eds. D. V. Glass and R. Revelle (London, 1972), pp. 331–46; J. A. Faber, H. K. Roessingh, B. H. Slicher van Bath, A. M. von der Woude, H. J. von Xanten, 'Population Changes and Economic Developments in the Netherlands: A Historical Survey', *A. A. G. Bijdragen*, 12 (1965), 47–113; B. H. Slicher van Bath, 'Contrasting Demographic Developments in some Parts of the Netherlands during the Depression Period of the 17th and 18th Centuries', *Population Growth and the Brain Drain*, ed. F. Bechhofer (Edinburgh, 1969), pp. 209–19; a remarkable chapter on population history is contained in W. Troeltsch, *Die Calwer Zeughandlungskompagnie und ihre Arbeiter. Studien zur Gewerbe- und Sozialgeschichte Altwürttembergs.* (Jena, 1897), pp. 394–430: Exkurs III: 'Zur altwürttembergischen Bevölkerungsstatistik, insbesondere im Schwarzwaldgebiet 1650–1800'; Summaries of research and the status of knowledge: Mendels, 'Industrialization and Population Pressure' (see n. 2 above), pp. 36–46 and W. Fischer, 'Rural Industrialization and Population Change', *Comparative Studies in Society and History*, 15 (1973), 158–70. For a remarkable research effort in regional history that is being conducted in Switzerland and in which questions of rural industry are considered as well, cf. M. Mattmüller, 'Demographische Studien am historischen Seminar der Universität Basel', *Historische Demographie als Sozialgeschichte. Giessen und Umgebung im 17. und 19. Jahrhundert*, vol. 2, ed. A. Imhof, Quellen und Forschungen zur hessischen Geschichte, vol. 31 (Darmstadt, 1975), pp. 1059–66, esp. 1063ff.

5 The classic formulation of the idea that population growth is a function of the demand for labour in A. Smith, *An Inquiry into the Nature and Causes of the Wealth of Nations*, Glasgow Edition of the Works and Correspondence of Adam Smith, ed. by R. Campbell and A. S. Skinner, vols. 1 and 2 (Oxford, 1976), vol. 1, Book 1, Ch. 8, p. 98: 'The demand for men, like that for any other commodity, necessarily regulates the production of men; quickens it when it goes on too slowly, and stops it when it advances too fast. It is this demand which regulates and determines the state of propagation in all the different countries of the world, in North America, in Europe, and in China.' A new version of this thesis, which however differentiates according to historical modes of production in S. H. Coontz, *Population Theories and the Economic Interpretation* (London, 1957), pp. 137ff.

6 Mendels, 'Industrialization and Population Pressure' (see n. 2 above), p. 210.

7 J. H. Boeke, *Economics and Economic Policy of Dual Societies as Exemplified by Indonesia* (Haarlem, 1953), p. 194.

8 For this concept, see G. Mackenroth, *Bevölkerungslehre. Theorie, Soziologie und Statistik der Bevölkerung* (Berlin, 1953), pp. 326ff., esp. 414ff.

9 J. Dupaquier, 'De L'animal à l'homme: le mécanisme autorégulateur des populations traditionelles', *Revue de l'Institut de Sociologie*, 45 (1972), 177–211; J. Dupaquier, 'Les débuts de la grande aventure démographique', *Prospectives*, 3 (1974), pp. 7–38, esp. 9ff. Wrigley, *Population and History* (see n. 1 above), pp. 45ff.: 'Agrarian Societies'; Mackenroth, *Bevölkerungslehre* (see n. 8 above), pp. 421ff.; P. Chaunu, *Histoire, science sociale. La durée, l'espace et l'homme à l'époque moderne* (Paris, 1974), pp. 325ff.

10 K. F. Helleiner, 'The Population of Europe from the Black Death to the Eve of the Vital Revolution', *Cambridge Economic History of Europe*, vol. 4 (Cambridge, 1967), pp. 1–95; survey in Wrigley, *Population in History* (see n. 1 above), pp. 76ff.

11 R. S. Schofield in a discussion on 10 April 1975.

12 Dupaquier, 'De l'animal à l'homme' (see n. 9 above), pp. 194ff.; formulated as a model in Schofield, 'Demographic Structure' (see n. 1 above); Wrigley, *Population and History* (n. 1 above), pp. 47ff. and esp. pp. 111ff.

13 Mackenroth, *Bevölkerungslehre* (see n. 8 above), pp. 422ff.; Dupaquier, 'De l'animal à l'homme' (see n. 9 above), pp. 204f.; Dupaquier, 'Débuts'. (n. 9 above), pp. 16ff.; J. Hajnal, 'European Marriage Patterns in Perspective', *Population in History. Essays in Historical Demography*, eds. D. V. Glass and D. E. C. Eversley (London, 1965), pp. 101–46.

14 P. Chaunu, *La civilisation de l'Europe classique* (Paris, 1966), p. 203; Chaunu, *Histoire* (see n. 9 above), p. 330.

15 Mackenroth, *Bevölkerungslehre* (see n. 8 above), p. 422; Dupaquier, 'De l'animal à l'homme' (n. 9 above), pp. 200ff.

16 For this interrelationship see W. Abel, *Agrarkrisen und Agrarkonjunkturen. Eine*

Geschichte der Land – und Ernährungswirtschaft Mitteleuopas seit dem hohen Mittelalter, 3nd ed. (Hamburg, 1978); M. M. Postan, 'The Economic Foundations of Medieval Society', in M. M. Postan, *Essays on Medieval Agriculture and General Problems of the Medieval Economy* (Cambridge, 1973), pp. 3–27; M. M. Postan, 'Medieval Agrarian Society in its Prime: England', *The Cambridge Economic History of Europe*, vol. 1 (Cambridge, 1966), pp. 548–632; E. le Roy Ladurie, Les Paysans de Languedoc, (Paris, 1966), esp. vol. 1, pp. 135ff., 415ff., 539ff.; concerning the function of class structure and political domination, see R. Brenner, 'Agrarian Class Structure and Economic Development in Pre-industrial Europe', *Past and Present*, 70 (1976), 30–75; but concerning Brenner cf. n. 48 to the Introduction above.

17 Wrigley, *Population and History* (see n. 1 above), p. 111.

18 Wrigley, *Population and History* (see n. 1 above), p. 111.

19 See the comments in Schofield, 'Demographic Structure' (see n. 1 above); cf. the evidence in Dupaquier, 'De l'animal à l'homme' (see n. 9 above), p. 206.

20 Cf. above pp. 17ff. and below pp. 95ff.

21 The categories for a discussion of these connections were first developed by T. R. Malthus, *An Essay on the Principle of Population*, rpt. from the 7th ed. of 1872 (New York, 1971), Book 3, Ch. 14, pp. 376ff.: 'General Observations'; the first edition of the *Essay*, which still pursued mostly propagandistic purposes, should not be used, but instead the completely revised second, or one of the later editions. Concerning Malthus, see the important article by H. Linde, 'Die Bedeutung von Th. R. Malthus für die Bevölkerungssoziologie', *Zs. für die gesamte Staatswissenschaft*, 118 (1961), 705–20; also J. Spengler, 'Malthus' Total Population Theory: A Restatement and Reappraisal', *Canadian Journal of Economics and Political Science*, vol. 11 (1945), 83–110, 234–64; R. Jones, *Literary Remains. Consisting of Lectures and Tracts on Political Economy*, ed. and introd. by W. W. Whewell (London, 1859), pp. 167ff. 'On the Effect of Fluctuations in the Real Wages of Labour on the Movement of Populations', and pp. 474ff., 517ff.; concerning Jones, who was Malthus's successor at the College of the East India Company in Hayleybury and one of the first theoreticians of the 'peasant economy', see W. Whewell, 'Prefatory Notice', in R. Jones, *Literary Remains*, pp. ix – xl and H. Weber, *Richard Jones. Ein Früher englischer Abtrünniger der klassischen Schule der Nationalökonomie*, Zürcher Volkswirtschaftliche Fonschungen, vol. 30 (Zürich, 1939); Concerning Jones's reception by later scholars, cf. D. Thorner, 'Old and New Approaches to Peasant Economics', *Subsistence Agriculture and Economic Development*, ed. C. R. Wharton (London, 1970), pp. 94–9, esp. 97.

22 See above, Ch. 1, pp. 33.

23 Linde, 'Bedeutung von Th. R. Malthus' (see n. 21 above), p. 707.

24 Cf. D. C. Coleman, 'Labour in the English Economy in the Seventeenth Century', *Econ. Hist. Rev.*, 8 (1956), esp. pp. 287ff.; generally: K. Marx, *Capital*, vol. 1, introd. by E. Mandel and transl. by Ben Fowkes (Harmondsworth, 1976), Ch. 25, section 1, pp. 762–72: 'A Growing Demand for Labour-Power Accompanies Accumulation if the Composition of Capital Remains the Same'; H. Grossmann, *Das Akkumulations- und Zusammenbruchsgesetz des kapitalistischen System* (1929), ed. W. Rosenbaum (Frankfurt, 1967), Ch. 14, pp. 396ff.: 'Ein historischer Rückblick: Das Bevölkerungsproblem im Frühkapitalismus. Der Charakter der frühkapitalistischen Kolonialpolitik; concerning Grossmann's early attention to the mercantilists' concern about the proto-industrial population-problem, cf. Grossmann, 'Aufgabe und geschichtliche Entwicklung der amtlichen Statistik in Österreich', *Statistische Monatsschrift* (Brünn), new ser. 21 (1916), 331–426 and 676–7; Coontz, *Population Theories* (see n. 5 above), pp. 108ff.

25 Cf. the exemplary controversy between J. H. G. v. Justi, *Vollständige Abhandlung von denen Manufacturen und Fabriken*, 2 vols. (Berlin, 1758–62), esp. vol. 1, pp. 13ff. and

J. P. Süssmilch, *Die göttliche Ordnung in den Veränderungen des menschlichen Geschlechts, aus der Geburt, dem Tod und der Fortpflanzung derselben erwiesen*, 2 vols., 2nd ed. (Berlin, 1761–2), vol. 2, ch. 16, pp. 45–70: 'Von den Vortheilen der Fabriken in Ansehung der Bevölkerung und des Reichthums' ('Concerning the advantage of manufactories from the standpoint of populousness and riches') and pp. 549–74: 'Zweyter Anhang: Prüfung der Gedanken des Herrn von Justi, von dem Einfluss der Manufakturen in die Bevölkerung eines Landes und ob selbige in solcher Absicht dem Ackerbau vorzuziehen?' ('Appendix II: an examination of the opinions of Herr von Justi regarding the influence of manufactures on the populousness of a province, and whether in this connection they are to be preferred to agriculture'); for the 'employment balance' dependent on external trade, which was one of the central concepts of mercantilist trade policy, cf. P. Mombert, *Bevölkerungslehre*, Grundrisse zum Studium der Nationalökonomie, vol. 15 (Jena, 1929), pp. 144f., 403f.

26 K. Marx, *Grundrisse. Foundations of the Critique of Political Economy*, transl. by M. Nicolaus (Harmondsworth, 1973), pp. 604ff., esp. 605; Marx, *Capital* 1 (see n. 24 above), Ch. 25, section 1, pp. 762ff.

27 Grossmann, *Akkumulations- und Zusammenbruchsgesetz* (see n. 24 above), p. 374.

28 Malthus, *Essay* (see n. 21 above), Ch. 14, pp. 376–88: 'General Observations', esp. pp. 377f.

29 For this central concept of Marx's only partially developed population theory: Marx, *Grundrisse* (see n. 26 above), p. 608.

30 The following construction is an attempt to apply to the specific 'generative structure' of proto-industrialization, which will be treated in detail in Ch. 3, pts. 2 and 3, the systematic demo-economic approach of Coontz, *Population Theories* (n. 5), pp. 137ff., esp. 148ff. and 166ff., to which have been added some aspects of the fertility theory of H. Leibenstein, *Economic Backwardness and Economic Growth. Studies in the Theory of Economic Development* (New York, 1957), Ch. 10, pp. 147ff.: 'Population Growth Theory and Economic Development', esp. pp. 159ff. and H. Leibenstein, 'An Interpretation of the Economic Theory of Fertility: Promising Path or Blind Alley?', *Journal of Economic Literature*, 12 (1974), 457–79 and *Journal of Economic Literature*, 13 (1975), 469–72. Coontz and, even more so, Leibenstein developed a theory of 'demographic transition', primarily in order to explain the secular decline in fertility in European and American societies since the end of the nineteenth century. See Coontz, *Population Theories* (see n. 5 above), pp. 137ff.; Leibenstein, 'Interpretation', pp. 458ff., esp. 460ff.; also H. Leibenstein, 'The Economic Theory of Fertility Decline', *Quarterly Journal of Economics*, 89 (1957), 1–31; if their theories are to be applied to the interrelationship between demographic and economic factors they must be modified in order to fit the different historical context. Both Coontz, *Population Theories*, pp. 145ff. and Leibenstein, *Economic Backwardness*, pp. 59ff. discuss the question which is crucial to the reproductive behaviour of the proto-industrial household, namely the household's function in the process of production and reproduction. This is not true for the attempts, which originated in the Chicago School of Economics, to establish a micro-economic theory of fertility; despite its name, the 'household *production* model' of the 'New Home Economics' is exclusively concerned with a micro-economic theory of consumer attitudes; see the controversy with Leibenstein: M. C. Keeley, 'A Comment on "An Interpretation of the Economic Theory of Fertility"', *Journal of Economic Literature*, 13 (1975), 161–8. M. Nerlove, 'Household and Economy: Toward a New Theory of Population and Economic Growth', *Journal of Political Economy*, 82 (1974), S200–S233; also G. S. Becker, 'An Economic Analysis of Fertility', *Demographic and Economic Changes in Developed Countries*, Universities National Bureau Series, vol. 11 (Princeton, N. J., 1960), pp. 209–40; G. S. Becker, 'A Theory of the Allocation of Time', *Economic Journal*, 75

(1965), 463–517; G. S. Becker, 'A Theory of Marriage', *Journal of Political Economy*, 81 (1973), 813–46 and *Journal of Political Economy*, 82 (1974), S11–S26; also see the systematic treatment of the subject in L. Tilly, J. W. Scott, M. Cohen, 'Women's Work and European Fertility Patterns', *Journal of Interdisciplinary History*, 6 (1975–6), 447–76, esp. 470ff.

31 See below, pp. 84ff.

32 For this concept see R. C. Geary, 'The Family in the Irish Census of Population Statistics', *Journal of the Statistical and Social Inquiry Society of Ireland* (1954).

33 See above, pp. 56ff.

34 S. Levine, *Family Formation* (see n. 4 above), pp. 66, 807. E. R. Green, 'The Cotton Hand-loom Weavers in the North-East of Ireland', *Ulster Journal of Archaeology*, 7 (1944), 30–41, esp. 36; the age- and sex-specific fluctuations in the prices for slaves and the incomes of the work of slaves show certain similarities; see the evidence in R. W. Fogel and St. Engermann, *Time on the Cross. The Economics of American Negro Slavery* (London, 1974), vol. 1, pp. 72ff.

35 Cf. above, p. 58ff.; in 1832, Fr. Schmidt calculated the subsistence minimum for a handloom weaver's family of five in the textile region of Saxon Upper Lusatia: Fr. Schmidt, *Untersuchungen über Bevölkerung, Arbeitslohn und Pauperismus in ihrem gegenseitigen Zusammenhang* (Leipzig, 1836), pp. 298f. That subsistence minimum was to allow them to 'provide for their bare necessities . . . at the most difficult period of the family economy, namely before the family could use the labour power of their first child'. It amounted to 60 Taler and 16 Groschen. The annual income of the weaver's family, depending on the stage in the family life-cycle, amounted to:

1. When no child can be used to wind bobbins
   a. in linen   60 T. 16 Gr.
   b. in cotton   65 T. –
2. When one child winds bobbins
   a. in linen   67 T. 4 Gr.
   b. in cotton   71 T. 12 Gr.
3. When two children wind bobbins
   a. in linen   73 T. 16 Gr.
   b. in cotton   78 T. –
4. When a child leaves school and weaves during the first year
   a. in linen   91 T. –
   b. in cotton   97 T. 12 Gr.
   in the second year
   a. in linen   121 T. 8 Gr.
   b. in cotton   130 T. –

36 Concerning child labour in general, see above, pp. 55; cf. the examples in E. P. Thompson, *The Making of the English Working Class*, 2nd ed. Pelican (Harmondsworth, 1968), pp. 367f.; for a description of the problem, though not for its explanation, see E. Shorter, 'Der Wandel der Mutter-Kind-Beziehung zu Beginn der Moderne', *Geschichte und Gesellschaft*, 1 (1975), 256–87, esp. 257ff.

37 Cf. Leibenstein, *Economic Backwardness* (see n. 30 above), p. 165; Tilly, Scott, Cohen, 'Women's Work' (n. 30 above), p. 472.

38 D. Levine attempted to falsify the hypothesis proposed here, using the data of his study of the proto-industrial population of Shepshed. Contary to his expectations, however, he arrived at a confirmation of the hypothesis established above, even for the difficult phase of de-industrialization in Shepshed between 1825 and 1851. Even under these adverse economic conditions, the framework knitters began to limit their families not immediately after marriage, but only after the survival of a sufficiently large number of children had been assured. See Levine, *Family Formation* (see n. 4 above), pp. 80ff.

39 H. Linde, 'Generative Strukturen', *Studium Generale*, 12 (1959), pp. 343–55; in this important work, Linde develops some central concepts which had originally been defined by G. Mackenroth. While Mackenroth had defined the concept of 'population structure' in a rather formal manner to characterize the interrelationship and interdependence between demo-statistical variables, Linde made the concept of 'population structure' central to his historical and sociological theory of population. At the centre of this theory lies the 'discovery of specific generative modes of population and their dialectic relation to modes of production' (p. 348).

40 Marx, *Capital*, vol. 1 (see n. 24 above), Ch. 25, sect. 4, p. 796. The same pattern of reproductive behaviour has been observed under similar social and economic conditions among the small peasant population in the Indian state of the Punjab; for the precise account of a participant observer see M. Mamdani, *The Myth of Population Control. Family, Caste and Class in an Indian Village* (New York, 1972), pp. 13ff., esp. 128ff.; Mamdani summarizes his observations: 'people are not poor because they have large families; they have large families because they are poor' (p. 14).

41 F. Galiani, 'Della Moneta', *Scrittori classici italiana de economia politica. Parte moderna* 3–4 (Milan, 1803), p. 78.

42 A. Imhof tries to explain the dynamic of reproduction of proto-industrial populations as a consequence of their financial reserves: A. E. Imhof, 'Demographische Stadtstrukturen der frühen Neuzeit. Giessen in seiner Umgebung im 17. und 18. Jahrhundert als Fallstudie', *Zs. Für Stadtgeschichte, Stadtsoziologie und Denkmalspflege*, 2 (1975), 189–227, esp. 194f., 220f. In view of what is argued here, this thesis is questionable, though the fact that it can be falsified in the majority of regional cases does not necessarily exclude its validity for population-groups who lived under special circumstances, like the domestically producing small peasants in Appenzell-Ausserrhoden and Toggenburg. Cf. the indications in Mattmüller, 'Demographische Studien' (see n. 4 above), pp. 1063, 1064f.; the particularities of the 'symbiosis between domestic industry and agriculture' in these areas was already pointed out by Braun, *Industrialisierung* (see n. 4 above), pp. 163ff., 201.

43 Mendels, 'Industrialization and Population Pressure' (see n. 2 above), esp. Ch. 5, pp. 220–77; Mendels, 'Protoindustrialization' (see n. 2 above), pp. 249ff; Mendels, 'Industry and Marriages' (n. 2), pp. 81ff.

44 Mendels, 'Industrialization and Population Pressure' (see n. 2 above), pp. 249ff.

45 A particularly significant example is provided by D. Levine, *Family Formation* (see n. 4 above), pp. 62f. for a local population of framework-knitters. During the depression of trade following the American Revolution, between 1776 and 1785, the average marriage-age of men rose considerably, but the crucial marriage age of women did not rise; to the contrary, it continued its secular decline; nuptiality, however, did not follow this trend, it distinctly went down during this period (p. 60). Levine observed similar lag of the female age at marriage in response to the highly unfavourable economic development during the final crisis of the domestic framework-knitting industry after 1815 (p. 61). A direct connection between a continuous population expansion and the long-term deterioration of the terms of trade was also observed by Friberg, 'Growth of Population' (see n. 4 above), p. 414, 415ff.

46 Leibenstein, *Economic Backwardness* (see n. 30 above), p. 160.

47 Ph. Deane, W. A. Cole, *British Economic Growth 1688–1959. Trends and Structure*, 2nd ed. (London, 1969); Chambers, *Vale of Trent* (see n. 4 above), p. 20; Blaschke, *Bevölkerungsgeschichte von Sachsen* (n. 4 above), pp. 79f., 85, 90ff., 100ff.; for Flanders: Deprez, 'Evolution démographique' (n. 4 above), pp. 49ff.; Mendels, 'Industrialization and Population Pressure' (see n. 2 above), pp. 83ff., 109ff., 124ff.; for the Netherlands: J. de Vries, *The Dutch Rural Economy in the Golden Age 1500–1700* (New Haven, Conn., 1974), pp. 113ff., 117ff.; Slicher van Bath, 'Historical Demography' (see n. 4 above), pp. 334ff.; W. Bickel, *Bevölkerungsgeschichte und Bevölkerungspolitik der Schweiz seit dem Ausgang des Mittelalters* (Zürich, 1947), pp. 52ff.; Braun, *Industrialisierung* (see n. 4 above), pp. 79ff.; new, though preliminary results from regional historical studies in M. Mattmüller, *Einführung in die Bevölkerungsgeschichte an Hand von Problemen aus dem Schweizerischen* (mimeographed lecture ms., 2 vols., Basel, 1973 and 1974/75; Mattmüller, 'Demographische Studien' (see n. 4 above), pp. 1063f.; for Bohemia: P. Horska, 'L'état actuel des recherches sur l'évolution de la population des pays tchèques aux XVIIIe et XIXe siècles', *Annales de Démographie Historique* (1967), 173–95, esp. 174ff. A. Klíma, 'The Role of Rural Domestic Industry in Bohemia in the Eighteenth Century', *Econ. Hist. Rev.*, 27 (1954), 48–56, here 50; the evidence of Horska and Klíma are based on the investigations of L. Kárniková, *Vývoj obyvatelstva v ceských zemích 1754–1914* (The population development in the Bohemian countries 1754–1914) (Prague, 1965); A. Petránová, 'L'influence de développement des centres industriels sur les structures économiques, démographiques et sociales en Bohème de seizième au dix-huitième siècle', *Troisième conférence internationale d'histoire économique*, congrès et colloques, vol. 10 (Paris, 1972), vol. 4, pp. 191–8.

48 G. Heitz, *Ländliche Leinenproduktion in Sachsen 1470–1555* (Berlin, 1961), pp. 44ff.; cf. the remarks in D. Sabean, 'Probleme der deutschen Agrarverfassung zu Beginn des 16. Jahrhunderts. Oberschwaben als Beispiel', *Revolte und Revolution in Europa*, ed. P. Blickle, Historische Zeitschrift, Beiheft, new ser. 4 (Munich, 1975), pp. 132–50, esp. 146f.; A. Wrasman, 'Das Heuerlingswesen im Fürstentum Osnabrück', *Mitteilungen des Vereins für Geschichte und Landeskunde von Osnabrück*, 42 (1919), 53–171 (will be cited as 'I') and *Mitteilungen des Vereins*, 44 (1921), 1–154 (will be cited as 'II'), esp. I, pp. 100ff.; A. Gladen, *Der Kreis Tecklenburg an der Schwelle des Zeitalters der Industrialisierung* (Münster, 1970), pp. 129ff.

49 Blaschke, *Bevölkerungsgeschichte von Sachsen* (see n. 4 above), p. 158; the so-called 'Heuerlingssystem' was particularly typical for the area of the north-west German *Grundherrschaft*. Here the village communities or the *Grundherr* exercised relatively firm control over land-ownership and partially also over an industrial labouring class that was excluded from the ownership of land. Cf. e.g. H. Riepenhausen, *Die Entwicklung der bäuerlichen Kulturlandschaft in Ravensberg* (Diss. mat. nat., Göttingen, 1936), pp. 107ff. Glade, *Kreis Tecklenburg* (see n. 48 above), pp. 129ff.

50 Concerning this pattern in regions of weak seigneurial and communal control, cf. J. Thirsk, 'Industries in the Countryside', *Essays in the Economic and Social History of Tudor and Stuart England*, ed. F. J. Fisher (Cambridge, 1961), pp. 70–88, esp. 76ff.; an exemplary analysis of population development in an 'industrial village' in Levine, *Family Formation* (see n. 4 above), esp. pp. 58ff; cf. also the summary by Levine, 'Demographic Implications', (n. 4 above), p. 179.

51 E. Hobsbawm, 'The Crisis of the Seventeenth Century' (1954), *Crisis in Europe 1560–1660*, ed. T. Ashton (London, 1965), pp. 5–58, esp. 28ff.

52 E. Jones, 'Agricultural Origins of Industry' (1968), in E. Jones, *Agriculture and the Industrial Revolution* (Oxford, 1974), pp. 128–42; E. Jones, 'Afterword', *European Peasants and their Markets. Essays in Agrarian Economic History*, eds. E. Jones and W. N. Parker (Princeton, N. J., 1975), pp. 327–60, esp. 337ff.

53 Deane and Cole, *British Economic Growth* (see n. 47 above), p. 105; Chambers, *Population, Economy and Society* (see n. 4 above), pp. 31f., 141ff.; Chambers says of the development in the intensively industrial regions of England since the middle of the seventeenth century that 'industry followed in the wake of demographic growth long before the conventional dates of the industrial revolution (p. 137); Blaschke, *Bevölkerungsgeschichte von Sachsen* (see n. 4 above), pp. 90ff., 149ff.; A. Kunze, 'Vom Bauerndorf zum Weberdorf. Zur sozialen und wirtschaftlichen Struktur der Waldhufendörfer der südlichen Oberlausitz im 16., 17. und 18. Jahrhundert', *Oberlausitzer Forschungen* (1961), 165–92, esp. pp. 184ff.; Mendels, 'Industrialization and Population Pressure' (see n. 2 above), pp. 97, 138ff.; Slicher van Bath, 'Historical Demography' (see n. 4 above), pp. 334ff.

54 Deane and Cole, *British Economic Growth* (see n. 47 above), p. 105; Blaschke, *Bevölkerungsgeschichte von Sachsen* (see n. 4 above), pp. 90ff., 149ff.; Slicher von Bath, 'Historical Demography' (n. 4 above), pp. 334ff.; De Vries, *Dutch Rural Economy* (see n. 47 above), pp. 107ff.; Mendels, 'Industrialization and Population Pressure' (see n. 2 above), pp. 109ff.

55 For the east-Prussian regions of *Gutsherrschaft*, Harnisch, 'Bevölkerung und Wirtschaft' (see n. 4 above), pp. 78ff. point out correctly that a new phase of population-expansion began in the second half of the eighteenth century with the introduction of new agricultural techniques, the disintegration of the traditional lord – peasant relationship, and the employment of wage-labour on the estates, long before the agrarian-reform legislation of the early nineteenth century. The growth-rates of this population expansion were quite similar to those of proto-industrial regions.

56 Deane and Cole, *British Economic Growth* (see n. 47 above), pp. 106ff., esp. 112ff.; Chambers, *Population, Economy and Society* (see n. 4 above), pp. 116f., 136f.; L. Bein, *Die Industrie des sächsischen Vogtlandes*, part 2: *Die Textilindustrie* (Leipzig, 1884), table 6.

57 For Prussian and Saxon industrial regions, cf. Harnisch, 'Bevölkerung und Wirtschaft' (see n. 4 above), pp. 70, 75ff.; Deane and Cole, *British Economic Growth* (see n. 47 above), pp. 128ff.; Chambers, *Vale of Trent* (see n. 4 above), pp. 53ff.; J. T. Krause, 'Some Aspects of Population Change 1690–1790', *Land, Labour and Population in the Industrial Revolution. Essays Presented to J. D. Chambers*, eds. E. L. Jones and G. E. Mingay (London, 1967), pp. 187–205, esp. 199f.

58 Deane and Cole, *British Economic Growth* (see n. 47 above), pp. 113, 120f; W. Koellmann, 'The Population of Barmen before and during the Period of Industrialisation', *Population in History. Essays in Historical Demography*, eds. D. V. Glass and D. E. C. Eversley (London, 1965), pp. 588–605, esp. 591ff.; K. Goebel, *Zuwanderung zwischen Reformation und Franzosenzeit. Ein Beitrage zur vorindustriellen Bevölkerungs- und Wirtschaftsgeschichte Wuppertals 1527–1808* (Wuppertal, 1966), esp. pp. 172ff.

59 A. P. Wadsworth and J. de Lacy Mann, *The Cotton Trade and Industrial Lancashire 1600–1780* (1931; rpt. Manchester, 1965), pp. 311f.; Blaschke, *Bevölkerungsgeschichte von Sachsen* (see n. 4 above), pp. 162ff., esp. 173f.; Troeltsch, *Calwer Zeughandlungskompagnie* (see n. 4 above), pp. 310f.; Slicher van Bath, *Een samenleving onder spanning* (see n. 4 above), Ch. 6.

60 De Vries, *Dutch Rural Economy* (see n. 47 above), pp. 115ff.

61 See above, p. 55.

62 Braun, *Industrialisierung* (see n. 4 above), pp. 27ff., 57; L. Stone, 'Social Mobility in England 1500–1700', *Past and Present*, 33 (1966), 16–55, esp. 31f. analyses lists of London apprentices and finds that the percentage of apprentices who migrated from north-western England to London fell sharply between the sixteenth and the end of the seventeenth centuries; it sank from over 50% to under 20% as rural industries established themselves in north-western England. Concerning the greater stability of residence at the local level, cf. H. Charbonneau, *Tourouvre-au-Perche aux XVIIe et XVIIIe siècles. Etude de démographie historique*, INED. Travaux et Documents, vol. 55 (Paris, 1970), pp. 39f.; E. Lais, 'Die Bevölkerung des Kirchspiels Schönau (i. Schwarzwald) und ihre Wirtschaft im 17. und 18. Jahrhundert' (Diss. rer. pol., Freiburg, 1921), pp. 43f.; Levine, *Family Formation* (see n. 4 above), pp. 35ff.

63 See above, p. 55 and the literature under n. 109 below; concerning the 'connection' which existed 'between the expansion of domestic industry in the countryside and the shortage of servants' in the industrial regions of Saxony before the 30-years-war, cf. R. Wuttke, *Gesindeordnungen und Gesindezwangsdienst in Sachsen bis zum Jahre 1835. Eine wirtschaftsgeschichtliche Studie.* (Leipzig, 1893), pp. 50ff., esp. 51; cf. also J. Ziekursch, *Hundert Jahre Schlesische Agrargeschichte. Vom Hubertusburger Frieden bis zum Abschluss der Bauernbefreiung*, 2nd ed. (Breslau, 1927), p. 135.

64 Especially the study by Levine, *Family Formation* (see n. 4 above); also the interesting work by a student of Louis Henri: Charbonneau, *Tourouvre-au-Perche* (see n. 62 above), important because this demographic micro-analysis distinguishes between occupational and social groups; important results are contained in the study stimulated by H. Linde and G. Ipsen: H. W. Rothe, *Lindhorst in Schaumburg-Lippe. Ein Beitrag zur Geschichte der ländlichen Gesellschaft des niedersächsischen Bergvorlandes zwischen Weser und Leine* (Diss. phil., Göttingen, 1953), esp. Ch. 8, pp. 173ff.: 'Agrarische Überbevölkerung' and Ch. 9, pp. 219ff.: 'Die Bevölkerungsbewegung von 1651–1871'; Lais, 'Bevölkerung des Kirschspiels Schönau' (see n. 62 above) is based on a most selective application of the micro-analytic methodology of O. K. Roller, *Die Einwohnerschaft der Stadt Durlach im 18. Jahrhundert in ihren wirtschaftlichen und kulturgeschichtlichen Verhältnissen dargestellt aus ihren Stammtafeln* (Karlsruhe, 1907); the results of the studies of P. Deprez partly rest on demographic micro-analyses according to the methodology developed by Louis Henri: Deprez, 'Demographic Development' (see n. 4 above), p. 609, notes 6 and 7; G. Heckh, 'Bevölkerungsgeschichte und Bevölkerungsbewegung des Kirchspiels Böhringen auf der Uracher Alb vom 16. Jahrhundert bis zur Gegenwart', *Archiv für Rassen- und Gesellschaftsbiologie*, 33 (1939), 126–69 is based on a simplified version of the family reconstitution method and is a careful statistical analysis, though without class-specific differentiations.

65 Charbonneau, *Tourouvre-au-Perche* (see n. 62 above), pp. 35ff.: a considerable portion of the population made clogs for supra-regional markets. Between 1715 and 1770, the industrial population comprised 20% of all married men, the great majority were employed in agriculture; Rothe, 'Lindhorst in Schaumburg-Lippe' (see n. 64 above), pp. 173ff.: a flax-spinning and linen-weaving cottager and lodger population in a north-west German 'Meierhof' settlement; Heckh, 'Bevölkerungsgeschichte . . . des Kirch-spiels Böhringen' (see n. 64 above): a considerable percentage of the population span flax and wove linen either as a primary or a subsidiary occupation in this south German partible-inheritance village since the eighteenth century; according to the *Beschreibung des Oberamts Urach* (Stuttgart/Tübingen, 1831), pp. 151ff., about 25% of Böhringen households were those of weaver masters; according to Heckh, p. 167, a much larger percentage of industrial households must be assumed for the period of the eighteenth and early nineteenth centuries: a census of 1810 mentions 29 household heads as farmers in a population of 657, i.e. 23% of all households if an average household size of 5 persons is assumed; 100 heads of households, i.e. 77% of all households, are designated as 'merchants, professionals, inn-keepers and artisans'.

66 Chambers, *Vale of Trent* (see n. 4 above), pp. 51f., see esp. the table on p. 52 which, for the marriage-ages of men, shows considerable differences between farmers, hus-bandmen, and labourers on the one hand, and framework knitters on the other. For women the age at marriage varies less between the different social groups, but here, too, that of the framework knitters is the lowest. Charbonneau, *Tourouvre-au-Perche* (see n. 62 above), p. 75: the wooden shoe makers have the lowest male age at marriage of all the social and occupational groups of the village; Rothe, *Lindhorst in Schaumburg-Lippe* (see n. 64 (above), pp. 223ff.: during industrial boom-periods, the age at marriage of the spinning and weaving cottager and lodger population rapidly declined below the marriage age of peasants and smallholders; Levine, *Family Formation* (see n. 4 above), pp. 64ff.; Krause, 'Aspects of Population Change' (see n. 57 above), esp, pp. 201ff.; Deprez, 'Demographic Development' (see n. 4 above), p. 615; for the partially industrial regions of Ireland, see Connell, *Population of Ireland* (see n. 3 above), pp. 26ff., 40, 42; Connell's hypothesis that there exists a connection between the low marriage age and rapid population expansion in Ireland since the second half of the eighteenth century has been much debated, see esp. the critique by M. Drake, 'Marriage and Population in Ireland, 1740–1845', *Econ. Hist. Rev.*, 16 (1963), 301–13. But even when Connell's data are disaggregated and analysed according to region, occupation, and social class, his thesis still holds; cf. J. Lee, 'Marriage and Population in Pre-famine Ireland', *Econ. Hist. Rev.*, 21 (1968), 283–95. This is particularly true for the intensively industrial districts of Ulster and Connaught. An interesting deviation from the historic European pattern was observed for the rural domestic rugmakers in Turkey; here the marriage-age of peasant daughters is relatively low owing to the brideprice which their parents get. But in villages with an intensive rugmaking industry, the female marriage age is considerably higher, since the daughters, by working in the houses of their parents, contribute more to the family income than can be achieved through the brideprice in the marriage-market; cf. E. Franz, *Das Dorf Icadiye. Ethnographische Untersuchung einer anatolischen lädlichen Gemeinde* (Diss. phil., Berlin, 1969), pp. 144ff. and esp. 304f.

67 Cf. the exemplary analysis and evidence in Levine, *Family Formation* (see n. 4 above), pp. 64ff; Deprez, 'Evolution démographique' (see n. 4 above), p. 51.

68 Levine, *Family Formation* (see n. 4 above), pp. 61ff., 80ff.; Deprez, 'Demographic Development' (n. 4 above), p. 615: a table about changes in the marriage-age of the rural industrial population near Ghent (Châtellenie le Vieuxbourg).

69 Levine, *Family Formation* (see n. 4 above), pp. 62f.

70 E. A. Wrigley draws the following general conclusion from his exemplary study of the conditions in Colyton (Devonshire) between 1538 and 1837: 'The male mean, medians and modes [of the age at marriage] were notably sticky. Men entered married life at much the same time for almost three hundred years [. . .] but they proved remarkably flexible in their judgement of what constituted an acceptable age in their brides', E. A. Wrigley, 'Family Limitation in Pre-industrial England', *Econ. Hist. Rev.*, 19 (1966), 82–109, esp. 88. Wrigley's study of the population of Colyton is especially interesting here, because D. Levine has followed up on the important unpublished thesis by W. G. Hoskins, *The Rise and Decline of the Serge Industry in the South West of England with Special Reference to the Eighteenth Century* (M.Sc. thesis, University of London, 1929), and established that the rise of the female age at marriage in Colyton since the second half of the seventeenth century which Wrigley had found, and the subsequent limitation of fertility were at least partially a response of an industrial rural cottager and smallholder population to the deindustrialization crisis of the 'Old Draperies' in southwestern England. Levine, *Family Formation* (see n. 4 above), Ch. 7: 'Colyton Revisited', pp. 103ff. Hoskins's and Levine's results increase the socio-economic plausibility of the demographic behaviour of Colyton's population, which had already been characterized as a 'cottar pattern of marriage' in Michael Drake, *Population and Society in Norway 1735–1865* (Cambridge, 1969), p. 159, n. 1; cf. E. A. Wrigley, 'The Changing Occupational Structure of Colyton over Two Centuries', *Local Population Studies* (1976).

71 Charbonneau, *Tourouvre-au-Perche* (see n. 62 above), p. 75; Rothe, *Lindhorst in Schaumburg-Lippe* (see n. 64 above), pp. 223ff.

72 Rothe, *Lindhorst in Schaumburg-Lippe* (see n. 64 above), p. 225; cf. also the data for the two villages Adegem and Elversele in Deprez, 'Demographic Development' (see n. 4 above), p. 615; these two villages are 'half industrial and half agrarian in character' (p. 621). In Elversele, the rise in the marriage-age during the eighteenth century coincides with the decline of rural industry and the turn towards agricultural labour (p. 623).

73 Cf. the data series in Chambers, *Vale of Trent* (see n. 4 above), p. 52; Levine, 'Demographic Implications' (n. 4), p. 108; Deprez, 'Demographic Development' (n. 4), p. 615 (Châtellenie de Vieuxbourg).

74 Charbonneau, *Tourouvre-au-Perche* (see n. 62 above), p. 75; Rothe, *Lindhorst in Schaumburg-Lippe* (see n. 64 above), pp. 225f.

75 Drake, *Population and Society in Norway* (see n. 70 above), pp. 133–49, esp. 138ff.; M. Drake, 'Age at Marriage in the Pre-industrial West', *Population Growth and the Brain Drain*, ed. E. Bechhofer (Edinburgh, 1969), pp. 196–208.

76 Cf. Rothe, *Lindhorst in Schaumburg-Lippe* (see n. 64 above), pp. 225ff.; the statistical data of group-specific marital behaviour in Charbonneau, *Tourouvre-au-Perche* (see n. 62 above), p. 87 shows a strong affinity between 'sabotiers' and the daughters of 'manouvres', but not between 'sabotiers' and the daughters of 'laboureurs' (relatively prosperous tillage farmers). In the weavers' village Vraiville, in Normandy studied by M. Ségalen, marriages between weavers and the daughters of full-scale farmers (Vollbaurn) frequently occurred at the beginning of proto-industrial development, but here, too, the marriages between weavers and the daughters of day-labourers ('journaliers') predominated. The expansion of industrial production was accompanied by a growing endogamy so that increasingly weavers married each other, and this behaviour did not change during the phase of deindustrialization; cf. M. Ségalen, *Nuptialité et alliance. Le Choix du conjoint dans une commune de l'Eure* (Paris, 1972), pp. 77f.

77 Levine, *Family Formation* (see n. 4 above), pp. 61, 65f., 78f. Cf. the remarkable stability of the female marriage-age in Böhringen during the crisis period 1800–1850 in Heckh, 'Bevölkerungsgeschichte ... des Kirchspiels Böhringen' (see n. 64 above), p. 152; for Ireland, cf. the evidence about the development of the marriage-age between 1830 and 1840 in the partially industrial, impoverished district of Connaught and in the agrarian districts of Munster and Leinster: Connell, *Population of Ireland* (see n. 3 above), p. 43; concerning the percentage of persons ever married, cf. the interesting tables in Gladen, *Kreis Tecklenburg* (see n. 48 above), p. 119; contrary to Gladen's own interpretation (pp. 199ff.), these tables do not indicate a consistent decline in the percentage of the married population, but a small rise during the crisis period after 1830, which suggests a 'generative structure' different from the structure that was 'typical during the pre-industrial phase'.

78 Levine, 'Demographic Implications' (see n. 4 above), pp. 185f.

79 See above, pp. 59f.

80 Concerning the fact that the emigration of families predominated over all other patterns of emigration, see Gladen, *Kreis Tecklenburg* (see n. 48 above), pp. 139ff., esp. 150; cf. Wrasman, 'Heuerlingswesen' II (n. 48), pp. 82ff.

81 Cf. the figures for marital fertility in Deprez, 'Demographic Development' (see n. 4 above), pp. 620, 622; cf. the interpretation in Fischer, 'Rural Industrialization' (n. 4), pp. 166ff.; Chambers, *Vale of Trent* (n. 4), p. 53; Harnisch, 'Bevölkerung und Wirtschaft' (n. 4), table 13, p. 76.

82 Heckh, 'Bevölkerungsgeschichte ... des Kirchspiels Böhringen' (see n. 64 above), p. 157; Levine, 'Demography of Rural Industrialization' (see n. 4 above), p. 185.

83 F. Lorimer, *Culture and Human Fertility* (New York, 1954), pp. 51ff.

84 Cf. the data in P. Goubert, 'Legitimate Fertility and Infant Mortality in France during the Eighteenth Century: a Comparison', *Population and Social Change*, eds. D. V. Glass and R. Revelle (London, 1972), pp. 321–30 for three communities in the interior of Brittany (La Guerche, Saint-Aubin, Saint-Méen) which were famous for their production of fine linen during the seventeenth and eighteenth centuries; for the socio-economic structure of these communities, cf. Mendels, 'Industrialization and Population Pressure' (see n. 2 above), pp. 41f. The data for the entire region in Y. Blàyo and L. Henri, 'Données démographiques sur la Bretagne et l'Anjou de 1740 à 1829', *Annales de*

Démographie Historique (1967), pp. 91–171, esp. 117ff. make it doubtful, however, that the high-average marriage-age in the three villages, assumed by Goubert, is characteristic for the rural industrial producers. Deprez, 'Demographic Development' (see n. 4 above), p. 617; concerning the lengthening of intervals between births and the reduction of marital fertility due to special working conditions, cf. Charbonneau, *Tourouvre-au-Perche* (see n. 62 above), pp. 107, 118f. and esp. 146f.

85 For this and the following theme see Levine, *Family Formation* (see n. 4 above), pp. 73ff., 79.

86 D. Levine, *The Demographic Implications of Rural Industrialization: a Family Reconstitution Study of Two Leicestershire Villages, 1600–1815* (Ph.D. Diss., Cambridge University, 1974), p. 118.

87 In general: H. J. Habakkuk, *Population Growth and Economic Development since 1750* (Leicester, 1971), pp. 35ff.; Krause, 'Aspects of Population Change' (see n. 57 above), pp. 193ff.; cf. the micro-analytic evidence in Levine, *Family Formation* (see n. 4 above), pp. 71ff.

88 Deprez, 'Demographic Development' (see n. 4 above), pp. 623f.; Heckh, 'Bevölkerungschichte . . . des Kirchspiels Böhringen' (see n. 64 above), pp. 137ff.; Troeltsch, *Calwer Zeughandlungskompagnie* (see n. 4 above), pp. 419ff.; for child mortality in particular: Goubert, 'Legitimate Fertility' (see n. 84 above), pp. 326ff.; Levine, *Family Formation* (see n. 4 above), pp. 68ff. cf. the table in Levine, *Demographic Implications* (see n. 4 above), p. 188.

89 See the comparative data in Goubert, 'Legitimate Fertility' (see n. 84 above), pp. 326ff.; Deprez, 'Demographic Development' (see n. 4 above), pp. 623ff.; Harnisch, 'Bevölkerung und Wirtschaft' (n. 4 above), pp. 66f.

90 Charbonneau, *Tourouvre-au-Perche* (see n. 62 above), pp. 172ff.: comments upon the near-absence of 'inégalité devant la mort' among the different population-groups of Tourouvre.

91 Cf. e.g. G. Schmoller, 'Die geschichtliche Entwicklung der Unternehmung, 5: Hausindustrie', *Jahrbuch für Gesetzgebung, Verwaltung und Volkswirtschaft*, 14 (1890), 1053–76, esp. 1061; G. Schmoller *Grundriss der allgemeinen Volkswirtschaftslehre*, 2nd ed. (1908), vol. 1, p. 490; but see also Fr. Engels who, in *The Condition of the Working Class in England* (1845) (Oxford, 1958), p. 10, views rural industry rather idyllically in contrast with the conditions of the early factories. Cf. all the evidence in W. Sombart, 'Die Hausindustrie in Deutschland', *Archiv für soziale Gestzgebung und Statitik*, 4 (1891), 103–56, esp. 148ff.

92 Deprez, 'Demographic Development' (see n. 4 above), pp. 624ff.; Levine, *Family Formation* (n. 4 above), pp. 72f.; Imhof, 'Demographische Stadtstrukturen' (see n. 42 above), p. 220.

93 Deprez, 'Demographic Development' (see n. 4 above), p. 625; Levine, *Family Formation* (n. 4 above), p. 72; cf. Heckh, 'Bevölkerungsgeschichte . . . des Kirchspiels Böhringen' (see n. 64 above), pp. 145f., in comparison with the data of the male population: Heckh, pp. 144f.

94 Levine, 'Demography of Rural Industrialization' (see n. 4 above), pp. 192ff.: 'Appendix: Calculating a Net Rate of Reproduction'.

95 Wrigley, 'Process of Modernisation' (see n. 1 above), p. 257.

96 Here especially Mendels, 'Industrialization and Population Pressure' (see n. 2 above), pp. 220ff. and the other works by Mendels listed under n. 2; the classic studies of the 'ancien régime démographique' are J. Meuvret, 'Les crises des subsistances et la démographie de la France d'Ancien Régime', in: J. Meuvret, *Etudes d'histoire économique*, Cahiers des Annales, vol. 32 (Paris, 1971), pp. 271–8, first in *Population*, 1 (1946); cf. also J. Meuvret, 'Les mouvements des prix de 1661 à 1715 et leur répercussions' (1944), in: Meuvret, *Etudes*, pp. 85–95, here 94f.

97 See the comments of P. Goubert, *Beauvais et le Beauvaisis de 1600 à 1730. Contribution à l'histoire sociale de la France du XVIIe siècle.* 2 vols. (Paris, 1960), vol. 1, pp. 604ff.; no systematic treatment, but empirical evidence in Chambers, *Population, Economy, Society* (see n. 4 above), pp. 128ff.

98 Cf. Meuvret, 'Crises' (see n. 96 above), p. 278.

99 C. E. Labrousse, *Esquisse du mouvement des prix et des revenues en France au XVIIIe siècle,* 2 vols., Collection scientifique d'économie politique, vol. 3 (Paris, 1933); C. E. Labrousse, *La crise de l'économie française à la fin de l'Ancien Régime et au début de la Révolution* (Paris, 1944); C. E. Labrousse, 'Les ruptures périodiques de la prospérité: les crises économiques du XVIIIe siècle', in C. E. Labrousse et al., *Histoire économique et sociale de la France,* vol. 2: *De derniers temps de l'âge seigneurial aux préludes de l'âge industriel (1660–1789)* (Paris, 1970), pp. 526–66.

100 Goubert, *Beauvais* (see n. 97 above), p. 46.

101 Meuvret, 'Crises' (see n. 96 above); also J. Meuvret, 'Réflexions d'un historien sur les crises démographiques aigues avant le XVIIIe Siècle', *Problèmes de mortalité. Actes du colloque international de démographie historique,* Congrès et colloques de l'Université de Liège, vol. 33 (Liège, 1965), pp. 93–7.

102 Goubert, *Beauvais* (see n. 97 above), pp. 45–59.

103 Labrousse, *Esquisse* (see n. 99 above); Labrousse, *Crise* (n. 99 above), pp. xiii–xvi and 172–84; Labrousse, 'Ruptures' (n. 99 above), pp. 529–63.

104 D. S. Landes, 'The Statistical Study of French Crises', *Journ. Econ. Hist.,* 10 (1950), 195–210, esp. 195.

105 J. Meuvret partially corrects the perceptions of Labrousse in Meuvret, *Etudes* (see n. 96 above), pp. 41ff. A good summary of the problems for France is provided by Louise Tilly, 'The Food Riot as a Form of Political Conflict in France', *Journal of Interdisciplinary History,* 2 (1971–2), pp. 35ff.

106 Abel, *Agrarkrisen und Agrarkonjunktur* (see n. 16 above), pp. 22f.; W. Abel, *Massenarmut und Hungerkrisen im vorindustriellen Europa. Versuch einer Synopsis* (Hamburg, 1974), pp. 279ff.; cf. already W. Abel, 'Wirtschaftliche Wechsellagen', *Berichte über Landwirtschaft,* N.F. (1936), pp. 7ff.

107 Labrousse, 'Ruptures' (see n. 99 above), pp. 545ff.; cf. also the examples in Abel, *Massenarmut* (see n. 106 above), pp. 191ff.

108 Goubert, *Beauvais* (see n. 97 above), p. 75.

109 Goubert, *Beauvais* (see n. 97 above), pp. 616ff.

110 For the difference between 'mortality crisis' and 'crisis mortality', see J. Ruwet, 'Crises de mortalité et mortalités de crise à Aix-la-Chapelle (XVIIe début du XVIIIe siècle)', *Problèmes de mortalité* (see n. 101 above), pp. 379–408.

111 Here esp. Goubert, *Beauvais* (see n. 97 above), pp. 604–17; cf. R. Lee, 'Population in Pre-industrial England: An Econometric Analysis', *Quarterly Journal of Economics,* 87 (1973), 582–607.

112 Adam Smith versus M. Messance, *Rècherches sur la population des généralités d'Auvergne, de Lyon, de Rouen, et de quelques provinces et villes du royaume, avec des réflexions sur la valeur de bled tant en France qu'en Angleterre, depuis 1674 jusqu'en 1764* (Paris, 1766), cit. in Smith, *Wealth of Nations,* vol. 1 (see n. 5 above), Book 1, Ch. 8. p. 102.

113 This was first pointed out to me by E. A. Wrigley; French historical demographers have devoted a considerable amount of attention to this problem, but they have been specifically interested in the difference in the behaviour patterns of city and countryside. Cf. esp. J. P. Bardet, 'La démographie des villes de la modernité (XVIe–XVIIIe siècles). Mythes et réalités', *Annales de Démographie Historique* (1974), 101–26, esp. 120ff.; F. Lebrun, 'Démographie et mentalités: les mouvements des conceptions sous l'Ancien Régime', *Annales de Démographie Historique* (1974), 45–50; cf. the general remarks, based on his own field studies, in A. E. Imhof, 'Die nichtnementliche Auswertung der Kirchenbücher von Giessen und Umgebung. Die Resultate', *Historische Demographie als Sozialgeschichte. Giessen und Umgebung vom 17. zum 19. Jahrhundert*, ed. E. A. Imhof, Quellen und Forschungen zur hessischen Geschichte, vol. 31 (Darmstadt, 1975), vol. 1, pp. 85–277, esp. 245ff.

114 Lais, 'Bevölkerung des Kirchspiels Schönau' (see n. 62 above), pp. 22ff. (births), pp. 29f. (marriages), p. 34 (adult mortality); Lais, p. 22: table of the long-term trends of seasonal fluctuations of births in the parish Schönau 1670–1810. The table shows the number of births in 1000 that occurred during different seasons:

Time periods	Jan. – March	April – June	July – Sept.	Oct.– Dec.	Winter	Summer	differ- ence
1670–1700	313	216	211	260	573	427	146
1700–1730	274	208	216	302	576	424	152
1730–1760	293	212	218	277	570	430	140
1760–1790	287	225	225	263	550	450	100
1790–1810	281	227	228	264	545	455	90

115 Cf. Lais, 'Bevölkerungsgeschichte des Kirchspiels Schönau' (see n. 62 above), pp. 56ff., esp. 70ff.: intensive cotton spinning done by women and children since the middle of the eighteenth century and industrial wood-working done by the men.

116 Bardet, 'Démographie des villes' (see n. 113 above), p. 123.

117 The great food crisis of 1771–4 in central Europe provides an example which ought to be pursued further in demographic case studies; in the industrial regions Minden, Ravensberg, Tecklenburg-Lingen, and Silesia, in any case, the effects of the crisis were weaker than in neighbouring agrarian regions. Cf. the interesting, though aggregate data in O. Behre, *Geschichte der Statistik in Brandenburg-Preussen bis zur Gründung des Königlich-Statistischen Bureaus* (Berlin, 1905), p. 450 (Minden, Ravensberg, and Tecklenburg-Lingen) and 452 (Schlesien); this case, however, is contrasted by the example of the industrial regions of Electoral Saxony: Blaschke, *Bevölkerungsgeschichte von Sachsen* (see n. 4 above), p. 127f.; Blaschke, remarkably, does not ascribe the distinctive · 'surplus of deaths' in the proto-industrial regions of Saxony to the downturn of the industrial conjuncture, i.e. to a crisis of the 'type ancien', but to the incomplete organization of the cereal markets and the bad regional transportation system which could not deal with the sudden rise in the demand for grain (pp. 126, 128f.). But this example should be clarified in the light of the possibilities outlined below on p. 93 and in n. 124, since the counter factual procedure chosen by Blaschke, which calculates the 'total losses' of the population, does not provide precise insights into the characteristics of the individual demographic variables during the hunger year of 1772. For England see Chambers, *Vale of Trent* (see n. 4 above), pp. 23ff; for France P. Goubert, 'Révolution démographique au XVIIIᵉ siècle', in Labrousse et al., *Histoire économique* (see n. 99 above), pp. 55–84, esp. 64f.; but cf. also the different opinion below, p. 118f. and Ch. 4, n. 140.

118 Chambers, *Vale of Trent* (see n. 4 above), p. 27.

119 J. Meuvret, 'Les oscillations des prix des céréales au XVIIᵉ et XVIIIᵉ siècles en Angleterre et dans les pays de bassin parisien', in Meuvret, *Etudes* (see n. 96 above), pp. 113–24, esp. 124; concerning the disappearance of the crises of the old type in general and its demographic consequences, cf. Meuvret, 'Crises' (see n. 96 above), pp. 275ff.; also Goubert, *Beauvais* (see n. 97 above), pp. 59ff. and esp. Goubert, 'Révolution démographique' (see n. 16 above), pp. 62ff.

120 Levine, *Family Formation* (see n. 4 above), pp. 100ff. provides a typical example for the subsistence crisis of 1727–30 in the agrarian regions of Leicestershire: in the rural 'industrial village' of Shepshed the crisis had almost no demographic consequences, whereas in the agrarian village of Bottesford it assumed all the classic characteristics of a 'crise démographique de type ancien'; but cf. also the deviating pattern in Nottinghamshire during the same period in Chambers, *Vale of Trent* (see n. 4 above), p. 30.

121 See below, pp. 119f.

122 Malthus, *Essay* (see n. 21 above), pp. 376ff., esp. 379; cf. Goubert, 'Révolution démographique' (see n. 117 above), pp. 64f.

123 Chambers, *Population, Economy and Society* (see n. 4 above), pp. 118ff.

124 Troeltsch, *Calwer Zeughandlungskompagnie* (see n. 4 above), p. 421; Goubert, *Beauvais* (see n. 96 above), vol. 1, pp. 47ff., 78f. and the graphs in *Beauvais*, vol. 2, pp. 56f.: the divergent 'conjunctural' patterns of the farming village Auneuil and the weavers' village Mouy during the crisis period at the end of the seventeenth century provide an early, very instructive example. While Auneuil develops all the characteristics of a crisis of the 'type ancien' in 1693–4, in Mouy these characteristics are partially concealed or modified: a distinct crisis mortality occurs in conjunction with a less clearly delineated decline in the number of marriages, and the curve of the conceptions – though their absolute number goes down markedly – declines less suddenly and more gradually, which indicates that the population in Mouy responded to the crisis more elastically than that of Auneuil. See the interpretation below, pp. 118f. and Ch. 4, n. 140.

Notes to Chapter 4

1 The younger historical school of German political economists has devoted considerable attention to the different phases and types of relations of production in 'domestic industry'. Cf. e.g. K. Bücher, 'Die gewerblichen Betriebssysteme in ihrer geschichtlichen Entwicklung', in K. Bücher, *Die Entstehung der Volkswirtschaft*, 11th ed. (Tübingen, 1919), vol. 1, pp. 161–96; K. Bücher, the article 'Gewerbe', in *Handwörterbuch der Staatswissenschaften*, 3rd ed. (1909), vol. 4, pp. 847–80; G. Schmoller, *Grundriss der allgemeinen Volkswirtschaftslehre*, 7th to 11th ed. (Leipzig, 1908), vol. 1, pp. 450–554; cf. also O. Schwarz, 'Die Betriebsformen der modernen Grossindustrie', *Zs. für die gesamte Staatswissenschaft* 25 (1869), 535–629, esp. 546–9, 616–23. Still stimulating: V. I. Lenin, *The Development of Capitalism in Russia* (Moscow, 1956), esp. Chs. 5 and 6 about the rural kustar' industries of Russia which during this period, however, stood already beside a fully developed industrial capitalism in other industries and other countries. General surveys in which considerable attention is paid to the relations of production: E. V. Tarlé, *L'industrie dans les campagnes en France à la fin de l'ancien régime*, Bibliothèque d'histoire moderne, vol. 11 (Paris, 1910). P. Mantoux, *The Industrial Revolution in the Eighteenth Century*, 2nd ed. (1961); Maurice Dobb, *Studies in the Development of Capitalism*, 2nd ed. (London, 1963); cf. P. M. Sweezy, M. Dobb et al., *The Transition from Feudalism to Capitalism* (1954) (Patna, 1957), republ.: R. Hilton, ed., *The Transition from Feudalism to Capitalism* (London, 1976). In the Soviet Union, scholars are working on a comprehensive and comparative study about the genesis of capitalism; see A. N. Chistozvonov, 'Über die Arbeit der Sektion "Genesis des Kapitalismus" . . .', *Jb. Wirtsch. G.* (1973), pt. 3, 225–39. – Concerning the relations of production in German industry during this period, see the interesting contributions made in the unpublished working papers of the 'Forschungsseminar Kuczynski 1952' (unpubl. working papers) J. Kuczynski and D. Lösche, 'Einleitung'; R. Berthold, 'Zur Geschichte der Entwicklung der Produktionsverhältnisse in der württembergischen Zeugmacherei von der Mitte des 16. bis zur Mitte des 18. Jahrhunderts', report 1; P. Stulz, 'Zur Geschichte der

Entwicklung der Produktionsverhältnisse in der ländlichen westfälischen Leinenproduktion in der Zeit von 1450 bis 1750', report 2; D. Lösche, 'Zur Geschichte der
Entwicklung der Produktionsverhältnisse in der Leinen- und Barchentproduktion
oberdeutscher Städte von 1450 bis 1750', report 3; H. Hoffmann, 'Diskussion über den
gesellschaftlichen Charakter des Verlages'; an extended version of another contribution
was published under G. Heitz, *Ländliche Leinenproduktion in Sachsen 1470–1555*, Deutsche
Akademie der Wissenschaften in Berlin. Schriften des Instituts für Geschichte, 2nd
series, vol. 4 (Berlin, 1961). – Although these questions have long been of concern to
scholars of different orientations, nobody, to my knowledge, has yet attempted to
establish explicit models for the relations of production which occur in different rural
industries. Such models would shed light on the laws of their functioning, on the
relationship of the different relations of production to each other – especially the
conditions under which a transition occurs from one set of relations to another – as well
as on the connection between the relations of production and other aspects of the socio-
economic process. Such explicit models are also lacking in E. März, *Einführung in die
Marxsche Theorie der wirtschaftlichen Entwicklung. Frühkapitalismus und Kapitalismus der freien
Konkurrenz* (Vienna, 1976).

2 Wallerstein, *The Modern World-System. Capitalist Agriculture and the Origins of the
European World-Economy in the Sixteenth Century* (New York etc. 1974), pp. 87–100, 126f.,
350f. Wallerstein overlooks the fact that, in spite of the basic connection between core
and periphery, the inner logic of the *Gutswirtschaft* is fundamentally different from that of
the capitalist system as analysed by Marx; see W. Kula, *Théorie économique du système
féodal. Pour un modèle de l'économie polonaise 16ᵉ–18ᵉ siècles*, Civilisations et sociétées, vol. 15
(Paris etc. 1970). Furthermore, by asserting that the world system was nothing but
'capitalist' from its very beginning in the sixteenth century, Wallerstein does little to
promote a thorough analysis of the great distance between merchant capitalism in the
sixteenth to industrial capitalism in the nineteenth and twentieth centuries.

3 Bücher, 'Gewerbe' (see n. 1 above), p. 867.

4 According to R. Wissell, *Des alten Handwerks Recht und Gewohnheit*, 2nd ed., ed. by
E. Schraepler, Einzelveröffentlichungen der Historischen Kommission zu Berlin, vol. 7
(Berlin, 1974), vol. 2, pp. 439–45 this was not originally true; but beginning in the
fifteenth and up to the seventeenth centuries, women were increasingly excluded from
the guild crafts. Since then, women worked as guild artisans only in exceptional cases,
and this situation was hardly at all changed by the occasional government decrees at the
end of the eighteenth century which specifically admitted women to the guilds.
Similarly, B. Brodmeier, *Die Frau im Handwerk in historischer und moderner Sicht*,
Forschungsberichte aus dem Handwerk, vol. 9 (Münster, 1963), pp. 11–51. The
cotton-lawn weavers of Hof in the sixteenth century provide an example of a craft that
consisted primarily of female masters and apprentices: E. Dietlein, *Das Textilgewerbe der
bayrischen Stadt Hof von 1500–1870. Eine wirtschaftsgeschichtliche Studie* (Diss. phil.,
Erlangen, 1921), pp. 138f., 141f. For purposes of comparison with concentrated rural
industry, it remains to investigate more closely to what extent – despite the more and
more strictly enforced exclusion of women from the guilds – the opportunity remained
for masters on the one hand to allow female members of their family to work alongside
them, and on the other hand to employ servant girls for ancillary and subordinate tasks.
In certain cities this kind of women's employment existed, in others it was prohibited:
Brodmeier, *Frau* (cited above), esp. pp. 20f.; cf. also L. Bittner, 'Das Eisenwesen in
Innerberg-Eisenerz bis zur Gründug der Innerberger Hauptgewerkschaft im Jahre
1625', *Archiv für österreichische Geschichte*, 89 (1901), 451–646, esp. 549, 551;
R. Stahlschmidt, *Die Geschichte des eisenverarbeitenden Gewerbes in Nürnberg von den ersten
Nachrichten im 12.–13. Jh. bis 1630*, Nürnberger Werkstücke zur Stadt-und Landesges-

chichte. Schriftenreihe des Stadtarchivs Nürnberg, vol. 4 (Nuremberg, 1971), pp. 182–4; E. Wiest, *Die Entwicklung des Nürnberger Gewerbes zwischen 1648 und 1806*, Forschungen zur Sozial- und Wirtschaftsgeschichte, vol. 12 (Stuttgart, 1968), pp. 68f., 70, 81f.

5 I. Pinchbeck, *Women Workers and the Industrial Revolution 1750–1850* (1930; rpt. London, 1969), pp. 7ff. on agriculture, pp. 111–47, 157–82, 202–35, 270–81 on rural industries.

6 The work of women and children was very common in rural industry. Little is known, however, about the shaping of production processes within the family, which must have differed according to industry and according to the level of the division of labour in the society. It seems exaggerated, though, to picture the proto-industrial family as a 'miniature factory', as is done by I. Pinchbeck, *Women Workers* (see n. 5 above), pp. 113f.; Pinchbeck is followed by N. J. Smelser, *Social Change in the Industrial Revolution* (London, 1959), p. 56. There is however an example which fits this picture in E. Gothein, *Wirtschaftsgeschichte des Schwarzwaldes und der angrenzenden Landschaften* (Strassburg, 1892), vol. 1, pp. 826f.; otherwise cf. below pp. 106f. One reason why the cooperative division of labour within the families of domestic producers was so little advanced during this time, probably lies in the fact that under the conditions of handicraft work, the division of labour increased in efficiency only when an optimal ratio between the number of workers who performed the different tasks could be achieved, and this was only rarely possible within the small unit of a family.

7 Cf. K. Marx, *Capital*, vol. 1, introd. by E. Mandel, transl. by Ben Fowkes (Harmondsworth, 1976), Ch. 10, pp. 344f.

8 Lately, a new discussion has arisen about this subject which has been guided by a strong interest in theory; see e.g. the models in E. J. Nell, 'Economic Relationships in the Decline of Feudalism', *History and Theory*, 6 (1967), 313–50; D. C. North, R. P. Thomas, 'The Rise and Fall of the Manorial System: A Theoretical Model', *Journ. Econ. Hist.*, 31 (1971), 777–803; but see also the critique in S. Fenoaltea, 'The Rise and Fall of a Theoretical Model: The Manorial System', *Journ. Econ. Hist.*, 35 (1975), 386–409; W. Rusinski, 'Über die Entwicklung der Fronwirtschaft in Mittel- und Osteuropa', *Studia Historiae Oeconomicae*, 9 (1974), 27–45; R. Brenner, 'Agrarian Class Structure and Economic Development in Pre-industrial Europe', *Past and Present*, 70 (1976), 30–75. – Cf. above pp. 6f. and n. 48, pp. 19ff.

9 Between these two extremes there existed a wide variety of other forms. The extent to which they promoted the emergence and growth of proto-industrialization is discussed above pp. 17–21.

10 This agrarian commodity-production on the basis of feudal labour-services is the central theme of the basic book by W. Kula, *Théorie économique du système féodal: pour un modèle de l'économie polonaise 16ᵉ–18ᵉ siècles*, Civilisations et sociétés, vol. 15 (Paris, 1970), although it deals only peripherally with *industrial* commodity-production within the *Gutswirtschaft*.

11 This question was especially debated for the case of Russia under the term 'feudal manufacture', which meant that more attention was paid to the centralized or partially centralized production facilities than to the dispersed rural production. The result of this debate appears to be that between the seventeenth and the middle of the nineteenth centuries, feudally-organized commodity-production was of considerable importance in Russian industry, but that it was by no means the only form of organization. Great differences existed between various periods, regions, and industries, and mixed forms were very common; for example, wages were often paid to personally unfree labourers. Summaries in B. Widera, 'Anfänge der industriellen Grossproduktion und Verbreitung der Lohnarbeit unter den Facharbeitern Russlands im 17. und 18. Jh.', *Genesis und*

272 Notes to pp. 96-8

Entwicklung des Kapitalismus in Russland. Studien und Beiträge, eds. P. Hoffmann and H. Lemke, Quellen und Studien zur Geschichte Osteuropas, vol. 17 (Berlin, 1973), pp. 96–127; N. M. Druzhinin, 'Besonderheiten der Genesis des Kapitalismus in Russland', *Genesis und Entwicklung*, pp. 26–62, esp. 47ff.; N. Pavlenko, 'Zum Problem der Struktur der russischen Manufaktur im 17.–19. Jh.', *Jahrbuch für Geschichte der sozialistischen Länder Europas*, 13, 2 (1969), 109–20; N. I. Pavlenko and B. B. Kafengaus, in: *Geschichte der UdSSR* (Berlin, 1962), vol. 1, pp. 443–6, 528–35; J. Blum, *Lord and Peasant in Russia from the Ninth to the Nineteenth Century* (Princeton, N. J., 1961; rpt. 1971), pp. 293, 297–9; P. I. Ljashchenko, *History of the National Economy of Russia to the 1917 Revolution* (1939; rpt. New York, 1949), pp. 283–306; critical about this discussion: A. Gerschenkron, *Europe in the Russian Mirror* (Cambridge, 1970), pp. 77–79. For the larger context in which this question is being discussed, cf. S. H. Baron, 'The Transition from Feudalism to Capitalism in Russia: A Major Soviet Historical Controversy', *American Historical Review*, 77 (1972), 715–29. – For Germany this question is discussed in Hoffmann, 'Verlag' (See n. 1 above).

12 H. Aubin, 'Die Anfänge der grossen schlesischen Leineweberei und -handlung', *VSWG*, 35 (1942), 169–74; cf. Kula, *Théorie* (see n. 10 above), pp. 31, 41f.

13 Cf. above pp. 20f. and 29f.; for Upper Lusatia also W. v. Westernhagen, *Leinwandmanufaktur und Leinwandhandel der Oberlausitz in der zweiten Hälfte des 18. Jh. und während der Kontinentalsperre* (Diss. phil., Leipzig, 1932), p. 11.

14 Kula, *Théorie* (see n. 10 above), pp. 85, 87.

15 Cf. e.g. Ljashchenko, *National Economy* (see n. 11 above), pp. 295f. – In the manufactures of Silesian and Bohemian feudal lords, labour services were mainly used for the unqualified auxiliary work: K. Hinze, *Die Arbeiterfrage zu Beginn des modernen Kapitalismus in Brandenburg-Preussen* (Berlin, 1927), pp. 80, 149–52; J. Purš, 'Struktur und Dynamik der industriellen Entwicklung in Böhmen im letzten Viertel des 18. Jahrhunderts', *Jb. Wirtsch. G.* (1965), part 1, 160–96, (1965), part 2, 103–24, esp. part 1, 191f.; cf. also H. Krüger, *Zur Geschichte der Manufakturen und der Manufakturarbeiter in Preussen. Die mittleren Provinzen in der zweiten Hälfte des 18. Jahrhunderts*, Schriftenreihe des Instituts für Allgemeine Geschichte an der Humboldt-Universität Berlin, vol. 3 (Berlin, 1958), pp. 58–63; H. Hoffmann, *Handwerk und Manufaktur in Preussen 1769. Das Taschenbuch Knyphausen*, Deutsche Akademie der Wissenschaften Berlin. Schriften des Zentralinstituts für Geschichte, 2nd ser., vol. 10 (Berlin, 1969), pp. 67f.

16 See above pp. 20f. and 29f. and the literature under n. 11 esp. with regard to the mixed forms. Similarly also A. Hoffmann, 'Die Grundherrschaft als Unternehmen', *Z. Agrarg. Agrarsoziol.*, 6 (1958), 123–31, esp. 126f.

17 Kula, *Théorie* (see n. 10 above), pp. 32–5, 96f.; cf. also below pp. 113–14.

18 Kula, *Théorie* (see n. 10 above), pp. 35, 107f.; cf. Lashchenko, *National Economy* (see n. 11 above), pp. 295f.

19 See also A. Kunze, *Die nordböhmisch-sächsische Leinwand und der Nürnberger Grosshandel. Mit besonderer Berücksichtigung des Friedland- Reichenberger Gebietes*, Forschungen zur sudetendeutschen Heimatkunde, vol. 1 (Reichenberg, 1926), pp. 50–2, 72–8; A. Klima, 'The Domestic Industry and the Putting-out-system (Verlagssystem) in the Period of Transition from Feudalism to Capitalism', *Deuxième Conférence Internationale d'Histoire Economique Aix-en-Provence 1962*, vol. 2 (Paris, 1965), pp. 477–81; A. Klima, 'The Role of Rural Domestic Industry in Bohemia in the Eighteenth Century', *Econ. Hist. Rev.*, 2nd ser., 27 (1974), 48–56, esp. 51–3; Krüger, *Manufakturen* (see n. 15 above), pp. 203f.; cf. also A. Kahan, 'The Infringement of the Market upon the Serf-economy in Eastern Europe', *Peasant Studies Newsletter*, 3 (1974), 7–13.

20 Westernhagen, *Leinwandmanufaktur* (see n. 13 above), p. 11; U. Lewald, 'Die Entwicklung der ländlichen Textilindustrie im Rheinland und in Schlesien. Ein

Vergleich', *Zs. für Ostforschung*, 10 (1961), 601–30, esp. 610; cf. Kunze, *Leinwand* (see n. 19 above), p. 47.

21 Cf. above, pp. 20, 29, and below pp. 114f., 125, 128f., 132ff., 143, 149f.; and Kisch below, pp. 178–200. Cf. already M. Weber, *Wirtschaft und Gesellschaft*, ed. by J. Winckelmann (Cologne and Berlin, 1964), pp. 823f.

22 Cf. also above, pp. 21f., and the literature cited there concerning the significance of the classic 'vent-for-surplus' theory for proto-industrialization.

23 This expression is taken from M. Dobb, *Studies* (see n. 1 above), p. 209, where it relates to foreign trade. The *Kaufsystem* was maintained until the end of proto-industrialization especially in linen-producing regions, and above all in those that were characterized by a large labour supply and low income for the direct producers, as well as by the local or nearby cultivation of flax or hemp, which often prevented them from making the switch to other textiles. Examples: E. Sabbe, *Histoire de l'industrie linière en Belgique*, Collection Nationale, 6th ser., vol. 67 (Brussels, 1954), pp. 39f., cf. p. 36; G. Jacquemyns, *Histoire de la crise économique des Flandres 1845–50*, Académie Royale de Belgique. Classe des lettres etc. Mémoires. Collection in 8°, 2nd ser., vol. 26, 1 (Brussels, 1929), pp. 196–202, cf. 29–42, 103–7, 130f.; P. Bois, *Paysans de l'Ouest. Des structures économiques et sociales aux options politiques depuis l'époque révolutionnaire dans la Sarthe* (Le Mans, 1960), pp. 516f., cf. 503ff.; but see also pp. 517f. and 521ff. for beginnings of capitalist relations of production in the late eighteenth century; H. Blumberg, 'Ein Beitrag zur Geschichte der deutschen Leinenindustrie von 1834 bis 1870', *Studien zur Geschichte der industriellen Revolution in Deutschland*, ed. H. Mottek, Veröffentlichungen des Instituts für Wirtschaftsgeschichte an der Hochschule für Ökonomie Berlin-Karlshorst, vol. 1 (Berlin, 1960), pp. 65–143, esp. 114f.; S. Kühn, *Der Hirschberger Leinwand- und Schleierhandel von 1648–1806* (Diss. phil., Breslau, 1936; printed 1938), pp. 21–4, cf. 7f.; H. Potthoff, 'Die Leinenleggen in der Grafschaft Ravensberg', *15. Jahresbericht des Historischen Vereins für die Grafschaft Ravensberg* (1901), 1–40, esp. 34f., 108f.; H. Potthoff, 'Das Ravensberger Leinengewerbe im 17. und 18. Jahrhundert', 35 *Jahresbericht des Historischen Vereins für die Grafschaft Ravensberg* (1921), 27–83, esp. 47, 61f., cf. 28–35. – Concerning the emergence of the putting-out system in the Irish linen industry, see C. Gill, *The Rise of the Irish Linen Industry* (Oxford, 1925), pp. 138, 144–7, 151–5, cf. 6f., 10; for Upper Lusatia cf. Westernhagen, *Leinwandmanufaktur* (see n. 13 above), pp. 12f., 17, cf. 8ff. – In other industries the *Kaufsystem* survived as long as guild organizations, which could exist outside of towns as well, were strong (see below p. 106, n. 74f.), e.g. in parts of the small metal industry in the Duchy Berg (Rhineland) where smiths still sold a portion of their products directly to consumers: W. Engels and P. Legers, *Aus der Geschichte der Remscheider und bergischen Werkzeug- und Eisenindustrie* (Remscheid, 1928), vol. 1, pp. 96ff., 119–23, 128, cf. 71–9, 8, 190f.; similarly for Sheffield: Mantoux, *Industrial Revolution* (see n. 1 above), pp. 277f.; cf. also M. B. Rowlands, *Masters and Men in the West Midland Metalware Trades before the Industrial Revolution* (Manchester, 1975), pp. 31f., 78, cf. 148f., 157. The Yorkshire woolen industry for a long time operated under a kind of *Kaufsystem* based on the interplay between merchants and small clothiers who worked predominantly with their own and their families' labour power. Especially in the eighteenth century, however, larger clothiers began to emerge who employed others for wages either in the putting-out system or in medium-to-large centralized manufactures, most of all in the production of worsted. Apparently it was they who made the transition to the factory system in the last quarter of the eighteenth century; at least they did so to a larger extent than the merchants; cf. below p. 107 and n. 86; H. Heaton, *The Yorkshire Woollen and Worsted Industries*, Oxford Historical and Literary Studies, vol. 10 (Oxford, 1920), pp. 92–101, 293–301; R. G. Wilson, *Gentlemen Merchants. The Merchant Community in Leeds 1700–1830*

(Manchester and New York, 1971), esp. pp. 53–60; D. T. Jenkins, *The West Riding Wool Textile Industry 1770–1835. A Study in Fixed Capital Formation*, Pasold Occasional Papers, vol. 4 (Edington, Wilts., 1975), pp. 5f., 191–205.

Concerning the limitation of competition among merchants: Kühn, *Hirschberger Leinwandhandel* (see above), pp. 5f., 28–32; H. Fechner, *Wirtschaftsgeschichte der preussischen Provinz Schlesien in der Zeit ihrer provinziellen Selbständigkeit 1741–1806* (Breslau, 1907), pp. 43–47, 715f.; A. Zimmermann, *Blüte und Verfall des Leinengewerbes in Schlesien* (1885), 2nd ed. (Oldenburg and Leipzig, n. d.), pp. 200–2; Gill, *Irish Linen* (see above), p. 140–2. In the area of Ravensberg (Westphalia), government regulations gave distinct privileges to native merchants at the expense of producers and foreign traders: Potthoff, 'Leinenleggen' (see above), esp. pp. 54ff., 62ff., 69ff., 74ff.; Potthoff, 'Ravensberger Leinengewerbe' (see above), pp. 54–61.

The term *Kaufsystem* in contrast to *Lohnsystem* (wage system) occurs already in Schwarz, 'Betriebsformen' (see n. 1 above), pp. 246f., cf. 619ff., and in Schmoller, *Grundriss* (n. 1 above), vol. 1, p. 485.

24 The construction of a model, which is attempted here, starts from Marx's analyses about 'simple commodity production' and 'merchant capital'. Marx however did not combine them to a model about a particular historical mode of production and circulation; instead Marx used these concepts in order to throw light on different aspects of the system of industrial capitalism; see esp. Marx, *Capital* 1, Chs. 3–6 and *Capital* 3, Chs. 16–20; cf. also K. Marx, *Grundrisse. Foundations of the Critique of Political Economy*, trans. by M. Nicolaus (Harmondsworth, 1973), pp. 856ff.

25 Taxes can be left out of consideration here.

26 A. V. Chayanov, 'On the Theory of Non-capitalist Economic Systems', in A. V. Chayanov, *The Theory of Peasant Economy*, eds. D. Thorner et al. (Homewood, Ill., 1966), pp. 1–28, here 6ff.

27 This is not to say, of course, that petty commodity producers did not make use of favourable terms of trade when the opporunity arose. It only means that, as a rule, the stimulus which motivated their economic activity was not the augmentation of the exchange value – in contrast to the stimulus behind the circuit of capital. Moreover, *in the long run*, only a small minority among them could ever obtain enough advantages in order to make the transition from petty commodity producers to capitalists.

28 See above, pp. 43, 54, 64ff., and below pp. 103 with n. 54, 108 with n. 87.

29 In quite a number of regions, periods, and industries the income of petty producers was hardly sufficient to cover the cost of their livelihood during normal times, and during bad periods they had to go into debt; even under favourable economic conditions, the income was still only just adequate to cover the cost of living. In these cases a 'backward bending supply of labour' could hardly have occurred. There are many contemporary reports about this phenomenon, but many of them – though not all – were designed to back up the argument that low prices or wages should be paid to the producers. Cf. Westernhagen, *Leinwandmanufaktur* (see n. 13 above), pp. 11f.; A. P. Wadsworth and J. de Lacy Mann, *The Cotton Trade and Industrial Lancashire 1660–1780* (1931; rpt. Manchester 1965), pp. 387–93; J. de Lacy Mann, 'Clothiers and Weavers in Wiltshire during the Eighteenth Century', *Studies in the Industrial Revolution*, ed. L. S. Presnell (London, 1960), pp. 66–96, esp. 76f.; T. S. Ashton, *An Economic History of England: The Eighteenth Century* (1955; rpt. London, 1972), pp. 204–6; D. S. Landes, *The Unbound Prometheus. Technological Change and Industrial Development in Western Europe from 1750 to the Present* (Cambridge, 1969), pp. 58–60; W. Sombart, *Der moderne Kapitalismus* (Munich, etc., 1928), vol. 1, pp. 802–8; Marx, *Capital* vol. 1, Ch. 10, pp. 385–8. But others say that the lower classes did respond to possibilities of increasing their consumption and that, since the middle of the eighteenth century, a growing number of observers and theoreticians in England considered high wages as an incentive toward more and better work: A. W. Coats, 'Changing Attitudes to Labour in the Mid Eighteenth Century', *Econ. Hist. Rev.*, 2nd ser., 11 (1958), 35–51; E. W. Gilboy, *Wages in Eighteenth Century England*, Harvard Economic Studies, vol. 45 (Cambridge, Mass., 1934), pp. 234–44. A first attempt to establish the backward-bending supply curve of labour empirically and statistically has not been successful: F. F. Mendels, 'Industrialization and Population Pressure in Eighteenth-Century Flanders' (unpubl. PhD. Diss., University of Wisconsin, 1969), pp. 273–6.

30 Schematically the circuit of merchant capital can be represented as follows: M(oney) – C(ommodity) – M(oney)′, where M′ > M. For the petty commodity producer, however, the circuit looks as follows: C(ommodity)–M(oney)–C(ommodity)′, where C′ is qualitatively different from C, i.e. its use value differs but not its exchange value. When the processes of production and reproduction are taken into account, the entire circuit for the petty commodity producer looks like this: C′ is divided into ms(means of subsistence) – which reproduces the labour power (L) – and the replacement and renewal of the means of production (mp); both together permit him to resume the P(roduction) of the C(ommodity):

$$\text{Petty commodity producer:} \quad C' \left\{ \begin{array}{c} ms \ldots L \\ mp \end{array} \right\} \ldots P \ldots C-M-C'$$

$$\text{Merchant capitalist:} \quad M-C-M'$$

Here, the direct producers exchange the finished product C for M with merchant capital and merchant capital has nothing to do with the production process.

31 The direct or indirect investment in land, estates, rights or privileges was probably especially important in countries with feudal agriculture; cf. below: Kisch, pp. 184f.

32 See above, pp. 21.

33 See above, pp. 14ff.

34 See above, pp. 74ff.

35 Employment figures which would provide reliable evidence for the progress of proto-industrialization in different regions are hardly available yet. The degree of industrial concentration around 1800, though, can be illustrated by a few German examples: in the Duchy of Berg, which specialized in textiles and metal products, only 25.3% of those gainfully employed worked in agriculture, fishing, and gardening, 59.5% in mining and industry, and 15.2% in the tertiary sector: F.-W. Henning, 'Die Wirtschaftsstruktur mitteleuropäischer Gebiete an der Wende zum 19. Jahrhundert mit besonderer Berücksichtigung des gewerblichen Bereichs', *Beiträge zu Wirtschaftswachstum und Wirtschaftsstruktur im 16. und 19. Jahrhundert*, ed. W. Fischer, Schriften des Vereins für Socialpolitik N.F. 63 (Berlin, 1971), pp. 101–67, esp. 129, cf. 103, n. 7. In the Eichsfeld (Central Germany; partly woolen manufacture, partly linen), 36 wool weaving looms and 54 looms altogether were counted for every 1000 inhabitants in 1802; in the woolen trade about 10 workers were employed per loom; K. Haendly, Bauern und Weber im Eichsfeld. Geschichte eines deutschen Kleinstaates, seiner Wirtschaft und der Menschen, die ihn bewohnten 897–1933 (Diss., Cologne, 1949), p. 205; cf. the more detailed figures for 1765 in W. Prochaska, Die Entwicklung des Textilgewerbes im Eichsfelde, *Eichsfelder Heimathefte*, Sonderheft 1963 (Worbis, 1963), pp. 11f., as well as the figures for 1796, 1802, 1804 in H. Godehardt, 'Zur Lage der Weber, Kämmer und Spinner des Eichsfeldes während der ersten preussischen Herrschaft (1802–1806)', *Eichsfelder Heimathefte* (1970), No. 1, 63–75, here 65ff., which indicate that in the most industrialized *Amt* (administrative district) almost the entire population was employed in weaving, carding, and spinning wool. In the county Tecklenburg (Westphalia; coarse linen), 179 looms existed for every 1000 inhabitants in 1785 : St. Reekers, 'Beiträge zur statistischen Darstellung der gewerblichen Wirtschaft Westfalens um 1800', *Westfälische Forschungen*, 19 (1966), pp. 70, 73. An example for the degree of industrial concentration in the English woolen industry at the beginning of the seventeenth century: R. H. Tawney and A. J. Tawney, 'An Occupational Census of the Seventeenth Century', *Econ. Hist. Rev.*, 5 (1934), 25–64. For the period 1660–1710, Rowlands, *Masters* (see n. 23 above), pp. 18ff. calculated that in the region of the West Midlands metal industry 61% of adult males were employed in industry, trade, and services (34% alone in the metal industry), and only 33% in agriculture.

36 Survey: C. T. Smith, *An Historical Geography of Western Europe before 1800* (London, 1967), pp. 543–81; H. Kellenbenz, 'Ländliches Gewerbe und bäuerliches Unternehmertum in Westeuropa vom Spätmittelalter bis ins 18. Jahrhundert', *Deuxième conférence* (see n. 19 above), vol. 2, pp. 377–427; H. C.Darby, 'The Age of the Improver, 1600–1800', *A New Historical Geography of England*, ed. H. C. Darby (Cambridge, 1973), pp. 302–88, esp. 355–70; Ashton, *Eighteenth Century* (see n. 29 above), pp. 91–7; P. Léon, in: *Histoire économique et sociale de la France*, eds. F. Braudel, E. Labrousse (Paris, 1970), vol. 2, pp. 525–8 and the maps on pp. 228–46; Tarlé, *L'industrie* (see n. 1 above), esp. pp. 5ff.; Purš, 'Struktur' (see n. 15 above), vol. 2, pp. 117–20; W. Zorn, 'Schwerpunkte der deutschen Ausfuhrindustrie im 18. Jahrhundert', *Jahrbücher für Nationalökonomie und Statistik*, vol. 173 (1961), pp. 422–47; cf. also H. Hahn and W. Zorn, eds., *Historische Wirtschaftskarte der Rheinlande um 1820*, Rheinisches Archiv, vol. 87 (Bonn, 1973).

37 In order to determine the significance of the individual factors which kept wage costs lower in the countryside than in towns, these factors must be analytically isolated, even though, in reality several of them tended to act together. This is especially important, because lower costs for the merchant or putter-out did not necesarily correspond to a lower *real* income for the industrial family. (Even less can one draw direct conclusions about the relative *profit*-situation of the merchant or entrepreneur from the income situation of the direct producers, for the former depended strongly on the entrepreneur's position among his – often international – competitors. If the production techniques of his competitors were superior, for example, the incomes of the direct producers and the capitalist's profits could both be low, cf. above, pp. 50–1). If the cost of living, and especially of food, in the rural areas was low, for example, the purchase prices or wage rates would be low, too, for the merchant or merchant-manufacturer; but this would not necessarily mean that the real income of the direct producers had to be lower than in town. Furthermore, if the guild-organization in towns assured the artisan family of a sufficient income without the labour of women and children, while in the countryside the entire family had to participate in industrial labour, the lower income per unit of labour in rural areas did not necessarily mean lower incomes per family. Where industrial labour was combined with agricultural labour, it must be taken into consideration that – if all other conditions were equal – less time was available for industrial work than in the case of a family that was exclusively employed in industry. When using these and other factors in order to explain actual developments (see above, pp. 22f., 44ff., 50ff.), one must be sure what is being compared in a given historical situation. For example, when production was first shifted from town to countryside, all three factors mentioned above are likely to have played a role. But once it had become normal for women and children to be involved in industrial work, a cost advantage could no longer have risen for the merchant or putter out, even less a 'differential profit' (see above, p. 23, but also p. 50). Concerning the combination of agricultural with industrial labour, see below pp. 105f. and n. 64).

38 Some examples: Ashton, *Eighteenth Century* (see n. 29 above), pp. 99ff.; W.

Bodmer, *Die Entwicklung der schweizerischen Textilwirtschaft im Rahmen der übrigen Industrien und Wirtschaftszweige* (Zürich, 1960), pp. 220f., 223; Gothein, *Schwarzwald* (see n. 6 above), pp. 723ff., 731f., 742, 753, 763f.; V. Hofmann, 'Die Anfänge der österreichischen Baumwollindustrie in den österreichischen Alpenländern im 18. Jh.', in V. Hofmann, *Beiträge zur neueren österreichischen Wirtschaftsgeschichte*, Archiv für österreichische Geschichte, vol. 110 (Vienna, 1926), vol. 2, pp. 415–742, esp. 525ff., 550; E. Barkhausen, *Die Tuchindustrie in Montjoie – ihr Aufstieg und Niedergang* (Aachen, 1925), pp. 64–66; H. Kisch, *Prussian Mercantilism and the Rise of the Krefeld Silk Industry: Variations upon an Eighteenth Century Theme*, Transactions of the American Philosophical Society n. s. 58, 7 (Philadelphia, 1968), pp. 27f.; G. Adelmann, 'Strukturwandel der rheinischen Leinen- und Baumwollegewerbe zu Beginn der Industrialisierun', *VSWG*, 53 (1966), 162–84, esp. 165–7.

39 In England, for example, three times as much cotton was processed in 1760–69 than in 1700–09, and in the woolen industry, which started at a higher level, twice as much was produced in the 1770s than at the end of the seventeenth century; Scotland's linen-production which had been unimportant before 1700 increased eightfold between 1710 and 1763; Ph. Deane and W. A. Cole, *British Economic Growth 1688–1959*, 2nd ed. (Cambridge, 1969), pp. 51–3; Ph. Deane, 'The Output of the British Woolen Industry in the Eighteenth Century', *Journ. Econ. Hist.*, 17 (1957), 207–23. A survey about the growth of a few industries in France during the eighteenth century: P. Léon, in: *Histoire économique* (see n. 36 above), vol. 2, pp. 514–22. Concerning the development of productivity, see below pp. 111ff.

40 A generally accepted definition of the term 'putting-out system' (Verlagssystem) does not exist. The definition here is similar to those in W. Sombart and R. Meerwarth, 'Hausindustrie (Verlagssystem)', *Handwörterbuch der Staatswissenschaften*, 4th ed. (1923), vol. 5, pp. 179–207, here 179f.; E. Schremmer, *Die Wirtschaft Bayerns. Vom hohen Mittelalter bis zum Beginn der Industrialisierung. Bergbau, Gewerbe, Handel* (Munich, 1970), pp. 472f.; cf. W. Sombart, 'Die Hausindustrie in Deutschland', *Archiv für soziale Gesetzgebung und Statistik*, 4 (1891), 103–56, esp. 117f. and n. 3. Bücher and Kulischer, on the other hand, speak of the 'putting-out system' when a trader intervenes between the producer and consumer: Bücher, *Betriebssysteme* (see n. 1 above), pp. 185f.; Bücher, 'Gewerbe' (n. 1), pp. 867–70; J. Kulischer, *Allgemeine Wirtschaftsgeschichte des Mittelalters und der Neuzeit*, 4th ed. (1929; rpt. Munich, 1971), pp. 113–37. According to their definition, no distinction is made between 'putting-out system' and *Kaufsystem*. A clear definition of the term 'putting-out system' helps to carefully analyse the relations between direct producers and the capitalist. Already G. Aubin called for such an analysis: G. Aubin, 'Zur Geschichte des Verlagssystems in der Periode des Frühkapitalismus', *Jahrbücher für Nationalökonomie und Statistik*, 127, 3rd. ser. (1927), 336–42, esp. 337.

41 For some authors this is included in their definition of the term 'putting-out system': Hoffmann, 'Verlag' (see n. 1 above), p. 6; Lösche, 'Produktionsverhältnisse' (n. 1), pp. 6f., 9, 13f.; Krüger, *Manufakturen* (see n. 15 above), pp. 179f.

42 An example: W. Troeltsch, *Die Calwer Zeughandlungskompagnie und ihre Arbeiter. Studien zur Gewerbe- und Sozialgeschichte Altwürttembergs* (Jena, 1897), pp. 55–135, esp. 89ff.; cf. Berthold, 'Produktionsverhältnisse' (see n. 1 above), pp. 21–6; B. Kirchgässner, 'Der Verlag im Spannungsfeld von Stadt und Umland', *Stadt und Umland*, eds. E. Maschke, J. Sydow, Veröffentlichungen der Kommission für geschichtliche Landeskunde Baden-Württemberg, vol. B 82 (Stuttgart, 1974), pp. 72–128, esp. 111–18.

43 Examples: Kulischer, *Wirtschaftsgeschichte* (see n. 40 above), vol. 2, pp. 113–16.

44 See above, p. 273, n. 22, counter-examples: notes 23 and 45. Examples of the form of the putting-out system in which the putter-out provided the yarn exist already for the south-German linen industry during the late Middle Ages: Kirchgässer, 'Verlag' (see n. 42 above), pp. 84–100, esp. 96f.; this form of putting-out system occurred even earlier in the south-German fustian trade.

45 Cf. J. D. Chambers, 'The Rural Domestic Industries during the Period of Transition to the Factory System, with Special Reference to the Midland Counties of England', *Deuxième conférence* (see n. 19 above), vol. 2, pp. 429–55, esp. 430f.; L. A. Clarkson, *The Pre-industrial Economy in England 1500–1750*, 2nd ed. (1972), pp. 99–103; Mantoux, *Industrial Revolution* (see n. 1 above), pp. 62–8; Ashton, *Eighteenth Century* (see n. 28 above), pp. 98–102; T. S. Ashton, *The Industrial Revolution 1760–1830* (London, 1948; rpt. 1970), pp. 22–4, 31; Pinchbeck, *Women Workers* (see n. 5 above), pp. 136ff.; Tarlé, *L'industrie* (see n. 1 above), pp. 48ff.; T. J. Markovitch, *L'industrie lainière à la fin du règne de Louis XIV et sous la Régence*, Economies et sociétés. Cahiers de l'I.S.E.A., 2, 8 (Geneva, 1968), pp. 1517–1697, esp. 1675ff.; Bodmer, *Schweizerische Textilwirtschaft* (see n. 38 above), pp. 145ff., 156, 162f., 181ff., 204ff., 216ff., 229; W. Zorn, in: *Handbuch der deutschen Wirtschafts- und Sozialgeschichte*, eds. H. Aubin and W. Zorn (Stuttgart, 1971), vol. 1, pp. 538–40. Some examples: – J. de Lacy Mann, *The Cloth Industry in the West of England from 1640 to 1880* (Oxford, 1971), pp. 89–119, esp. 104, 115f.; Mann, 'Wiltshire' (see n. 28 above), esp. pp. 68ff.; Wadsworth and Mann, *Cotton Trade* (n. 29 above), esp. pp. 78–91, 273–7; W. H. B. Court, *The Rise of the Midland Industries 1600–1838*, 2nd ed. (Oxford etc., 1953), pp. 199–204 (about nail-making); Rowlands, *Masters* (see n. 23 above), pp. 27f., 35f., 78ff., 156ff. (several branches of the small metal-goods industry); J. Kaplow, *Elbeuf during the Revolutionary Period*, The Johns Hopkins University Studies in the Historical and Political Science, vol. 81, 2 (Baltimore, Md., 1964), pp. 25–33 (woolen cloth); J. Sion, *Les paysans de la Normandie orientale* (Paris, 1908), pp. 181ff.; L. K. Berkner, *Family Social Structure and Rural Industry. A Comparative Study of the Waldviertel and the Pays de Caux in the Eighteenth Century* (Diss., Harvard University, 1973), pp. 259ff. (cotton and linen); P. Deyon, *Amiens. Capitale provinciale. Etude sur la société urbaine au XVIIe siècle* (Paris etc., 1967), pp. 209ff. (woollen cloth); Ch. Tilly, *The Vendée* (London, 1964), pp. 139f., 217ff. (linen); H. Hasquin, *Le 'Pays de Charleroi' aux XVIIe et XVIIIe siècles* (Brussels, 1971), p. 146, cf. 58–61, 150f., 327–9 (nail-making); H. Kisch, 'From Monopoly to Laissez-faire: The Early Growth of the Wupper Valley Textile Trades', *Journal of European Economic History*, 1 (1972), 298–407, esp. 328, 341f., 350f.; Gothein, 'Schwarzwald' (see n. 6 above), pp. 723–70 (cotton, silk and others); Westernhagen, *Leinwandmanufaktur . . . Oberlausitz* (see n. 13 above), p. 17; H. Eberhardt, *Goethes Umwelt. Forschungen zur gesellschaftlichen Struktur Thüringens*, Thüringsiche Archivstudien, vol. 1 (Weimar, 1951), pp. 73–85 (framework knitting); for the making of needles in the area of Iserlohn (Westphalia), see below, p. 288 n. 105.

46 See below, pp. 109f. and n. 98.

47 In general: Clarkson, *Pre-industrial Economy* (see n. 45 above), p. 99; specifically for handloom weaving: H. Blumberg, *Die deutsche Textilindustrie in der industriellen Revolution*, Veröffentlichungen des Instituts für Wirtshaftsgeschichte and der Hochschule für Ökonoie Berlin-Karlshorst, vol. 3 (Berlin, 1965), pp. 48f.

48 See e.g. F. F. Mendels, 'Proto-industrialization: The First Phase of the Industrialization Process', *Journ. Econ. Hist.*, 32 (1972), 241–61, esp. 243.

49 Dobb, *Studies* (see n. 1 above), pp. 145–8; Mantoux, *Industrial Revolution* (n. 1 above), pp. 64–6; Tarlé, *L'industrie* (n. 1 above), p. 50f. Examples: J. D. Chambers, *Nottinghamshire in the Eighteenth Century* (1932; rpt. London, 1966), pp. 101–36 (framework knitting); S. D. Chapman, 'The Genesis of the British Hosiery Industry, 1300–1750', *Textile Industry*, 3 (1972), 7–38f.; Deyon, *Amiens* (n. 45), p. 210 (woollen weaving); Bodmer, *Schweizerische Textilwirtschaft* (see n. 38 above), pp. 193, 213 (ribbon weaving in Basel); Kisch, *Mercantilism* (n. 38 above), esp. 32–4 (Krefeld silk industry); cf. M. Barkhausen, 'Staatliche Wirtschaftslenkung und freies Unternehmertum im westdeutschen und im nord- und südniederländischen Raum bei der Entstehung der neuzeitlichen Industrie im 18. Jahrhundert', *VSWG*, 45 (1958), 168–241, esp. 199f.; G. Schmoller and O. Hintze, *Die preussische Seidenindustrie im 18. Jahrhundert und ihre Begründung durch Friedrich den Grossen*, Acta Borussica, vol. 3 (Berlin, 1892), pp. 101f.

50 Here I deal only with the 'formal subsumption of labour under capital'; concerning 'real subsumption', see below, p. 107 and n. 83.

51 It could happen that the producers' living quarters were the property of the entrepreneur as well: S. D. Chapman, 'Industrial Capital before the Industrial Revolution: An Analysis of the Assets of a Thousand Textile Entrepreneurs c. 1730–50', *Textile History and Economic History. Essays in Honour of Miss J. de Lacy Mann*, eds. N. B. Harte and K. G. Ponting (Manchester, 1973), pp. 113–37, esp. 134ff.; Dobb, *Studies* (see n. 1 above), pp. 147f.; E. Barkhausen, *Montjoie* (see n. 38 above), p. 62.

52 E.g. Chambers, *Nottinghamshire* (see n. 49 above), pp. 119ff.; D. C. Levine, *Family Formation in an Age of Nascent Capitalism*, Studies in Social Discontinuity (New York, 1977), pp. 24f.; cf. also below, p. 289, n. 113.

53 Chambers, 'Rural Industries' (see n. 45 above), pp. 437ff.; Ashton, *Eighteenth Century* (see n. 29 above), pp. 100–3; Wadsworth and Mann, *Cotton Trade* (n. 29 above), pp. 78–91; Chambers, *Nottinghamshire* (see n. 49 above), pp. 125–32; Levine, *Family Formation* (see n. 52 above), pp. 23ff.; Court, *Midland Industries* (see n. 45 above), pp. 200ff.; P. Lebrun, *L'industrie de la laine à Verviers pendant le XVIIIᵉ et le début du XIXᵉ siècle*, Bibliothèque de la Faculté de Philosophie et Lettres de l'Université de Liège, vol. 114 (Liège, 1948), pp. 350–5; L. Dechesne, *Industrie drapière de la Vesdre avant 1800* (Paris and Liège, 1926), pp. 47f.; Hofmann, 'Österreichische Baumwollwarenindustrie' (see n. 38 above), pp. 526f., 552, 619f., 624ff., 648f.; Bodmer, *Schweizerische Textilwirtschaft* (see n. 38 above), pp. 147f., 184f., 191, 208ff., 224; R. Braun, *Industrialisierung und Volksleben: die Veränderungen der Lebensformen in einem ländlichen Industriegebiet vor 1800 (Zürcher Oberland)* (Zürich etc., 1960), pp. 14f.; Gothein, *Schwarzwald* (see n. 6 above), pp. 746f.; A. Kunze, 'Der Weg zur kapitalistischen Produktionsweise in der Oberlausitzer Leineweberei im ausgehenden 17. und zu Beginn des 18. Jahrhunderts', *E. W. v. Tschirnhaus und die Frühaufklärung in Mittel- und Osteuropa*, ed. E. Winter, Quellen und Studien zur Geschichte Osteuropas, vol. 7 (Berlin, 1960), pp. 207–13; A. Kunze, 'Vom Bauerndorf zum Weberdorf. Zur sozialen und wirtschaftlichen Struktur der Waldhufendörfer der südlichen Oberlausitz im 16., 17. und 18. Jahrhundert', *Oberlausitzer Forschungen. Beiträge zur Landesgeschichte*, ed. M. Reuther (Leipzig, 1961), pp. 165–92, here 178f.

54 For the effects during a crisis, see below p. 123. Especially during a crisis situation, which is not taken into consideration above on p. 53, it is apparent that, the penetration of capital into the sphere of production diminished the power of the proto-industrial family economy to determine the course of production, despite the fact that the household and family continued to be the location of production. But if the interest of the entrepreneur was to dominate production completely, he had to provide all the means of production and impose greater discipline; see above p. 100 and below p. 108 with n. 87. Schematically, the processes of production, reproduction, and circulation in this form of putting-out system can be represented as follows: a portion of the means of production (mp_1) belongs to the direct producers, the other portion (mp_2) to the putter-out, see above p. 275, n. 30:

$$\text{direct producer:} \quad C' \left\{ \begin{array}{c} ms \ldots L \\ mp_1 \end{array} \right\} C - M - C'$$

$$\text{putting-out capitalist:} \quad M - C \left\{ \begin{array}{c} L + mp_1 \\ mp_2 \end{array} \right\} \ldots P \ldots C' - M'$$

The commodity C which the direct producers exchange against M with the putter-out is no longer the finished product because that is the property of the putter-out from the beginning; the commodity C consists of the labour power L and the means of production mp_1. The production process P is made possible when the capital of the putter-out joins $L + mp_1$ and mp_2 together.

If one considers the process of circulation in isolation, the differences between the *Kaufsystem* and the putting-out system are not apparent (nor those between the *Kaufsystem* and industrial capitalism, cf. below, p. 286 n. 88). For the direct producer, the process of circulation always has this form: $C - M - C'$, where C′ is qualitatively, i.e. according to its use value, different from C; for the capitalist, it always has the form $M - L - M'$, where $M' > M$, i.e. quantitatively according to the exchange value.

55 Fr. Engels makes this clear in his postscript to the 3rd volume of *Das Kapital*, Marx-Engels Werke, vol. 25 (Berlin, 1964), pp. 914f.

56 See above, pp. 99ff.

57 This, of course, does not mean that the income of such putting-out labourers was necessarily lower than that of independent petty producers. If the productivity of labour was higher in the putting-out system than in the *Kaufsystem*, the merchant-manufacturer could pass on part of this advantage to the direct producers (as a work incentive). The annual income of the direct producers, of course, also depended on their level of employment. Concerning these questions, cf. the following pages with n. 63.

58 This question is not clarified in Engels (see n. 55 above). In the next few pages, I shall discuss the *economic* causes of the penetration of capital into the sphere of production. As regards the *non*-economic conditions and the violence of the methods used – on which Marx deliberately placed the main emphasis – in his chapter about the 'So-Called Primitive Accumulation' (see *Capital*, vol. 1, pp. 871ff.), see the section below, pp. 126ff.

59 See above pp. 99 and n. 23. There were of course also agreements among putters-out to keep wages low and to regulate the working conditions in their own interests, see Mann, 'Wiltshire' (see n. 28 above), pp. 71, 75; Levine, *Family Formation* (see n. 51 above), p. 26f.

60 See below, p. 106 and n. 74f.

61 These considerations as well as the empirical evidence (cf. e.g. above, p. 101 and n. 38) contradict the assumption of an oversupply of labour or an unlimited labour supply for proto-industrialization in general (see above, pp. 28f., 75); instead this question must be examined for each individual phase and region. Furthermore, this is not merely a demographic question, but one that concerns the *relationship* between economic *and* demographic development: it is not necessarily by the demographic behaviour of their populations that regions with an oversupply of labour were distinguished from those with a relative shortage of labour. Neither can I support the thesis (see above, p. 74) that the demographic behaviour of proto-industrial populations was one of the *causes* of de-industrialization, as long as evidence is not available about the differences between the demographic development of proto-industrial regions which shifted to industrial capitalism rapidly and those which succumbed to de-industrialization. Given our present state of knowledge, I believe it more plausible that the competition of advanced regions led to the de-industrialization of others; although once the de-industrialization crisis had begun, it was probably aggravated if the population continued to expand; cf. below, pp. 145ff., 150. Such considerations lead to a critique of a development policy which sees its main object merely in lowering the birth rate, see G. Hohorst, 'Bevölkerungsentwicklung und Wirtschaftswachstum als historischer Entwicklungsprozess demo-ökonomischer Systeme', *Dynamik der Bevölkerungsentwicklung*, eds. R. Mackensen and H. Wewer (München, 1973; rpt. 1974), pp. 91–118, esp. 115. Cf. also below pp. 117f. and n. 131.

62 E.g. J. Koch, 'Geschichte der Aachener Nähnadelzunft und Nähnadelindustrie bis zur Aufhebung der Zünfte in der französischen Zeit (1798)', *Zs. des Aachener Geschichtsvereins,* 41 (1920), 16–122, esp. 140f.; cf. also H. Aubin, 'Formen und Verbreitung des Verlagssystems in der Altnürnberger Wirtschaft', *Beiträge zur Wirtschaftsgeschichte Nürnbergs,* Beiträge zur Geschichte und Kultur der Stadt Nürnberg, vol. 11 (Nuremberg, 1967), vol. 2, pp. 620–68, esp. 627f., 647f.

63 Concerning the tendency of capital to progressively dominate industrial commodity production in England during the late seventeenth century, when prices were falling or stagnating, see C. Wilson, *England's Apprenticeship 1603–1763* (London, 1965), pp. 185ff. It is very difficult to compare *incomes* between different relations of production, industries, and regions for labourers employed in domestic production; for it is problematic to calculate the income of producers from prices per unit or piece-wages. Some data are given in Jacquemyns, *Flandres* (see n. 23 above), pp. 205–10; H. Schmidt, *Die Entwicklung der Bielefelder Firmen E. A. Delius, E. A. Delius und Söhne und C. A. Delius und Söhne . . . 1787 bis 1925* (Diss. rer. pol., Göttingen, 1926), pp. 189f.; a detailed discussion of incomes is contained in Troeltsch, *Calwer Zeughandlungskompagnie* (see n. 42 above), pp. 200–46; Krüger, *Manufakturen* (see n. 15 above), pp. 300–62; Fechner, *Wirtschaftsgeschichte* (see n. 23 above), pp. 699–724; L. Schneider, *Der Arbeiterhaushalt im 18. und 19. Jahrhundert, dargestellt am Beispiel des Heim- und Fabrikarbeiters,* Beiträge zur Ökonomie von Haushalt und Verbrauch, vol. 4 (Berlin, 1967), pp. 33–45; Chambers, *Nottinghamshire* (see n. 49 above), pp. 291–8; Levine, *Family Formation* (see n. 52 above), pp. 20ff. Mann, *Cloth* (see n. 45 above), pp. 102–7, 322–9; Rowlands, *Masters* (see n. 23 above), pp. 158–64; Pinchbeck, *Women Workers* (see n. 6 above), pp. 138–47; Mendels, 'Industrialization' (see n. 29 above), pp. 171, 201–9. With the emergence of capitalist relations of production the truck system became a common means of lowering wage costs, not least in the putting-out system; see e.g. Ashton, *Eighteenth Century* (see n. 29 above), pp. 101f.; Mann, 'Wiltshire' (n. 29 above), pp. 67f., 73f., 88f.; Mann, *Cloth* (n. 45 above), pp. 105, 108; Levine, *Family Formation* (n. 52 above), pp. 25f.; Dechesne, *Vesdre* (see n. 53 above), pp. 204f., 207; Bodmer, *Schweizerische Textilwirtschaft* (see n. 38 above), pp. 151f.; Gothein, *Schwarzwald* (see n. 6 above), pp. 716, 746f.; Koch, 'Aachener Nähnadelzunft' (see n. 62 above), pp. 76–99.

64 Wadsworth and Mann, *Cotton Trade* (see n. 29 above), pp. 316f.; cf. above, pp. 23, 45ff. It must be taken into consideration that – all other conditions being equal – a family who combined agricultural with industrial labour had less time to devote to industrial activity than a family who did nothing but industrial work (see above, p. 276, n. 37). Therefore, for the labourers on the periphery, the combination of agricultural with industrial labour could lead to lower wage-rates than were paid to full-time industrial labourers in the centres only under two conditions: (1) the acceptance of a low remuneration could be *enforced* because an oversupply of labourers existed on the periphery, possibly in the form that agriculture provided part of the inhabitants' livelihood but not all of it; (2) the acceptance of a low remuneration was *made possible* because for the producers on the periphery the real income per unit of labour-time was higher in agriculture than in industry. Apart from crises, only under this second condition were industrial incomes possible which would have been below subsistence level, *if* they had been the only income. On the average the total income had to be sufficient for survival or else the labourers would have starved to death. It must be assumed hat the real income per unit of labour was higher in agriculture than in industry wherever the producers were the owners of their plot of land, and often where they rented it as well. The situation of smallholders under feudal obligations must be examined from case to case, and for agricultural wage-labour, this was true in some regions (e.g. Jacquemyns, *Flandres* [n. 23 above], pp. 207ff., 240ff., cf. 29ff., 197ff.; Bois, *Paysans de l'ouest* [n. 23 above], p. 520) but not in others (cf. above p. 27 also for the possible causes of this difference). In the latter regions, therefore, the landless population pursued industrial work only: see Sion, *Normandie orientale* (see n. 45 above), pp. 177ff., 187ff.; Berkner, *Family* (n. 45 above), pp. 269f., 287; Tilly, *Vendée* (n. 45), p. 136; Tarle, *L'industrie* (see n. 1 above), pp. 34ff.; cf. Gothein, *Schwarzwald* (see n. 6 above), pp. 764f.; Rowlands, *Masters* (see n. 23 above) p. 9, cf. 41ff., 156f. The smaller the plot of land became, or the higher its rent rose due to the growth of the population (cf. below, Mendels, pp. 173f.), or the lower – for the same reason – the wages for seasonal agricultural labour fell, the weaker this effect of the combination of agriculture and industry must have become, until the point was reached where the industrial producers no longer rented any land and no longer did seasonal agricultural labour (unless feudal obligations limited their freedom of operation). Cf. above, p. 27f.

65 E. G. Heaton, *Yorkshire* (see n. 23 above), pp. 93, 293f. Similarly Dobb, *Studies* (see n. 1 above), pp. 149–51; cf. also Sée, 'Remarques sur le caractère de l'industrie rurale en France et les causes de son extension au XVIIIe siècle', *Revue historique*, 142 (1923), 47–53, here 48–50; Rowlands, *Masters* (see n. 23 above), pp. 80, 158, 161. Concerning the political discussion of the nineteenth and twentieth centuries about such agrarian questions, cf. J. Wysocki, 'Landwirtschaftlicher Nebenerwerb und soziale Sicherheit', *Agrarisches Nebengewerbe und Formen der Reagrarisierung im Spätmittelalter und 19./20. Jahrhundert*, ed. H. Kellenbenz, Forschungen zur Sozial- und Wirtschaftsgeschichte, vol. 21 (Stuttgart, 1975), pp. 125–40.

66 Hasquin, *Charleroi* (see n. 45 above), pp. 288f.; Jacquemyns, *Flandres* (see n. 23 above), pp. 197f.; Wadsworth and Mann, *Cotton Trade* (see n. 29 above), pp. 314–23; Rowlands, *Masters* (see n. 23 above), pp. 41–3; Braun, *Industrialisierung* (see n. 55 above), pp. 62f., 155ff.; Bodmer, *Schweizerische Textilwirtschaft* (see n. 38 above), pp. 205, 227; E. L. Shorter, *Social Change and Social Policy in Bavaria 1800–60* (Diss., Harvard University, 1967), pp. 397ff., 423; cf. O. Dascher, *Das Textilgewerbe in Hessen-Kassel vom 16. bis 19. Jahrhundert*, Veröffentlichungen der Historischen Kommission für Hessen und Waldeck, vol. 28, 1 (Marburg, 1968), p. 157; C. F. Müller, *Choragraphie von Schwelm. Anfang und Versuch einer Topographie der Grafschaft Mark* (1789), ed. by W. Crone, Crones Heimatbücher zwischen Ruhr und Wupper, vol. 3 (Schwelm, 1922), p. 19.

67 Cf. above, p. 273, n. 23.

68 J. Thirsk, 'The Fantastical Folly of Fashion: The English Stocking-Knitting Industry 1500–1700', *Textile History and Economic History* (see n. 51 above), pp. 50–73; cf. e.g. also E. Barkhausen, *Montjoie* (see n. 38 above), pp. 34–6, 60–4; Kirchgässner, 'Verlag' (see n. 42 above), pp. 80f.; K. Schmid, *Die Entwicklung der Hofer Baumwollindustrie 1432–1913*, Wirtschafts- und Verwaltungsstudien mit besonderer Berücksichtigung Bayerns, vol. 60 (Erlangen etc., 1923), pp. 10f.; Rowlands, *Masters* (see n. 23 above), pp. 150ff.

69 See below pp. 111ff., esp. 113.

70 Troeltsch, *Calwer Zeughandlungskompagnie* (see n. 42 above), pp. 89ff.; F. Dransfeld, *Solinger Industrieverhältnisse im 18. Jahrhundert* (Solingen, 1914), pp. 7f., 12f., 36–9: in this urban case, the cutlery-makers were split around 1777: the smaller ones agreed to give up the opportunity to market their own products in return for higher wages whereas the large ones resisted the change (p. 39). A similar split occurred in the beginning of the seventeenth century among the producers of small metal wares in the West Midlands: Rowlands, *Masters* (see n. 23 above), pp. 9f.

71 Wissell, *Handwerk* (see n. 4 above), vol. 2, pp. 298–303; Bodmer, *Schweizerische Textilwirtschaft* (see n. 38 above), pp. 140f., cf. 89f., 121, 154; cf. Schmidt, *Firmen* (see n. 63 above), pp. 114ff.

72 See below, pp. 114ff.

73 See e.g. Koch, 'Aachener Nähnadelzunft' (see n. 62 above), p. 39, 75–85,

95–111; P. Dirr, 'Augsburgs Textilindustrie im 18. Jh.', *Zs. des Historischen Vereins für Schwaben*, 37 (1911), 1–106, here 46ff., 68ff.; cf. W. Zorn, *Handels- und Industriegeschichte Bayerisch-Schwabens 1648–1870*, Veröffentlichungen der schwäbischen Forschungsgemeinschaft bei der Kommission für bayerische Landesgeschichte, vol. 1, 6 (Augsburg, 1961), pp. 52ff., 64f.

74 E.g. Engels and Legers, *Remscheider Werkzeugindustrie* (see n. 23 above), vol. 1, pp. 71–165, 203–20. cf. 240 (scythe-making); Wadsworth and Mann, *Cotton Trade* (see n. 29 above), esp. pp. 325f. (ribbon-weavers).

75 Engels and Legers, *Remscheider Werkzeugindustrie* (see n. 23 above), vol. 1, pp. 176–89, 198–202 (small smithies); K. Spannagel, 'Die Gündung der Leineweberzunft in Elberfeld und Barmen im Oktober 1738', *Zs. des Bergischen Geschichtsvereins*, 30 (1894), 181–99; cf. Kisch, 'Wupper Valley' (see n. 45 above), pp. 351ff., 401ff.; E. Barkhausen, *Montjoie* (see n. 38 above), pp. 80–122; J. Kermann, *Die Manufakturen im Rheinland 1750–1833*, Rheinisches Archiv, vol. 82 (Bonn, 1972), pp. 135, 145.

76 See above, pp. 104ff.

77 The tendency seems to have been as follows: as the workforce who, as independent petty producers, had left only the trade in the hands of merchants, gradually lost their independence and became the wage-labourers of merchant-manufacturers, so the goals and forms of their organizations no longer followed the examples set by the guilds but approached those of the later labour movement. But this tendency was slow and often interrupted and needs to be examined as thoroughly as E. P. Thompson has studied it in England for the period of the emergence of industrial capitalism: E. P. Thompson, *The Making of the English Working Class*, 2nd ed. (Harmondsworth, 1968); see also Wilson, *England* (see n. 63 above), pp. 291f.; W. J. Shelton, *English Hunger and Industrial Disorders. A Study of Social Conflict during the First Decade of George III's Reign* (London, 1973), pp. 7f.; Shelton, *Eighteenth Century* (see n. 29 above), pp. 228–31; Mantoux, *Industrial Revolution* (see n. 1 above), pp. 74–83; Mann, *Cloth* (see n. 45 above), pp. 108–15; Mann, 'Wiltshire' (see n. 29 above); Heaton, *Yorkshire* (see n. 23 above), pp. 316–21; Wadsworth and Mann, *Cotton Trade* (see n. 29 above), 340–53, 361–85; Chambers, *Nottinghamshire* (see n. 49 above), pp. 35–44, 104–14; Rowlands, *Masters* (see n. 23 above), pp. 83, 162–4; Gill, *Irish Linen Trade* (see n. 23 above), pp. 138–44; Dechesne, *Vesdre* (see n. 53 above), pp. 199–220; Lebrun, *Verviers* (see n. 53 above), vol. 2, pp. 257–67. See also below p. 118 and n. 135 about the participation of proto-industrial labourers, working under different relations of production, in food riots. Cf. also below p. 122: for the petty commodity producers in the *Kaufsystem*, the high prices of raw materials in the face of falling prices for finished products were an incentive to riot; in the putting-out system, with its capitalist features, that incentive would have been provided by the wage rates. Concerning the forms, causes and significance of violence in industrial riots, see E. J. Hobsbawm, 'The Machine Breakers', *Past and Present*, 1 (1952), 57–70, esp. 59ff.; cf. also G. Rudé, *The Crowd in History. A Study of Popular Disturbances in France and England 1730–1848* (New York etc., 1964), pp. 66–78.

78 Cf. Smelser, *Change* (see n. 6 above), esp. 54ff.; N. J. Smelser, 'Mechanisms of Change and Adjustment to Change', *Industrialization and Society*, eds. B. F. Hoselitz and W. E. Moore (The Hague etc., 1963), pp. 32–54, esp. 35–7; Pinchbeck, *Women Workers* (see n. 5 above), pp. 121ff., 134ff.; Schremmer, *Bayern* (see n. 40 above), p. 474; M. Godelier, *Rationality and Irrationality in Economics* (London, 1972), pp. 267f.

79 For the normal case: Potthoff, 'Ravensberger Leinengewerbe' (see n. 23 above), pp. 37f., 45, 47; E. Schönfeld, 'Herford als Garn- und Leinenmarkt in zwei Jahrhunderten', *43. Jahresbericht des Historischen Vereins für die Grafschaft Ravensberg* (1929), 1–172, here 23–60; Kühn, 'Hirschberger Leinwandhandel' (n. 23 above), pp. 8f.; cf. Fechner, *Wirtschaftsgeschichte . . . Schlesien* (n. 23 above), pp. 710–24; Bois,

Paysans de l'Ouest (n. 23 above), pp. 507f., cf. 533f. For exceptions: H. Wiemann, 'Die Osnabrücker Stadtlegge', *Mitteilungen des Vereins für Geschichte und Landeskunde von Osnabrück*, 35 (1910), 1–76, here 57f.; Jacquemyns, *Flandres* (see n. 23 above), pp. 32f., 130f., 196–202; cf. Mendels, 'Industrialization' (see n. 29 above), pp. 23f., 200f., 203f. For a comparison with the production for home consumption ('Hauswerk'), see Bücher, 'Gewerbliche Betriebssysteme' (see n. 1 above), pp. 168–74; cf. K. Bücher, 'Die Entstehung der Volkswirtschaft', in K. Bücher, *Entstehung* (n. 1 above), pp. 83–160, esp. 92ff. Cf. above, p. 95 and n. 6.

80 E.g. Troeltsch, *Calwer Zeughandlungskompagnie* (see n. 42 above), pp. 98–102, 125f.; Westernhagen, 'Leinwandmanufaktur' (see n. 13 above), pp. 17f.; Kaplow, *Elbeuf* (see n. 45 above), pp. 27, 31; cf. Ashton, *Industrial Revolution* (n. 45 above), p. 37.

81 Wadsworth and Mann, *Cotton Trade* (see n. 29 above), pp. 325–7, 332, 336; Levine, *Family Formation* (see n. 52 above), pp. 27f., cf. 50ff. Braun, *Industrialisierung* (see n. 53 above), pp. 24–6, 30–2.

82 Chambers, *Nottinghamshire* (see n. 49 above), pp. 295f.; Kaplow, *Elbeuf* (see n. 45 above), pp. 26f., 31; Mann, 'Wiltshire' (see n. 29 above), pp. 92f., cf. 90; Braun, *Industrialisierung* (see n. 53 above), pp. 83–9. Since the degree to which the members of a family cooperated in industrial work varied, a *general* necessity, based on the nature of the proto-industrial production process, to contract early marriages and to have many children hardly existed. The proto-industrial family was usually not a 'miniature factory' (cf. above, p. 95, n. 6). In my opinion it is therefore problematic to construct a *specific* demo-economic *system* which embraces *all* of proto-industrialization and *nothing but* proto-industrialization (see above, pp. 74ff.). Even if one assumes that an economic benefit was derived from an early marriage and a large number of children, one would still have to explain why this would have been different from the situation of labourers in centralized manufactures or of the early factory workers, as long as the women and children of their families were employed in large numbers as well. Therefore the model still appears valid which explains population-growth during proto-industrial-ization – though not during proto-industrialization *alone* – on the basis of the 'pro-letarianization' of the population. On the one hand, the controls which lords and communities exercised over population-growth loosened; on the other hand, it became possible to earn an income without property and inheritance. This model is to be found in Levine, *Family Formation* (see n. 52 above), esp. pp. 146ff.; Braun, *Industrialisierung* (see n. 53 above), pp. 59–73; Ch. Tilly and R. Tilly, 'Agenda for European Economic History in the 1972', *Journ. Econ. Hist.*, 31 (1971), 184–98, esp. 189, 191. This explanatory model is supported by Hasquin's observation that the domestic nail-makers had the same demographic behaviour as the workers in larger production units in coal mining and iron production: Hasquin, *Charleroi* (see n. 45 above), pp. 287–95. It would be interesting to investigate whether this demographic pattern existed among agricul-tural labourers and among early factory workers as well. For the agricultural labourers, see Levine, *Family Formation* (see n. 52 above), pp. 116ff.; H. Harnisch, 'Bevölkerung und Wirtschaft. Uber die Zusammenhänge zwischen sozialökonomischer und de-mographischer Entwicklung im Spätfeudalismus', *Jb. Wirtsch. G.* (1975), pt. 2, 57–88, esp. 73ff., 75ff., 83ff.

Questions concerning the internal structure of the household and family during proto-industrialization must be seen in connection with the family members' participation in the production process, i.e. with the quantity and kind of work they performed. Ultimately, such questions must be placed in the context of different relations of production as well. These questions concern the distribution of functions within the household – such as consumption, the socialization of children, possibly work in the fields or the garden – as well as the hierarchy within the family. Cf. above, pp. 61ff.

83 As the production-processes were restructured, the direct producers sometimes lost the ability to manufacture a saleable product; this can be regarded as the beginning of the process which Marx occasionally called the 'real subsumption of labour under capital' (in contrast to its precondition, namely the emergence of wage labour relations which he called the 'formal' subsumption of labour under capital; see Marx, *Capital*, vol. 1, Chs. 13, 16, 28, pp. 453, 645f., 899f., cf. Chs. 11 and 12, pp. 424f., 431ff., 447ff.). In greater detail: K. Marx, *Resultate des unmittelbaren Produktionsprozesses*, Archiv sozialistische Literatur, vol. 17 (Frankfurt, 1969), pp. 45–64; cf. L. Althusser and E. Balibar, *Reading Capital* (London, 1977), pp. 213ff. concerning the distinction between 'property relations' and 'labour process'. However, it is problematic to build on this distinction a general theory of transitional modes of production as Althusser and Balibar do; cf. the criticism in B. Hindess and P. Q. Hirst, *Precapitalist Modes of Production* (London etc., 1975), pp. 264ff. and the revised position of E. Balibar, 'Sur la dialectique historique', in E. Balibar, *Cinq études du matérialisme historique* (Paris, 1974), pp. 203–45, esp. 238ff.

84 It was pointed out earlier that here only those centralized manufactures are dealt with which are directly related to rural industries, i.e. those which either replaced rural industries or supplemented them (see above, p. 8). As regards the question of whether the mines and ironworks had their origins in the peasant economy, see M. Mitterauer, 'Produktionsweise, Siedlungsstruktur und Sozialformen im österreichischen Montanwesen des Mittelalters und der frühen Neuzeit', *Österreichisches Montanwesen. Festschrift A. Hoffmann*, ed. M. Mitterauer (Vienna and Munich, 1974), pp. 234–315, esp. 285–315.

85 On the question of 'feudal manufactures' see above, pp. 271f., notes 11 and 15. Workhouses, poorhouses and houses of correction were more frequent, see below, p. 130 and n. 1991. But their share is not very large either: Hoffmann, *Handwerk* (see n. 15 above), pp. 68f. In contrast to common usage, the term 'manufacture' here means all the production facilities which clearly exceeded the size of the family work unit or artisanal workshop. It includes production units which emerged when the workshops of petty producers were enlarged and began to employ more wage labourers than family members so that the head of the household ceased to do directly productive labour.

86 Concerning the question of whether this second road contributed more than the first to revolutionizing the mode of production, see the debate which follows Marx's remark in *Capital*, vol. 3, Ch. 20, pp. 334ff.: Dobb, *Studies* (see n. 1 above), pp. 123ff., 277ff.; P. M. Sweezy, M. Dobb, H. K. Takahashi, G. Lefèbvre in *The Transition* (n. 1 above), pp. 17ff., 27ff., 47ff., 57f., 77ff. Empirical evidence supporting this hypothesis is provided by Wilson, *Merchants* (see n. 23 above), pp. 33f., 56–60, 90–135; Jenkins, *West Riding* (n. 23 above), pp. 191–205; Wadsworth and Mann, *Cotton Trade* (see n. 28 above), pp. 172, 322f.; Lebrun, *Verviers* (see n. 53 above), pp. 361ff., 388f. Cf. S. D. Chapman, *The Early Factory Masters. The Transition to the Factory System in the Midlands Textile Industry* (Newton Abbot, Devon, 1967), esp. pp. 77ff.

87 This is true even for the wage-labourers in industrial capitalism: P. M. Sweezy, *The Theory of Capitalist Development – Principles of Marxian Political Economy* (New York, 1942), p. 139. Cf. also below, pp. 293f., n. 158. Therefore it is not surprising that, even under the conditions of the capitalist factory, complaints continued to be voiced to the effect that the work-effort declined when real wages rose. Beyond the transformation of the means of production into capital and their withdrawal from the control of the direct producers, many incentives, threats of punishment and re-education measures were required in order to submit the labourers to the interest of capital and to eliminate such dysfunctional elements – dysfunctions, that is, from the point of view of capital – as the 'backward bending supply of labour'. S. Pollard, *The Genesis of Modern Management. A Study in the Industrial Revolution in Great Britain* (London, 1965), pp. 160–208, esp. 181ff.

88 Cf. above, pp. 100 and 279f. with n. 54. Although the capitalist manufacture differs substantially from the capitalist factory with regard to the technical aspects of the production process, (concerning the question of 'real subsumption', see above, p. 285, n. 83), the capitalist character of the relations of production is the same in the factory as in centralized manufacture. Therefore, the formula of the capitalist production process can be applied to the latter as well. Cf. Marx, *Capital*, vol. 2, transl. by B. Fowkes (Harmondsworth, 1978), Ch. 1, p. 124:

$$\text{Capitalist:}\ \ M - C \left\{ {mp \atop L} \right\}\ \ \ldots P \ldots C' - M'$$

$$\text{Worker:}\ \ C'\ \{ms \ldots L\}\ \ C-M-C'$$

The direct producer sells to the capitalist the commodity C which is his labour power L. For a comparison see above, pp. 275f., n. 30, pp. 279f., n. 54.

89 It is crucial to define accurately the socio-economic group to which a certain behaviour pattern is attributed, if one wants not only to describe economic behaviour but explain it as well. In my opinion, this can be done most fruitfully by further developing the categories which are contained, in rudimentary form, in the *Critique of Political Economy* (concerning the reasons see above, p. 210f., n. 58). It seems to me especially important to define precisely the socio-economic group which manifests the economic behaviour that Chayanov observed for the Russian peasantry from the abolition of serfdom to the October Revolution, and that he described in terms of marginal utility. For a critical assessment of the concept of marginal utility, see W. Hofmann, *Sozialökonomische Studientexte* (Berlin, 1964–5), vol. 1, 116–83, vol. 2, 161–239.

90 See above, p. 95, 276, n. 37; pp. 106f.; but cf. also above, pp. 50ff.

91 See above, pp. 102f., 107f.; differently above, pp. 41ff.

92 See above, pp. 101, 105; cf. above, 21ff., 33ff., 44ff.

93 Pollard, *Management* (see n. 87 above), pp. 160–6; Mann, *Cloth* (see n. 45 above), p. 115; Wadsworth and Mann, Cotton Trade (see n. 29 above), pp. 302, 304, cf. pp. 499f.; Chambers, *Nottinghamshire* (see n. 49 above), pp. 41f. Bodmer, *Schweizerische Textilwirtschaft* (see n. 38 above), p. 213; Kisch, 'Wupper Valley' (see n. 45 above), pp. 401ff., 405ff.; Troeltsch, *Calwer Zeughandlungskompagnie* (see n. 42 above), pp. 169f.; cf. Hobsbawm, 'Machine Breakers' (see n. 77 above), pp. 61ff. concerning the phase of the Industrial Revolution.

94 Nevertheless, before the Industrial Revolution fixed capital continued to comprise a relatively small share of total capital: S. Pollard, 'Fixed Capital in the Industrial Revolution in Britain', *Journ. Econ. Hist.*, 24 (1964), 299–314, esp. 301f.; Clarkson, *Pre-industrial Economy* (see n. 45 above), pp. 97–9; Lebrun, *Verviers* (see n. 53 above), pp. 374ff., 382f.; Gothein, *Schwarzwald* (see n. 6 above), p. 770; G. Slawinger, *Die Manufaktur in Kurbayern*, Forschungen zur Sozial- und Wirtschaftsgeschichte, vol. 8 (Stuttgart, 1966), pp. 39–41; Schmoller and Hintze, *Preussische Seidenindustrie* (see n. 49 above), vol. 2, pp. 585ff.; W. Kurschat, *Das Haus Friedrich und Heinrich von der Leyen in Krefeld . . . 1794–1814* (Frankfurt/M., 1933), Appendix. Chapman, 'Capital' (see n. 51 above) emphasizes that entrepreneurs preferred to invest fixed capital in such buildings which could be used for several purposes; this way they tried to remain flexible in cases of changing demand.

95 See below, pp. 111, 113.

96 In the textile industry, preparatory processes (carding, washing, and dyeing of wool as well as twisting, dyeing, and sometimes warp-shearing in the silk industry) and the finishing processes (bleaching linen, printing cotton, fulling and finishing cloth) were often carried out in centralized manufactures, but only very valuable fabrics were woven in centralized manufactures. Since such centralized manufactures were mostly located in the towns and the domestic workshops in the countryside, town and countryside often came to complement each other in the production process.

97 Spinning and weaving, for example, in the textile industry.

98 Sombart, *Der moderne Kapitalismus* (see n. 29 above), vol. 2, pt. 2, pp. 766ff.; Pollard, *Management* (see n. 87 above), pp. 34–7, 51–60; Chambers, 'Rural Industries' (see n. 45 above), pp. 439–41; S. D. Chapman, 'The Textile Factory before Arkwright: A Typology of Factory Development', *Business History Review*, 48 (1974), 451–78; Chapman, *Factory Masters* (see n. 86 above), pp. 34–45; Ashton, *Eighteenth Century* (see n. 29 above), pp. 115ff.; Wadsworth and Mann, *Cotton Trade* (see n. 29 above), pp. 105–8, 284–310, 325f.; Rowlands, *Masters* (see n. 23 above), pp. 149–156; Léon, in: *Histoire économique* (see n. 36 above), vol. 2, pp. 257–66; Kaplow, *Elbeuf* (see n. 45 above), pp. 25–32; Lebrun, *Verviers* (see n. 53 above), pp. 213–20, 276–87, 342; Hasquin, *Charleroi* (see n. 45 above), pp. 100–3, 146f.; Bodmer, *Schweizerische Textilwirtschaft* (see n. 38 above), p. 212; Hoffmann, *Handwerk* (see n. 15 above), pp. 66, cf. pp. 58f., 92; Krüger, *Manufakturen* (see n. 15 above), pp. 192–206; Kühn, 'Hirschberg' (see n. 23 above), pp. 11–13; Kisch, *Mercantilism* (see n. 38 above), pp. 24f., 27–9, 31–3; concerning the pin-making industry of Iserlohn see n. 105; R. Forberger, *Die Manufaktur in Sachsen vom Ende des 16. bis zum Anfang des 19. Jahrhunderts*, Deutsche Akad. d. Wiss. Berlin, Schriften des Instituts für Geschichte, ser. 1, vol. 3 (Berlin, 1958), pp. 58–61, 153–205; Kunze, 'Produktionsweise' (see n. 53 above), pp. 211f.; Kermann, *Manufakturen* (see n. 75 above); Kisch, 'Wupper' (see n. 45 above), pp. 401ff.; Barkhausen, *Montjoie* (see n. 38 above), pp. 48, 60–4; Koch, 'Aachener Nähnadelzunft' (see n. 62 above), pp. 37–50; W. Freitag, *Die Entwicklung der Kaiserslauterner Textilindustrie seit dem 18. Jahrhundert* (Diss. rer. pol., Mannheim, 1960), pp. 22–41; Troeltsch, *Calwer Zeughandlungskompagnie* (see n. 42 above), pp. 57f., 89f., 167–72; Schremmer, *Bayern* (see n. 40 above), pp. 473–6, 487–91; Slawinger, *Manufaktur in Kurbayern* (see n. 94 above), esp. p. 159; Zorn, *Bayrisch-Schwaben* (see n. 73 above), pp. 42–70; Wiest, *Nürnberger Gewerbe* (see n. 4 above), pp. 94, 103f.; O. Reuter, *Die Manufaktur im fränkischen Raum*, Forschungen zur Sozial- und Wirtschaftsgeschichte, vol. 3 (Stuttgart, 1961), esp. pp. 142ff.; Klíma, 'Role' (see n. 18 above), pp. 53f.; A. Klíma, 'English Capital in Bohemia in the Eighteenth Century', *Econ. Hist. Rev.*, 2nd ser., 12 (1959/60), 34–48, esp. 42ff.; H. Hassinger, 'Der Stand der Manufakturen in den deutschen Erbländern der Habsburgermonarchie am Ende des 18. Jahrhunderts', *Die wirtschaftliche Situation in Deutschland und Österreich um die Wende vom 18. zum 19. Jahrhundert*, ed. F. Lütge, Forschungen zur Sozial- und Wirtschaftsgeschichte, vol. 6 (Stuttgart, 1964), pp. 110–76, esp. 119ff.; Berkner, 'Family' (see n. 45 above), pp. 135ff., 259f.; Hofmann, 'Österreichische Baumwollwarenindustrie' (see n. 38 above), pp. 524ff., 618ff., 624ff., 638, 644f., 648f., 655f.; G. Grüll, 'Die Strumpffabrik Poneggen 1763–1818', *Mitteilungen des oberösterreichischen Landesarchivs*, 6 (1959), 5–135.

99 This was already emphasized by Marx, *Capital*, vol. 1, Ch. 12, pp. 490–1, Ch. 30, pp. 911–12. For a distinction between manufacture and factory see below, p. 300, n. 9.

100 See below, pp. 138,140,156f.

101 In eastern Europe some industries were apparently organized on the basis of centralized manufactures from the very beginning, while in the developed countries of western Europe the same industries had evolved on the basis of dispersed artisanal or rural production: A. Spiesz, *Die Manufaktur im östlichen Europa*, Kölner Vorträge zur Sozial- und Wirtschaftsgeschichte, vol. 2 (Cologne, 1969), pp. 4f.; cf. J. Kocka, *Unternehmer in der deutschen Industrialisierung*, Kleine Vandenhoeck-Reihe, vol. 1412 (Göttingen, 1975), pp. 23f.

102 This trend was observed in the older literature as well though its conditions, causes and consequences were not really analyzed. See W. Roscher, 'Nationalökonomie des Handels und Gewerbefleisses', in W. Roscher, *Das System der Volkswirtschaft*, vol. 3 (Stuttgart, 1881), pp. 541ff.; Schmoller, *Grundriss* (see n. 1 above), pp. 481ff., esp. 485; Bücher, 'Betriebssysteme' (n. 1 above), pp. 185f., 190f.; Kulischer, *Wirtschaftsgeschichte* (see n. 40 above), vol. 2, pp. 120ff., 125ff.; Dobb, *Studies* (see n. 1 above), pp. 143ff.; Chambers, *Rural Industries* (see n. 45 above), pp. 437ff.

103 This was already noted by Sée, 'Remarques' (see n. 65 above), when he distinguished between two types of rural industry in France in the eighteenth century. This thesis will be substantiated in the following section, pp. 111ff.

104 L. White, *Medieval Technology and Social Change* (Oxford, 1962).

105 Cf. above, pp. 95, 106f.; see also Clarkson, *Pre-industrial Economy* (see n. 45 above), pp. 101f. Thus the division of labour in the making of needles in Iserlohn (Westphalia), where most of the workers were employed in the putting-out system by the owners of grinding and scouring mills, reached the degree which Adam Smith observed in a centralized manufacture: Adam Smith, *An Inquiry into the Nature and Causes of the Wealth of Nations*, ed. by R. H. Campbell, et al., The Glasgow Edition of the Works and Correspondence of Adam Smith, vol. 2 (Oxford, 1976), vol. 1, Book, 1, Ch. 1, pp. 14ff., see F. Schulte, *Die Entwicklung der gewerblichen Wirtschaft in Rheinland-Westfalen im 18. Jahrhundert*, Schriften zur rheinisch-westfälischen Wirtschaftsgeschichte, vol. 1 (Cologne, 1959), pp. 91–3; W. Schulte, *Iserlohn. Die Geschichte einer Stadt* (Iserlohn, 1937), vol. 1, pp. 110–13. Cf. also G. Schanz, *Zur Geschichte der Colonisation und Industrie in Franken. Die Fürstentümer Ansbach und Bayreuth*, Bayerische Wirtschafts- und Verwaltungsstudien, vol. 1 (Erlangen, 1884), vol. 1, pp. 303ff.; F. Morgenstern, *Die Fürther Metallschlägerei* (Tübingen, 1890), p. 33f.

106 The classic statement in Marx, *Capital*, vol. 1, Ch. 14, pp. 455–91. The attempt has been made to quantify and compare the productivity of guild artisans, non-guild artisans, and centralized manufactures: Krüger, *Manufakturen* (see n. 15 above), p. 186–9; cf. Troeltsch, *Calwer Zeughandlungskompagnie* (see n. 41 above), 172; cf. also Landes, *Prometheus* (see n. 28 above), pp. 56–60 concerning the disadvantages of the putting-out system.

107 The latter are emphasized in D. C. Coleman, 'Textile Growth', *Textile History and Economic History* (see n. 51 above), pp. 1–21, esp. 10ff.

108 For the technological development see Ch. Singer et al., *A History of Technology*, vol. 3 (Oxford, 1957); A. P. Usher, *A History of Mechanical Inventions*, 2nd ed. (Cambridge, Mass., 1954). A survey also in P. Léon in *Histoire écon.* (see n. 36 above), vol. 2, pp. 233–50; D. Sella, 'European Industries 1500–1700', in *Fontana Economic History of Europe*, vol. 2 (London, 1974), pp. 354–426, esp. 397–9; Landes, *Prometheus* (see n. 29 above), pp. 80–6; Sombart, *Der moderne Kapitalismus* (n. 29 above), vol. 1, pt. 2, pp. 480–512; cf. J. A. Schumpeter, *Konjunkturzyklen* (1939, rpt. Göttingen, 1961), vol. 1, pp. 253; cf. Chambers, *Nottinghamshire* (see n. 49 above), pp. 90f.; Court, *Midland Industries* (see n. 45 above), pp. 103ff.; Rowlands, *Masters* (see n. 23 above), pp. 138f., pp. 154f.; Engels and Legers, *Remscheider Werkzeugindustrie* (see n. 23 above), pp. 56–70, 131–9, 145–7, 153–5, esp. pp. 82, 135. Greater detail is provided in the quantitative analysis about productivity increases: W. Endrei, *L'évolution des techniques du filage et du tissage du Moyen Age à la révolution industrielle*, Industrie et artisanat, vol. 4 (Paris, 1968).

109 See above, pp. 278f. n. 49.

110 Wadsworth and Mann, *Cotton Trade* (see n. 29 above), pp. 105f., 284–6; Chapman, *Factory Masters* (see n. 86 above), pp. 34–40; Chapman, *Genesis* (see n. 49 above), pp. 19, 34.

111 Sombart, *Der moderne Kapitalismus* (see n. 29 above), vol. 2, pt. 2, pp. 734ff.;

Ashton, *Eighteenth Century* (n. 29 above), p. 116; Wadsworth and Mann, *Cotton Trade* (n. 29 above), pp. 106–8, 301–8, 411–48; Chapman, *Factory Masters* (see n. 86 above), pp. 40–3, cf. 43–5; Court, *Midland Industries* (see n. 45 above), pp. 103ff., 194ff.; Bodmer, *Schweizerische Textilwirtschaft* (see n. 38 above), pp. 191ff., 210f., 213; Schmoller and Hintze, *Seidenindustrie* (see n. 49 above), vol. 3, pp. 101f.; Kisch, *Mercantilism* (see n. 38 above), p. 25; Kermann, *Manufakturen* (see n. 75 above), pp. 145ff., 236ff., 253, 284ff., 555ff.; E. Strutz, 'Wirtschaftsgeschichte', in J. Hashagen, K. J. Narr et al., *Bergische Geschichte* (Remscheid, 1958), pp. 346–55; Koch, *Aachener Nähnadelzunft* (see n. 62 above), pp. 38f., 41–50.

112 Landes, *Prometheus* (see n. 28 above), pp. 81f.

113 Even the first jennies, which were hand operated and had a small number of spindles, were largely installed in domestic workshops: Wadsworth and Mann, *Cotton Trade* (see n. 29 above), p. 499; but they were the property of putting-out capitalists who rented them out to spinners for money: Forberger, *Manufakturen* (see n. 98 above), p. 289.

114 Kula, *Théorie* (see n. 10 above), pp. 85ff., 90–4, 96f.; cf. W. Abel, *Geschichte der deutschen Landwirtschaft vom frühen Mittelalter bis zum 19. Jahrhundert*, Deutsche Agrargeschichte, vol. 2, 2nd ed. (Stuttgart, 1967), pp. 330–5; W. Abel, 'Die Lage der deutschen Land- und Ernährungswirtschaft um 1800', in *Die wirtschaftliche Situation* (see n. 98 above), pp. 238–54, esp. 252f.; R. Forster, 'Obstacles to Agricultural Growth in Eighteenth-Century France', *American Historical Review*, 75 (1970), 1600–15, esp. 1611ff.; Brenner, 'Agrarian Class Structure' (see n. 8 above), pp. 48f.

115 Cf. above, pp. 96f., 97f.

116 Cf. above p. 199ff.

117 See the literature below, under n. 120; Wadsworth and Mann, *Cotton Trade* (see n. 29 above), pp. 353f., 416–18, 451. In general see also Schumpeter, *Konjunkturzyklen* (see n. 108 above), vol. 1, pp. 154f.

118 Here the progress of industry was also hindered by the fact that the merchants and putters-out had to share the profit they made from the industrial production of the rural population with the feudal lord who received rent from that production. Furthermore, the direct or indirect investment of money in feudal estates may have competed considerably with investment opportunities in trade and industry; cf. Kisch, below, esp. pp. 184f.

119 Wadsworth and Mann, *Cotton Trade* (see n. 29 above), pp. 451–5 and cf. p. 105 concerning the higher expense for the Dutch loom as opposed to the traditional loom and its importance in goading the weavers to resistance.

120 Kulischer, *Wirtschaftsgeschichte* (see n. 40 above), vol. 2, pp. 111, 172–4; Wadsworth and Mann, *Cotton Trade* (see n. 29 above), pp. 98–106; Chambers, *Nottinghamshire* (see n. 49 above), pp. 89–92; Bodmer, *Schweizerische Textilwirtschaft* (see n. 38 above), pp. 154f. H. Mottek, *Wirtschaftsgeschichte Deutschlands. Ein Grundriss* 5th ed. (Berlin, GDR, 1968), vol. 1, pp. 272f.; Forberger, *Manufaktur* (see n. 98 above), pp. 138–41.

121 Wissel, *Handwerk* (see n. 4 above), vol. 2, pp. 312–22. Cf. above, p. 106.

122 Engels and Legers, *Remscheider Werkzeugindustrie* (see n. 23 above), vol. 1, pp. 131–9, cf. also pp. 56ff., 69, 223f.

123 Cf. above pp. 99ff., also with regard to the following exposition.

124 Cf. above, pp. 105f. and n. 64.

125 Cf. below, pp. 121f.

126 Cf. Marx, *Capital*, vol. 3, Ch. 16, pp. 279f.

127 Cf. Hobsbawm, 'Machine Breakers' (see n. 77 above), concerning the reasons why the direct producers – even under industrial capitalism – rejected 'technical progress' and the extent to which they did so. Concerning the reason why the behaviour of wage labourers resembled that of petty commodity producers, see above, p. 108.

128 See above, pp. 104ff., 108f.

129 Cf. below, p. 123. A well-documented example for the lowering of wages by the putter-out in the face of marketing difficulties and for the introduction of improved methods of production (probably the flying shuttle) in the face of labour scarcity is provided for the West Riding woolen industry at the beginning of the 1770s: T. S. Ashton, *Economic Fluctuations in England 1700–1800* (Oxford, 1959), pp. 158f.

130 Cf. above, pp. 280, n. 61.

131 E.g. S. D. Chapman, 'Enterprise and Innovation in the British Hosiery Industry, 1750–1850', *Textile History*, 5 (1974), 14–37, esp. 28ff. Cf. the evidence for Lancashire where the tendency of rising wages was particularly marked during the eighteenth century compared with other English regions; the rise was accelerated from about 1760 onward: Gilboy, *Wages* (see n. 29 above), esp. pp. 176–90, 219ff., 240ff.; E. W. Gilboy, 'The Cost of Real Wages in Eighteenth Century England', *The Review of Economic Statistics*, 18 (1936), 134–43; these works, however, do not contain wage-series from the textile industry.

The argument I have developed here stands outside the controversy as to whether the development of relative factor prices is decisive, for the process of substitution only or also for technological progress in the narrow sense, in determining whether more labour or more capital is saved.[Concerning this controversy see W. E. G. Salter, *Productivity and Technical Change*, 2nd ed., University of Cambridge. Department of Applied Economics. Monographs, vol. 6 (Cambridge, 1966), pp. 41–5 against J. R. Hicks, *The Theory of Wages* (London, 1932), pp. 123–5; cf. N. Rosenberg, 'The Direction of Technological Change: Inducement Mechanisms and Focusing Devices', *Economic Development and Cultural Change*, 18 (1969–70), pp. 1–24, esp. 1ff.] For the productivity of labour, which is here used as the most important indicator, can be raised by substitution *or* technological progress. For the early phases of industrialization when human strength was replaced by mechanical power Salter (p. 43) recognizes a 'labour-saving bias' of technological progress. Cf. also Rosenberg's argument concerning the 'most restrictive constraint' or 'bottleneck' (esp. pp. 12–17 concerning the availability of labour). More than in H. J. Habakkuk, *American and British Technology in the Nineteenth Century. The Search for Labour-Saving Inventions* (Cambridge, 1962) the factor prices and bottlenecks are here considered as mechanisms which determine merely the concrete manifestations of innovations, the time of their application etc. It is a more fundamental problem to determine why some economies make a productive response to such a challenge and why others fail to do so (Rosenberg, p. 5f., nn. 19f.). The relative stagnation of urban crafts, for example, where the guilds guaranteed relatively high wages, demonstrates that high wages were not a sufficient precondition for raising the productivity of labour; on the contrary, they could lead to an industry's stagnation and decline. I see the reasons why an economy could or could not make positive responses to economic challenges in the relations of production: in the period under discussion emerging capitalist relations of production offered more favourable conditions than the older relations of production.

In any case, the argument that the relative factor prices and bottlenecks challenged the economy to industrialize cannot be applied generally but applies primarily to England: the countries which industrialized subsequently had to deal with her competition and not with labour shortage and high wages. If, despite minimal wages, those countries which industrialized later had to offer their products for a higher price than the advanced region, their only alternative to decline was the transition to the advanced technology. For example in the Ravensberg (Westphalia) linen industry, machine-spinning was introduced after the price of hand-spun yarn and the incomes of spinners had drastically declined owing to the competition of imported machine-spun yarn: G. Adelmann, 'Strukturelle Krisen im Textilgewerbe Nordwestdeutschlands zu Beginn der Industrialisierung', *Wirtschaftspolitik und Arbeitsmarkt*, ed. H. Kellenbenz (Munich, 1974), pp. 110–28, esp. 116f., 126f.; G. Engel, *Ravensberger Spinnerei AG Bielefeld* (Bielefeld, 1954), pp. 46ff.; cf. Schmidt, *Firmen* (see n. 63 above), pp. 148f., 206–49; in general terms, and arguing on the basis of the situation of the labourers: W. E. Moore, *Industrialization and Labor* (Ithaca, New York, 1951), pp. 55ff., 304ff. Other mechanisms which stimulate innovations, esp. in the advanced industrial capitalism of the late nineteenth and twentieth century, are dealt with in D. Felix, 'Technological Dualism in Late Industrializers', *Journ. Econ. Hist.*, 34 (1974), 194–238.

132 Kula, *Théorie* (see n. 10 above), p. 110; W. Abel, *Massenarmut und Hungerkrisen im vorindustriellen Europa. Versuch einer Synopsis* (Hamburg etc., 1974), pp. 291ff., 300f. Cf. above, pp. 31f., 96f., 114f.

133 See above, pp. 30–3.

134 W. Achilles, 'Getreidepreise und Getreidehandelsbeziehungen europäischer Räume im 16. und 17. Jahrhundert', *Z. Agrarg. Agrarsoziol.*, 7 (1959), 32–55; Kula, *Théorie* (see n. 10 above), pp. 65–70, 98f., 159f.; C. W. J. Granger and C. M. Elliott, 'A Fresh Look at Wheat Prices in the Eighteenth Century', *Econ. Hist. Rev.*, 2nd ser., 20 (1967), 257–65; L. A. Tilly, 'The Food Riot as a Form of Political Conflict in France', *Journal of Interdisciplinary History*, 2 (1971), 23–57, esp. 35–45; cf. Abel, *Massenarmut* (see n. 132 above), pp. 216–26, 272, 295–300, cf. also 39–41, 158–66, 169–74, 177f., 179–83, 195–7, 202f., 258f.; C. -E. Labrousse, *Esquisse du mouvement des prix et des revenues en France au 18e siècle*, Collection scientifique d'économie politique, vol. 3 (Paris, 1933), pp. 6–9, 93f., 103–13, 531; C. -E. Labrousse, 'Prix et structure régionale: le froment dans les régions françaises 1782–1790', *Annales d'histoire sociale*, 1 (1939), 382–400; C.-E. Labrousse, 'Comment contrôler les mercuriales? Le test de concordance', *Annales d'histoire sociale*, 2 (1940), pp. 117–30.

135 Wadsworth and Mann, *Cotton Trade* (see n. 29 above), pp. 355–83; Shelton, *Hunger* (see n. 77 above), esp. 36ff., 141–6; Kaplow, *Elbeuf* (see n. 45 above), pp. 126ff.; Berkner, *Family* (n. 45 above), pp. 274ff.; Bois, *Paysans de l'Ouest* (see n. 23 above), pp. 524ff.; Tilly, *Vedée* (see n. 45 above), pp. 219ff.; Jacquemyns, *Flandres* (see n. 23 above), pp. 324–9. Cf. also R. B. Rose, 'Eighteenth-Century Price Riots and Public Policy in England', *International Review of Social History*, 6 (1961), 277–92; Rudé, *Crowd* (see n. 77 above), pp. 21ff., 35ff., 47ff., esp. 37; Thompson, *English Working Class* (see n. 77 above), pp. 67ff.; Thompson, 'The Moral Economy of the English Crowd in the Eighteenth Century', *Past and Present*, 50 (1971), 76–136.

136 Both the grain *and* flax harvests were bad in Ireland, for example, in 1800: Gill, *Irish Linen Industry* (see n. 23 above), pp. 340f., Abel, *Massenarmut* (see n. 132 above), p. 184 and Labrousse, *Esquisse* (see n. 134 above), pp. 315–17 observe that in times of dearth flax and wool prices did usually not move parallel with food prices.

137 Ashton, *Fluctuations* (see n. 129 above), p. 39f. (concerning wool); cf. Westernhagen, 'Leinwandmanufaktur' (see n. 13 above), pp. 9f. (concerning flax); Lebrun, *Verviers* (see n. 53 above), pp. 290–310, 326–340 (in detail about the movement of wool-prices, cloth-prices, and the volume of sales). But also see Kühn, 'Hirschberger Leinwandhandel' (see n. 23 above), p. 54; Labrousse, in: *Histoire économique* (see n. 36 above), vol. 2, p. 552.

138 Cf. below, p. 122 and Troeltsch, *Calwer Zeughandlungskompagnie* (see n. 42 above), pp. 213–18, cf. 101; Kaplow, *Elbeuf* (see n. 45 above), p. 47; Bodmer, *Schweizerische Textilwirtschaft* (see n. 38 above), pp. 206f.; cf. also Mann, *Cloth* (see n. 45 above), pp. 260ff., 269ff.

139 Ulrich Bräker, 'Lebensgeschichte und natürliche Ebenteuer {sic} des armen

Mannes im Tockenburg' (1789), in: Bräker, *Werke in einem Bande*, ed. H. -G. Thalheim, Bibliothek deutscher Klassiker (Berlin etc., 1964), p. 221 (Eng. tr. U. Bräker, *The Life Story and Real Adventures of the Poor Man of Toggenburg* (Edinburgh, 1970), pp. 162–5); Bodmer, *Schweizerische Textilwirtschaft* (see n. 38 above), pp. 206, 221, 229, but cf. 135f.

140 Labrousse, *Esquisse* (see n. 134 above), pp. 554, 560, cf. pp. 528–67, concerning the relatively smaller fluctuations of industrial commodity prices, see pp. 315–20, 325–30; also Abel, *Massenarmut* (see n. 132 above), pp. 204, 206, 260–4. Concerning the effects of harvest-fluctuations on the industrial population in general cf. above, pp. 31f., 89ff. Important however the qualifications in P. Dardel, 'Crises et faillites à Rouen et dans la Haute-Normandie de 1740 à l'an V', *Revue d'histoire économique et sociale*, 27 (1948), 53–71; D. Landes, 'Statistical Study of French Crises', *Journ. Econ. Hist.*, 10 (1950), 195–211.

141 According to K. Blaschke, *Bevölkerungsgeschichte von Sachsen bis zur industriellen Revolution* (Weimar, 1967), 126–9. Concerning the crisis mortality in the woolen region of Eichsfeld (Central Germany) in 1770–2 see Haendley, 'Bauern' (see n. 33 above), pp. 194f. In the wool-weaving village of Mouy in 1693–4 the number of marriages declined less than in the agrarian village Auneuil (though the number of cases is very small), conceptions declined equally, and deaths surged particularly high: P. Goubert, *Beauvais et les Beauvaisis de 1600 à 1730*, Démographie et sociétés, vol. 3 (Paris, 1960), vol. 1, pp. 47f., 50, 52f., 78f., vol. 2, 56f. The number of marriages declined, though the female marriage-age did not rise, in the framework knitter village of Shepshed under bad economic conditions: Levine, *Family Formation* (see n. 52 above), pp. 60, cf. 63. The thesis that proto-industrial regions generally show no significant demographic reactions to economic crises (Mendels, 'Proto-Industrialization' {n. 48 above}, pp. 251f.; cf. also above, pp. 81f., 91ff.) needs to be more carefully examined in the light of what is argued here. The development in proto-industrial regions should also be seen in conjunction with the fact that the demographic consequences of crises declined in many agricultural regions as well in the eighteenth century.

142 Labrousse, *Esquisse* (see n. 134 above), pp. 531f., 555–61, 564–7; F. F. Mendels, 'Industry and Marriages in Flanders before the Industrial Revolution', *Population and Economics*, ed. P. Deprez (Winnipeg, 1970), pp. 81–93, esp. 88f. See also the remarks in Smith, *Wealth of Nations* (see n. 105), vol. 1, Bk. 1, Ch. 8, pp. 102f.

143 Calculated on the basis of 'Nachweisung wieviel leinene Waare von 1748/49 bis 1789/90 in Schlesien, und zwar in byden Cammer-Departments ausser Landes versandt worden', *Schlesische Provinzialblätter*, 31 (1800), 9–12 (concerning this source, see above, p. 232, n. 131); cf. Zimmermann, *Blüte* (see n. 23 above), pp. 462–5; Kühn, 'Hirschberger Leinwandhandel' (n. 23 above), p. 150. For 1772/73 the value of the linen exports from Silesia is missing. The value of linen exported from Hirschberg, which had amounted to 39% of the total Silesian linen export during the two preceding years, declined by 3.8% from 1771–2 to 1772–3. The quantity of linen export from Landeshut rose by 1.1% in the same year (calculated according to Kühn, p. 150). The year 1772 was a year of 'scarcity and dearness' in Silesia as well: Fechner, *Wirtschaftsgeschichte* (n. 23 above), p. 706; Kühn, p. 53f.

144 Fechner, *Wirtschaftsgeschichte* (see n. 23 above), pp. 704–7; Westernhagen, 'Leinwandmanufaktur' (see n. 13 above), pp. 19f.

145 Cf. above, pp. 91ff.

146 Mendels, 'Industry' (see n. 141 above), p. 83; Mendels, 'Industrialization' (see n. 29 above), p. 9.

147 Cf. below, pp. 130f.

148 Calculated according to 'Nachweisung wieviele leinene Waare' (see n. 143 above). See also Kühn, *Leinwandhandel* (see n. 23 above), p. 52.

149 See below, p. 122.

150 Calculated according to O. Schumann, *Die Landeshuter Leinenindustrie in Vergangenheit und Gegenwart*, Abhandlungen des wirtschaftlichen Seminars zu Jena, vol. 19, pt. 1 (Jena, 1928), p. 128. Concerning the impact of the Napoleonic Wars and the Continental Blockade on the development of European industry see below, pp. 147f. Other examples of crises caused by war: Kaplow, *Elbeuf* (see n. 45 above), pp. 45f., pp. 112–20, 123–6; Deschesne, *Vesdre* (see n. 53 above), pp. 172–81, 192–8; Heaton, *Yorkshire* (see n. 23 above), pp. 41–4, 47–9; Court, *Midland Industries* (see n. 45 above), pp. 206–12; Gill, *Irish Linen* (see n. 23 above), pp. 179f.; Dascher, *Hessen-Kassel* (see n. 66 above), pp. 149–51; cf. also below, p. 122, n. 161, p. 295, n. 172; but also below pp. 125, 130f.

151 K. Marx, *Theories of Surplus Value* (London and Moscow, 1969), vol. 2, Ch. 17, pp. 492–535; cf. Sweezy, *Theory* (see n. 87 above), pp. 138ff.; K. Kühne, *Ökonomie und Marxismus* (Neuwied etc., 1974), vol. 2, pp. 361ff.; V.-M. Bader et al., *Krise und Kapitalismus bei Marx*, 2 vols. (Frankfurt, A. M., 1975).

152 Kühn, *Hirschberger Leinwandhandel* (see n. 23 above), pp. 41f.; Schmidt, 'Firmen' (see n. 63 above), pp. 33–5. Concerning the long periods of the turnover of capital in the putting-out system as well see Mann, 'Wiltshire' (see n. 29 above), pp. 81f.; Kisch, 'Wupper' (see n. 45 above), pp. 377f.; E. Barkhausen, *Montjoie* (see n. 38 above), p. 34.

153 Wilson, *Merchants* (see n. 23 above), pp. 78ff.; Lebrun, *Verviers* (see n. 53 above), pp. 378ff., 383f.

154 Cf. above, pp. 99ff.

155 B. E. Supple, *Commercial Crisis and Change in England 1600–1642* (1959; rpt. Cambridge, 1970), pp. 10ff.; cf. Bodmer, *Schweizerische Textilwirtschaft* (see n. 38 above), p. 241.

156 The concept 'trading goods crisis' (Handelswarenkrise) comes from M. Bouniatian, *Wirtschaftskrisen und Überkapitalisation. Eine Untersuchung über die Erscheinungsformen und Ursachen der periodischen Wirtschaftskrisen* (Munich, 1908), pp. 30–7; cf. A. Spiethoff, *Die wirtschaftlichen Wechsellagen* (Tübingen etc., 1955), vol. 1, pp. 60f. Examples are to be found in Kühn, *Hirschberger Leinwandhandel* (see n. 23 above), pp. 52–6, 59; Schmidt, *Firmen* (see n. 63 above), pp. 30, 32–4, 48f.; A. Wrasmann, 'Das Heuerlingswesen im Fürstentum Osnabrück', pt. 2, *Mitteilungen des Vereins für Geschichte und Landeskunde von Osnabrück*, 44 (1921), p. 17.

157 Cf. above, pp. 100f.

158 See Wrasmann, 'Heuerlingswesen', pt. 2 (see n. 156 above), p. 17f., though he gives only aggregate figures for the entire region and explains the rising output during the crisis by the growth of that part of the population which depended on spinning and weaving. Cf. below p. 158 and n. 127. Guilds, wherever they existed, could attempt to limit the output per producer: Engels and Legers, *Remscheid* (see n. 23 above), vol. 1, pp. 82–5. The reason why the consequences of the crisis in the area of petty commodity-production differed from its consequences in capitalist commodity-production does not lie in the subjective attitudes of the direct producers, but in the objective relations of production (cf. above p. 108). The wage-labourer under capitalism must sell his labour power, just as the petty producer must sell his product, in order to earn his livelihood. Consequently the former, like the latter, can be forced by a lower income to make more of his commodity available: his labour-power as well as that of his wife and children in the former case; products in the latter case. Concerning the wage-labourer see M. Dobb, *Wages* (London, 1956), pp. 125f., 147f. Hicks, *Wages* (see n. 131 above), pp. 97–102. The difference between the two lies in the fact that the petty commodity-producer (with the qualifications outlined on the following pages) himself decides whether he wants to manufacture a product or not, while under capitalist conditions the direct producer's 'willingness to work' leads to the manufacture of a product only if he is employed by a capitalist who anticipates a profit. In contrast to this, see the interpretation above, pp. 42f., 45ff., 51.

159 One example out of many: Rowlands, *Masters* (see n. 23 above), pp. 82f. Cf. the statements cited above, p. 274f., n. 29, which considered high wages as an incentive to better work.

160 Detailed calculations, which are based on the same considerations, were made by W. Achilles, 'Die Bedeutung des Flachsanbaus im südlichen Niedersachsen für Bauern und Angehörige der unterbäuerlichen Schicht im 18. und 19. Jahrhundert', *Agrarisches Nebengewerbe* (see n. 65 above), pp. 109–24 about the cost–profit relationships in the cultivation and processing of flax. This relationship varied from large estates to peasant farms to sub-peasant holdings.

161 The linen export from Landeshut fell by 36% in 1793 compared with the previous year. Calculated according to Zimmermann, *Blüte* (see n. 23 above), pp. 470f.; Fechner, *Wirtschaftsgeschichte* (n. 23 above), p. 710; Schumann, *Landeshuter Leinenindustrie* (see n. 150 above), p. 128. Since the weavers were subject to feudal obligations, their revolts tended to combine with peasant revolts and took on anti-feudal characteristics; they were also stimulated, up to a degree, by impressions of the French Revolution: Zimmermann, *Blüte*, pp. 188–207; Fechner, *Wirtschaftsgeschichte*, pp. 710–21; J. Ziekursch, *Hundert Jahre schlesischer Agrargeschichte. Vom Hubertusburger Frieden bis zum Abschluss der Bauernbefreiung*, 2nd ed. (Breslau, 1927), pp. 228–37.

162 Wilson, *Merchants* (see n. 23 above), p. 48.

163 Supple, *Crisis* (see n. 155 above), pp. 53–58; Mann, *Cloth* (see n. 45 above), p. 102, cf. pp. 89ff.; Mann, 'Wiltshire' (see n. 29 above), pp. 67–72, 94f.; Levine, *Family Formation* (see n. 52 above), pp. 22f.; Kisch, *Mercantilism* (see n. 38 above), p. 12, 33f.; Koch, 'Nähnadelzunft' (see n. 62 above), p. 82; Kisch, 'Wupper' (see n. 45 above), pp. 403f.; Kaplow, *Elbeuf* (see n. 45 above), pp. 45–8, 106–8, 124–6; Tilly, *Vendée* (see n. 45 above), pp. 217ff.; Deschesne, *Vesdre* (see n. 53 above), pp. 206–8; T. Geering, *Handel und Industrie der Stadt Basel. Zunftwesen und Wirtschaftsgeschichte bis zum Ende des 17. Jahrhunderts* (Basel, 1886), pp. 622f.

164 Kisch, *Mercantilism* (see n. 38 above), pp. 33f.; H. Botzet, 'Die Geschichte der sozialen Verhältnisse in Krefeld und ihre wirtschaftlichen Zusammenhänge' (WiSo Diss., Cologne, 1954), pp. 20–39.

165 Schumpeter, *Konjunkturzyklen* (see n. 108 above), vol. 1, pp. 242–63; Spiethoff, *Wechsellagen* (see n. 156 above), vol. 1, 86–110; Sombart, *Der moderne Kapitalismus* (see n. 29 above), vol. 2, pt. 1, pp. 208–28; Mendels, 'Proto-Industrialization' (see n. 48 above), pp. 256f.; M. Bouniatian, *Geschichte der Handelskrisen in England . . . 1640–1840* (Munich, 1908), pp. 127–50; Labrousse, in: *Histoire économique* (see n. 36 above), vol. 2, pp. 545–63; Supple, *Crisis* (see n. 155 above), pp. 8–18; Ashton, *Fluctuations* (see n. 129 above), esp. pp. 138–78; St. Skalweit, *Die Berliner Wirtschaftskrise von 1762 und ihre Hintergründe*, VSWG Beiheft 34 (Stuttgart, 1937), esp. pp. 38–48.

166 From 1748–9 to 1789–90 between 71 and 83% of the Silesian linen export went to 'England, Holland, France, Spain, Portugal, the West Indies and other parts of the world'; only 5 to 14% went to Austria, Switzerland, Saxony, the other states of the Empire, and Prussia. 2.5 to 5.5% went to Prussia alone, while the consumption in the province Silesia is unknown; calculated for 5-year periods according to the tables about the value of linen exported from Silesia: 'Nachweisung wieviele leinene Waare' (see n. 143 above). Cf. also above, pp. 35f.

167 See above, pp. 18, 31f.

168 See above, p. 18.

169 Even during proto-industrialization, when the industries working for luxury demand were of considerable importance, the development of luxury demand could hardly replace that of mass demand. This is illustrated by the fact that the continuously-growing Krefeld silk-industry was not built on the demand of the feudal nobility of the eastern half of Prussia – it was indeed cut off from this market – while the Berlin silk-industry which had a monopoly on this market survived only as long as it was supported by state subsidies and privileges. Kisch, *Mercantilism* (see n. 38 above), esp. p. 8f.; Krüger, *Manufakturen* (see n. 15 above), pp. 161–4; M. Barkhausen, *Wirtschaftslenkung* (see n. 49 above), pp. 203–5.

170 Cf. above, p. 113.

171 Here Sombart's theses need to be revised: W. Sombart, *Luxus und Kapitalismus* (Munich etc., 1912; rpt. 1922); W. Sombart, *Krieg und Kapitalismus* (Munich etc., 1913). Concerning the limited importance of luxury demand compared with mass demand, also see the discussion in D. E. C. Eversley, 'The Home Market and Economic Growth in England 1750–1780', *Land, Labour and Population in the Industrial Revolution. Essays presented to J. D. Chambers*, eds. E. L. Jones and G. E. Mingay (London, 1967), p. 206–59; concerning the demand generated by the state, see the scepticism in Schumpeter, *Konjunkturzyklen* (see n. 108 above), vol. 1, pp. 247f.

172 Thus, in England, the volume of processed cotton could grow much more (by 37%) than the export of cotton products (by 9%) between the decade 1760–9 and 1770–9, i.e. during the crucial phase of the transition to machine spinning: Eversley, 'Home Markets' (see n. 171 above), p. 255; the figures are calculated on the basis of Deane and Cole, *Growth* (see n. 39 above), pp. 51, 59. Concerning the export crisis during the War of the American Revolution see Eversley, 'Home Markets', pp. 247–9; Ashton, *Fluctuations* (see n. 129 above), pp. 160–4; Chambers, *Nottinghamshire* (see n. 49 above), pp. 97f.

173 From 1700–9 to 1760–9 the English exports of iron and steel rose eightfold, those of linen 42-fold, those of cotton products more than 17-fold; according to Deane and Cole, *Growth* (see n. 39 above), p. 59.

174 A. H. John, 'Wars and the English Economy 1700–63', *Econ. Hist. Rev.*, 2nd ser., 7 (1955), 329–44; cf. Ashton, *Fluctuations* (see n. 129 above), pp. 49–83. Cf. below, pp. 130f.

175 Concerning the importance of the domestic market and the export market, see the balanced discussion in E. J. Hobsbawm, *Industry and Empire*, The Pelican Economic History of Britain, vol. 3 (London, 1968), pp. 40–8; Landes, *Prometheus* (see n. 29 above), pp. 46–56. Cf. above, pp. 33f. and below, pp. 144f.

Notes to Chapter 5 (Excursus)

176 This excursus owes much to D. C. North and R. P. Thomas, *The Rise of the Western World. A New Economic History* (Cambridge, 1973), whose theory places the interrelationship between the economic growth process and institutional change in the context of secular crises and upswings, as well as the expansion of markets. In trying to determine the institutions which promoted growth, however, they are biased and fall back on the positions of classic economic liberalism (see e.g. p. 91). Cf. H. Medick, *Naturzustand und Naturgeschichte der bürgerlichen Gesellschaft. Die Ursprünge der bürgerlichen Sozialtheorie als Geschichtsphilosophie und Sozialwissenschaft bei Samuel Pufendorf, John Locke und Adam Smith*, Kritische Studien zur Geschichtswissenschaft, vol. 5 (Göttingen, 1973), pp. 262ff.; J. S. Mill, *Principles of Political Economy*, Book 5, esp. Chs. 1, 8 and 11, in J. S. Mill, *Collected Works*, vol. 3 (Toronto and London, 1965), pp. 799ff., 880ff., 936ff.; cf. also W. Roscher, 'Grundlagen der Nationalökonomie', in W. Roscher, *System der Volkswirtschaft*, 18th ed. (Stuttgart, 1886), vol. 1, pp. 148–214.

177 This ambivalence which was pointed out in the critique of political economy but is ignored by North and Thomas must be taken into consideration. See, on one side, Marx, *Grundrisse* (see n. 28 above), pp. 239–43; Marx, *Capital*, vol. 1, Ch. 2, pp. 178ff.; on the other side, Marx, *Capital*, vol. 1, Chs. 26–32, pp. 873–930.

178 Weber, *Wirtschaft und Gesellschaft* (see n. 21 above), vol. 2, p. 663; cf. P. Anderson, *Lineages of the Absolutist State* (London, 1974), esp. pp. 18ff., 428f.

179 The connection between power politics and economic policy is also emphasized by C. H. Wilson, 'Trade, Society and the State', *Cambridge Economic History*, vol. 4 (Cambridge, 1967), pp. 487–575, esp. 495f., 498f., 516, 521, 556ff., 570.

180 Cf. above p. 25.

181 Also in Wilson, 'Trade', pp. 570ff., cf. 527f.

182 Also in North and Thomas, *Rise* (see n. 176 above), esp. pp. 98–101. This is also emphasized by G. Ardant, 'Financial Policy and Economic Infrastructure of Modern States and Nations', *The Formation of National States in Western Europe*, ed. Ch. Tilly, Studies in Political Development, vol. 8 (Princeton, N. J., 1975), pp. 164–242.

183 See the attempt in H. Gerstenberger, 'Zur Theorie der historischen Konstitution des bürgerlichen Staates', *Probleme des Klassenkampfes*, 8/9 (1973), 207–26, although this article overemphasizes the need to support mercantile interests *abroad*; cf. also H. Gerstenberger, *Zur politischen Ökonomie der bürgerlichen Gesellschaft. Die Bedingungen ihrer Konstitution in den USA* (Frankfurt, a. M., n.d.), esp. pp. 119–34.

184 This direction has been followed by the more recent literature, esp. in the case of Prussia, see below, pp. 298f. n. 217.

185 North and Thomas, *Rise* (see n. 176 above), pp. 1ff., 91, 146–56. This implies that the comprehensive analysis of the economic development of a specific society must include the non-economic conditions of growth in addition to the economic stimuli and impediments to growth (concerning the latter, see above, pp. 104ff.).

186 Cf. Schmoller, *Volkswirtschaftslehre* (see n. 1 above), vol. 1, pp. 313ff.

187 See above pp. 22f. and the literature under n. 52 above. In the internationally-important cotton industry of eighteenth-century Augsburg, the urban, guild-organized weavers preserved a strong position, because they specialized in certain products and because they had a strong guild organization; but the cotton-entrepreneurs, in hard and protracted struggles, succeeded in assuring the processing of enough cotton cloth that was woven outside the city: Zorn, *Bayerisch-Schwaben* (see n. 73 above), pp. 42–6, 51–8, 62–6, 68f.; Dirr, 'Augsburgs Textilindustrie' (n. 73 above), pp. 46–95.

188 See above pp. 17ff., 26f., also with regard to the role of the collective institutions of the village community. Rights in communal resources were often part of the agrarian basis of the land-poor population that shifted to industry.

189 Cf. Berkner, 'Family' (see n. 45 above), pp. 164ff., 169ff., 177ff., 194ff. Cf. above pp. 17f.

190 Purš, 'Struktur' (see n. 15 above), vol. 2, pp. 121f.; cf. Pavlenko and Kafengaus, in: *Geschichte der UdSSR* (see n. 11 above), vol. 1, pt. 2, pp. 436, 440, 532f.; cf. also above pp. 18ff., 96ff. Cf. also the discussion about the reasons why an intensive linen industry did not exist in the southern parts of Ireland in Gill, *Irish Linen Trade* (see n. 23 above), pp. 20–7, 165.

191 See above, pp. 20f., 29, 97f., and below, pp. 115,125 142f., 149f.

192 Cf. Purš, 'Struktur' (see n. 15 above), vol. 2, pp. 104f., 120–2.

193 Cf. already Weber, *Wirtschaft und Gesellschaft* (see n. 21 above), vol. 1, pp. 254f., cf. 624f.; vol. 2, pp. 717–21.

194 E. F. Heckscher, *Der Merkantilismus* (Jena, 1932), vol. 1, pp. 27–90.

195 See e.g. above p. 122 and the literature under n. 161.

196 Heckscher, *Merkantilismus* (see n. 194 above), vol. 1, pp. 138–48, 243–50; Potthoff, 'Leinenleggen' (see n. 23 above), pp. 36–54.
197 Wadsworth and Mann, *Cotton Trade* (see n. 29 above), pp. 395–400; Pollard, *Management* (see n. 87 above), pp. 33f.; Bodmer, *Schweizerische Textilwirtschaft* (see n. 38 above), p. 255; Hofmann, 'Österreichische Baumwollwarenindustrie' (see n. 38 above), pp. 521f.; E. Barkhausen, *Montjoie* (see n. 38 above), pp. 102–12.
198 Wadsworth and Mann, *Cotton Trade* (see n. 29 above), pp. 340–83; Chambers, *Nottinghamshire* (see n. 49 above), pp. 35–44; Gill, *Irish Linen Trade* (see n. 23 above), pp. 138–44; Léon, in: *Histoire économique* (see n. 36 above), vol. 2, pp. 679–81; E. Barkhausen, *Montjoie* (see n. 38 above), pp. 80–102 (also pp. 81f. about the closed organization of putters-out); Kisch, 'Wupper' (see n. 45 above), 401–7; cf. Krüger, *Manufakturen* (see n. 15 above), 438–43.

199 Sombart, *Der moderne Kapitalismus* (see n. 29 above), vol. 1, pt. 2, pp. 814–24, cf. 811; Pollard, *Management* (see n. 87), pp. 163–6; Wilson, *England* (see n. 63 above), pp. 346–52; Levine, *Family Formation* (see n. 52 above), pp. 20f., 30f.; Hinze, *Arbeiterfrage* (see n. 15 above), pp. 155–71; H. Eichler, 'Zucht- und Arbeitshäuser in den mittleren östlichen Provinzen Brandenburg-Preussens', *Jb. Wirtsch. G.* (1970), pt. 1, 127–47; W. Wolf, *Zur Geschichte des Armen- und Arbeitshauses in Potsdam 1774–1800*, Veröffentlichungen des Bezirksheimatmuseums in Potsdam, vol. 2 (Potsdam, 1963); Krüger, *Manufakturen* (see n. 15 above), pp. 139–48; Forberger, *Manufaktur* (see n. 98 above), pp. 154, 158–60, 215–18; Slawinger, *Manufaktur* (see n. 94 above), pp. 76–81; Reuter, *Manufaktur* (see n. 98 above), pp. 22f., 25f., 69f., 123, 149f.

200 But there were also very unequal trading contracts; a particularly flagrant example is the trade agreement between Prussia and Poland of 1775, see Krüger, *Manufakturen* (see n. 15 above), pp. 98f.; H. Rachel, 'Der Merkantilismus in Brandenburg-Preussen', *Forschungen zur Brandenburgischen und Preussischen Geschichte*, 40 (1927), p. 258; M. Herzfeld, 'Der polnische Handelsvertrag von 1775', *Forschungen zur Brandenburgischen und Preussischen Geschichte*, 32 (1919), 57–107, vol. 35 (1923), 45–82, vol. 36 (1924), 210–20; see the data in H. Rachel, *Handels- Zoll- und Akzisepolitik*, Acta Borussica, vol. 3, 2 (Berlin, 1928), pp. 487–506.
201 Also in Wilson, 'Trade' (see n. 179), pp. 535ff., 562.
202 North and Thomas, *Rise* (see n. 176), pp. 17, 94ff.
203 John, 'Wars' (see n. 174 above); Wilson, *England* (see n. 63 above), pp. 276–87. Cf. also above, p. 120.
204 See above, pp. 34ff.
205 Hobsbawm, *Industry* (see n. 175), p. 50; cf. also Wilson, *England* (see n. 63 above), pp. 263–87; also above pp. 125f. and below pp. 144f.
206 Cf. the discussion about the 'social foundations of absolutism': F. Hartung and R. Mousnier, 'Quelques problèmes concernant la monarchie absolue', *10. Congresso internazionale di scienze storiche Roma 4.–11.9.1955*, Relazioni 4 (Florence, n.d., Biblioteca Storica Sansoni, n. s. vol. xxv), pp. 1–55 and 429–43; E. Molnar, 'Les fondements économiques et sociaux de l'absolutisme', *12e Congrès international des sciences historiques Vienna 29.8. à 5.9.1965*, (Vienna, n. d.), vol. 4, pp. 155–69 and vol. 5, pp. 675–716; R. Vierhaus, 'Absolutismus', in *Sowjetsystem und demokratische Gesellschaft. Eine vergleichende Enzyklopädie*, ed. C. D. Kernig (Freiburg i.B., 1966), vol. 1, columns 17–37 and the literature cited there. The differences in the socio-economic foundations of absolutism in eastern and western Europe have recently been emphasized in Anderson, *Absolutist State* (see n. 178 above), esp. pp. 18ff., 43ff., 159ff., 221ff., 428ff.
207 North and Thomas, *Rise* (see n. 176 above) in principle include the discussion of the tax system, the governmental structure, and economic development in their theory,

but they make a rather crude distinction between absolutist states and those which were governed by representative bodies, without pursuing the question of whose interests were represented in the latter; see esp. pp. 98, 127.

208 See the interesting study by R. Braun, 'Taxation, Sociopolitical Structure, and State Building: Great Britain and Brandenburg-Prussia', *Formation of National States* (see n. 182 above), pp. 243–327; Ardant, 'Financial Policy' (n. 182 above).

209 Heckscher, *Merkantilismus* (see n. 194 above), vol. 1, pp. 28–38.

210 North and Thomas, *Rise* (see n. 176 above), pp. 147–9, 152–5; Dobb, *Studies* (see n. 1 above), pp. 161–76; Wilson, *England* (see n. 63 above), pp. 269ff.; Clarkson, *Pre-industrial Economy* (see n. 45 above), pp. 159–83. Concerning the monopolies and privileges which became obstacles to growth at an advanced stage of development, see also Troeltsch, *Calwer Zeughandlungskompagnie* (see n. 42 above), pp. 165ff., 322–30; Gothein, *Schwarzwald* (see n. 6 above), pp. 715–22, cf. 791–801; Kisch, 'Wupper' (see n. 45 above); Kisch, *Mercantilism* (see n. 38 above), pp. 5, 8ff.; Engels and Legers, *Remscheid* (see n. 23 above), pp. 71–153, 165–228.

211 P. G. M. Dickson, *The Financial Revolution in England. A Study in the Development of Public Credit 1688–1756* (London etc., 1967); Clarkson, *Pre-industrial Economy* (see n. 45 above), pp. 187–91; Wilson, *England* (see n. 63 above), pp. 206–25, 313–36.

212 Wilson, 'Trade' (see n. 179 above), pp. 503ff., 520ff.; Wilson, *England* (see n. 63 above), pp. 160–84, 266–9, 297; R. Davis, 'The Rise of Protection in England 1689–1786', *Econ. Hist. Rev.*, 2nd ser., 19 (1966), 306–17; cf. Wadsworth and Mann, *Cotton Trade* (see n. 29 above), pp. 116ff.; N. B. Harte, 'The Rise of Protection and the· English Linen Trade 1690–1790', *Textile History and Economic History* (see n. 51 above), pp. 74–112.

213 Already stated by Mirabeau in 1788, see Krüger, *Manufakturen* (see n. 15 above), pp. 201f.; also Ch. Tilly and R. Tilly, 'Emerging Problems in the Modern Economic History of Western Europe' (Unpubl., 1971), pp. 38f., 41; Ch. Tilly, 'Food Supply and Public Order in Modern Europe', *Formation of National States* (see n. 182 above), pp. 380–455, esp. 445f., 453f.; Kula, *Théorie* (see n. 10 above), p. 27.

214 G. Schmoller, 'Die Epoehen der preussischen Finanzpolitik bis zur Gründung des deutschen Reiches', in G. Schmoller, *Umrisse und Untersuchungen zur Verfassungs-, Verwaltungs- und Wirtschaftsgeschichte* (Leipzig, 1898), pp. 104–246, esp. 151–8; Krüger, *Manufakturen* (see n. 15 above), pp. 30, 106–11; Fechner, *Wirtschaftsgeschichte ... Schlesien* (see n. 23 above), pp. 34–7; Rachel, *Handels- Zoll- und Akzisepolitik* (see n. 200), vol. 1, pp. 505–642. In the region of Ravensberg (Westphalia) it was the combined effect of the *Akzise* (excise) system and the public institutions which controlled the quality of linen *(Legge)* that limited the linen trade to the towns, see Potthoff, 'Leinenleggen' (see n. 23 above), pp. 44–51. The way in which such limitations functioned as an obstacle to growth is also demonstrated by Berkner, 'Family' (see n. 45 above), pp. 167ff., in this case in an Australian example; cf. also above p. 99 with n. 23 and p. 104.

215 Cf. above p. 287, n. 101.

216 Gerschenkron himself, who originally developed this thesis for the process of industrialization, applied it to mercantilism: see A. Gerschenkron, *Economic Backwardness in Historical Perspective* (Cambridge, Mass., 1962); Gerschenkron, *Russian Mirror* (see n. 11 above), pp. 62–96, esp. 86f.

217 See above pp. 20f., 29, 97f., 115, 125, 128f., and below pp. 142f., 149f. The example of Prussia makes this particularly clear: the mostly positive evaluations of the older pro-Prussian historiography and its successors have largely been replaced by a more critical approach which sees the country's explicit economic policy within this broader context; see, on the one side, Schmoller, *Volkswirtschaftslehre* (see n. 1 above), vol. 2, pp. 549–99; Rachel, 'Merkantilismus' (see n. 200 above); W. Treue, in B.

Gebhardt, *Handbuch der deutschen Geschichte*, ed. H. Grundmann, 9th ed. (Stuttgart, 1970), vol. 2, pp. 521–3, 533–5; on the other hand, Krüger, *Manufakturen* (see n. 15 above), esp. 148–56; M. Barkhausen, 'Wirtschaftslenkung' (see n. 49 above); Kisch, below; Kisch, *Mercantilism* (see n. 38 above); Tilly and Tilly, 'Problems' (see n. 213 above), pp. 39, 44; Braun, 'Taxation' (see n. 208 above), pp. 281, 300ff.

218 O. Büsch, *Militärsystem und Sozialleben im alten Preussen 1713–1807*, Veröffentlichungen der Berliner Historischen Kommission beim Friedrich-Meinicke-Institut der FU Berlin, vol. 7 (Berlin, 1962).

Notes to Chapter 6

1 R. Tilly and Ch. Tilly, 'Agenda for European Economic History in the 1970s', *Journ. Econ. Hist.*, 31 (1971), 184–98, here 186. It should be emphasized that the following is a discussion about the contribution of proto-industry to the emergence of factory industry; this chapter cannot deal with the theory of the Industrial Revolution as such. Accordingly, it is not the growth process as such which stands at the centre of this approach, e.g. the 'unbalanced growth' model of W. W. Rostow and A. O. Hirschman, or the 'balanced-growth' model of R. M. Hartwell, *The Industrial Revolution and Economic Growth* (London, 1971), both of which determine the literature in economic history; instead, the approach here will centre on a theory of transition from the proto-industrial system to the system of factory industry (see above Ch. 1, n. 1).

2 W. Hoffmann, *Stadien und Typen der Industrialisierung. Ein Beitrag zur quantitativen Analyse historischer Wachstumsprozesse*, Probleme der Weltwirtschaft, vol. 54 (Jena, 1931), pp. 19–23; Ph. Deane, *The First Industrial Revolution* (Cambridge, 1965), pp. 101f.

3 Cf. the substitution theory of A. Gerschenkron, 'Die Vorbedingungen der europäischen Industrialisierung im 19. Jahrhundert', *Wirtschafts- und sozialgeschichtliche Probleme der frühen Industrialisierung*, ed. W. Fischer, Einzelveröffentlichungen der Historischen Kommission zu Berlin, vol. 1 (Berlin, 1968), pp. 21–28; A. Gerschenkron, 'Reflections on the Concept of "Prerequisites" of Modern Industrialization', in A. Gerschenkron, *Economic Backwardness in Historical Perspective. A Book of Essays* (Cambridge, Mass., 1962), pp. 31–51; A. Gerschenkron, 'The Approach to European Industrialization: A Postscript', in A. Gerschenkron, *Economic Backwardness*, pp. 353–64 and other works.

4 See above pp. 54,100.

5 D. S. Landes, *The Unbound Prometheus. Technological Change and Industrial Development in Western Europe from 1750 to the Present* (Cambridge, 1969), pp. 55f.; D. S. Landes, 'Introduction', *The Rise of Capitalism*, ed. D. S. Landes (New York, 1966), pp. 1–25, esp. 13f.; F. F. Mendels, 'Proto-industrialization: The First Phase of the Industrialization Process', *Journ. Econ. Hist.*, 32 (1972), 241–61, esp. 243f. Though the law of diminishing returns has been disproved, it is valid under special circumstances, for example in the case of a decentralized system of production such as the putting-out system.

6 Landes, *Prometheus* (see n. 5 above), pp. 56–60; S. Pollard, *The Genesis of Modern Management. A Study in the Industrial Revolution in Great Britain* (London, 1965), pp. 30–7; A. P. Wadsworth and J. de Lacy Mann, *The Cotton Trade and Industrial Lancashire, 1600–1780* (Manchester, 1931), pp. 395–400.

7 Landes, *Prometheus* (see n. 5 above), pp. 57f.; P. Mantoux, *The Industrial Revolution in the Eighteenth Century. An Outline of the Beginnings of the Modern Factory System in England* (London, 1928; rpt. 1961), pp. 208f.; M. M. Edwards, *The Growth of the British Cotton Trade, 1780–1815* (Manchester, 1967), pp. 3f. Rising wages in West Riding and Lancashire: E. W. Gilboy, *Wages in Eighteenth-Century England*, Harvard Economic Studies, vol. 45 (Cambridge, Mass., 1934), pp. 176–90, 210–15, 240–3.

8 H. Freudenberger and F. Redlich, 'The Industrial Development of Europe.

Reality, Symbols, Images', *Kyklos*, 17 (1964), 372–403, esp. 378; cf. also G. Stedman-Jones, 'Class Struggle and the Industrial Revolution', *New Left Review*, 90 (1975), 35–69, esp. 49f. Concerning the putting-out system see above Ch. 4, pt. 1, c.

9 For a distinction between 'manufacture' (here 'proto-factory') and the factory properly speaking, see S. D. Chapman, 'The Textile Factory before Arkwright: A Typology of Factory Development', *Business History Review*, 48 (1974), 451–78, esp. 468–73. Chapman is critical of the conceptualization in Freudenberger and Redlich, 'Development' (see n. 8 above), pp. 382–97, which hardly makes a distinction at all between 'proto-factory' and factory; but unfortunately, he does not relate his thoughts to Marx's concept of 'manufacture'. For Chapman, the distinctive feature of the factory is what he calls 'flow production', in contrast to the 'batch production' of the 'proto-factory'. For an evaluation of 'manufacture', cf. the perceptive observations by K. A. Wittfogel, *Wirtschaft und Gesellschaft Chinas. Versuch der wissenschaftlichen Analyse einer grossen asiatischen Agrargesellschaft*, Schriften des Instituts für Sozialforschung, vol. 3 (Leipzig, 1931), vol. 1, pp. 674f.; see also above, Ch. 4, pt. 1, d.

10 The most recent survey of the large specialized literature: S. C. Chapman, *The Cotton Industry in the Industrial Revolution* (London, 1972); also Mantoux, *Revolution* (see n. 6 above), pp. 220–61; Wadsworth and Mann, *Cotton Trade* (n. 6 above), pp. 472–503; in particular see Edwards, *Growth* (see n. 7 above), pp. 4ff.

11 D. Bythell, *The Handloom Weavers. A Study in the English Cotton Industry during the Industrial Revolution* (Cambridge, 1969), pp. 26f., 66–93.

12 E. J. Hobsbawm, 'History and "The Dark Satanic Mills"', in E. J. Hobsbawm, *Labouring Men. Studies in the History of Labour* (1964; rpt. London, 1968), pp. 105–19, esp. 116; also E. P. Thompson, *The Making of the English Working Class* (1963; rpt. Harmondsworth, 1968), pp. 288f. Thus, the last phase of the expansion of handloom weaving constitutes the beginning of modern domestic industry which is closely linked to the process of capitalist industrialization. Beside the domestic workshops, however, there existed some centralized manufactures with a large number of looms; cf. Bythell, *Handloom Weavers* (see n. 11 above), pp. 33f.

13 For a survey: Pollard, *Genesis* (see n. 6 above), pp. 94–6; J. D. Chambers, *The Workshop of the World. British Economic History 1820–1880* (Oxford etc., 1961), pp. 26–8; specialized studies: D. T. Jenkins, *The West-Riding Wool Textile Industry, 1770–1835. A Study of Fixed Capital Formation* (Edington, Wilts., 1975), pp. 124–7, 133; J. de Lacy Mann, *The Cloth Industry of the West of England from 1640 to 1880* (Oxford, 1971), pp. 157–222; Ch. Erickson, *British Industrialists. Steel and Hosiery, 1850–1950*. Economic and Social Studies, vol. 18 (Cambridge, 1959), pp. 78–99, 171–87; for ribbon-weaving: J. Prest, *The Industrial Revolution in Coventry* (Oxford, 1960), pp. 93–135 (here also the transitional form of the 'cottage factory').

14 Pollard, *Genesis* (see n. 6 above), pp. 80–2.

15 F. Crouzet, 'Angleterre et France au XVIIIe siècle. Essai d'analyse comparée de deux croissances économiques', *Annales E.S.C.*, 21 (1966), 254–91, esp. 285–90; M. Lévy-Leboyer, 'Les processus d'industrialisation: le cas d'Angleterre et de la France', *Revue Historique*, 239 (1968), 281–98, esp. 283–5; E. J. Hobsbawm, 'Le origini della revoluzione industriale britannica', *Studi storici*, 2 (1961), 496–516, esp. 507f.; T. S. Ashton, *The Industrial Revolution in England 1760–1830* (1948; rpt. Oxford, 1969), pp. 62–4; T. S. Ashton, *The Eighteenth Century*, An Economic History of England, vol. 3 (London, 1955), pp. 108f. For the interpretation of technological change 'in terms of bottleneck analysis': N. Rosenberg, 'The Direction of Technological Change: Inducement Mechanisms and Focusing Devices', *Economic Development and Cultural Change*, vol. 18 (1969–70), 1–24, esp. 17–24; also R. Nelson et al., *Technology, Economic Growth and Public Policy* (Washington, D.C., 1967), pp. 28–34 (a 'demand-pull model' of technological progress); J. Smookler, *Invention and Economic Growth* (Cambridge, Mass., 1966).

16 For France: Crouzet, 'Angleterre' (see n. 15 above), pp. 285–90; Lévy-Leboyer, 'Processus' (n. 15 above), pp. 285–7. The level of German development is underestimated in F. -G. Dreyfus, 'Bilan économique des Allemagnes en 1815', *Revue d'histoire économique et sociale*, 43 (1964), 433–64, esp. 433f., 454–9.

17 Landes, *Prometheus* (see n. 5 above), pp. 137f.; L. Bergeron, 'Remarques sur les conditions de développement industriel en Europe occidentale à l'époque napoléonienne', *Francia*, 1 (1973), 537–56, esp. 541–9, and above all H. Kisch, 'The Impact of the French Revolution on the Lower Rhine Textile Districts. Some Comments on Economic Development and Social Change', *Econ. Hist. Rev.*, 2nd ser., 15 (1962–3), 304–27. For Saxony (in comparison with Westphalia): W. Fischer, '"Stadien und Typen" der Industrialisierung in Deutschland. Zum Problem ihrer regionalen Differenzierung', in W. Fischer, *Wirtschaft und Gesellschaft im Zeitalter der Industrialisierung. Aufsätze, Studien, Vorträge*, Kritische Studien zur Geschichtswissenschaft, vol. 1 (Göttingen, 1972), pp. 464–73, 534; A. Kunze, 'Vom Frühkapitalismus zur industriellen Revolution', *Beiträge zur Heimatgeschichte von Karl-Marx-Stadt*, 13 (1965), 7–51, esp. 23–38.

18 J. Kermann, *Die Manfakturen im Rheinland 1750–1833*, Rheinisches Archiv, vol. 82 (Bonn, 1972), pp. 117–91 and in addition for Verviers: P. Lebrun, *L'industrie de la laine à Verviers pendant le XVIIIe et le début du XIXe siècle. Contribution à l'étude des origines de la révolution industrielle*, Bibliothèque de la Faculté de philosophie et lettres de l'Université de Liège (Liège, 1948), pp. 276–87.

19 G. Adelmann, 'Strukturwandlungen der rheinischen Leinen- und Baumwollgewerbe zu Beginn der Industrialisierung', *VSWG*, 53 (1966), 162–84, esp. 164–7.

20 M. Barkhausen, 'Staatliche Wirtschaftslenkung und freies Unternehmertum im westdeutschen und nord- und südniederländischen Raum bei der Entstehung der neuzeitlichen Industrie im 18. Jahrhundert', *VSWG*, 45 (1958), 168–241, esp. 239.

21 Concerning the expansion of domestic industry in the first half of the nineteenth century cf. Landes, *Prometheus* (see n. 5 above), pp. 188–90. For France: M. Lévy-Leboyer, *Les banques européennes et l'industrialisation internationale dans la première moitié du XIXe siècle*, Publications de la Faculté de lettres et sciences humaines de Paris. Série Recherches, vol. 16 (Paris, 1964), pp. 66ff., 130ff.; J. Sion, *Les paysans de la Normandie orientale. Etude géographique sur les populations rurales du Caux et du Bray, du Vexin normand et de la vallée de la Seine* (Paris, 1908), pp. 304–12; R. Lévy, *Histoire économique de l'industrie cottonnière en Alsace. Etude de sociologie descriptive* (Paris, 1912), pp. 92 and 145. In the silk industry of Lyon, the percentage of rural workshops rose from 4 to 75% between 1810 and 1872, according to Lévy-Leboyer, *Les banques*, p. 43. For a similar development in Bas-Dauphiné cf. P. Léon, *La naissance de la grande industrie en Dauphiné (fin du XVIIe siècle–1869)*, Université de Grenoble. Publications de la Faculté des lettres, vol. 9 (Paris, 1954), vol. 2, pp. 597–602. For Germany, see G. Schmoller, *Zur Geschichte der deutschen Kleingewerbe im 19. Jahrhundert* (Halle, 1870), pp. 269–87, 504–10, 515–28, 561–72, 591–614; O. Büsch, *Industrialisierung und Gewerbe im Raum Berlin/Brandenburg 1800–1850. Eine empirische Untersuchung zur gewerblichen Wirtschaft einer hauptstadtgebundenen Wirtschaftsregion in frühindustrieller Zeit*, Einzelveröffentlichungen der Historischen Kommission zu Berlin, vol. 9 (Berlin, 1971), pp. 98–102; W. Fischer, *Der Staat und die Anfänge der Industrialisierung in Baden 1800–1850*. Vol. 1: *Die staatliche Gewerbepolitik* (Berlin, 1962), pp. 287–91; E. Shorter, *Social Change and Social Policy in Bavaria, 1800–1860* (Diss., Harvard University, 1967), vol. 2, pp. 390–402. An estimation of the employment figure for domestic industry in Germany: F. -W. Henning, 'Industrialisierung und dörfliche Einkommensmöglichkeiten. Der Einfluss der Industrialisierung des Textilgewerbes in Deutschland im 19. Jahrhundert auf die Einkommensmöglichkeiten in den ländlichen Gebieten', *Agrarisches Nebengewerbe und Formen der Reagrarisierung im Spätmittelalter und 19./20. Jahrhundert*, ed. H. Kellenbenz, Forschungen zur Sozial- und Wirtschaftsgeschichte, vol. 21 (Stuttgart, 1975), pp. 155–75, esp. 159f. For Russia see the classic study of M. Tugan-Baranovskii, *Geschichte der russischen Fabrik*, Sozialgeschichtliche Forschungen, 5/6 (Berlin, 1900), pp. 252–318. In many places the decline of hand-spinning led to the expansion of hand-weaving; cf. for the mountainous area above Zürich R. Braun, *Sozialer und kultureller Wandel in einem ländlichen Industriegebiet (Zürcher Oberland) unter Einwirkung des Maschinen- und Fabrikwesens im 19. und 20. Jahrhundert* (Erlenbach and Zürich etc., 1965, pp. 19f., 25.

22 In Prussia, the index of operating looms did not rise faster between 1816 (= 100) and 1846 (= 181) than the number of artisans (1846 = 188); the rise in the latter number is likely to be due to population growth (1846 = 156): K. H. Kaufhold, 'Das preussische Handwerk in der Zeit der Frühindustrialisierung. Eine Untersuchung nach den preussischen Gewerbetabellen 1815–1858', *Beiträge zu Wirtschaftswachstum und Wirtschaftsstruktur im 16. und 19. Jahrhundert*, ed. W. Fischer, Schriften des Vereins für Socialpolitik, n.F. 63 (Berlin, 1971), pp. 169–93, esp. 189f.; but the number of looms must be differentiated according to different branches of textiles. The index of silk handlooms, for example, rose to 227 during that period (1816 = 100), and the index of cotton handlooms rose to 529; calculated according to C. F. W. Dieterici, *Der Volkswohlstand des preussischen Staates* (Berlin etc., 1846), p. 186; 'Übersicht der in den verschiedenen Provinzen des preussischen Staates für Gewerbe aller Art bestehenden Fabriken und der mit denselben in Verbindung stehenden Bleicherei, Färberei und Druckerei; nach der für das Jahr 1846 aufgenommenen Gewerbetabelle der Fabrikations-Anstalten und Fabrik-Unternehmungen aller Art', *Mitteilungen des statistischen Bureau's in Berlin*, 1 (1848), 149–96, esp. 193; slightly changed figures appear for 1816 in T. Ohnishi, *Zolltarifpolitik Preussens bis zur Gründung des Deutschen Zollvereins. Ein Beitrag zur Finanz- und Aussenhandelspolitik Preussens* (Göttingen, 1973), p. 239, app. 4.

23 Lévy-Leboyer, *Banques* (see n. 21 above), pp. 65f., 169–75, 409–11; Lévy-Leboyer, 'Processus' (see n. 16 above), pp. 287–92, 295f.; S. Pollard, *European Economic Integration, 1815–1970* (London, 1974), pp. 17–23; S. Pollard, 'Industrialization and the European Economy', *Econ. Hist. Rev.*, 2nd ser., 26 (1973), 636–48, esp. 640–3; Mendels, 'Proto-industrialization' (see n. 5 above), p. 260. Generalizing from the Alsatian case, Lévy-Leboyer (Lévy, *Histoire* (see n. 21 above), pp. 7–10, 178–87) formulated the theory that while in England industrialization was a process of 'intégration vers l' aval', proceeding in the direction of the course of production from spinning to weaving, in France it was a process of 'intégration vers l'amont', i.e. it proceeded from printing to weaving to spinning. The validity of this theory for industrialization in Germany deserves to be examined.

24 The 'Chambre consultative des arts et manufactures' of Mulhouse estimated in 1827 that spinning doubled the value of one pound of cotton from 1.25 fr. to 2.5 fr.; weaving doubled it again to 5 fr.; and printing once again to 10 fr.: P. Leuillot, *L'Alsace au début du XIXe siècle. Essais d'histoire politique, économique et religieuse* (1815–1830), vols. 1–3 (Paris, 1959–60), vol. 2, pp. 423 and see also Lévy-Leboyer, *Banques* (see n. 21 above), p. 65. For the value of the gross production in German cotton-spinning and weaving cf. the aggregate data in G. Kirchhain, *Das Wachstum der deutschen Baumwollindustrie im 19. Jahrhundert. Eine historische Modellstudie zur empirischen Wachstumsforschung* (Diss. rer. pol., Münster, 1973), pp. 146–52, tables 42 and 43.

25 Pollard, *Integration* (see n. 23 above), p. 17.

26 Lévy-Leboyer, *Banques* (see n. 21 above), pp. 116ff., 169f.

27 Kirchhain, *Wachstum* (see n. 24 above), pp. 29–33.

28 Pollard, 'Industrialization' (see n. 23 above), p. 643; M. Kutz, *Deutschlands Aussenhandel von der französischen Revolution bis zur Gründung des Zollvereins*. VSWG Beiheft 61 (Wiesbaden, 1974), pp. 256f., 261; B. von Borries, *Deutschlands Aussenhandel 1836 bis 1856. Eine statistische Untersuchung zur Frühindustrialisierung*, Forschungen zur Sozial- und Wirtschaftsgeschichte, vol. 13 (Stuttgart, 1970), pp. 220f., 246f.; H. Blumberg, *Die deutsche Textilindustrie in der industriellen Revolution*, Veröffentlichungen des Instituts für Wirtschaftsgeschichte an der Hochschule für Ökonomie Berlin-Karlshorst, vol. 3 (Berlin, 1965), pp. 156–8, 170–80, 209–15; H. -J. Teuteberg, 'Das deutsche und britische Wollgewerbe um die Mitte des 19. Jahrhunderts. Ein Beitrag zur quantitativ-komparativen Wirtschaftsgeschichte', *Vom Kleingewerbe zur Grossindustrie. Quantitativ-regionale und politisch-rechtliche Aspekte zur Erforschung der Wirtschafts- und Gesellschaftsstruktur im 19. Jahrhundert*, ed. H. Winkel, Schriften des Vereins für Socialpolitik n.f. 83 (Berlin, 1975), pp. 9–103, esp. 94–7. For the development of textile exports see G. Hermes, 'Statistiche Studien zur wirtschaftlichen und gesellschaftlichen Struktur des zollvereinten Deutschlands', *Archiv für Sozialwissenschaft und Sozialpolitik*, 63 (1930), 121–62, esp. 136–41.

29 C. Fohlen, *L'industrie textile au temps du Second Empire* (Paris, 1956), pp. 161–249; Blumberg, *Textilindustrie* (see n. 28 above), pp. 95–105; W. Bodmer, *Die Entwicklung der schweizerischen Textilwirtschaft im Rahmen der übrigen Industrien und Wirtschaftszweige* (Zürich, 1960), pp. 291–9, 305–11, 313–19; T. J. Markovitch, *Le revenu industriel et artisanal sous la Monarchie de Juillet et le Second Empire*, Histoire quantitative de l'économie française, vol. 8 = Economies et sociétés, *Cahiers de l'Institut de Sciences Economiques Appliquées*, vol. [1]4 (Paris, 1967), pp. 81–83 estimates that during the time of the July monarchy and the second Empire domestic industry comprised 20 to 25% of the entire industrial product.

30 Fohlen, *Industrie* (see n. 29 above), pp. 455–61; Blumberg, *Textilindustrie* (see n. 28 above), pp. 47–52, 62–6, 88–92, 97–101, 105–32; Teuteberg, 'Wollgewerbe' (see n. 28 above), pp. 83–94. It must be taken into consideration, however, that the number of handlooms in comparison with the total number of looms can be taken as an indicator for the continuous existence of the domestic mode of production only with great reservations, since a large part of the handlooms were installed in centralized manufactures; cf. the tables according to the industrial census of 1875 in Blumberg, *Textilindustrie* (see n. 28 above), pp. 65, 132.

31 R. Spree and J. Bergmann, 'Die konjunkturelle Entwicklung der deutschen Wirtschaft 1840 bis 1864', *Sozialgeschichte heute. Festschrift für H. Rosenberg zum 70. Geburtstag*, ed. H. -U. Wehler, Kritische Studien zur Geschichtswissenschaft, vol. 11 (Göttingen, 1974), pp. 289–325, esp. 302–4, 319. Concerning the slow growth of the French textile industry – and not only of its traditional branches – and its role as an obstacle to the growth process of French industry in general, see F. Crouzet, 'Essai de construction d'un indice annuel de la production industrielle française au XIXe siècle', *Annales E.S.C.*, 25 (1970), 56–99, esp. pp. 73–6, 85f. On the continent, the tendency toward a divergent development of the industrial and agrarian cycles, which had begun with proto-industrialization (see above pp. 119f.), was temporarily reversed during the early phase of industrialization after many of the overseas markets had been lost.

32 A. Gerschenkron, 'Economic Backwardness in Historical Perspective', in Gerschenkron, *Backwardness* (see n. 3 above), pp. 5–30; Gerschenkron, 'Approach' (see n. 3 above), pp. 353–64; concerning specifically the insignificance of the consumer-goods industry among late industrializers, see Gerschenkron, *Backwardness*, pp. 15 and 354; a critical appraisal in S. L. Barsby, 'Economic Backwardness and the Characteristics of Development', *Journ. Econ. Hist.*, 29 (1969), 449–72, esp. 456–64.

33 Spree and Bergmann, 'Entwicklung' (see n. 31 above), pp. 305–21;

R. Fremdling, *Eisenbahnen und deutsches Wirtschaftswachstum 1840–1879. Ein Beitrag zur Entwicklungstheorie und zur Theorie der Infrastruktur.* Untersuchungen zur Wirtschafts-, Sozial- und Technikgeschichte, vol. 2 (Dortmund, 1975), pp. 12–85, esp. 83–5; C. -F. Holtfrerich, *Quantitative Wirtschaftsgeschichte des Ruhrkohlenbergbaus im 19. Jahrhundert. Eine Führungssektoranalyse,* Untersuchungen zur Wirtschafts-, Sozial- und Technikgeschichte, vol. 1 (Dortmund, 1973), pp. 155–68; H. Wagenblass, *Der Eisenbahnbahnbau und das Wachstum der deutschen Eisen- und Maschinenbauindustrie 1835 bis 1860. Ein Beitrag zur Geschichte der Industrialisierung Deutschlands,* Forschungen zur Sozial- und Wirtschaftsgeschichte, vol. 18 (Stuttgart, 1973), pp. 237–75. France, too, experienced an acceleration of industrial growth around the middle of the nineteenth century, but it did not last; cf. Crouzet, 'Essai' (see n. 31 above), pp. 88–91. Concerning the slow economic growth in France in the second half of the nineteenth century, cf. the explanation in M. Lévy-Leboyer, 'La déceleration de l'économie française dans la seconde moitié du XIXe siècle', *Revue d'histoire économique et sociale,* 49 (1971), 485–507; this explanation is not entirely convincing and would benefit from a comparative perspective.

34 Fr. Engels, 'Preface to the Second German Edition', *The Housing Question* in Karl Marx and Fr. Engels, *Selected Works* (London and Moscow, 1958), vol. 1, pp. 546–635, esp. p. 550. For a survey of German domestic industry around 1900 see the investigations of the Verein für Socialpolitik: *Die deutsche Hausindustrie,* vols. 1–4, Schriften des Vereins für Socialpolitik, vols. 39–42 (Leipzig, 1889–90); also *Hausindustrie und Heimarbeit in Deutschland und Österreich,* vols. 1–4, Schriften des Vereins für Socialpolitik, vols. 84–7 (Leipzig, 1899); for the domestic industries of other countries cf. W. Sombart and R. Meerwarth, 'Hausindustrie', in *Handwörterbuch der Staatswissenschaften,* 4th ed. (1923), vol. 5, pp. 179–207, here 191–204. The older domestic industries must be distinguished from the modern domestic industry which existed primarily in the large cities and worked predominantly for the clothing industry, although the former gradually took on many of the features of modern domestic industry. Marx expressively described modern domestic industry as the 'external department of the factory, the manufacturing workshop or the warehouse' and as a 'sphere, in which capital conducts its exploitation against the background of large-scale industry': K. Marx, *Capital,* vol. 1, introd. by E. Mandel and transl. by Ben Fowkes (London, 1977), pp. 595–9, footnotes on pp. 591 and 595. Modern domestic industry distinguishes itself from the older domestic industries by its new social foundation, namely the population of large cities, as well as by the fact that it is an integral part of the process of capitalist industrialization. Cf. Landes, *Prometheus* (see n. 5 above), pp. 118ff.; L. Baar, *Die Berliner Industrie in der industriellen Revolution,* Veröffentlichungen des Instituts für Wirtschaftsgeschichte an der Hochschule für Ökonomie Berlin-Karlshorst, vol. 4 (Berlin, 1966), pp. 73–87; Büsch, *Industrialisierung* (see n. 21 above), pp. 102–9; P. G. Hall, *The Industries of London since 1861* (London, 1962), pp. 53–70; G. Stedman-Jones, *Outcast London. A Study in the Relationship between Classes in Victorian Society* (London, 1971), pp. 23, 85–7. For a distinction between the old and new domestic industries, see the approach in Sombart and Meerwarth, 'Hausindustrie' (see above), pp. 182–4 and especially in A. Weber, 'Die Hausindustrie und ihre gesetzliche Regelung', Schriften des Vereins für Social-politik, vol. 88 (Leipzig, 1900), pp. 12–35, esp. 14–29.

35 For the following discussion cf. Mendels, 'Proto-industrialization' (see n. 5 above), pp. 244f.; Ch. and R. Tilly. 'Emerging Problems in Modern Economic History in Western Europe' (Unpubl., 1971), pp. 15f.

36 The mechanization of yarn and cloth production has been dealt with in greater detail than is possible here in Braun, *Wandel* (see n. 21 above), pp. 24–36; cf. Blumberg, *Textilindustrie* (see n. 28 above), pp. 303–12. In 1858, a notice appeared in Berlin for the purpose of founding a joint stock company in cotton spinning and weaving in Sagan (now Żagań), Lower Silesia; it contained the following remark: 'The necessary labourers will come from the numerous weaver families of the surrounding places and are therefore already partially trained in this kind of work' (quoted in Baar, *Industrie*, n. 34, p. 46).

37 Pollard, *Genesis* (see n. 6 above), pp. 160–208; E. P. Thompson, 'Time, Work-discipline, and Industrial Capitalism', *Past and Present*, 38 (1967), 56–97, esp. 79–86.

38 Braun, *Wandel* (see n. 21 above), pp. 66–108; S. D. Chapman, *The Early Factory Masters. The Transition to the Factory System in the Midlands Textile Industry* (Newton Abbot, Devon, 1967), pp. 77–124, esp. 99f.; J. Foster, *Class Struggle and the Industrial Revolution. Early Industrial Capitalism in three English Towns* (London, 1974), pp. 9–13; Léon, *Naissance* (see n. 21 above), vol. 2, pp. 513–15; Blumberg, *Textilindustrie* (see n. 28 above), pp. 132–9; Adelmann, 'Strukturwandlungen' (see n. 19 above), p. 183; A. König, *Die sächsische Baumwollenindustrie am Ende des vorigen Jahrhunderts und während der Kontinentalsperre*, Leipziger Studien aus dem Gebiet der Geschichte, vol. 5, 3 (Leipzig, 1899), pp. 337–9; W. Zorn, *Handels- und Industriegeschichte Schwabens 1648–1870. Wirtschafts- Sozial- und Kulturgeschichte des schwäbischen Unternehmertums*, Veröffentlichungen der Schwäbischen Forschungsgemeinschaft bei der Kommission für Bayerische Landesgeschichte, vol. 1, 6 (Augsburg, 1961), pp. 206–10 Surveys: J. Kocka, *Unternehmer in der deutschen Industrialisierung*, Kleine Vandenhoeck-Reihe, vol. 1412 (Göttingen, 1975), pp. 19–34, 42–50; H. Kaelble, *Berliner Unternehmer während der frühen Industrialisierung. Herkunft, sozialer Status und politischer Einfluss*, Veröffentlichungen der Historischen Kommission zu Berlin, vol. 40: Publikationen zur Geschichte der Industrialiserung, vol. 4 (Berlin, 1972), pp. 109–19.

39 Statistically proved for the first time on the basis of 'Sun Fire Office insurance-policy registers' by S. D. Chapman, 'Industrial Capital before the Industrial Revolution: An Analysis of the Assets of a Thousand Textile Entrepreneurs c. 1730–1750', *Textile History and Economic History. Essays in Honour of Miss J. de Lacy Mann*, eds. N. B. Harte and K. G. Ponting (Manchester, 1973), pp. 113–37.

40 Braun, *Wandel* (see n. 21 above), p. 67; concerning the great importance of the clothiers for the rise of the West Riding cloth industry in the eighteenth century and its industrialization (in contrast to the West Country and East Anglia), see R. G. Wilson, 'The Supremacy of the Yorkshire Cloth Industry in the Eighteenth Century', *Textile History* (see n. 39 above), pp. 225–46, esp. 236–9; R. G. Wilson, *Gentlemen Merchants. The Merchant Community in Leeds 1700–1830* (Manchester, 1971), pp. 5, 28–34, 52–60, 93–97; cf. also Crouzet, 'Capital Formation in Great Britain during the Industrial Revolution', *Capital Formation in the Industrial Revolution*, ed. F. Crouzet (London, 1972), pp. 162–222, esp. 164–70. It was characteristic of the early factory industry that little fixed capital was necessary, which accounts for the frequent rise to industrial entrepreneurs of the members of these social groups.

41 K. Marx. *Capital*, vol. 3 (London and Moscow, 1971), Ch. 20, p. 393 and in addition the Dobb-Sweezy controversy: M. Dobb, *Studies in the Development of Capitalism*, 2nd ed. (London, 1963), pp. 123–51 and P. Sweezy et al., *The Transition from Feudalism to Capitalism* (London, 1976), pp. 52–5, 64f., 87–97, 100f., 107, 124–6, 137–41.

42 Chapman, 'Capital' (see n. 39 above), p. 136; cf. Chapman, 'Textile Factory' (see n. 9 above), p. 456.

43 See above Ch. 1, pt. 3, a and Ch. 1, pt. 3, b; also Mendels. 'Proto-industrialization' (see n. 5 above), p. 245.

44 See above Ch. 1, pt. 3, c.

45 M. Weber, *General Economic History* (Glencoe, Ill., 1927), pp. 276–7.

46 Here esp. D. C. North and R. P. Thomas, *The Rise of the Western World. A New Economic History* (Cambridge, 1973), pp. 1–8.

47 R. Forster, 'Obstacles to Agricultural Growth in Eighteenth Century France', *American Historical Review*, 75 (1969–70), 1600–15; E. Hinrichs, 'Die Ablösung von Eigentumsrechten. Zur Diskussion über die droits féodaux in Frankreich am Ende des Ancien Régime und in der Revolution', *Eigentum und Verfassung. Zur Eigentumsdiskussion im ausgehenden 18. Jahrhundert*, ed. R. Vierhaus, Veröffentlichungen des Max-Planck-Instituts für Geschichte, vol. 37 (Göttingen, 1972), pp. 112–78, esp. 122–7, 167–78; R. Berthold, 'Einige Bemerkungen über den Entwicklungsstand des bäuerlichen Ackerbaus vor den Agrarreformen des 19. Jahrhunderts', *Beiträge zur deutschen Wirtschafts- und Sozialgeschichte des 18. und 19. Jahrhunderts*, Schriften des Instituts für Geschichte, vol. 1, 10 (Berlin, 1962), pp. 81–131, esp. 93–7, 109–112. Concerning the key role of the agrarian sector, cf. P. Bairoch, *Révolution industrielle et sous-développement*, 3rd ed. (Paris, 1969), pp. 73–84; P. Bairoch, 'Agriculture and the Industrial Revolution 1700–1914', *The Fontana Economic History of Europe*, ed. C. M. Cipolla, vol. 3: *The Industrial Revolution* (London, 1973), pp. 452–506; F. Crouzet, 'Agriculture et Révolution industrielle. Quelques réflexions', *Cahiers d'histoire*, 12 (1967), 67–86; A. Gerschenkron, 'The Typology of Industrial Development as a Tool of Analysis', in A. Gerschenkron, *Continuity in History and Other Essays* (Cambridge, Mass., 1968), pp. 77–97, esp. 87f. Concerning the role – limited though it was – of proto-industrialization in the process of agrarian transformation, see above p. 142.

48 See esp. L. Stone, 'Social Mobility in England, 1500–1700', *Past and Present*, 33 (1966), pp. 16–55; cf. also R. Braun, 'Zur Einwirkung sozio-kultureller Umweltbedingungen auf das Unternehmerpotential und das Unternehmerverhalten', *Probleme*, ed. Fischer (see n. 3 above), pp. 247–84.

49 A neo-classical theory of the infrastructure: R. Jochimsen, *Theorie der Infrastruktur. Grundlagen der marktwirtschaftlichen Entwicklung* (Tübingen, 1966); for a theory of the general conditions of production, see the somewhat inadequate work by D. Läpple, *Staat und allgemeine Produktionsbedingungen. Grundlagen zur Kritik der Infrastrukturtheorien* (Berlin, 1973).

50 P. Lundgreen, *Bildung und Wirtschaftswachstum im Industrialisierungsprozess des 19. Jahrhunderts. Methodische Ansätze, empirische Studien und internationale Vergleiche*, Historische und pädagogische Studien, vol. 5 (Berlin, 1973), pp. 127–32.

51 F. C. Lane, 'Economic Consequences of Organized Violence', *Journ. Econ. Hist.*, 18 (1958), 401–17, esp. 402–8; F. C. Lane, 'The Role of Governments in Economic Growth in Early Modern Times', *Journ. Econ. Hist.*, 35 (1975), 8–17, esp. 12–17.

52 E. Labrousse, 'The Evolution of Peasant Society in France from the Eighteenth Century to the Present', *French Society and Culture since the Old Regime*, eds. E. M. Acomb and M. L. Brown (New York etc., 1966), pp. 44–64; C. Fohlen, 'France 1700–1914', *The Fontana Economic History of Europe*, ed. C. M. Cipolla, vol. 4, 1: *The Emergence of Industrial Societies* (London, 1973), pp. 7–75, esp. 28–31; F. -W. Henning, 'Kapitalbildungsmöglichkeiten der bäuerlichen Bevölkerung in Deutschland am Anfang des 19. Jahrhunderts', *Beiträge*, ed. Fischer (see n. 22 above), pp. 57–73, esp. 68–73.

53 E. J. Hobsbawm, 'The Crisis of the Seventeenth Century', *Crisis in Europe, 1560–1660*, ed. T. Aston (London, 1965), pp. 5–58, esp. 47–9; concerning the importance of London in the growth-process of the English economy see E. A. Wrigley, 'A Simple Model of London's Importance in Changing English Society and Economy', *Past and Present*, 37 (1967), 44–70.

54 E. J. Hobsbawm, *Industry and Empire*, The Pelican Economic History of Britain, vol. 3 (Harmondsworth, 1969), p. 49; also above pp. 34 and n. 110.

55 Crouzet, 'Wars, Blockade and Economic Change in Europe, 1792–1815', *Journ. Econ. Hist.*, 24 (1964), 567–88, esp. 587f.

56 D. C. Coleman, 'Textile Growth', *Textile History*, eds. Harte and Ponting (see n. 39 above), pp. 1–21, here 8–10.

57 E. Schremmer, in *Handbuch der bayerischen Geschichte* 3, 2, ed. M. Spindler (München, 1971), pp. 1084–87.

58 B. E. Supple, *Commercial Crisis and Change in England, 1600–1642. A Study in the Instability of a Mercantile Economy* (Cambridge, 1959), pp. 135–62; P. J. Bowden, *The Wool Trade in Tudor and Stuart England* (London, 1962), pp. 43–56; Ch. Wilson, *England's Apprenticeship, 1603–1763* (London, 1965), pp. 69–79, 188–94, 289–96.

59 For the following discussion cf. Mendels, 'Proto-industrialization' (see n. 4 above), p. 246; Tilly and Tilly, 'Problems' (see n. 35 above), p. 17; Ch. Tilly, 'Clio and Minerva', *Theoretical Sociology*, eds. J. C. Kinney and E. A. Tiyakian (New York, 1970), pp. 434–66, esp. 455–9.

60 This is discussed in greater detail in Coleman, 'Textile Growth' (see n. 56 above), pp. 2–7; also with modifications above Ch. 4, pt. 2.

61 H. Blumberg, 'Ein Beitrag zur Geschichte der deutschen Leinenindustrie von 1834 bis 1870', in H. Motteck et al., *Studien zur Geschichte der industriellen Revolution in Deutschland*, Veröffentlichungen des Instituts für Wirtschaftsgeschichte an der Hochschule für Ökonomie Berlin-Karlshorst, vol. 1 (Berlin, 1960), pp. 65–143, esp. 107f., 124–6, 134f., 138–40; cf. also Schmoller, *Geschichte* (see n. 21 above), pp. 498–510.

62 J. D. Chambers, *Nottinghamshire in the Eighteenth Century. A Study of Life and Labour under the Squirearchy*, 2nd ed. (1932, rpt. London, 1966), pp. 132–6; J. D. Chambers, *The Vale of Trent 1670–1800. A Regional Study of Economic Change*, Econ. Hist. Rev. Supplements, vol. 3 (Cambridge, 1957), pp. 59f.; Erickson, *Industrialists* (see n. 13 above), pp. 79–99, 171–87; D. C. Levine, *Family Formation in an Age of Nascent Capitalism*, Studies in Social Discontinuity (New York, 1977), pp. 21–34.

63 Tilly and Tilly, 'Problems' (see n. 35 above), pp. 45–51. The British competition is placed into a broader context below, p. 150.

64 F. Crouzet, 'Les conséquences économiques de la Révolution. A propos d'un inédit de Sir Francis d'Ivernois', *Annales historiques de la Révolution Française*, 34 (1962), 182–217 and 336–62, esp. 199–214; Crouzet, 'Wars' (see n. 55 above), pp. 568–74; F. Crouzet, 'Les origines du sous-développement économique du Sud-Ouest', *Annales du Midi*, 71 (1959), 71–9, esp. 73–5; also Ch. Tilly, *The Vendée* (London, 1964), pp. 215–22; F. Dornic, *L'industrie textile dans la Maine et ses débouchés internationaux (1650–1815)* (Le Mans, 1955), pp. 268–71; R. Musset, *Le Bas-Maine. Etude géographique* (Paris, 1917), pp. 270–2; J. Tanguy, 'La production et le commerce des toiles "bretagnes" du XVIe au XVIIIe siècle. Premiers résultats', *Actes du 91e Congrès national des Sociétés savantes, Rennes 1966. Section d'histoire moderne et contemporaine*, 1 (Paris, 1966), pp. 105–41, esp. 136; V. Prévot, 'Une grande industrie d'exportation. L'industrie linière dans le Nord de la France, sous l'Ancien Régime', *Revue du Nord*, 39 (1957), 205–26, esp. 226. For the crisis of the French foreign trade before 1789, see above p. 136 and n. 129. For the southern Netherlands, see E. Sabbe, *Histoire de l'industrie linière en Belgique*, Collection Nationale, vol. 6, 67 (Brussels, 1945), pp. 49–51.

65 M. Kossok, 'Die Bedeutung des spanisch-amerikanischen Kolonialmarktes für den preussischen Leinwandhandel am Ausgang des 18. und zu Beginn des 19. Jahrhunderts', *Hansische Studien H. Sproemberg zum 70. Geburtstag*, Forschungen zur mittelalterlichen Geschichte, vol. 8 (Berlin, 1961), pp. 210–18, esp. 217f.; S. Kühn, *Der Hirschberger Leinwand- und Schleierhandel von 1648–1806*, Breslauer historische Forschungen, vol. 7 (Breslau, 1938), pp. 56–9; W. v. Westernhagen, *Leinwandmanufaktur und Leinwandhandel der Oberlausitz in der zweiten Hälfte des 18. Jahrhunderts und* *während der Kontinentalsperre* (Diss. phil., Leipzig, 1932), pp. 55–84; G. Karr, *Die Uracher Leinenweberei und die Leinwandhandlungskompagnie. Ein Beitrag zur Wirtschaftsgeschichte Alt-Württembergs,* Tübinger wirtschaftswissenschaftliche Abhandlungen, vol. 7 (Stuttgart, 1930), pp. 86–9; O. Dascher, *Das Textilgewerbe in Hessen-Kassel vom 16. bis 19. Jahrhundert,* Veröffentlichungen der Historischen Kommission für Hessen und Waldeck, vol. 28 (Marburg, 1968), p. 156.

66 O. Schumann, *Die Landeshuter Leinenindustrie in Vergangenheit und Gegenwart. Ein Beitrag zur Geschichte der schlesischen Textilindustrie,* Abhandlungen des wirtschaftswissen-schaftlichen Seminars zu Jena, vol. 19, 1 (Jena, 1928), p. 128 or Dascher, *Textilgewerbe* (see n. 65 above), p. 156. The linen production in Upper Lusatia fell from 2,035,076 Taler 20 Groschen in 1806 to 1,535,300 Taler 4 Groschen in 1807 (1811:735, 333 Taler 12 Groschen); see R. Forberger, 'Beiträge zur statistischen Erfassung der gewerblichen Produktion Sachsens in der Frühzeit des Kapitalismus', *Jb. Wirtsch. G.* (1962), pt. 4, 224–46, esp. 245.

67 Kutz, *Aussenhandel* (see n. 28 above), pp. 60–4; Ohnishi, *Zolltarifpolitik* (see n. 22 above), pp. 11–14; Pollard, 'Industrialization' (see n. 23 above), 639f. For the beginning of the English export offensive: F. Crouzet, *L'économie britannique et le blocus continental (1860–1813),* vols. 1–2 (Paris, 1958), vol. 2, pp. 845–8.

68 For the development of export cf. Ohnishi, *Zolltarifpolitik* (see n. 22 above), pp. 218–25; Hermes, 'Studien' (see n. 28 above), pp. 126f., 139–41, 159; Blumberg, 'Beitrag' (see n. 61 above), pp. 93–104; for France see T. J. Markovitch, *L'industrie française de 1789 à 1964. Analyse des faits,* Histoire quantitative de l'économie française, vols. 5–6 = *Cahiers de l'I.S.E.A.* 173–174 (Paris, 1966), esp. vol. 5, pp. 147–51 and vol. 6, tables 16; for Belgium see Sabbe, *Histoire* (see n. 64 above), pp. 51–7.

69 Blumberg, 'Beitrag' (see n. 61 above), p. 97; C. Gill, *The Rise of the Irish Linen Industry* (Oxford, 1925), pp. 315–34; Ph. Deane and W. A. Cole, *British Economic Growth, 1688–1959. Trends and Structure,* 2nd ed. (Cambridge, 1969), pp. 201–6. The develop-ment of the machine-spinning of flax in Britain was at least partially a response to the declining yarn-imports imposed by the Napoleonic blockade: Schmoller, *Geschichte* (see n. 21 above), p. 459; for the development of English yarn-imports see E. B. Schumpeter, *English Overseas Trade Statistics 1697–1808* (Oxford, 1960), tables 16 and 17; N. B. Harte, 'The Rise of Protection and the English Linen Trade, 1690–1790', *Textile History,* eds. Harte and Ponting (see n. 39 above), pp. 74–112, esp. 103–5; Crouzet, *Economie* (see n. 67 above), vol. 1, pp. 60f., vol. 2, p. 891, table 10.

70 K. A. Wittfogel, 'Die natürlichen Ursachen der Wirtschaftsgeschichte', *Archiv für Sozialwissenschaft und Sozialpolitik,* 67 (1932), 466–92, 579–609, 711–31, esp. 482–5.

71 P. Chaunu, 'Malthusianisme démographique et malthusianisme économique. Réflections sur l'échec industriel de la Normandie à l'époque du démarrage', *Annales E.S.C.,* 27 (1972), 1–19, esp.13–19; under a different title this article also appeared in P. Léon et al., eds., *L'industrialisation en Europe au XIXᵉ siècle. Cartographie et typologie* (Paris, 1972), pp. 285–314 (including a discussion).

72 Regional examples: A. Armengaud, *Les populations de l'Est-Aquitaine au début de l'époque contemporaine. Recherches sur une région moins développée (vers 1845–vers 1871)* (Paris, 1961), pp. 77–109, 126; L. Wiatrowski, *Przemiany gospodarki folwarcznej i chłopskiej na Śląsku w okresie reform agrarnych w XIX w.* (Changes in the manorial and peasant economy in Silesia at the time of the agrarian reforms in the nineteenth century), Acta Universitatis Wratislaviensis, vol. 225 = Historia 25 (Wrocław, 1974), pp. 86f., 92, 117, 138f., 154f., 198.

73 H. Kisch, 'The Textile Industries in Silesia and the Rhineland: A Comparative Study in Industrialization', *Journ. Econ. Hist.,* 19 (1959), 541–64, esp. 554 (= below p. 187); J. H. Clapham, 'The Transference of the Worsted Industry from Norfolk to the

West Riding', *Economic Journal*, 20 (1910), 195–210, esp. 210; Chapman, *Factory Masters* (see n. 38 above), pp. 213–15. For the concept of 'external economies' cf. among others R. Nurkse, *Problems of Capital Formation in Underdeveloped Countries* (Oxford, 1953), p. 14f.; T. Scitovsky, 'Two Concepts of External Economies', *Journal of Political Economy*, 32 (1954), 143–51; R. B. Sutcliffe, 'Balanced and Unbalanced Growth', *Quarterly Journal of Economics*, 78 (1964), 621–40, esp. 630–4.

74 Crouzet, *Origines* (see n. 64 above), pp. 77f.; A. Corbain, *Archaïsme et modernité en Limousin aux XIX^{e}siècle. 1845–1880*, vols. 1–2 (Paris, 1975), vol. 1, pp. 119–51; Musset, *Bas-Maine* (see n. 64 above), pp. 420f.; E. Barkhausen, *Die Tuchindustrie in Montjoie, ihr Aufstieg und Niedergang* (Aachen, 1925), p. 172.

75 W. Troeltsch, *Die Calwer Zeughandlungskompagnie und ihre Arbeiter. Studien zur Gewerbe- und Sozialgeschichte Altwürttembergs* (Jena, 1897), p. 326; the role of the Urach linen trading company is judged too favourably in Karr, *Leinenweberei* (see n. 65 above), pp. 93–5.

76 V. Loewe, 'Zur Geschichte des hausindustriellen Leinengewerbes in Schlesien. Der Weberzins', *Zs. des Vereins für Geschichte Schlesiens*, 59 (1925), 90–101, esp. 97–100; J. Ziekursch, *Hundert Jahre schlesischer Agrargeschichte. Vom Hubertusburger Frieden bis zum Abschluss der Bauernbefreiung*, 2nd ed. (Breslau, 1927), pp. 297f., 305f., 365f.; H. Bleiber, *Zwischen Reform und Revolution. Lage und Kämpfe der schlesischen Bauern und Landarbeiter im Vormärz 1840–1847*, Schriften des Instituts für Geschichte, vol. 2, 9 (Berlin, 1966), pp. 31–56 but cf. the critique of this work by L. Wiatrowski and St. Michalkiewicz in *Jb. Wirtsch. G.* (1970), pt. 2, 253–72.

77 T. Welp (= E. Pelz), *Über den Einfluss der Fabriken und Manufakturen in Schlesien*, vols. 1–2 (Leipzig, 1844), vol. 2, pp. 40–4; W. Wolff, 'Das Elend und der Aufruhr in Schlesien', in W. Wolff, *Gesammelte Schriften*, ed. by F. Mehring, Sozialistische Neudrucke, vol. 3 (Berlin, 1909), pp. 38–60, esp. 46f.; in addition S. B. Kan, *Dva vosstaniya silezskich tkachei (1793–1844)* (Moscow etc., 1948), here according to the Czech translation: *Dvě povstání slezských tkalců 1793–1844* (Two revolts of the Silesian weavers 1793 to 1844), Socialistická věda, vol. 23 (Praha, 1952), pp. 219f.; also A. Schneer, *Über die Noth der Leinen-Arbeiter in Schlesien und die Mittel ihr abzuhelfen. Ein Bericht* (Berlin, 1844), pp. 46–54, 73–6.

78 Schneer, *Noth* (see n. 77 above), pp. 8–10; in addition Kisch, 'Textile Industries' (see n. 73 above), p. 553 (= below p. 186).

79 Kisch, 'Textile Industries' (see n. 73 above), pp. 549–54 (= below pp. 183–7) and in addition U. Lewald, 'Die Entwicklung der ländlichen Textilindustrie im Rheinland und in Schlesien. Ein Vergleich', *Zs. für Ostforschung*, 10 (1961), 601–30, esp. 617–25. Some of the results of Kisch's article must be qualified. A number of misconceptions would have been avoided if Silesia had been compared with a west-European linen-region instead of with the highly developed textile industry of the Rhineland. In addition, a careful appraisal should have taken into account that the development of the Silesian textile industry differed greatly from region to region in the first half of the nineteenth century; for example, the linen industry around Hirschberg (now Jelenia Góra) declined, while the cotton industry around Reichenbach (now Dzierżoniów) rose steeply (see below, n. 99). It is also likely that the Silesian textile industry would have been sustained better, had Silesia belonged to a customs union that extended to the East. The rise of the textile industry of Łódź seems to support this assumption: it owed its emergence primarily to petty producers from Great Poland and Silesia who found a new field of activity and very different conditions of competition beyond the customs barriers, after the textile industries had declined in their home regions; cf. W. Kula, *Kształtowanie się kapitalizmu w Polsce* (The formation of capitalism in Poland) (Warsaw, 1955), pp. 54–62; G. Missalowa, *Studia nad powstaniem łódzkiego okręgu* *przemyslowego 1815–1870* (Studies in the emergence of the industrial region of Łódź), vols. 1–2 (Łódź, 1964–7), vol. 1, pp. 60–72, 74–83 for the immigration from Saxony and Bohemia, see also the maps and vol. 2, pp. 43–55.

80 A. Gerschenkron, 'Agrarian Reform and Industrialization, Russia 1861–1917', *The Cambridge Economic History of Europe*, vol. 6, 2 (Cambridge, 1966), pp. 706–800, esp. 714f.; J. Kulischer, 'Die kapitalistischen Unternehmer in Russland (insbesondere die Bauern als Unternehmer) in den Anfangsstadien des Kapitalismus', *Archiv für Sozialwissenschaft und Sozialpolitik*, 65 (1931), 309–55, esp. 354; H. Rosovsky, 'The Serf Entrepreneur in Russia', *Explorations in Entrepreneurial History*, 6 (1953/54), 207–33, esp. 229f.

81 Gerschenkron, 'Reform' (see n. 80 above), pp. 717–63, 798–800; A. Gerschenkron, 'Russia: Patterns and Problems of Economic Development, 1861–1958', in Gerschenkron, *Backwardness* (see n. 3 above), pp. 119–51, esp. 119–24; A. Gerschenkron, 'The Early Phases of Industrialization in Russia: Afterthoughts and Counterthoughts', *The Economics of Take-off into Sustained Growth*, ed. W. W. Rostow (London, 1963), pp. 151–69 and in addition M. E. Falkus, *The Industrialization of Russia, 1700–1914* (London, 1972), pp. 47–50.

82 G. Myrdal, *Economic Theory and Under-developed Regions* (London, 1957), pp. 23–38; a summary of the Myrdal thesis in H. Hesse, 'Die Entwicklung der regionalen Einkommensdifferenzen im Wachstumsprozess der deutschen Wirtschaft vor 1913', *Probleme*, ed. Fischer (see n. 22 above), pp. 261–79, esp. 265–8; Ch. Tilly, 'Clio' (see n. 59 above), pp. 451–66 and the quotation on p. 459.

83 A. Weber, 'Industrielle Standortlehre (Allgemeine und kapitalistische Theorie des Standorts)', *Grundriss der Sozialökonomie*, vol. 6, 2nd ed. (Tübingen, 1923), pp. 58–86, here 76f.; H. Ritschl, 'Reine und historische Dynamik des Standortes der Erzeugerzweige', *Schmollers Jahrbuch*, 51, 2 (1927), 813–70, esp. 868.

84 Esp. Léon, *Naissance* (see n. 21 above), vol. 2, pp. 452–4, 554–6, 638–41; however, the large-scale use of water-power in Dauphiné led to a 'reconquête de la montagne', Léon, pp. 821–33.

85 For the cloth industry in Dauphiné see Léon, *Naissance* (see n. 84 above), vol. 2, pp. 570–5: 'Elle mourait, tuée par son archaïsme, par la disparition de l'écran protecteur que constituait la difficulté des communications, par la concurrence de centres mieux équipés' (p. 575).

86 E. von Böventer, 'Die Struktur der Landschaft. Versuch einer Synthese und Weiterentwicklung der Modelle J. H. von Thünens, W. Christallers und A. Löschs', in R. Henn et al., *Optimales Wachstum und optimale Standortverteilung*, Schriften des Vereins für Socialpolitik n.F. 27 (Berlin, 1962), pp. 77–133, esp. 124; cf. also E. von Böventer, *Theorie des räumlichen Gleichgewichts*, Schriften zur angewandten Wirtschaftsforschung, vol. 5 (Tübingen, 1962), pp. 13–20; W. Isard, *Location and Space-economy. A General Theory Relating to Industrial Location, Market Areas, Land Use, Trade and Urban Structure* (New York, 1956), pp. 7f.; P. Lebrun, 'La rivoluzione industriale in Belgio. Strutturazione e destrutturazione delle economie regionali', *Studi storici*, 2 (1961), 548–658, esp. 555f., 559–80, 654–6; following F. Perroux, Lebrun tries to conceptualize the problems discussed here, but despite his use of the terms 'strutturazione' and 'destrutturazione' he does not treat the phenomenon of deindustrialization in any detail. Concerning the border as a location-factor cf. G. Adelmann, 'Die deutsch-niederländische Grenze als textilindustrieller Standortfaktor', *Landschaft und Geschichte. Festschrift für F. Petri* (Bonn, 1970), pp. 9–34.

87 Clapham, 'Transference' (see n. 73 above), pp. 195–210; Wilson, 'Supremacy' (see n. 40 above), pp. 235–46; Clapham, *Gentlemen Merchants* (see n. 40 above), pp. 5, 52–4; for the decline of the woolen industry in the West Country see Mann, *Industry* (see

n. 13 above), pp. 157–222; cf. also the remarks by Chapman, *Factory Masters* (see n. 38 above), pp. 210–18 concerning the decline of the early spinning-mills in the Midlands.

88 Gill, *Rise* (see n. 69 above), pp. 320–2; L. M. Cullen, *An Economic History of Ireland since 1660* (London, 1972), p. 108; for the role of the cotton industry see Gill, pp. 234–6 and Cullen, p. 106.

89 Gill, *Rise* (see n. 69 above), pp. 323–5; Cullen, *History* (see n. 88 above), pp. 119–21, 130–3.

90 F. Crouzet, comment in: *Industrialisation*, eds. Léon et al. (see n. 71 above), p. 301; cf. P. Mathias, contribution in: *Industrialisation*, eds. Léon et al. (n. 71 above), p. 302.

91 Chaunu, 'Malthusianisme' ed(see n. 71 above), pp. 12f.; T. W. Freeman et al., *Lancashire, Cheshire and the Isle of Man*, Regions of the British Isles (London, 1966), pp. 66–77, 94–109.

92 The terms of trade between cotton cloth and linen yarn (1913:100) fell between 1800 and 1850 from 634 to 193, and until 1870 to 159, according to Kirchain, 'Wachstum' (see n. 24 above), pp. 228f., table 65 and graph 18; for production-costs at the beginning of the twentieth century in France: A. Aftalion, *La crise de l'industrie linière et la concurrence victorieuse de l'industrie cotonnière* (Paris, 1904), pp. 131–5; the pure production-costs (without raw materials) were three times as high, despite the fact that the wages were lower in the linen industry than in the cotton industry (Aftalion, pp. 81–90, 123–5, 134).

93 Here esp. Aftalion, *Crise* (see n. 92 above), pp. 57–131; this is one of the main reason why even at the beginning of the twentieth century, the productivity of labour in the linen industry, which had meanwhile been mechanized, was considerably lower than in the cotton industry (Aftalion, pp. 103–9, 119–21).

94 See above, p. 146 and n. 61.

95 H. Sée, 'Remarques sur le caractère de l'industrie rurale en France et les causes de son extension au XVIIIe siècle', *Revue Historique*, 142 (1923), 47–53, esp. 48f.; Musset, *Bas-Maine* (see n. 64 above), p. 267; P. Bois, *Paysans de l'Ouest. Des structures économiques et sociales aux options politiques depuis l'époque révolutionnaire dans la Sarthe* (Le Mans, 1960), pp. 521–3; Tanguy, 'Production' (n. 64), pp. 116f.; Sabbe, *Histoire* (n. 64), pp. 49f.; Adelmann, 'Strukturwandlungen' (see n. 19 above), p. 165; H. Potthoff, 'Das Ravensberger Leinengewerbe im 17. und 18. Jahrhundert', *Jahresbericht des Historischen Vereins für die Grafschaft Ravensberg*, 35 (1921), 27–83, esp. 61f.; Kisch, 'Textile Industries' (see n. 73 above), pp. 552f. (and below, pp. 186). In the West Riding, the petty producers promoted the restructuring of the woolen industry on their own initiative, but in the linen industry during the first half of the nineteenth century the preconditions for such a course of action did not exist.

96 Blumberg, 'Beitrag' (see n. 61 above), pp. 115–23; G. Adelmann, 'Die Stadt Bielefeld als Zentrum fabrikindustrieller Gründungen nach 1850', *Die Stadt in der europäischen Geschichte. Festschrift E. Ennen* (Bonn, 1972), pp. 884–94, esp. 890f.; Schumann, *Leinenindustrie* (see n. 66 above), pp. 49–53.

97 Gill, *Rise* (see n. 69 above), pp. 330–4; Fohlen, *Industrie* (see n. 29 above), pp. 223–41; C. Zarka, 'Un exemple de pôle de croissance. L'industrie textile du Nord de la France 1830–1870', *Revue Economique*, 9 (1958), 65–106, esp. 81–103; Lévy-Leboyer, *Banques* (see n. 21 above), pp. 106–9; Sabbe, *Industrie* (see n. 64 above), pp. 78–88; S. Reekers, 'Beiträge zur statistischen Darstellung der gewerblichen Wirtschaft Westfalens um 1800. 2: Minden-Ravensberg', *Westfälische Forschungen*, 18 (1965), 75–130, esp. 105f.; Adelmann, 'Bielefeld' (see n. 96 above), pp. 884–94; C. Frahne, *Die Textilindustrie im Wirtschaftsleben Schlesiens. Ihre wirtschaftlichen und technischen Grundlagen, historisch-ökonomische Gestaltung und gegenwärtige Bedeutung* (Diss. rer. pol., Tübingen, 1905), pp. 133–50; Schumann, *Leinenindustrie* (see n. 66 above), pp. 51–74. For the German linen-industry around the turn of the century see H. Potthoff, 'Die Leinenindustrie', in *Die Hauptindustrien Deutschlands, Handbuch der Wirtschaftskunde Deutschlands,* vol. 3 (Leipzig, 1904), pp. 555–66; H. Potthoff, 'Die Leinenindustrie (Leinen, Wäsche, Hanf und Jute)', *Die Störungen im deutschen Wirtschaftsleben während der Jahre 1900ff.* Vol. 1: *Textilindustrie,* Schriften des Vereins für Socialpolitik, vol. 105 (Leipzig, 1903), pp. 1–126. During this period Silesia still occupied the leading position in the German linen industry.

98 Fohlen, *Industrie* (see n. 29 above), pp. 164–75 and pp. 501, 503, 510; Musset, *Bas-Maine* (see n. 64 above), pp. 270–2, 416–20; H. Sée, 'L'industrie textile et le commerce du Bas-Maine pendant le premier Empire et la Restauration d'après les papiers des Guyard-Moricière (1800–1815)', *Mémoires et documents pour servir à l'histoire du commerce et de l'industrie en France,* 12 (1929), 291–337, esp. 313–37; H. Sée, 'L'industrie rurale des toiles en Ille-et-Vilaine au XIXe siècle', *Mémoires et documents,* 10 (1926), 129–48; Tanguy 'Production' (see n. 64 above), p. 137; Dascher, *Textilgewerbe* (see n. 65 above), pp. 156–60; K. Schäfer, 'Die wirtschaftliche Entwicklung des Hochstifts Fulda unter Kurhessen', *Jahrbuch für hessische Landesgeschichte,* 2 (1952), 134–70, esp. 151–7; A. Gladen, *Der Kreis Tecklenburg an der Schwelle des Zeitalters der Industrialisierung,* Veröffentlichungen der Historischen Kommission Westfalens, vol. 22a = Geschichtliche Arbeiten zur westfälischen Landesforschung. Wirtschafts- und sozialgeschichtliche Gruppe 2 (Münster, 1970), pp. 54–67; in my opinion, the developments which can be observed in Tecklenburg (p. 174) do not form part of the process of early industrialization. A. Wrasman, 'Das Heuerlingswesen im Fürstentum Osnabrück', *Mitteilungen des Vereins für Geschichte und Landeskunde von Osnabrück,* 42 (1919), 53–174, vol. 44, 1–154, esp. vol. 44, 16–21, 123f.; G. Adelmann, 'Strukturelle Krisen im ländlichen Textilgewerbe Nordwestdeutschlands zu Beginn der Industrialisierung' *Wirtschaftspolitik und Arbeitsmarkt,* ed. H. Kellenbenz (München, 1974), pp. 110–28.

99 Harte, 'Rise' (see n. 69 above), pp. 110–12; on p. 112, Harte speaks of an 'oedipal relationship' between the linen and cotton industries in England. Silesia provides an example that this dynamic union was not afforded everywhere, despite the initially very rapid development of cotton weaving, especially in the country of Reichenbach (now Dzierżoniów) and its bordering regions. The following percentages of cotton-looms in Prussia were found in Silesia: 1816: 23.8%, 1831: 33.2%, 1846: 40.1%, 1861: 39.5%, 1875: 42.7%, 1901: 17.5%, according to Ohnishi, *Zolltarifpolitik* (see n. 22 above), pp. 239, appendix 4; Dieterici, *Volkswohlstand* (n. 22), p. 186; 'Übersicht' (n. 22), pp. 189 and 193; *Tabellen der Handwerker, der Fabriken, sowie der Handels- und Transportgewerbe im Zoll-Vereine. Nach den Aufnahmen im Jahre 1861 vom Central-Bureau des Zoll-Vereins zusammengestellt* (n. p., n. d.), p. 100; *Statistik des deutschen Reiches,* vol. 34, 1 (Berlin, 1879), pp. 404, 409f.; K. Kuntze, 'Die Baumwollindustrie', *Hauptindustrien* (see n. 97 above), pp. 578–621, esp. 586. Already in 1846, 193 cotton-looms existed in Silesia for every 100 fully employed linen-looms; if the partially employed linen-looms are included, the cotton-looms amount to 110 ('Übersicht', p. 183). In the end, the cotton industry in Silesia was subject to the same restrictive conditions as the linen industry. The mechanization of cotton-weaving was not introduced early enough; really efficient cotton-spinning factories were never established: in 1843, Silesia had 23.9% of the cotton spindles of Prussia, in 1861: 17.8%, in 1901: 4.6%; A. Bienengräber, *Statistik des Verkehrs und Verbrauchs im Zollverein für die Jahre 1842 bis 1864* (Berlin, 1868), pp. 197f.; tables: 'Übersicht', p. 98; Kuntze, p. 589; cf. also H. Roemer, *Die Baumwollspinnerei in Schlesien bis zum preussischen Zollgesetz von 1818,* Quellen und Darstellungen zur schlesischen Geschichte, vol. 19 (Breslau, 1914), pp. 37–50; Frahne, 'Textilindustrie' (see n. 97 above), pp. 150–69, 238–44; St. Michalkiewicz, in: *Historia Sląska. Opracowanie zbiorowe* (History of Silesia. Collected Essays) (Wrocław etc., 1970), vol. 2, 2, pp. 233–6.

100 Similarly: Tilly, 'Clio' (see n. 59 above), p. 458.

101 A. J. Taylor, 'Concentration and Specialization in the Lancashire Cotton Industry, 1825–1850', *Econ. Hist. Rev.*, 2nd ser., 1 (1949/50), 114–22, esp. 114–16.

102 Silesia for example in Tilly and Tilly, 'Problems' (see n. 35 above), p. 50; Mendels, 'Proto-industrialization' (see n. 4 above), p. 246.

103 E. P. Thompson, 'The Moral Economy of the English Crowd in the Eighteenth Century', *Past and Present*, 50 (1971), 76–136, esp. 79–91 and in addition L. A. Tilly, 'The Food Riot as a Form of Political Conflict in France', *Journal of Interdisciplinary History*, 2 (1971/72), 23–57, esp. 45–7.

104 See in particular W. Abel, *Agrarkrisen und Agrarkonjunktur. Eine Geschichte der Land- und Ernährungswirtschaft Mitteleuropas seit dem hohen Mittelalter*, 2nd ed. (Hamburg, 1966), pp. 226–42; W. Abel, *Massenarmut und Hungerkrisen im vorindustriellen Europa* (Hamburg etc., 1974), pp. 25–9, 302–9, 397–9.

105 None of the existing explanations of pauperism do justice to the historical reality; these explanations can be grouped into three categories: (1) pauperism was brought about by the conditions of the final stages of the agrarian age. This position is put forth by W. Abel in the works listed under n. 104 and in W. Abel, 'Der Pauperismus in Deutschland. Eine Nachlese zu Literaturberichten', *Wirtschaft, Geschichte und Wirtschafts- geschichte. Festschrift zum 65. Geburtstag von F. Lütge* (Stuttgart, 1965), pp. 284–98. (2) Pauperism was caused by rapid population growth: W. Conze, 'Vom "Pöbel" zum "Proletariat". Sozialgeschichtliche Voraussetzungen für den Pauperismus in Deutschland', *VSWG*, 41 (1954), 333–64; W. Köllmann., 'Bevölkerung und Arbeitskräftepotential in Deutschland 1815–1865. Ein Beitrag zur Analyse der Problematik des Pauperismus', in W. Köllmann, *Bevölkerung in der industriellen Revolution. Studien zur Bevölkerungsgeschichte Deutschlands*, Kritische Studien zur Geschicht- swissenschaft, vol. 12 (Göttingen, 1974), pp. 61–98, esp. 77–9 (this work also discusses the crisis in domestic industry); these works stand in the same general context as the conservative interpretation of pauperism as emancipation crisis by C. Jantke, 'Zur Deutung des Pauperismus', *Die Eigentumslosen. Der deutsche Pauperismus und die Emanzipationskrise in Darstellungen und Deutungen der zeitgenössischen Literatur*, eds. C. Jantke and D. Hilger (Freiburg etc., 1965), pp. 7–47, esp. 14–26; F. Seidel, *Die soziale Frage in der deutschen Geschichte. Mit besonderer Berücksichtigung des ehemaligen Fürstentums Waldeck- Pyrmont. Ein lehrgeschichtlicher Überblick* (Wiesbaden, 1964). (3) Pauperism was a result of the development of industrial capitalism: among others, H. Stein, 'Pauperismus und Assoziation. Soziale Tatsachen und Ideen auf dem europäischen Kontinent vom Ende des 18. bis zur Mitte des 19. Jahrhunderts unter besonderer Berücksichtigung des Rheingebiets', *International Review of Social History*, 1 (1936), 1–120. Surveys of the contemporary literature and collections of contemporary documents about pauperism in Germany: P. Mombert, 'Aus der Literatur über die soziale Frage und über die Arbeiterbewegung in Deutschland in der ersten Hälfte des 19. Jahrhunderts', *Archiv für die Geschichte des Sozialismus und der Arbeiterbewegung*, 9 (1921), 169–236; Jantke and Hilger, eds., *Eigentumslose* (see above); J. Kuczynski, *Bürgerliche und halbfeudale Literatur aus den Jahren 1840 bis 1847 zur Lage der Arbeiter. Eine Chrestomathie*, vol. 9 of J. Kuczynski, *Geschichte der Lage der Arbeiter unter dem Kapitalismus* (Berlin, 1960). The English discussion about the standard of living during the Industrial Revolution has only peripherally touched the problem which is placed at the centre here; the English discussion is documented in A. J. Taylor, ed., *The Standard of Living in Britain during the Industrial Revolution* (London, 1975).

106 M. Reinhard et al., *Histoire générale de la population mondiale*, 3rd ed. (Paris, 1968), pp. 241ff., 287ff., 315ff.; E. Shorter, 'Illegitimacy, Sexual Revolution, and Social Change in Modern Europe', *Journal of Interdisciplinary History*, 2 (1971), 237–72; E. Shorter, 'Female Emancipation, Birth Control, and Fertility in European History',

American Historical Review, 78 (1973), 605–40 (both of these articles are rather speculative). It is difficult to determine the extent to which the relatively slow French population growth, based on the spread of birth-control practices, limited the effects of pauperism in France; for population growth in France, see J. Dupâquier. 'Les débuts de la grande aventure démographique', *Prospectives*, 3 (1974), 7–38, esp. 30–8; for pauperism in France cf. L. Chevalier, *Classes laborieuses et classes dangereuses à Paris dans la première moitié du XIXᵉ siècle* (Paris, 1958) and the following regional studies: Armengaud, *Populations* (see n. 72 above), pp. 150–66; Corbin, *Archaisme* (see n. 74 above), vol. 1, pp. 485–94.

107 See above Ch. 3; Levine, *Family Formation* (see n. 62 above), pp. 79–83.

108 H. Harnisch, 'Bevölkerung und Wirtschaft. Über die Zusammenhänge zwischen sozialökonomischer und demographischer Entwicklung im Spätfeudalismus', *Jb. Wirtsch. G.* (1975), pt. 2, 57–87, esp. 73–85; H. Linde, *Preussischer Landesausbau. Ein Beitrag zur Geschichte der ländlichen Gesellschaft Süd-Ostpreussens am Beispiel des Dorfes Piasutten/Kreis Ortelsburg*, Beiheft zum Archiv für Bevölkerungswissenschaft und Bevölkerungspolitik, vol. 7 (Leipzig, 1939), pp. 53–70; H. Linde, 'Die soziale Problematik der masurischen Agrargesellschaft und die masurische Einwanderung in das Emschergebiet', *Soziale Welt*, 9 (1958), 233–46, esp. 239–44; G. Ipsen, 'Die preussische Bauernbefreiung als Landesausbau', *Bevölkerungsgeschichte*, eds. W. Köllmann and P. Marschalck, Neue wissenschaftliche Bibliothek, vol. 54 (Cologne, 1972), pp. 154–89 (this article does not recognize that this process set in before the peasant emancipation).

109 G. F. Knapp, *Die Bauernbefreiung und der Ursprung der Landarbeiter in den älteren Theilen Preussens*, 2nd ed. (Munich etc., 1927), vol. 1, pp. 303–6; W. Conze, 'Die Wirkungen der liberalen Agrarreformen auf die Volksordnung in Mitteleuropa im 19. Jahrhundert', *VSWG.* 38 (1949/51), 2–43, esp. 14f., 20f.; W. Conze, *Die liberalen Agrarreformen Hannovers im 19. Jahrhundert*, Agrarwissenschaftliche Vortragsreihe, vol. 2 (Hanover, 1946), pp. 15f.; Wrasman, 'Heuerlingswesen' (see n. 98 above), vol. 44, pp. 7–9; Gladen, *Tecklenburg* (n. 98 above), pp. 30–3.

110 Köllmann, 'Bevölkerung' (see n. 105 above), pp. 76–85; Köllmann's attempt to develop an indicator of the level of pauperization by contrasting the number of vacancies with the number of labourers is not convincing. The assumptions on which the number of positions is based are too speculative (as the author himself agrees, p. 87), and, furthermore, pauperism was characterized not so much by open as by disguised unemployment.

111 Mantoux, *Revolution* (see n. 6 above), pp. 399–408; G. D. H. Cole and R. Postgate, *The Common People, 1746–1946*, 4th ed. (London, 1949), p. 134; I. Pinchbeck, *Women Workers in the Industrial Revolution, 1750–1850* (1930; rpt. London, 1969), pp. 147–56; too uncritical: Bythell, *Handloom Weavers* (see n. 11 above), p. 42.

112 The prices of cotton yarn No. 100 fell from an index of 100 to 17 between 1786/90 and 1811/15 in England (if 1780, for which a single note exists, is taken as the base year with the index of 100, it fell to 10; calculated according to Edwards, *Growth* [n. 7 above], p. 254, appendix D). During the same period the prices of raw cotton fell only to 79, calculated according to B. R. Mitchell with the Collaboration of Ph. Deane, *Abstract of British Historical Statistics* (Cambridge, 1962), p. 490; cf. also Edwards, *Growth*, p. 253, appendix C/5.

113 Mantoux, *Revolution* (see n. 6 above), pp. 410–12; Chapman, *Factory Masters* (see n. 38 above), pp. 165f.; Léon, *Naissance* (see n. 21 above), vol. 2, pp. 743–5; Braun, *Wandel* (see n. 21 above), pp. 28–30; König, *Baumwollenindustrie* (see n. 38 above), p. 330; Bythell, *Handloom Weavers* (see n. 11 above), p. 42.

114 Chapman, *Cotton Industry* (see n. 10 above), p. 59f. with table 8.

115 See above, p. 300 cit. 12.

116 Bythell, *Handloom Weavers* (see n. 11 above), pp. 105, 107; Thompson, *Making* (see n. 12 above), pp. 315f., 345.

117 Bythell, *Handloom Weavers* (see n. 11 above), pp. 275f., appendix 1 and pp. 94–138. Nevertheless, it must be taken into consideration that the cost of living fell, too, during this period though not as steeply; the so-called 'Silberling'-index fell from 100 in 1815 to 81 in 1840 (Bythell, p. 279, appendix 2, table 2).

118 Cf. the different view points of Thompson, *Making* (see n. 12 above), p. 333–5 and Bythell, *Handloom Weavers* (see n. 11 above), pp. 251–72, and in addition Chapman, *Cotton Industry* (see n. 10 above), p. 61.

119 Evidence in R. Strauss, *Die Lage und die Bewegung der Chemnitzer Arbeiter in der ersten Hälfte des 19. Jahrhunderts*, Schriften des Instituts für Geschichte, vol. 2, 3 (Berlin, 1960), pp. 15–25; cf. Braun, *Wandel* (see n. 21 above), pp. 31–5.

120 C. F. G., 'Der Pauperismus und dessen Bekämpfung durch eine bessere Regelung der Arbeitsverhältnisse', *Deutsche Vierteljahrsschrift* (1844), part 3, 315–40, esp. 318.

121 C. F. G., 'Der Pauperismus' (see n. 120 above), p. 316.

122 In Germany, the index of flax prices rose between 1792/1800 (= 100) and 1841/50 to 140, the yarn prices fell to 53, while the prices of rye (1791/1800 = 100) sank only to 96; calculated according to A. Jacobs and H. Richter, *Die Grosshandelspreise in Deutschland von 1792 bis 1934*, Sonderhefte des Instituts für Konjunkturforschung, vol. 37 (Berlin, 1935), p. 68 and Abel, *Agrarkrisen* (see n. 104 above), p. 289, appendix 2, table 2; for the yarn prices see C. Biller, *Der Rückgang der Hand-Leinwandindustrie des Münsterlandes*, Abhandlungen aus dem staatswissenschaftlichen Seminar zu Münster, vol. 2 (Leipzig, 1906), pp. 47f. Those spinners who processed their own flax were not affected by the rising flax prices. The catastrophic extent of the decline in the spinners' incomes is particularly apparent when the fluctuations in their purchasing power are considered which were produced by the harvest cycle; concerning this problem in general: D. Saalfeld, 'Handwerkereinkommen in Deutschland vom ausgehenden 18. bis zur Mitte des 19. Jahrhunderts', in W. Abel and associates, *Handwerksgeschichte in neuer Sicht*, Göttinger handwerkswirtschaftliche Studien, vol. 16 (Göttingen, 1970), pp. 65–115; D. Saalfeld, 'Lebensstandard in Deutschland 1750–1860. Einkommensverhältnisse und Lebenshaltungskosten städtischer Populationen in der Übergangsperiode zum Industriezeitalter', *Wirtschaftliche und soziale Strukturen im säkularen Wandel. Festschrift für W. Abel zum 70. Geburtstag*, Schriftenreihe für ländliche Sozialfragen, vol. 70 (Hannover, 1974), vol. 2, pp. 417–43.

123 G. Weerth, 'Die Armen in der Senne', *Deutsches Bürgerbuch für 1845*, ed. H. Püttmann (Darmstadt, 1845), pp. 266–71, esp. 266.

124 C. H. Bitter, 'Bericht über den Nothstand in der Senne zwischen Bielefeld und Paderborn, Regierungsbezirk Minden, und Vorschläge zur Beseitigung desselben, auf Grund örtlicher Untersuchungen angestellt', *Jahresbericht des Historischen Vereins für die Grafschaft Ravensberg*, 64 (1966), 1–108, here 26–9; for Silesia, cf. Schneer, *Noth* (see n. 77 above), pp. 13–16.

125 Schmoller, *Geschichte* (see n. 21 above), pp. 459–66; Blumberg, 'Beitrag' (see n. 61 above), pp. 129f.; Adelmann, 'Krisen' (see n. 98 above), p. 116.

126 Schmoller, *Geschichte* (see n. 21 above), pp. 547–51; Blumberg, 'Beitrag' (see n. 61 above), pp. 128, 131–3; Adelmann, 'Krisen' (see n. 98 above), pp. 116f.; for Silesia esp. Schneer, *Noth* (see n. 77 above), pp. 32–55. For the decline in the price of linen cloth see F. von Reeden, *Der Leinwand- und Garnhandel Norddeutschlands* (Hanover, 1838), pp. 11–30; F. von Reeden, *Das Königreich Hannover statistisch beschrieben, zunächst in Beziehung auf Landwirtschaft, Gewerbe und Handel* (Hanover, 1839), vol. 1, pp. 342–50;

H. Schmidt, *Vom Leinen zur Seide. Die Geschichte der Firma C. A. Delius & Söhne und ihrer Vorgängerinnen und das Wirken ihrer Inhaber für die Entwicklung Bielefelds 1722–1925* (Lemgo, 1926), p. 125 (documents the decline of the prices for linen cloth by 20 to 25% between 1840 and 1848); below n. 127.

127 Schneer, *Noth* (see n. 77 above), p. 15; Adelmann, 'Krisen' (see n. 98 above), p. 117. The quantity of linen cloth exhibited at the Osnabrück Legge (an official cloth inspection) increased by 70.3% between 1838 and 1843, while its value fell by 46.7% during the same period. After 1843, the quantity of linen declined as well, a short-lived recovery notwithstanding (1847–1850); calculated according to H. Wiemann, 'Die Osnabrücker Stadtlegge', *Mitteilungen des Vereins für Geschichte und Landeskunde von Osnabrück*, 35 (1910), 1–76, esp. 60. Nothing comparable seems to have occurred in the county Tecklenburg; here not only the price but also the quantity of linen brought to the Legge declined since 1838: Biller, *Rückgang* (see n. 122 above), pp. 90, 112–17; Gladen, *Tecklenburg* (see n. 98 above), pp. 199f., appendix tables 13 and 14.

128 Kisch, 'Textile Industries' (see n. 73 above), p. 549 (and below p. 183); Kan, *Povstání* (see n. 77 above), pp. 273–310; B. Radłak, 'Rozwój przemysłu tkackiego na Śląsku i powstanie tkaczy w 1844 roku' (The development of the weaving industry in Silesia and the weavers' uprising of 1844), *Szkice z dziejów Śląska*, ed. E. Maleczyńska (Warsaw, 1956), vol. 2, 73–102, esp. 87–96. The classic account of W. Wolff, 'Elend' (see n. 77 above), pp. 38–60 is completely confirmed by the judgement of 31 August 1844, which is partially printed in J. Kuczynski, *Zur politökonomischen Ideologie in Deutschland vor 1850 und andere Studien*, vol. 10 of J. Kuczynski, *Die Geschichte der Lage der Arbeiter unter dem Kapitalismus* (Berlin, 1960), pp. 90–8. There exists no evidence at all that 'the so-called weavers' uprising of 1844 was a revolt of cotton yarn spinners against the installation of spinning-machines', as is stated in Henning, 'Industrialisierung' (see n. 21 above), pp. 162 and 170 with reference to G. Meinhardt, 'Der schlesische Weberaufstand von 1844', *Jahrbuch der schlesischen Friedrich-Wilhelms-Universität zu Breslau*, 17 (1972), 91–112, where nothing on the subject appears, however. For the pre-history of the weavers' uprising of 1844 cf. the extremely important article by W. Długoborski, 'Wystąpienia tkaczy w Dzierżonowskim w latach 1830–1831' (Weavers' uprisings in the area of Dzierżoniów [formerly: Reichenbach] in the years 1830–1), *Kwartalnik Historyczny*, 63, 6 (1956), 1–36.

129 Ch. H. Pouthas, *La population française pendant la première moitié du XIXᵉ siècle*, INED. Travaux et documents, vol. 25 (Paris, 1956), pp. 219–25; Fohlen, 'France' (see n. 52 above), p. 27.

130 Abel, *Massenarmut* (see n. 104 above), pp. 359–96; E. Labrousse, 'Panoramas de la crise', *Aspects de la crise et de la dépression de l'économie française au milieu du XIXᵉ siècle*, Bibliothèque de la révolution de 1848, vol. 19 (La Roche-sur-Yon, 1956), pp. iii–xxiv and the other contributions in that volume; Léon, *Naissance* (see n. 21 above), vol. 2, pp. 791–804; Armengaud, *Populations* (see n. 72 above), pp. 171–80; G. Jacquemyns, *Histoire de la crise économique des Flandres (1845–1850)*, Académie Royale de Belgique. Classe des lettres et des sciences morales et politiques. Mémoires, vol. 26, 1 (Bruxelles, 1929), pp. 229–69; J. Kuczynski, *Studien zur Geschichte der zyklischen Überproduktionskrisen in Deutschland 1825–1866*, vol. 11 of J. Kuczynski, *Die Geschichte der Lage der Arbeiter unter dem Kapitalismus* (Berlin, 1961), pp. 71–109; W. Schulte, *Volk und Staat. Westfalen im Vormärz und in der Revolution 1848/49* (Münster, 1954), pp. 149–57; G. Missalowa, 'Les crises dans l'industrie textiles au Royaume de Pologne à l'époque de la révolution industrielle (dans l'optique des crises mondiales)', *Studia Historiae Oeconomicae*, 8 (1973), 285–303, esp. 287–95.

131 Abel, *Massenarmut* (see n. 104 above), pp. 374–7; Labrousse, 'Panoramas' (see n. 130 above), pp. x–xiii; M. Perrot, 'Aspects industriels de la crise: Les régions textiles du Calvados', *Aspects*, ed. Labrousse (see n. 130 above), pp. 164–99, esp. 177–88; Kuczynski, *Studien* (see n. 130 above), pp. 85–96; concerning the 'Janus face' of the crisis, i.e. the fact that it was a crisis of the old as well as the new type, see Léon, *Naissance* (see n. 21 above), vol. 2, pp. 803f.

132 Cited in Kuczynski, *Ideologie* (n. 128), p. 109; the linen-cloth exports from Landeshut (now Kamienna Góra) fell from 28,570 in 1845 to 19,012 in 1847, to 7,820 pieces in 1848: Schumann, *Leinenindustrie* (see n. 66 above), p. 129; concerning the general misery in Silesia see A. Zimmermann, *Blüthe und Verfall des Leinengewerbes in Schlesien. Gewerbe- und Handelspolitik dreier Jahrhunderte*, 2nd ed. (Oldenburg etc., 1892), pp. 381f.; Bleiber, *Reform* (see n. 76 above), pp. 121–33.

133 Jacquemyns, *Histoire* (see n. 130 above), pp. 160–4, 301–10.

134 Cullen, *History* (see n. 88 above), pp. 119–22, 130–3; for the regional distribution of mortality, see the maps in S. H. Cousens, 'The Regional Variation in Mortality during the Great Irish Famine', *Proceedings of the Royal Irish Academy* C 63, 3 (Dublin, 1963), pp. 127–49.

135 Henning, 'Industrialisierung' (see n. 21 above), p. 169; also E. J. T. Collins, 'Labour Supply and Demand in European Agriculture, 1800–1880', *Agrarian Change and Economic Development. The Historical Problems*, eds. E. L. Jones and S. J. Woolf (London, 1969), pp. 61–94, here 61–74; E. J. T. Collins, 'Harvest Technology and Labour Supply in Britain, 1790–1870', *Econ. Hist. Rev.*, 2nd ser., 22 (1969), 453–73.

136 U. Troitzsch, 'Staatliche Bemühungen um die Einführung der Strohflechterei in Kurhessen in der Mitte des 19. Jahrhunderts – ein Beispiel verfehlter Nebenerwerbsförderung', *Nebengewerbe*, ed. Kellenbenz (see n. 21 above), pp. 141–54; Reekers, *Beiträge* (see n. 97 above), vol. 2, pp. 105f.

137 The most thorough study was done for three cantons: Ph. Pinchemel, *Structures sociales et dépopulation rurale dans les campagnes picardes de 1836 à 1936*, Centre d'Etudes Economiques. Etudes et Mémoires, vol. 35 (Paris, 1957), pp. 69, 99, 104–28, 203–12; A. Demangeon, *La plaine picarde. Picardie, Artois, Cambrésis, Beauvaisis. Etude de géographie sur les plaines de craie du nord de la France* (Paris, 1905), pp. 404–10; Sion, *Paysans* (see n. 21 above), pp. 441–3; Armengaud, *Populations* (see n. 72 above), pp. 240f., 256–9; in general: Pouthas, *Population* (see n. 129 above), pp. 121–41; Jacquemyns, *Histoire* (see n. 130 above), pp. 381–6; Gladen, *Tecklenburg* (see n. 98 above), pp. 139–55; K. Kiel, 'Gründe und Folgen der Auswanderung aus dem Osnabrücker Regierungsbezirk, insbesondere nach den Vereinigten Staaten, im Lichte der hannoverschen Auswanderungspolitik betrachtet (1823–1866)', *Mitteilungen des Vereins für Geschichte und Landeskunde von Osnabrück*, 61 (1941), 85–176, esp. 103–13; T. Ładogórski, in *Historia Śląska*, vol. 2, 2 (see n. 99 above), pp. 108f.; in general: P. Marschalck, *Deutsche Überseewanderung im 19. Jahrhundert. Ein Beitrag zur soziologischen Theorie der Bevölkerung*, Industrielle Welt, vol. 14 (Stuttgart, 1973), pp. 34–44, 62–71, 75–84. The fact that the emigration figures, i.e. the number of emigrants per 1,000 inhabitants, were highest in Germany in the middle of the nineteenth century is evidence for the functional connection between emigration and the final crisis of proto-industry (Marschalck, pp. 35–40; cf. also the remarks on pp. 82f. and in n. 19 concerning the characteristics of the first phase of the German emigration movement in the nineteenth century, which lasted until 1865); see also K. Obermann, 'Die deutsche Auswanderung nach den Vereinigten Staaten von Amerika im 19. Jahrhundert, ihre Ursachen und Auswirkungen (1830 bis 1870)', *Jb. Wirtsch. G.* (1975), pt. 2, 33–55.

138 Tilly, 'Clio' (see n. 59 above), pp. 455–9; D. R. Mills, 'Introduction', *English Rural Communities. The Impact of a Specialized Economy*, ed. D. R. Mills (London, 1973), pp. 9–27, esp. 15; R. Lawton, 'Rural Depopulation in Nineteenth Century England', *English Rural Communities*, pp. 195–218, esp. 215; Pinchemel, *Structures* (see n. 137

above), pp. 208f.; Henning, 'Industrialisierung' (see n. 21 above), pp. 171f.; P. Fried, 'Reagrarisierung in Südbayern seit dem 19. Jahrhundert', *Nebengewerbe*, ed. Kellenbenz (n. 21 above), pp. 177–94, esp. 184–93.

139 A. Hoffmann, 'Zur Problematik der agrarischen Nebengewerbe und der Reagrarisierung', *Nebengewerbe*, ed. Kellenbenz (see n. 21 above), pp. 29–37, esp. 36f.; A Hoffmann, 'Die Agrarisierung der Industriebauern in Österreich', *Z̧. Agrarg. Agrarsoziol.*, 20 (1972), 66–81.

Notes to Part II

Agriculture and peasant industry in eighteenth-century Flanders

by Franklin F. Mendels

This article was originally published in *European Peasants and their Markets: Essays in Agrarian Economic History* by William N. Parker and Eric L. Jones (eds.) (© 1975 by Princeton University Press), pp. 179–204. It is here reprinted with slight revisions by permission of Princeton University Press.

This paper has greatly benefited from the contributions made by Iris Mendels and Lutz K. Berkner.

I have followed the Anglo-American custom concerning Flemish place names. When an English translation does not exist, the French version, if available, is used.

1 G. Ch. Faipoult, *Mémoire statistique du département de l'Escait* (1805), ed. by Paul Deprez (Ghent, 1960), p. 165. I would like to acknowledge my debts to the work of Professor Paul Deprez, of the University of Manitoba. I hope my footnotes will reflect this debt adequately. I should also mention that the rarely cited but superb piece by Professor Jan Craeybeckx, 'De agrarische wortels van de industriele omwenteling' (The agrarian roots of the Industrial Revolution), *Revue belge de philologie et d'histoire*, 41 (1963), 398–448, anticipated some of my thoughts.

2 Louis Varlez, *Les salaires dans l'industrie gantoise*. II, *L'industrie de la filature du lin* (Brussels, 1904), p. xxii; H. Coppejans-Desmedt, 'De Gentse vlas industrie vanaf het einde van de XVIIIe eeuw tot de oprichting van de grote mechanische bedrijven (1838)', *Handelingen der Maatschappij voor Geschiedenis en Oudheidkunde te Gent* (*HMGOG* hereafter), new ser. 22 (1968), 179–202.

3 'Tabelle van de getauwe bevonden binnen de naerschreven parochien, . . . 1792', ed. by D. Berten, *Coutumes des pays et comté de Flandre, quartier de Gand*, VII, *Coutumes du Vieuxbourg de Grand* (Brussels, 1904), pp. 97–8; P. Deprez, *De Kasselrij van de Oudburg in de XVIIIe eeuw* (Ph. D. dissertation, University of Ghent, 1960), p. 63. Source for figures 1 and 2: J. Bastin, 'De Gentse lijnwaadmarkt en linnenhandel in de XVIIe eeuw', *HMGOG*, new ser. 21 (1967), 131–62.

4 Deprez, 'Kasselrij' (see n. 3 above), p. 74; A. de Vos, *Geschiedenis van Ertvelde* (Ertvelde, 1971), p. 456; J. de Brouwer, *Geschiedenis van Lede* (Lede, 1963), p. 235; de Brouwer, *Geschiedenis van Impe* (Ghent, 1958), pp. 70–1; de Brouwer, 'Zo groeide Hofstade', *Tijdschrit van de Heemkundige Vereniging 'Het Land van Aalst'*, 10 (1958), p. 20; de Brouwer, 'Bijdrage tot de geschiedenis van Henderleeuw', *Tijdschrift van de Heemkundige Verenigung 'Het Land van Aalst'*, 12 (1960), p. 30.

5 In Ertvelde almost a half of the households had a loom at the end of the eighteenth century, but there were only 53 weavers, or 7% of the heads of households in the labour force. De Vos, *Ertvelde* (see n. 4 above), p. 717.

6 These figures refer to year IX (1801–2): East Flanders, 10.5 million francs; West Flanders, 7.3 million francs; South Flanders, 7 9 million france (arrondissements of

Bergues, Hazebrouck, and Lille), Dieudonné, *Statistique du Département du Nord* (Douai, 1804) vol. 2, p. 216; C. Viry, *Mémoire Statistique du Département de la Lys* (Paris, 1804), p. 174.

7 Viry, *Mémoire Statistique* (cit. 6).

8 Natalis Briavoinne, *Mémoire sur l'état de la population, des fabriques, des manufactures et du commerce dans les provinces des Pays-Bas depuis Albert et Isabelle jusqu'à la fin du siècle dernier*, Académie Royale de Belgique, Mémoires Couronnés, vol. 14 (Brussels, 1840); H. Coppejans-Desmedt, *Bijdrage tot le studie van de gegoede burgerij to Gent in de XVIII^de eeuw*, Verhandelingen van de Koninklijke Vlaamse Academie voor de Letteren, Wetenschappen en Schone Kunsten van België (VKVA hereafter), vol. 14 (Brussels, 1952).

9 C. Van Hoobrouck-Mooregem, *Exposition des produits de l'industrie du départment de l'Escaut reçus à la mairie de Gand, à l'occasion du passage du Premier Consul en cette ville en Thermidor an VI* (1803), Rijksarchief, Ghent.

10 J. G. van Bel, *De linnenhandel van Amsterdam in de XVIIIe eeuw* (Amsterdam, 1940), p. 49 and *passim*. Figures showing the impressive growth of the Irish and Scottish linen production are available in John Horner, *The Linen Trade of Europe* (Belfast, 1902). For other references, see F. Mendels, *Industrialization and Population Pressure* in *Eighteenth-Century Flanders* (New York, forthcoming).

11 For comments by a Ghent merchant, see those quoted by J. Lefèvre, *Etude sur le commerce de la Belgique avec l'Espagne au XVIIIe siècle*, Académie Royale de Belgique, Mémoires, Coll. in-8°, 2nd ser., 16 (Brussels, 1922), p. 179. Paul Deprez has found a relationship between fluctuations in seignorial rents and conditions in the linen market. Deprez, 'De inkomsten van het Land van Nevele', *Bijdragen tot de geschiedenis der Stad Deinze en van het Land aan Leie en Schelde*, 32 and 33 (1965 and 1966), 45–75 and 55–72.

12 A. J. L. van den Bogaerde, *Proef op de Aanmoediging en uitbreiding der linnenweveryen in Oost-Vlaanderen, gevolgd an de tienjarige optelling van al de op de markten van Oost-Vlaanderen verkochten lynwaeden* (Ghent, n. d. [ca. 1825]).

13 'Tabelle van de getauwe, 1792' (see n. 3 above).

14 Mendels, *Industrialization* (see n. 10 above), pp. 200ff., based on J. F. D. Lichtervelde, *Mémoire sur les fonds ruraux du Département de l'Escaut* (Ghent, 1815), pp. 114–15; G. Willemsen, 'Contribution à l'histoire de l'industrie linière en Flandre', *HMGOG*, 7 (1906), p. 255; P. Deprez, 'Prijzen te Sint-Niklaas-Waas', in Charles Verlinden et al., eds., *Dokumenten voor de geschiedenis van prijzen en lonen in Vlaanderen en Brabant (XV–XVIIIe eeuw)* (Bruges, 1959), pp. 121–3.

15 This concept was popularized by H. Myint, 'The "Classical" Theory of International Trade and the Underdeveloped Countries', reprinted in Myint, *Economic Theory and the Underdeveloped Countries* (London, 1971), pp. 118–46.

16 Willemsen, 'Industrie linière' (see n. 14 above), p. 229; Deprez, 'Oudburg' (see n. 3 above); Denise de Weerdt, 'Loon en Levensvoorwarden van de fabrieksarbeiders, 1789–1850', in Jan Dhondt, ed., *Geschiedenis van de socialistische arbeidersbeweging in België* (Antwerp, 1960), pp. 71–3.

17 Archives Nationales, Paris, F20 139 (1801–1802).

18 P. C. van der Meersch, 'De l'état de la mendicité et de la bienfaisance dans la province de Flandre Orientale, 1740–1850', *Bulletin de la Commission centrale de statistique*, 5 (1853), 25–268; P. Bonenfant, *Le problème du paupérisme en Belgique à la fin de l'Ancien Régime*, Académie Royale de Belgique, Mémoires, Coll. in-8° (Brussels, 1934), pp. 33ff.

19 In V. Prévôt, 'L'industrie linière du Nord de la France sous l'Ancien Régime', *Revue du Nord*, 39 (1957), p. 214.

20 In the polders proper, they were only 1.1%. D. Dalle, 'De bevolking van de stad en van de Kasselrij Veurne in 1796', *Album Archivaris Jos. De Smet* (Bruges, 1964), p. 130;

D. Dalle, 'De volkstelling van 1697 in Veurne-Ambacht en de evolutie van het Veurnse bevolkingscijfer in de XVIIe eeuw', *Handelingen van het Genootschap voor Geschiedenis te Brugge*, 40 (1953), 95–130 and 41 (1954), 18–54.

21 E. Coornaert, *La draperie-sayetterie d'Hondschoote (XIV–XVIIIe s.)* (Rennes, 1930); D. Dalle, *Pogingen tot het heropbeuring van de wolnijverheid te Veurne (15de–17de eeuw)* (Ghent, 1960), pp. 77–86.

22 Text of 1765 quoted in Willemsen, 'Industrie linière' (see n. 14 above), p. 291.

23 Mendels, *Industrialization* (see n. 10 above), pp. 192ff.; Willemsen, 'Industrie linière' (see n. 14 above), pp. 255, 269, 281; P. Lenders, S.J., *De politieke crisis in Vlaanderen omstreeks het midden der achttiende eeuw*, VKVA, vol. 25 (Brussels, 1956).

24 P. J. Bouman, *Geschiedenis van de Zeeuwschen landbouw in de negentiende en twintigste eeuw* (Wageningen, 1946), pp. 17–18.

25 G. De Rammelaere, 'De beroepsstructuur van de plattelandse bevolking in Zuidoost-Vlaanderen gedurende de 18e eeuw', *Tijdschrift voor sociale wetenschappen*, 4 (1957), 225–43.

26 Results of a study of the family and social structure of these two villages and others will appear shortly.

27 Viry, *Mémoire* (n. 6); J. N. H. Schwerz, *Anleitund zur Kenntnis der belgischen Landwirtschaft* (Halle, 1808–1811), vol. 3, pp. 123ff.; Emile de Laveleye, *Essai sur l'économie rurale de la Belgique* (Paris, 1875), p. 25; Raoul Blanchard, *La Flandre* (Paris, 1906); M.A. Lefèvre, *L'habitat rural en Belgique* (Liège, 1926).

28 In Lede (Interior), there were 6.2% in 1796. De Brouwer, *Lede* (see n. 4 above), p. 240; Dalle, 'Bevolking 1796' (see n. 20 above), p. 30.

29 Faipoult, *Mémoire* (see n. 1 above), p. 30.

30 Dieudonné, *Statistique* (see n. 6 above); R. Blanchard, *La densité de la population du départment du Nord au XIXe siècle* (Lille, 1906).

31 J. Peuchet and P. G. Chanlaire, *Description topographique et statistique de la France* (Paris, 1811), vol. 17.

32 Archives Nationales, Paris, F 20 435 Lys; Rijksarchief Ghent, Escaut 1636 (1805); T. Radcliff, *A Report on the Agriculture of Eastern and Western Flanders* (London, 1819), p. 192; D. Dalle, *De bevolking van Veurne-Ambacht in de 17^e eeuw*, VKVA, vol. 49 (Brussels, 1963), p. 100.

33 Whereas Deprez shows evidence of the construction of cabins in the sandy areas of the interior, Dalle has shown the stiff resistance on the part of the local authorities to such construction, as witnessed by regulations and prohibitions in the course of the eighteenth century. Deprez, 'De boeren in de 16de, 17de, en 18de eeuw', in J. L. Broeckx et al., eds., *Flandria nostra*, vol. 1 (Antwerp, 1957), Dalle, *Veurne-Ambacht* (see n. 32 above), pp. 83–8. Similarly, for Zealand-Flanders, see M. T. Boerendonk, *Historische Studie over den Zeeuwschen landbouw* (The Hague, 1935), pp. 322–4.

34 Dalle, *Veurne-Ambacht* (see n. 32 above), p. 180.

35 Faipoult, *Mémoire* (see n. 1 above), pp. 29–30.

36 Viry, *Mémoire* (see n. 6 above), p. 50; Abbé Mann, *Mémoire sur les moyens d'augmenter la population et de perfectionner la culture dans les Pays-Bas Autrichiens*, Mémoires de l'Academie Impériale et Royale des Sciences et Belles Lettres, vol. 4 (Brussels, 1783), p. 171.

37 It would have been impossible for small farms to share in the use of ploughs because it was the practice to enclose the fields with ditches, hedges, bushes, or rows of trees. C. Petit, 'Clôtures et forme des champs en Belgique', *Bulletin de la Société Belgé d'Etudes Géographiques*, 12 (1942), 125–222; F. Dussart, 'Les types de dessin parcellaire et leur répartition en Belgique', *Bulletin de la Société Belge d'Etudes Géographiques*, 30 (1961), 21–65.

38 Viry, *Mémoire* (see n. 6 above), pp. 26–7; G. G. Dept, 'Note sur le défrichement dans le comté de Flandre au XVIIIe siècle', *Bulletin de la Société Belge d'Etudes Géographiques*, 3 (1933), 120–9; H. Coppejans-Desmedt, 'Economische opbloei in de Zuidelijke Nederlanden', in J. A. Van Houtte et al., eds., *Algemene geschiedenis der Nederlanden*, vol. 8 (Antwerp, 1955), p. 266; P. J. Bouman, *Zeeuwsche landbouw* (see n. 24 above), p. 14.

39 Faipoult, *Mémoire* (see n. 1 above), p. 149.

40 By 1820, in the province of East Flanders (now amputated of most of Zealand-Flanders) 250,000 hectares were productive. Algemene Rijksarchief, The Hague, Nationale Nijverheid N 3394b. Rapport sur le défrichment des terres incultes, des landes, et des bruyères de la Flandre Orientale, 1819.

41 Richard Weston, *A Discourse of Husbandrie used in Brabant and Flanders shewing the Wonderful Improvements* . . . (London, 1652); Lindemans, *Geschiedenis van de lanbouw in België* (Antwerp, 1952), vol. 1, pp. 117ff.; B. H. Slicher van Bath, 'The Rise of Intensive Husbandry in the Low Countries', in J. S. Bromley and E. H. Kossman, eds., *Britain and the Netherlands* (London, 1960), pp. 130–53.

42 In Meigem a sandy village west of Ghent, the number of small farms did not increase as rapidly, although the population also doubled. P. Deprez, 'Uitbatingen en grondbezit in Meigem (1571–1787). En methodologisch artikel', *HMGOG*, new ser. 10 (1956), 159–65; see also C. D. Ramelaere, 'Bijdrage tot de Landbouwgeschiedenis in Zuid-Oostvlaanderen (1570–1790)', *HMGOG*, new ser. 16 (1962), 21–40; de Brouwer, 'Denderleeuw' (see n. 4 above), p. 42; de Brouwer, 'Hofstade' (n. 4 above), p. 32; de Brouwer, *Impe* (n. 4 above), pp. 76ff.

43 P. Deprez, 'De boeren' (see n. 33 above), pp. 141–2. Also, I. Delatte, 'L'évolution de la structure agraire en Belgique de 1575 à 1950', *Annales du Congrès de la fédération archéologique et historique de Belgique, Tournai, 1949* (Brussels, 1951), vol. 1, pp. 480–8.

44 D. Dalle, 'Lanbouwbedrijven in het Iperse in 1695', *Handelingen van het Genootschap 'Société d'Emulation' te Brugge*, 101 (1964), 240–7.

45 De Rammelaere, 'Zuid-Oostvlaanderen' (see n. 42 above), pp. 38–40; de Brouwer, *Lede* (see n. 4 above), p. 208.

46 Deprez, 'De boeren' (see n. 33 above), p. 142.

47 Dussart, 'Dessin parcellaire' (see n. 37 above), p. 36.

48 De Brouwer, *Lede* (see n. 4 above), p. 219.

49 A. E. Verhulst, *Histoire du paysage rural en Flandre* (Brussels, 1966).

50 Deprez, 'Meigem' (see n. 42 above); H. van Houtte, *Histoire économique de la Belgique à la fin de l'Ancien Régime* (Ghent, 1920), pp. 405ff.

51 Van Houtte, *Histoire économique* (see n. 50 above), pp. 509–10. See also Deprez, 'De hypothekaire grondrente in Vlaanderen gedurende de 18de eeuw', *Tijdschrift voor Geschiedenis*, 79 (1966), pp. 141–9.

52 Deprez, 'Meigem' (see n. 42 above), p. 169.

53 Coppejans-Desmedt, *Gegoede Burgerij* (see n. 8 above), pp. 117–19.

54 Deprez, 'Hypothekaire grondrente' (see n. 51 above). New estimates of land-rent, based on a much larger sample than previously used, confirm Deprez's figures. See F. de Wever, 'Pachtprijzen in de streek rond Gent (18^e eeuw)', in Verlinden, *Dokumenten* (see n. 14 above), vol. 3 (1972), pp. 222–86. See also de Wever, 'Pachtprijzen in Vlaanderen en Brabant in de achtiende eeuw. Bijdrage tot de konjunktuurstudie', *Tijdschrift voor Geschiedenis*, 85 (1972), 180–204 (this article came to my attention after the final draft of this paper was written). My thanks to Vernon Ruttan and J. Verhelst for their critique.

55 *L'agriculture belge*, Congrès International de Paris, 1878 (Paris, 1878), P. xxxiii; J. Yver, 'Les deux groupes de coutumes de Nord', *Revue du Nord*, 35 (1953) and 36 (1954); F. van de Walle, *Le régime successoral dans les coutumes de Flandre* (Lille, 1902);

E. M. Meijers, *Het Oost-Vlaamsche erfrecht* (Haarlem, 1939); *Het West-Vlaamsche erfrecht* (Haarlem, 1952).

56 P. Thuysbaert, *Het Land van Waes. Bijdrage tot de geschiedenis der landelijke bevolking in de XIXe eeuw* (Courtrai, 1913), pp. 70–1.

57 B. Verhaegen, *Contribution à l'histoire économique des Flandres* (Louvain, 1961), vol. 1, pp. 127ff.; De Laveleye, *Essai* (see n. 27 above), pp. 51–52; G. Jacquemyns, *Histoire de la crise économique des Flandres*, Académie Royale de Belgique, Mémoires, Coll. in-8°, 26 (Brussels, 1929), p. 233; S. Seebohm Rowntree, *Land and Labour. Lessons from Belgium* (London, 1911), p. 49.

58 Except that one would expect them to interrupt their efforts when the utility of this (small) marginal income became smaller than the gain in utility obtainable by taking some rest instead. This takes effect once the family is past the subsistence level.

59 C. Vandenbroeke, 'Cultivation and Consumption of the Potato in the 17th and 18th Century', *Acta Historiae Neerlandica*, 5 (Leiden, 1971), p. 38 (translated from 'Aardappelteelt en aardappelverbruik in de 17^e en 18^e eeuw', *Tijdschrift voor Geschiedenis*, No. 82, 1969, p. 67).

60 De Brouwer, *Lede* (see n. 4 above), p. 245.

61 P. Deprez, 'Pachtprijzen in het Land van Nevele (17e en 18e eeuw)', in *Dokumenten* (see n. 14 above), I, pp. 181ff.

62 Mendels, 'Industrialization' (see n. 10 above), pp. 130ff.

63 Faipoult, *Mémoire* (see n. 1 above), pp. 104–5; C. Vandenbroeke and W. Vanderpijpen, 'De voedingsgewassen in Vlaanderen tijdens de XVIIIe en XIXe eeuw (1700–1846)', *Revue Belge d'Histoire Contemporaine*, 2, no. 2 (1970), 47–82.

64 Since a hectare planted with potatoes can support twice as many people as a hectare planted with wheat, a 100% substitution theoretically allows a 100% population growth, and so forth.

65 H. van Houtte, *Histoire économique* (see n. 50 above), pp. 255ff.; C. Vandenbroeke, 'De graanpolitiek in den Oostenrijken Nederlanden', *Revue Belge de Philologie et d'Histoire*, 45 (1967), 369–87.

66 The same source reveals a growth of turnip cultivation and a decline of beans. De Brouwer, *Lede* (see n. 4 above), pp. 232–3.

67 Faipoult, *Mémoire* (see n. 1 above), p. 107 finds 43% and W. Wanderpijpen 25% (after animal and industrial consumption). 'De landbouwstatistiek in Vlaanderen onder het Frans bewind', *Revue Belge d'Histoire contemporaine*, 2, no. 2 (1970), p. 43.

68 Bonenfant, *Paupérisme* (see n. 18 above); J. Craeybeckx, 'De arbeiders voor de industriele omwenteling', in J. Dondt, *Arbeidersbeweging* (see n. 16 above) J. Craeybeckx, 'De arbeiders in de XVIIe en de XVIIIe eeuw', *Flandria Nostra* (see n. 33 above), vol. 1, pp. 281–328; P. Deprez, 'Evolution démographique et évolution économique en Flandre au dix-huitième siècle', *Third International Conference of Economic History, Munich, 1965*, Vol. 4, ed. D. E. C. Eversley (Paris, 1972) pp. 49–53.

69 Lichtervelde, *Mémoire* (see n. 14 above).

70 Calculated from Faipoult, *Mémoire* (see n. 1 above), pp. 26, 36–46, 104; P. Vandermaelen, *Dictionnaire géographique de la Flandre Orientale* (Brussels, 1834), p. 121; and Institut d'Etudes Economiques et Sociales des classes moyennes, *Le lin* (Brussels, 1951), p. 23.

71 F. F. Mendels, 'Proto-Industrialization: The First Phase of the Process of Industrialization', *Journ. Econ. Hist.*, 30 (1972), 241–61.

72 Mendels, 'Industrialization' (see n. 10 above), Ch. 5; F. F. Mendels, 'Industry and Marriages in Flanders before the Industrial Revolution', in P. Deprez, ed., *Population and Economics, Proceedings of Section 5 (Historical Demography) of the 4th Congress of* the International Economic History Association, *1968* (Winnipeg, 1970), pp. 81–93; Mendels, 'Proto-Industrialization' (see n. 71 above).

73 G. Jacquemyns, *Histoire* (see n. 57 above); A. de Vos, 'Bloei en verval der plaatselijke Handweefnijverheid te Evergem (1794–1880)', *HMGOG*, new ser. 13 (1959), 113–62.

74 Faipoult, *Mémoire* (see n. 1 above), p. 30.

75 Vandenbroeke, 'The Potato' (see n. 59 above), p. 38.

76 Faipoult, *Mémoire* (see n. 1 above), p. 107; Vandenbroeke, 'The Potato' (see n. 59 above), p. 37.

77 Vandenbroeke, 'The Potato' (see n. 59 above), p. 38.

Notes to

The textile industries in Silesia and the Rhineland: A comparative study in industrialization

By Herbert Kisch

[This article was first published in the *Journal of Economic History*, 19 (1959), 541–64. It is here reprinted with the permission of the author and the Economic History Association in New York.

The author is grateful to the Social Science Research Council for a post-doctoral fellowship (1958–1959) which enabled him to complete the research necessary for this study.]

1 For an elaboration of the thesis '. . . the textile crafts . . . occupied a central position in economic history. . .' see George Unwin's introductory chapter to G. W. Daniels, *The Early English Cotton Industry*, University of Manchester Historical Series, No. XXXVI (Manchester, 1920), pp. xx – xxi.

2 L. Brentano, 'Über den grundherrlichen Charakter des hausindustriellen Leinengewerbes in Schlesien', *Zeitschrift für Sozial- und Wirtschaftsgeschichte*, 1 (1893), p. 323.

3 J. Horner, *The Linen Trade in Europe during the Spinning-Wheel Period* (Belfast, 1920), p. 389.

4 G. Croon, 'Zunftzwang und Industrie im Kreise Reichenbach', *Zeitschrift des Vereins für Geschichte und Altertum Schlesiens*, 43 (1909), p. 104.

5 H. Aubin, 'Die Anfänge der grossen schlesischen Leinenweberei und -handlung', *VSWG*, xxxv (1942), 169–70.

6 Croon, 'Zunftzwang' (see n. 4 above), pp. 106–10.

7 E. Zimmermann, 'Der schlesische Garn- und Leinenhandel im 16. und 17. Jahrhundert', *Economisch-Historisch Jaarboek-Bijdragen tot de economische geschiedenis van Nederland*, 26 (1956), 208–13 and 247–52.

8 H. Myint, 'The "Classical Theory" of International Trade and the Under-developed Countries', *Economic Journal*, LXVIII (1958), 317–37.

9 E. Zimmermann, 'Garn- und Leinenhandel' (see n. 7 above), p. 237.

10 Aubin, 'Anfänge' (see n. 5 above), pp. 162f.

11 P. J. Marperger, *Schlesischer Kauffmann oder Ausführliche Beschreibung der schlesischen Commercien und deren jetzigen Zustandes . . .* (Breslau and Leipzig, 1714), pp. 65–7.

12 A. Zimmermann, *Blüte und Verfall des Leinengewerbes in Schlesien* (Oldenburg etc., 1885), p. 60.

13 For an account of these peasant revolts during the late 17th century see S. Michalkiewicz, 'Einige Episoden aus der Geschichte der schlesischen Bauernkämpfe im 17. und 18. Jahrhundert', *Beiträge zur Geschichte Schlesiens*, ed. E. Maleczyńska, German translation from the Polish (Berlin, 1958), pp. 365–81.

14 A. Zimmermann, *Blüte und Verfall* (see n. 12 above), p. 64.

15 R. Gottwald, *Das alte Wüstewaltersdorf – Ein Beitrag zur Geschichte des Eulengebirges* (Breslau, 1926), pp. 25–27.

16 Regarding the special position enjoyed by the linen trades see Croon, 'Zunftzwang und Industrie' (see n. 4 above), pp. 112–17.

17 200 new villages were founded and 13,000 foreigners were brought into the Province. J. F. Zöllner, *Briefe über Schlesien, Krakau, Wieliczka und die Grafschaft Glatz* (Berlin, 1793), vol. 2, p. 389.

18 Horner, *Linen Trade* (see n. 3 above), pp. 393–5 and A. Zimmermann, *Blüte und Verfall* (see n. 12 above), pp. 75–90.

19 J. Ziekursch, *Beiträge zur Charakteristik der preussischen Verwaltungsbeamten in Schlesien bis zum Untergang des friderizianischen Staates – Darstellungen und Quellen zur schlesischen Geschichte* (Breslau, 1907), vol. 4, pp. 3–12.

20 C. Frahne, *Die Textilindustrie im Wirtschaftsleben Schlesiens – Ihre wirtschaftlichen und technischen Grundlagen, historisch-ökonomische Gestaltung und gegenwärtige Bedeutung* (Tübingen, 1905), p. 94.

21 Zöllner, *Briefe über Schlesien* (see n. 17 above), pp. 387–8.

22 This movement was already noted by Marperger, *Schlesischer Kauffmann* (see n. 11 above), p. 65, early in the 18th century.

23 J. Ziekursch, *Hundert Jahre schlesischer Agrargeschichte – vom Humbertusburger Frieden bis zum Abschluss der Bauerbefreiung – Darstellungen und Quellen zur schlesischen Geschichte* (Breslau, 1915), vol. 20, pp. 109ff.

24 von Klöber, *Von Schlesien vor und seit dem Jahre MDCCXXXX* (Freiburg, 1785), p. 228.

25 Horner, *Linen Trade* (see n. 3 above), Ch. 27.

26 A. J. Warden, *The Linen Trade Ancient and Modern*, 2nd ed. (London, 1867), pp. 436ff.

27 H. Fechner, *Wirtschaftsgeschichte der preussischen Provinz Sahlesien in der Zeit ihrer provinziellen Selbständigkeit 1741–1806* (Breslau, 1907), pp. 537–8 and 700–1.

28 For an account of the circumstances leading up to the weavers' revolt in 1793 see the important study by the Soviet historian S. B. Kan, *Dva vosstaniya silezskich tkachei* (Two revolts of the Silesian weavers) (Moscow and Leningrad, 1948). Here the Czech translation *Dvě Povstaní Slezskýh Tkalců 1793–1844* (Prague, 1952) is used, pp. 95–107.

29 C. Grünhagen, ed., 'Monatsberichte des Ministers von Hoym über den schlesischen Handel', *Zeitschrift des Vereins für Geschichte und Alterthum Schlesiens*, 28 (1894), 346–407. Regarding the detrimental effects of the Continental system, see the report of State Secretary Kunth in F. and P. Goldschmidt, *Das Leben des Staatsrath Kunth*, 2nd ed. (Berlin, 1888), p. 190.

30 G. von Gülich, *Geschichtliche Darstellung des Handels, der Gewerbe und des Ackerbaus* (Jena, 1830), vol. 2, p. 489.

31 Gülich, *Geschichtliche Darstellung* (see n. 30 above), pp. 413 and 489.

32 Frahne, *Die Textilwirtschaft* (see n. 20 above), pp. 121 and 195–6.

33 G. Schmoller, *Zur Geschichte der deutschen Kleingewerbe im 19. Jahrhundert* (Halle, 1870), pp. 21 and 464.

34 Frahne, *Die Textilwirtschaft* (see n. 20 above), p. 156.

35 F. W. von Reden, *Erwerbs- und Verkehrsstatistik des Königsstaats Preussen* (Darmstadt, 1853), vol. 1, pp. 590–5.

36 Kan, *Dva vosstaniya* (see n. 28 above) 28, pp. 231–2.

37 The most interesting account of this famous revolt was given by Wilhelm Wolff in

Das Elend und der Aufruhr in Schlesien – Gesammelte Schriften, ed. by F. Mehring (Berlin, 1909). Also see Kan, *Two Revolts* (see n. 28 above), pp. 273–99.

38 A. Schneer, *Über die Noth der Leinenarbeiter in Schlesien und die Mittel ihr abzuhelfen* (Berlin, 1844), pp. 73–6.

39 V. Loewe, 'Zur Geschichte des hausindustriellen Leinengewerbes in Schlesien. Der Weberzins', *Zeitschrift des Vereins für Geschichte und Alterthum Schlesiens*, 59 (1925), p. 100.

40 Schneer, *Noth der Leinenarbeiter* (see n. 38 above), p. 73 and Wilhelm Wolff's pamphlet *Die Schlesische Milliarde* (Hüttingen-Zürich, 1886).

41 F. V. Grünfeld, *Streiks in der Schlesischen Leinen- und Baumwollindustrie – Ein sozialhistorischer Beitrag zur Geschichte des schlesischen Weberelends* (Greifswald, 1920), pp. 70–5.

42 M. Weyrmann, *Zur Geschichte des Immobiliarkreditwesens in Preussen mit besonderer Nutzanwendung auf die Theorie der Bodenverschuldung*, Freiburger Volkswirtschaftliche Abhandlungen (Karlsruhe, 1919), pp. 75ff.

43 H. Maurer, *Das landschaftliche Kreditwesen Preussens agrargeschichtlich und volkswirtschaftlich betrachtet*, Abhandlungen aus dem staatswirtschaftlichen Seminar zu Strassburg, vol. 22 (Strassburg, 1907), pp. 21–3.

44 Weyermann, *Zur Geschichte des Immobiliarkreditwesens* (see n. 42 above), pp. 75ff.

45 Zöllner, *Briefe über Schlesien* (see n. 17 above), vol. 2, pp. 397–9.

46 H. Myint, 'The Gains from International Trade and the Backward Countries', *Review of Economic Studies*, 1954–5, 22 (1958), 133–6.

47 L. Brentano, 'Über den Einfluss der Grundherrlichkeit und Friedrichs des Grossen auf des schlesische Leinen-Gewerbe', *Zeitschrift für Social- und Wirtschaftsgeschichte*, 2 (1894), p. 298.

48 Brentano, 'Grundherrlichkeit' (see n. 47 above), p. 310.

49 W. Sombart, 'Zur neueren Literatur über Hausindustrie', *Jahrbücher für Nationalökonomie und Statistik*, 3rd ser., 6 (1893), 756–66.

50 Goldschmidt and Goldschmidt, *Staatsrath Kundt* (see n. 29 above), pp. 202–3.

51 'Journal of a tour through Silesia' appeared anonymously as an article-series in the Philadelphia weekly *The Port Folio*, January to June 1801. See especially vol. 1, no. 6 (7 Feb. 1801) and vol. 1, no. 16 (18 April 1801).

52 Schneer, *Noth der Leinenarbeiter* (see n. 38 above), pp. 25 and 88.

53 von Klöber, *Von Schlesien* (see n. 24 above), p. 322.

54 The report of this commission is summarized by Christian Noback, *Die Leinenindustrie in Deutschland* (Hamburg, 1850), pp. 31–6.

55 Von Reden, *Erwerbs- und Verkehrsstatistik* (see n. 35 above), vol. 1, p. 592.

56 T Scitovsky, 'Two Concepts of External Economies', *Journal of Political Economy*, 62 (1954), 143–51.

57 H. K. Takahashi, 'A Contribution to the Discussion' in *The Transition from Feudalism to Capitalism* (New York, 1954), pp. 51–2, esp. n. 68.

58 B. Kuske, *Die Volkswirtschaft des Rheinlands in ihrer Eigenart und Bedeutung* (Essen, 1925), pp. 69–70.

59 M. Barkhausen, 'Staatliche Wirtschaftslenkung und freies Unternehmertum im westdeutschen und im nord- und südniederländischen Raum bei der Entstehung der neuzeitlichen Industrie im 18. Jahrhundert', *VSWG*, 45 (1958), esp. pp. 174–5.

60 Barkhausen, 'Staatliche Wirtschaftlenkung' (see n. 59 above), pp. 170–3.

61 H. Aubin, 'Agrargeschichte', *Geschichte des Rheinlands von der ältesten Zeit bis zur Gegenwart*, eds. H. Aubin et al. (Essen, 1922), vol. 2, pp. 125–35.

62 B. Kuske, 'Gewerbe, Handel und Verkehr', *Geschichte des Rheinlands* (see n. 61 above), vol. 2, pp. 189–90.

63 M. Barkhausen, 'Der Aufstieg der rheinischen Industrie im 18, Jahrhundert und die Entstehung eines industriellen Grossbürgertums', *Rheinische Vierteljahresblätter*, 19 (1954), pp. 137–8.

64 W. Kurschat, *Das Haus Friedrich und Heinrich von der Leyen in Krefeld. Zur Geschichte de Rheinlands in der Zeit der Fremdherrschaft 1794–1814* (Frankfurt, 1939), pp. 9–20.

65 W. von Humboldt, *Tagebücher 1788–1789*, ed. by A. Leitzmann (Berlin, 1916), vol. 1, pp. 80–81.

66 Comte de Mirabeau, *De la Monarchie Prussienne sous Fréderic le Grand* (London, 1788), vol. 3, pp. 239–40.

67 H. Dahn, 'Verluste der jülich-bergischen Landmiliz im Dreissigjährigen Kriege', *Düsseldorfer Jahrbuch*, 45 (1951), p. 286.

68 E. F. Wiebeking, *Beiträge zur Kurpfälzischen Staatengeschichte vom Jahre 1742 bis 1792 vorzüglich in Rücksicht auf die Herzogtümer Jülich und Berg* (Heidelberg and Mannheim, 1973), pp. 21ff.

69 F. O. Dilthey, *Die Geschichte der niederrheinischen Baumwollindustrie* (Jena, 1908), pp. 3–5.

70 E. Barkhausen, *Die Tuchindustrie in Montjoie, ihr Aufstieg und Niedergang* (Aachen, 1925), pp. 70ff. and 112–13.

71 B. Kuske, 'Die rheinischen Städte', *Geschichte des Rheinlands* (see n. 61 above), vol. 2, p. 70.

72 F. Schnabel, *Deutsche Geschichte im Neunzehnten Jahrhundert* (Freiburg, 1934), vol. 3, pp. 271–2.

73 J. Hashagen, 'Das Rheinland beim Abschlusse der französischen Fremdenherrschaft', *Die Rheinprovinz 1815–1915.Hundert Jahre preussischer Herrschaft*, ed. Joseph Hansen (Bonn, 1917), pp. 1–21.

74 F. Engels, 'The campaign for the German Imperial Constitution', *Marx-Engels Collected Works* (London, 1978), vol. 10, p. 156.

75 A. Thun, *Die Industrie am Niederrhein und ihre Arbeiter, Staats- und socialwissenschaftliche Forschungen* (Leipzig, 1879), vol. 2, sect. 2, pp. 19ff.

76 Thun, *Industrie am Niederrhein* (see n. 75 above), pp. 89–90.

77 W. Schumacher, *Untersuchungen über die Entwicklung der bergischen Seidenindustrie* (Heidelberg, 1919), p. 23.

78 Dilthey, *Niederrheinische Baumwollindustrie* (see n. 69 above), pp. 8–9.

79 W. Treue, *Wirtschaftszustände und Wirtschaftspolitik in Preussen 1815–1825*, VSWG supplement 31 (Stuttgart, 1937), pp. 67–113.

80 P. Benaerts, *Les origines de la grande industrie allemande* (Paris, 1933), p. 100.

81 Goldschmidt and Goldschmidt, *Staatsrath Kundt* (see n. 29 above), pp. 255–7; W. E. Lindner, *Das Zollgesetz von 1818 und Industrie und Handel am Niederrhein* (Trier, 1911), pp. 46 and 50.

82 Goldschmidt and Goldschmidt, *Staatsrath Kundt* (see n. 29 above), p. 265 and Lindner, *Zollgesetz* (see n. 81 above), p. 46.

83 Goldschmidt and Goldschmidt, *Staatsrath Kundt* (see n. 29 above), pp. 255–7.

84 *Werden und Wachsen eines Wirtschaftsgebietes am linken Niederrhein. Festschrift zur Feier ihres* [the Industrie- und Handelskammer = Chamber of Commerce] *100-Jährigen Bestehens* (Mönchen-Gladbach, 1937), p. 41.

85 Regarding the importance of the United States see Schumacher, *Entwicklung* (see n. 77 above), p. 29 and Thun, *Industrie am Niederrhein* (see n. 75 above), vol. 2, p. 25.

86 Thun, *Industrie am Niederrhein* (see n. 75 above), vol. 2, p. 30.

87 G. Schmoller, *Kleingewerbe* (see n. 33 above), pp. 477–8.

88 T. C. Banfield, *Industry of the Rhine* (London, 1848), vol. 2, pp. 243–6.

89 In a letter to P. V. Ann'enkov on November 28, 1846.

90 *Werden und Wachsen* (see n. 84 above), pp. 36 and 90.

91 W. Köllmann, *Sozialgeschichte der Stadt Barmen im 19. Jahrhundert,* Soziale Forschung und Praxis, vol. 21 (Tübingen, 1960), pp. 24ff.

92 Schumacher, *Entwicklung* (see n. 77 above), p. 30.

93 Regarding the difficult conditions of the wage-earners during this period, A. Thun's book is still the classic.

94 G. W. F. Hallgarten, *Imperialismus vor 1914* (Munich, 1951), vol. 1, pp. 114–21.

95 H. Rosenberg, *Die Weltwirtschaftskrise von 1875–1859,* 2nd ed. (Göttingen, 1974), p. 15.

96 K. Marx, 'Affairs in Prussia', *New-York Daily Tribune,* 1 Feb. 1859 'Die Lage in Preussen', *Marx-Engels Werke* (Berlin, 1969), vol. 12, p. 686.

97 H. J. Habakkuk, 'Free Trade and Commercial Expansion 1853–1870', *Cambridge History of the British Empire. The Growth of the New Empire* (Cambridge, n. d. [1940]), vol. 2, pp. 770–6.

98 Hallgarten, *Imperialismus* (see n. 94 above), vol. 1, pp. 124–5 and 158.

Notes to

Postscriptum

by H. Kisch

1 R. Tilly, 'Das Wachstumsparadigma und die europäische Industrialisierungs-geschichte. Rezension: Fontana Economic History of Europe Hg. C. Cipolla, Bde 1–4, London 1972–4, *Geschichte und Gesellschaft,* vol. 3 (1977), 93–108, for an extended discussion regarding the strengths and limitations of that post World War II generation of economic historians.

2 For that characteristic interaction between economic history and economic growth see the anthology edited by B. Supple, *The Experience of Economic Growth. Case Studies in Economic History* (New York, 1963).

3 R. Tilly, 'Wachstumsparadigma' (see n. 1 above), esp. pp. 97ff.

4 The most distinguished names that come to mind are R. H. Tawney and the Hammonds.

5 In many ways symptomatic for that period, W. W. Rostow's *The Stages of Economic Growth* (1960) and the subsequent response by economists and economic historians to that book. See W. W. Rostow, ed., *The Economics of Take Off into Sustained Growth* (London, 1963).

6 P. A. Baran, 'On the Political Economy of Backwardness', originally published in *Manchester School,* January 1952, and reprt. in A. N. Agarwala and S. P. Singh, eds., *The Economics of Underdevelopment* (New York, 1963), pp. 75–92, was one of the first essays to emphasize the institutional barriers to economic progress.

7 G. Myrdal, *An International Economy. Problems and Prospects* (New York, 1956), esp. Ch. 12. In this book and subsequently in many other publications, Myrdal never tired in demonstrating that the colonial countries, because of their peculiar political and social structures, experienced only the 'backwash effects of capitalist development'.

For an argument along similar lines, see the early writings of H. Myint notably his article 'The Gains from International Trade and the Backward Countries', republished in Myint's collection of essays *Economic Theory and Underdeveloped Countries* (Oxford, 1971), pp. 92–117. Also see a more recent study by K. Griffin, *Underdevelopment in Spanish America* (Cambridge, Mass., 1969), esp. 22ff.

8 The project was to be known as 'The Inter-University Study in Labor Problems in Economic Development' and its perspectives and purposes are elaborated in C. Kerr, et al., *Industrialism and Industrial Man. The Problems of Labor Management in Economic Growth* (Cambridge, Mass., 1960).

9 See Appendix of Kerr, *Industrialism* (see n. 8 above), for the work that was done under aegis of that project.

10 Many years later, F. Crouzet was to put so well the importance of regional investigations: 'What is most needed is a close analysis of the local or regional level, since to speak of English society and French society as a whole only leaves one with dubious generalities. After all, the industrial revolution was not made in England but in a few small districts of England.' 'England and France in the Eighteenth Century: A Comparative Analysis of Two Economic Growths', rpt. in R. M. Hartwell, ed., *The Causes of the Industrial Revolution in England. Debates in Economic History* (London, 1967), p. 159.

11 S. A. Mosk, 'Latin America versus the United States', *American Economic Review* (Papers and Proceedings), 41 (1951), 367–83.

12 Most of what I know about Latin American development I largely owe to David Felix who was also in Berkeley and at that time began his distinguished and lifelong research into issues pertaining to South American development; see for example his 'Monetarists, Structuralists and Import-Substituting Industrialization: A Critical Appraisal', *Inflation and Growth in Latin America*, eds. W. Baer and I. Kerstenetzky (Homewood, Ill., 1964), pp. 370–401.

13 See J. Purš, 'K probematice průmyslove revoluce v ČSR' (The industrial revolution issue in the CSR), *Československý Časopis Historický*, 4 (1956), 1–27. This article compares the industrial development in Bohemia and Moravia with that in Slovakia. This essay was on my mind when I turned to my comparison of Silesia with the Rhineland.

For the usefulness of the comparative analysis in trying to probe the transition from feudalism to capitalism see the excellent piece by R. Brenner, 'Agrarian Class Structure and Economic Development in Pre-Industrial Europe', *Past and Present*, 70 (1976), 30–75.

14 U. Lewald, 'Die Entwicklung der ländlichen Textilindustrie im Rheinland und in Schlesien', *Zeitschrift für Ostforschung*, 10 (1961), 601–31.

15 Lewald, 'Entwicklung' (see n. 14 above), pp. 606–9.

16 J. Thirsk, 'The Farming Regions of England', *Agrarian History of England and Wales*, vol. 4, ed. J. Thirsk (Cambridge, 1967).

17 On the noxious impact of various feudal forms of landholding in underdeveloped countries, see Ch. 22 ('Labor Utilization in Traditional Agriculture') in vol. 2 of G. Myrdal's *Asian Drama* (New York, 1968). As regards how far the Silesian aristocracy (in this instance the Hochbergs) was to be involved in the linen trades (e.g. finishing), see the interesting essay by S. Michalkiewicz, 'Z dziejów Wykańczalnej tkackiej W Gluszyzy na Pogórzu Sudeckim' (The History of the Weaver's Finishing Operations in Głuszyca along the Foothills of the Sudeten Mountains), *Studia i materiały z Dziejów Śląska*, 4 (1961), esp. 68–9 and 102–3.

18 That in many of these industrial mountain villages the position of these rural weavers was one of feudal dependence is clearly brought out by the account of Theodor von Schön who travelled through these parts in the last two years of the eighteenth century. He writes on July 28, 1797: 'In the morning I drove to the longest village of Silesia, and most likely of all of Germany, namely Langenbielau. It is over a mile long and belongs to the Count of Sandretzky. It is divided into two parts. The larger part used to belong to the Cathedral and contains 3,000 inhabitants, among them 49 farmers. These 3,000 people owe no services at all, every house pays 16ggr. yearly, every lodger 8ggr. Nevertheless, the people are subject to their lord. They must pay 10% *Laudemium* not only when they move out of the village altogether, but also when they move from one part of it to the other. When they move away from the estates, men must pay 2 Dukaten and women one.'

Von Schön then goes on to say that in this instance these dues were relatively light, though, of course, they do demonstrate that serfdom had not as yet been abolished, at least not by 1800. See T. von Schön, *Studienreisen eines jungen Staatswirths in Deutschland* (Leipzig, 1879), pp. 488–9. Also see pp. 490–1 which show that even as late as 1815 the civic freedom of these Silesian inhabitants from feudal interference was not as yet quite secure.

19 That during the 1830s, and indeed until 1848, the weavers *qua* cottars (Häusler) were paying feudal dues which, considering their plight, were excessive, has been emphasized in an important article (which I somehow missed 20 years ago) by W. Długoborski, 'Wystąpienia tkaczy w Dzierżonowskim w latach 1830–1831' (Weavers' Revolts in the Dzierżoniów Area during the Years 1830–31), *Kwartalnik Historyczny*, 63, 6 (1956), esp. pp. 14–15.

20 Since the above article was written I have tried to describe in great detail the rise to industrial eminence of the two Rhenish textile districts, 'From Monopoly to Laissez-Faire: The Early Growth of the Wupper Valley Textile Trades', *Journal of European Economic History*, 1 (1972) and 'Prussian Mercantilism and the Rise of the Krefeld Silk Industry: Variations upon an Eighteenth Century Theme', *Transactions of the American Philosophical Society*, new ser., 58, pt. 7 (1968). Both these areas were originally linen districts. S. B. Kan, *Dvě Povstání Slezských Tkalců 1793–1844* (Prague, 1952), pp. 57–59 and 181–4.

21 Kan, *Povstání* (see n. 20 above), 184–6.

22 Kan, Povstáni (see n. 20 above), pp. 184–6.

23 The strategic importance of the merchant producer as 'quality control agent' and purveyor of market information within the framework of putting-out system has recently been demonstrated for another area and another part of the world: K. Chao, 'The Growth of a Modern Cotton Textile Industry and the Competition with the Handicrafts', *China's Modern Economy in Historical Perspective*, ed. D. H. Perkins (Stanford, Calif; 1975), pp. 190–1. I am indebted to Franklin Mendels for steering me to this valuable article.

24 By the turn of the century, a cotton manufacture was to be introduced to the linen districts of Lower Silesia. But the spread of this particular industry was to be very slow. Kan, *Povstání* (see n. 20 above), pp. 126–32 is very specific about the feudal barriers that hampered the development of cotton production.

25 The need of an 'open society' – where 'new men' can emerge as entrepreneurs because they have access to the necessary capital – has been emphasized by one scholar as the key to the dynamic of the West-Riding woolen trades, see R. G. Wilson, 'The Supremacy of the Yorkshire Cloth Industry in the Eighteenth Century', *Textile History and Economic History. Essays in Honour of Miss Julia de Lacy Mann*, eds. N. B. Harte and K. G. Ponting (Manchester, 1973), pp. 237–8.

26 Kan, *Povstání* (see n. 20 above), pp. 88–94 and 175 and W. Długoborski's chapter, 'Przemysł i górnictwo' (Industry and Mining), in *Historia Śląska*, vol. 2, part 1, 1763–1850, ed. W. Długoborski (Wrocław, 1966), pp. 169–77.

27 I am, of course, aware that even in western Europe some of the older textile districts declined and disappeared (e.g. Wiltshire and Brittany) for other reasons than the persistence of a feudal structure. See *idem and H.* Sée, 'Remarques sur le caractère de l'industrie rurale en France et les causes de son extension au XVIII siècle', *Revue Historique*, 142 (1923), pp. 47–53.

Index

Abel, W. 90

accumulation, process of 37, 53; and class 15, 44, 121, 188; and population 78–9, 81; and capitalism 114–15, 141, 160, 184

agrarian cycle 66, 82, 83, 91; *see also* harvest

agrarian economy 95, 117, 176; changes in 7, 13–14, 21, 40; crises in 76, 78, 82, 90, 118, 160

agrarian producers 17, 25, 28, 30, 31, 37, 44, 45

agrarian specialization 25–6; *see also* crops

agrarian surplus 12, 27, 29, 30, 38–9, 41, 96, 175, 177; *see also* productivity, agricultural

agriculture 12, 14, 16–17, 27, 96–8, 160, commercial 8, 21, 24, 27, 83, 153, 167, 169, 176, 185, 193; crises of 32, 76–7, 89–91, 118, 146; organization of 14, 17–18, 25–6, 27, 167, 169, 171, 174–5, 188; and rural industry 1, 4, 5, 8, 14, 16, 21, 24, 26–7, 29, 30–2, 44, 59, 83, 91, 96, 105, 117, 142, 143, 165–6; *see also* cereal agriculture

agricultural productivity 6, 12, 17, 30, 31–2, 44–5, 97

artisans, rural: *see* rural industrial producers

Aubin, H. 22

authority, seigneurial 15, 17–18, 28, 39, 70; *see also* feudalism

Bardet, J.-P. 91

Berkner, L. K. 55

birth control 76

Bitter, C. H. 49

birth rate 19, 85, 87, 91–2, 119, 155

births, surplus of 83; *see also* population, increase in

Bloch, Marc 21

Boeke, J. H. 75

Bohannan, P. 12

Bois, G. 44

Braun R. 49, 60, 63, 69, 83, 196

Brunner, O. 38

Bücher, K. 3, 47, 53, 69

capital: agricultural 167; merchant 94, 149; importance of 7, 9, 13, 21–3, 24, 27, 29, 33, 37, 78, 98, 100ff, 115, 121, 141, 187, 200; and family economy 27, 41, 50, 52, 53, 128, 185; v. putter-out 123–4, 128; rural producers' 49–50, 53, 55, 63, 78–81, 108; *see also* property; production, capitalization of

capital–labour relationship 105, 146

capital market 129; *see also* market economy

capitalism, development of 5, 9, 37, 52, 53, 94, 107–11; agrarian 148; industrial 5, 8, 9–10, 37, 54, 138–41, 144, 154, 159; see *also* industrialization

capitalists, industrial 101, 138

cattle farming; *see* stock raising

centralization 107, 109, 111, 123, 150; *see also* factory system; workshops, centralized

cereal agriculture 24, 30, 83, 89–91, 96, 174–5; *see also* agriculture

Chambers, J. D. 17, 92

Chapman, S. D. 142

Charbonneau, H. 88

Chaunu, P. 76, 148

Chayanov, A. V. 16, 40, 41, 42, 43, 44, 51, 58, 79

children 44, 55, 58, 60, 70, 79, 80, 84, 88, 91, 95; *see also* labour, child

circulation process: and capital 10, 13, 99–102, 141; interruption of 10, 121; *see also* trade

class 3, 67, 129–30; development of 44, 188, 193; and population 76, 83, and taxation 133, 184

climate, importance of 15, 118; *see also* agrarian crises; agricultural crises; harvest

coal, importance of 30, 151

Coleman, D. C. 22, 65, 145

330